W9-CHX-383

THE KNOWLEDGE MANAGEMENT TOOLKIT

THE KNOWLEDGE MANAGEMENT TOOLKIT

PRACTICAL TECHNIQUES FOR BUILDING A KNOWLEDGE MANAGEMENT SYSTEM

AMRIT TIWANA

To learn more about this title, point to:
www.kmtoolkit.com

ISBN 0-13-012853-8

90000

9 780130 128539

PRENTICE HALL PTR,
UPPER SADDLE RIVER, NJ 07458
WWW.PHPTR.COM

Library of Congress Cataloging-in-Publication Data

Tiwana, Amrit, —
    The knowledge management toolkit: practical techniques for building a
knowledge management system/Amrit Tiwana.
      p. cm.
    Includes bibliographical references and index.
    ISBN 0-13-012853-8
    1. Knowledge management. I. Title.
    HD30.2.T59 2000
    658.4'038--dc21   99-049321
                                        CIP

Editorial/Production Supervisor: *Kerry Reardon*
Project Coordinator: *Anne Trowbridge*
Acquisitions Editor: *Miles Williams*
Editorial Assistant: *Noreen Regina*
Manufacturing Manager: *Alexis Heydt*
Marketing Manager: *Kate Hargett*
Art Director: *Gail Cocker-Bogusz*
Cover Designer: *Anthony Gemmellaro*
Cover Design Director: *Jerry Votta*

© 2000 Prentice Hall PTR
Prentice-Hall, Inc.
Upper Saddle River, NJ 07458

Prentice Hall books are widely used by corporation and
government agencies for training, marketing, and resale.
The publisher offers discounts on this book when ordered
in bulk quantities. For more information, contact

    Corporate Sales Department,
    Prentice Hall PTR
    One Lake Street
    Upper Saddle River, NJ 07458
    Phone: 800-382-3419; FAX: 201-236-7141
    E-mail (Internet): corpsales@prenhall.com

Printed in the United States of America

10 9 8 7 6 5 4 3

ISBN 0-13-012853-8

Prentice-Hall International (UK) Limited, *London*
Prentice-Hall of Australia Pty. Limited, *Sydney*
Prentice-Hall Canada Inc., *Toronto*
Prentice-Hall Hispanoamericana, S.A., *Mexico*
Prentice-Hall of India Private Limited, *New Delhi*
Prentice-Hall of Japan, Inc., *Tokyo*
Pearson Education Asia Pte. Ltd., *Singapore*
Editora Prentice-Hall do Brasil, Ltda., *Rio de Janeiro*

Credits for Chapter-opening Quotes
Chapter 3: Simon, H.A. (1988). "Managing
in an information-rich world." In Y.K. Sketty
and V.M. Buehler (eds.), *Competing Through
Productivity and Quality.* Cambridge, MA:
Productivity Press. **Chapter 5:** Foreword by
Arthur C. Clarke, "Intelligent Software
Agents" by Richard Murch, Tony Johnson,
Prentice Hall (1998). **Chapter 6:** "What Life
Means to Einstein: An Interview by George
Sylvester Viereck," for the October 26, 1929
issue of *The Saturday Evening Post.*
Chapter 8: "The Speaker's Electonic
Reference Collection," AApex Software, 1994.
Chapter 9: Rita Mae Brown. **Chapter 11:**
From THE ART OF WAR by Sun Tzu, trans-
lated by Samuel B. Griffith. Translation copy-
right ©1963 by Oxford University Press, Inc.
Used by permission of Oxford University Press,
Inc. **Chapter 12:** As quoted by Richard
Murch and Tony Johnson in "Intelligent
Software Agents: Prentice Hall (1998).
Chapter14: L. Lodish, "Vaguely Right
Approach to Sales Force Automation,"
Harvard Business Review, 52, 119–124 (1979).

To Sherry

BRIEF CONTENTS

Contents

PART II   THE ROAD AHEAD: IMPLEMENTING KNOWLEDGE MANAGEMENT

PART IIA THE FIRST PHASE: INFRASTRUCTURE EVALUATION AND LEVERAGE

PART IIB THE SECOND PHASE: KM SYSTEM ANALYSIS, DESIGN, AND DEVELOPMENT

PART IIC THE THIRD PHASE: KMS DEPLOYMENT

PART IID THE FINAL PHASE AND BEYOND: MEASURING ROI AND PERFORMANCE

PART III SIDE ROADS: APPENDICES

PREFACE

Real knowledge is to know the extent of one's ignorance—Confucius

In the quest for sustainable competitive advantage, companies have finally come to realize that technology alone is not that. What sustains is knowledge. It is in unchaining knowledge that lies in your company's people, processes, and experience that the hope for survival rests. Peter Drucker warned us years ago, but it's only now that companies have finally woken up to the value of managing their knowledge and bringing it to bear upon decisions that drive them up or out of existence.

If your organization is confused by vendor buzz and consultant pitches about how they and their products can solve all your knowledge problems, be forewarned: It's not that easy. Knowledge management (KM) is just about 35 percent technology. While technology is the easy part, it's the people and processes part that is hard.

The Knowledge Management Toolkit will provide you with a strategic roadmap for knowledge management and teach you how to implement KM in your company, step by step. Technology should not always be mistaken for computing technology; the two are not synonymous. Chapter 1, rather than this preface, introduces you to KM and to this book. Before you begin, a notational warning would be in order. You'll find a lot of citations because of the cumulative tradition that this book follows by choice. However, do not let this distract you; all that you need to comprehend a topic being discussed is footnoted on the same page. You can safely ignore all endnotes without losing any information (unless you want to trace bibliographic history). When a URL is mentioned in the text, you will likely find further information on it in Appendix D.

You'll hear about the *silver bullet,* a term rooted in folklore of the American Civil War. It supposedly emerged from the practice of encouraging a patient who was to undergo field surgery to bite down hard on a lead bullet "to divert the mind from pain and screaming" (*American Slang,* Harper & Row, New York, 1986). You'll soon realize that you've found the silver bullet of business competitiveness.

Think of this book as a conversation between you and me. Remember to visit the companion site at www.kmtoolkit.com. I would love to hear your comments, suggestions, questions, criticisms, and reactions. Feel free to email me at atiwana@acm.org.

Amrit Tiwana
Atlanta

ACKNOWLEDGMENTS

Robert Dubin pointed out as early as 1976 (*Theory Building in Applied Areas,* Rand McNally College Publishing Co., Chicago, 17-26) that there is probably a five- to ten-year lag between the time a theoretical model—which KM for a large part is—becomes *fashionable* in the real world. It's the thinkers who prepare the revolution and the bandits who carry it out. I could not even begin to truly acknowledge the intellectual debt that I owe to thinkers like Ikujiro Nonaka, Karl Wiig, Tom Davenport, Bob Buckman, Peter Drucker, Michael Zack, Andrew Inkpen, Wanda Orlikowski, Marco Iansiti, and James Brian Quinn, who prepared the knowledge revolution and have long influenced my own thinking. Special thanks are also due to Herbert Simon for his insightful comments. It is on the shoulders of these giants that this book stands.

I would like to thank the people from the industry who made that initial leap of faith and embraced the value of knowledge management in their work, products, services, and as a centerpiece of their businesses. Among the many people I wish to thank for their support are Elaine Viscosi at Intranetics Inc. for permission to use a sample Intranet deployment described as Urban Motors in Chapter 9; Michael Zack of Northeastern University; Chuck Sieloff of Hewlett Packard; Johanna Rothman of Rothman Consulting; Joni Schlender of Plumtree Corporation; Steve Shattuck of Alpha Microsystems; Jean Heminway of Xerox Corporation for her zealous support for the DMA/WebDAV standards and the inputs that she provided; Susan Hanley at AMS Inc; Michael Davis of OSIS; Ray Edwards of Lighthouse Consulting; Joni Schlender of Plumtree Software; Harry Collier of Infornotics, England; Jim Eup of Powerway; Mark Turner of the Natural Language Processing Lab at Thomson; Jeff Barton of Texas Instruments for his insightful analysis of this book; Glenn Shimkus of Platinum Technology, Inc.; Rick Dove of ParadigmShift International; Thomas Davenport of Andersen Consulting and Boston University; Mark Montgomery of GWIN; Fanuel Dewever of Newcom, Belgium; Steve Singer of CIO; Gord Podolski of Nortel Networks; Bettina Jetter of MindJet LLC for extensive information on mind mapping; Simon Tussler of the Boston Consulting Group; Mark Kawakami and others who I have inadvertently left out.

I would also like to acknowledge the invaluable suggestions and unfailing support that I have received from my colleagues including Arjan Raven; Bala Ramesh, my mentor; and especially Ashley Bush, who "lived through" several drafts of this book and helped me through the many software crashes that come exactly in the middle of your best ideas in a Windows world. Thanks are also due to my close associates, Smiley and Tommy, without whose help this book would have been a more formidable task.

I would also like to thank Mark Keil, Daniel Robey, Richard Baskerville, and Vijay Vaishnavi at the J. Mack Robinson College of Business, from whom I have much learned to strike the balance between rigor and relevance in research. Built upon the shoulders of the giants in information systems research, this book is my humble attempt at proving that there is more relevance in the cumulative body of research that comes out of the ivory towers than we usually get credit for.

This book would have been an impossible task without the enthusiasm of my editor, Miles Williams, his able assistant Noreen Regina, and my initial contact at PHPTR, Mark Taub. The quality of this book also owes a lot to my technical reviewers including Corinne Gregory of Data Dimensions, Chuck Fay of FileNet Corporation, and to my anonymous initial reviewers, for their suggestions. The credit for the readability of this book goes largely to my development editor, Mary Lou Nohr, whose insights, arguments, and suggestions helped me see the forest when all I could see were the trees. The visual appeal of this book owes much to the skills of Kerry Reardon.

Most importantly, I would like to acknowledge the support and encouragement that my family has provided me. Without them, this book would have been far from possible.

THE KNOWLEDGE MANAGEMENT TOOLKIT

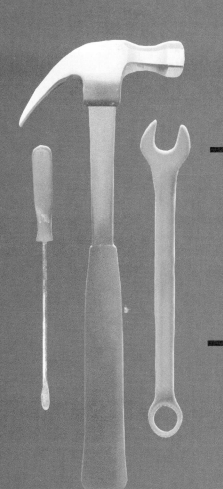

PART I
THE RUBBER
MEETS THE ROAD

CHAPTER 1
INTRODUCTION

IN THIS CHAPTER

- ✔ Define knowledge management (KM).
- ✔ Understand the noise about knowledge management. Understand why now.
- ✔ Evaluate knowledge management's value proposition
- ✔ Look beyond the buzz to see if there is anything "real" behind KM.
- ✔ Define what knowledge management is not.
- ✔ Understand if your company is ready for knowledge management.

AS WE GAIN MORE KNOWLEDGE, WE DO NOT BECOME CERTAIN,
WE BECOME CERTAIN OF MORE.
—AYN RAND

Data. At first we had too little. We asked for more and we got it. Now we have more than we want. Data led to information, but what we were looking for in the first place was knowledge.

As an increasing number of companies now realize that knowledge is their key asset, they want to turn to managing this asset to deliver business results. Maybe you want to introduce knowledge management (KM) in your own company.

But where and how do you begin? What is behind the buzz? What is KM's value proposition? What types of companies can actually begin knowledge management? Is it a technology problem or a management problem? What happens to the millions that your company has invested in information technology (IT) if it is replaced by yet another hyped "fix-it-all" technology? Can you build upon existing IT investments? What kinds of people, skills, and organizational structures are necessary to pull it off? How can KM be aligned with your business's strategy? Is there an architecture that you can use? How can you deploy KM in your own company? Are there any business metrics for it? How can you maximize payoff if you implement KM? Can your small business without deep pockets afford it? How do you know if your business is even ready for it? These are some of the questions that this book will help you answer.

KNOWLEDGE MANAGEMENT: A GOLDMINE OR AN EMPTY PIGGY-BANK?

Knowledge management might be "hot" as of today, but successful managers have always realized its value. Long before terms such as *expert systems, core competencies, best practices, learning organizations,* and *corporate memory* were in vogue, these managers knew that their company's key asset was not its buildings, its market share, or its products, but it lay in its people, their knowledge, and skills. After having tried everything else—from the greatest products and the best technology to virtual monopolies—in their respective markets, more businesses have finally come to the realization that the only sustainable source of competitive advantage is their knowledge. As Drucker fittingly warns us, "those who wait until this challenge indeed becomes a 'hot' issue are likely to fall behind, perhaps never to recover."[1]

WHY KNOWLEDGE?

Far from vendor sales pitches, a crying need for knowledge management is evident. This need is a growing reality, worldwide: from Antigua to Zaire. *The Scotsman* reports that 98 percent of senior managers in a KPMG survey believe that knowledge management was more than just a passing fad.[2] The London *Times* calls it the "fifth discipline" after business strategy, accounting, marketing, and human resources and called upon British companies to harness it to improve their performance and profitability.[3] The need is evident in Singapore, where *The Strait Times* reports that "organizations lack a strategy to manage knowledge sharing among their staff."[4] Some organizations there, *The Strait Times* reports, are not even sure *what* a knowledge management strategy is or how to develop one. Of 75 senior managers interviewed in Singapore, only 3 of whom felt that their companies were even moderately effective at knowledge sharing, unequivocally voice their intent to make knowledge management their number one priority.[5]

This sounds very much like the opinion that we've been hearing in the United States. For good reason: forty percent of the U.S. economy is directly attributable to the creation of intellectual capital.[6] As companies fail to solve KM problems by plugging in "fix-it-all" technology solutions, echoes of the cultural complement needed to make these solutions actually work are resounding far beyond the United States. David Hewson writes in the *Sunday Times,* "the problem is cultural...where the idea of making information available to all, at every level throughout the company, frequently is anathema to managers."[7]

WHAT'S KNOWLEDGE?

Knowledge and knowledge management are lofty concepts—debated by academics and managers and even doubted by some analysts—one that only a few businesses have mastered.[8] The few big businesses that have are the ones that now top the *Fortune 500* list and the few small ones top the *Inc. 100 hot companies to watch* list. Before we continue, here is a *working* definition of knowledge suggested by Thomas Davenport and Laurence Prusak, which we will refine as we proceed:

> Knowledge is a fluid mix of framed experience, values, contextual information, expert insight and grounded intuition that provides an environment and framework for evaluating and incorporating new experiences and information. It originates and is applied in the minds of knowers. In organizations, it often becomes embedded not only in documents or repositories but also in organizational routines, processes, practices, and norms.[9]

So What's Knowledge Management?

Next, let's try getting a temporary handle on what knowledge management means. In the simplest terms it means exactly that: management of knowledge. In the context of our discussion, it can be extended to "management of organizational knowledge for creating business value and generating a competitive advantage." Knowledge management enables the creation, communication, and application of knowledge of all kinds to achieve business goals.[10] Kirk Klasson elucidates, "Knowledge management is the ability to create and retain greater value from core business competencies." Knowledge management addresses business problems particular to your business—whether it's creating and delivering innovative products or services; managing and enhancing relationships with existing and new customers, partners, and suppliers; or administering and improving work practices and processes.

KM'S VALUE PROPOSITION

The ability of companies to exploit their intangible assets has become far more decisive than their ability to invest and manage their physical assets.[11] As markets shift, uncertainty dominates, technologies proliferate, competitors multiply, and products and services become obsolete rapidly, successful companies are characterized by their ability to consistently create new knowledge, quickly disseminate it, and embody it in their new products and services. In the postindustrial era, the success of a corporation lies deeply embedded in its intellectual systems, as knowledge-based activities of developing new products, services, and processes become the *primary* internal function of firms attempting to create the greatest promise for a long-term competitive advantage. Kirk Klasson suggests that companies can reap an immense payoff when a knowledge management solution makes it easier for practitioners to reach out to other practitioners who share common problems or have experience to share. Why all this noise about knowledge management and why now? There are nine reasons for this:

1. *Companies are becoming knowledge intensive, not capital intensive.* Knowledge is rapidly displacing capital, monetary prowess, natural resources, and labor as the quintessential economic resource.[13] Knowledge is the only input that can help your company cope with radical change and ask the right questions before you attempt to find the answers,[a] for without this knowledge you might never even realize how your industry's competitive environment is changing until it's a little too late. It is this knowledge that brings quality into any company's product and service offerings.[b] Further, product life cycles and service time-to-market can be accelerated in unprecedented ways through knowledge. Knowledge management is the only way to reach and apply this knowledge in time.

   eBay (market value, $22 billion), eFax ($200 million), CISCO ($190 billion), Pfizer ($150 billion), and Microsoft ($400 billion) are a few of several hundred thousand examples.

2. *Unstable markets necessitate "organized abandonment."* Your target markets might undergo radical shifts, leaving your company in a disastrous position of being with the wrong product, at the wrong time, and in the wrong place. The impact of these forces is witnessed most prominently in high-technology environments[c] and financial markets, and increasingly in other markets as well. KM lets you undertake what Drucker calls *organized abandonment:*[14] reshape products, get out of projects and product lines that can pull your business down, and get into others that maximize growth potential.

   National Semiconductors, an excellent example, closed down its division Cyrix Corporation, the well-known manufacturer of low-end Intel-clone microprocessors in 1999 when it realized that it was pulling the entire company down as it tried to withstand price-based assaults from mighty Intel, which had pockets deeper than those of National.

---

[a]Asking the right questions and taking action based on such knowledge, Peter Drucker adds, usually double or triple knowledge worker productivity, and usually fast.

[b]Drucker also points out that unlike in the production economy, quality of work, decisions, and processes is *at least* as important as their quantity.

[c]Just-in-time (JIT) manufacturing, the driver of Toyota's success, for example, is more knowledge based than it is resource based. Also see B. Ramesh and A. Tiwana, Supporting Collaborative Process Knowledge Management in New Product Development Teams, *Decision Support Systems* (forthcoming), for an analysis of KM's role in high-technology businesses.

3. *KM lets you lead change so change does not lead you.* KM is no longer needed by service-based businesses and consultants alone. Even conventional retailers like Wal-Mart consider their competence in logistics management—a knowledge-intensive activity—to be their primary driver of business success. Drucker warns that no industry or company has a natural advantage or disadvantage; the only advantage it *can* possess is the ability to exploit universally available knowledge. He describes knowledge as "the window of opportunity."[d] After all, the next critical piece of critical information could take any form—an evolving social trend affecting customer preferences, a new management practice, a nascent technology, or a political or economic development in a remote manufacturing location.[15] You cannot manage this change, Drucker reminds. You can only *lead* change, and stay ahead of it.

   In a data-obsessed business environment where only 2 percent of grocery store scanner data collected is ever analyzed,[16] knowledge management can help you determine those points and see opportunities through these "windows" in processes where change needs to be led, before your competitors do.

4. *Only the knowledgeable survive.* "The survival of the fittest firm" is an outmoded thought in the knowledge-based economy. The ability to survive and thrive comes only from a firm's ability to create, acquire, process, maintain, and retain old and new knowledge in the face of complexity, uncertainty, and rapid change.[17] It becomes deterministic in the firm's long-term survival. Drucker points out that knowledge is productive only if it is applied to make a difference (rather than simply exist) and suggests that it is this productivity that is going to be the deterministic factor in the competitive position of any company, or industry.[18] Knowledge management can make that a reality.

   When your company *can* apply its past experience for accelerating future work, why should you start every project with a blank sheet and then work feverishly, sometimes even desperately, to make the deadline on budget? Yet companies do it all the time, Connie Moore notes in *CIO*,[19] and in that mass stupidity lies the opportunity to differentiate your company's processes.

5. *Cross-industry amalgamation is breeding complexity.* Drucker warns us that complexity, uncertainty, and ambiguity are the hallmarks of today's production and business systems irrespective of the nature of business or type of industry. Knowledge management has allowed many companies such as Bay Networks to turn this complexity to their advantage.[20]

6. *Knowledge can drive decision support like no other.* Providing effective decision support by making knowledge about past projects, initiatives, failures, successes, and efforts readily available and accessible can make a significant contribution toward convalescing this process. Drucker lists four diagnostic tools for decision making that we will focus on: foundation, productivity, competence, and resource allocation knowledge. KM solutions that are capable of effectively supporting collaboration and knowledge sharing enable individual knowledge workers, teams, and communities to collaboratively make better decisions faster—and act on those decisions to create more economic value for their company.

---

[d]Drucker (1999, page 84) also indicates that many such opportunities arise from unexpected failure of competitors (such as in a sales pitch) and unexpected successes on your company's side.

7. *Knowledge requires sharing; IT barely supports sharing.* KM requires a strong culture of sharing that information systems do not inherently support. In the United States, Tom Davenport has been feverishly supporting the idea of figuratively creating "water cooler cultures" in the same way as the Europeans have been demanding "coffee machine cultures":[21] environments that allow and systems that support social informality. Knowledge, as any witness to artificial intelligence research knows, "is not about machines, but about culture."[22] Principles that have traditionally driven IT design, though with moderate success, no longer apply in designing KM systems.

8. *Tacit knowledge is mobile.* Too often when someone leaves your firm, his or her experience leaves too. This knowledge, skills, competencies, understanding, and insight then often go to work for a competitor. Knowledge management can save your company from losing critical capabilities when that happens.

9. *Your competitors are no longer just on the West Coast.* We are becoming increasingly global, Drucker notes. Keeping up with developments and ensuing threats or opportunities in other countries is a tedious, time-consuming, and difficult process. Knowledge management technology, when given the right source feeds, can deliver relevant and timely knowledge.

As companies shift from a product-centric form to a knowledge-centric form, it becomes essential to support various dimensions of this knowledge as a critical asset. Companies—big or small—cannot afford to underinvest in using, reusing, and not losing knowledge that they already have. Knowledge management is therefore an imperative for companies that do not operate in *purely* cost-driven markets anymore.

WHY NOW?

Strategy driven by knowledge can help your company be what Drucker calls *"purposefully opportunistic."* Peter Drucker rightly points out that the most valuable assets of the twenty-first-century company are its knowledge and knowledge workers.[e] Drucker, like many others saw this coming for over 50 years. The recognition that the value of complex products rests not in the factories and buildings used for fabrication, but in the minds of people who created them, has been pronounced in the business world well before Thorstein Veblen wrote about it in *The Engineers and the Price System.*

Figure 1-1 shows the darling tools of managers as they evolved from the 1950s to the 2000s. Some of these died much anticipated deaths as fads, and some live till this day. Notably, one consistent and pervasive thread runs through all these—about leveraging knowledge, experience, intellectual assets, and their management. And this consistent thread has led businesses to what we now call knowledge management.

---

[e]Drucker also compares these to production equipment and capital that were key to business success in the twentieth century.

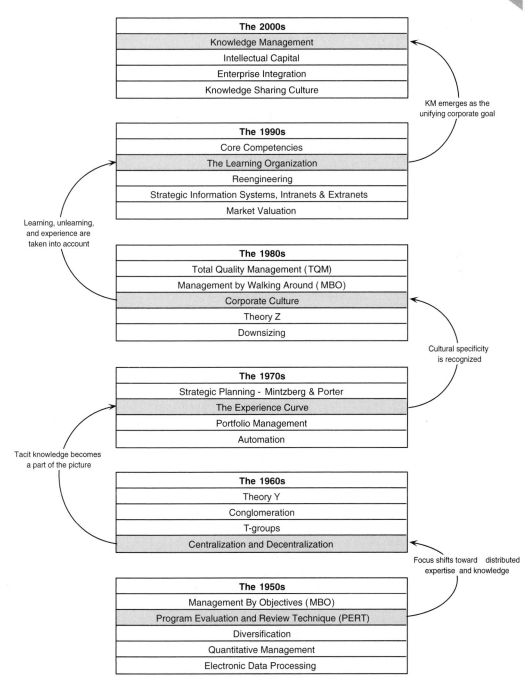

Figure 1-1   Managers' tools through the decades: Knowledge management has been coming since the 1950s.

In a global economy, Davenport and Prusak suggest, "Knowledge many be your company's greatest competitive advantage." Having exhausted all other sources of competitive advantage such as technology and market dominance—none of which have sustained their promises—companies are befittingly placing all hopes in knowledge and its effective management. The value proposition of knowledge management is now stronger than ever, as it is no longer a rare competitive differentiator but the *only* differentiator.

Who Should Be Pursuing Knowledge Management?

Two types of companies should be pursuing knowledge management. The first type is one that has realized the need to keep up with its competitors and remain a legitimate player through the process of maintaining knowledge that is core to its line of business. Core knowledge is the basic level of knowledge required before you can even "play the game."[23] The second type is one step ahead: It already has the core knowledge necessary. This company realizes that what is innovative knowledge today will be commonplace, core knowledge tomorrow. Such companies are struggling with their ability to keep ahead, not just viably compete. Drucker rings the warning bell and reminds us that knowledge workers have mobility unlike ever before.[24] Since your company's capabilities rest *between the ears* of such knowledge workers, its competencies can, and often do, walk out, lured into your competitor's corner office. Productivity of your company's knowledge workers, and in effect productivity of their knowledge, determines the productivity of your company. Effective knowledge management will allow you to unleash that productivity.

Knowledge management can deliver equally astounding results in both small companies and large. A survey of over a hundred CEOs in Ireland reported in *The Irish Times,* indicates how small-sized businesses are betting on knowledge management to get their companies in the otherwise minuscule Ireland ahead in international markets.[25] The same shift resonates in large companies. Gartner Group estimates that by the year 2003, over 50 percent of Fortune 1000 companies will depend on knowledge management and knowledge management systems to widen the gap between them and their competitors.[26]

WHAT'S BEHIND THE BUZZ?

As with any other concept that businesses rush to adopt, KM has its share of consultants out to make the "quick bucks." You've probably heard vendors of photocopiers, printers, word processors, search engines, desktop PCs, wireless services, scanners, removable high-capacity disks, and enterprise software all make the same claim: Here's the ultimate knowledge management tool that will solve all your company's knowledge problems. Nonsense. Knowledge management is not a technology problem; it is a process problem. Technology is only an enabler. And this enabler can rarely, if ever, produce the same results in two different organizations.

Within the noise however, is a concrete reality that has been around and will be long after most of these vendors have gone out of business. The business drivers behind the move to knowledge management are so compelling that most industry analysts insist that if your company has not already started exploring knowledge management tools to harness its intellectual assets, it soon must.[27]

Knowledge management is here to stay; you either adopt it or begin counting the years to the closure of your business as your competitors who accept its value leave you far behind. This book hopes to separate the chaff from the grain.

Under the Magnifying Glass

Knowledge management is much more than mere technology: It is a potent competitive tool for an ever more brutally competitive age of shrinking margins, shorter product development times, and fickle customers.[28] Competing on knowledge requires either aligning strategy to what your company knows or developing knowledge management capabilities required to support a desired strategy. Michael Zack warns that knowledge management, to deliver competitive advantage, must be grounded solidly in the context of business strategy. Only through such strategic grounding can your company effectively prioritize its investments in knowledge management and come out ahead of competitors who have not grounded their efforts in business strategy.

What Knowledge Management Is Not About

Knowledge management is not solely a technology problem; it is partly a management problem. Only by aligning the two can you build knowledge management technology that will truly enable effective knowledge management. This focus will be evident throughout the rest of the pages in this book. To cleanse you of vendor sales pitches, let me first clarify what knowledge management is *not*.

- *Knowledge management is not knowledge engineering.* Knowledge engineering has been a vital part of computer science but is barely even related to knowledge management. Knowledge management is a business problem and falls in the domain of information systems and management, not in computer science. Knowledge management needs to meld information systems *and people* in ways that knowledge engineering has never been able to.

- *Knowledge management is about process, not just digital networks.* Management of knowledge has to encompass and improve business processes.[29] Agreed that IT is the biggest enabler for effective knowledge management if used correctly. However, Drucker warns that focusing on the *T* and not the *I* in *IT* will deliver little. The *T* will never be used effectively if the people who are supposed to use it are not in the equation right from the start.

  "Without a way of capturing and integrating past knowledge, any development process can quickly dissolve into chaos."[30] Evidence from companies "loudly" suggests one thing: KM needs a knowledge culture driven by a performance-linked-to-reward system that encourages these knowledge workers to both pass along what they know and says "it's okay to admit that you don't know something."[31]

- *Knowledge management is not about building a "smarter" intranet.* A knowledge management system can use your company's intranet as its front end, but one should never be mistaken for the other. Saying that your intranet is your knowledge management system is something as senseless as saying that a jetliner is the cockpit. The "just-add-water" approach traditionally used with packaged intranets collapses face down when used for knowledge management. The intranet is, however, a part of the equation that provides a stable messaging and collaboration platform.[32]

- *Knowledge management is not about a one-time investment.* Knowledge management, like any other future-oriented investment, requires consistent attention over a substantial period of time even after it begins to deliver results.[f] KM critically requires metrics that allow businesses to measure its impact, provide room for improvement, and to provide a robust basis for resource allocation.[33]

- *Knowledge management is not about enterprise-wide "infobahns."* While enterprise integration helps, the primary focus of KM is on creating, getting, importing, delivering, and most importantly helping the *right* people apply the *right* knowledge at the *right* time. Knowledge management solutions must, therefore, reflect the way individuals and organizations have managed and shared information, albeit more effectively.

- *Knowledge management is not about "capture."* Document management vendors would have you believe otherwise, but knowledge management is not about capturing "knowledge." An inevitable loss of context occurs when documents are "sanitized" for use across the company. While a document management system lacks context, experience, and insight, it still has a marginal place in knowledge management technology. Knowledge, in its entirety, cannot be captured.[g]

WHAT THIS BOOK IS ABOUT

A survey of 92 U.S. companies by the *Giga Information Group* reported in *CIO* in late 1998 reveals panic as many business managers ask their IS (information systems) organization to "do something" about knowledge management because they've heard that KM will become the next big competitive differentiator.[34] Dead wrong. Knowledge management is not the "next big differentiator"; it is the *only* competitive differentiator left. Where do managers like

---

[f]Peter Drucker recommends that this attitude be carried on in new services and technology innovations as well.

[g]The artificial intelligence community has been trying to capture tacit knowledge since the past 40 years with little luck.

this turn? To software vendors or management consultants. Neither management tools nor software solutions are comprehensive solutions; they are generalized treatments created for generalized problems. They are not created with your company in mind. They do not come bundled with an intimate knowledge of your company's history, culture, experience, goals, realities, or problems. If shrink-wrapped solutions like Windows do not "plug-and-play" perfectly in your company, it is far-fetched to assume that either these "trademarked theories" or software tools will.

Thank You, Dr. Davenport

Tom Davenport's 1998 bestseller, *Working Knowledge: How Organizations Manage What They Know* (Harvard Business School Press), was perhaps the key to a surging business interest in knowledge management. Ever since the Japanese scholar Ikujiro Nonaka popularized the idea in his 1995 book, *The Knowledge Creating Company* (Oxford University Press) and a 1991 *Harvard Business Review* paper by the same name, companies had been toying with the idea, but only a few realized early on that knowledge management was coming. Amidst Peter Drucker's cry for a knowledge focus in his 1993 book, *The Post Capitalist Society* (HarperBusiness Press), companies were still struggling to compete with technology. Herbert Simon's drum beat is being heard twenty years too late.

Nonaka's treatment, although a seminal contribution, unfortunately was too philosophically theoretical for business to actually apply. Davenport's book—the pioneer in business knowledge management—provided an initial direction to businesses that actually wanted to adopt knowledge management. Davenport stresses the need for linking knowledge management to business goals but does not show how to do it. It illustrates excellent applications of technology but does not provide companies guidance on how to build knowledge management solutions for themselves. It does not describe knowledge metrics and teaming. In short, it provides an excellent overview of knowledge management but provides little guidance on how companies can actually do it. Nor were these pragmatics objectives of that book, but they are the objectives of this book. I continue where Tom Davenport left off.

WHAT THIS BOOK WILL DO

This book seeks to bridge the gap between knowledge management theory and practice. It shows you how you can implement both a knowledge management strategy and a knowledge management system in *your* company. It helps you ask the right questions—not attempting to give you generic answers to unasked generic questions. It provides you with practical guidance on linking knowledge management to business strategy rather than approaching KM from a technically biased or impossible-to-implement philosophical perspective. A 10-step roadmap, each step of which is illustrated with real-life examples, guides you through the process of *actually* implementing knowledge management in your company.

The 10-Step Roadmap Helps You—

This book walks you through a road map with four phases involving 10 different steps that will help you leverage your company's existing infrastructure; design, develop, and deploy a knowledge management system that is aligned with your business strategy, on top of existing infrastructural capabilities; undertake cultural and organizational changes that can make knowledge management succeed in your company; and show you ways to evaluate both its effectiveness and return on investment.

Identify Knowledge That Is Critical to Your Business

This book helps you understand how knowledge management contributes to your company's economic value and competitiveness. It explains the difference between information management and knowledge management, guides you through the process of identifying knowledge that is critical to your own business processes, helps you identify opportunities for exploiting this knowledge through its effective management and application. KM, however important, is not for every company: This book will help you determine whether or not your company is ready for knowledge management.

Align Business Strategy and Knowledge Management

Business vision operates at a high level of abstraction, and systems development needs low-level details and specifications. This book helps you raise knowledge management system design to the level of business strategy and pull strategy down to the level of systems design—without undermining either. Through an analysis of the nature of your business, this book helps you balance codification versus personalization, knowledge exploration versus exploitation. It will also guide you through the process of making a strong case for knowledge management to effectively "sell" it to both your potential users and senior management.

Analyze Knowledge Existing in Your Company

You must begin with knowledge that already exists in your company in various forms. This book will describe the process of assembling an appropriate knowledge audit team, the actual steps involved in the audit process, and the methods for analyzing implications of those results on the system's design.

Build Upon, Not Discard, Existing IT Investments

The value of supporting knowledge management with technology comes from leveraging existing IT investments. This book shows you how you can build further upon these infrastructural pieces and identify which components can be used *as is* and which need further development. We discuss how existing networks, GroupWare, intranets, data mining tools, collaborative platforms, and data warehouses differ from the knowledge management system itself and how these might fit. We will also examine emerging technologies such as intelligent agents and their potential use in your system, the level of complexity associated with their development, and cost-reduction alternatives.

Focus on Processes, and Tacit, Not Just Explicit Knowledge

Tacit knowledge is perhaps the most important component of knowledge that exists in your company and one that is least supported by IT. This book helps you incorporate support for tacit knowledge sharing and transfer, rather than repeat the same old mistake of ignoring it as information systems design has done to this point.

Design a Future-Proof, Adaptable KM System Architecture

This book describes the seven-layer knowledge management system architecture and guides you through the process of customizing it specifically for your own company through a series of diagnostic iterations. We will also analyze the appropriate choice of collaborative platform based on your project's strategic leanings and past investments. This book further helps you "future-proof" this blueprint so that it is immune to technological changes that could threaten its usability a few years down the road.

Build and Deploy a Results-Driven KM System

This book shows you how to use results-driven incrementalism (RDI methodology) so that each increment in your system is based on the previous increment's results. In other words, the entire system is driven by business results, avoiding common pitfalls—both cultural and technical—that such a system is vulnerable to. We'll also analyze the process of selecting pilot deployments before the system is introduced on an organization-wide scale.

Implement Reward Structures, Leadership, and Cultural Enablers Needed to Make KM Work

This book shows you that having a chief knowledge official (CKO) is not always a great idea. It will help you evaluate the need or lack of need for a CKO or equivalent manager. It will help you determine the type of knowledge-sharing culture and KM-friendly reward structure that is needed to make knowledge management work in your company. Through several examples of companies that have been very successful even with moderate technology and those that have failed miserably even with the best technology, I illustrate the criteria that might work in your own company.

Calculate ROI and Apply Knowledge Metrics

A common myth is that knowledge management returns on investment (ROI) cannot be calculated. This book shows you that both the long-term and in the short-term benefits of KM can be accurately calculated, although with difficulty. Many managers whom I have informally surveyed have complained that without tangible short-term results, it is difficult to sustain senior management support for knowledge management. This book demonstrates how ROI from KM can be calculated both in dollar figures for the short term and in terms of tangible competitive gains in the long term. We'll analyze the balance that needs to be struck between these two temporal measurements and ways of determining that balance point for your own company.

Learn From War Stories

And, yes, this book does include "war stories" from managers who have struggled with the concept of knowledge management—some have become KM legends and some still need this book! There are high-profile knowledge management pioneers, and then there are market leaders who fell victims to disruptive technologies and practices. Such war stories and results from early adopters are interesting examples but dangerous strategies for reasons that I will soon describe.

Why Not the "M" Word?

The following chapters provide a roadmap that I will refrain from calling a methodology. The term *methodology* connotes a process that can be carried out in almost the same way in just about any company and still deliver the same results. No two companies are exactly the same. Calling the process of knowledge management implementation a methodology undermines both its company specificity and its complexity. Every phase and, in turn, step on this roadmap will help you develop a knowledge management strategy in the context of *your* own company. By focusing on the right questions, you can arrive at answers that are right for your situation.

GENERAL WARNING: "MANAGERIAL INSTINCT NOT INCLUDED"

The 10-step roadmap provides you with a tool, a mechanism, an enabler to which you need to add the most important ingredient: your instinct. This includes intimate knowledge of your own company, its existing culture, its strategic focus, and its unique problems. Through every step on this roadmap, you'll find the answers to both developing KM strategy and a strategically aligned KM system by asking the right questions. Every step is illustrated with examples of both successes and failures.

These are not examples to blindly follow but examples to help you comprehend the intricacies of the KM design process. You will find recommendations for design. You must take these recommendations and judge their fit relative to your own company. This book serves you as a toolkit, but no one else but your own team can use this toolkit to develop a knowledge management solution that works in *your* company. Implementing knowledge management sounds easier than it actually is, but don't let this keep your company from starting now. There might never be a second chance.

HOW TO USE THIS BOOK

In spite of the hyperlinked, Weblike world we live in, I highly recommend that you go against that notion and read this book in a linear fashion: Begin with Chapter 1 and continue through Chapter 4. Once you reach Chapter 4, if you have a strong reason to jump to any other chapter, do so. Chapters 5 through 14 make the most sense if you read them *after* you've read Chapter 4. The reason for this recommendation is simple: Each of Chapters 5 through 14 represent one step of the 10-step roadmap that I introduce in Chapter 4. The 10-step roadmap appears at the beginning of each of Chapters 5 through 14, with details of the current step highlighted in the respective chapters. As with any roadmap, this serves the purpose of a "you are here" sign. The accompanying CD-ROM includes an interactive version of the road map and customizable analysis forms that appear throughout this book. Every chapter but Chapter 1 ends with a "Lessons Learned" section that summarizes the key points covered in that chapter. This might be useful as a checklist when this book is not gathering dust on your bookshelf.

Chapter 16 discusses software tools that might be relevant to your own knowledge management system. Some of these are also included on the companion CD-ROM. Most, though not all, tools on the CD-ROM have feature restrictions of some type. They are there not to give you entire software suites to help you cut down the expense of building a knowledge management system or to charge you an extra five dollars for a CD-ROM that cost only 50 cents to produce. These tools are here because I believe that they add value and help you make better sense. They are here for you to actually be able to see the technologies that we talk about in the chapters that follow.

How This Book Is Organized

Table 1-1 summarizes the organization of this book. An additional table in Chapter 4 (Table 4-1) leads you through the individual phases and steps of the knowledge management roadmap.

Table 1-1 How this book is organized

Chapter	What is covered
PART I: THE RUBBER MEETS THE ROAD	
Chapter 1	Introduction, KM's value proposition.
Chapter 2	Imperatives for KM, its need, potential business benefits of KM.
Chapter 3	How to make the transition from IM to KM, topologies of knowledge, differences between IT tools and KM tools, why KM is difficult to implement.

Table 1-1 How this book is organized (cont.)

Chapter	What is covered
PART II: THE ROAD AHEAD: IMPLEMENTING KNOWLEDGE MANAGEMENT	
Chapter 4	10-step roadmap for implementing knowledge management in your company.
PART IIA: THE FIRST PHASE: INFRASTRUCTURE EVALUATION AND LEVERAGE	
Chapter 5	The role of IT in KM, tools and enabling technologies that can be used to build a knowledge management system upon your existing IT infrastructure.
Chapter 6	How to align business strategy and knowledge management in *your* company, creating knowledge maps, analyzing strategic knowledge gaps to fill with KM, how to "sell" KM in your company.
PART IIB: THE SECOND PHASE: KM SYSTEM ANALYSIS, DESIGN, AND DEVELOPMENT	
Chapter 7	How to lay the infrastructural foundations of your company's knowledge management system and choose the collaborative platform, the seven layers of the KM architecture.
Chapter 8	Audit, analyze, and identify existing knowledge assets and candidate processes in your company.
Chapter 9	How to design a right-sized and well-balanced knowledge management team.
Chapter 10	How to create a knowledge management system blueprint customized for your company, define the seven layers of the KMS architecture, "future-proof" your design.
Chapter 11	How to develop the knowledge management system, understand how it can be integrated with existing technology standards such as WebDAV and DMA.
PART IIC: KMS DEPLOYMENT	
Chapter 12	How to deploy the system using the results-driven incrementalism methodology, select pilot projects, maximize payoffs, avoid common pitfalls.
Chapter 13	Understand the reward structures, cultural change, and leadership needed for making knowledge management successful; in your company, decide if you need a CKO or equivalent manager.

Table 1-1 How this book is organized (cont.)

Chapter	What is covered
PART IID: THE FINAL PHASE AND BEYOND: MEASURING ROI, EVALUATING PERFORMANCE	
Chapter 14	Decide which metric(s) to use for knowledge management in your company—balanced scorecards, quality function deployment, Tobin's q—and how to use it, arrive at lean metrics that help you calculate ROI on your KM project.
Chapter 15	Case studies and examples of knowledge management projects in U.S. and European companies, early adopters, successes, and failures.
Appendix A	Knowledge management assessment kit and CD-ROM forms.
Appendix B	Alternative structural approaches for the knowledge management front end.
PART III: SIDE ROADS: APPENDICES	
Appendix C	Software tools and CD-ROM documentation.
Appendix D	Web resources and pointers.
Appendix E	Bibliography and further reading.

ASSUMPTIONS ABOUT YOUR COMPANY

There are certain assumptions that I make about you as a reader of this book. I would hope that most, if not all, of these are true if this book (which is written with these assumptions about you as a reader in mind) is to help you and your company with implementing knowledge management.

My first assumption is that you are neither a diehard propeller-head nor a manager who can't remember how to check his e-mail every morning. In other words, irrespective of your technical or managerial background, I assume that you at least have an appreciation for both the significance and limitations of technology and corporate culture. KM requires an appreciation of the fact that neither culture nor technology can independently provide a strong KM solution. KM design and strategy formulation is at least as much a management issue as it is a technical one. I am assuming an open mind there. And yes, a diehard PalmPilot user qualifies as an acceptable reader!

I also assume that your company already has a company-wide network in place and that everyone is probably connected to the Web at work. If this assumption is violated, you will need to do some serious work on creating such a network to build the transport layer of the KMS architecture in your company.

I also assume that your company is not at a stage where information paucity itself is the problem. If that is the case, then you are probably not ready for knowledge management as approached in this book. I further assume—since you are reading this book—that you have been previously exposed to the idea of knowledge management or at least have heard that companies are beginning to invest in knowledge management. I further assume that you realize that most of the information flowing through and stored in your company's information systems is explicated.

My Vocabulary: More than Words Can Say

This book also rests on some of my own assumptions and vocabulary nuances. This book uses the terms *firm, company,* and *business unit* interchangeably. The techniques described in this book need not always be applied across the organization; they can be applied at the level of *communities of practice.*[h] These communities can be as small as a specific department or a division, intermediate such as several departments, or as large as an entire enterprise. In any case, by calling your business unit a firm, I assume that your business operates at least *like* a for-profit organization.

I also assume that you will use the process described in the 10 steps of the four phases to arrive at your knowledge management design and not flip directly to Chapter 15 and try using a case as your KM strategy's basis. A roadmap is like a map—it provides direction but you do the driving. In contrast, a methodology is like a shortcut to arriving at the destination. Figuratively speaking, it's like taking a flight (that flies all its 300 passengers in exactly the same way) rather than going the harder and longer way, i.e., driving. But, just an activity as highly structured and "shrink-wrapped" as taking a flight gets you *and everyone else* to the same destination—the airport, a methodology gets you to the same place as your competitors. A uniquely tailored roadmap helps you take your own company into account to build a KM system and KM strategy that is hard for your competitors to imitate.

I use the term *CKO* with much disdain for the title. Since this term is an easy descriptor, I use it to refer to anyone in your company who plays the CKO's role, whether it's you, a senior manager, a senior IT manager, a knowledge champion, a strategist, or any one else in your company who *actually* plays the lead role of a knowledge management evangelist or proponent.

WHAT THIS BOOK IS NOT ABOUT

I have explained what this book is about. Let me also explain what this book is not about and what it is that distinguishes this book's approach.[35] This book is:

---

[h]Communities of practice, a description proposed by Etienne Wenger, refers to informal networks of people who share common objectives, interests, or solutions.

- *Not about trends*: This book is not about trends. Trends change: That is why they are called trends. The principles that this book is based on come from years of cumulative research that has withstood the test of time. You've probably heard that organizations are now becoming decentralized, dis-intermediated, organic, flattened and T-shaped. You've probably heard this in knowledge management conferences and books that attempt to forecast the future. The methodology for such forecasts is often an extrapolation from recent developments and past data. Such extrapolation, as all research, weather forecasts, and stock markets suggest, is rarely an accurate predictor of the future. What you'll learn in this book will probably still apply when organizations supposedly become e-shaped, intermediated, or inorganic. Rather than being a trend in itself, this book will help you benefit from those trends.

- *Not about new vocabulary:* This book is not out to invent new buzzwords. You won't hear about the *infobahn, just-about-anything.com, cyber-space, cyber-economy, cyber-knowledge,* or *cyber-anything.* Buzzwords come and go, knowledge management is here to stay.

- *Not about the silver bullet:* This book is not the silver bullet for knowledge management and does not claim to be one either. It is not about trademarked methodologies that promise the world but scarcely deliver a village. If you are actually reading this book, then you have probably already found the silver bullet that you've been looking for: knowledge.

- *Not about socialism:* This book assumes that you are in business because you are out to achieve "something" beyond the general good of society. For most businesses this good is cold hard cash, for some it is not. My assumption is that your company is out to survive and compete.[i]

- *Not about analogies:* Business strategy is business strategy. Analogies can sometimes be helpful but can also be very misleading. Analogies are an effective way of communicating strategies, but a *very* hazardous way of analyzing them. This book is not about analogies for running your business. Nowhere in the following pages will you find a discussion about how knowledge management is like ecology, bungee jumping, war, or making love. The same holds true of the cases discussed in this book. Cases are instances of strategies, not strategies themselves.

- *Not about* my *opinion:* Opinions can be wrong. Sometimes totally wrong. If Peter Drucker can have an opinion that was dead wrong,[j] so can your latest Armani-clad $800-per-hour consultant whom you might be betting your company's future on. This

---

[i]Government and nonprofit organizations are not excluded by this characterization: The U.S. Postal Service, for example, is a competitive not-for-profit capitalist "company" that competes against the likes of FedEx and UPS. Knowledge, as this book deals with it, is not without a purpose and a business objective.

[j]See Peter Drucker's own discussion in *Management Challenges for the 21st Century,* Harper Business, New York (1999).

book is not built upon a couple of "best-practices adopted from my company" or *my* "brainchild" thoughts about how *you* should run *your* business, but on lessons learned from years of cumulative research spanning several countries and hundreds of companies, big and small, in diverse industries. Wherever there is an opinion, I'll tell you it's an opinion and that opinion is not necessarily a fact.

Let us begin by taking a closer look at how knowledge and knowledge management are generating a competitive edge for some companies, in the next chapter.

CHAPTER 2
THE KNOWLEDGE EDGE

IN THIS CHAPTER

- ✔ See how knowledge contributes to market valuation and corporate prosperity.
- ✔ Understand why knowledge can deliver a sustainable competitive advantage and increasing returns.
- ✔ Know the key drivers of knowledge management.
- ✔ Realize how knowledge management helps avoid reinvention of solutions, loss of know-how, and repetition of mistakes.
- ✔ Understand how knowledge management can help companies deal with complex expectations, intricate processes, compressed life cycles, deregulation, globalization, the need for predictive anticipation, and product-service convergence.

A LITTLE KNOWLEDGE THAT ACTS IS WORTH INFINITELY MORE THAN
MUCH KNOWLEDGE THAT IS IDLE
—KHALIL GIBRAN

When engineers at Ford[1] looked back at their record-breaking bestseller, the Ford Taurus, no one in the entire company could really place his finger on the reason why the car had become such a runaway success. PalmPilot, the nifty little personal digital assistant (PDA) made by 3COM,[a] became an instant bestseller as soon as it was introduced, gained a market share of several million and growing, and a huge following of loyal and diehard fans that beats even that of the original Apple Macintosh (and since, the iMac). Two major companies, Texas Instruments[2] and Sharp,[3] released feature-richer, more powerful, and faster PDAs competing hard on prices, features, and value for the consumer's dollar. Texas Instruments' Avigo, a PalmPilot lookalike, had all the features of the PalmPilot plus some more, cost one-third as much and came with more software and an infrared wireless data link to connect to laptops.

With all those features, better prices, and arguably better value for money, it still could not stand up against the PalmPilot. If it was not price, features, or value for money, what is the basis of competition between these products?

Getting to Why: The New World

With an incredible $155 billion in sales, Ford Motor Company (www.ford.com) came second to General Motors (www.gm.com) on the 1998 Fortune 500 list. Taking classical value determinants into account, all off the assets of this company add up to $280 billion.[4] This makes it a rather immoderately wealthy company. Chrysler came seventh on the list, with $62 billion in sales and $60 billion in assets. Interestingly, even on a global level, Mitsubishi Corporation came in around the top of the Global 500 list with $179 billion in sales and $72 billion in assets.

The Missing Pieces

Microsoft ranked 137th on the Fortune 500 list, with $12 billion in sales and $14 billion in assets. On first thought, it might seem almost unimpressive compared to giants like GM and Ford. But a look at the market valuation of Microsoft reveals the other side of the story: It runs up to about $400 billion, far exceeding the market valuation of General Motors, Ford, and Mitsubishi combined. Other companies include Microsoft's longtime partner, Intel, which ranked thirty-seventh on the Fortune 500 list. With $25 billion in sales and a hard asset base of $28 billion, most of which is in the form of factories and semiconductor chip "fabs"[b] in addition to factory and office buildings around the world; its market valuation comes close to $130 billion.

Accounting for Abnormal Differences

Monsanto, a company whose main line of business is drugs and artificial sweeteners, happens to be another one in the same league. Monsanto had $9 billion in sales, built on its asset base of $10 billion, yet the market value of $32 billion was approximately three times any of these figures. IBM's value, contributed in part by its acquisition of Lotus and Lotus Notes, was $20 billion more than its annual sales of $78 billion.

---

[a] The PalmPilot™ was originally manufactured by US Robotics and later acquired by 3COM. In late 1999, Palm devices owned 70 percent of the hand-held computing device market share.

[b] *Fabs* is a semiconductor industry term used to describe clean-room factories that manufacture microchips.

Table 2-1   Top U.S. Companies Based on Capital-Based Products and Their Hard Assets

Company	Annual sales ($ billions)	Hard assets ($ billions)	Fortune Rank in 1998
Ford	155	280	2
Chrysler	62	60	7
Mitsubishi	179	72	2 (Global rank)

Source: All figures are quoted from 1998 Fortune 500 ranks.

However, if you take a closer look at how the value of a company is determined, you will notice another measure called *market valuation.* In simple terms, this represents *the* measure of value that the investors and markets associate with a company. It is only when you take into account these figures that you realize that the prosperity level of a firm is not what it seems to be on the surface. These companies, even with assets running into tens or hundreds of billions, are less well off than they might seem at a first glance. A cursory glance at Tables 2-1 and 2-2 reveals the startling absence of companies with the highest market valuations from the Fortune capital asset-based list. Market value, and not capital assets or sales, drives the long-term health of a company.

Table 2-2   Top Fifteen U.S. Companies With the Highest Market Values

Company	Market valuation ($ billions)
Microsoft	$375
General Electric	$335
Intel	$200
Merck	$195
Wal-Mart	$194
Pfizer	$172
Exxon	$161
IBM	$159
Coca-Cola	$158
Cisco Systems	$155
MCI WorldCom	$152
AT&T	$149
American International Group	$141
Lucent Technologies	$134
Citigroup	$133

Source: Forbes Inc. Data from TableBase.com, Feb 1999, updated June 1999.

As Table 2-2 reveals, neither Ford, Chrysler, nor Mitsubishi even appears on the list of the top 15 companies with the highest market values. This ranking implies that neither investors nor the markets perceive these capital-intensive, production-oriented companies as having more value than even Citigroup, which comes last on the list.

At first these observations seem quite contradictory and out of the ordinary. But consider the businesses that these companies are in: Microsoft makes operating systems such as Windows, Intel makes microprocessors that run Windows PCs, Merck and Pfizer produce innovative drugs, Coke has enough loyal fans like me who refuse to drink Pepsi, Lucent invented the transistor and now produces, among other things, semiconductor chips, and Citigroup operates in the financial markets, and Citibank is a major issuer of credit cards. None of these are "Internet" companies riding the fabled Internet stock bubble. These are all companies with "real" assets such as buildings, manufacturing facilities, equipment, and offices far lesser in value than their market valuation. Even the few odd ones here have something in common with the rest: They are capital intensive but not capital centric anymore. Wal-Mart, for example, is not viewed as a discount store by investors and not valued on the basis of what is on its shelves.

Then what is the basis of their value?

A COMMON THEME

You might argue that our 15 leaders are all companies that have been around for a while. True, but let's take a look at Table 2-3. These are companies that are relatively new, many of them started well after 1997. Several have market values approaching several tens of billions. Not all of them are Internet companies either.

In 1998, Amazon.com, the leading online retailer of books, paid well over $100 million to acquire a smaller Web-based company, PlanetAll (www.planetall.com). Amazon itself had yet to make money, yet its market value is approaching $20 billion, and its stock price has been touching unbelievably high levels.

One common theme that brings together all these companies and their very different reasons for being successful. Companies like Microsoft, Intel, AMD, Cyrix, Netscape, Coca-Cola, eBay, eFax, and Yahoo share something that cannot be shown on the balance sheets and cannot be accounted for by the taxation department! Their intangibles:

- Brand recognition
- Industry-driving vision
- Patents and breakthroughs
- Customer loyalty, their reach
- Innovative business ideas
- Anticipated future products

Table 2-3 Market Valuation of Some Recently Founded Companies

Company	Market Valuation ($ millions)
eBay	$24,000
Amazon.com	$18,024
Priceline.com	$15,000
eToys Inc.	$6,000
Broadcast.com	$4,000
Infospace	$2,300
Go2Net (formerly MetaCrawler)	$1,400
Value America	$1,034
Marketwatch.com	$712
Xoom	$700
eFax	$139

Source: Yahoo Finance. Figures are as of June 8, 1999.

- Past achievements
- Ground-breaking strategies

Whether it is the creation of a new retail channel for books through the Web (Amazon), the creation of a graphical Web browser (Netscape), a technological application breakthrough that can potentially kill the existing facsimile market (eFax),[c] or owning the entire market share for PC operating systems and perceivably future operating systems as well (Microsoft)— the achievement that might *now* seem very doable and feasible. But what counts is the fact that they did it first and they did it almost right when it was the least expected. These companies are driven by and valued for their knowledge, not their capital assets.

These are business that both threaten to destroy existing businesses by competing in ways that were never anticipated, or they are businesses that have created entirely new markets by themselves. Just as Amazon-like businesses have the *potential* to replace brick-and-mortar bookstores, eFax has the potential to replace personal fax machine retailers, Value America has the potential to replace your local computer and appliance store, Marketwatch.com has the potential to replace your stockbroker, Priceline.com has the potential to replace your travel agent, and Broadcast.com has the potential to replace all of your cable companies, neighborhood video rental libraries, and your television manufacturers; their likes have the potential to replace your business. Worse still, they have the potential to eliminate your entire market.

---

[c]eFax allows its customers to send fax messages through conventional fax machines and delivers them through e-mail without charging the customer even a penny.

INTELLECTUAL CAPITAL

Companies with high levels of market valuation are often companies with high levels of intangible assets, often referred to as their *intellectual capital*. Intellectual capital might be any asset that cannot be measured but is used by a company to its advantage. Knowledge, collective expertise, good will, brand value, and patent benefits fail to directly show up on conventional accounting documents. No wonder very few companies (like Microsoft with $14 billion in sales) with the highest levels of intellectual and intangible knowledge assets never make it to the upper echelons of the Fortune sales-based ranking list.

A company's skilled people, and their competencies, market position, good will, recognition, achievements, patents, contacts, support, collaborators, leadership, "tuned-in" customer base, and reputation are some of those key intangible assets that are hard to put a dollar figure on, yet they represent most of the market value that these companies have. Even some intangible assets such as reputation can do little to sustain your business if you are Atlanta's most reputable travel agent who still can't match Priceline.com's price *and* service—in other words, value. In the end, the only competitive advantage that sustains is knowledge. Knowledge management provides you the "window," as Drucker describes it, to see opportunity coming and act upon it by applying knowledge that is otherwise idle.

KNOWLEDGE, MARKET VALUE, AND PROSPERITY

As businesses shift from an asset-centric environment to a knowledge-centric environment, traditional value measures become increasingly fallible. When Netscape Corporation (later acquired by America Online) went public a few years back, the market valued this $17 million company at $3 billion at the end of the very first day of trading. Considering the fact that the average company on Wall Street has a market-to-book value ratio of 3, Netscape's opening day trade ratio was a whopping 175. The reasons for this are obvious. The market did not value the company on the basis of its buildings and computers but on the basis of its knowledge assets: its invention of the Web browser, its innovative projects, its patented technology, and its employee-founder Marc Andeersen (who invented the Web browser and continues to work for America Online since that company acquired Netscape in 1998).

Market value also matters to startups or growing small companies. Borrowing capital for expansion into the rapidly opening international markets is not usually easy, since the *typical* company cannot always offer compelling assurances to venture capitalists and external financiers. In a knowledge-based economy, this security is the value of its intangible assets and their perceived future value—which carry more weight than last year's balance sheet or income statement. Market valuation is a pervasive though risky determinant of its

MICROSOFT AND KNOWLEDGE APPLICATION

Knowledge management can make a difference when it enables the application of knowledge. In the technology industry, companies that have prospered are not the companies that invented new technology, but those that applied it. Microsoft is perhaps a good example of a company that had first relied on good marketing, then on its market share, and now on its innovative knowledge—mostly external.

The customer base it built for its Windows operating system was probably its strongest asset when it decided to seriously compete in the Web browser market. Microsoft, a latecomer to the Internet market, came to the sweeping realization that the Internet was going to change everything, including its own product markets. Its strategy took a U-turn in 1995 when it began focusing on the Internet (every software product that Microsoft made in 1999 worked with the Internet in some manner). Microsoft's reputation and strong skills base, coupled with its cash flow provided it with all it needed to compete in the car retail business (www.carpoint.com), then the travel business (www.expedia.com), and more recently in the toy business as well. Besides a strong brand recognition, the company leveraged its existing collective skills to plan for the future.

When Microsoft began delving into the toy market in late 1998 with its Actimates™ series of electronic toys (including Barney and Arthur), it brought together its competitive advantage from manifold sources within Microsoft: marketing abilities, software capabilities, hardware skills, and its brand value.

Bob Ingle, president of new media for Knight-Ridder, commented in Fortune that "Microsoft is like Godzilla—it screws up but keeps coming!" A good example of a failed attempt was Microsoft's online services division, Microsoft Network, which failed to replace either America Online or *the* Internet. But the company learned. Microsoft is led by the richest man in the world; a fierce, tireless competitor who hires people with the same qualities. The company has $10 billion in cash, more than three times Knight-Ridder's annual revenues. With approximately $6 billion invested in research and development in 1999, Microsoft is an exemplary case of a company that is learning to leverage the biggest competitive advantage of all: knowledge.

Even though there is no publicized KM agenda within Microsoft, it has been essentially managing knowledge all along. The critical difference between Xerox's legendary Palo Alto Research Center (PARC) and Microsoft is that PARC created a lot of knowledge but Microsoft (and Apple) actually applied it to make the difference, create new markets, and generate economic value.

future potential and explains why companies like Apple[d] and Netscape ever got financed in the first place.

The Back of the Envelope at Ford Motor Company

Ford manufactures a broad range of cars and trucks targeted at various consumer segments. A study done at Stanford University reveals how knowledge utilized in the conceptual design stage of a typical Ford car drives between 70 to 90 percent of its final life-cycle cost.[5] Even though design accounts for only 5 percent of the final cost of a typical car, it influences 70 percent or more of the vehicle's final cost. Similarly, material (as shown in Figure 2-1) constitutes 50 percent of the final cost of a typical car, but its influence on the final cost is only about 20 percent.

Most conceptual design and decision making are done with canonical tools and "low technology media" such as *paper and pencil on the back of an envelope*[6] because of their flexibility and agility. Even with seemingly labor, and raw-material-intensive products, Ford's major cost drivers are its decisions in the design process. By perfecting the design process, Ford can ensure that the price tags on its cars remain competitive. It is in companies like this, that we have always taken for granted in the conventional economy, there lies the potential for effectively leveraging past experience and process knowledge to generate a sustainable advantage that can keep them far ahead of their pack.

THE 24 DRIVERS OF KM

Knowledge has been the staple source of competitive advantage for some classic companies (such as Coke) for hundreds of years—not exactly a new concept.[7] Turbulently changing environments, rapidly evolving technologies, and a different breed of knowledge workers create the demand for an entirely new organizational structure that is process oriented, team based, brain rich, but asset poor. Except for rare cases of intangible assets (such as Coke's formula) that do not grow if shared, knowledge grows in value if it is appropriately shared.

In the long run, technology, laws, patents, and market share fail; nothing provides an advantage beyond temporary. Technology provided Citibank only a temporary competitive advantage when it first introduced the automated teller machine (ATM). Duplicating pieces of differentiating technology might be expensive, but not impossible. Before long, any technology that provides a competitive advantage to one business becomes a staple component of the services and products offered by any firm engaged in that business. Citibank lost its advan-

---

[d]The three-part PBS (www.pbs.org) documentary, *Triumph of the Nerds,* provides an interesting story about Apple's financing, as told by its original venture capitalist. This series was later followed by another three-part series by Robert Cringley, *Nerds 2.0,* which provides a historical account of the emergence of the Internet-centric computing business models that have driven several successful multi-billion-dollar startups.

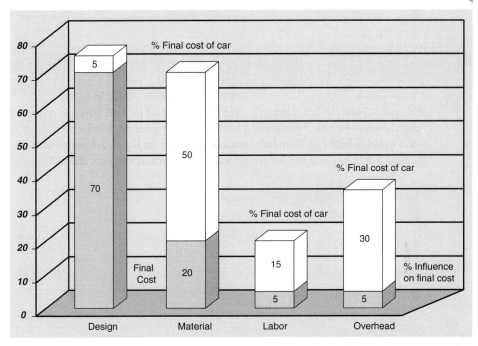

Figure 2-1   Seventy percent of Ford's costs are driven by decisions made in the conceptual design stage, even though this process accounts for only five percent of
the actual cost of its typical car.

tage when other banks started providing ATM services. ATMs were then no longer considered
an added value but expected value.

Microsoft's Hotmail service popularized e-mail systems that allowed users to check their
e-mail through a conventional Web browser. Soon copied, the Web-based interface is now a
norm for most Internet service providers. What was originally an innovative technology application soon became a basic expectation in the consumer market.

Let us examine 24 key drivers that make knowledge management a compelling case for
businesses. Several, if not all, will probably apply to your business, irrespective of your industry. These drivers can be grouped into six broad categories as described below:

Knowledge-Centric Drivers

1. The failure of companies to know what they already know.

2. The emergent need for smart knowledge distribution.

3. Knowledge velocity and sluggishness.

4. The problem of knowledge walkouts and high dependence on tacit knowledge.

5. The need to deal with knowledge-hoarding propensity among employees.

6. A need for systemic unlearning.

Technology drivers
7. The death of technology as a viable long-term differentiator.

8. Compression of product and process life cycles.

9. The need for a perfect link between knowledge, business strategy, and information technology.

Organizational structure-based drivers
10. Functional convergence.

11. The emergence of project-centric organizational structures.

12. Challenges brought about by deregulation.

13. The inability of companies to keep pace with competitive changes due to globalization.

14. Convergence of products and services.

Personnel drivers
15. Widespread functional convergence.

16. The need to support effective cross-functional collaboration.

17. Team mobility and fluidity.

18. The need to deal with complex corporate expectations.

Process focused drivers
19. The need to avoid repeated and often-expensive mistakes.

20. Need to avoid unnecessary reinvention.

21. The need for accurate predictive anticipation.

22. The emerging need for competitive responsiveness.

Economic drivers
23. The potential for creating extraordinary leverage through knowledge; the attractive economics of increasing returns.

24. The quest for a silver bullet for product and service differentiation.

Many of these drivers fall in to multiple categories, a cross-tabulation of domains of influence—illustrated using a wagons and horses metaphor—is shown in Table 2-4.

Let us analyze each of these drivers in order to understand why they make a compelling business case for knowledge management.

Table 2-4   KM Wagons, Their Contents, and Their Horses

Wagons (Category)	Contents (factors)	Horses (drivers)
Knowledge-Centric	Awareness Distribution Emergence Preservation Application Creation Validation	{1}, {2}, {3}, {4}, {5}, {6}, [7], [13], [14], [19], [20], [23], [24]
Technology	Pressures Failures Influence Strategic use	{7}, {8}, {9}, [8], [23], [24]
Organizational Structure	Convergence Structural emergence Effects on structure Moderating influence of IT Impact of knowledge flow Deregulation Globalization of divisions Strategy	{10}, {11}, {12}, {13}, {14}, [15], [17], [22]
Personnel	Cross-functional collaboration Functional convergence Mobility Fluidity Levels of management Levels of employees Decision hierarchies	{15}, {16}, {17}, {18}, [22], [10], [11], [2], [3], [5]
Process	How-to Know-How ➜ Know-what Reuse and accuracy Responsiveness Strategy implementation	{19}, {20}, {21}, {22}, [24], [23], [14], [8], [9]
Economics	Bottom line effects Extraordinary leverage Increasing returns Long- short-term considerations Long- short-term goals	{23}, {24}, [1], [2], [4], [7], [8], [12], [16], [19], [21]

Legend: Numbers in brackets represent drivers in the list: {Primary drivers} [Secondary drivers]. Each broad category is shown as a wagon, and each wagon is pulled by several horses (third column, representing drivers).

KNOWLEDGE-CENTRIC DRIVERS

Knowledge-centric drivers for knowledge management emerge from the recognition of the business value of knowledge. The failure of companies to know what they already know, the need to improve work processes through improved distribution of knowledge, the need for overcoming barriers to flow and retention of knowledge, the need to unlearn what is no longer valid, and the culture of knowledge hoarding dominant in most companies are a few of these drivers that we discuss next.

FAILURE TO KNOW WHAT YOU ALREADY KNOW

Companies often don't know what they *already* know. This is almost always the root cause of companies reinventing old wheels. The British patent office uses an interesting story that makes this point. A major British chemicals company was developing a process that had gone through several iterations in its pilot tests a few years ago. As the company scaled up this process to its full production level, a flaw in the seemingly perfect solution showed up: A sludge deposit was produced at the bottom of the process tank. The company, attempting to salvage its development, invested in further research hoping to eliminate this problem. Soon, the researchers realized that it was going to be a time-consuming and expensive proposition. As plans for an initiative were being finalized, a junior team member decided to investigate existing patents just in case some other company had already encountered a similar problem. Licensing the process, they thought, might be cheaper than developing it from scratch. The patent office searched through all its patents and found one that was a perfect fit. You guessed it: The patent belonged to the very same company! No one in the company knew about it until the patent office clued them in. Knowledge management can help companies know what they do know.

THE EMERGENT NEED FOR SMART KNOWLEDGE DISTRIBUTION

Every day, companies and their knowledge workers are faced with problems stemming from lack of smart knowledge distribution. How familiar do these scenarios sound?[8]

- *Employees can't find critical existing knowledge in time.* Your consulting company is asked to tender a quote for a major client. Collating the necessary information from the company's records or tracking down your own consultants with relevant experience becomes an unrealizable task in the allowable time frame. You do meet the deadline, but your tender documents are far from perfect. Your company loses the bid to a competitor.

- *Lessons are learned but not shared.* You notice that your office in Atlanta is bringing in far less revenue than your office in Boston, even though they are essentially doing the same job and servicing an identical customer base. Lessons learned and best practices followed by your Boston office employees are being learned over again by those in Atlanta. There is neither a sufficient process nor the requisite infrastructure that allows either sharing or transfer of best practices across the two offices. Swapping employees for a few months did not help, even though your company thought it would.

- *Your company can't keep up with competition.* Your biggest competitor seems to be gaining new customers at a faster rate than your company. They also seem to be losing fewer customers to you than you lose to them. Your company does not seem to be learning from its recent mistakes, and your competitors seem to be learning both about your mistakes and about new opportunities at a faster rate than you.

These are common problems that almost any manager will aver that he has seen in his own company. They are typical of companies that have not yet focused on sharing, distributing, nurturing, and managing their only sustainable asset: their knowledge. Even though our examples are from a knowledge-intensive consulting company, we will soon see that these service companies are no different from other manufacturing companies that produce "hard" goods and physical products.

The ability to "smartly" distribute knowledge across the entire organization is therefore another compelling driver for knowledge management.

KNOWLEDGE SLUGGISHNESS

Don't undervalue knowledge gained from failures. Knowledge management initiatives that support active and complete transfer of knowledge from successful projects to new ones could reduce the extent of repeated wasteful expenditure of resources and effort put into solving problems that might have already been solved. Failed approaches and decisions often provide equally useful insights into what *not* to do. Retaining and actively using this knowledge of failures can steer resource allocation into promising directions. Without learning from failures and their analyses, workers pursuing current projects might unknowingly repeat past mistakes.

Lacking a mechanism to find the information they need, people often tend to use incomplete information that they already possess, with the result that designs are generated without the benefit of the related information and expertise that exists within the enterprise, or maybe even within the same department. Two detailed research studies suggest that this often occurs because there is no reliable record of discussion or deliberation.[9] The problem lies solely in the lack of knowledge or its inaccessibility. Knowledge is of little value if it cannot be found when it's needed.

Knowledge asset management looks like a promising neutralizer for this rather expensive exigency.

CAPITALIZING ON PAST EXPERIENCE

Sluggish and nonobvious knowledge can provide some deep insights that can give your business an edge. My poster child case is Wal-Mart's experience with mining its data warehouse. Wal-Mart did data mining on its repositories a few years back and found that a specific item sold in larger than usual quantities along with beer on Friday nights throughout the United States. What was this other item? Every time I have asked my students at the J. Mack Robinson College of Business (where I teach business data communications, intelligent systems, and management information systems,) I get responses that range from being off-the-wall to obscene. But never quite the right one. It was diapers. Baby diapers. Sometimes trends exist, but companies are just not aware of them and fail to leverage them. Data mining might not always reveal such startling pieces of knowledge, but, if done properly, it occasionally comes close.

KNOWLEDGE VELOCITY

Successful companies develop *knowledge velocity,* which helps them overcome knowledge sluggishness, to apply what they learn to critical processes at a faster rate than their competitors. Underlying this concept is the integration of a company's knowledge processes with its business processes to substantially enhance business process performance. The quality and celerity of decisions are anchored directly to employees' ability to access *key* actionable information.

Effective knowledge management systems allow people to learn from past decisions, both good and bad, and to apply the lessons learned to complex choices and future decisions.[10]

TACITNESS OF KNOWLEDGE

While a lot of facts about a firm may be documented in its plans, documents, designs, and databases, much of its experience resides in its employees' heads. Very often, the largest part of a firm's intellectual prowess is not in its organizational intellect, but its human intellect. When the person having that critical piece of knowledge quits to join a competitor, that knowledge also walks out the door. A study conducted by KPMG in 1998 showed that in over 40 percent of the cases it examined, an employee departure caused loss of key clients, suppliers, loss of best practices in his/her area of specialization, and in many cases, a significant loss of income.[11]

Knowledge Walks Out of the Door

Knowledge professionals play a critical role in the knowledge economy. They can demand better working conditions, greater freedom, increased job satisfaction. This means that the knowledge professional will not be easily bound to one company. Certainly, the idea of employment for life is alien to this new breed of professionals. They will job-hop unhesitatingly and go where they can achieve greatest satisfaction.

The banking industry provides an outrageous example of how knowledge that walks out of your company's door can become an instant threat: 60 of the 140 analysts working for ING Baring left the bank and reappeared in the trading room of its competitor, Deutsche Morgan Granfell. Companies wanting to stay on the top must develop a way of revitalizing themselves, not simply by attracting young and fresh people, but rather by renewing and rejuvenating their existing workforce. At the same time, companies need to combat internal inefficiencies in systems, people, and processes that create competitive bottlenecks.

Knowledge management is not the total solution for this problem, but it offers a part of the solution.

KNOWLEDGE = POWER

Most of us, because of the limitations of our very human nature, have a strong knowledge-hoarding propensity. Hoarding is symptomatic of old thinking that does not harmonize in the knowledge-based economy and can undermine a company's ability to move quickly into new markets or compete effectively. But hoarding is a human tendency[12] that can be overcome only by providing an irresistible incentive to share. Bringing in performance measures and incentives that reward knowledge sharing strengthens the benefits of sharing knowledge throughout the organization. Individuals, being task focused, might not have the luxury of available time even if they want to share knowledge that they possess. The solution to this dilemma mandates a culture where knowledge workers are also given the time and space needed to enable knowledge sharing, growth, and the interaction that accompanies it.

Knowledge management, when not obsessed with technology alone, can provide the cultural enablers that overcome knowledge-sharing propensity and foster a knowledge-sharing environment.

SYSTEMIC UNLEARNING REQUIREMENTS

As complex interrelationships within and between companies evolve, the assumptions, rules-of-thumb, heuristics, and processes associated with the ways of doing business and creating products and services change as well. Companies are often caught up in the past and continue to apply old practices, methods, and processes that no longer apply. Companies must learn to unlearn (a term borrowed from knowledge engineering) what they have learned from past experience if it does not apply anymore.

The need for such unlearning is difficult to identify in a complex business environment; knowledge management can potentially provide the devices for recognizing such a need.

CASE IN POINT: AMERICAN AIRLINES

When American Airlines realized that it was making more money selling ticket reservation and routing information through its SABRE reservation system, it had to stop thinking like an airline. It needed to stop believing that its business was focused on selling air tickets and flying its own planes. It needed to focus on itself as an information broker, not as an airline. Realizations like this that allow companies to realign their strategic focus do not come easy and are often too easy to miss. Knowledge management can help identify such shifts, encourage systemic unlearning by monitoring internal and external data, and sift out trends that deserve immediate attention. Data warehousing proponents had high hopes that data warehousing could fill these needs. Unfortunately, data warehousing primarily provides a technology-driven internal focus and often fails to integrate and capitalize on the wealth of external competitive knowledge that abounds.

TECHNOLOGY DRIVERS

Technology drivers from knowledge management are either motivated by new opportunities that have arisen for companies to compete through knowledge process differentiation using technology or through their failure to compete sustainably using technology. Next, we examine technology's trials and failures, influence of product, and service life cycle compression caused by technology,

TECHNOLOGY—TRIALS, TRIUMPHS, AND TRIBULATIONS

Technological impetus has revolutionized the way we communicate, store, and exchange data at low cost and high speed. The proliferation of PCs on every employee's desktop has made more information readily available than ever was. Far more work—at all levels and in all industries—is now done in front of computer monitors, keyboards, wireless PalmPilots, laptops, and around coffee tables rather than in the manufacturing shop.

With a typical high-end personal computer costing under $700 in late 1999, processing power is not an issue or financial limitation for any company—big or small—anymore. Of all the touted benefits of technology, the two components that directly affect our ability to manage knowledge are storage and communications capabilities. These storage and communication technology tools, not the enviable processing power that comes with them, enable smart distribution of knowledge. Technology, by itself, is simply an entry-precursor and core-capability *leveler,* not a competitive differentiator.

Knowledge and its effective management hold promise as a robust differentiator, unlike technology.

COMPRESSION OF PRODUCT AND PROCESS LIFE CYCLES

Information, service, and physical product life cycles in most markets have significantly shortened, thereby compressing the available window for recouping the expenses associated with their development. Time-to-market is a critical factor in the development of both services and products. The high-technology industry provides an obvious example of the do-or-die imperative that a fast time-to-market poses, but other industries are not too far behind.

Look at the cellular-phone-enabled personal digital assistant industry. It has experienced the introduction of a flood of competing products, several real-time operating systems (RTOs), convergence of functionality of hand-held devices, palm devices, small phones (such as 3Com's Palm VII), and car communication systems within a short span of about two years (1997–1999). Frequent changes in the software, communication protocols supported, and communication and computing hardware and software are common as prices of products plummet in this market.

As complex and often irreversible decisions need to be made fast, accurately, and repeatedly, knowledge management holds the promise for accelerating this process.

THE NEED FOR A PERFECT LINK BETWEEN KNOWLEDGE, BUSINESS STRATEGY, AND IT

As we move further into the information age, the interesting counterintuitive shift that becomes evident is that of the firm's anthropocentricity—dependence on people. While computing power can move information and data from Boston to Bombay faster than a click on a keyboard, it's the people who turn that information into good decisions. These people in turn depend on their intelligence and experience. Drucker points out that "knowing how a typewriter works does not turn [someone] into a writer!" As knowledge replaces capital as a driver of a firm, it's all too easy to confuse information technology with information and information with knowledge.

The companies that will truly thrive are those that can use their information technology assets to leverage their people's knowledge in ways that are immediately applicable. Ways this could happen include improved processes, decentralized decision making, better performance, beating deadlines, reducing (if not eliminating) mistakes, and satisfying the right customers in the right way at the right time. The list could go on and on.

One common theme throughout all these factors is that a company's ability to help its employees do their job better, faster, and more effectively comes largely through the levers of knowledge. Knowledge management, as Chapter 6 describes, if grounded in business strategy, can provide a perfect bridge between strategy and technology investments.

ORGANIZATIONAL STRUCTURE-BASED DRIVERS

The effect of organizational structure changes moderated by technology proliferation and process changes reverberates a clear need for effective knowledge management. Next, we examine some drivers grounded in organizational structure including the effect of functional convergence, a visible shift toward project-centered forms in companies, effects of deregulation and globalization, and product and service convergence.

FUNCTIONAL CONVERGENCE

Uncertainties inherent in new product and service development processes lead to complex dependencies among and between different functional areas (such as marketing, production, finance, etc.) and require inputs and cooperation from different departments to accomplish joint objectives.[13] In addition to the traditional functional barriers that exist between marketing, design, purchasing, and manufacturing that can be observed in most industrial organizations, the diversity of the expertise needed for complex projects creates serious barriers for commonly accepted and agreed-upon shared understanding. Knowledge management can answer questions about the knowledge assets, trust, and ownership, both before and after the work is done.

EMERGENCE OF THE PROJECT-CENTRIC COMPANY

Companies rely on ad hoc project-centered teams for the sole purpose of bringing together the best of their talent and expertise. While teaming up undoubtedly helps, it also brings other problems. The team involved in a success is often moved to the next high-profile project (and unsuccessful teams might be moved to the lowest-profile project). Expertise gained during development of the product or service is not readily available to project teams working the subsequent versions of the product during its evolution.[14]

In a project-oriented, team-based organizational structure, skills developed during the collaboration process might be lost after the team is broken up and redistributed among other newly formed teams. When such a team is disbanded, the process knowledge acquired by the team and needed for tasks such as product modification, service development, or maintenance is lost for future use.[15] The rapid growth in many skills markets and the shortage of highly specialized skills are critical factors contributing to the severe shortage of qualified personnel and high turnover, especially in high technology and areas of fringe specialization.

Knowledge management provides an opportunity for retaining project knowledge in ways that allow it to be reapplied.

DEREGULATION

Deregulation increases competition like nothing else can. As firms shoot for a more varied product line, converge businesses, experiment with a variety of delivery channels, their margins keep becoming increasingly thinner than razor thin. As margins drop, there is only one way the firm can keep from going broke: cost reduction. At a national level, cost reduction is accomplished through deregulation. Deregulation, not just a U.S. phenomenon, can have the most profound effects here if it occurs in other countries. It's being seen all over the world, from Eastern Europe to the Pacific Rim. If one of your suppliers is in Korea and your competitor's supplier in India was just deregulated, your competitor might have gained an edge over your cost structure just about overnight. The difference between cost reduction by brute force, such as downsizing, and cost reduction by brain force, such as knowledge and skills management, is similar to that between trying all possible combinations of a combination lock and knowing how to pick a lock!

As firms race toward more competitive positions, knowledge becomes a significant driver of competitive advantage under a globally deregulated business environment.

GLOBALIZATION

As national barriers disappear, managing knowledge is becoming the key to accessing timely information about international competitive environments, regional growth rates, economic and cultural issues—information necessary to build a solid global business portfolio. Telecommuting and the penetration of the Internet are catalysts that are speeding up this process unlike anything witnessed before. Twenty years ago, who would have expected that India would be a software powerhouse or that Malaysia would be chock full of semiconductor and hard disk drive factories?

An increase in virtual collaboration and remote teaming among highly distributed teams and partnering firms needs explicit and tacit knowledge sharing. Businesses that once were organized along geographic lines are now reorienting themselves according to markets, products, processes. Companies such as Lotus, Verifone, and Microsoft are using this phenomenon to their advantage by shifting "mental labor" intensive software development and coding to their programmers in India and Russia, who do a good job at one-tenth the wage that a programmer would demand in Redmond, while retaining design and strategic planning at their base offices.

PRODUCT AND SERVICE CONVERGENCE

Strategic innovation occurs when a company identifies gaps in its industry's positioning map[16] and decides to fill them; and the gaps grow into mass markets. Gaps might imply new emerging customer segments that competition might have neglected, new and emerging needs of old customers, or just new ways of delivering products and services. This is a risky business in

WALT DISNEY AND MICKEY MOUSE

Walt Disney has seen the value of intangible assets since the early 1970s. In 1978, the film *Star Wars* generated $25 million from its box office receipts and a whopping $22 million from the sales of Star Wars logo merchandise. In 1979, the retail value of goods using characters owned by Walt Disney was estimated to be over $3 billion. Walt Disney happens to be among a few of the luckier companies that have actually converted their intangible assets into dollar profits. Consistently. Recent successes have only increased the company's income from such royalties even though the figures are not officially available.

which companies like Netscape filled such gaps and made itself a fortune before being bought out by America Online in 1998 for over $4 billion. eFax, a startup company valued at over $140 million, filled such a gap by providing consumers a mechanism for receiving faxes at home without requiring a second telephone line. eBay fueled a latent market for two-way auctions for over six million consumers who were eager to sell and buy just about anything.

Companies that consider themselves producers of "hard" (i.e., physical) products are actually as dependent on a service focus as a consulting company might be. And at the point of gyration of such business lies knowledge: knowledge that is derived from information that flows in and around such businesses. Many companies that manufacture computer parts do not actually own the plants that manufacture these parts: All they do in-house is the design.

These ideas were not born yesterday. This convergence between products and services has been going on for over 100 years, if not more. Hal Rosenbluth, CEO of Rosenbluth Travel, a $1.3 billion[e] global travel management company, was quoted in *Sloan Management Review* as saying that his company was not in the travel business but in the information business. Their biggest competitive advantage was to have understood and applied their knowledge and intuition of how deregulation would change their business. This is not knowledge about the company's product itself but the process that delivers that product. Hence the term *process knowledge.*

The convergence of product-based and service-based companies means that knowledge management cannot and must not be ignored by product or service companies alike. Rosenbluth's forefathers, who started his business generations back, understood this as well, when they realized and believed that they were not in the business of selling ship passages to people who wanted to cross the Atlantic but were in the business of getting whole clans of people successfully settled in then-emerging America.

---

[e]This figure was current as of 1990, when this quote was made. The company is worth a lot more now.

WAL-MART AND SUPPLIER PROXIMITY

Companies that sell towels in Wal-Mart do not own terry towel weaving plants. Their business runs on the information and strategic knowledge pulled from their markets and retailers. That is their primary asset. All the manufacturing actually is done at mills in places like Bangalore and Shanghai to which production is outsourced.

Arkansas offers a perfect snapshot of this, where Wal-Mart's small suppliers have based their offices along the periphery of Wal-Mart's own buildings. Is it the case of being literally close to the customer? It's not being close to the customer; it's being close to the source of information—information that could suddenly becomes useful and turn into knowledge that any small company needs to keep its only customer happy.

Companies that have succeeded on the basis of such a belief abound. Apple Computer, for one: Steve Jobs (the founder of Apple) never considered himself in the computer business but in the "change-the-world business." Howard Schultz, the president of Starbucks (my favorite caffeine overdose spot!) still believes that he is in the "romance-theatrics and community" business and not in the coffee business! Silly as it might sound, these companies have succeeded beyond a trace of doubt, simply because they realized the process knowledge focus (e.g., knowing what the romance or change-the-world business means and doing what it takes to bring substance to that seemingly esoteric perception) and worked hard to keep it in continuous or long view.[f] These companies have successfully reused, recalibrated, and expanded competencies—some of the things that knowledge management sets out to do in the less visionary (than Apple and Starbucks) companies of our times.

BLOWING AWAY THE FREE WEB SERVICE MODEL

Whether it a "hard" physical product such as a BIOS chip (which was reverse engineered to create Compaq Computer Corporation), a methodology (such as methodologies used by consulting companies and the one proposed in this book), a service (such as the pizza delivery concept, which has been copied by every mom-and-pop pizzeria), or a service-product combination (such as Starbucks coffee), it is rarely possible to protect innovation using the law as a primary defense mechanism.

---

[f]Focusing present performance to drive long-term plans of the business.

> ## WAL-MART, DIAPERS, AND BEER
>
> Wal-Mart, for example, used data mining technology to gain critical sales-related knowledge of how beer and diapers sold together on Friday nights, and used it—the knowledge not the information technology—for better inventory management. Wal-Mart's example, although deceptively close, is not that of market research but that of knowledge application. On that account, knowledge and its strategic management are not just an imperative for service companies like consulting firms but also for product-based companies.

Knowledge management can help keep multiple, and oft-changing objectives in mind when the product itself is defined by the service that goes with it, i.e., the two converge almost indistinguishably.

PERSONNEL-FOCUSED DRIVERS

Personnel-focused drivers of knowledge management include the need for improved knowledge transfer, sharing, and creation in cross-functional teams of knowledge workers; the need to deal with complex expectations from such workers; and the need to prevent loss of knowledge as fluid teams emergently form and re-form. Let's take a look at some of these personnel-focused drivers.

CROSS-FUNCTIONAL COLLABORATION

To respond to competitive challenges, otherwise-independent firms have become more closely coupled than in the past, often working in parallel to complete assignments spanning traditional boundaries and functional areas. The creation of today's complex systems of products requires melding of knowledge from diverse disciplinary and personal skills-based perspectives where creative cooperation is critical for innovation. Expertise and skills that are needed for a project might be distributed both within and outside the responsible company; therefore, people from different companies often need to work together to bring in the entire skill set that a product or service might demand. In the development of complex products and services, it is a sine qua non to draw needed expertise from a variety of functional areas such as technical design, engineering, packaging, manufacturing, and marketing.

Different cultures and backgrounds might lead to issues that even an effective knowledge-sharing strategy might not resolve in its entirety. The team members drawn from different disciplines often lack understanding of the critical process factors for areas other than their own. The process of creating, sharing, and applying knowledge requires varying degrees of collaboration. Brainstorming, strategy planning, competitive response, proactive positioning—all need collaboration, often across multiple functional areas, departments, and companies with differing notions, values, and beliefs.

Knowledge management shows promise here because it encourages conversation and discussion, which is the first step toward effective collaboration and effective sharing of knowledge.

TEAM MOBILITY AND FLUIDITY

Fluid "flash" teams or on-the-fly, ad hoc teams formed for specific projects or engagements are often disbanded at the end of the project.[17] Team members are often assigned to other projects over time and across phases where their functional expertise is valued more than their knowledge gained during the process of collaboration with members of other functional areas.

A major threat to the collective knowledge in firms is personnel turnover, since much tacit knowledge is situated (not stored) in the minds of these individual employees. The departure of such employees leads to a reduction in the organizational knowledge and collective firmwide competency. Making employees write a manual or bringing them back in as consultants might not solve the problem. Manuals can be internally inconsistent, invalidated, out of date, and difficult to maintain; and what good does an external consultant do if she has forgotten a good part of what she was trained for four years earlier!

Knowledge management provides processes to capture a part of tacit knowledge through informal methods and pointers and a fairly high percentage of explicit knowledge, reducing loss of organizational knowledge and collective firmwide competency.

COMPLEX EXPECTATIONS

Most businesses today have limited, defined objectives, and they deliver measurable value within strongly imposed structures and rules, but because of their close coupling to unstable markets, they are subject to radical change. They contend with unnatural time scales, unexpected innovations from competitors, shifting markets, and severe mismatches of internal and external pace.

Better, timely,[18] accurate and *just the right* knowledge is what it takes to make strategic decisions that keep such businesses ahead of their competition.

PROCESS DRIVERS

Process drivers are focused on improving work processes through knowledge management.

REPEATED MISTAKES AND REINVENTION OF SOLUTIONS

Talk to any management consultant. It might surprise you how many times companies repeat *exactly* the same mistakes. David Teece reported in the *California Management Review* that the annual aggregate reinvention costs in the United States range between $2 billion and $100 billion.[19] Learning from the past is how things *should* work, but they rarely do. Organizations have been disconcerted by reinventing solutions and repeating mistakes because they could not identify or transfer best practices and experiential knowledge from one location to another or from one project to another. The level to which this problem invades daily work was evident in the show of hands in an informal survey of an incoming graduate business school class that I recently asked, "Have you worked on a project only to realize that you did a lot of exactly the something that someone had done before you?"

Starting from scratch with each new project indicates that knowledge is neither being retained nor shared. When such knowledge—both explicit and tacit—is not retained, a potentially competitive knowledge asset has been squandered and the company incurs unnecessary expense to relearn the same lessons.

PREDICTIVE ANTICIPATION

The ability to anticipate and respond to market trends is a critical capability required of any company. To be truly competitive, a company must be able to see the bigger picture and not just react to trends (reactive) but actually anticipate them (proactive). It is important to recognize in advance the forces that will shape the markets in which your company is operating. It is sometimes too easy for even the best companies to miss a beat here and fall far behind. Microsoft, for example, did not anticipate the explosive rise of the Internet and soon found that Netscape, a seemingly insignificant startup company, had entered a market niche and secured a dominant position.

Barnes & Noble is another good example. The company responded to Amazon.com by using its expertise as a traditional "brick-and-mortar" book retailer. The question is whether the largest U.S. bookseller may actually be cannibalizing its own bookstores by offering its books at a discount through its Web-based store. It's important to recognize that a strong ability to respond does not necessarily imply a strong ability to anticipate.

The ability to integrate external knowledge with internal expertise can provide companies with the capability to proactively anticipate changing markets and respond ahead of time.

RESPONSIVENESS OF COMPETITORS

Reacting quickly to market changes is one of the biggest challenges for companies, and also one of the biggest opportunities.[20] Wal-Mart is a frequently cited example of a company that has put the just-in-time (JIT) inventory management system to good use. Wal-Mart is in the same line of business as many other competitors such as K-mart and Target stores. Wal-Mart is the only retailer that comes on the Fortune 10 list because it delivers value to the customers not just through better products but through exemplary logistics based on knowledge gained from its sales data—and applied to make the difference.

As competitors become increasingly responsive to customer needs, companies must match the effort, using the right application of knowledge within the proper structures and processes. Responsiveness that exceeds that of competitors then becomes the key to differentiation. This often means using knowledge to control processes, many of which are highly complex, demanding literally hundreds of contributing participants and suppliers, each with their own stipulations.

Knowledge management allows companies to apply knowledge in ways that makes them more responsive, and gives them agility.

CASE IN POINT: ASEA BROWN BOVERI

The Swedish company Asea Brown Boveri (ABB)[21] is a global company that makes and markets electrical power generation and transmission equipment, high-speed trains, automation and robotics, and control systems. The company has over 200,000 employees who are led by only 250 senior managers. When formed by the merger of the Swedish ASEA and the Swiss firm Brown Boveri in 1987, one of the key strategies was to move power from the center to its operating companies. The head office staff was reduced from a total of 6,000 to a total of 150 people with a matrix management structure worldwide. Several layers of middle management were stripped out, and directors from the central headquarters were moved into regional coordinating companies. The company was split into 1,400 smaller companies and around 5,000 profit centers functioning as closely as possible to independent companies. At the same time, a new group-coordination arrangement was introduced where everyone in the company had a country manager and a business sector manager, and about 65 global managers ran the eight business sectors.

ECONOMIC DRIVERS

Knowledge defies traditional economics of organizational assets by creating superordinary returns and added value as it's increasingly used. The promise of increasing returns indeed makes KM a more promising investment than many "hard" assets.

EXTRAORDINARY LEVERAGE AND INCREASING RETURNS

Basic economics theory suggests that most assets are subject to diminishing returns, but this does not apply to knowledge.[22] A bulk of the fixed cost in knowledge-intensive products and services usually lies in their creation rather than in manufacturing or distribution. Once such knowledge-intensive products have been created, their initial development cost can be spread out across mounting volumes. In traditional industries, assets decline in value as more people use them. Knowledge assets, in contrast, grow in value as they become a standard used by more and more people, standards on which others can build. Their users can simultaneously benefit from this knowledge and increase its value as they add to, adapt, enhance, enrich, and validate it.

THE OCTICON STORY

Around 1988, Octicon, the Danish manufacturer of hearing aids, had seen its market share and profitability decline as competitors introduced more advanced and cheaper products. When Lars Kolind became CEO in 1990, he set out to create an environment that would promote the flow of knowledge and encourage entrepreneurial behavior because he realized that technological innovation and time-to-market would be critical success factors. Organization charts, offices, job descriptions, and formal roles were abandoned, and company employees were expected to choose their own projects and work in fast-moving, cross-functional teams. Did all this help? One might be inclined to think it did, as these changes produced dramatic results: Return on equity climbed from the low single digits in the late 1980s to over 27 percent in the 1990s as Octicon developed and rapidly commercialized innovative products like its digital hearing aid.

Beyond Economics: Increasing Returns on Knowledge

Knowledge has very different economics from what governs the physical world. Peter Drucker gives the example of a book: When you give a book (a physical asset) away or sell it, you lose it.[23] You cannot sell it again. Conversely, you can sell the same knowledge again and again. Similarly, you can use the same knowledge again and again. This is what economists call the law of *increasing returns:* The more you use it, the more value it provides—thereby creating a self-reinforcing cycle. Knowledge is the only variable that explains the widening gap between a successful company's market value and asset base. Very unlike the economist's finite resources like land, capital, and labor, knowledge and intellectual capital are infinite resources that *can* generate increasing returns through their systematic use and application. Sustainability of a knowledge-based competitive advantage comes from knowing more about the same things than your competitors.[24] It comes from creating time constraints for competitors that keep them from acquiring similar knowledge regardless of how much they invest to catch up. Time, decidedly, is the next source of competitive advantage after knowledge. Knowledge management provides a unique opportunity to integrate knowledge in a manner that lets your company create a time-based advantage that keeps your competition on a consistent lag[25] and in turn, create incontestable economic and market value. Newcomers such as eFAX (valued at over $200 million) and eBay (valued at $22 billion) are not the only examples, Microsoft, SAP, and Nintendo fall into the same category as well.

Overdependence on IT for Competitive Breakthroughs

Companies out to compete on the basis of information technologies have started out on the wrong foot. Information technology can separate the gems from the glut of information that abound in and around an organization, identify new opportunities, and find how the business environment in which you are operating is changing in ways that will affect you. Information—actionable information, a.k.a. knowledge—not IT, can be used for competitive breakthroughs. Information technology is just a part of the means, not an end.

Knowledge management removes this illusory overdependence on IT, and instead focuses on the *I* in IT by getting the right, and relevant, information to the right people in time.

Is It Just High-Technology Companies?

Browning Ferris Industries (BFI) is a solid waste management company spread out across 48 states and 15 foreign countries. With revenues exceeding $6 billion, BFI has been on an acquisition run and has acquired over 1,000 smaller companies. Its 40,000 employees range from managers who manage a multi-million-dollar waste disposal plant to those who throw waste into the back of dump trucks.

When BFI chose 18 of its best managers and gave them a free hand to turn the company inside out, the two significant points of agreement that emerged were the need to revitalize human resources to assess, and to improve what they knew and to accelerate that process. Tapping into the knowledge of the people they work with everyday, across 500 different locations, has enabled BFI to achieve breakthrough results and improvements.

THE QUEST FOR A SILVER BULLET

Companies must constantly look for ways in which they can keep their *knowledge spiral*[26] steadily moving upward. Any competitive advantage that is not based on knowledge can be, at most, temporary. Achieving the upward trend largely depends on a company's ability to create new knowledge. It might mean using R&D to create new products by using existing knowledge in a new way, or it might mean gaining new knowledge about customers. Customer loyalty programs such as the many frequent flyer airline clubs or frequent shopper cards given away by grocery stores provide valuable insight into the spending habits of major target customer groups. In the pharmaceutical industry, for example, companies are using information technology to transform their raw and untapped data resources into competitive tools to provide customers with critical information and value-added services.

Pfizer Inc., a $10 billion firm based in New York, has launched a massive sales-force automation program that enables its 2,700 sales representatives to customize their sales pitches using readily accessible information about any specific drug while providing doctors with accurate details of dosage, side effects, and treatment regulations.

Knowledge management can help companies accelerate the knowledge spiral and, in effect, accelerate both creation and application of new knowledge.

CREATING THE KNOWLEDGE EDGE

Several other companies have tried their hand at managing their knowledge and competencies to effectively compete in a busy, noisy, and cut-throat marketplace. Taking a closer look at some of the more successful efforts (in Chapter 6) will provide us a good starting point to dig deeper into the strategic and design aspects of a business-driven knowledge management strategy and a well-designed knowledge management system. For now, we preview some of those ideas.

COMPETING THROUGH PROCESS

Arthur Andersen is an international accounting, tax, and business consulting firm with revenues exceeding $4 billion. Its employees are spread across its 400 offices in over 70 countries. When a consultant comes across a problem that a client is facing, it is often likely that some other client—maybe in some other country—has faced a similar problem in the past. Rather than have consultants start every new project with a blank slate, AA decided to implement a system called the Global Best Practices™ in mid-1992. The system helps employees share best practices and collaborate as they work with their clients in different parts of the world. The Global Best Practices knowledge base is only one component of the company's knowledge-sharing network. It is complemented by highly specialized knowledge bases and discussion databases resulting from conversations and network-based discussions.

If Arthur Andersen believed that the knowledge base was the end in itself, this highly successful effort might have never gone very far. To keep the quality of the information stored in this knowledge base high, AA screens incoming information in a variety of ways. Hotlines are staffed by what AA calls *librarians,* who perform custom searches on the knowledge base and return the results to the consultant. AA now commercially markets a derivative product called "Knowledge Space." What this case demonstrates is that creation of the technical infrastructure is only the beginning. What becomes critical from that point onward is the skillful management of the process that fosters an environment conducive to knowledge creation and sharing, which the company nurtures, grows, and incrementally improves.

ELIMINATING THE WRONG TRADEOFFS

Although the concept of knowledge has been around since Adam and Eve, its business significance has been recognized on a large scale relatively recently. While discussing this subject at a philosophical level will further develop it at a more conceptual level, your company probably can't be run at a philosophical or conceptual level! Companies desperately trying to implement a knowledge management system often stray from the business strategy perspective to either a technologically obsessed strategy or a deeply philosophical perspective, neither of which does much good in the real world. As a result, either the focus of their plan is too constricted, often to the advantage of the product vendor trying to help them build a knowledge management strategy, or is too broad to be actually implemented. In an ideal world, we would like to have an all-encompassing and theoretically perfect implementation, in the real world, we end up making choices and tradeoffs. Making the wrong tradeoffs could potentially kill not just the knowledge management initiative but your company as well.

BEWARE OF RELABELED CANS OF WORMS

Managing the knowledge assets of a capitalist company is a relatively new and undeveloped area, although research in adjacent areas such as corporate memory systems, organizational learning and rationale capture has been going on for decades. The emergence of knowledge management has opened up a new can of worms, and as we try to cluster them in a smaller number of cans—organizational, technical, managerial, strategic etc—vendors seem to be pointing only to the original big can. This is no different from the kind of problem that was rampant in 1970 when two of the founders of IS wrote about similar problems in electronic data processing (EDP).[g] As companies like Monsanto, Microsoft, and Skandia have started talking more about knowledge management, companies with products from all related areas such as data warehousing, intranets, discussion list tools, and object-oriented database systems have been involved in a relabeling frenzy, touting their products as the ultimate knowledge management solutions. The fact is, however, that there is no one single, canned approach to managing knowledge. What you need is a good understanding of your business, and a convincing business case; only then can you even think of beginning a knowledge management initiative.

THE ROAD AHEAD

In many service industries, the ability to identify best practices and spread them across a dispersed network of operations or locations is a key driver of added value. Such a strategy can create powerful brands that are continually refreshed as knowledge about, say, how to serve customers better, travels across the network. This often results in a commonly encountered dilemma: it may be all but impossible to tell whether value has been created by the brand or by knowledge. How much does McDonald's brand depend on, say, network-wide knowledge of how best to cook french fries?

---

[g]Jones, Malcolm M, and Ephraim R. McLean, Management Problems in Large-Scale Software Development Projects, *Industrial Management Review,* vol. 11 (Spring 1970) 1–15.

> ## X-MILLION SOLD: DEVELOPING
> ## AND TRANSFERRING BEST PRACTICES
>
> McDonald's, for example, gets comparable outlets to work together to benchmark performance, set aspirations, and make product mix and service decisions. These peer groups are supported by a real-time information system that transmits sales to headquarters hourly. The system enables corporate headquarters to keep a tight grip on the valuable knowledge that links its outlets.
>
> However, McDonald's is based on a model in which the corporation defines rigid standards not only for its products but for the processes that deliver them. The company's squabbles with franchisees over its 1999 introduction of the Arch Deluxe product and the 29 cent Wednesday hamburger promotion illustrate the degree to which this formula can conflict with entrepreneurship. There are indications that McDonald's may devolve more decision making to franchisees and seek to learn more from them, particularly about new business development.

LESSONS LEARNED

Knowledge is the key differentiator of companies that have learned to survive and thrive. Intangible assets derived from processes based on the application of knowledge are the key determinants of market valuation of companies—old and new, big and small. To summarize these relationships, I offer a few key points about how knowledge gives today's companies the edge to successfully compete:

- *Market valuation is largely based on intangible assets.* Market valuation refers to the value that investors and stock markets place on your company. In companies that have learned to leverage their intangible assets well, this value might be several times (or even hundreds of times) more than their capital assets. We discussed the example of Microsoft, which has sales of about $14 billion, assets of about $10 billion, but market valuation in the range of $400 billion. We also looked at how eBay, a small startup, catapulted to a market value of $22 billion. This intangibles-driven valuation is not just the case in technology or Internet companies; it is true of any industry.

- *Technology is dead as a source of competitive advantage. Long live knowledge!* Many companies have unsuccessfully tried to differentiate themselves solely through the use of innovative technology. Technology, unfortunately, is too easy to copy. Even if you have patent protection for your new technology, it can either be copied by global competitors in countries where domestic patent laws are difficult to enforce or your patent will provide you a temporary competitive advantage for 17 years (the life of a typical U.S. patent). Knowledge, unlike technology that can be copied or market share that can be threatened by price cutting, provides a source of competitive advantage that is hard for competitors to copy. Even if they do manage to copy your knowledge management technology, they can never reuse it without the context that drives such systems toward successful results.

- *KM has 24 compelling drivers that make it a strong business case.* We discussed 24 points that can help you make a compelling case for knowledge management when you need corporate support and funding to initiate it.

- *Knowledge, unlike any physical asset, delivers increasing returns.* Physical assets—both production-oriented and technological—lose value as they are used. Knowledge, however, increases in value. For example, if you have a small software development business, you can have only so many employees using your workstations, which when being used, cannot be used by others. Similarly, advertising dollars, once spent, cannot be respent. This idea that applies to assets such as equipment and capital also applies to just about any other tangible asset such as buildings, land, factories, etc. Returns provided by knowledge move in the other direction: an enigma that has long perplexed economists.

- *KM helps avoid unnecessary work duplication, expensive reinvention, and repeated mistakes.* Almost any experienced manager has encountered these woes. Effective knowledge management can provide channels for smart knowledge distribution.

- *KM can save your company from "knowledge walkouts."* When an experienced employee leaves your company, two threats emerge. The first threat is that she might have intricate tacit knowledge from which your company derived a fair part of its competitive capabilities. Since tacit knowledge is located between her ears and is difficult to articulate, that knowledge leaves the company with her. The second threat is that she could join your competitor. The critical piece of knowledge that worked for you will then begin working against your company. Knowledge management provides an opportunity to mitigate the effects of such walkouts.

- *KM can compress delivery schedules and help you deliver ahead of time.* Schedules for delivery of products and services have become compressed, and the shelf life of products in many industries is a fraction of what it might have been a few years ago. Where companies try to differentiate themselves through fast delivery, knowledge management can serve two purposes: Through process competence development, it can help your company deliver in the shortest possible time frame and through reuse of existing knowledge; it can do so at a fraction of the cost of starting with a "blank sheet."

- *KM promotes intelligent collaboration.* Collaboration is the centerpiece of knowledge work. Teams often consist of people brought together from different functional areas and companies This practice makes effective collaboration even more difficult. Knowledge management centers on collaborative work in organizations that might be distributed. The principles of knowledge management system design can provide a platform for collaboration that is unlike the constricted information systems in use today.

- *KM can make your company a proactive anticipator.* Mahatma Gandhi once commented, "We must become the change we want to see." The problem with today's business environment is that change occurs so fast that companies barely have a chance to realize that change is occurring until it's too late. Applying knowledge, as opposed to letting it sit idle, lets you proactively anticipate change and strategically react to it. Examples abound. UPS never anticipated that fax machines would drop to $50 when it began offering fax transmission services in the late 1980s. Fax machine manufacturers did not anticipate that companies like eFax would replace their product and take over their target market with some service previously unthought of. Change can take any form: changing consumer preferences, new products, emerging markets, or political changes in countries that are 12 time zones away. Knowledge management provides an opportunity to anticipate such change, realize that it's coming, and lead it.

- *KM can help your company become purposefully opportunistic.* KM is a fountainhead for companies that want turn business environment turbulence into opportunity. With every change in the business environment that can affect your line of business comes an opportunity. Not only does application of knowledge let your business react to change, it also lets you see emerging opportunities for future growth. Knowledge management, by integrating otherwise dispersed knowledge, lets you apply your company's collective knowledge to these emerging opportunities.

- *KM creates process competence.* In the knowledge economy, you cannot compete on the basis of superior products but only on the basis of superior processes. Through process knowledge management, such processes can be incrementally perfected. Examples of Wal-Mart, Starbucks, eBay, eFax, and Netscape described in this chapter can be too easily mistaken for competitive advantage based on market research, best practice transfer, or automation. They are, in fact, examples of applied process knowledge that helped these companies do what they did in the first place.

- *KM has a two-way relationship with corporate agility.* The ability of companies to react comes from their knowledge, and this agility reinforces their ability to apply such knowledge.

In the next chapter, we see how this data → information → knowledge transformation (and a corresponding shift from data management [DM] → information management [IM] → knowledge management [KM] takes place and the enabling conditions plus technology that make it happen. We also take a look at some companies that have been very successful at this transformation and some that have unexpectedly failed. And we look at the corporate determinants of technology choice.

CHAPTER 3
FROM INFORMATION TO KNOWLEDGE

WHAT INFORMATION CONSUMES IS RATHER OBVIOUS: IT CONSUMES THE ATTENTION OF ITS RECIPIENTS. HENCE, A WEALTH OF INFORMATION CREATES A POVERTY OF ATTENTION, AND A NEED TO ALLOCATE THAT ATTENTION EFFICIENTLY AMONG THE OVERABUNDANCE OF INFORMATION SOURCES THAT MIGHT CONSUME IT.
—HERBERT SIMON

Numerous debates have been raised in company boardrooms, industry consortia, conferences, and academia on the true meaning of knowledge. Since I do not intend to contribute any further to this debate, I will take a more conservative approach and attempt to build upon an understanding of what knowledge means to different firms and people. First, though, we must pin down the meaning of data and information, which normally precede knowledge. Without this background, we cannot reach consensus on what we are trying to manage in the context of knowledge management.

Before you can understand and apply the 10-step knowledge management roadmap introduced in the next chapter, you must clearly appreciate the distinction between data management, information management, and knowledge management, relate KM to organizational learning, describe processes used to convert data and information into knowledge, describe knowledge flows, and categorize various types and components of knowledge. This understanding is essential because certain types of knowledge can heavily benefit from information technology (IT), whereas some other critical types are not supported by even the best of technology.

To a man whose only tool is a hammer, almost every problem looks like a nail. The last thing you want to do is to mix up these categories and end up trying to solve a nontechnology problem with an expensive piece of technology while failing to apply the same technology where immediate benefits could have been drawn.

I will use the *knowledge leveragibility* framework to explain various stages of knowledge on a knowledge map. This discussion will provide you the basis to make an initial judgment about your company's readiness for knowledge management. With all the lip service given to knowledge management, very few companies have been able to successfully do it. The few that have, have demonstrated enviable gains in both profitability and competitiveness. The ones that have failed have left us with lessons that I use in this chapter to describe problems, hurdles, and challenges in implementing knowledge management.

FROM DATA TO INFORMATION TO KNOWLEDGE

Let us begin with where we want to go—knowledge—then look at its predecessors: information and data.

KNOWLEDGE

Many of us have an intuitive feel for what knowledge means. I provided an initial definition of knowledge in Chapter 1. With the intention of staying away from esoteric notions of knowledge and using an applicable yet complete description of the terms *knowledge* and *knowledge management,* let us survey formal definitions of knowledge.

- Webster's dictionary gives the following description:

knowledge: 1. applies to facts or ideas acquired by study, investigation, observation, or experience 2. rich in the knowledge of human nature 3. **learning** applies to knowledge acquired especially through formal, often advanced, schooling 4. a book that demonstrates vast learning.

The first definition implies that knowledge extends beyond information. It has something to do with facts and ideas that have been acquired mostly through experience and includes formal and informal learning.[a]

- *Roget's Thesaurus* provides a set of synonyms for knowledge:

  Knowledge.—N. cognizance, cognition, cognoscence; acquaintance, experience, ken, privity, insight, familiarity; comprehension, apprehension; recognition; appreciation ; judgment; intuition; conscience; consciousness; perception, precognition.

  The synonyms give a better description of Webster's highly constricted definition above. The inclusion of intuition, recognition, ken, art, perception, and precognition define knowledge in a more complete manner. Knowledge is deeper, richer, and more expansive than information.

- For consensus, let us stick with Davenport and Prusak's definition of knowledge, which best captures both its valuable and almost impossible-to-manage characteristics.

  Knowledge is a fluid mix of framed experience, values, contextual information, expert insight and grounded intuition that provides an environment and framework for evaluating and incorporating new experiences and information. It originates and is applied in the minds of knowers. In organizations, it often becomes embedded not only in documents or repositories but also in organizational routines, processes, practices, and norms.[1]

  To put it more simply: Knowledge is simply actionable information. Actionable refers to the notion of *relevant, and nothing but the relevant* information being available in the right place at the right time, in the right context, and in the right way so anyone (not just the producer) can bring it to bear on decisions being made every minute. Knowledge is the key resource in intelligent decision making,[2] forecasting,[3] design, planning, diagnosis, analysis, evaluation, and intuitive judgment making. It is formed in and shared between individual and collective minds. It does *not* grow out of databases but evolves with experience, successes, failures, and learning over time.

How Is It Different From Information?

The key link between knowledge and information is probably best expressed in the commonly accepted idea that knowledge in the business context is nothing but *actionable information.* If you can use it to do what you are trying to do, information, arguably, becomes knowledge. One way of looking at knowledge is that it is information stored or captured along with its

---

[a]Formal and informal learning could be through past experience, failures, and successes both within and outside your own company.

context. Knowledge allows for making predictions, casual associations, or predictive decisions about what to do, unlike information, which simply gives us the facts.

Knowledge is not clear, crisp, or simple. Instead, it's muddy,[4] fuzzy, partly structured, and partly unstructured. It's intuitive, hard to communicate and difficult to express in words and illustrations, and a good chunk of it is *not* stored in databases, but in the minds of people who work in your organization. It lies in connections, conversations between people, experience-based intuition, and people's ability to compare situations, problems, and solutions. Only a minuscule portion of this tacit knowledge gets formalized in databases, books, manuals, documents, and presentations; the rest of it stays in the heads of people. While there is nothing wrong with that, it means that the very moment people who have that knowledge walk out of your company, all that knowledge goes with them! In contrast, information can be explicitly stored; it remains behind when people move on.

Knowledge is supported by both formal *and informal*[5] processes and structures for its acquisition, sharing, and utilization. Knowledge workers or employees broadly communicate and assimilate values, norms, procedures, and data beginning with early socialization[6] (when they first fit into the organization and slowly become more willing to share), and the process is continued through ongoing formal and informal group discussions and exchanges. Information, in contrast, is more devoid of such owner dependencies.

TACIT KNOWLEDGE

Breezing past the philosophical underpinnings of knowledge, it's essential to realize at the outset that knowledge management is as much a cultural challenge as a technological one.[7] To be on the safer side, it's better to assume that it is more a cultural issue than a technological one. So any system that is designed to support this endeavor must extend well beyond enterprise-wide technology and take into account the people who will actually use it[8] and contribute to its success.

Knowledge emerges in the minds of people, through their experiences and jobs.[9] While some parts of this knowledge are explicitly captured in an electronic form or hardcopy documents, a more significant portion is not. The portion that does not lend itself to easy capture and storage is the *tacit* component of knowledge. Whatever portion of this knowledge is formalized, captured, or explicated can easily be converted and packaged into a reusable and searchable form. This knowledge is then converted back into tacit knowledge that is learned and absorbed by others in the organization.

As long as your job security and my job security depends on what we know—our skills and level of understanding—it makes you and me more reluctant to share our basic, critically exclusive knowledge and understanding with others, either directly or through networked databases. So any knowledge management initiative that assumes "if we build it, they will come," is predestined doomed for failure. Whatever the design strategy is, it must be devised around the acceptance that knowledge hoarding, to a fair extent, is basic human nature. Without a very strong incentive to do so, we are usually reluctant to give away all that we know.

AN EXAMPLE: TAKING A FLIGHT

Let me give a simple example of typical decision-making "content, " wherein the boundaries between knowledge and its predecessors are, at best, hazy. Suppose I am trying to take an urgent flight from Atlanta, Georgia, to Shanghai, China. If I look up information in the time table shown on a travel agent's Website, I move through the stages of data gathering to knowledge application in the following steps:

1. The Website provides me a flight map along with departure times for flights that currently have seats available. Assuming that there are no restrictions such as visa controls that I might need for my trip to China, I must be able to read and interpret what shows up on the page, to effectively collect the raw data needed.

2. I know that the flight will stop over in London. The flight that leaves in an hour is a British Airways flight that stops over at Heathrow Airport in London. The flight that leaves in another two hours is a Delta flight that stops over at Gatwick Airport in London. Comparing the current time with the departure times, I have the necessary information.

3. I know, however, from a previous trip to New Delhi via London, that flights originating in North America have to transfer passengers over to Gatwick Airport for their connecting flights to the Asian continent. I also know that the bus ride from Heathrow to Gatwick airports takes over an hour. So I realize that the plane that leaves first will not arrive before the one that leaves later. I applied what I knew from previous experience, made a judgment based on this knowledge, and took the later flight, which gave me enough time to pack and shave.

Data and information are essential, but it's the knowledge that can be applied, experience that comes into context, and skills that are used at that moment that make the difference between a good and a bad decision.

Since much of the knowledge that is created in an organization, whether its a 5-employee small business or a 100,000-employee behemoth, is created during the act of collaboration and action, supporting collaborative efforts is a critical part of a KM initiative.

FROM DATA TO KNOWLEDGE

There has been an emerging shift in firms beginning with a focus on data, much evident in the early interest in electronic data processing (EDP) and further refining into information management (IM), and information systems (IS). As firms are beginning to get comfortable with both data and percolated data (i.e., information), the next challenge that comes into the picture is that of making sense of this overwhelming amount of information itself. Where does this process begin?

DATA

Every time you check out at a grocery store, each beep on the cash register adds yet another piece of data to the grocery store's database. The transaction records information from the UPC (Universal Product Code): what product you bought, at what time, and in what quantity. What it does not tell the grocery store is why you bought it, why that specific brand, why at that time, and why so much.

From the perspective of a firm, *data is a set of particular and objective facts about an event or simply the structured record of a transaction.* The event might be the purchase of your favorite beer at the grocery store or a change in the stock price of the stock you might be betting your life's savings on. Such figures, in themselves, do not say anything meaningful. A transaction at a grocery store, for example, does not tell you whether the brand of beer you bought is selling more than the others today—in this store or nationwide—and whether it did so yesterday. In a similar fashion, stock prices do not tell you whether the company is doing better than it was doing yesterday, or whether you would have reaped a windfall had you sold your stock this morning. Such meaning comes to these raw facts and figures once they are converted into some form of information. Though raw data in itself has purpose, it might have little or no relevance.

While there are firms and organizations whose very survival rests solely on their effectiveness and efficiency in handling and keeping this raw data. Thomas Davenport[10] calls these "data cultures," or cultures whose lifeblood is keeping records. The Internal Revenue Service (IRS), the Social Security Administration (SSA), the Census Bureau are examples of organizations with strong data cultures.

The terms *knowledge, data,* and *organizational learning* are subject to varied interpretation and use. Davenport and Prusak suggest that data should not be stored per se into a system for managing knowledge; instead, it should be stored as *value-added information*—by the addition of historical context.

When we talk about managing data, our judgment is mostly quantitative.[11] How much data can be processed in an hour, how much it costs to capture a transaction, how much capacity we have, and so on. Qualitative measures are considered secondary. These measures address issues such as the timely availability of data when we need it and whether the data we need is easily retrievable.

The More, the Better?

The quantity of data captured often gives firms a false illusion of rigor and accuracy.[12] The often false belief that firms tend to stick with is that having collected a lot of data means that ensuing decisions will be good, accurate, objective, and rational. With the extent of technology in place in most businesses, collecting large volumes of data is rarely, if ever, a problem. In fact, a great deal of an effective executive's time is spent seeking out knowledge—not information but knowledge. The fundamental point to note before accumulating a ton of data is that data, in itself, possesses no inherent meaning. Moreover, collecting too much data often makes it even more difficult to make sense of it.

Let's take a simple example. How many times do you think that you could manage your budget better? If you're like me, then it might be often. Take two different approaches. In one approach you know what your income is, and you have a rough idea of how much you spent on major purchases, say, over the past six months. You can then immediately make sense of where major chunks of your money are going and possibly take steps to control them. An alternative data-rich approach would be to take each and every gas, rent, utility, restaurant, and phone bill over the past six months and try to make sense out of all that information put together. You will probably be able to make more sense when you are dealing with a smaller amount of data, as in the first case.

Running even a small business often involves larger volumes of data than a typical family's household budget. As businesses grow, the amount of data that might have been gathered might become so overwhelming that they might end up in an insurmountable *data glut*. Data, although important to firms, has little use by itself unless converted into information. Though raw data might be archived for record-keeping purposes, there is little or no need for that once the information in it has been squeezed out. The point here is that focusing on data for the sake of being accurate and specific is useless if done so at the cost of generating information from it.

INFORMATION AND NOISE

As Peter Drucker describes it, *"information is data endowed with relevance and purpose."* Information has its root in *inform,* which means something that changes or shapes the person who gets it. It is the recipient of this information who decides whether it is truly information or purely noise. If someone told you that Microsoft stock went up by two dollars, and in fact you do own some of it, that information shapes your idea of how well Microsoft is probably doing. However, if someone told you that the Hong Kong stock exchange took a downward plunge, it might have little meaning for you sitting in the United States without a stake in the Hong Kong market, and you might consider that noise rather than information. On the other hand, a person running a company in Hong Kong might find the same message very relevant and will not perceive it as noise. What qualifies as useful information in different situations is a subjective judgment. Fig 3-1 illustrates the conversion process. And that is where the entire problem of generating useful information, information that can help a manager run a busi-

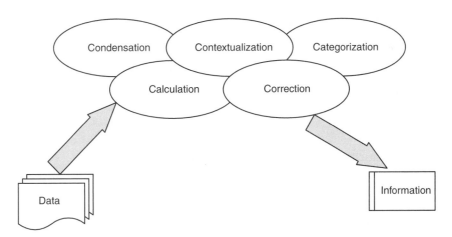

Figure 3-1 The five C's that differentiate data from information.

The five C's, as applied to knowledge management, were originally suggested by Davenport, Thomas H, and Laurence Prusak, *Working Knowledge: How Organizations Manage What They Know,* Harvard Business School Press, Boston (1998). This figure further builds upon that discussion.

ness better, make effective decisions and change things in the right direction, comes into the picture.

Information moves around both in electronic and hard format, through electronic networks and social networks. As the volume of information that flows through our desks grows, we approach the same problem that we once had with data: information overload. This means that there is more relevant and irrelevant information around us than we want to have to deal with. Having too much information is, in some respects, better than having too little, since we can then figure out how to focus only on the information that is relevant and currently applicable. On the other hand, having an overwhelming amount of information that makes it difficult to make sense of it is often no better than having none at all.

Table 3-1 shows different ways in which meaning can be added to data to transform it into information.

The Data-Rich and Information-Poor Society

Look at your checkbook. How frequently do you update its balance register? If you're like most of us, you use the balance register quite frequently. But how frequently do you use it to *actually* make changes in your spending patterns. Rarely? This is exactly is the problem with many organizations and businesses. They tend to collect a lot of data, hoping that it will give them that imaginary esoteric notion of the fountainhead of competitive advantage that any firm yearns for.

The Big Slip Between the Swipe and the Refrigerator

At every swipe that each product at your local grocery goes through and before it ends up in your refrigerator, there is a wealth of captured data. The (UPC) and the accompanying bar code scanner tell the store about the product, its date of manufacture, the time and date the sale was made, who sold it, how it was charged, etc. Although it's exciting to see how much data is captured in one swipe, the threat comes from that very ability: the collection of too

Table 3-1 Different Ways of Creating Information by Adding Meaning to Data: The Five C's

Addition to Data	Result
Condensed	Data is summarized in more concise form and unnecessary depth is eliminated.
Contextualized	We know why the data was collected.
Calculated	Analyzed data, similar to condensation of data.
Categorized	The unit of analysis is known
Corrected	Errors have been removed, missing "data holes" have been accounted for.

Source: Based on a discussion by Davenport, Thomas H., and Laurence Prusak, *Working Knowledge: How Organizations Manage What They Know*, Harvard Business School Press, Boston (1998).

much data all too easily. As firms overcome their inability to gather data by using pieces of technology, they often begin to make an overkill in the amounts of data and information that they capture. The result is that firms end up with overwhelming volumes of data—so overwhelming that they have a hard time figuring out just what to do with it.

Examples of the data-hoarding mentality are not just seen in large businesses. Government-run census data contains invaluable information, much of which is never extracted. Companies running surveys often collect every iota of information, just hoping that each additional piece of data collected *might* be useful for *something* later on. The meaning and purpose of much of the collected data are not clear to the firms that collect it.[13]

Not being able to make sense of a good chunk of data that firms collect is the underlying reason why they try to desperately make sense of it through data mining and similar techniques. The hope driving that is just a two-sided question:

— Can this help us run our business any better?

— Does this tell us what, if anything, is wrong with what we are doing?

The advantage that a firm gains is not from its data riches but from its knowledge riches.

Shared Data

The same piece of data that might represent a piece of useful information to one person might represent nothing more than a meaningless element of data to another. Very often, when data is shared and distributed among people within a firm, it starts to become increasingly useful as some people perceive it as useful, as illustrated in Figure 3-2.

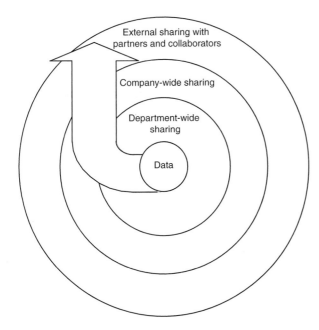

Figure 3-2 Data becomes increasingly useful as it is shared within the department, throughout the company, and beyond the organizational boundaries with suppliers and partners.

As we begin sharing data, value gets added to. Later, we will see in how information technology both enables and supports such value addition to data.

Information Flow Is Not Knowledge Flow

Most managers readily recognize that getting knowledge to move around in a company can be difficult. But, often, as several studies have found, after being convinced by tool vendors and for other reasons, they, *very* inaccurately reduce this problem to an issue of information flow. As a result, a number of companies have invested in intranets with great hopes. Intranets do have their own benefits and, beyond a doubt, add value to the organization. But the value added is that due to the improved information flow, not knowledge flow. While technology has pushed us beyond the point where information flow is not a problem, as people begin to use this information, act upon it, and rely on it for making decisions, it takes a form that resembles actionable information—information that leads to knowledge. Merely making information flow smoothly does not guarantee that it will actually be used. The idea of retrieving locally developed knowledge for use elsewhere does not address the whole issue. Intranets, by themselves, can only help ensure that this information flows.

Companies that have implemented intranets that allow users to provide feedback, add to the content, and validate what is posted have probably taken their first steps toward building an infrastructure for knowledge management. But an intranet, by itself, is not a knowledge management system as some vendors would like you to believe.

BEYOND INFORMATION FLOW

Restricted search and retrieval paths are a significant issue but are not the only issue. Bringing locally created knowledge, say, from a specific department, into view is only the first step toward making that knowledge useful elsewhere. For example, if a company thinks that making its sales figures for its PDA available to its engineering and product development department is covering a lot of ground in sharing knowledge, that company is unfortunately mistaken.

A good case in point is Hewlett-Packard (HP). HP pursued a strategy of making its best practices available throughout the company. Although HP was quite successful in identifying its best practices, it was not successful in moving them from one location to another.

When an intranet, for example, moves the knowledge without the practice, what actually gets moved is the *know-what* without the *know-how*. What does not move this way is the warranting mechanisms and standards of judgment on which people distinguish the valid and the worthwhile from the useless pieces of "knowledge."

The fundamental mistake that companies repeatedly make is that of equating information and knowledge. While the former can be handled well by information technology tools such as intranets alone, the latter is not.

CLASSIFYING KNOWLEDGE

Knowledge—whether it is about your customers, your company's own markets, its products and services, its competitors, its processes, its employee skills, regulatory environments, or methods—can be classified along four key dimensions, as shown in Figure 3-3. These four dimensions are:

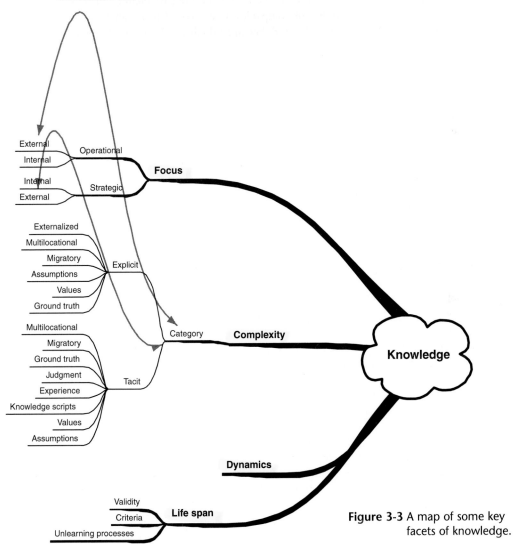

Figure 3-3 A map of some key facets of knowledge.

- Complexity, which includes categories and types, and specifies the degree of context needed to give it meaning and make it useful
- Life span
- Dynamics
- Focus: operational or strategic

As Figure 3-3 only partially illustrates, the complexity of knowledge is closely related to other dimensions. One way of looking at knowledge from a pragmatic viewpoint is to consider one key subdimension, category of complexity. We deal with this next.

CATEGORIES OF KNOWLEDGE

Knowledge can be classified into two broad categories: tacit and explicit. These categories can be subdivided into types. Further, each category consists of various components such as intuition, experience, ground truth, judgment, values, assumptions, beliefs, and intelligence, which must be supported. We discuss types and components in the next sections.

- Tacit knowledge is personal, context-specific knowledge that is difficult to formalize, record, or articulate; it is stored in the heads of people. The tacit component is mainly developed through a process of trial and error encountered in practice.

- Explicit knowledge is that component of knowledge that can be codified and transmitted in a systematic and formal language: documents, databases, webs, e-mails, charts, etc.

Ikujiro Nonaka, in his cornerstone book *The Knowledge Creating Company*,[c] indicated that the essence of knowledge creation is the substantiate distinction between the age-old concepts of tacit and explicit knowledge.

Knowledge creation processes can be thought of as those activities that surround the conversion of subjective tacit knowledge (based on experience) to objective explicit knowledge, also called *externalization*. The problem with this process is that tacit knowledge based on experience is often difficult to articulate, formalize, and encode.

For example, when you drive on an interstate, you make a complex set of decisions based on traffic patterns, your position relative to other vehicles ahead of and behind you, traffic speed, local speed limits, etc. Using experience, you can subconsciously make these decisions in split seconds, often without fatal errors. However, it would be extremely difficult if you were to codify this series of decision processes or transfer them to another person.

---

[c]This book's philosophical foundation builds upon Nonaka and his colleagues' previous research, notably on Nonaka, Ikujiro, The Knowledge Creating Company, *Harvard Business Review*, November–December (1991), 2–9.

The process of externalization results in the conversion from a tacit, unarticulated form to an explicit form of representation, which is easier to move across communication networks when compared to tacit forms that cannot be penned down in any readily explicated form. Externalization is often driven by metaphors and analogy. Seeing how a new project in your company is similar to another unrelated project that your company undertook in the past is an example of such analogy.

TYPES OF KNOWLEDGE

Tacit and explicit knowledge interact in these types:

- *Externalized knowledge.* Knowledge is complex and initially tacit; however, it can be externalized and embedded in a company's products and processes.[d] One of the aspects of tacit knowledge is the cognitive dimension that comprises beliefs, ideals, values, schemata, and mental models that are deeply ingrained in participants, often taken for granted by the possessors. While this cognitive component, like any other aspect of tacit knowledge, is difficult to articulate, it shapes the perception of the participants. This cognitive component should be extracted to retain context and fullness of the captured explicit knowledge.

- *Multilocational knowledge.* Knowledge might be resident both within the organization and outside it. Knowledge management encompasses activities surrounding the integration of this knowledge from different sources in different forms and maintaining it. Knowledge management creates value by actively leveraging the know-how, experience, and judgment resident within and outside an organization. The initial key to knowledge creation thus lies in mobilization and conversion of this tacit knowledge into a form of explicit knowledge.

- *Migratory knowledge.* Migratory knowledge is knowledge that is independent of its owner or creator. As knowledge becomes more and more extensively codified, its capacity to move increases. Codification implies some kind of capture—in documents, databases, pictures, illustrations, spreadsheets on a disk, e-mails, video tapes, or on a Web page on the corporate intranet. Codification however does not imply that capture has to be electronic. It could be on paper, on tape, or on film. Converting these to an electronic format that is more amenable to easy transfer is rarely a challenge these days. When we talk about the movement of knowledge, we are talking about our ability to transfer knowledge from one person or organization to another without losing its context and meaning.

---

[d]Ikujiro Nonaka, who, in my opinion, is truly the father of knowledge management as we know of it today, recognized this years ago. But the first recognition of tacit versus explicit knowledge in written form was expressed by Michael Polyani in 1967. If you go beyond the boundaries of the Western world, Chinese and Indian scholars have recognized this subtle yet important difference for thousands of years now.

COMPONENTS OF KNOWLEDGE

Intuition, ground truth, judgment, experience, values, assumptions, beliefs, and intelligence—a knowledge management strategy and a knowledge management system must support all of these components.

Ground Truth and Truth Maintenance

Projects and investments made in companies are often based on a set of assumptions: These assumptions might be about markets, customers, the business environment, consumer preferences, competition, etc. Often, the entire set of decisions that might have been made earlier might not hold in future situations, because these assumptions might have changed. Discovering, recording, and maintaining these assumptions and the *ability* to do a what-if analysis akin to scenario analysis with spreadsheets is a critical component of a complete knowledge management system.

The problem, however, is that these assumptions are often deeply embedded in individuals from a specific functional area; they almost seem so natural and obviously ingrained that they never explicitly surface. Getting employees to talk about these assumptions and recording them is often very difficult. In a research study I did with a colleague, we found that companies involved in highly cross-functional product development are often victims of this problem.[14] For example, assumptions that an engineering department never questions might have come from the marketing department without the engineering team realizing the source. Engaging in a conversational mode of communication rather than in information transfer provides a partial solution to this problem. On that account, an emphasis on conversation and discussion as an integral part of the knowledge management system is well placed.

Judgment

Very unlike information, which is facts, and data, which is factoids, knowledge has a component of judgment attached to it. While a colorful and precise stock ticker and a real-time graph are excellent information for any stockbroker, it means nothing if he can't act upon it or make a decision based on the data they provide. Unactionable information is *not* knowledge. However, if our stockbroker recognizes that he needs to sell like a madman when the trend chart looks like "this" or needs to hold when it looks like "that," he is making judgments based on it. Judgment allows knowledge to rise above and beyond an opinion when it reexamines itself and refines every time it is applied and acted upon.

A number of tools in information technology's Pandora's box including case-based reasoning (CBR) and machine learning systems can be used to make these kinds of judgments very accurately and in real time. But these come only when the business case has been evaluated and the preceding data-cleansing stages have been accomplished perfectly.

Experiential Knowledge and Knowledge Scripts

Knowledge is largely derived from experience. Being able to transfer knowledge implies that a part of experiential knowledge also gets transferred to the recipient. The benefit of experience lies in the fact that it provides a historical perspective that helps better understand present situations. Experienced people are usually valued in a company (and are often paid more) because they possess this historical perspective from which they can view current situations—something that a typical newcomer will almost never have. This perspective allows them to make connections with what is happening now with what might have happened earlier, and evaluate decisions in that light.

As people's experience in their jobs increases, they begin to figure out *shortcut solutions* to problems they have seen before. When they see a new situation, they match it to compare patterns that they are aware of. An experienced car driver, for example, recognizes that excessive rattle in the car *could* mean a flat tire. Similarly, a computer technician can match a computer that fails to boot up with a pattern that he might have seen before, say, a bad hard drive or a failed power supply. With experience, these *scripts* guide our thinking and help avoid useless tracks[e] that we might have followed earlier. Such *rules of thumb* or *heuristics* provide a single option out of a limited set of specific, often approximate, approaches to solving a problem or analyzing a situation accurately, quickly, and efficiently.

Likewise, in the complex, yet seemingly easy task of driving described earlier, there are little actions that take place without an effort or initiative: They play out as scripts. Our experience teaches us these scripts.

Beyond simplistic situations like these, in the complex business environment, it is the subconscious repertoire of scripts and rules of thumb that make experienced managers more valuable than new hires.

Although computer systems with *machine-learning* capabilities exist, the possibility of implementing them as a part of a knowledge management system is not only prohibitively expensive but also tedious, and with uncertain outcomes. Fortunately, many of these rules of thumb are in people's heads as tacit knowledge, providing the power that decades of machine-learning research have been unable to give to businesses.

Contrast this with information. Is there anything like this associated with information that flows through your company's information systems? Tacit knowledge, however complex to understand and manage, holds the promise for long-lasting impact, if we can successfully tap into even a fraction of what is available. Information is, at best, a source of temporary advantage.

Values, Assumptions, and Beliefs

Very often, business processes are based on a set of assumptions. These are so natural to and so deeply ingrained within the minds of the people who hold them that they find their way into most of the decisions that people make, but they are almost never expressed. Engineers, such as I, *assume* that anything that is behaving strangely has to have an underlying rationale. Managers, often mistakenly, might assume that their ordinate goal is to maximize their profit center's financial profits. One level above this, people might assume that companies are rational and neutral. And for a good reason, after the widespread influence of Nobel Prize winner Herbert Simon's research on the concept of *bounded rationality.*[15]

---

[e]Tracks, in this context, refer to decision paths or known problem-solving methods.

Companies, however, are often shaped by the beliefs of a few key people working there. Just as the culture of having fun is ingrained in Southwest Airline's work environment, and environment in the Starbucks coffeeshop culture, creating "insanely great" (such as the iMac and iBook) products in Apple's, and profits and market dominance in Microsoft's; these beliefs, values, and assumptions are brought into the very character of the firm, very often by its founders.

Such values, assumptions, and beliefs are integral components of knowledge. Such values probably explain why different companies have varying reactions to the same development. Why Barnes and Noble initially interpreted other businesses selling books on the Web as a threat to its very existence—a situation that Jeff Bezos[f] and Amazon.com viewed as nirvana. These values, assumptions, and beliefs differentiate a risk-taking competitor from a risk-averse one. And knowing, capturing, and sharing this component of knowledge can make all the difference between complete knowledge and incomplete, unactionable information. Not all beliefs can be "captured" explicitly. This is still an area of ongoing research, and initial results show promise in terms of mechanisms for capturing beliefs. Until more can be done about this area in a systemic manner, we must rely on people who hold the critical beliefs that drive processes. It is for this reason that you will see repeated emphasis on providing systemic pointers to people holding such components.

Intelligence

When knowledge can be applied, acted upon when and where needed, and brought to bear on present decisions, and when these lead to better performance or results, knowledge qualifies as intelligence. When it flows freely throughout a company, is exchanged, grows, is validated,[g] it transforms an *informated*[16] company into an *intelligent enterprise.*[h]

INTEGRATION OF KNOWLEDGE SOURCES

So what are the primary feeds to a knowledge management system? Where does knowledge come into the system from? A quick roundup of the sources from which knowledge comes is presented in Table 3-2.

---

[f]Jeff Bezos is the founder of Amazon.com, a leading online bookstore with physical presence in the United States, Great Britain, and Germany. Amazon has distribution centers and warehouses in many locations worldwide. Amazon's Website can be found at www.amazon.com, www.amazon.co.uk, and www.amazon.de. Bezos also was one of the early stakeholders in eBay— the online auction site that was valued at $22 billion in the second quarter of 1999.

[g]Validation refers to the process of repeated confirmation stemming from ongoing applicability or rejection from lack of such acceptability.

[h]The term *intelligent enterprise* refers to organization-wide intelligence, and was coined by James Brian Quinn in *Intelligent Enterprise: A Knowledge and Service Based Paradigm for Industry.* Free Press, New York (1992).

Table 3-2 Sources of Knowledge That Feed a Knowledge Management System

Source	Explicit/Codifiable	Tacit/Needs Explication
Employee knowledge, skills, and competencies	✔	✔
Experiential knowledge (both at an individual and group level)	✔	✔
Team-based collaborative skills		✔
Informal shared knowledge	✔	✔
Values		✔
Norms		✔
Beliefs	✔	✔
Task-based knowledge	✔	✔
Knowledge embedded in physical systems	✔	✔
Human capital		✔
Knowledge embedded in internal structures		✔
Knowledge embedded in external structures	✔	✔
Customer capital	✔	✔
Experiences of the employee	✔	✔
Customer relationships	✔	✔

Although the list in Table 3-2 is a partial one, it is clear that much of the knowledge can be explicated, put into systems, and reused. However, some critical pieces of tacit knowledge are extremely difficult, if not impossible, to externalize in such a manner.

THE THREE FUNDAMENTAL STEPS

Three basic steps are involved in the knowledge and learning process. Taking a closer look at these three basic steps, which many researchers like Nonaka and Takeuchi have expanded, will give us a better feel for what type of information technology functionality will support this effort. These three fundamental steps, illustrated in Figure 3-4, are:

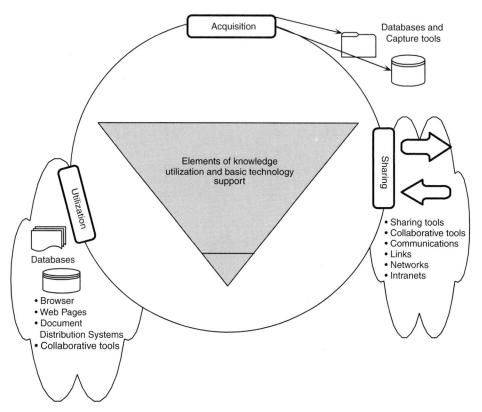

Figure 3-4 The basic elements of knowledge utilization and typical technology tools that can be used to support each stage.

- Knowledge acquisition
- Knowledge sharing
- Knowledge utilization

An important aspect in these stages is that they need not be in a sequence. They can, and often do, run in parallel.

KNOWLEDGE ACQUISITION

Knowledge acquisition is not to be confused with information acquisition. Knowledge acquisition is the process of development and creation of insights, skills, and relationships. For example, when an experienced stockbroker can see the trend line on a computer monitor and tell which way the market is headed—that is an example of intuition or acquired knowledge. It is this type of knowledge in which information technology components surrounding this process need to focus. Data-capture tools with filtering abilities, intelligent databases, keyboard scanners, CrossPad type note-capture tools and electronic white boards are examples of information technology components that can support knowledge acquisition.

Professional Intellect: Know-What to Care-Why

James Brian Quinn and his colleagues describe intellect and knowledge in an organization on four bases or levels in their landmark 1996 *Harvard Business Review* article.[17] A company's knowledge, in the order of importance, can be viewed at four levels. Not all these stages stand to benefit from a knowledge management system. An understanding and appreciation of technology's limitations will help your team place reasonable expectations on your knowledge management system. Lack of support by the knowledge management system does not mean that the knowledge management strategy cannot support those levels. The four levels of professional intellect, in the decreasing order of momentousness are, care-why, know-why, know-how, and know-what. Technology support possibilities are illustrated in Figure 3-5.

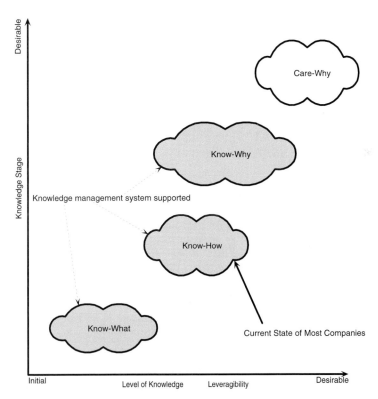

Figure 3-5 The four levels of knowledge, levels of leverage derived, and possibilities of technology support.[1]

1. *Care-why:* Care-why represents self-motivated creativity that exists in a company. This happens to be the only level that cannot be supported by a knowledge management system. Care-why explains why highly motivated, creative, and energetic groups and companies outperform larger corporations with more money and resources. This level of knowledge exists in a company's culture, and after we have done all we can to provide technology support for the other three levels, we must give this one our best shot, since technology is of little or no help at this level. Beliefs, in some respects, fall into this category—hence the difficulty in comprehensively supporting beliefs with a knowledge management system, about which I have cautioned you.

2. *Know-why:* A system's understanding represents the know-why aspect of knowledge. It's the deep knowledge of the complex slush of cause-and-effect relationships that underlie an employee's range of responsibilities. This knowledge enables individuals to move a step above know-how and create extraordinary leverage by using knowledge, bringing in the ability to deal with unknown interactions and unseen situations. Examples include a stockbroker who intuitively knows just when to sell and buy, or a baseball player who knows the perfect moment to hit.

    Most companies are at one stage below this level of understanding—the know-how stage, where they can use known rules and apply them well. But the knowledge economy demands more than just that ability. To be able to move knowledge workers from the know-how level, a knowledge management system must support extensive discussion and conversation so that the participants and employees get a feel for the problems rather than simply apply well-known rules that have worked in most situations. Conversation is stressed in meetings and brainstorming sessions, but an alarmingly small number of firms support the same types of conversations in systems intending to leverage their corporate knowledge.

    Perhaps, we have bought into the concept of expert systems and conventional decision support systems a little too much. Value creation from knowledge is enhanced if experimentation in the course of problem solving increases know-why and if incentive structures stimulate care-why, rather than solely focusing on know-how.

3. *Know-how:* Know-how represents the ability to translate bookish knowledge into real-world results. Marketing departments, for example, know that advertising during the Superbowl is expensive, but the payoffs are huge. This is a general rule that can be applied very well by a marketer. Being able to compete beyond these rules, which *might* be common knowledge, requires a shift from a know-how information-oriented environment to know-why, that is, knowledge orientation. Professional know-how is developed most rapidly through repeated exposure to real-world, complex problems. Any networking or knowledge support system that intends to move workers from this level to the know-why level must enable extensive exposure to problem solving.

4. *Know-what:* This represents cognitive knowledge. This is an essential but insufficient basis for competing. An analogy would be the kind of detailed knowledge a college graduate might have when he graduates with a degree in his discipline. He might know what should be done but might not have ever done it in real life.

KNOWLEDGE SHARING

Knowledge sharing is the next component. As Figure 3-4 shows, this stage comprises disseminating and making available what is already known. An expert system that helps a novice technical support person answer tech support calls at the help desks of Microsoft is a good example of knowledge that is being shared with that person.

The Collaborative Nature of Knowledge

One characteristic that distinguishes a firm's knowledge from its information assets is the foundation on which knowledge is primarily built. Collaborative problem solving, conversations, and teamwork generate a significant proportion of the knowledge assets that exist within a firm.

In today's dynamic environments and industries, even the knowledge about the process of doing things is incomplete at the outset and develops gradually over time, through various kinds of learning. These processes, as Marco Iansiti demonstrates with Netscape's case,[19] consist of a series of interdependent solutions, each of which adds something to what a firm knows.

Knowledge involved in deliberation on alternative decisions that could have been made is typically lost in the process, once the job is done. Knowledge utilization is inherently a collaborative process, and neither within-firm nor cross-firm utilization and transfer of knowledge can succeed without effectively supporting collaboration. This focus on collaboration and collaborative support is perhaps one of the primary distinguishing factors that differentiates knowledge support systems from information systems. A simple question such as "Has anyone seen something like this before?" can perhaps generate an amazingly rich array of responses, all but one of which will soon be forgotten once the problem is solved. Fortunately, this happens to be one of the easiest avenues for capturing knowledge electronically, as illustrated in Figure 3-6. Inclusion of learning allows deliberate actions *before* relevant processes are completed.

KNOWLEDGE UTILIZATION

Knowledge utilization comes into the picture when learning is integrated into the organization. Whatever is broadly available throughout the company can be generalized and applied, at least in part, to new situations. The example of the tech support guy at Microsoft is a perfect case of this: Sharing and utilization are taking place simultaneously. Any computer-supported facility to enhance these functions, in part or as a whole, will have to keep these three broad concepts in clear view before successful implementation can begin.

The Telephone as a Role Model for KM Systems Design

When we begin thinking of technology support for knowledge management, the first technology that comes to the minds of most managers is their intranet. But what often is forgotten is a device as common as their coffeepot and arguably more useful than their PalmPilot:

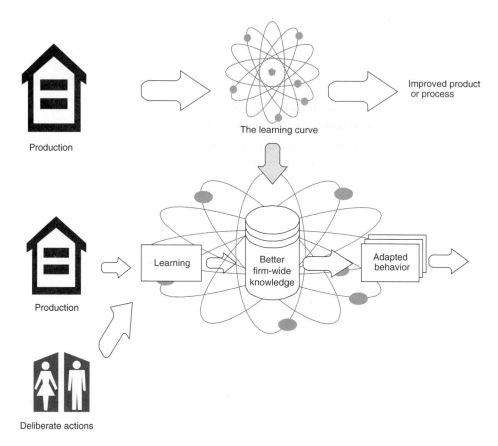

Production

The learning curve

Improved product
or process

Production

Learning

Better
firm-wide
knowledge

Adapted
behavior

Deliberate actions

Figure 3-6 Key differences between the concept of a learning company and a knowledge-leveraging company.

the telephone. The telephone represents the best set of characteristics that one could wish for in a system that supports knowledge flow effectively. As you speak into the telephone, you can convey context, meaning, an attitude, and tone, along with information and data.

The telephone, the fax, and the newspaper are successful devices not because they carry information but because they are deeply embedded in the communities within a company. For this reason, the telephone is perhaps the best role model for a knowledge management system. Any successful knowledge management system will have to possess the characteristics and communication richness of a telephone; as it is embedded in the organization, its use is almost transparent, rarely formal, natural, and hesitation free. The telephone provides us with a laundry list of basic characteristics that any system supporting knowledge must possess:

- The system should be well accepted in the community that will actually use it, not just the community that creates it.

- The system should allow and support rich communication.

- Context, meaning, opinions, tone, and biases should have a way to move through the system.

- The user should not feel as if she were using something she would not use if given a choice.

- The system should support informal communication and multiple ways of expressing ideas, thoughts, and communication.

- The system should be transparent to the user. A good example of a relatively powerful tool that has emerged recently is the CrossPad. The CrossPad is a digital device that resembles a clipboard on which the user can place a regular legal scratch pad and take notes just as he normally would. The pen that he uses digitally captures everything he writes on the page. This data can then be transferred to a personal computer.

    A transparent technology must allow the user to do things the way he would normally do them, such as taking notes on an OfficeMax® yellow legal pad. A technology that requires the legal-pad-loving user to key in all the notes that he takes during a meeting is unlikely to be accepted easily because it requires a fundamental shift in the way the user had been trained to do things—the way he is comfortable doing them.

- The system should support the informal *slang* used in the company or department. The informal language that people use to communicate with colleagues is often very different from the formal language used in presentations to senior management or clients. The system needs to support that and ensure that the users are comfortable using it on the system. The telephone, for the most part, offers a certain degree of confidentiality that makes people comfortable using this "slang." This is an imperative to prevent the system from decaying into a formality that no one actually cares to use—but still uses it because it is mandated.

Supporting Informal Knowledge

Knowledge sharing and utilization necessitate support for informal technology: something that most information technology is not designed to handle. The demand for formality made by technologists and their technologies often disrupts the more productive informal relations between knowledge workers. Search engines and electronic library catalogs are a good example of how formality constricts and severely limits our ability to either capture or support retrieval of informal knowledge. You can use keywords, for searching, but if a document, Web page, or book does not closely match the keywords they might never show up in your results. Narrowing down searches is fine, but then a lot remains to be easily missed. In terms of retrieval in the context of knowledge management, intelligent agents, which I discuss in Chapter 11, look very promising. But they will not help if you cannot capture informal knowledge. The problem with information systems today is that the user must know where to look, what to ask for it, and how to ask. Information overload is probably more descriptive of this situation than information abundance: Iterative keyword searching, for example, is frustrating and often ends up retrieving too much noise. Too much information is about as dangerous as too little. In stark contrast with how much an information system can help you find, say, a book in a library, a knowledgeable librarian would perhaps be a better bet.

The Perils of Excessive Formalization

Excessive formalization prevents people from behaving in ways other than those that are negotiated ahead of time and constrained by technology. In a research study involving a major personal digital assistant accessories manufacturer, a colleague and I found that the same idea described as an optimized design by an engineer in the company was described very differently by a marketing manager, even though they meant exactly the same thing: a good product that the consumer liked. Excessive focus on formal knowledge leaves little room for informal, tacit, and socially embedded knowledge, which is where the *know-why* lies and the most significant work gets accomplished.

Amazon.com is a company that has recognized this fact. Amazon realizes that people can mean something else when they are describing something, just because of a difference in vocabularies. Figure 3-7 shows that a search for Tom Davenport's knowledge management

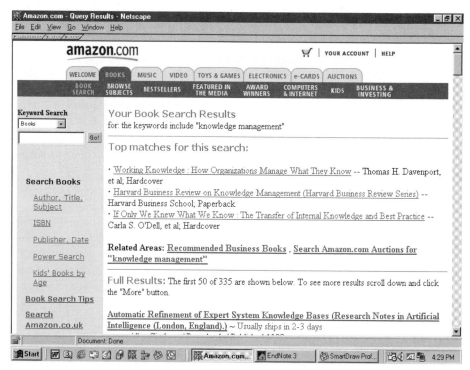

Figure 3-7 Amazon.com's Website uses intelligent agents to pull up related concepts, ideas, or documents from an expansive repository even when retrieval is based on highly formalized and structured requests for information.

classic creates a context for the search by informing a potential shopper about the other titles that people with similar interests to hers have bought. The search results list three more books that people who bought this book also bought.

At the same time, recognizing that the shopper might have searched on the keywords *knowledge management* in a context totally different from the one that the system interpreted, it listed related and similar keywords that could possibly be used to better describe what she *thought* she was looking for. This is shown in Figure 3-8.

The underlying technology is a set of intelligent agents that keep track of the other books that people buying this book have purchased in the past. It also lists other interpretations that might have been intended. This situation is a good example of overcoming, at least in part, the limitations that a community, department-specific description, or vocabulary might impose on the retrieval process. Informal and unrestricted comments that can follow each book provide a ground for informal communication, where the contributors can choose whether or not to identify themselves. We discuss details of how intelligent agents can be used to deliver similar functionality in your own company's knowledge management system.

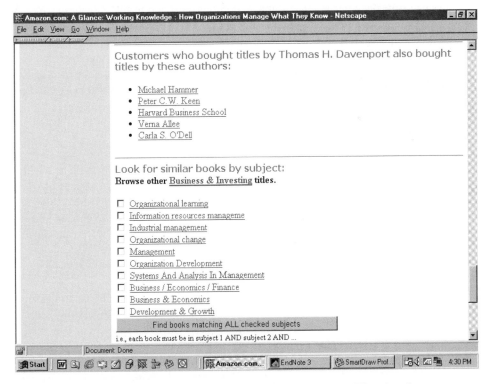

Figure 3-8 Amazon.com provides a workaround for vocabulary differences between users describing a concept or an idea.

KNOWLEDGE MANAGEMENT SYSTEMS AND EXISTING TECHNOLOGY

In this section, we will examine how a knowledge management system differs from an intranet, extranet, data warehouse, GroupWare systems, and project management tools. We will also see how and which of these existing pieces of technology can harmonize with a knowledge management system.

DIFFERENCES BETWEEN A KM SYSTEM AND A DATA WAREHOUSE

What makes a knowledge management system any different from a data warehouse, you might ask. The key differentiators are as follows:

Types of Information Managed

A data warehouse focuses more on highly structured content, whereas a knowledge management system needs to support both informal and formal (highly unstructured as well as highly structured) content and everything in between. A data warehouse does not and cannot support informal content such as video content, audio recordings, scribbles, conversations, doodles on notepads, etc., like a knowledge management system needs to be able to support. This implies that a data warehouse can be a part of a knowledge management system, only as a source of structured data that is input to the complex collaborative filtering mechanisms of the knowledge management system.

Context

A data warehouse is arguably a resource of unquestionable value when you need to mine factual data. When such data is mined and interpreted, it provides value. But the need for interpretation is a fuzzy idea; data warehouses, by themselves, are devoid of context. Some products, such as Intraspect and Digital Knowledge Asset's SceneServer™, allow some degree of context to be "wrapped" with the data that goes into a data warehouse; a knowledge management system depends on much higher contextual focus than that typically provided by data warehouses.

Size

Since a data warehouse primarily focuses on clean, structured, and organized data, the size of a data warehouse is *always* large. Raw data, often in its native form, is stored here, so high storage capacity is a must. Unlike this, a knowledge management system might have storage system sizes ranging from very small to extremely large. As support for multimedia content grows, storage needs skyrocket. However, a knowledge management system never has raw data stored in it: Everything there is at least at the information stage of condensation. So size requirements for pure content (excluding multimedia) are often low.

Content Focus

The content focus of a knowledge management system is on highly filtered information and on knowledge, whereas that of a data warehouse is on scrubbed, raw, clean, and organized data.

Performance

Because of the complex nature of retrieval and classification requests that a KM system must be able to handle, performance requirements and computing power needed for a knowledge management system are much higher than those of a data warehouse. At the same time, if multimedia is digitally supported, processors need to be able to handle the additional processing burden of graphic renditions as well. With multimedia-enhanced technology that has been around for a few years on personal computer platforms and parallel processing capabilities of Pentium-class microprocessors, this is not a significant cost or technological feasibility concern.

Networks

A data warehouse does not need to be on a live network to function properly; however, this live network is imperative for a knowledge management system that is trying to draw from resources available throughout the entire enterprise and beyond it—from the Internet and collaborative, extended enterprise.

DIFFERENCES BETWEEN A KM SYSTEM, AN INTRANET, AND AN EXTRANET

An intranet certainly is a building block of a knowledge management system that must never be confused for one. Intranets rely on firewalls to delineate TCP/IP-based communication networks with regular, hypertext, Web-page-type content within organizational boundaries. The choice of the word *organizational* is probably incongruous here: A more descriptive and precise designation is *extended-enterprise-wide*. Intranets often include the company's allies, partners, suppliers, and major customers and allow knowledge exchange within this extended enterprise. Since an extranet can also be viewed as an extended version of an intranet, for this analysis, I will make no explicit distinction between the two.

HP has used its intranet, which includes over 2,700 servers that, together, move close to 8 Terabytes of data in a given month. By allowing its main customers access to this intranet, HP is building customer knowledge that is enhanced by a two-way information flow both within and beyond the company's immediate boundaries. Even with congruent objectives, there are differences. The key differences between an intranet and knowledge management system are as follows:

Content Focus

Intranets focus more on efficient information delivery and publishing. The focus is often more on fast, low-cost delivery throughout the enterprise and the extended enterprise. However, knowledge management systems focus more on actionable information, in other words, knowledge.

Performance

Performance demands on knowledge management systems are often higher than on basic intranets, both in terms of network bandwidth requirements and processing power demands. While processing power is rarely the problem, network bandwidth often is.

Broader Base

A typical intranet often has a broader base and a more open face to the outside world such as the firm's major customers and partners. This is usually not the case with critical knowledge management systems a company uses to gain a competitive edge and to leverage business processes across an extended enterprise and the firm's value chain.

Productizing Knowledge

Because intranets have a broader user base, they do not *productize* knowledge as much as knowledge management systems do. A typical knowledge management system, especially if it uses push delivery, has to do individual iteratively improved content customizations unlike mass customization on which a typical intranet depends. However, these functionalities can be merged with relative ease, and as we shall discover in the rest of this book (specifically, Chapter 11), the intranet provides one of the best choices for the knowledge management system front end.

Reciprocity

Information technology, the Internet, and the Web are far reaching. However, the assumption that knowledge networks aided by these information networks will spread the same way is fundamentally flawed. A knowledge network is not limited by its reach and the extent to which it can be used to communicate but rather by the extent to which it supports reciprocity. The ability to support a multidirectional, complex mechanism for negotiation is required to enable this reciprocity. Users of a knowledge management system will contribute only if they feel they are gaining something *valued by them* in reciprocation. This idea is very different from the primarily publishing-oriented model that intranets commonly seem to follow.

Lave and Wenger, who developed the notion of communities of practice, stress the need to limit, though not cut off, reciprocity to enable "legitimate peripheral participation." For example, employees should be allowed to "lurk" in electronic mailing lists and discussion groups. Technologies that understand this subtle difference and can parse how relationships between communities where reciprocity is cultivated differ from those within communities where reciprocity is inherent can actually help extend the reach between communities without disrupting the balance of reciprocity that exists within them.

Differences Between a KM System and GroupWare

GroupWare products such as Lotus Notes are often mistaken for knowledge management systems. While Lotus Notes is an excellent product, there are numerous other group collaboration products that must not be taken at face value on the basis of vendors' claims of having created the ultimate knowledge management solution! Since this is an area of significant misunderstanding and misdirected expenditure in companies, we look at this comparison very closely in Part II of this book. Our focus on the differentiation between GroupWare and knowledge management systems is built around the following characteristics:

- Focus—function and content
- Archival versus generation functionality
- Internal versus external sources
- Relationship with knowledge generated from activities of the firm

DIFFERENCES FROM PROJECT MANAGEMENT TOOLS

Although project management tools allow for the capture of formal structured knowledge, a system needs to support some form of informal knowledge as well to "capture" at least some portion of tacit knowledge. To transfer tacit knowledge from individuals to a repository, you need to support some form of community-based electronic discussion. A key feature that would differentiate a knowledge management support tool from a project management tool's organizational memory store which is the ability to capture and retrieve uncodified or tacit knowledge that can be slow and costly to transfer.[20]

An example of such an IT tool is a competence database that could efficiently find articulated knowledge or links to the knowledge source used in an earlier development effort. To ensure efficiency and accuracy, such systems must frequently be updated to reflect changes in skills.

Tacit knowledge, like all other types of knowledge, can become outdated, hence invalid; therefore, it is critical to ensure the applicability of tacit knowledge to *current* situations. The maintainability aspect, for this reason, is not significant only for explicit and formalized knowledge but also for tacit knowledge. Providing support for partial capture of such knowledge, using an IT tool, could help ensure its currency and relevance.

Retrofitting Knowledge to Information Technology

Knowledge must be treated as a driver for technology choice, not vice versa. Table 3-3 shows how technology can be fitted to knowledge that it is meant to support.

TAMING THE TIGER'S TAIL

In undertaking to manage knowledge, you might find yourself holding the tail of a tiger. In this section, we examine why we need this tiger in the first place, and then how we tame it. Finally we look at some companies that have succeeded in the knowledge jungle.

Table 3-3 Retrofitting knowledge to the choice and implementation of IT and IT support functions

Aspect	Asset and Outcome	Technology as a Secondary Asset-Based Choice
What is managed?	Knowledge Knowledge creation Knowledge reuse Knowledge half-life	Hardware Software Systems life cycle Communications network
Why manage it?	Deliver knowledge to consumers Provide historical basis for decisions Enable rigor based decisions Provide a sustaining competitive edge Increase decision and choice efficiency	Implement reliable and high-quality hardware, software, and communication systems
How do we manage it?	Integrated, cross-functional approach Include the entire extended enterprise, i.e., suppliers, consumers, consultants, vendors, and buyers	Integrate existing systems Control costs Make processes more efficient Learn from mistakes Reuse, not reinvent Inventorize[i]
Metrics and success criteria	Financial, tangible and intangible gains realized Impact on performance Impact on competitiveness Timeliness Benchmark performance	A working knowledge management system A well-used knowledge management system A growing knowledge management system Users increasingly contribute and demonstrate reciprocity.

Who manages it?	The CKO j equivalent manager	or	The CKO or equivalent managerial employee
	Individual organizational units using it		The information technology function
			Network service providers.
			Practice leaders

iInventorize refers to the concept of taking knowledge into account and formally recording its existence.

jThe CKO title can be a misleading role definer. Many companies are structured in ways that do not allow a CKO, per se, to oversee knowledge management. Numerous companies have scrapped the CKO title and assigned the role to equivalent high-level managerial workers such as competence managers and practice area specialists.

THE SURVIVAL IMPERATIVE

The obvious question is why? The simple answer: survival. In the knowledge-based economy, survival depends on the best possible response to a multitude of challenges. Managing knowledge means more than just introducing powerful databases or intranets. Managing it means adding or creating value by actively leveraging know-how, judgment, intuition, and experience resident within and outside the company with a focus on:

- *Generating new knowledge:* Creating new knowledge that provides process competence and a hard-to-copy competitive advantage to your company.

- *Using accessible knowledge in making decisions:* Making decisions based on knowledge that already exists in the company and bringing existing, but often unreachable, knowledge to bear upon new decisions.

- *Embedding it in products, services, and processes:* Delivering value to the customer by integrating knowledge in products, services, and processes. This will result in higher-quality outcomes at a lower cost than what your competitors incur.

- *Facilitating knowledge growth:* This is best done through rewards, incentives, a knowledge-sharing culture, and recognition.

- *Transferring existing knowledge:* Transferring existing knowledge into other parts, departments, and locations of the company.

- *Integrating competitive intelligence:* Accessing valuable knowledge from competitors and external sources.

- *Driving strategy:* Using it to support strategic business drivers.

Surprisingly enough, a survey over 400 U.S. and European firms conducted by Ernst and Young found that a very few companies considered themselves to be doing well on any of these fronts.[21]

The business drivers for knowledge management, listed in Chapter 2, make KM an essential survival imperative in the knowledge-based economy. Reasons include the following:

1. *Changing requirements for success:* Requirements for success of product lines and service offerings are very different from what they were in the 1980s. It is harder than ever to guess what makes one product successful and the other a flop. Ford's Taurus, 3Com's PalmPilot, and more recently Apple's iMac and iBook are distinct examples of recent successes that many competitors have tried to emulate with little success. KM creates greater corporate coherence and improves decision making in such unstable environments, while bringing congruence between business strategy and IT investments.

2. *The quest for better, faster, and cheaper:* Cost and performance-based competition is almost a given in the current business environment. Personal computers are perhaps an extreme example of a commodity that is always cheaper than the year before, always better, and always faster. When eMachines introduced its first sub-$600 PC, a flurry of competitors such as Hewlett Packard, IBM, Gateway and Compaq entered the market that eMachines had just opened. Cost, which was the distinguishing factor for eMachines' success, could no longer be its source of competitive advantage. Knowledge, unlike cost and technology, cannot be copied and can be used to deliver value to your customers in ways that your competition cannot emulate. This brings in the need for three-dimensional positioning along the following, often contradicting requirements for success:

   - **Time-to-market:** Most products, whether physical goods or services, do not have the luxury of extended time for development.

   - **Quality maximization:** Quality is no longer defined as a minimum benchmark level that needs to be met. Quality, Drucker notes, is a major component that defines the value of the end product. KM provides a unique opportunity to build quality into your company's products and services by leveraging past experience and knowledge gained from preceding projects and products.

   - **Cost minimization and cost cutting:** Short times-to-market, the demand for the highest level of quality, and cost-based competition can be simultaneously satisfied by bringing in the ability to reuse existing knowledge,

3. *Avoiding the infinite loop of work duplication:* KM provides the unique opportunity so that the resources otherwise expended in duplication are instead funneled to beat the three-way tension between cost minimization, quality maximization, and fast delivery.

4. *Competing through process:* Process, not the ingredients used to deliver a product or service to the consumer, differentiates successful companies from unsuccessful ones. For example, companies that distinguish themselves in terms of customer service do not do so solely on the basis of the possibly smarter people that they hire, but on the process used to support customers. Starbucks distinguishes the taste of its coffee through the process of brewing coffee and not by the better quality of coffee beans, which its competitors can also import. KM helps you develop and refine these processes in ways that allow their application long after an existing contract or product line has been archived or discontinued.

5. *Convergent engineering:* As products and services become increasingly complex, boundaries between functional areas in all types of companies blur and diffuse. KM provides support for cross-functional collaboration and the cultural change needed to make such collaboration work.

6. *Functional decomposition:* Tasks of developing products and services are increasingly being decomposed between functional areas. KM provides a mechanism for dealing with the process complexities that arise from this decomposition.

7. *Assumptions, assumptions, assumptions:* Delivering products and services unscientifically depends on the assumptions of the people who work to develop them. These assumptions about markets, customers, and business environments can change as quickly as the stock market. KM tracks and maintains knowledge regarding the validity of assumptions before critical decisions are made on the basis of flawed assumptions.

8. *Timely information delivery:* An attempt to avoid the information glut is perhaps one of the key motivations of companies that have decided to get out of it by sieving knowledge, resulting in increased responsiveness to changing environmental conditions, dynamic competitive scenarios, evolving markets, competing products, and rival innovations. Just as information management was a natural successor to data management, knowledge management is a natural successor to information management.

   KM provides a mechanism for push delivery of information that might otherwise never reach the right person in the organization. With methods such as profiling, information that might be relevant in near-term decisions can reach the right people ahead of time.

9. *Tangible asset creation:* Managing knowledge provides opportunities for creating more tangible tradable assets that are built with the aid of corporate knowledge.

10. *Preventing knowledge walkouts:* Job mobility coupled with high levels of tacit knowledge in companies are a lethal combination. Losing a few key people to your competitor means not only losing that competence but also means that your competitor gained the same competence.

DIFFICULTIES AND COPING MECHANISMS FOR KNOWLEDGE MANAGEMENT

Knowledge management has not (until this book) lent itself to any existing clear-cut strategy or technique. The same initiatives that might succeed in one firm might fail miserably in another. Implementing an initiative for managing knowledge is inherently difficult for several reasons, most of which have to do with the way firms have been run—more or less successfully—in more traditional settings, past eras, and structures. There is no knowledge management silver bullet. As I forewarned you, a knowledge management project is specific to *your* company and can be successful only if it is built with your company in mind. We don't know exactly why it cannot be easily or successfully copied. In this section, we examine barriers inherent to knowledge management and ways around them.

Knowledge Management Is Expensive

One of the biggest barriers to implementing a knowledge management initiative in a company is that of selling the idea to senior management and to end users. Knowledge management is often an expensive proposition; it's not just the expense of the technology infrastructure to enable it but also the expense involved in implementing corporate culture changes and revitalizing employee reward structures. If your knowledge management strategy is improperly planned, there is no immediate tangible outcome that can be easily demonstrated, and this further raises skepticism among upper management that controls the budget.

Incompatible Combinations of Technology and People

Firms that have experimented with technology as a primary enabler for managing knowledge have learned a painful lesson. Managing knowledge requires a level of participation that defies the fundamental knowledge-hoarding sentiment that exists, among knowledge workers—most of whom derive their job stability from their knowledge, experience, and skills. Building a knowledge exchange mechanism with fancy pieces of technology does nothing to motivate employees to part with their valuable and sustenance-critical knowledge assets. The feasible solution lies in an amicable synthesis of people with technology, and cultural change with technological change. The catch phrase is "People first, technology next." It's the *building people to work around technology* mentality that leads many initiatives of this type down the road to failure.

Sharing Knowledge: The New Way of Thinking

"Build it and they will come" might be an idea that does apply to many other things in business, but not to knowledge management. Knowledge workers often tend to use all knowledge that's easily accessible but do not always give out all knowledge that they own. After all, one might argue, if all the skills of a CEO could be captured in a decision support system, why would you need to keep a CEO who takes home $200,000 a year! "Unnecessary expenditure," some might say.

There need to be strong reasons and cogent incentives for knowledge workers to share the knowledge that they have. This is where a new way of thinking, a new approach to rewarding employees on the basis of their contribution to the firm's knowledge and not just performance, needs to be put into place. And that, among other roles, is a key role that the senior manager masquerading under the much-despised title of the knowledge manager, a.k.a. the CKO, needs to play, and play well.

Knowledge Markets, Not Hierarchies

Knowledge thrives in markets where knowledge is allowed to grow, is exchanged, is validated, and is added to. Knowledge does not thrive in hierarchies of traditional business structures. As a corollary, systems that support traditional businesses might have their structures and information flows that are inadequate and unsuited for the needs of knowledge flow and knowledge growth. Three observations regarding knowledge support, using knowledge markets rather than hierarchies, are in order:

COMPANIES THAT MANAGE KNOWLEDGE WELL

Throughout this book, we look at good examples from small and large companies. We close this section with a brief look at companies that have reaped significant financial and customer satisfaction gains by managing specialized internal knowledge. Even though these companies have not implemented full-fledged, organization-wide knowledge management programs, the gains from highly circumscribed versions of such programs show that there is a *lot* to be gained.

- Price Waterhouse used Lotus Notes and formed a central group to identify, capture, and document best practices throughout the company.
  - Collaborative work was significantly improved.
  - Information flows throughout the firm became frictionless.

  Price Waterhouse measures the return on its investments in terms of the gain in revenue generated through the use of such a system.

- Kaiser Permanente has leveraged its best practices extensively. In one case, the company implemented an open access program a year earlier than expected just because it transferred best practices from one location to another across regions within the United States. The success of a best practice at one location makes it easier to sell its value to senior management at another location.

- Texas Instruments (TI) was low on its customer satisfaction rankings in 1992 because of the company's unusual failure to deliver semiconductors on time. TI's worldwide wafer fabrication team adopted and transferred best practices internally across several locations, effectively creating additional wafer fabrication capacity that would have needed a $500 million investment in a new fabrication plant. Besides saving half a billion dollars in additional investments, this knowledge-sharing initiative pulled up the company from the bottom to the top position on its industry's customer satisfaction rankings.

1. *Knowledge access is only the beginning of knowledge management.* Truly leveraging knowledge means that knowledge flows around your company freely, just the right knowledge is available when a decision is to be made, there are no inefficiencies, and knowledge hoarding is down to zero. At that level, knowledge management will be so transparent and invisible, so much a part of an organization's culture that there will be no place for a discipline or area of concern such as knowledge management. And, in my best guess, such perfection, thanks to our human nature, is impossible to achieve. However, a lot of inefficiencies can be removed to add competitive strength to the firm. Enabling access to knowledge is only the beginning.

2. *Knowledge management is an infinite loop that never ends.* There is always room for incremental and continuous improvement that is created by three factors:
   - Imperfections in knowledge assessment
   - Changing user needs
   - Changing business climate

3. *Organizational politics come into play when knowledge exists, is used, and is exchanged.* Politically charged environments in companies are ill suited to knowledge management, exchange, and development, and nothing but strong cultural initiatives can prevent them from negatively affecting knowledge development in the enterprise.

BUSINESS AND KNOWLEDGE

The firm, taken for granted in the conventional economy, appears to have a doubtful future in the knowledge economy. Well-established firms that were probably doing very well, innovating, and leading their industries, have gradually begun to fade out. Examples abound. Netscape Corporation, which literally created the Web browser market, was bought out by America Online. CompuServe, one of the oldest online service companies that had flourished even before the mass advent of the Internet, was bought out by AOL. The diminishing competitive power of leading firms, the global competitive demands faced, and the ever-changing business scenarios, coupled with everyday examples of failures and bankruptcies among companies that once led their markets have convinced many organizations facing a highly unpredictable business environment, of survival instincts inherent in managing their primary, or should I say, only competitive asset—their knowledge and their ability to learn faster than their competitors.

How Companies Learn to Learn

While knowledge is thought of as the property of individuals, a great deal of knowledge is both produced and held collectively.[22] Such knowledge is produced when people in a company work together in tightly knit groups or communities of practice. Even though the employees and the knowledge they carry around in their heads are beginning to play the most significant part in the success of companies, it's unfortunate that companies fail to recognize this early enough—before it's too late.

Managing an organization's collective, and largely tacit knowledge has become the critical survival factor for companies that intend to maintain or improve performance based on their experience. Gaining new knowledge, managing it, and applying it have become as much an imperative as the ability to produce quality goods and services.

KNOWLEDGE-FRIENDLY COMPANIES

Knowledge-friendly companies are those that realize that their knowledge can be the only asset from which they can hope to draw a long-term competitive advantage. Technology by itself, owing to its relative ease of replicability, has failed to provide this advantage. Core competencies are more than just "know-what." They go beyond the typical form of explicit knowledge, such as a manual or a cookbook approach, and depend on the singular ability to put the *know-what* into action. And that is what distinguishes it from information.

Having detailed information of yesterday's sales in your store located in Richmond, Virginia, is information. Putting it into action, knowing what to do with it, interpreting it, and acting upon it are where the challenge lies. And that is where knowledge comes in. Nevis, DiBella, and Gould, in their 1995 article in *Sloan Management Review,* identified three factors that distinguish such companies from others:[23]

1. *Leveraged core competencies:* Companies such as Canon make significant investments in developing knowledge in the key areas of core competency (there are eight such areas in the case of Canon). This investment has paid off in the long term: Canon attributes 30 of its very successful products to this ability. Companies that have a knowledge management mindset use their well-developed core competencies as the launch pad for their new product and service offerings. This means that these companies are willing and able to make the commitment toward both identification and management of knowledge around the key areas in which their core competencies lie. At the heart of any successful knowledge management project lies the focus on knowing what the firm needs to prioritize. As intuitive and commonsensical as it might seem, companies miss this point over and over. It's only after you get beyond this point that you can even think of building a knowledge management system. Starting the other way around—fitting people to the latest technology that you want to introduce in your company—is predestined for failure.

2. *Continuous improvement of the value-added chain*: Wal-Mart is a great example of a company that continuously experiments with an eye on improvement. The company conducts ongoing experiments in its stores throughout the country. Wal-Mart is often discussed as the poster child example of a successful just-in-time (JIT) inventory management implementation in business schools. Wal-Mart, realizing the value of information flows between its suppliers and stores, thought to leverage it. It effectively leveraged information to create knowledge, adding context and meaning to the numbers generated by its checkout counter cash registers. The captured data is automatically converted into well-summarized information that is further converted into knowledge of its safe-stock levels for each product in its multitudes of product lines. The summary automatically informs and authorizes the supplier to replenish stocks in each of its stores. This entire process reflects an attitude that supports constant learning and addition to Wal-Mart's existing knowledge.

3. *Ability to fundamentally revitalize*: Another characteristic that distinguishes a company that is ready for knowledge management is the ability to fundamentally revitalize itself. This might mean dropping old ways of doing things altogether or challenging the fundamental ways in which the company does business. Motorola is a classic example. The company simply drops entire product lines and enters new lines when the markets seem to be making fundamental shifts. This flexibility is perhaps the primary reason for Motorola's enviable success in the cellular telephone market.

    Barnes & Noble has been selling books the traditional way, in its plush carpeted bookstores. Direct competition from the Web-based newcomer Amazon.com required it to question its belief in the traditional approach. So the company went through a fundamental shift and began selling books over the Internet. And it was very successful at that, with its 1999 initial public offering (IPO) marking of that success.

    Egghead, a U.S. software retail chain, similarly closed down all its 80 stores around the country and moved its entire operation to its Website (www.egghead.com), again changing the way it did its business in a very fundamental way.

Companies that want to actually apply knowledge that they gain should be ready to accept such fundamental shifts that such knowledge might demand.

KNOWLEDGE-SHARING COMPANIES

Knowledge is one the few resources that demonstrates increasing returns to scale: The more you share it, the more it grows. In 1997, Netscape saw a rapid decline in its share of the Internet browser market as Microsoft's Internet Explorer gained market share at the expense of its Netscape Communicator and Navigator browser products. In March 1998, Netscape made the source code of its browser products available, at no cost and under licensing provisions, to anyone who cared to download it from Netscape's Web site (www.netscape.com). The company apparently gave away knowledge that cost millions of dollars to generate—an asset that any company would conceivably guard with its life.

Now, why in the world would Netscape do this? First, by making its products widely available, accepted, and used, it hopes to secure the market share of a complementary product: its own Web server software. Second, it hopes that millions of software developers will adopt, adapt, and enhance its products. Netscape is betting that the efforts of many programmers outside the company will turn its products into a valuable standard.

The software industry is not an exception. Our second example comes from the pharmaceuticals industry, since this, like the software industry, is highly knowledge intensive in nature. Incyte Pharmaceuticals, which achieved a market capitalization of over $600 million in under six years, followed a similar strategy by licensing its gene-sequencing knowledge nonexclusively to large pharmaceutical companies. This initiative helped it gain access to knowledge assets of its partners and created a standard platform for the provision of all gnome data that becomes increasingly valuable as more and more companies begin to utilize it. Table 3-4 summarizes some reasons and frequently encountered impediments for sharing knowledge.

IS YOUR COMPANY READY FOR KNOWLEDGE MANAGEMENT?

We've looked in depth at knowledge and its value to businesses. We've looked superficially at companies that employ knowledge management to their advantage (in Chapter 6 we look in depth at other companies that have successfully institutionalized knowledge management). Now it's time to look at your company.

A number of facilitating factors are required for any knowledge management effort to succeed. You will notice that most successful adopters share many of these underlying facilitators that indicate their readiness for knowledge management:

- *Scanning imperative:* This is the first facilitator for successful knowledge management. Three simple questions can help you determine if such a scanning imperative exists in your own company:

Table 3-4 Sharing Knowledge: Reasons and Impediments

Enablers	Impediments
High levels of trust	Fear and suspicion
Rewards for sharing	Unintentionally rewarded for hoarding
Team-based collaborative work	Individual effort without recognition and reward
Aligned mission, vision and values, and strategy	Individual accountability and reward
Joint team-wide accountability and rewards	Functional focus
Group accountability and rewards	Employee-owner interest conflicts.
Process focus	Lack of alignment
Focus on customer satisfaction	Not-invented-here syndrome
Open to outside ideas	Too busy to share
Eye on competition	Internal competition
Collaborative and cross-functional work	Incompatible IT
Need to share	Compartmentalization of functional groups
Localized decision making	Centralized top-down decision making

1. Does your company truly understand the environment in which it functions?

2. Does it gather information about practices and conditions outside the organization?

3. Is there awareness about how your company's internal operations compare with those of your competitors?

- *Shared perception of performance gaps:* Is there a shared and relatively well agreed upon perception of how things are in your company and of how they actually need to be? Maybe your customer response times are too long? Maybe the quality of your services is below the mark? There needs to be a fairly high degree of consensus on issues relating to performance gaps. Only then can you begin addressing the issues of primary concern and make an effort toward reducing those performance discontinuities and closely associated knowledge gaps. Recognizing these gaps also means that you can initially focus knowledge management on addressing issues where the benefits could be most compelling.

- *Metrics:* There should be a considerable focus on how things are measured. Is everything measured solely on the basis of financial outcomes? If so, you need to incorporate a better set of metrics that measures knowledge assets also. And that is the hardest part. Without an explicitly recognized set of measures, how can you attribute any part of improved performance to your company's knowledge?

A major consulting firm measures the value it gains from its knowledge management system to the number of additional consulting contracts completed and signed that result directly from what already exists in its portfolio of past projects. Even though there might be no perfect measure, there needs to be *some* way of measuring knowledge assets and the gains that the company realizes by leveraging them (Chapter 14 addresses this issue in detail).

- *Corporate culture:* Knowledge management is *at least* as much about a company's culture as it is about underlying technology. No technology, by itself, can take care of the often-ignored cultural part. Examples abound of companies that failed to realize any benefits from their knowledge management systems just because the culture was just not right. You need to realize the significance of nurturing a conducive corporate culture before you begin to attempt leveraging knowledge. Figuratively speaking, technology can lead the horse to the water but cannot make him drink it.

  A sharing culture in which problems, errors, omissions, successes, and disasters are shared and not penalized or hidden, is mandatory. You must accept debate and conflict as ways of solving problems. In Chapter 7, where we discuss the design of the technology infrastructure, you will see how different computer-based tools can be used to actually resolve conflict and debate by using past knowledge. But such tools will be of no help if debates and conflict are discouraged and failures hidden. Chapter 13 takes on this issue.

- *Knowledge champions:* Unlike what most prior management ideas suggest, having just one champion for knowledge management might just not cut it. New ideas and methods suggested by employees at all levels have to make it into the design. Because of the highly cross-functional nature of corporate knowledge, you need champions from different functional areas. The CIO or CKO alone might not be inertial enough as a champion. Champions can define the vision, but everyone else in the company needs to support, agree upon, refine, or even challenge it. Without this support, your company might be better off sticking to its old ways and avoid the bother of trying to implement a system that no one will *really* use.

  Knowledge activists serve as catalysts of knowledge creation and as the *connectors* of present initiatives with those in the future. Present initiatives represent projects being pursued in the organization at any given point in time; future initiatives refer to projects that follow either directly or indirectly from these present efforts. The underlying element of a knowledge management system is a supporting infrastructure of both IT applications as well as organizational measures that facilitate creation, capture, reuse, maintenance, and transfer of knowledge.

- *Strategic alignment:* Like any information technology strategy, knowledge strategy needs to be closely tied to the company's business strategy. If the company's primary goal is to sell low-cost products, then knowledge management strategy must be aligned to support that goal. If the ultimate goal is customer satisfaction, then the knowledge strategy needs to have a comparable and endorsing focus. A misalignment implies that your company is still missing a crucial facilitator to support knowledge use, application, and reuse.

- *Begin with what you know:* Before your company decides to become something new, evaluate what you are now. Without full awareness of what assumptions your company runs on now, you cannot gauge what needs to be done and where you need to begin. Rather than creating "new knowledge" in an attempt to breathe new life into your company's competitiveness, accept your current data and information assets and begin by leveraging those first.

Finally, use the toolkit in Appendix A (and the enclosed CD-ROM) to assess your company's readiness for knowledge management.

LESSONS LEARNED

Knowledge is best defined as actionable information—deeper, richer, and more expansive. Actionable implies that it is available when and where it is needed to make the right decisions, and in the right context. It is valid information endowed with meaning, context, and purpose that brings it to habitually bear upon decisions. Management of knowledge, not data or information, is therefore the primary driver of a firm's competitive advantage.

- *There are two primary types of knowledge.* Tacit knowledge is knowledge in the minds of employees that cannot be easily codified or explicated (therefore hard to manage or support with technology), and explicit knowledge is knowledge that can be stored and transferred, say, electronically. Using the process of externalization, subjective tacit knowledge based on experience is converted into objective explicit knowledge. Tacit and explicit knowledge can further be organized as strategic and operational, multilocational and centralized, migratory and situated. These include components such as experience, ground truth, judgment, heuristics, values, assumptions, and beliefs.

- *Experiential knowledge is stored as scripts.* Knowledge is largely derived from experience. Being able to transfer knowledge implies that a part of experiential knowledge—scripts, intuition, rules of thumb, heuristics, and methods—get transferred to the recipient as well.

- *Knowledge is essentially collaborative and falters with a data-hoarding mentality.* New knowledge is created, in part, through the collaborative processes that employees pursue as a part of their work. The threat to enabling such collaboration comes from the "more is better" data-hoarding mentality inherited from data processing and data management eras.

- *The five Cs:* Data is converted to information through condensation, contextualization, correction, categorization, and correction.

- *Managing knowledge is essential.* Knowledge management can help your company deal with market pressures; avoid the infinite, expensive loop of work duplication; precinct reinvention; and deal with the threat of job mobility of employees holding critical parts of your firm's tacit knowledge drivers.

- *Managing knowledge effectively can produce enviable results.* KM holds many promises for increased efficiency of processes, and proactively responsive corporate capabilities.

- *Beyond know-how, toward care-why.* Professional intellect can be thought of as a moving scale that begins with know-what and proceeds through know-how, know-why to care-why. The first three stages are well supported by a knowledge management system. First bring your company to the know-why stage using technology and cultural enablers. Most companies are still at a know-how driven stage.

- *Intranets and extranets can be a starting point for building a KMS.* An intranet is not a knowledge management system but can be built upon further to create the most suitable front end for one. A knowledge management system has a different content focus, has higher performance demands, uses a narrow base, and productizes knowledge.

- *Success of a knowledge management system depends on reciprocity.* Knowledge management depends on knowledge sharing, reciprocity, and a supporting culture. Reciprocity drives people's willingness to share knowledge, and such reciprocity can be introduced only through appropriate reward systems and corporate culture change.

- *Is your company ready for knowledge management?* Companies that have successfully deployed knowledge management share seven characteristics that can help you decide if your company is ready for it.

With this background, let us proceed to the 10-step knowledge management "methodology" that provides a road map for planning, developing, aligning, and successfully implementing both a knowledge management system and an incremental knowledge management strategy in your company.

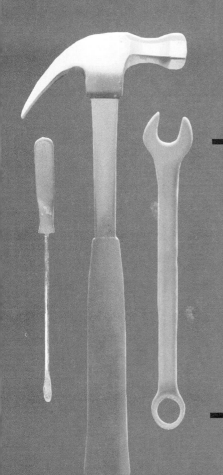

PART II
THE ROAD AHEAD:
IMPLEMENTING
KNOWLEDGE
MANAGEMENT

CHAPTER 4
THE 10-STEP
KM ROADMAP

IN THIS CHAPTER

✔ Understand the 10-step knowledge management roadmap and how it applies to *your* company.

✔ Understand the four phases constituting these 10 steps: infrastructural evaluation; KM system analysis, design, and development; deployment; and evaluation.

✔ Understand where each step takes you.

✔ Articulate a clear link between KM and business strategy to maximize performance and impact on your company's bottom line.

✔ Learn how to prioritize KM processes to maximize business impact.

✔ Understand the key steps involved in knowledge auditing, knowledge mapping, strategic grounding, deployment methodology, teaming, change management, and ROI metrics formation.

THEY COPIED ALL THAT THEY COULD FOLLOW BUT THEY COULD NOT COPY MY MIND,
AND I LEFT 'EM SWEATING AND STEALING AND A YEAR AND HALF BEHIND
—RUDYARD KIPLING.

Knowledge management is a complex activity, and like anything else that cannot deliver business impact without a concrete plan, it needs a perfect plan. This chapter introduces that plan: the 10-step knowledge management roadmap that will guide you through the entire process of creating a business-driven knowledge management strategy, designing, developing, and implementing a knowledge management system and effecting the soft changes that are required to make them work—with *your* company in mind. I chose to describe this plan as a roadmap rather than relegating it to the status of a methodology. A methodology undermines the level of complexity that is actually involved in managing knowledge and gives it a deceptive look of a cookie-cutter formulation.

May your competitors who thought that bleeding-edge technology was their nirvana rest in peace. For *nothing*—no technology, no market share, no product, and no monopoly—can ever provide a competitive advantage that is anything but temporary: They can all be copied, sometimes easily and sometimes with a little effort. Knowledge is the only resource that cannot be easily copied. Knowledge is much like *copy protection:* Even if your competitors get to it, they cannot apply it, for knowledge is protected by context in as copy-protected software is protected by encryption.

This strengthening idiosyncrasy of knowledge also has a negative implication for you: You cannot easily copy a competitor's knowledge management strategy and system. Examples from your industry's leaders can be useful for understanding knowledge management, but they cannot show you the right way to do it. For these reasons, your knowledge management system and knowledge management strategy will have to be unique to your company.

What follows in the next four sections of this book is an explication of the roadmap—not imitable methodology—that will help focus on your own company and develop a knowledge strategy whose results are hard hitting, but one that no competitor can easily duplicate. They can copy your KM technology but can never copy its context, let alone make it work in theirs. KM's deep grounding in corporate context comes from the fact knowledge management is lesser of a technology problem and more of an organizational problem. However, the technology that enables it and the culture that makes it work are so closely linked that separating the two will make neither work.

THE 10-STEP KNOWLEDGE MANAGEMENT ROAD MAP

Each of the next 10 chapters that follow will describe one each of the 10 steps in the knowledge management road map. These steps and their sequence are described in Figure 4-1.

To grasp the bigger picture, look at the four phases of the 10 steps of the road map. These comprise:

1. Infrastructural evaluation
2. KM system analysis, design, and development
3. System deployment
4. Evaluation

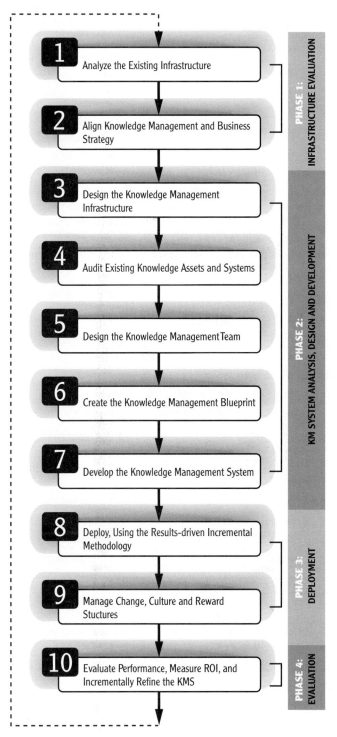

Figure 4-1 The 10-step knowledge management roadmap.

These four phases are described in Parts IIA, IIB, IIC and IID of this book. Table 4-1 describes how each of these steps is logically arranged in these chapters.

PHASE 1: INFRASTRUCTURAL EVALUATION

The first phase of the 10-step technique involves two steps. In the first step you analyze your existing infrastructure, then you identify concrete steps that you can take to leverage and build your knowledge management system upon. In the second step you analyze knowledge gaps by creating knowledge maps for your company. You further use these knowledge maps to create a high-level strategic link between business strategy and knowledge management. You then use this link develop both the knowledge management strategy and system in a manner that aligns them with business performance and objectives.

Table 4-1 Organization of Chapters Describing The Four Phases
of The 10-Step KM Roadmap

Part	Chapter	Step
PHASE 1: INFRASTRUCTURAL EVALUATION		
IIA	5	Step 1: Analyzing existing infrastructure
	6	Step 2: Aligning knowledge management and business strategy
PHASE 2: KM SYSTEM ANALYSIS, DESIGN, AND DEVELOPMENT		
IIB	7	Step 3: Designing the knowledge management architecture and integrating existing infrastructure
	8	Step 4: Auditing and analyzing existing knowledge
	9	Step 5: Designing the knowledge management team
	10	Step 6: Creating the knowledge management blueprint
	11	Step 7: Developing the knowledge management system
PHASE 3: DEPLOYMENT		
IIC	12	Step 8: Deploying with RDI methodology
	13	Step 9: Change management, culture, reward structure design, and choice of the CKO
PHASE 4: PERFORMANCE EVALUATION		
IID	14	Step 10: Measuring results of knowledge management, devising ROI metrics, and evaluating system performance

Step 1: Analysis of Existing Infrastructure

In this first step, you gain an understanding of various components that constitute the knowledge management strategy and technology framework. By analyzing and accounting for what is already in place in your company, you can identify critical gaps in the existing infrastructure. Consequently, you will be able to build upon what already exists. The key lies in accurately identifying *and fixing* what will work as a part of the knowledge management system and what will not. There is no silver bullet for knowledge management: Anything making that claim is fraught with immense risk. Instead of *telling* you what components to build upon, I will guide you through the process of making those decisions specifically in the context of your company. Although leveraging existing infrastructure is the logically, scientifically, rationally, theoretically, commonsensically, and financially right approach, it also stands a better chance of generating stronger management support for your knowledge management project because of the perception that you are not completely abandoning the "old" existing investments.

Specifically, as a part of this first step, we focus on the following:

1. Understanding the role of your company's existing networks, intranet, and extranets in knowledge management. You will analyze, leverage, and build upon data mining, data warehousing, project management, and decision support system (DSS) tools that might already be in place.

2. Understanding the knowledge management technology framework and its components.

3. Considering the option of using knowledge servers for enterprise integration, and performing a preliminary analysis of business needs that match up with relevant knowledge server choices.

4. Integrating existing intranets, extranets, and GroupWare into your knowledge management system.

5. Understanding the limitations of implemented tools and identifying existing gaps in your company's existing technology infrastructure.

6. Taking concrete steps to leverage and build upon existing infrastructural investments.

Step 2: Aligning KM and Business Strategy

Knowledge drives strategy, and strategy drives knowledge management. Without a clearly articulated link between knowledge management and business strategy, even the world's best knowledge management system will deliver zilch. Business strategy is usually at a high level, and, dare I say, with lofty goals. Developing systems is always at a low level: Specifications and features are needed, not abstractions, visions, or business ideas. The second step in the 10-step road map allows you to make the connection between these two: Raise knowledge management system design to the level of business strategy and pull strategy down to the level of systems design. As a part of the process of creating this alignment between knowledge management and business strategy, Chapter 6 describes what you must do:

1. Shift your company from strategic programming to strategic planning.

2. Move your systems design practices and business decisions away from the seemingly rigorous, fallacious notion of making predictions using extrapolations from past data. You must shift this critical decision-making dependency on knowledge that is both within and outside your company.

3. Perform a knowledge-based SWOT (strengths, weaknesses, opportunities, and threats) analysis and create knowledge maps for your own company, your main competitors, and your industry as a whole.

4. Analyze knowledge gaps and identify how knowledge management can fill those gaps. Do a cost-benefit analysis to prioritize filling such gaps.

5. Determine whether a codification or personalization focus is better suited for your company

6. Balance exploitation, exploration, and just-in-time (JIT) and just-in-case (JIC) delivery supported by your KM system.

7. Before you can design your knowledge management system, determine the right diagnostic questions to ask.

8. Translate your strategy-KM link to KM system design characteristics. You must articulate a clear strategy-KM link and incorporate the 24 critical success factors in KM design that we have learned from some exemplary knowledge management projects worldwide.

9. Mobilize initiatives to help you "sell" your KM project internally. Chapter 6 also describes how such initiatives can be selected.

10. Diagnose and validate your strategy-KM link, and use it to drive the rest of the design process.

When such alignment between your knowledge management and business strategy is clearly established from the outset, you can be sure that your knowledge management system is moving in a direction that holds promise for long-lasting competitive advantage and that it will *actually* benefit both your company's employees and its bottom line.

PHASE 2: KNOWLEDGE MANAGEMENT SYSTEM ANALYSIS, DESIGN, AND DEVELOPMENT

The second phase of knowledge management implementation involves analysis, design, and development of the knowledge management system. The five steps that constitute this phase are:

*   Knowledge management architecture design and component selection
*   Knowledge audit and analysis

- Knowledge management team design
- Creation of a knowledge management blueprint tailored for your organization
- Actual systems development

Let us briefly examine each of these steps and understand the key tasks that need to be accomplished at each step.

STEP 3: KNOWLEDGE MANAGEMENT ARCHITECTURE AND DESIGN

As the third step toward deploying knowledge management, you must select the infrastructural components that constitute the knowledge management system architecture. Knowledge management systems use a seven-layer architecture, and the technology required to build each layer is readily available. Integrating these components to create the knowledge management system model requires thinking in terms of an *infostructure* rather than an infrastructure.

Your first big choice is the collaborative platform. You can choose to use an open standard, such as the Web, or opt for a packaged solution such as Lotus Notes or a similar proprietary group support platform. We will reason through the choice of the preferred collaborative platform to decide whether the Web or Notes is better suited for your company. You must also create profiling mechanisms for push- and pull-based knowledge delivery while balancing cost versus value-added for each additional enabling component. Specifically, as a part of this third step, you must:

1. Comprehend various components of the knowledge infostructure
2. Identify internal and external knowledge source feeds that must be integrated
3. Choose IT components to find, create, assemble, and apply knowledge
4. Identify elements of the interface layer: clients, server, gateways, and the platform
5. Decide on the collaborative platform: Web or Notes?
6. Identify and understand components of the collaborative intelligence layer: artificial intelligence, data warehouses, genetic algorithms, neural networks, expert reasoning systems, rule bases, and case-based reasoning
7. Optimize knowledge object molecularity with your own company in mind
8. Balance cost against value-added for each enabling component
9. Balance push- and pull-based mechanisms for knowledge delivery
10. Identify the right mix of components for searching, indexing, and retrieval
11. Create knowledge tags and attributes: domain, form, type, product/service, time, and location tags
12. Create profiling mechanisms for knowledge delivery
13. Retrofit IT on the SECI knowledge management model to validate your choices

You do this after considering the ways in which work is done in your own company. The choice of these components will vary according to the different corporate cultures and work norms that exist in different companies.

STEP 4: KNOWLEDGE AUDIT AND ANALYSIS

A knowledge management project must begin with what your company already knows. In the fourth step, you audit and analyze knowledge, but first you must understand why a knowledge audit is needed. Then you assemble an audit team representing various organizational units as described in Chapter 8. This team performs a preliminary assessment of knowledge assets within your company to identify those that are both critical and the weakest.

As a part of this step you will:

1. Use Bohn's Stages of Knowledge Growth framework to measure process knowledge.
2. Identify, evaluate, and rate critical process knowledge on an 8-point scale.
3. Select an audit method out of several possible options.
4. Assemble a preliminary knowledge audit team.
5. Audit and analyze your company's existing knowledge.
6. Identify your company's K-spot.
7. Choose a strategic position for your knowledge management system that is in line with the strategic gaps identified in step 2.

STEP 5: DESIGNING THE KNOWLEDGE MANAGEMENT TEAM

In the fifth step on the KM road map, you design the knowledge management team that will design, build, implement, and deploy your company's knowledge management system. To design an effective knowledge management team, you must identify key stakeholders both within and outside your company and identify sources of expertise that are needed to successfully design, build, and deploy the system while balancing the technical and managerial requirements.

We examine the issues of correctly sizing the knowledge management team, managing diverse and often divergent stakeholder expectations, and applying techniques for both identifying and avoiding critical failure points in such teams. Specifically, you must take the following steps to design an effective team for implementing knowledge management:

1. Identify key stakeholders: IT, management, and end users; manage their expectations.
2. Identify sources of requisite expertise.
3. Identify critical points of failure in terms or unmet requirements, control, management buy-in, and end user buy-in.

4. Balance the knowledge management team's constitution—organizationally, strategically, and technologically.

5. Balance technical and managerial expertise that forms a part of this team.

6. Resolve team-sizing issues.

STEP 6: CREATING THE KNOWLEDGE MANAGEMENT SYSTEM BLUEPRINT

The knowledge management team identified in step 5 builds upon a knowledge management system blueprint that provides a plan for building and incrementally improving a knowledge management system. As you work toward designing a knowledge management architecture, you must understand its seven layers specifically in the context of *your* company and determine how each of these can be optimized for performance and scalability as well as high levels of interoperability.

Specifically, you will address the following issues in this step:

1. Customize the details of the seven layers of the knowledge management architecture to your own company.

2. Understand and select the components required by *your* company: integrative repositories, content centers, knowledge aggregation and mining tools, the collaborative platform, knowledge directories, the user interface options, push delivery mechanisms, and integrative elements.

3. Design the system for high levels of interoperability with existing IT investments; optimize for performance and scalability.

4. Understand and execute repository life-cycle management.

5. Understand and incorporate the seven key user interface (UI) considerations.

6. Position and scope the knowledge management system to a feasible level where benefits exceed costs.

7. Make the build-or-buy decision and understand the tradeoffs.

8. *Future proof* the knowledge management system so that it does not "run out of gas" when the next wave of fancy technology hits the market.

This step integrates work from all preceding steps so that it culminates in a strategically oriented knowledge management system design.

STEP 7: DEVELOPING THE KNOWLEDGE MANAGEMENT SYSTEM

Once you have created a blueprint for your knowledge management system (step 6), the next step is that of actually putting together a working system.

If you choose the Internet rather than depend on a proprietary collaborative platform, you can convert your company intranet to a front end for your system.

Web-friendly document standards such as DMA (Document Management Alliance) and WebDMA provide a great opportunity to build collaborative document systems to industry standards. Even though users will see a familiar intranet interface that they are probably already used to, the fundamental shift caused by the knowledge management system at the back end is the reorientation from a client/server architecture to an agent-computing architecture.

We will look at occasionally feasible approaches to integrate an array of hardware (including copiers, printers, and scanners) built around these standards into the knowledge management system itself. In this step, you will specifically:

1. Develop the interface layer. Create platform independence, leverage the intranet, enable universal authorship, and optimize video and audio streaming.

2. Develop the access and authentication layer. Secure data, control access, and distribute control.

3. Develop the collaborative filtering and intelligence layer, using intelligent agents and collaborative filtering systems. We look at options to buy intelligent agents versus easy and free tools that can be used to build your own.

4. Develop and integrate the application layer with the intelligence layer and the transport layer.

5. Leverage the extant transport layer to take advantage of existing networks that are already in place in your company.

6. Develop the middleware and legacy integration layer to connect the knowledge management system both to true legacy data and "recent," inconsistent legacy data repositories and databases left behind by custom systems that your company needs to retire for reasons of cost or lack of functionality.

7. Integrate and enhance the repository layer.

PHASE 3: DEPLOYMENT

The third phase in the 10-step road map involves the process of deploying the knowledge management system that you built in the preceding stages. This phase involves two steps:

1. Deployment of the system with a results-driven incremental technique, more commonly known as the RDI method. This step also involves the selection and implementation of a pilot project to precede the introduction of a full-fledged knowledge management system.

2. Cultural change, revised reward structures, and the choice of using (or not using) a Chief Knowledge Officer (CKO) to make knowledge management produce results. This is

perhaps the most important complementary step that is critical to the acceptance, and the consequent success, of a knowledge management system in any company.

Let us take a brief look at these two steps.

STEP 8: PILOT TESTING AND DEPLOYMENT USING THE RDI METHODOLOGY

A large-scale project such as a typical knowledge management system must take into account the *actual* needs of its users. Although a cross-functional KM team can help uncover many of these needs, a pilot deployment is the ultimate reality check. In the eighth step on the knowledge management road map, you must decide how you can select KM releases with the highest payoffs first.

Specifically, the deployment step requires you to:

1. Understand the need for a pilot knowledge management system deployment, and evaluate the need to run one; if it is needed, select the right, nontrivial, and representative pilot project
2. Identify and isolate failure points in pilot projects
3. Understand the knowledge management system life cycle and its implications for knowledge management system deployment.
4. Eliminate the "big-bang" information packaging methodology, the waterfall methodology, and systems development life cycle (SDLC) orientation
5. Understand the scope of knowledge management system deployment
6. Use the RDI methodology to deploy the system, using cumulative results-driven business releases
7. Decide when to use prototypes, and when not to use them
8. Convert factors to processes
9. Create *cumulative* results-driven business releases by selecting releases with the highest payoffs first
10. Identify and avoid the traps in the RDI methodology

Well-executed deployment will ensure that the knowledge management system is well received by the users for whom it is built.

STEP 9: THE CKO, REWARD STRUCTURES, TECHNOLOGY, AND CHANGE MANAGEMENT

The most erroneous assumption that many companies make is that the intrinsic value of an innovation such as a knowledge management system will lead to its enthusiastic adoption and use by their employees. Knowledge sharing cannot be mandated: Your employees are not like troops; they are like volunteers. Encouraging use and gaining employee support require integration of business processes with knowledge management system use, and new reward structures that motivate employees to use the system and contribute to its infusion, championing, and training. Above all, it requires enthusiastic leadership that sets an example to follow.

As part of this one but last step on the knowledge management road map, you need to:

1. Understand the role of a chief knowledge officer and decide whether your company—big or small—needs to formally have a CKO at all. This decision further requires an understanding of how a CKO relates to the CIO, CFO, and CEO. If you decide not to appoint a CKO, who else can best play that evangelist's role?

2. Organize the four broad categories of the CKO's or knowledge manager's responsibilities. To do so, you must understand the CKO's technological and organizational functions. We examine the backgrounds most successful CKOs come from.

3. Enable process triggers for knowledge management system success.

4. Plan for knowledge management success using the knowledge evangelist as an agent for selling foresight. Selling foresight is as hard as selling oxygen, but not as hard as selling the Brooklyn Bridge: It is difficult, but it can be done.

5. Manage and implement cultural and process changes to make your knowledge management system as well as your knowledge management strategy succeed.

Many companies hastily appointed CKOs out of a fear of being left behind, only to realize later that they did not really need one. You do not always need a CKO, per se, and Chapter 13 guides you through that choice.

PHASE 4: METRICS FOR PERFORMANCE EVALUATION

The last phase involves one step that most companies have been struggling with: measuring business value of knowledge management. When pushed for hard data, managers have often resorted to ill-suited and easily misused approaches, such as cost-benefit analysis, net present value (NPV) evaluation, vague ROI measures, or at best Tobin's q. Chapter 14 describes the seven pitfalls that companies are most vulnerable to and suggests ways to avoid them while devising a robust set of company-specific metrics for knowledge management.

STEP 10: METRICS FOR KNOWLEDGE WORK

The tenth step—measuring return on knowledge investment (RoKI)—must account for both financial and competitive impacts of knowledge management on your business. This step guides you through the process of selecting an appropriate set of metrics and arriving at a lean but powerful composite.

In this last iterative step on the 10-step knowledge management road map, you will do the following:

1. Understand how to measure the business impact of knowledge management, using a set of lean metrics

2. Calculate returns-on-investment (ROI) for knowledge management investments

3. Decide when to use benchmarking as a comparative knowledge metric

4. Evaluate knowledge management ROI using the Balanced Scorecard (BSC) method

5. Use quality function deployment for creating strategic knowledge metrics

6. Identify and stay clear of the seven common measurement pitfalls, and identify what *not* to measure

7. Review and select software tools for tracking complex metrics, QFDs, and BSCs

We also look at ways to classify and evaluate processes using *The APQC Process Classification Framework*. We also see how successful companies have approached metrics, what errors they have made in the past, and how you can learn from their mistakes.

Being able to measure returns serves two purposes: It arms you with hard data and dollar figures that you can use to prove the impact of effective knowledge management, and it lets you refine knowledge management design through subsequent iterations.

LESSONS LEARNED

The 10-step road map is built on years of cumulative research involving small and large companies in a variety of industries worldwide. It can help you create a link between business strategy and knowledge management. It can further help you design, develop, and deploy a knowledge management system that delivers actual business results. It is a road map that—unlike a cookie-cutter methodology—will help you build both a knowledge management strategy and a knowledge management system that are tailored to *your* company.

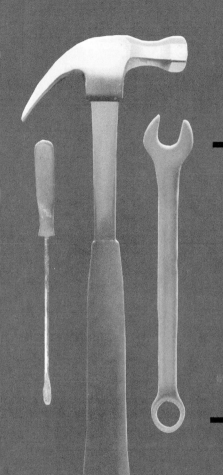

PART IIA
THE FIRST PHASE:
INFRASTRUCTURE
EVALUATION
AND LEVERAGE

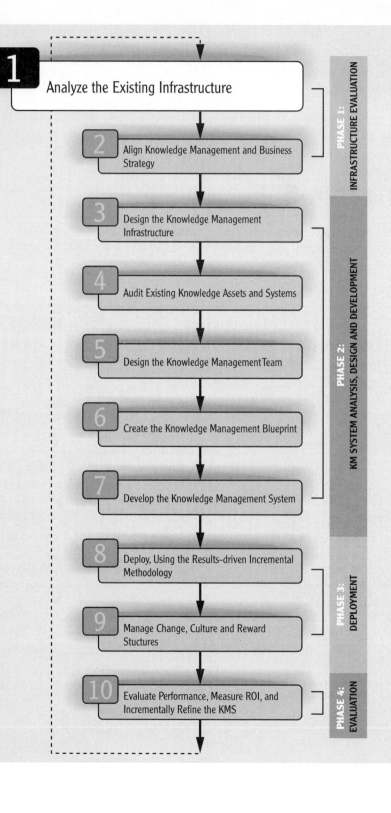

Chapter 5

The Leveraged Infrastructure

IN THIS CHAPTER

✔ Link your company's existing networks, intranet, and extranets to your knowledge management strategy.

✔ Comprehend the knowledge management technology framework and its components.

✔ Analyze, leverage, and build upon data mining, data warehousing, project management, and DSS tools that might already be in place.

✔ Deploy knowledge servers for enabling enterprise integration.

✔ Integrate existing intranets, extranets, and GroupWare into your knowledge management system.

✔ Perform a preliminary business needs analysis to evaluate relevant knowledge server choices.

✔ Identify the limitations of implemented tools and identify existing gaps in your company's existing infrastructure.

✔ Take definite steps to leverage and build upon existing infrastructural investments.

GREAT IDEAS OFTEN HAVE THREE STAGES OF REACTION—FIRST, "IT'S CRAZY AND DON'T WASTE MY TIME." SECOND, "IT'S POSSIBLE, BUT IT'S NOT WORTH DOING." AND FINALLY, "I'VE ALWAYS SAID IT WAS A GOOD IDEA."
—ARTHUR C. CLARKE

What would be your reaction if a consultant tried to convince you that knowledge management would make your company the most competitive firm in existence? But in exchange for this lofty promise, you were asked to abandon your existing practices, your communication systems, your networks, and your infrastructural investments and start building a knowledge management system from scratch. I, not alone, would almost be confident that his ideas would be a hard sell. Rightly so. But interestingly enough, in the exuberant rush to be the provider of the ultimate knowledge management tool, many companies and vendors selling everything from Web conferencing systems, data warehousing solutions, and GroupWare systems to Intranet toolkits are making precisely those claims. If we are to believe the unbelievable and exaggerated sales pitch of a data mining tool developer, their data mining tool is, *supposedly*, the ultimate knowledge management solution! But, we know better.

Ignoring the economic theory of sunk costs, the hard fact is that you cannot afford to abandon what you have, or for the most part, afford to substantially change what is working for your company right now—just on the premise of a distant rainbow! Knowledge management efforts and initiatives that will gain management support, continue funding, and keep risks low will have to build upon existing systems.[1] We call this concept *the leveraged infrastructure*. You build your entire knowledge management system over and above the existing infrastructure; you put in parts and tools that integrate what already exists. What works for Ford, Microsoft, and Monsanto need not work for your company. After all, losing a couple of hundred million dollars is only a small dent in Microsoft's budget. What about yours?

This chapter helps you through the analysis and evaluation of your company's existing infrastructure. By understanding components that constitute the knowledge management technology framework, you can identify gaps in your present infrastructure. A good part of this infrastructure will be usable for building your knowledge management system. But the key lies in accurately identifying *and fixing* what will work as part of the knowledge management system and what will not. There is no perfect recipe for knowledge management, and prescribing one is fraught with risk. Instead, we will walk through the process of making those decisions specifically in the context of your company. We examine technologies and assess their relative fit in the planned knowledge management system. I will introduce the concept of a knowledge server and provide guidelines to help you decide if you need one and criteria for selecting one if you do.

The greatest difficulty, as John Maynard Keynes[2] notes, lies not in persuading people to accept new ideas (such as knowledge management) but persuading them to abandon the old ones. The ability to leverage is, therefore, critical for knowledge management, as support from your higher-ups will probably depend on how well this is done.

THE APPROACH: LEVERAGE, LEVERAGE, LEVERAGE

Technology's most valuable role in knowledge management is broadening the reach and enhancing the speed of knowledge transfer.[3] Computing resources and processing power are no longer a limitation. The role of technology in knowledge management primarily lies in two aspects that assist it the most—storage and communications.[4] The primary role that computing has to play in knowledge management is therefore that of storing, which includes searching, retrieval, and networking. The key to successful knowledge management lies in leveraging the *existing* infrastructure: Tie in what already exists, integrate it, and begin there. Emerging technologies enable such integration.[5] Beginning from scratch is just not an option.

Knowledge, and the benefits of domesticating it, are old concepts. Technology puts us in an able position to harness it. Perhaps the biggest blessing is the advent of the Internet and the World Wide Web. However, knowledge management technology is a broader concept than just the Web and related technologies; most of the technologies that support KM processes and activities[6] have been around for many years.[7]

Bear in mind the following ideas when you are looking at what can be leveraged:

- *From the machine to the mind:* Innovation, generation of new ideas, and exploitation of a firm's intellectual prowess: These are keystones that a KM system needs to support.

- *Collaborative synergy and support:* Successful knowledge management is anchored to collaboration and collaborative success. If the KM system cannot support collaboration, knowledge sharing, learning, and continuous improvement, it's not worth the bother—it's destined to die for lack of use.

- *Real knowledge, not artificial intelligence:* A good knowledge management system is not about capturing your smartest employee's knowledge in a knowledge base or expert system. Even though that was the original intent of the artificial intelligence community, the possibility of that has now become a joke. While considering components to leverage, count out technology investments that solely focus on codification of tacit knowledge.

- *Conversation as a medium for thought:* A knowledge management system lives and thrives on conversation. Free, unrestricted, and easy conversation must be supported. The medium itself should not be a stricture.

- *Sources and originators, not just information:* A good knowledge management system must make it easy to find sources of know-how, not just know-how itself, locate people and expertise, and reuse what exists either in a tangible form, or in someone's head.

- *The golden rule:* A good knowledge management system is built around people.[8] Any proposed system must effectively recognize the primary mechanisms by which workers "work," and build technology solutions to leverage and facilitate these processes. People are not built to work around the way your system is designed. This golden rule—building systems around people instead of molding people to work with systems—is a concept that I teach every business school undergraduate!

- *Decision support:* Decision-making quality and accuracy should be enhanced by the historical perspective that a knowledge management system has to support.

- *Flexibility and scalability:* A well-designed knowledge management system is not written in stone. It has and needs room to grow and change with the business that it supports. Such flexibility in design will ensure future leverageablity.

- *Pragmatism, not perfection:* A knowledge management system should focus on pragmatism. Begin with what you have, and then incrementally improve it. Trying to get everything in place before you get ready to get on board will most likely cause you to miss the boat. As many managers I've talked to will attest, beginning in the most likely place, or with the most promising critical process is better than not beginning at all.

- *The user is king:* In concert with significant changes in both applications and technology architecture is greater awareness of user-defined requirements within this environment. A key success factor in a knowledge management system is the ability of end users to define and control interaction with numerous sources of information, and decide how information is classified, organized, and prioritized to suit perceived business needs and strategy.

- *Ease of use:* A knowledge management system has to be easy to use. Leveraging our knowledge of "good" Web design can partially ensure that. The role model is the telephone. Really.

LEVERAGING THE INTERNET

A fleeting glimpse of existing technology in most companies reveals a transformative addition—the Internet. It offers hope for true integration of the islands of information and knowledge that dot the organizational landscape. Even though Lotus Notes, by itself, is very promising, it is the Internet that will truly make enterprise-wide knowledge integration possible.[9] We next discuss some of the characteristics that make the Internet an inevitable choice.

GLOBAL REACH

The Internet was intended to be free for all. The value of this is akin to having free long distance in your home! You can use it all you want, yet pay nothing. All you pay for is the local line. Just as in case of free long distance (there is no such thing as truly free long distance!), all you really pay for is the monthly fee to get on the Internet. In the context of knowledge management, the Internet's global reach has five key implications:

1. *A cost-effective global network backbone:* In reality, the Internet, albeit cheaper than an equivalent leased network, is still an expensive proposition in some respects. Companies pay for access to the Internet and the Web, partly in hard dollars and partly in soft dollars (including time lost by employees who get too caught up in surfing the Web)!

2. *Anyplace, anywhere:* The value of the Internet primarily lies in its ability to connect users anyplace and anywhere, as long as they have access to the Web. You could be in Atlanta and log on to a company intranet in Bangkok, and vice versa. What would have

once cost hundreds of thousands of dollars—connecting five offices in five countries—can now be done for a minuscule fraction of that cost with technologies such as virtual private networks (VPNs).

3. *Distributed connectivity:* Similarly, distributed resources and databases can be interconnected cost effectively and reliably, using virtual networks tunneled within the Internet. Web browsers provide a ubiquitous interface that easily is customized to support multiple languages, regional preferences, and features across the enterprise, which might span national boundaries.

4. *Robust global data path:* The Internet is a robust global connection mechanism. Unlike a leased line that can bring the network down at any one point of failure, the Internet offers multiple paths for moving time-sensitive data reliably, even if networks fail at multiple points. The inherent nature of the Internet offers unprecedented redundancy and robustness.

5. *Cheaper, faster, and directly usable global competitive intelligence:* The Internet makes it possible to reach other sites, such as competitor portals, as easily as your own. This open accessibility reduces the cost of having to keep up with what competition is up to. In the context of knowledge management, the Internet makes it viable and cost effective to tap into readily available, continuously and invisibly importable external electronic information on competitive businesses.

THE SOUL OF THE NETWORK

Ignoring the soft costs for the time being, let's look at the hard costs, such as monthly access fees. Usually, this money goes to the Internet service provider (ISP) which charges you for connecting to an access point that lets you connect to the backbone networks. The U.S. portion of the Internet can be thought of as having three levels. At the bottom are local-area networks (LANs); for example, campus networks. Usually the local networks are connected to a regional or mid-level network. The mid-levels connect to one or more backbones. A backbone is an overarching network to which multiple regional networks connect and that generally does not serve directly any local networks or end users. The U.S. backbones connect to other backbone networks around the world. A few years ago the primary backbone was the NSFNET. On April 30, 1995, the NSFNET ceased operation, and now traffic in the United States is carried on several privately operated backbones. The new "privatized Internet" in the United States is becoming less hierarchical and more interconnected. The separation between the backbone and regional network layers of the current structure is blurring as more regional companies are connected directly to one another through network access points (NAPs) and as traffic passes through a chain of regional networks without any backbone transport.

PLATFORM INDEPENDENCE

Data in the enterprise is often available in a multitude of formats and platform-dependent forms. Even if we ignore the platform compatibility issues that people might have with different versions of Windows alone, a typical company is still left with several, often incompatible platforms across which its data is spread out. Knowledge management must begin by taking stock of what information and knowledge already exists.[10] But the range of formats in which explicit knowledge alone exists makes this a formidable task. Paper documents are not a problem to begin with, as they come into the picture once we know how to deal with electronic ones first. Paper can always be scanned into the primary repository format that a company uses.

However, electronic data, as shown in Figure 5-1, exists on PCs, UNIX workstations, proprietary systems, Linux machines, Apple Macintosh systems, iMacs, and Palm OS devices.[11] As organizations grapple with technology decision chains, increasing attention comes to bear on identifying an integrated solution that can meet current and emerging user needs. Business information no longer comes from or resides in a single place; it is derived from disparate information streams—collaborative documents, Web pages, newsfeeds, e-mail, etc. At the same time as firms, enterprises, and knowledge workers are seeking integrated solutions to managing and using information resources, the emergence of intranet technology has presented enormous opportunities for information sharing and content delivery to enterprise workers and collaborative audiences. More than the benefit of global reach that the Internet brings with it, its ability to integrate data and documents across almost all platforms is its strongest, undeniably great characteristic.

The Internet, or more accurately, the Web, provides this integrative ability through the use of a common, relatively standardized hypertext markup language commonly known as HTML and the complementary HTTP protocol. These provide that *magical binding glue* that we have always wished for.

ENABLING TECHNOLOGIES FOR THE KNOWLEDGE MANAGEMENT TECHNOLOGY FRAMEWORK

Many of the technologies that support the management of knowledge have been around for a long time.[12] The Internet has finally provided the ether to meld these. In this section, we examine enabling technologies that make the knowledge management technology framework possible. Following an analysis of these extant technologies, many of which might be already in place—albeit fragmented—in your own company, we can make judgments about what can be taken as is, and what more needs to be added to leverage existing infrastructure.

Figure 5-2 illustrates the five meta components of the knowledge management technology framework.

To understand how these components interrelate, it is essential to understand their key functions. The primary set of functions (and cross-category secondary functions) of these meta components are as follows:

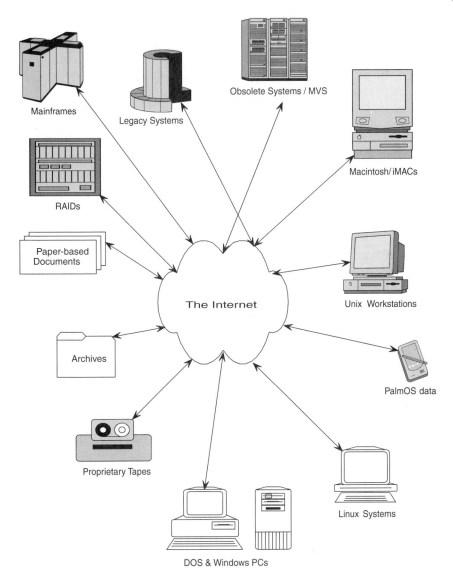

Figure 5-1 The Internet provides the common base that allows data exchange across all platforms. The number of independent, often incompatible platforms has not decreased even as the desktop-computing environment has standardized itself on Windows.

1. *Knowledge flow:* These components facilitate knowledge flow within the knowledge management system.
2. *Information mapping:* These link and map the flow of information that might later be converted to knowledge across the enterprise.

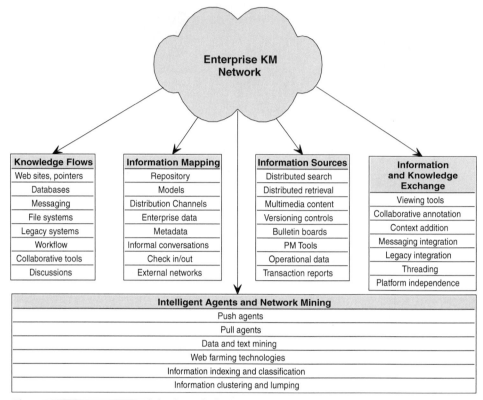

Figure 5-2 Components of the knowledge management technology framework.

3. *Information sources:* Data sources feed raw data and information into the knowledge management system.

4. *Information and knowledge exchange:* Tools and nontechnological facilitators that enable exchange of information across tacit (such as people) and explicit (such as databases, transaction processing repositories, and data warehouses) sources, help create and share context (the process itself is called *contextualization*), and facilitate sensemaking.[a]

5. *Intelligent agent and network mining:* Knowledge mining, linking, retrieval, and intelligence tools facilitate finding knowledge using intelligent agents and pattern mining tools.

Figure 5-3 illustrates how these technology components tie in together. Let's examine each of these technologies as we build upon this understanding in the following chapters.

---

[a]Sensemaking refers to the ability of a person, or group to comprehend knowledge and interpret it in its context. The term was popularized by Chun Wei Choo in *The Knowing Organization,* Cambridge University Press, New York (1998).

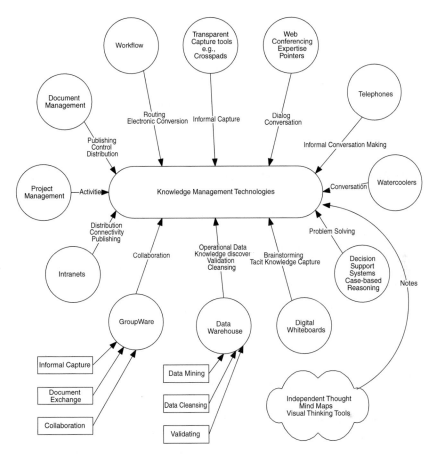

Figure 5-3 The framework of technologies required to support knowledge management and their functionality.

KNOWLEDGE FLOW META COMPONENT

The knowledge flow meta component constitutes subcomponents that facilitate the flow of information and knowledge across the organization. Intranets and extranets provide paths for explicated knowledge, group support mechanisms and collaborative platforms provide paths for both explicated content and tacit context, and knowledge pointers provide directions to locations where actual tacit knowledge is situated.

Collaborative Environments and GroupWare

The process of creating, sharing, and applying knowledge inherently involves collaboration.[13] Knowledge-based activities related to innovation and responsiveness are intensively collaborative. For example, brainstorming sessions, problem solving, idea generation, and strategy planning meetings are usually highly interactive, involving multiple people, often from different locations, functional mixes, and operational bases. The basic technological element to support such collaboration is GroupWare.[b]

GroupWare tools provide a document repository, remote integration, and a base for collaborative work. Unfortunately, the term *GroupWare* is not always associated with collaborative work, since such tools are often underutilized and relegated to the limited status of document management and routing tools. Lotus Notes is perhaps the most widely used GroupWare tool in use today. Other examples include Netscape Collabra, Microsoft's freebie NetMeeting, Novell GroupWise, Webflow, etc.

COLLABORATIVE ENVIRONMENTS AT THE CHASE MANHATTAN BANK

Chase Manhattan has developed a Notes-enabled collaborative system that manages client portfolios by drawing together information from disparate systems and presenting it in a number of views. The bank's relationship managers use the system to make decisions that benefit both Chase and its customers.

Figure 5-4 provides a deeper overview of this component and how it fits into a knowledge management system. I would include e-mail in this category as well because it is the primary driver of conversation on the Internet.

Intranets and Extranets

Given the wealth of information available within and outside an organization, some of the explicit knowledge that enterprises need already exists.[14] The primary concern is to find an effective way to access it and distribute it as required.[15] Thus, internal and external access and distribution has become a priority for knowledge workers.

Before the Internet entered the mainstream of computing, communication networks had to be either built or leased. While building a dedicated communications link from one building to the next is not a very expensive proposition, building one from Atlanta to New York or Sacramento to Singapore surely is. Until the advent of the Internet as a public medium, the ability of larger companies to afford such networks provided them a temporary competitive advantage. Now, Intranets allow the same networks to be constructed over the Internet. Virtual private networks allow secure, cost-effective, and unrestricted communication across regional and national boundaries. While intranets have been in use for a while and many companies have used them effectively for improving information flow throughout their enterprise, the true value of intranets as a tool for collaboration is yet to be realized. Similarly, extranets, which are farther reaching, more expansive, transorganizational versions of Intranets, allow companies to efficiently tap into knowledge-based resources of partners and those of ally firms.

---

[b]GroupWare is a trademarked term that is now loosely used to describe only group support systems, including collaborative workspaces such as Lotus Notes.

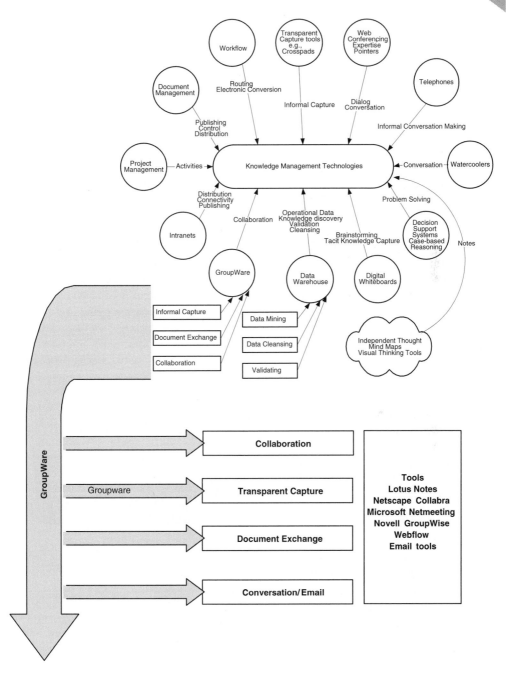

Figure 5-4 GroupWare tools form an essential component of a knowledge management system and include common collaborative tools such as electronic mail and document routing systems.

One of the most important aspects of information access is that of being able to view content of documents regardless of file format, operating system, or communications protocol. Intranets, owing to their consistent, platform-independent access formats such as rich HTML, and a common, consistent protocol (HTTP), make this possible. Besides information distribution and publication, intranets provide the backbone platform for push delivery of information to user's desktops.[16] If this information is well filtered and cleansed by collaborative filtering tools such as GrapeVine, it will be a key source of actionable, timely, and immediately relevant information—knowledge. You nevertheless have to buy into the idea of push knowledge delivery before you actually do implement methods for this approach. Figure 5-5 shows how intranets fit into the knowledge management technological framework.

Pointers to Expertise

Besides their basic roles as publishing and information distribution platforms, intranets are the primary platform for the creation of *electronic yellow pages*. As Thomas Davenport and Laurence Prusak suggest in *Working Knowledge,*[17] there is a limit to the extent of information that is humanly possible to put into electronic format, say, on an intranet. There is also a limit on the knowledge that can be actually elicited from an individual with the necessary expertise.[c] Beyond this fatigue point, pointers to the person who actually contributed that knowledge are needed to facilitate knowledge flow. Knowledge yellow pages and skills directories provide that link. Yellow pages are simply a Web-searchable electronic version of skills lists, albeit with a lot more context added to them by past users. When a key resource person is needed or when a person with specific skill sets or expertise is required, keyword and attribute tag searching can pull up pointers with contact information about persons who qualify, both inside (such as employees in local and foreign offices) and outside the organization (such as consultants and researchers). While this has been a popular concept in academia, where work is typically knowledge intensive, it is gaining increasing popularity in many skills-fueled, knowledge-intensive companies such as Microsoft.

Figure 5-6 shows such a Web-based directory that lists people with their primary areas of expertise. It further allows users to search for persons with specific skills, experience, and knowledge, as shown in Figure 5-7. The actual example in Figure 5-7 shows a contact telephone number. It would be a good idea to make an e-mail address, possibly a fax number, and related contacts available as well. The results screen shows these data listed for a fictitious entry.

INFORMATION MAPPING META COMPONENT

Subcomponents of the information mapping meta component map paths for both the origins and destinations influencing information. We look at document management systems (which are often integrated with workflow tools) in this section. Repositories with context, information distribution channels, meta-data, data associated with informal conversations, and paths of external networks constitute other subcomponents of the information mapping component.

---

[c]This is, arguably, the primary reason for the lackluster success of expert systems.

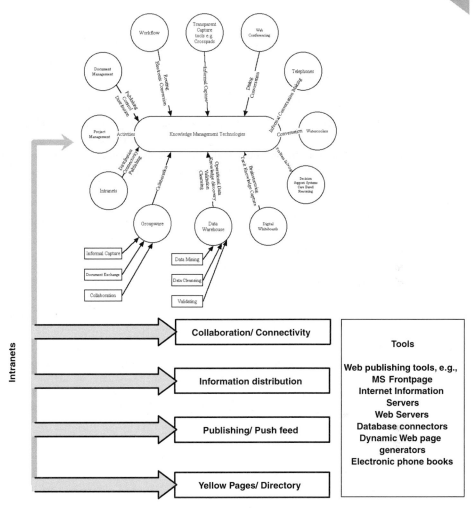

Figure 5-5 How intranets fit into the bigger picture of a knowledge management technological framework. Specific examples of tools listed here allow extension of
the capabilities of the traditional information-centric model of the corporate
intranet to support knowledge management.

Document Management

A lot of crucial information often exists primarily on paper. Companies try to convert
this information into a more easily transferable and searchable electronic format by scanning
these documents. This laudable effort should be pursued in moderation. It should not be the
focus of a knowledge management initiative, because this often sanitizes information of its
context. Convert only those pieces of information that are needed. Simply cataloging information is often sufficient.

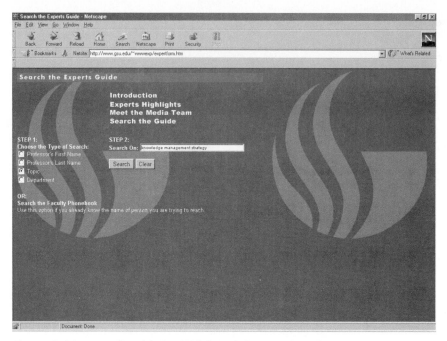

Figure 5-6 An expert's guide is a Web-based directory that allows users to search through its employee database on the basis of skills and areas of expertise.

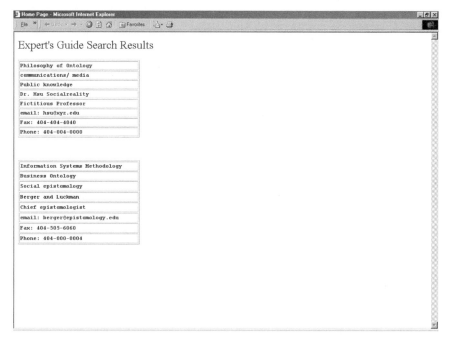

Figure 5-7 After an expert is located, key contact information should be made available as well.

If teams collaboratively work on documentation or creation of documents, tools that support versioning are very helpful. They ensure that everyone has access to the latest updated version of the document, instead of different people working on different and often inconsistent versions of these documents. GroupWare often fills this need, at least in part. At a commercial level, a number of other tools and standards based on standards such as DMA WebDAV allow tighter integration with knowledge management systems. We look at such tools later.

Document management (DM) also includes the ability to develop a database of documents and classify them, automatically. This makes document searching a painless job. PC Docs, FileNet, Documentum, and Hyland are popular vendors in this product market. See Chapter 9 for an in-depth discussion of the relationship between knowledge management and document management. Figure 5-8 illustrates document management in the knowledge management technology framework.

Emerging DM standards, such as WebDAV and DMA, that allow document management solutions to be tightly integrated with some knowledge management systems hold a lot of promise.

INFORMATION SOURCE META COMPONENT

The information source meta component comprises subcomponents that provide information feeds to the knowledge management system. Distributed search and retrieval mechanisms, multimedia content containing informal content (such as speech or video clips), electronic bulletin boards, summaries of transactional and operational data, transaction reports, project management tools, etc., constitute this category. In this section, we look at project management tools and multimedia content because they call for further explanation.

Project Management Tools

Project management tools, such as Microsoft Project[18], provide a fairly high degree of organization to activities that surround creation of knowledge. Very often, these tools allow users to trace back documents and artifacts that might have resulted from an earlier project. Microsoft Project (see Figure 5-9) is a good example of a tool that integrates well with the rest of the enterprise tool suite, in this case, Microsoft Office 2000.

Although the role of project management tools in the actual creation of knowledge is limited, these tools can provide a good basis for organizing and storing documents, records, notes, etc., coming out of a single project engagement. Project management tools often allow users to link the resources they use to the project management document, generate a variety of reports, and trace referenced hyperlinks. Such tools are quite novel, but they have a long way to go before they truly become useful in organizing knowledge. Another aspect of their relegation to the status of mere data sources comes from the inconsistent manner in which they are used. Many companies populate these tools in a postproject phase, leaving the accuracy of project history traceability open to questions. Only the tools that support the common Web-based interface will truly fit into the overall knowledge management system architecture.

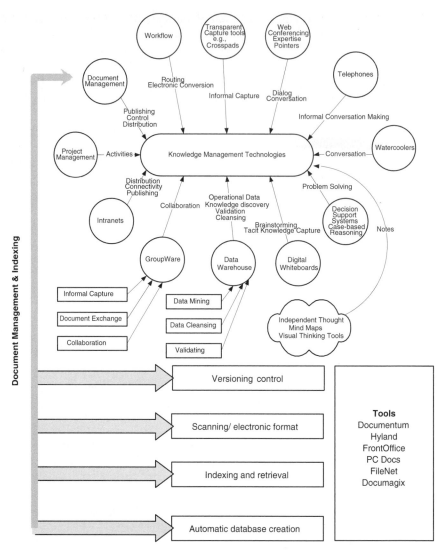

Figure 5-8 The role of document management tools in the knowledge management
system and infrastructure

Multimedia

The worth of multimedia reaches far beyond fancy Websites. In a knowledge management system, multimedia allows the system to capture informal content that would otherwise
be lost for ever. Multimedia content is classified as an information source because, by itself, it
is devoid of context and needs interpretation. A multimedia clip of, say, a moving machine
part, when stored in an information repository, conveys a complex operation that would be

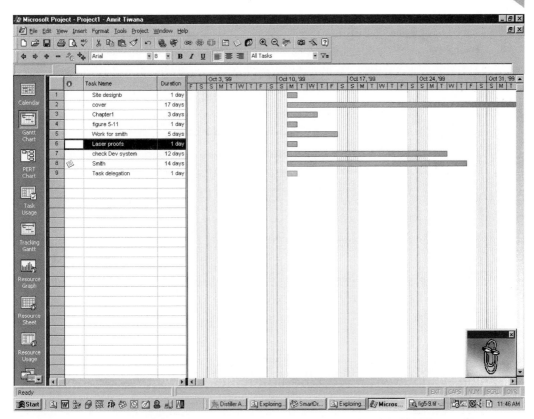

Figure 5-9 Project management tools such MS Project allow consistent and conflict-free control of various activities surrounding projects. The ability to link to information sources across the enterprise, incorporate pointers at dead ends, and easy integration with the Web-based interface used by the KM system are crucial choice factors.

complicated, time-consuming, and expensive to describe in explicated words. Multimedia, especially video content, bypasses limitations of language—an occasional barrier to knowledge sharing when you are working in transnational project teams. If a picture is worth a thousand words, a full-motion multimedia video clip is perhaps worth even more.

INFORMATION AND KNOWLEDGE EXCHANGE META COMPONENT

The information and knowledge exchange meta component comprises computer-based tools and nontechnological facilitators that allow people and systems to exchange, contextually share, transfer explicit and tacit forms of knowledge. The subcomponents constituting this component include collaborative annotation tools, messaging integrators, legacy integrating middleware, conversation threading mechanisms, and information beading tools on the explicit end of the spectrum; and context addition mechanisms, rich-media Internet conferencing systems, video conferencing tools, electronic water coolers, community building networks, the telephone, mind maps, visual thinking software, white boards (both wooden and electronic) on the tacit end of the spectrum. We look at transparent capture enabling tools, Web conferencing systems, mind mapping software tools, and electronic water coolers in this section.

COLLABORATIVE KNOWLEDGE SHARING AT DOW CHEMICAL

Dow Chemical demonstrates how simple desktop collaborative tools can result in enviable paybacks, without significant upfront investments. Dow Chemical Company realized by late 1996 that it was becoming increasingly difficult for its 40,000 employees to collaborate across its 115 locations in 37 countries. Traveling had been extensive until virtual teams began meeting by telephone. A presentation, plan, or other document would be put out on a machine running Windows NT server (now Windows 2000), and each person in the conference would bring up the document at the desktop. The problem was that as changes were made, each person would have to make them in his/her individual document, which left the door open to errors and inconsistencies.

The company then, very successfully, tried Microsoft NetMeeting conferencing software and made it available to its 28,000 desktop users at 250 sites around the world. Dow has enabled these virtual, globally distributed teams to exchange data, confer, share presentations, and collaborate on the same document at the same time, irrespective of their location. John Deere and Ford Motor Company have also had positive experiences with Web conferencing tools for encouraging and enabling knowledge exchange and sharing.

Transparent Capture Enablers

Managers and project team members often take notes during meetings and brainstorming sessions.[d] White boards and legal pads, both of which now have electronic equivalents, are perhaps the most widely used nontechnology tools used in such sessions. For this reason, Figure 5-10 shows an additional component, independent thought (and notes associated with these thoughts), that is integrated into the rest of the framework in subsequent discussions. A lot of information, ideas, possible directions, approaches get thrown on the table in such meetings. When specific solutions are chosen, others are discarded. These discarded solutions are often valuable in other projects or helpful in revising strategies when changes in product target markets occur.

---

[d]Even if some of these participants are doodling, organizational theorists argue that their context is associated with the doodles. In any case, being able to keep track of all such "notes" is relevant and potentially helpful.

For example, a Web development team might have chosen not to use graphics-intensive Macromedia Flash™ on its Website, knowing that a typical customer does not have high-speed Internet access. If this assumption changed one year later, the company would go through the time-wasting grunt of deliberating exactly the same issue. Unfortunately, decisions in product and service development teams are not as simple as this example.

Technologies like the Crosspad[19] (by Cross, the pen manufacturer) allow such informal notes, including doodles, to be electronically captured without affecting the way participants *ordinarily* go around their regular jobs. The Crosspad and similar products capture whatever is drawn on regular paper notepads, and store as images on a personal computer. Scanners attached to whiteboards can scan entire contents of a white board and convert them into an electronic file that can then be distributed, posted, printed, exchanged, or emailed.

Similarly, tools such as electronic whiteboards (including the basic form of white board technology that comes as a part of Microsoft NetMeeting for Windows 98 and Windows

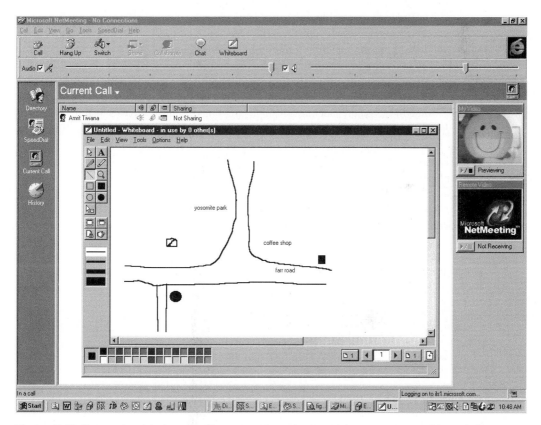

Figure 5-10 Electronic whiteboards allow users to exchange tacit components of knowledge across highly distributed networks. The screenshot above shows how a Microsoft NetMeeting user exchanges directions and sketches with a collaborator in another country in real time.

2000) allow such exchanges to take place in real time, over highly distributed networks, and among geographically dispersed participants. Tools like this are indispensable in moving a company from a structured information-based focus to a formal and informal knowledge-centric focus.

Web Conferencing, Water Coolers, and Telephones

The telephone is perhaps the best example of a system that has some of the characteristics highly desirable in an *effective* knowledge management system. As we saw in the previous chapter, a critical component that promotes knowledge sharing, creation, and transfer but is missing in most information technology tools is the component that supports informal collaboration, discussion, and chat. While not all desktop systems in your company need to be chat enabled, it does have other implications on knowledge management technology design. There must be a way to encourage *and enable* informal chat and conversations (even office gossip) that are a part of work life in most nonvirtual office settings.

The technologies to enable that have been with us for a few years now and only need to be put to effective use. While people who have felt the need to collaborate in such a manner have been doing so, using the fax and telephone together. Simply fax a document, drawing or illustration to the person on the other end, then pick up the phone and talk about it! This has been successful in creating a medium for a two-way, albeit highly constricted collaborative work. For example, if the person on one end makes a change to a drawing or illustration or expresses something visually (such as a scribble or a line diagram), she will be limited only to the degree (richness) of communication that a telephone allows—highly limited. But recent advances in computing, along with the advent of higher-speed, high-bandwidth networks have made it possible to allow this in a richer fashion through the Web. This has the following implications for knowledge management system design:

1. *Virtual meetings:* Web conferencing enables virtual meetings where users from different locations connect, conduct meetings, and share information as if everyone were in the same room. Participants can share virtually any Windows-based application, including program screens, presentation graphics, word processing, and spreadsheet software, and all meeting participants can see the same information in real time.

2. *Document collaboration:* Web-based, real-time, distributed collaboration lets team members work together with many other participants on documents or information in real time, or share an application running on one single computer with other people in a meeting. Everyone can view the information shared by the application, and any participant can take control of the shared application to edit or paste information in real time. This technology brings collaborative work to a new level that resembles two people working on a task on the same personal computer at a given time—the closest that you can come to working together physically.

3. *Informal communication:* Since conversations can take place in natural voice and with electronic (visual) presence, informality, like that possible with a telephone, is possible

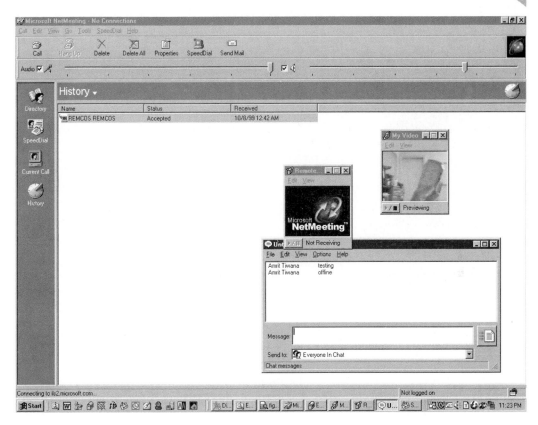

Figure 5-11 Microsoft's NetMeeting allows real-time communication with participants connected through the Internet. Tools like this allow users to converse—through video, audio, sharing, and controlled collaboration.

to achieve. A lot of research in academia has shown that people who can see one another face to face establish trust more easily[20]—and trust is a prerequisite for effective knowledge sharing and uninhibited collaboration.

Microsoft NetMeeting is an excellent example of a Web-based conferencing tool that allows people to collaborate and conference through the Web. Figure 5-11 shows how participants from across the world can collaborate, share a document, and add content to it in real time, at virtually no incremental cost. Chat-rooms are the electronic version of *water coolers* that Davenport and Prusak talked about in *Working Knowledge.* Participants can hang around, take part in discussions, argue, disagree, converse, and deliberate.

AMERICA ONLINE'S MOST WIDELY SHARED SECRET

For the believers of capitalist free markets, the best proof of the value of real-time collaborative environments comes from America Online. If market acceptance is the litmus test for real-time collaboration, America Online has been passing it with flying colors for a long time, years before even Windows became mainstream.

America Online had about 18 million customers as late 1999. Even Microsoft's own online service could not compete with AOL for one simple reason—AOL had the best conversation tools built into its interface. These have, since AOL's inception, been called chat rooms and have been the favorite feature among AOL users and a primary reason for its continued success and popularity despite the higher price that it charges for its services. *The New York Times* (July 24, 1999) reports that AOL had over 80 million registered users of its AOL messenger and ICQ chat tools, who exchanged almost 800 million messages every day. Microsoft, embracing the value of real-time chat over the Internet, introduced a competing product, Microsoft Messenger* in June 1999.

---

*A free copy can be downloaded at http://messenger.msn.com/.

Other tools that fall under this category of enablers include Caucus, Web Crossing, Notes discussion databases, REMAP[e], Optimus, and Netscape's AOL Instant Messenger[f] add-on for Web browsers.

Mind Mapping

Knowledge sharing can be synchronous or asynchronous. Software developers and programmers have used concept maps to organize logical thought, for several years. Mind mapping,[g] a visual thinking technique popularized by Tony Buzan, falls into the category of independent thought in Figure 5-3. Mind maps, very close to concept maps, can be used to organize individual or collective thought and represent it visually.

---

[e]REMAP is a tool developed by a colleague. See Balasubramaniam, Ramesh, and Vasant Dhar, Supporting Systems Developing Using Knowledge Captured During Requirements Engineering, *IEEE Transactions on Software Engineering* (1992). This tool has been extensively developed further to support knowledge management in distributed teams collaborating over the Web.

[f]This tool is available for free. Download on America Online's Website at www.aol.com.

[g]An excellent discussion of the mind-mapping concept can be found in Tony and Barry Buzan's *The Mind Map Book,* Plume, New York (1996). Detailed descriptions of software tools for collaborative mind mapping can be found in Chapter 16. A software tool based on this idea is included on the companion CD-ROM.

Mind mapping can be an excellent knowledge creation and organization tool, especially with the advent of excellent software supporting it. Some of these tools have most of the features of real-time collaboration software integrated in them, and allow for collective deliberation over the Internet. Figure 5-12 shows a mind map used in the early stages of writing this book.

A full version of the popular mind mapping tool, Mind Man Personal, is included on the companion CD-ROM.

INTELLIGENT AGENT/NETWORK MINING META COMPONENT

The intelligent agent and network mining meta component comprises subcomponents such as intelligent decision support systems, search engines, content aggregation tools, push- and pull-based intelligent agents, content mining, Web farming, clustering, automatic indexing, and tag-based cybernetic classification tools. We look at intelligent decision support systems and intelligent agent-based content aggregation and clustering tools, both of which warrant more discussion in the context of knowledge management.

Intelligent Decision Support Systems

Decision support systems, case-based reasoning (CBR) systems, and contextual information retrieval systems provide the needed historical base from past experience that help make both minor and major decisions fast and accurately. Popular tools in this category include those from Inference Inc. and Brightware technologies. Data mining tools help extract trends and patterns from data warehouses. External information retrieval systems provide the key financial and nonfinancial indicators of the company's health. Later chapters in Part IIB of this book discuss these topics in detail.

Intelligent Agent-Based Tools

Filtering, editing, searching, and organizing pieces of knowledge, collectively called *packaging,* are essential though frequently overlooked components of successful knowledge management. Packaging knowledge ensures that what is sieved proves useful, provides value, encourages application of that knowledge to address actual business issues, and figures into critical decisions. Search tools need to integrate knowledge latently existing in a company's transaction databases, data warehouses, discussion databases, documents, informal media, and, most importantly, in people's minds. While plumbing the last source is not an easy or direct job, yellow pages and skills directories provide that capability to a moderate extent.

Search tools have to go beyond the basic keyword-based search capabilities in common use in businesses today. Conventional search mechanisms are of limited value in a knowledge management system for three reasons:

1. *Excessive query matches:* Search engines such as Yahoo and AltaVista use simple keyword matching to find matches between target documents and keywords contained in a user's query, often returning hundreds, if not thousands, of irrelevant "hits." Due

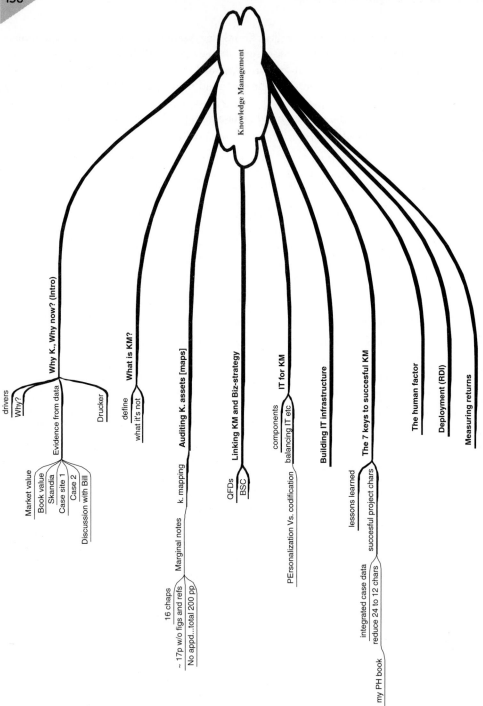

Figure 5-12 A typical mind map consists of visual associations between logical units of individual thought. Collaborative software tools make this a valuable technique in group knowledge sharing processes.

to the sheer simplicity of keyword matching (even with relevance rankings and boolean AND/OR filtering), there is often the risk of finding information that is no longer valid. Date-based sorting provides little respite, since "new" information can also be invalid, stale, or outright wrong.

2. *Breadth tradeoffs:* Information retrieval tools such as Verity and Fulcrum provide relevancy rankings with query results. Although such tools mitigate the problem of excessive hits, they often limit their searches to certain data types.

3. *Failure to understand meanings of words and exact context of use:* The most severe limitation of search engines and information retrieval tools lies in their inability to understand the *meanings* of words that users *intend* to convey.

   For example, if the user asked a question with "blow" as a part of it, a conventional search engine is unable to determine whether the user meant an air current, flower blossoms, an explosion, an act of fleeing, bragging, an unexpected attack, or enlargement (all of which are defined as acceptable meanings of the word by *Webster's New Riverside Desk Dictionary*).

Emerging developments in intelligent agent-based search mechanisms allow synchronous and asynchronous searches to be performed in an intelligent manner, while simultaneously reducing the bandwidth requirements typically demanded by conventional search mechanisms. Mobile agents—which depart from a "home" location, hop across networked servers scouring for information, and return home when they find it—are perhaps the most interesting development to watch as they make their way into commercial products on a mass scale.

Information-based assets and, in turn, knowledge extend across a number of systems and operating platforms. These systems and resources include document management systems, database management systems—relational, such as Oracle or Access—and flat-file; spatial information systems; distributed and open hyperconnected systems such as intranets, VPN-connected enterprise nets, discussion forums, collaborative tools, help desk technologies, and informally captured information (such as video clips, audio, and electronic notes on mobile note-capture devices). In spite of the limitations of basic search tools, off-the-shelf tools such as Excalibur[21] provide acceptable solutions based on semantic networks (that use built-in thesauri, dictionaries, and lexical databases) that help distinguish between multiple meanings and contexts of a single word or phrase. Tools based on adaptive pattern recognition processing (APRP), if well integrated into a knowledge management system, further enhance the system's ability to recognize fuzzy queries and questions.

Although such tools are far from providing a perfect solution to the problem of understanding meanings intended by the user, they are one step closer to that goal. Alas, the limitation of technology becomes apparent: Being able to search through all these, at best, still taps into only a fraction of the explicit knowledge—leave alone tacit—assets that a company owns. Table 5-1 describes types of repositories, the level of formality of their content, and the content of interest that a knowledge management system's agents must be able to extract.

Without powerful search and retrieval tools that support meta information creation, a system will never go past the characteristic set of a traditional information system. Valuable, actionable information that is part of your underutilized intangible assets can be obtained

Table 5-1 Agent-Based Tools Must Scan a Variety of Repositories

Type of Repository	Types of Knowledge Supported	Content Examples
External knowledge	Formal and informal	Competitive intelligence
Structured, internal knowledge	Formal	Techniques, methods, and reports
Informal, internal knowledge	Informal	Discussion databases, "lessons learned"

See the discussion by Tiwana and Ramesh[22] for details on this categorization.

through the tracking and assessment of knowledge production, manipulation, and processing. Defined as *meta information,* this information about information assists in defining, categorizing, and locating knowledge sources and resources. In essence, this function provides data about *who is doing what with what.* Meta information provides insight into information users, types of data and information being accessed, where and which information repositories are being most frequently accessed. Your company probably stored meta information all along; now your KM system can leverage that asset to provide awareness and control of knowledge flows and a feedback mechanism for knowledge development—and in the future, to provide continuous insights to the CKO's support staff, for improving information acquisition, management, aggregation, conversion, and dissemination functions.

AltaVista, CompassWare, InText, Lycos, Microsoft Index Server, Oracle, Thunderstone, and Verity are some products that for enabling enterprise-wide keyword and meta attribute searching; and Netperceptions, Alexa, Firefly, GrapeVine, and NetPerceptions for collaborative filtering.

INTEGRATING TECHNOLOGY

A large set of technology components around which a knowledge management system is built is often already in place. The key driver of an effective knowledge management system is the proper leverage and tight integration (e.g., using knowledge servers) of existing technology, tools, and information resources.

KNOWLEDGE SERVERS

While a significant volume of information is spread out across the enterprise and the intranet provides a medium for integrating it to some extent, new information generated every day adds to the chaos. The KM technology components discussed in the preceding sections must be integrated into a seamless whole, so that the process of adding new content to the repository is then as painless and efficient as possible. A knowledge server can be the basis for such integration. A good knowledge server allows smooth integration across multiple enterprises that use the same knowledge server. Since the concept of a knowledge server is still emergent and developing, I cannot make this claim for all such servers: However, Plumtree Server is an exceptionally good product example in this category.

Figure 5-13 shows how a knowledge server can connect islands of data in situations where the intranet is not expansive and new information is being generated at a high rate. We examine knowledge servers in depth, in Chapters 10 and 11.

A knowledge server, as Table 5-2 illustrates, provides an extensible architecture for unifying and organizing access to disparate corporate repositories and Internet data sources as a first affirmative step toward building content for the knowledge management system. In a typical knowledge server, plug-in components or accessors periodically poll remote data sources for new content.

The knowledge server creates a reference to each new document that is similar to a card in a library card catalog. Each card captures key meta data such as author, subject, and title as

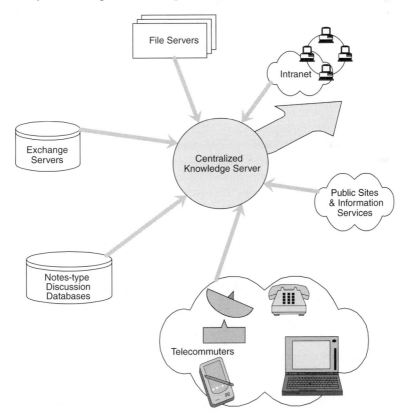

Figure 5-13 Connecting islands of data with a knowledge server.

Table 5-2 How Knowledge Servers Integrate Enterprise-Wide Information and Explicit Knowledge

Before	After
Cumbersome to integrate.	Partly automated.
Employees unaware of postings and documents.	Personalized push channels provide periodic updates to users.
Multiple versions of documents result in inconsistencies.	Multiple versions are minimized.
Scope of content limited to application.	Enterprise-wide scope.

a standard set of properties, and maintains a link to the original content, which the knowledge server indexes in a text-search engine. On the basis of the text index and the meta data properties captured for each card, the knowledge server automatically organizes cards in a hierarchy of administrator-defined categories that users can browse via a Web browser, typically on the intranet. Products such as Plumtree offer features that allow users to subscribe to briefings delivered via plug-in modules (Plumtree calls these *delivery methods)*. Knowledge servers provide several business benefits as a direct result of the high level of integration that they make possible (see Table 5-3).

The strength of knowledge servers comes from their ability to integrate existing repositories without having to start from scratch. Furthermore, the knowledge management team can then take existing explicit knowledge into account efficiently, allowing more time and resources to deal with the harder part of managing tacit knowledge.

Extensive research[23] has warned us: Good technology does not necessarily translate to good information or knowledge. Since knowledge servers do not have a systems administrator decide what information everyone else needs, they overcome a frequently encountered barrier faced by information management tools by putting that choice in the hands of end users. Figure 5-14 shows the integrative concept behind a knowledge server.

LESSONS LEARNED

We examined how, as the first step in the knowledge management methodology, the existing infrastructure can be leveraged. You need to take several material steps to analyze and leverage existing infrastructure and enabling technology components. The key points to keep in mind while analyzing existing infrastructural components are summarized here.

- *There is no one best way of managing knowledge.* Analogies are useful for communicating knowledge management strategies but a dangerous way of analyzing them. What works for one company need not work for you. It *might.* Simply copying a

Table 5-3 Business Needs and The Characteristics of Knowledge Servers That Meet Those Needs

Business Need	Technical Characteristics of Knowledge Servers
Adaptability	Plug-in modules provide support for new data formats and delivery mechanisms as they emerge. This provides unprecedented extensibility and adaptability.
Automated tracking	Intelligent agents and Web crawlers navigate through integrated internal repositories and external sources to inform users of new content as it becomes available. New content can either be delivered through push mechanisms or made available at personalized pull-based portals on the company intranet.
Determination of emergent structure within large volumes of new and often chaotic information.	Meta information provides automated content aggregation and electronically catalogs new information as it gets added to the system.
Extant content utilization	Since knowledge servers build upon existing repositories, they can take existing content into account and organize it to make it more amenable to browsing and searching.

competitor's knowledge management strategy or system can be a very risky move even if you are in an identical line of business.

- *Understand the role that your existing networks play in knowledge management.* Technology—in its limited role—helps in knowledge management in primarily two respects: by connecting knowledge and by storing, retrieving, and distributing it. Begin with the technology and network infrastructure investments that you already have in place.

PLUMTREE KNOWLEDGE SERVER

A product that epitomizes the ideals shown in Figure 5-14 is the Plumtree Server (www.plumtree.com). This software provides integrated Web access to the most important repository within many large companies: the Lotus Notes Server. The Plumtree Server can query Lotus Notes databases distributed throughout the enterprise for new documents, records, and attachments, organizing access to diverse Notes content by subject matter rather than by server. This approach allows Notes content from different databases together with documents, Web pages, and data warehousing reports on the same topic to be viewed all in one place (see Figure 5-15).

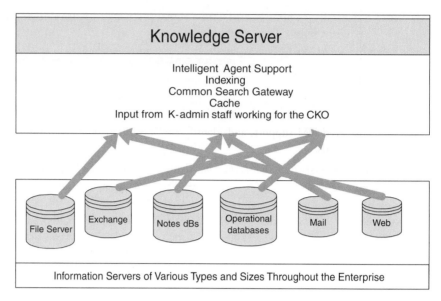

Figure 5-14 The concept of a knowledge server.

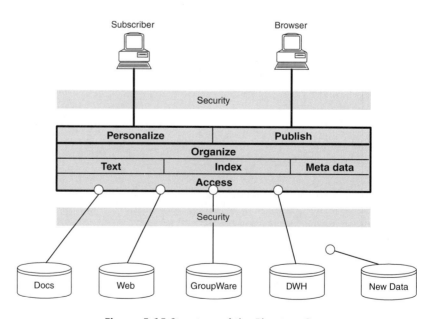

Figure 5-15 Structure of the Plumtree Server.

- *Integrate, build upon, and leverage enterprise resources.* Technology's most valuable role in knowledge management is broadening the reach and enhancing the speed of knowledge transfer. The key to successful knowledge management lies in leveraging the *existing* infrastructure, primarily communications and storage capabilities that are already in place.

- *Look before you leap.* Understand the knowledge management technological framework and its components. Examine your needs and determine the processes that most need KM support, and identify existing infrastructure can (or cannot) meet those needs.

- *Focus on pragmatism, not perfection.* Identify extant explicit knowledge, take stock of what information and knowledge already exists beginning with explicit knowledge sources. Analyze and build upon data mining, data warehousing, project management, and DSS tools that are already in place.

- *Remember the golden rule.* A good knowledge management system is built around people. The people who use it, their work practices, and the company culture should govern choice of technology. Don't try to force people into the knowledge management system mold.

- *Go beyond the intranet.* Knowledge management technology is a broader concept than just the Web and related technologies. Provide process support for collaborative synergy, real knowledge, informal conversation, intelligent decision support, and visual team thinking.

- *Use knowledge servers to integrate the islands of information and create new knowledge.* Examine your business needs and determine the feasibility of a knowledge server as an enabler.

- *Plan for flexibility and scalability.* A well-designed knowledge management system design must be flexible and scaleable, and not written in stone. The Web-based approach holds the greatest promise for system scalability, flexibility, and longevity.

In the next chapter, we take a look at the second step in the 10-step knowledge management roadmap and see how knowledge management and business strategy can be aligned right from the start.

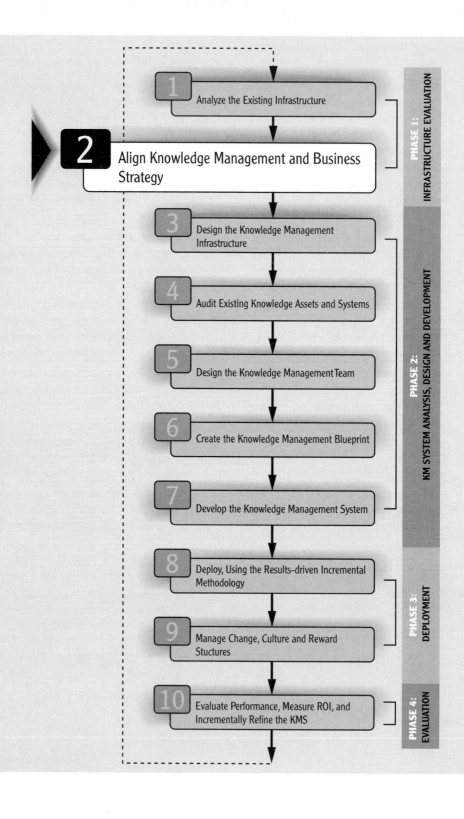

1 Analyze the Existing Infrastructure

2 Align Knowledge Management and Business Strategy

3 Design the Knowledge Management Infrastructure

4 Audit Existing Knowledge Assets and Systems

5 Design the Knowledge Management Team

6 Create the Knowledge Management Blueprint

7 Develop the Knowledge Management System

8 Deploy, Using the Results-driven Incremental Methodology

9 Manage Change, Culture and Reward Stuctures

10 Evaluate Performance, Measure ROI, and Incrementally Refine the KMS

PHASE 1: INFRASTRUCTURE EVALUATION

PHASE 2: KM SYSTEM ANALYSIS, DESIGN AND DEVELOPMENT

PHASE 3: DEPLOYMENT

PHASE 4: EVALUATION

CHAPTER 6

ALIGNING KNOWLEDGE MANAGEMENT AND BUSINESS STRATEGY

IN THIS CHAPTER

✔ Understand how to shift KM in your company from strategic programming to strategic planning.

✔ Perform a *knowledge-based* SWOT analysis to create knowledge maps: internal, competitive, and industry-wide.

✔ Analyze knowledge gaps and relate them to strategic gaps.

✔ Articulate, diagnose, and validate a clear link between strategy and KM.

✔ Translate your strategy-KM link to KM system design characteristics.

✔ Determine the right diagnostic questions to ask, package knowledge, and reduce noise.

✔ Mobilize initiatives to "sell" your KM project internally

✔ Balance exploitation versus exploration, JIT versus JIC delivery, and codification versus personalization using your KM system.

✔ Incorporate the 24 critical success factors in KM design.

IMAGINATION IS MORE IMPORTANT THAN KNOWLEDGE
—ALBERT EINSTEIN

If knowledge creation is to be successfully directed, there must be an indisputable link between your company's business strategy and its knowledge management strategy. I have researched several companies that have had a fair degree of success in their efforts directed toward the management of knowledge. The focus of most knowledge management projects has primarily been on developing new IT applications for supporting digital capture, storage, retrieval, and distribution of an organization's explicitly documented knowledge.[1] Michael Zack, of the Northeastern University business school, notes that "a smaller number of organizations, on the other hand, believe that the most valuable knowledge is the tacit knowledge existing within people's heads, augmented or shared via interpersonal interaction and social relationships" that exist within and between organizations.[2] An effective knowledge management strategy is not simply a technology strategy but a well-balanced mix of technology, cultural change, new reward systems, and business focus that is perfectly in step with the company's business strategy. Technical and organizational initiatives, when aligned and integrated, can provide a comprehensive infrastructure to support knowledge management processes.

As companies clamor to jump on the knowledge management bandwagon, this critical linkage between business strategy and knowledge strategy, while much talked about, is often ignored in practice.[3] Technology is *almost* like magic, but every so often we place our hopes too high. It's wise to know the limitations and understand where technology fits into knowledge management rather than seeing every problem as a nail when all you have is a hammer. Technology, after all, still isn't magic.

In this chapter, we see how high-level business strategy can be translated into pragmatic and doable goals that can drive knowledge management strategy and design. We examine how knowledge maps can translate strategic vision into action and further translate this into a supporting knowledge management system design. We apply Michael Zack's pioneering *knowledge strategy model* to develop a knowledge management system that truly delivers results in your company. Twenty-four key lessons learned from dozens of successful knowledge management projects worldwide supply implications to guide the design of your knowledge management system.

FROM STRATEGIC PROGRAMMING TO STRATEGIC PLANNING

Knowledge drives strategy. Strategy drives knowledge management. Henry Mintzberg, one of the foremost management thinkers of our times, warns us that companies are too easily driven by strategic plans, not strategic visions. Strategic planning has not lived up to the irrational expectation of providing step-by-step instructions (i.e., strategic programming) for managers to execute strategies. Mintzberg cautions that strategic thinking cannot be done as strategic programming. Companies need to take a 180° turn and move from strategic programming to strategic thinking. Managers and businesses need to capture what they learn both from the soft insights and experiences and from hard market data, and then synthesize that learning into a vision of the direction that the business should pursue.[4] Such strategic orientation requires knowledge of the complex environment in which your company operates and comprehension of the complex processes that it undertakes. This requirement brings in the role of knowledge and knowledge management.

Effective knowledge management is to knowledge what the spreadsheet is to financial analysis: Both can be underused and abused, but when put into action properly, they provide the widest window into the future.

MOVING BEYOND FALLIBLE DATA PATTERNS

Data alone, lacking qualitative richness and being aggregated (therefore missing important nuances), provides, at most, just half of the true picture.[a] Strategic choices based solely on such data often involve serious commitments of capital, people, and resources, and once the company is heading down a particular path, it might be very costly, time-consuming, or simply impossible to change course. The problem is that most of us tend to recognize patterns and then try to interpret new situations and problems in the context of such patterns that we have seen before. "Our drive to see patterns is so strong that we will see then even in perfectly random data."[5]

We also often tend to *assume* linear relationships between cause and effect and extrapolate current trends to future events. In a path-dependent world, such extrapolation can prove *dead wrong*.

Knowledge provides opportunism that can drive novel strategies. Knowledge management provides pathways for that knowledge. Knowledge management can support, but not replace, the individuals in your company who provide breakthroughs and innovations in day-to-day aspects of how you run the business. Systems do not think, and when used for more than the facilitation of human thinking, they can actually prevent thinking. Mintzberg further suggests that strategic competition is driven not by finding the right answers but by posing the right questions. Knowledge management discovers and provides the opportunity for asking those questions. Knowledge-based competitive advantage is sustainable because the more an organization already knows, the more it can learn.[6]

MOVING BEYOND SWOT ANALYSIS

The strengths, weaknesses, opportunities, and threats (SWOT) framework, put forward by Michael Porter, has been the mainstay of business strategy for over 30 years. SWOT analysis involves an assessment of the company's strengths and weaknesses relative to the opportunities and threats, brought about by the environment in which your company operates. The objective is to sustain the company's strengths, mitigate its weaknesses, avoid threats and grab oppor-

---

[a]For those of us who have been drenched in an unexpected shower or those who have seen their hard-earned dollars vaporize during a stock market "low," weather forecasting and stock market predictions are perfect examples of such failures. Knowledge, not data, needs to be the driver of such commitments.

ASKING THE RIGHT QUESTION: THE EMERGENCE OF POLAROID

The success of well-known companies such as Microsoft, Starbucks, Southwest Airlines, and eBay comes from their ability to ask the right questions. This is nothing new: only that the recognition of knowledge management makes this more likely. Polaroid, whose instant camera virtually created an entire market in itself, began with such a simple application of knowledge: knowledge that was soon converted into action, a product, and a very successful company. It all began one day in 1943 when Edwin Land's three-year-old daughter asked why she could not immediately see the picture that he had taken of her. Within an hour, Land conceived the camera that would take an industry by storm and transform then-small Polaroid into one of the most successful companies of our time. Land's vision was evoked by the synthesis of the insight evoked by his daughter's question and his extensive technical knowledge.

tunities. Porter's five forces model, though much respected, has recently been criticized for its focus on entire industries instead of individual companies. Companies, for the most part, compete with their competitors. Porter's model does not provide guidance as to how companies can compete *within* their industry. As Michael Zack notes, unique characteristics of individual companies can make a difference in terms of profits and performance within their industry. Zack adds that any company, given what it knows, must identify the best products and market opportunities for exploiting that knowledge. Since knowledge management focuses specifically on your company and not your industry, Zack's model, not Porter's SWOT analysis framework, provides the key to aligning business strategy and knowledge management.

CODIFICATION OR PERSONALIZATION?

Before we turn to mapping business strategy to knowledge management, let us look at two expansive knowledge management approaches: codification and personalization. There is no right or wrong approach—both are required in the right balance. The right balance is determined by your company's objectives in pursuing knowledge management. For any knowledge management initiative to be successful, both approaches *must* be present in the knowledge orientation of the firm, but not with equal weightage. If a company decides to use codification as its primary strategy, it should direct, for example, 80 percent of its efforts toward codification and the remaining 20 percent toward personalization. Table 6-1 compares these two focal choices. (See Appendix A for a checklist).

Table 6-1 Comparison of Codification and Personalization KM Strategies

Business Strategy Question	Codification	Personalization
What type of business do you think your company is in?	Providing high-quality, reliable, fast, and cost-effective services.	Providing creative, rigorous and highly customized services and products.
How much old material, such as past project data, existing documents, and archived projects, do you reuse as a part of new projects?	You reuse portions of old documents to create new ones. You use existing products to create new ones. You know that you need not begin from scratch to deliver a new product or service.	Every problem has a high chance of being a "one-off" and unique problem. Although cumulative learning is involved, highly creative solutions are often called for.
What is the costing model used for your company's products and services?	Price-based competition.	Expertise-based pricing; high prices are not detrimental to your business; price-based competition barely (if at all) exists.
What are your firm's typical profit margins?	Very low profit margins; overall revenues need to be maximized to increase net profits.	Very high profit margins.
How best can you describe the role that IT plays in your company's work processes?	IT is a primary enabler; the objective is to connect people distributed across the enterprise with codified knowledge (such as reports, documentation, code, etc.) that is in some reusable form.	Storage and retrieval are not the primary applications of IT; IT is considered a great enabler for communications; applications such as e-mail and video conferencing age considered the most useful applications; conversations, socialization, and exchange of tacit knowledge are considered to be the primary use of IT.
What is your reward structure like?	Employees are rewarded for using and contributing to databases such as Notes discussion databases.	Employees are rewarded for directly sharing their knowledge with colleagues and for assisting colleagues in other locations/offices with their problems.
How is knowledge exchanged and transferred?	Employees refer to a document or best practices database that stores, distributes, and collects codified knowledge.	Knowledge is transferred person to person; intrafirm networking is encouraged to enable sharing of tacit knowledge, insight, experience, and intuition.

Table 6-1 Comparison of Codification and Personalization KM Strategies (cont.)

Business Strategy Question	Codification	Personalization
Where do your company's economies of scale lie?	Economies of scale lie in the effective reuse of existing knowledge and experience and applying them to solve new problems and complete new projects.	Economies rest in the sum total of expertise available within the company; experts in various areas of specialization are considered indispensable.
What are your typical team structure demographics?	Large teams; most members are junior-level employees; a few project managers lead them.	Junior employees are not an inordinate proportion of a typical team's total membership.
What company's services do your company's services resemble?	Andersen Consulting, The Gartner Group, Delphi Consulting, ZDNET, Delta Airlines, Oracle.	Boston Consulting Group, McKinsey and Company, Rand Corporation.
What company's products do your company's products resemble?	Pizza Hut, Dell Computer, Gateway, Microsoft, SAP, People Soft, Baan, America Online, Bell South, Air Touch Cellular, Lotus, SAS Institute, IBM, Hewlett-Packard, Intranetics, 3COM.	A custom car or bicycle manufacturer, Boeing, a contract research firm, a private investigator.

The classification of knowledge management strategies was first discussed in Hansen, M., N. Nohria, and T. Tierney, What's Your Strategy for Managing Knowledge?, *Harvard Business Review,* March–April (1999), 106–116. This table further builds on it to provide diagnostic analysis. Enterprise Resource Planning (ERP) vendors appear in my codification strategy examples since most of the software that is implemented is based on preprogrammed modules.

As Table 6-1 illustrates, the personalization strategy is more focused on connecting knowledge workers through networks and is better suited to companies that face *one-off* and unique problems that depend more on tacit knowledge and expertise than on codified knowledge. The codification strategy is more focused on technology that enables storage, indexing, retrieval, and reuse. This strategy is better suited to companies that have to deal with similar problems and decisions over and over. And remember, it's foolish to try using both approaches to the same degree. It is equally unsound to use only one. As one would suspect, the incentives needed to make either one work are very different.[8] Focus on those incentives that help you get the *primary* strategy right.

KNOWLEDGE MAPS TO LINK KNOWLEDGE TO STRATEGY

Systematically mapping, categorizing, benchmarking, and applying knowledge with the help of a knowledge management system cannot only make such knowledge more accessible, but also prioritizes and focuses knowledge management. The idea of knowledge maps as applied to KM comes from research by Michael Zack, who also describes this process as knowledge-based SWOT analysis. Effective knowledge management strategies using such knowledge maps can help companies build a defensible competitive knowledge position—a long-term effort that requires foresight, hindsight, careful planning, alignment, as well as luck.

Let's examine the process, moving from a high level to the level of action that you would use to create such knowledge maps.

STARTING AT THE TOP

To articulate the strategy-knowledge link, a company must explicate its strategic intent, identify knowledge required to actually execute that strategic choice, and reveal its strategic knowledge gaps by comparing these to its actual knowledge assets. The strategic choices that your company makes regarding technology, markets, products, services, and processes have a direct impact on the knowledge, skills, and competencies that it needs to compete in its intended markets.[9] Later, we will translate the links into actionable goals. Such a linkage is illustrated in Figure 6-1.

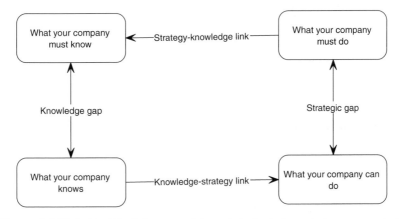

Figure 6-1 High-level Zack framework-based strategic knowledge gap analysis.

Assessing your company's present knowledge position necessitates documenting its existing knowledge assets—the fourth step of the 10-step KM roadmap (Chapter 8).

For our initial *high-level* analysis, we can categorize knowledge into three classification "buckets":[10]

1. *Core knowledge:* Core knowledge is the basic level of knowledge required just to *play the game.* This is the type of knowledge that creates a barrier for entry of new companies. Since this level of knowledge is expected of all competitors, you must have it even though it will provide your company with no advantage that distinguishes it from its competitors.

    Let's take two examples: One from the consumer electronics (hard product) business and one from Internet programming (soft product). To enter the modem manufacturing market, a new company must have extensive knowledge of these aspects: a suitable circuit design, all electronic parts that go into a modem, fabricating surface mount (SMD) chip boards, how to write operating system drivers for modems, and familiarity with computer telephony standards. Similarly, a company developing Websites for, say, florists, needs server hosting capabilities, Internet programming skills, graphic design skills, clearly identified target markets, and necessary software. In either case, just about any competitor in those businesses is assumed to have this knowledge in order to compete in their respective markets; such essential knowledge therefore provides no advantage over other market players.

2. *Advanced knowledge:* Advanced knowledge is what makes your company *competitively viable.* Such knowledge allows your company to differentiate its product from that of a competitor, arguably, through the application of superior knowledge in certain areas. Such knowledge allows your company to compete head on with its competitors in the same market and for the same set of customers.

    In the case of a company trying to compete in modem manufacturing markets, superior or user-friendly software or an additional capability in modems (such as warning online users of incoming telephone calls) represents such knowledge. In case of a Website development firm, such knowledge might be about international flower markets and collaborative relationships in Dutch flower auctions that the company can use to improve Websites delivered to its customers.

3. *Innovative knowledge:* Innovative knowledge allows a company to lead its entire industry to an extent that clearly differentiates it from competition. Michael Zack points out that innovative knowledge allows a company to change the rules of the game.

    Patented technology is an applicable example of changing the rules. Innovative knowledge cannot always be protected by patents, as the lawsuit between Microsoft and Apple in the 1980s should serve to remind us. Apple sued Microsoft for copying the look and feel of its graphical user interface (GUI). The Supreme Court ruled that things like look and feel cannot be patented; they can only be copyrighted. Microsoft won the case, since it copied the look and feel but used entirely different code to create it in the first place.

CREATING A KNOWLEDGE MAP

Knowledge is not static.[11] What is innovative knowledge today will become the core knowledge of tomorrow. The key lies in staying consistently ahead of the competition. The knowledge map we'll create (see Figure 6-2) provides a snapshot of where your company is at any given time (such as today) relative to its competitors.

Here's how it works. Categorize each market player including yourself as an innovator, leader, capable competitor, straggler, or risky player. Next, identify your own business' strengths and weaknesses on various facets of knowledge to see where you lag or lead your competitors. Use that information to accordingly reposition either your knowledge or strategic business focus.

For example, if you are analyzing customer support knowledge in a competing company and realize that your competitor is an innovator and your own company is only a capable competitor, you can choose either to invest in catching, or simply decide to compete in a different market segment.

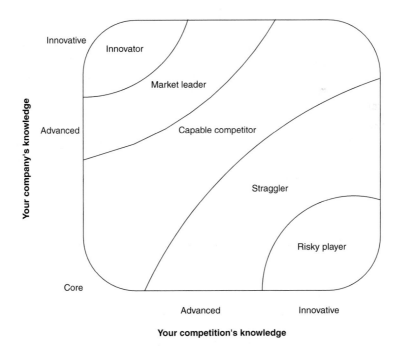

Figure 6-2 Creating a knowledge map to evaluate corporate knowledge.

Analyzing Knowledge Gaps

The gap between what your company is doing and what it should be doing represents its strategic gap, as illustrated by Figure 6-1. Similarly, your company's knowledge gap is represented by what your company *should* (and possibly can) know and what it does know in order to support the competitive position that it has adopted. These two gaps must be aligned and must feed into each other to bridge existing gaps.

Knowledge management strategy must then address how your company's knowledge gaps in identified critical processes are best bridged. In addition to balancing personalization and codification, you must then balance the level of exploration and exploitation that you want your company to engage in.

Exploration implies the intent of your company to develop knowledge that helps it create new niches for its products and services. This intent has profound implications for the design of both the knowledge management strategy and system: Exploration alone cannot be supportively pursued or financially sustained for too long without having a negative impact on the company's bottom line results.

Exploitation implies the intent to focus on deriving financial and productivity gains from knowledge that is already existing, both inside and outside, your company. Your company must simultaneously pursue exploitation (which results in short-term benefits) and exploration (which accumulates long-term benefits), varying the balance with strategic focus. In either case, integrate external knowledge into the knowledge management strategy—only those companies that possess the best learning capability and absorptive capacity for external knowledge hold long-run viability.[b]

Use knowledge to create value, that is, to innovate. Consider a variety of companies that have used their knowledge to create value: Enron in energy, Wal-Mart in discount retailing, eMachines and Compaq in low-end computers, IKEA in home products retail, Barnes & Noble in book retail, Airtran in short-haul travel, Charles Schwab in investment management. These companies have been so successful not because they hired Web masters with long ponytails, were dynamic young startups, monopolized their markets, or had the latest technology; they were successful because they used their knowledge to innovate and create value.

Being an innovator on the knowledge map is of little help if you are not an exploiter, you must first be an exploiter (at least of your internal knowledge) before trying to be an explorer. The implications of this on knowledge management system design are significant: Your knowledge management system must support exploitation of available and accessible knowledge before it can begin supporting exploration.

---

[b]Zack has also suggested an aggressive versus conservative strategy for managing knowledge. Since we are trying to draw implications of knowledge strategy on knowledge management system design, this is not within the scope of our analysis. For details, I highly recommend reading (especially page 30) Michael Zack's seminal research paper, Developing a Knowledge Strategy, *California Management Review,* vol. 41, no. 3, Spring (1999), 125–145.

Innovate or Imitate?

Intel has long enjoyed dominance in the microprocessor business that fuels growth in the personal computer industry. Even though cost-based competition has provided some of its competitors, notably AMD and Cyrix (a National Semiconductor Division that went out of business in May 1999, and was soon acquired by VIA Technologies of Taiwan) a short-term advantage, Intel chose to adopt an innovative rather than an imitative strategy. By choosing to do so, it introduced its line of low-cost Celeron™ (identical to its high-end processors, less the cache memory) processors coupled with extensive price cuts. This forced Cyrix out of business, since what it possessed was core knowledge. Cyrix's ability to reverse engineer or emulate the Intel processor, avoid the high costs of developing the Intel Pentium chip, further refine it, and sell it at a fraction of Intel equivalents (although consistently behind Intel's release schedules) allowed it to enjoy market dominance in the sub-$1,000 PC market for a few years. As Intel introduced its own line of low-end processors, Cyrix's market share began to dwindle, ultimately causing the company huge losses that forced it to exit the market.

AMD, which had originally adopted Cyrix's strategy of creating low-cost Pentium clones finally moved from an imitative strategy to an innovative strategy. Rather than simply accept what its competitor Intel was doing and striving to do it better,[12] AMD made a departure with the introduction of its K6-3D-2 and K-7 series microprocessors that use a different but compatible architecture called Super 7 (derived from the industry standard, Socket 7, that preceded Intel's introduction of the Slot 1 architecture). AMD was still surviving as a strong contender against Intel as of late 1999 primarily because it chose a proactive rather than a reactive competitive position[13]—it moved from being a capable competitor to an innovator. A noteworthy historical parallel in Intel's story is that the company had used a very similar *value subtraction* strategy for creating a low-end 486sx spin off for its i486 series microprocessor about a decade earlier.

Adding Up the Numbers

To make sense of it all, look at Figure 6-3, which illustrates the linkages between a company's strategic context, knowledge management strategy, and knowledge management technology.

The competitive environment—a combination of technical opportunities, competitive threats, and regulatory controls—impacts both your company's strategic context (and in turn its products, services, markets, customers, and allocation of resources) and its knowledge management strategy. KM technology (which includes the knowledge management system)

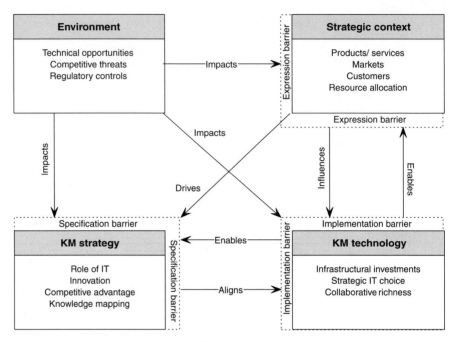

Figure 6-3 Aligning knowledge and business strategy.

enables the realization of your company's chosen knowledge strategy. KM strategy in turn aligns KM technology design. It's your company's business strategy that drives its knowledge management strategy, and not the other way around. Similarly, KM technology choices enable its strategic context and are in turn influenced by it.

Strategic context has an *expression barrier* surrounding it. Your company breaches the barrier by articulating its business strategy, based on its vision and translated into actionable targets and goals. Knowledge strategy has a *specification barrier:* the need to specify critical knowledge that supports and refines your company's business strategy. I would recommend using Michael Zack's knowledge mapping scheme to overcome the specification barrier that shields KM strategy. Knowledge management technology, itself, has an *implementation barrier* surrounding it. This barrier is primarily related to technology choice and design and is rarely a hardy deterrent because it can often be copied easily by your competitors.

SUMMARY

The process of creating a well-articulated link between business strategy and knowledge strategy is summarized in Figure 6-4.

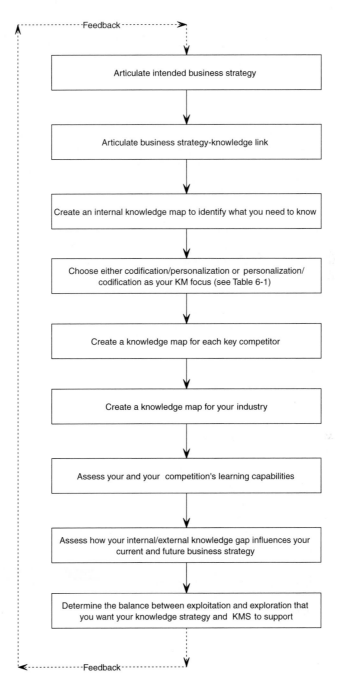

Figure 6-4 The process of articulating the link between business and knowledge strategy.

Based on a synthesis of suggestions by Michael Zack (1999) and M. Hansen et al. (1999).

STRATEGIC IMPERATIVES FOR A SUCCESSFUL KM SYSTEM

Knowledge management holds the potential to help your company not just outcompete within given industry conditions but to create fundamentally new and superior value that makes competitors *irrelevant*.[14] A core and quintessential tenet of any initiative that supports knowledge management that is developed without the detection and correction of errors in "what we know" and how we learn becomes obsolete over a relatively short period of time.[15] The only thing that is likely to emerge from such a mechanism is bad and inaccurate decisions, since the efforts aimed at managing knowledge are themselves based on faulty knowledge principles and ideas. As we begin to plan for managing knowledge in an organization, we must focus our undivided attention on a key set of attributes. These attributes have been extracted from studies of exemplary knowledge management project successes and abysmal failures in several U.S. and foreign companies.

TWENTY-FOUR LESSONS: CRITICAL SUCCESS FACTORS

Before we actually devise a blueprint for a knowledge management system, we need to identify the bare essentials that must be supported in any successful knowledge management system deployment. Before you unintentionally end up repeating some of the devastating mistakes that other companies have made in the past, let us probe the 24 key lessons that successful knowledge management projects have taught.

In a study of over two dozen companies that have successfully managed their knowledge assets, I found that a unique set of characteristics, values, and strategic leanings distinguished these companies from those that had failed to leverage their knowledge or knowledge management systems to create a sustainable competitive advantage within their industry.

The 24 key lessons include the following:

1. There is no silver bullet for knowledge management. In spite of what consultants eyeing your checkbook might say, all research suggests that there is no *one right way* to do it.[c]

2. Successful knowledge management projects begin with a working definition of knowledge that is accepted equivocally throughout the company.

3. A process focus is required, not a technology focus.

---

[c]The 10-step roadmap based on years of cumulative research consequently helps you devise a knowledge management strategy and translate it into a knowledge management system with the singular case of your own company in focus.

4. Successful projects begin with the acceptance that there are no perfect measures or metrics for knowledge work. However, *some* metrics, even if vague, are needed to gauge the effectiveness of knowledge management.

5. Selling knowledge management to both managers and end users requires demonstration of at least *some* short-term impact.

6. Effective knowledge management must count in tacit knowledge right from the outset, even if the primary focus is on codification. Codification with no personalization is bound to fail.

7. Shared knowledge requires the creation of a shared context.

8. A successful knowledge management project must begin with knowledge that already exists, deliver initial results, and then continue to expand. Without such orientation, your knowledge management project risks being stifled in its early days.

9. Accommodation for reasoning and support for assumption surfacing must be an integral part of knowledge management.

10. KM projects that succeed have an eye on the future and not the past or present. In contrast, information management handles the present, and data archives document the past.

11. Knowledge management systems must minimize *unnecessary* routing re-transmissions— a common source of noise and distortion.

12. What your employees need are incentives, not faster computers. Technology provides many enablers except the biggest one of all: an incentive to share knowledge.

13. A knowledge management system must allow everyone to both contribute and access knowledge. However, critical knowledge that represents confidential, competitive and innovative process knowledge or private records must be protected.

14. Effective systems for knowledge management respect confidentiality of users by allowing them to choose not to identify themselves. Although anonymity goes contrary to the idea of linking contributions to their originators, this balance is necessary.

15. Most successful knowledge management systems allow users to access, read and contribute from anywhere and at any time. Remote connectivity therefore becomes necessary.

16. If the system is used extensively, its technical design should be such that its users can see updates and additions in real time without having to manually refresh content. This is a trivial technical problem that is often overlooked—with disastrous results.

17. As explicated content and tacit knowledge pointers within a knowledge management system grow, resource maps must be provided to help users navigate through them.

18. Best practice databases are essential, but they are not the primary component of an effective knowledge management system.

19. Ongoing management support is needed for both the knowledge strategy and the knowledge management system.

20. Effective knowledge management systems must support collaborative work and *internal* consulting. Knowledge management must also focus on product and service development processes.

21. Knowledge management systems need to be informal and communicatively rich. Effective knowledge management systems are easy to use. Extensive features that make the system cumbersome to use or less intuitive can discourage its use.

22. Packaging knowledge is a goal that must be supported by knowledge management systems right from the outset. Remember that less (volume) is more when it comes to knowledge and its effective management.

23. Knowledge management technology should provide a logical extension for business units, and its choice should create a win-win situation primarily for its users, not your company's technologists.

24. Different users prefer different delivery mechanisms. This distinction implies that users of a knowledge management system should be able to choose whether they will pull content or it will be pushed to them. Similarly, users must not be bombarded by all-inclusive content.

Let us now analyze the implications of each of these characteristics on the design of your own knowledge management system.

Lesson 1: There Is No "One Right Way"

There is no one right way to implement knowledge management. What works well for one company often fails to produce results in another. Effective KM is situated in organizational context: *your* organization's context.

Lesson 2: Reach a Working Definition of Knowledge

Difficult as it is to define knowledge, agreeing on a *working definition* ensures that everyone involved in the initiative is exactly on the same wavelength and understands *what* is being talked about.

Many managers seem reluctant to distinguish between what constitutes data, information, and knowledge.[16] If we were to argue over the exact definition of knowledge, we could carry on the debate throughout the rest of this book! What is critical here is agreeing upon a *consensual* [d] definition of what comprises knowledge.

Failure to grapple with a working definition of knowledge creates a dysfunctional environment for knowledge work and the knowledge workers and is often the factor that leads companies down the wrong track. It is better to deal with the tough job before you begin than deal with it several million dollars later!

---

[d]*Consensual* refers to a definition that all people involved in the project can agree upon. The trap to define knowledge in an extremely broad sense is one that many companies fall into. The results achieved by such politically correct definitions rarely get knowledge management teams into positions that are any better than those without any definition at all.

Executives have become skeptical toward new approaches to work that they have tried in the past—in most cases, approaches that promised a lot but delivered zilch; to avoid the déjà vu, you need to narrow down the scope of what *you* define as knowledge.

Lesson 3: Focus on Processes and Not Just Technology

Knowing the community and understanding the information needs within the enterprise are critical. The focus should be on the process of adding, searching, filtering, validating, retrieving, and maintaining information and knowledge—both tacit and explicit. These needs are often innate to the organization's overall business strategy. Without a clearly defined business problem, the knowledge management project will not stand even a remote chance of success. What you need to do is learn to manage a balanced portfolio of KM projects to keep the business *alive and kicking*.

Knowledge management embodies the dream that when one employee learns something, everybody else in the company knows it. The effectuating process of knowledge sharing and transfer is quintessential to the success of a knowledge management system. The system's design must account for the people who will actually use the system, harmonize with their work processes, and be simple and easy to use.

Lesson 4: Live with Vague Knowledge Measures

Companies that have had some degree of success in their initiatives in managing knowledge have learned to live with the fact that there are no accurate or perfect measures of knowledge, knowledge work, and knowledge effectiveness. Any reasonable and sensible manager, when confronted with a request for a few million dollars for managing the intangible asset that knowledge is, will bring up the question about what the expected payoff is.

To prepare for this expected question, plan to go deep rather than broad and start by picking a few initiatives and doing them well.

Next, educate your company's CFO. Henry Mintzberg reminds us that many business decisions or investments cannot be made solely on the basis of hard data such as financial numbers; neither can knowledge investments. Conventional metrics fail to do justice to the measurement of *return on knowledge investments* (RoKI), so agree on the acceptability of more innovative approaches, such as balanced scorecard (BSC) analysis, Quality Function Deployment (QFDs), and benchmarking. No amount of analysis can eliminate the uncertainty associated with decisions, but analysis using approaches similar to the balanced scorecard can reduce these uncertainties and help quantify returns. In many cases, senior managers have to fall back on their business judgment and experiential tacit knowledge, to set their (and your) expectations.

Some firms that have been very successful in leveraging their intellectual capital use proxy measures, such as patent counts, process innovation metrics, product development cycle-time gains, and defect reduction to evaluate the consequences of knowledge-based work. Other possible surrogate measures (see cases in Chapter 15) that can be used in a company include the stability of its workforce, the stability and longevity of the customer base, and the development of competence in knowledge workers. While these surely do a better job at approximating gains emerging from effective handling of knowledge, they still underestimate the actual gain as they measure "knowledge stock" and not knowledge flows.

There is no *one good way* of measuring the benefits that result from effective management of knowledge within a company. In fact, no correct and complete way even exists yet. Due to the extensive differences that exist between firms of a similar nature, a measure that might apply to one might not apply well to another. A well thought out initiative should recognize this and leave room for changes in the proxy metrics for success.

Skandia,[17] the Swedish company, uses an innovative technique to decompose its market value into two categories: capital assets and knowledge assets (see Figure 6-5). Skandia has devised a method for putting a dollar figure on its knowledge assets as a way of measuring return on its knowledge investments. The company reports this on the balance sheet in hard figures (see Figure 6-6) that are further reported to its stockholders.

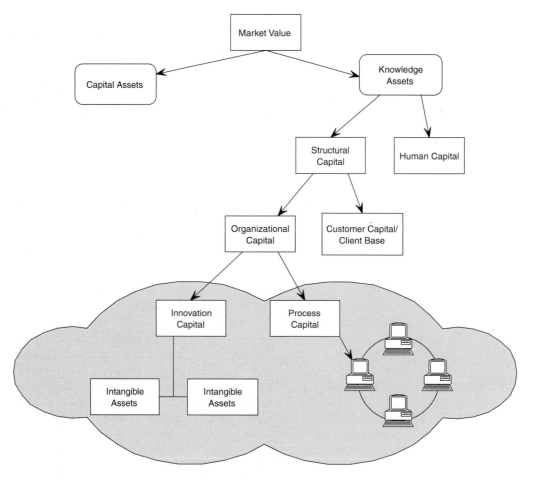

Figure 6-5 Skandia's breakdown of market value.

Skandia Navigator

DIAL

Dial is Europe's second-largest telemarketing insurance company and offers primarily motor, householders, homeowners, vacation homeowners, boat and personal lines of insurance.

	1996	1995	1994*
FINANCIAL FOCUS			
Gross premiums written (MSEK)	935	880	667
Gross premiums written/employee (SEK 000s)	3,832	3,592	3,586
CUSTOMER FOCUS			
Telephone accessibility (%)	95.8	92.5	90.0
Number of individual policies	320,139	275,231	234,741
Satisfied customer index (max. value = 5)	4.36	4.32	4.15
Sweden's Customer Barometer (max. value = 100)	65	69	n.a.
HUMAN FOCUS			
Average age	40	40	37
Number of employees	244	245	186
Time in training (days/year)	7	6	3.5
PROCESS FOCUS			
IT-employees/total number of employees (%)	7.4	7.3	8.1
RENEWAL & DEVELOPMENT FOCUS			
Increase in gross premiums written (%)	6.3	31.9	28.5
Share of values in claims assessment system (%)	20.5	9	n.a.
Number of ideas filed with Idea Group	175	n.a.	n.a.

SKANDIABANKEN

SkandiaBanken is Sweden's leading distance bank, offering customers a range of banking services with a high degree of

Figure 6-6 An excerpt from Skandia's 1996 annual report shows dollar figures associated with its knowledge assets.

However, companies, especially American ones, should be cautious about actually using this approach, as it could bring about some unwelcome tax liabilities! Skandia's approach—a true innovation back in 1996—provides a good, informal, internal measure to provide a snapshot of the health of the company in terms of its knowledge assets. Thanks to pioneering research by Michael Zack, we can now use knowledge maps instead.

Lesson 5: Salability Necessitates Demonstration of Short-Term Impact

Metrics aside, continuing support for knowledge management projects in the real world often depends on the demonstration of some tangible and short-term results. An approach some companies have adopted in the past is one where a very tangible productivity gain measure is used along with proxy measures. The proxy measure guides the knowledge management champions and the knowledge management project, and the tangible measures demonstrate direct benefits to upper management. Showing benefits in a demonstrable form is a very tricky part of the job and often comes at a cost to the actual KM initiative itself.

Showing short-term benefits is akin to another more technical but badly executed activity: documentation of programming code. Although it is well established that program documentation is essential, anyone who has spent even a little time behind a computer screen on a programming job knows that most documentation is done after the fact (and rarely captures the process that it originally intended to capture). Time spent writing this documentation is often time that could have been better used having your programmers move on to the next programming job.

However, it *can* be done. Platinum Technology, Inc., illustrates this point very well (see the case described in Chapter 15). Platinum further demonstrates how this need not be a useless activity but one that actually accumulates direct financial benefits if planned carefully at the outset.

Lesson 6: Count in Tacit Knowledge

A *fair* chunk of knowledge can be embedded in processes,[18] repositories, databases, manuals, documents and videos—but not all of it. Yet when companies talk about implementing solutions for managing knowledge, they exclusively seize explicit content as though it had a life of its own.

Dubbing mundane databases and object repositories as knowledge management tools, and search engines as human brain-power does little justice to the complexity and completeness of corporate knowledge. This ignores a very critical component of knowledge: knowledge that lies in the head of employees.[19] As product vendors make vigorous attempts to dress up old-time technologies such as databases, search engines, and discussion lists as knowledge management solutions, the threat of ignoring this critical completing component of knowledge becomes even more serious.

To truly support management and reuse of knowledge, tacit components too need to be counted in—and counted in very strongly. Such tacit knowledge includes many "things":

- *Perspectives,* such as a Japanese manager's view of his American parent company's customers (that is framed by his experience with Japanese customers)

- *Perceptions,* such as a salesperson's perception that apartment residents are willing to talk to him when they see him in his blue company uniform

- *Values,* such as a customer service representative's belief that she must satisfy the customer at any cost (a value that runs strong in the corporate cultures of Office Depot and Gateway)

- *Beliefs,* such as a product designer's belief that a teal-colored case for his company's personal digital assistant will help achieve higher sales in, say, South America

How often do you hear of values, beliefs, perceptions, and experience stored in a data warehouse? My guess would be: rarely.

Almost every rigorous survey of companies and entire industries reveals that managers realize that tacit knowledge is out there, but managers grapple with the concept and increase their investment on the explicable knowledge capture technology infrastructure either hoping to compensate for their inability to deal with tacit knowledge or wishing that it would "go away." Eventually, they ignore the tacit parts! And in that critical mistake, we lose the very basis of success of a new knowledge management initiative. So count tacit knowledge into any major strategy geared toward the management of knowledge.

Lesson 7: Create a Shared Context

Tacit knowledge cannot be explicated formally, easily, or at all. It is difficult to put into documents or embed in databases. Key decisions driving companies are most often made by

KNOWLEDGE RESOURCE MAPS AND POINTERS

Knowledge management is not solely technology-driven. Still, the trend in KM seems to be focusing more on making the professional's knowledge explicit and turning it into codified organizational knowledge (stored in databases and repositories), rather than finding ways to retain the professionals themselves and creating value by making them accessible. Put the development of knowledge about knowledge (like a yellow pages guide or expert resource database) at the top of your priority list. Use IT only as a connector, an enabler, instead of building a standalone knowledge base, or as an end it in itself. Building this common language helps spread the skills and competencies available within the organization itself.

Capturing all types of relevant actionable information and knowledge is a time-constrained activity that cannot really be completed.[e] This process is continuous: There is a beginning of the process, but no clear-cut end. And, very often, some critical parts of the knowledge that a user needs might have not been captured by the system. The solution is to provide a pointer such as an e-mail address, telephone number, or contact information for the person who originally contributed that piece of knowledge to the KM system. Such pointers must provide functionality and context exceeding traditional skills databases. Call it what you will: resource maps, yellow pages, skill bases, and competency databases.

[e]*Completed*, in this context, refers to a state where no further modifications are needed for a considerable period of time.

people who actually use their tacit knowledge to do their jobs. As products get complex, people from various functional areas get involved in a project. In the absence of a shared context, people coming from different backgrounds, with different values, beliefs, assumptions, and views, are most likely to collide and immobilize the possiblities of reaching consensus or making decisions.[20]

Every effective effort targeted at managing knowledge needs some mechanism that allows open, supportive, critical, and reflective conversations[21] between participants; this mechanism allows them to challenge, align, and establish a shared context. Without this context, the knowledge that flows within the company would be no different from its information flows along disjointed data points.[f] Conversations can be through discussion groups, chat

[f]Several studies Such as Fahey, Liam, and Laurence Prusak's, The Eleven Deadliest Sins of Knowledge Management, *California Management Review,* vol. 40, no. 3 (1998), 265–276, have found that the decision relevance and usefulness of data and information at hand becomes evident only after a significant amount of discussion and dialogue. Without such conversations and dialogue, the road from information to knowledge could be a misleading one.

> ### COMMUNITY-CENTRIC SHARED CONTEXT BUILDING APPROACHES
>
> IDEO, the industrial design firm, has some 300 professionals worldwide, but operates a total of 10 offices (including four in the Palo Alto/San Francisco Bay area alone) in order that none should have more than 50 people. Similarly, the Swedish software company WM-data employs 3,800 people but mandates that there be no more than 50 people in a single unit. Limiting the size of work groups is a commonly used successful approach for creating shared context.

rooms, video conferencing, or bulletin boards: any technology that roughly equals its chalk-and-board equivalent in the electronically connected virtual and distributed world.

We studied a company that was developing an add-on card that allowed personal digital assistants similar to the PalmPilot to receive messages over wireless paging networks. The people involved belonged not only to the company that was developing the product but also those outside it—the operating system developer, the company that wrote software drivers for the device, the marketing department that sold the product, and the company that provided the paging network services. To get these people to *talk* required a shared vision of what the product was to *supposed* be. Since the various people involved in the project came from different functional groups, different organizations, and different backgrounds, it was no surprise that they talked at different wavelengths. For such a team to be effective, it was essential to create a shared context.

Lesson 8: Begin with What You Have

Instead of grappling with the notion of knowledge in the dark, it's better to begin with what you already have. It is essential that you know what is already out there before you can even attempt to begin managing it. Recognizing knowledge gaps implies ensuring that quality, depth, and tone of the knowledge pool content evolve with the organization. This assurance includes regularly updating the information and sustaining the ability to identify and fill knowledge gaps. As Figure 6-4 illustrates, without knowing what the firm already knows, it can be hard, if not impossible, to identify critical gaps in knowledge and competencies.

When Mercer Management Consulting (www.mercermc.com) realized that it was growing too fast to continue relying on informal networks of its consultants, it created a repository that it calls its Knowledge Bank™. In 1996, the company appointed a manager, Jacques Cesar, to lead the effort. Cesar's team started out to serve as a catalyst, communicator, and a clearinghouse for knowledge that existed within the company's offices and practices in 25 different countries. Throughout 1996, the team interviewed all the firm's partners, and collected documentation, reports, white papers, and other documents to construct a bigger picture of the company's existing and germinating intellectual assets.

In 1997, Mercer launched its Knowledge Bank. This was a humble beginning in an information system that catalogued all existing documents that the company had worldwide and included a yellow pages–type directory that listed the areas of expertise, past projects, and experience of each of the company's consultants.

The same approach is evident in many other successful knowledge-intensive companies that we examined. The key lesson to take away is that the best place to begin a knowledge management project is collecting and sorting out the existing knowledge, albeit in more tangible forms, such as documents, reports, and project documentation. At the same time, compiling expertise of each employee will give you a good feel for who knows what throughout the organization. Once this starting step is accomplished, you can begin to address the *softer* and *fuzzier* aspects of information that flows and resides within the firm.

Lesson 9: Accommodate Reasoning and Assumptions

Data warehouses and decision support systems promised a lot but have delivered little. Maybe we set our expectations too high. A critical failure point lies in the fact that managers have some deeply held, extensively shared, often believed, but rarely tested assumptions about the key decisions they make and the basis on which they make them. Like many other things in a dynamic environment that firms operate in, these assumptions can, and often do, change.

When a major manufacturer of a personal digital assistant rethought the assumption that the size of the device needs to be no larger than the competitor's product, he gave a free hand to the design team. The design team looked at the most popular brand of shirts sold to the target buyer market and measured their pocket sizes, and resized the product so that it comfortably slid into a typical shirt pocket. This meant reexamining the very assumption that the size of the device needed to mirror the competitor's. It meant rethinking the underlying criteria for the sizing decision. But it worked. The market share of the device grew substantially after a few of these retested assumptions were applied to the design decisions for the next version of the product.

Starfish Software (www.starfish.com), the developer of the personal information utility (PIU), Sidekick™ for Windows, did something similar. One single successful product has allowed this company to thrive ever since the introduction of MS-DOS in the early 1980s. In a recent product revision, the company, which had been integrating an increasing number of features to keep up with competing products, rethought two basic assumptions. The first assumption was the need to compete with the feature-rich products in its market. The second assumption was to keep the newer releases of the product compatible with the older versions so that existing customers could easily upgrade. When Starfish asked its existing customers for suggestions, it realized that those assumptions were quite misplaced. So the company scrapped all but the basic functionality in the product that the users said they "never used" and gave them exactly what they asked for—a "light and fast" program. Even though the program has half the number of the features that competing products have, a loyal customer base willing to pay for a product whose competitors were giving theirs away for almost free, only grew. And it grew exponentially.

> ### OO METHODOLOGY: AN UNTESTED ASSUMPTION OR DIEHARD BELIEF
>
> For years, people believed that object-oriented (OO) software development methodologies make software development more efficient. On the basis of a fair amount of anecdotal evidence, developers bought into the idea and blindly embraced it. But the validity of this assumption has never been thoroughly tested. Some recent studies have shown that the assumption might not always be valid.[20]

Lesson 10: Future Think

Knowledge-centric initiatives and projects must look to the future and not at the past or present, except to see how past decisions, experience, successes, and failures can help make better decisions in the future. The ability to test assumptions and their effects adds much more to the quality of decisions than do well-documented past decisions alone. An effective knowledge management system should allow key decision makers to test-run scenarios and juggle with what-if analysis with assumptions and outcomes.

Any new knowledge that is created by a company *must add value* to the company. If knowledge creation is to be successfully directed, there must be an indisputable and absolute link between the business strategy of your company and the development and use of knowledge within it. Although it is difficult to project the immediate benefits of such efforts, estimates using newer approaches such as the balanced scorecard approach can be of value. Alternative projections of the future, especially when dealing with inputs that do not lend themselves to numerical analysis, provide better direction for both immediate and the future decisions.

Lesson 11: Minimize Routing Retransmissions

As actionable information moves from one recipient to the next, two things get added to it: noise and value (see Figure 6-7). First, noise or distortion gets added to it, depending on the way it is interpreted by the recipient. Second, some value gets added to it. Depending on whether the noise added is lesser or greater than the value added to it, the usefulness and accuracy of the original transmission might increase or decrease. It is often safer to assume that the distortion is more than the value, especially when rerouting is nonessential. So it is better to retain the original context in which the piece of information was generated or created. The design of your knowledge management system should minimize the number of transmissions of knowledge between individuals to achieve the least distortion of that knowledge.

Lesson 12: Give Incentives, Not Faster Computers

Many among us believe that all problems can be solved by an intranet, an intelligent search engine–enabled site, or a Lotus Notes database. But reality is far from this belief. None

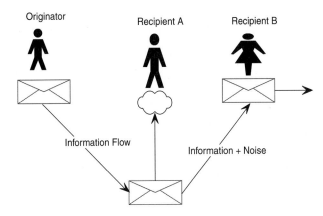

Figure 6-7 As information flows from the originator to others within and outside the company, noise is added to it.

of these can ever solve the fundamental problem of relationships within a company, and the supposed ability to be *able* to share knowledge will not break down a determination of people to keep it to themselves. An intranet will not cause people to work for the good of the company rather than for the good of themselves.

In classic management theory, this problem has often been addressed as *agency-agent conflict*, where a manager tries to maximize her gain even if it is opposed to maximizing that

---

CASE: BUCKMAN LABORATORIES

Buckman Laboratories is a good example of a company that limits rerouting transmissions. Buckman is a multinational chemicals company that invents, develops, and manufactures specialty chemicals for industrial and agricultural uses. The 1,200-employee company is based in Memphis, Tennessee, with offices and representatives in 82 countries. A company with offices in as many countries such as Buckman is, understandably, faced with barriers of time, culture, language, and distance.

The company realized that empowering its employees to truly satisfy customer needs needed both a customer knowledge-sharing environment and easy access to customer information. The knowledge management program in the company is targeted at helping its employees get all the knowledge they need to help do business with and satisfy the needs of its customers more effectively. Minimizing transmissions not only allows Buckman to retain accuracy in its knowledge repository but also increases the span of communication of each and every employee in the company.

of the company. The only solution is to tie the two together. In other words, give incentives that are too attractive to be ignored! In most Western countries, these incentives equal financial rewards; in other countries such as Japan and India, they primarily hinge on performance recognition.

Arthur Andersen, a management consulting firm, has successfully implemented this strategy by making an employee's contribution to the internal knowledge repository an essential evaluation criteria for promotion.

Lesson 13: Allow Everyone Access, and Allow Everyone to Contribute

Everyone in the organization should be able to access most, if not all, sources of knowledge that exist within the company. The greater the span of communication, the greater the employee's influence in taking the company in the intended direction.

As the ability of the individual to access available information expands, so does that of the company as a whole. At the same time, confidential information can be controlled or restricted within the same system, without the need to resort to alternative delivery channels.

Similarly, allow everyone to help solve the problem at hand.[23] As pieces of knowledge begin to fit together, the most insightful part might come from the most unexpected source or employee. A successful knowledge management system does not restrict employees from contributing what they know and want to contribute irrespective of their positions.

If yours is a global company, you may need to break language barriers. If employees feel comfortable contributing in their native language, the system should allow them to do so. Though multilingual support might not be easy or even possible to implement in the very first attempt, keep it on the drawing board. Until automated translation becomes feasible, keep posted content in the original language or have someone translate it (without massacring the original meaning). A good approach is to keep the content posted in the original language and add a pointer with contact information to the person who made the contribution.

Lesson 14: Allow Confidentiality

Allow users to contribute to the system without the fear of being reprimanded for their words. This is occasionally possible only if there is a venue or outlet through which employees can post content without disclosing their identity. As important as it is to be able to trace back to contributors of knowledge, allowing free expression under anonymity is also critical.

There are obvious downsides to this. For example, employees might post obscene content or damaging competitor job listings, etc. But this content can be controlled or removed by the support staff who operate under the CKO. Publicly declared policies against extreme abuse can further serve as effective deterrents.

A good example is Amazon.com's Website where readers can freely, and anonymously, post negative comments about a book without fearing that the content will not be posted. Obscene, personally targeted, or racially directed content is an exception. Figure 6-8 shows an example of a system that enters the contributor's identity by default, giving him the option to conceal it. This arrangement further saves the contributor from having to manually type that repetitive information every time he wants to add something while revealing his identity.

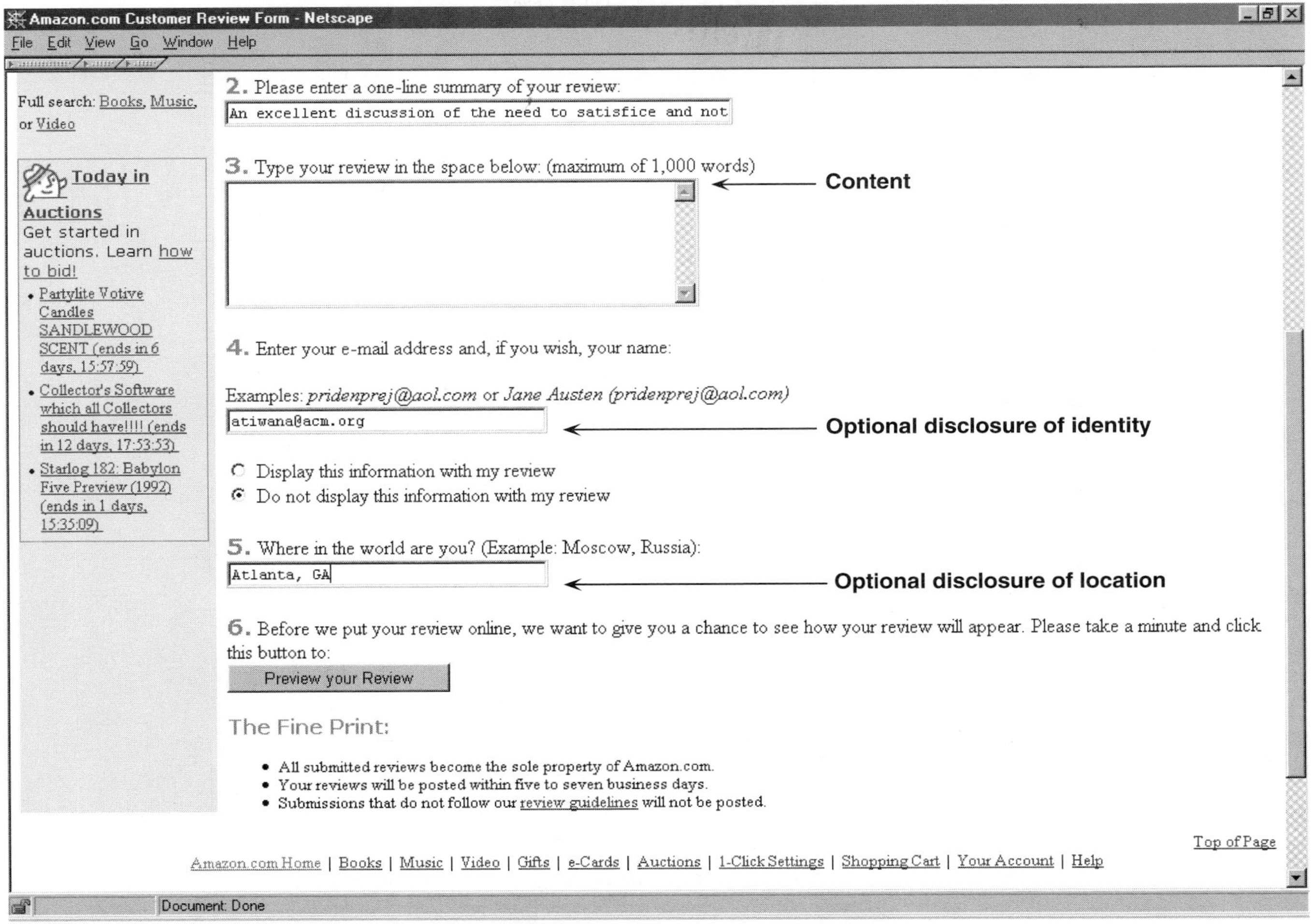

Figure 6-8 Amazon.com's interface enters the contributor's identity in the user field by default, giving him the option to conceal it if he wants to.

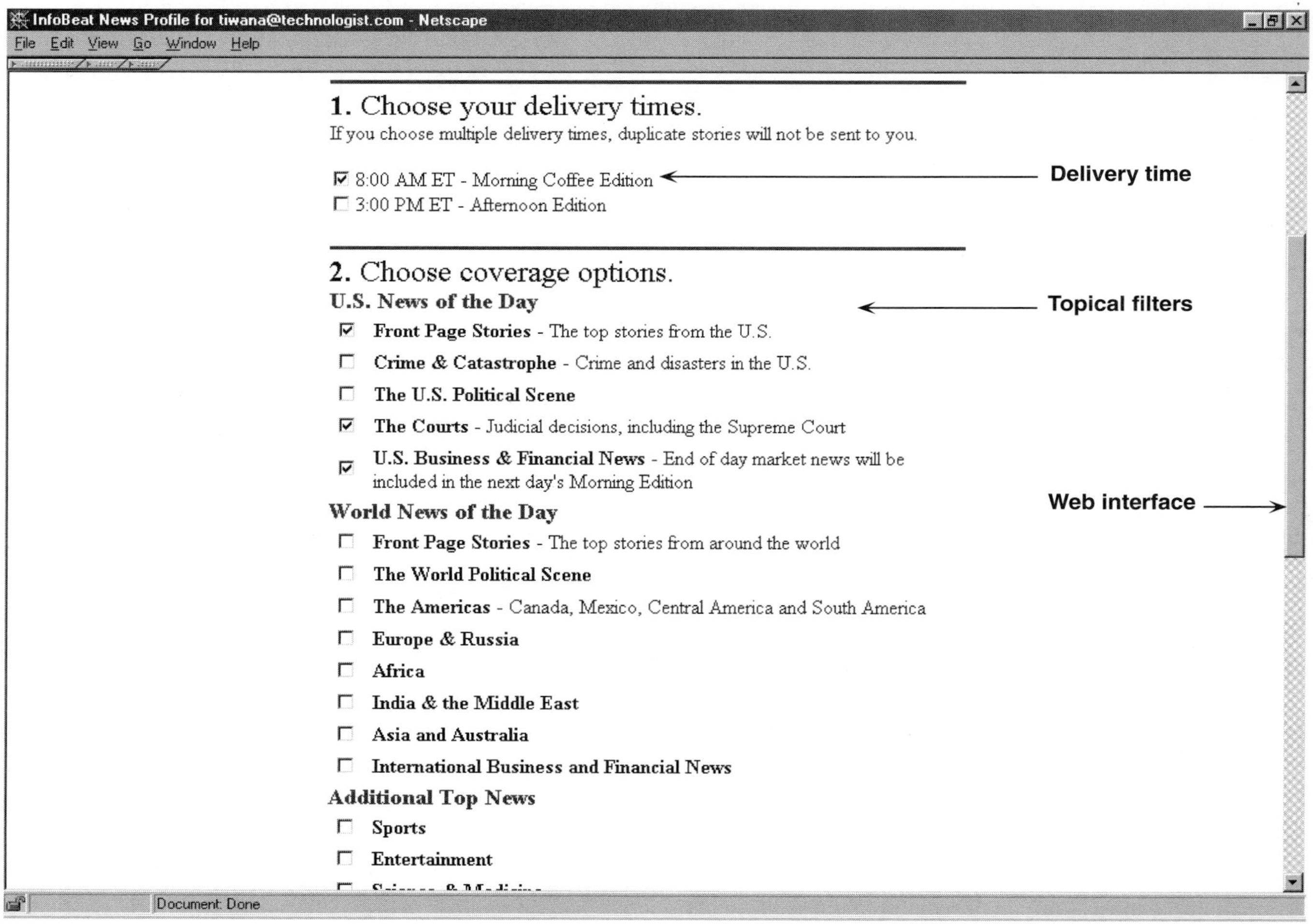

InfoBeat News Profile for tiwana@technologist.com - Netscape

File Edit View Go Window Help

1. Choose your delivery times.

If you choose multiple delivery times, duplicate stories will not be sent to you.

☑ 8:00 AM ET - Morning Coffee Edition ——————→ **Delivery time**

☐ 3:00 PM ET - Afternoon Edition

2. Choose coverage options.

U.S. News of the Day ——————→ **Topical filters**

☑ **Front Page Stories** - The top stories from the U.S.

☐ **Crime & Catastrophe** - Crime and disasters in the U.S.

☐ **The U.S. Political Scene**

☑ **The Courts** - Judicial decisions, including the Supreme Court

☑ **U.S. Business & Financial News** - End of day market news will be included in the next day's Morning Edition

World News of the Day

☐ **Front Page Stories** - The top stories from around the world

☐ **The World Political Scene**

☐ **The Americas** - Canada, Mexico, Central America and South America

☐ **Europe & Russia**

☐ **Africa**

☐ **India & the Middle East**

☐ **Asia and Australia**

☐ **International Business and Financial News**

Additional Top News

☐ **Sports**

☐ **Entertainment**

☐ **Science & Modicine**

——————→ **Web interface**

Document: Done

Figure 6-9 Illustrates the same idea implemented in a push-delivery system.

Lesson 15: Allow Access Anytime, Anywhere

The way in which you connect to a central repository or database is a critical determinant of how much it will actually be used. Since a lot of us spend at least as much time away from our desks as we do at them, actionable information, and in turn knowledge, should be accessible from any location, and at anytime. While the *anytime* factor is not much of a problem with information that is stored electronically, the *anywhere* aspect can sometimes cause the problem. If a Lotus Notes database in Cincinnati, Ohio, is not accessible to a salesperson hotelling in Lincoln, Nebraska, it is probably close to useless.

Although a system where users can dial in from remote locations using dial-up connections is not too hard to implement, long distance connection costs for international dial-up connections can quickly add up to enormous dollar figures.

The obvious choice then narrows down to the Web. Use an existing network such as the Internet to keep costs involved in *anywhere* access down to a minimum. Connecting to virtual private networks (VPNs) can be a major advantage of basing access mechanisms on the Web.[g] The advantage of using such a mechanism is that users with an account can often find local access numbers not only throughout the United States but also in other countries. America Online is a good example, as are other major online services or ISPs that have nationally, or even globally distributed dial-up network access points (NAPs).

There are obvious speed limitations inherent in dial-up connections as they currently exist, but the savings and advantages balance them out rather well. Windows 98, for example, has built-in functionality that allows it to make secure VPN connections without the need for any additional software, and you can expect this functionality in most of the upcoming versions such as Windows 2000 and other flavors of Windows-based products.

Lesson 16: Update Automatically

As discussions take place on a common forum, your system must reflect these additions—questions, searches, and answers—automatically and in real time. For Web browser–based interfaces, the browser's content should be automatically refreshed at regular time intervals. This can be done by programming the refresh function in browsers to execute at periodic intervals. While this feature is useful, the user must be able to optionally deactivate this feature.

Lesson 17: Supply Resource Maps to Ease Navigation

All successful knowledge management systems share the common characteristic of easy navigability. There are two parts to this: ease of use and ease of retrieval. Most employees, even in technical companies, have little interest in dealing with a system that uses a cryptic and hard-to-use interface. Keep the process for sharing or tapping into the knowledge pool simple, straightforward, and efficient, lest you discourage people from contributing to or tapping into your overall corporate body of knowledge.

Using the Web as a base platform makes sense in a large organization. Ease of use comes with an intuitive interface (including a ubiquitous application that most employees have already used—the Web browser) where the user does not get lost too easily, and gets to where

---

[g]Buckman Labs, for example, has for long used CompuServe to connect to its own system.

she wants to go. Nevertheless, be forewarned: Using the Web does not automatically imply an easy interface. Examples of companies that have blundered by creating hard-to-use interfaces on the Web abound.

You need to be careful about the user's ability to search through content. If you are using the Web browser as the primary interface for your knowledge management system, you can partially ease this worry by using some of the powerful search engine tools, available as out-of-the-box solutions, in the market. In addition, you must:

- Map knowledge and give it quicker access formats

- Capture knowledge in a way that is meaningfully representative of employees' experience

- Provide a feedback mechanism that emergently allows the format and general structure to evolve with general consensus of the actual users

Good examples of easy-to-use interfaces come from some popular electronic commerce sites such as Amazon.com. Such a site allows users to either search the entire site on the basis of a keyword or to delve deeper into the advanced search menu by specifying multiple criteria. When you are thinking about the features supporting search and retrieval from a repository of knowledge, following Amazon.com's example can save you a lot of thinking (alternative structures are described in Appendix B).

When people get value from the knowledge management system, they will spend their time and energy using it and will simultaneously be more inclined to add to it. Ask users to rate the usefulness of resources, documents, and content included; publish these results actively, and if possible, in real time.

Are companies doing this? At first glance, it almost seems intuitive. But a survey by KPMG found that such resources in most companies were not as easily accessible as it might seem.[24] Typical respondents in U.S. companies who said that they could find the telephone number for a colleague in Europe in 5 minutes actually spent up to 15 minutes tracking down the contact number!

Whatever you decide to call it, it is essential that general pointers to the sources be stored along with the captured knowledge wherever possible.[h] Sometimes this is impossible if you have pledged to maintain confidentiality of the contributor. In that case, give the contributor the choice to respond selectively.

Lesson 18: Use Other Databases in Addition to Corporate Best Practices Databases

As a company's size grows, keeping track of what another department of division or the company is doing can itself be a daunting challenge. Many companies use Lotus Notes as a platform for creating databases of best practices within the organization across all its locations.[25] When the enterprise is widely spread out, this is perhaps the best way to identify and transfer best practices across far-flung units of the enterprise. Follow the lead of companies that have successfully demonstrated both use and sharing of best practices:

---

[h]The concept itself is similar to business objects and the object-oriented design methodology.

CHEVRON'S CASE

Chevron has something it calls its best practices resource map. The map is organized by Baldrige Award criteria and further divided into business processes. This index or rolodex-type approach directs people to resources across the entire company. For a 50,000-employee company with over $50 billion in revenues, finding another person within the company itself was a challenge. Such a resource map lets employees find knowledgeable people, experts, contacts, and resources that could range from something like a database, an e-mail, a brochure, a newsletter, or a person. Each resource area has an owner, and this owner is cited on the map. So, if looking for something that just cannot be found, a Chevron employee could do straight to the owner of that resource and ask him.

Chevron saved millions of dollars by identifying and making available its own best practices across all its locations, units, and offices. By sharing its best practices on energy use management, Chevron managed to save about $150 million on its annual fuel and power bills in 1996 alone.

MONSANTO'S CASE

At Monsanto, a radical decentralization has resulted in the creation of a number of business units, one of which has been given the task of focusing purely on growth. Its mission is to *grow existing businesses and create new business by exploiting "white spaces" where core competencies exist to increase the overall profitability of the enterprise.* To address this, Monsanto created a web of knowledge teams, tasked with creating and maintaining a yellow pages–type of directory of the company's knowledge and serving as points of contact for people seeking information about different areas of specialization.

- Integrate the sharing of knowledge with their business strategy.
- Build a culture that supports knowledge exchange and learning. Knowledge management is more than the simple use of databases and information technology; it is about creating an enterprise-wide learning culture that permeates every aspect of the business.
- Build awareness and eagerness among employees on the value of creating, sharing, and using knowledge.
- Develop and maintain human networks that share current knowledge and create new knowledge while keeping the social and human side of information technology in focus.
- Share knowledge and best practices, regardless of proximity, through virtual collaboration and distributed decision making, often tapping into the original knowledge contributor's expertise.

THE FATE OF INNOVATIVE NONEXPLOITERS

As the legend goes in the Silicon Valley, it's not the innovators but the exploiters who make the billions. Apple Computer, Inc., was born in its most successful form by momentary knowledge link established (evoked as a realization) by Steve Jobs, its co-founder, when he was seeing a demonstration of a crude version of the embryonic idea of a GUI (graphical user interface) at Xerox PARC in the early 1980s. Jobs asked the right question: how could he use this immature technology to change the future of computing? The GUI—a driver of Apple's stellar success—is now the de facto interface in almost all computer operating systems including Windows.

Apple figured out its GUI from PARC, Microsoft exploited the Mac operating system to create Windows; Xerox created the computer mouse, which is produced by hundreds of other companies *other than Xerox*. Sony, which is often wrongly credited for the invention of the VCR, exploited Ampex's 1950s innovation of video recording, and the semiconductors industry is built around Bell Labs Nobel prize–winning invention of the transistor.

Lesson 19: Provide Management Support

To sort corporate priorities in the right order, senior management must address a set of critical questions that provide some direction to guide knowledge management effectively:

1. What intellectual assets satisfy your company's strategic needs the most?
2. Can you leverage what you have right now?
3. What does it cost to leverage that?
4. Is the cost worth the benefit, given the time and financial constraints we face?
5. How will it help?

In trying to gain commitment from top managers, you, as a champion of knowledge management, must realize that many, if not most, managers have been trained to handle industrial companies and not knowledge-based ones. Senior managers are often concerned with the potential impact that investments in knowledge management initiatives might directly have on bottom-line results. These concerns often tend to outweigh the other, less tangible, and arguably longer-term results of managing this asset. After all, what good is the world's best knowledge management system when the company is on the verge of bankruptcy? So get real and demonstrate in surrogate measures how the speed and quality of service to your clients will gain from, say, exchanging best practices. Such pitches might be more salable arguments.

Top management's active support and understanding of the role that knowledge has to play, whether your company is a small business or a multinational business, are critical for its success. Most companies that I talked to seem to view establishing management support as the biggest challenge. How do you convince senior management that money spent on managing the company's knowledge is more important than some other seemingly critical expenses that the company needs to incur? It is an uphill battle to convince top management of the need for such operational knowledge management. They demand dollar values and hard figures, neither of which can be easily provided. *Establish top management sponsorship with ongoing involvement during the design, development, and implementation stages of your knowledge management system.*

This brings us back to the question of metrics and surrogate metrics. Having clear-cut deadlines and projections, even if they are surrogate measures, helps convince senior management. A major company that I investigated had successfully leveraged the knowledge of sales employees to reap very strong competitive positions for the company in various markets that it competed in. However, the knowledge management project leader demonstrated the entire benefit of the project in terms on savings in package delivery expenditures that resulted from the use of the supporting "intranet" until the senior management bought into his idea that the management of knowledge was actually helping the entire company in a larger way.

Dow Chemical and Management Support

Dow Chemical Company, a company that employs approximately 50,000 people across its 115 manufacturing sites located in over 30 countries, sells over $20 billion of its products that belong to its 2,400 product families. Upper management began its knowledge management efforts with the firm belief that its intellectual assets needed to be managed as seriously as its hard assets. The company owns approximately 30,000 patents. In a highly research oriented company like Dow, typically 1 out of 15 new projects succeeds. The company's senior management formulated a clear-cut vision for its knowledge management project with a definite target: to increase this success rate from 1-15 to 1-5. This end needed a system that strategically directed existing knowledge into new ventures and projects. With assets like patents, the intellectual property of the company is well articulated.

In cases like this, it is always better to shoot toward leveraging those assets that are most suited for strategic business purposes before trying to implement a theoretically complete and encompassing effort to manage *all* forms of knowledge.

Lesson 20: Focus on Technology and Internal Consulting Support for Collaboration

Information technology is a great facilitator but it should not be equated to face-to-face (FTF) contact. Promote face-to-face meetings, and given that geographical distances exist, use technology like audio and video streaming to get as close as you can get to FTF collaboration. Knowledge is primarily a function and consequence of the meeting, collaboration and interaction of minds.[26] Research has shown that electronic communication still does not fully substitute for actual meetings, but definitely include video and audio support in your KM project's infrastructural plans. Depending on textual and passive exchange through e-mail, discussion groups, and intranets leads to frustration among the project's champions and often results in added expense in a desperate attempt to fix problems. No wonder the telephone, a seemingly old-fashioned and unsophisticated piece of technology, is still a popular piece of collaborative and conversational equipment!

As businesses become more and more complex—so complex that tracking knowledge as fast as it grows and diversifies becomes a mammoth effort—a group of internal consultants can help support proper channeling, storage, exchange, transfer, and capture of knowledge. A number of questions then begin to arise:

- Can KM systems keep up-to-date with the rapid development of knowledge in a specific area?

- Does the system really support and keep talented knowledge workers?

- Does it contribute to greater coherence both within and between various divisions and departments?

- Does it lead to better use of knowledge in unstructured processes and problems where information management is incommensurate and mechanization is not germane?

Any knowledge management system being designed in your company must potentially support an internal consulting group—very knowledgeable experts drawn from various ranks within the company—to assist other employees with proper use and reuse of knowledge that is to go into the system.

INTERNAL CONSULTING SUPPORT AT HP

As companies expand, their divisions and operating units begin to operate more and more like independent businesses. These units often tend to be highly autonomous and decentralized. As the lines of business expand either through acquisitions or through planned diversification, any company's knowledge begins to fragment. Hewlett-Packard is one such company. With over 100,000 employees generating over $35 billion in revenues, the company operates in 110 countries. The solution to its increasingly complex problem of fragmentation of skills and knowledge was addressed by a management team at HP when they formed a unit called PPO, or the Product Process Organization, within HP. This division is an internal consulting group that leverages best practices in new product development processes among the company's highly decentralized and autonomous operating businesses. The PPO serves as an internal consulting group and draws its employees from a diverse cross-functional pool. Members come from engineering, quality, change management, manufacturing, marketing, information systems, etc.

Lesson 21: Support Informality

A successful knowledge management system also supports the ways that people naturally share information.

Anthropologists at the Xerox Palo Alto Research Center observed, for example, that whenever field representatives gathered, they exchanged horror stories about the problems that they had encountered, their bad experiences, and how they resolved them. Xerox initially discouraged these informal get-togethers because it wanted to eliminate employee downtime. But when the company recognized the value of the knowledge exchanged, it equipped the reps with telephone headsets so they could continue their conversations even on the road. The system has since been expanded to include a database that captures information submitted by Xerox's representatives.

Lesson 22: Remember that Less Is More—The Art of Packaging Knowledge

An abundance of unfiltered data renders most knowledge management systems ineffective and practically useless. Volume might have been king in the electronic data processing (EDP) ages that ended in the late 1970s.[27] Not now. Knowledge bases are filled with meaningless documents, anecdotes, mundane discussion threads, and other material of little practical use to anyone. Sensing that it is a waste of time and effort, many employees stop contributing to or relying on knowledge databases, consequently nullifying the potential value of these databases. To capitalize on the wealth of intelligence available in an organization, knowledge must be packaged in such a way that it's insightful, relevant, and useful. Knowledge is generally shared with employee groups[28] in teams with differing priorities, skill sets, training, functional responsibilities, and backgrounds; therefore, knowledge packaging efforts require several rounds of review and revision.

Ask selected end users to evaluate the material and provide ideas for how to improve its content, value, quality, and style so that it increases the perceived credibility and value of such content. The time required to do this does not come out of thin air. Allow employees the necessary time to package knowledge for further use.

To make content useful, include:

1. *Identification:* Identify general domains of knowledge applicable to your company or business unit.

2. *Segmenting:* Identify segments and target users and classify them into broad groups. Identify a small number of mutually exclusive groups.

3. *Mass customization:* Mass-customize content to suit each audience. Let the audiences further tailor the content targeted toward them through collaborative filtering mechanisms and choice-enabling software such as Grapevine.

4. *Format:* Select an appropriate format. Consider the bandwidth through which it will be delivered. If you are trying to send video clips to telecommuters connected through slow dial-up lines or ISDN connections, you will probably frustrate them more than anything else. Use indexes, groupings, site maps, mind maps, and tables of contents for easy navigation.

5. *Tests:* Don't assume that your end users want what you think they want. Test and refine the steps described above, and use user feedback as a positive indicator of perceived usefulness and incremental improvement.

Lesson 23: Provide Logical Business Extensions

When you begin to build or propose a knowledge management project for your company, there is bound to be skepticism about its short-term value. Build the system one logical component at a time. This practice not only makes the entire effort more credible, but improves and overcomes the shortfalls before the next logical extension is implemented. Conventional systems development methodologies fail to work well with KM projects. Instead, use alternative techniques such as the results-driven incrementalism (RDI) methodology (see Chapter 12).

Companies such as Platinum Technologies have built their knowledge management system as logical extensions of the current business to maintain credibility and ensure value. They began with the marketing department, moved on to support their field sales representatives, and gradually extended the system to include other parts of the company.

Another aspect of business extensions is vendor choice. When you partner with a vendor or reseller to buy the technology around which you plan to build your company's knowledge management system, don't decide purely on cost. Partner with vendors that really get what you are trying to do, not with those that are out to sell you as many site licenses of their product as they possibly can!

A serious problem, observed in many companies, is only getting worse as technology gets more sophisticated and complex: Too many choices are being made by the wrong people. Technologies that would ideally enable the organization to leap to a new level of performance are being ignored in favor of more appealing, faddish, or popular tools and platforms. Many technologists are ill equipped to select appropriate enterprise-wide technologies. Make sure that nontechnical management is included in the evaluation phase of product selection or that the technologists assigned to the task have actually had substantial experience managing a strategic profit center "out" in your company.

When it comes to vendor choices for technology, look beyond existing contractual arrangements and benefits to explore the long-term potential for suppliers to create win-win situations. When such a match can be made, the supplier can look forward to increased revenues by providing services and products that increase your company's revenues.

Lesson 24: Determine Your Knowledge Delivery *Weltanschuung*

The design philosophy—*Weltanschuung,*[i] of your knowledge management system dictates how actionable information or knowledge is delivered. This brings us to several key choices that must be made.

---

[i] *Weltanschuung,* a German term for "world view" or philosophy, has no close equivalent in English. This term has been in favor, especially with management researchers, who have been critical of how logical positivist epistemologists construe the reality of organization science as being completely free of human judgment.

Case Study: How KM Was Implemented at Heineken NV, Holland

When Heineken NV, the Dutch company that brews a popular brand of beer by the same name, designed a number of scenarios to see whether its corporate office could become more process oriented, it realized that three questions needed to be answered:

- What is the added value of the corporate office?
- What strategic processes does it apply?
- How can the corporate office be organized around these processes?

The main purpose of the corporate office was defined as providing effective support to the executive board in formulating and realizing the strategy of the company as a whole. The corporate office's role was therefore thought of as the creator of strategic and operational knowledge that exists above the business units; that knowledge is easily accessible and adds value that is evidenced by the competitive advantage of Heineken.

The next step was to define the companywide strategic processes and related goals of the corporate office.

- Those directly related to the strategy of the company
- Those semipermanent in character, changing only when the strategy of the company "as a whole" changed
- Those making a multifunctional contribution to the entire company that rises above the business units and were divisible into separate strategic processes

Heineken then created several scenarios with specific outcome objectives:

- Strengthening worldwide market presence
- Stimulating operational excellence
- Optimizing management performance
- Maximizing company financial leverage

In these scenarios, the corporate office was no longer organized by functional disciplines. Instead, many people would be organized in teams around the company's strategic processes. Corporate office professionals could work on several teams both as team members and team leaders. So one day a financial controller could work in a team on the acquisition of an Asian brewer and contribute to the strengthening of the worldwide market presence. The next day the same specialist could work in a team advising on the fiscal plan of a specific operating division. A board member would no longer be responsible only for a specific function. Besides their operational responsibilities, they would also be responsible for one of the strategic processes such as corporate process responsibilities. The delivery of this responsibility and therefore the added value and accountability would become more explicit and clearly defined.

The teams were eventually connected in what the company described as "smart networks," where workers work together in soft networks of people and knowledge. They are supported by hard networks forming an electronic performance system with productivity tools, communication tools, etc.

DELIVERY OPTIONS

Push versus Pull

Pull system: A pull system requires a user to actively seek information.

- *User choice:* Users proactively seek knowledge as and when they need it.

- *No distraction:* Pull systems do not distract users with unwanted updates but require user initiative. Users actually need to *go and get* what they need to know.

Push systems: Distribute and deliver knowledge to their audience, after filtering it through highly customized filters.

- *Noticeability:* Push systems deliver information to users' desktops or electronic mail accounts and are more likely to get noticed.

- *Ease of use:* Within a work group, there might be some that might actually prefer receiving push, rather than have to deal with the effort of going and looking for the pieces of information that they might need to complete their task

- Tools—examples of systems that implement push delivery include Grapevine (www.grapwvine.com), Firefly (www.firefly.com), and Alexa (www.alexa.com).

An administrator first tells Grapevine where to look for useful information and knowledge. Grapevine then monitors those Websites, file servers, and databases and checks all information that has been recently added. Using an organization-specific taxonomy or category tree, it classifies new documents in those categories. Each user creates an interest profile. Once Grapevine finds some information that matches that interest profile, it will alert the user by sending an e-mail. The user can validate this by attaching a rank to the document—from

The first choice is the method of delivery—when users want the knowledge (the pull approach) or when you want them to have it (the push approach). You can make both options available to every user without adding much complexity to the system itself—the push system can simply deliver the final content from the pull-based system. Be aware that how information is filtered can be an issue with the push system: Filters may not be consistent with users' needs, so ask them what categories of filtering they want. Some filtering tools use intelligent agents to learn from each user's habits; users may consider this a violation of privacy. It's even possible, if the system is not powerful enough, that the filter may filter out wrong, possibly critically needed content. For example, a user who reads reports about her company's competitor's products will begin receiving more of competitive intelligence reports. The problem begins, however, when she starts receiving job postings, say, after having checked Steve Jobs's official title once.

Another decision is how much information should be delivered: all or selected portions. *Selective* delivery of content is the only way push mechanisms can be effectively used to push content through a knowledge management system.

You may also consider when to deliver knowledge: when needed ("just-in-time") or when created or acquired ("just-in-case"). A middle path is not an option, but anecdotal evidence (e.g., a customer study Lotus) suggests that just-in-time delivery is more valuable than just-in-case. Certainly, just-in-case systems have their problems: Information, not knowledge, is delivered; users become inured to the flow of irrelevant information and simply ignore it; users pursue interesting threads not applicable or useful to their work.

"Useless" to "Must read!"—that is, escalate it and pass it on to others. Escalated items are those that another participant has flagged as particularly useful; other users whose profiles indicate an interest in the item will be alerted and have a chance to collaborate on how to characterize the item's significance.

All versus Some

All-inclusive: Unlike a filtering approach, all-inclusive systems deliver content in its entirety.

- *Suited for information management, not knowledge management:* Volume, as Davenport and Prusak describe it, is data's friend. A few decades back when the focus of technology was electronic data processing, it was this lack of data volume that companies were trying to address. The problem today is the excess of information.

- *Data slam:* The onslaught of meaningless pieces of data, often called *data slam*, that attack and clog corporate intranet sites and databases not only mucks up internal databases; it can also dangerously slow down management decision making by making systems slow, unwieldy, and difficult to navigate.

Selective: Selective delivery takes a minimalist approach. Selective delivery of content is the only way push delivery can be used effectively to push content through a knowledge management system.

- *Useful, contextually applicable pieces:* Selective delivery mechanisms specifically extract useful and contextually applicable pieces from an enormous volume of processed data and information. Too many databases, too many documents, and too many categories can prevent users from efficiently finding information that they need.

THE KNOWLEDGE-STRATEGY LINK REVISITED

The key characteristics identified from leading companies that have successfully leveraged their knowledge assets provide a fertile ground for developing a knowledge management strategy. Companies that want to leverage this asset must approach knowledge management with a focus on their core competencies and tie those in very tightly to the business strategy and vision. Many research studies, cases, and management books have found that company mission statements often do not have much to do with what the companies actually do! Even though the mission statement might not be descriptive of the firm's actual strategy and vision, a clear-cut and well-defined business strategy is required before an investment in knowledge management can be successfully realized. Figure 6-10 summarizes this linkage as based on our preceding discussion.

An integrative approach for identifying knowledge areas, specializations, and knowledge links has been successfully embraced by the pharmaceutical giant Hoffman-LaRoche. Success in the pharmaceutical industry depends on the speed of new product launches more than anything else. The faster a product is brought to market, the faster a company can recoup its development costs and generate higher profits. Hoffman-LaRoche, for example, calculated that every day gained in market availability represented a gain of $1 million.

Knowledge management often supports the development of a product—physical, information, or service—and your company must never lose sight of that outcome focus. Create a strong relationship between the outcomes of the knowledge management system and the regular business cycle of your organization.

- *Specifically analyzed information, contextual knowledge and business intelligence:* Instead of dumping entire content of articles and reports into the system, it limits online content to abstracts and directs interested readers to the original sources and authors for more information. Instead of a flood of data, decision makers need knowledge. This approach ensures that.

Tradeoffs: One might argue that this might cause some critical piece of information—that could have helped—not to reach the consumer or knowledge worker requiring it. But that is a necessary tradeoff. Not having something reach the user is better than having too much reach him. In the latter case, little or nothing will actually be used.

- Tools—Web-based Infobeat (www.infobeat.com) is a good example of a tool that uses a selective push approach.

Just-in-time versus Just-in-case

- JIT: Lotus has been studying its customers and has found that knowledge is more valuable when it is delivered at the moment its needed—"just-in-time"—rather than being available at all times, "just-in-case" it might be needed.

- JIC: Just-in-case systems devalue knowledge as users become used to receiving information (this is not knowledge due to possible lack of action-ability) that is not relevant to their immediate work or task in hand. They may ignore the messages or spend time following threads that are interesting but not applicable or useful to them in their work.

 # ASSESSING FOCUS

The challenge of business and knowledge management is to address the three-way strategic alignment between business, knowledge, and technology used to support the first two. A company must consistently focus information technology and knowledge management to support the primary business strategy.

Companies that are new to knowledge management must address some "first" questions that often surface:

1. How can we turn the knowledge we have into something that adds value to the markets in which we operate?

2. What do we know, or think we know, about different aspects of our customers? Are we actually doing something with what we know about them?

3. How can we generate meaningful knowledge, rather than simply flooding our organization with indiscriminate information?

4. How can we create a knowledge-supportive organizational culture in which everybody is convinced of the contribution that knowledge can make to the success of the company?

5. Can we cut costs, reduce time-to-market, improve customer service, or increase margins by more effectively sharing knowledge and leveraging what we already know? Could such knowledge be applied to the activities of other divisions of our company, in other locations, and in foreign manufacturing sites? How can we ever transfer them and then make them work?

6. Are there any fundamental errors in what we *think* we know as a company? What will be the consequences of these errors? How can these be proactively fixed?

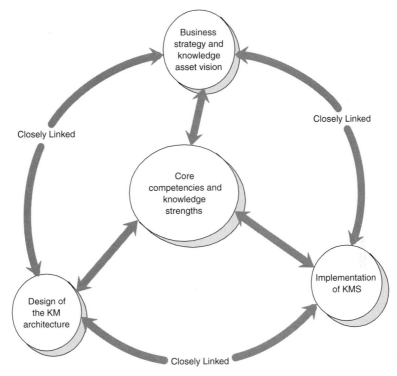

Figure 6-10 Enduring challenges in knowledge management must have a strong focus on your business strategy and KM.

GIVING IT AWAY FOR FREE GENERATES PROFITS TOO

The fragmented nature of knowledge and its characteristic of increasing returns means that the value of a knowledge-based business can occasionally be boosted by actions that might appear to destroy value. To the extent that information can create standards, a company might choose to give it away, as Netscape has recently done with its Web browser, or sell it at the cost of transmission, as Microsoft has done in the past with products like Microsoft Outlook and its Web browser, Internet Explorer.* This practice ties customers to its other, more profitable, knowledge services and products.

*Microsoft charges customers only for the cost of burning the CD and mailing it. Alternatively customers can download a free copy from its Website.

7. How can we manage our people, who will increasingly become knowledge workers motivating them to generate knowledge and share it with their peers?

8. Which of these people actually play critical roles in developing and testing new knowledge and information that gets used here?

9. Are exciting ideas emerging within the company but failing to be commercialized? If these ideas are not reaching the market, what incentives, structures, or management processes seem to be blocking them? How can valuable knowledge that exists within the company be applied to produce benefits?

10. Maybe our company has more money than ideas. Are there opportunities to form partnerships with companies that may be more in the flow of innovative ideas and knowledge? Given different cultures, how can this ever work?

11. Is the "not invented here" syndrome so strong that we are missing attractive business opportunities? Could knowledge-based collaboration (i.e., integration of external knowledge) with a wider range of innovative companies increase our value?

12. How does tacit knowledge—skills, intuitive abilities, employee experience—affect the generation and transfer of explicit forms of knowledge in our company?

The design of the knowledge management architecture must be closely linked to the actual areas of expertise and competency that a business possesses. At the same time, it must address the fundamental question of how it adds value and agility to the business strategy, at each stage of development. This necessitates the creation of a coherent blueprint that responds to the present and future needs of the company. While this makes a long-term vision for a knowledge management system an imperative, it also has a prerequisite of a pragmatic, short-term orientation.

A future-oriented focus necessitates selection of a proper set of team players that will actually develop the knowledge management system, as shown in Table 6-2 and discussed further in Chapter 9.

LESSONS LEARNED

Lessons learned from the analysis of many successful knowledge management projects allow us to further explicate the knowledge-strategy link formation process described in Figure 6-4, as illustrated by the example in Figure 6-11.

To summarize the main point raised in this chapter: Knowledge management and business strategy must drive each other. This is possible only if the two are in perfect alignment. When you are devising this critical link and using it as a basis for your knowledge management system, keep in mind these points:

*   *An effective knowledge management strategy begins with a vision.* Knowledge drives strategy and strategy drives knowledge management. Effective knowledge manage-

Table 6-2: Criteria for Selecting Key Players in the Implementation of a KM System

Core Capability	Business Skills Needed	Technical Skills Needed	Interpersonal Skills Needed	Focus Time Frame	Strategy Motivation	Structure Motivation	Technology Motivation	User Needs Fulfillment Motivation
CKO and team leaders	High	Medium	High	Present and future	✓	✓		✓
Business systems analysis	High	Medium	Medium	Future	✓			
Knowledge management system architecture planning	Low	High	Medium	Future			✓	
Vendor selection	High	Medium	High	Present and future	✓	✓		
Monitoring	Medium	Medium	Low	Future			✓	
Technology implementation	Low	High	Low	Present			✓	

Based on an adaptation from I. Feeny and J. Wilcocks, Core IS Capabilities for Exploiting Information Technology, *Sloan Management Review*, Spring (1998), 9–21. The discussion has been extended to apply to knowledge management systems and their underlying development processes.

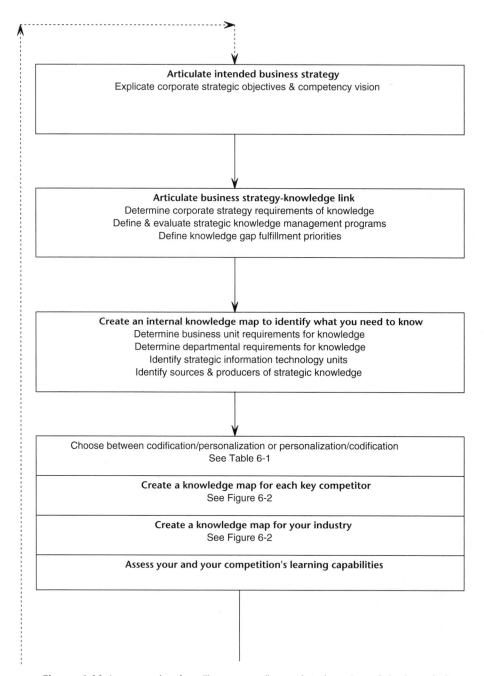

Figure 6-11 An example of an "in progress" populated version of the knowledge-strategy link.

Assess how your knowledge gap influences your current and future business strategy

INTERNAL

Current cultural & knowledge sharing norms
Current conversation practices
Current communication channels
Current collaborative & IT platforms
Identify Knowledge gaps, inefficiencies & failures
Identify enterprise wide best practices

EXTERNAL

Identify market leaders in your industry
Identify integrative IT solutions
Determine effect of leverage on Industry
"Steal" best practices from competitors

Determine the balance between exploitation and exploration

Choose to be primarily an exploiter or explorer
Define metrics for evaluation of success & strategic alignment
Develop IT architecture with an eye on the future
Define fit within your leveraged existing infrastructure
Define short-term goals & long-term goals with definite milestones
Allocate budgets, resource distribution, &
expenditure control guidelines
Address cultural issues
Advertise, promote, & motivate system usage
Reward contribution
Implement management procedures

ment must begin with a strategic vision and a clear definition of what knowledge is critical for your company.[j]

- *Shift from strategic programming to strategic planning.* Managers and businesses need to capture what they learn from both the soft insights and experiences as well as hard data from the markets, then synthesize that learning into a vision of the direction that the business *should* pursue. This also implies that knowledge management and strategy drive each other; that is, the link is two way.

- *Data extrapolation is a fallible predictor.* Don't assume linear relationships and look for patterns in data. Data is often random and is a poor means for predicting future opportunities and conditions. Use knowledge instead of data patterns when you are making decisions about serious financial and resource commitments.

- *Use knowledge-based SWOT analysis.* The strengths, weaknesses, opportunities, and threats framework has been well adapted to knowledge-based analysis. Read the must-read paper by Michael Zack in *California Management Review.* Spring 1999   125-146. "Developing a knowledge Strategy"

- *Create internal, competitive, and industry-wide knowledge maps to give you a reality check.* These maps will help you figure out which areas of knowledge are empty, slightly lacking, or weak beyond hope. Accordingly, orient your knowledge management system to strengthen strategic-gap knowledge in those areas in which your company will compete.

- *Focus on one but don't choose between codification and personalization.* Codification and personalization are two "equally right" knowledge management strategies: Use Table 6-1 to compare your own business unit to the companies exemplified; then focus primarily on one that matches your own company.

- *Balance exploitation and exploration.* Both must be supported, but one without the other can be a death blow.

- *Articulate a clear strategy-KM link.* It's a tough job that must be done. Use the process flow method described in Figure 6-4 to create this two-way link step by step. Creative without strategy is called art; creative with strategy is called good design. Translate this link to draw two sets of implications: implications for business strategy, change management, reward structures, and those for the design features that a knowledge management system must support. Validate this link so that users can feed back into the original strategy and incrementally or even radically change it.

---

[j]The word *vision* evokes a negative response in managers who often see their company's vision statement as a useless placeholder on its annual report. The vision that drives knowledge management strategy must be the one that *actually* drives your business. A vision can be translated to actionable "to-dos" with the aid of knowledge maps and gap analysis; and then translated into low-level KM system design features that support this high-level vision. Without such vision, the strategy-KM link can, at best, be force-fitted.

- *Incorporate the 24 critical success factors in KM design.* Each factor has profound implications on the design of your knowledge management system. Take these into account as you go through the actual process of KM team, system, and change management design.

- *Determine the right diagnostic questions to ask.* Knowing the right answers to the wrong questions will not serve your knowledge management project.

- *Mobilize initiatives to help you "sell" your KM project internally.* Even after all the noise about the "long view," most companies still look for short-term results. Balancing tangible short-term gains with long-term gains is the only way you can sell the project to your end users and top management. Your company's sudden introduction of a KM system to the surprise of end users is like an 800,000-ton aircraft carrier trying to make a sudden U-turn in the high seas.

The elegance of the techniques described in this chapter lies in their ability to take something as high level as your company's vision and, through a series of clear, iterative steps, translate it into low-level strategic steps, and subsequently into knowledge management system functionalities/features.

Having identified the key characteristics that are needed in a knowledge management system for it to be successfully aligned with your business strategy, we have made it through the second step on our 10-step roadmap. Let us now examine and understand the third step in the next chapter: infrastructural components of the knowledge management architecture that can allow you to realize the system to support this strategic link.

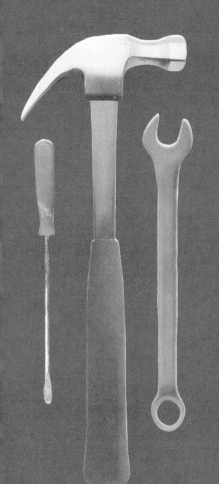

PART IIB

THE SECOND PHASE: KM SYSTEM ANALYSIS, DESIGN, AND DEVELOPMENT

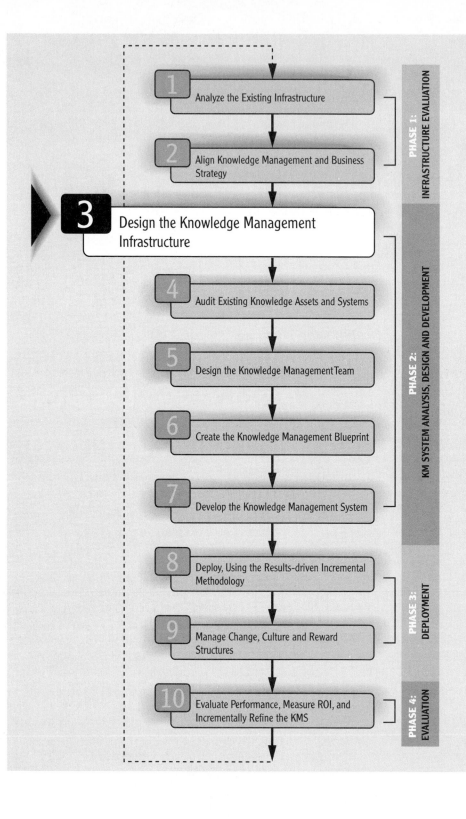

1. Analyze the Existing Infrastructure

2. Align Knowledge Management and Business Strategy

PHASE 1: INFRASTRUCTURE EVALUATION

3. Design the Knowledge Management Infrastructure

4. Audit Existing Knowledge Assets and Systems

5. Design the Knowledge Management Team

6. Create the Knowledge Management Blueprint

7. Develop the Knowledge Management System

PHASE 2: KM SYSTEM ANALYSIS, DESIGN AND DEVELOPMENT

8. Deploy, Using the Results-driven Incremental Methodology

9. Manage Change, Culture and Reward Structures

PHASE 3: DEPLOYMENT

10. Evaluate Performance, Measure ROI, and Incrementally Refine the KMS

PHASE 4: EVALUATION

CHAPTER 7

INFRASTRUCTURAL FOUNDATIONS

IN THIS CHAPTER

✔ Choose IT components to find, create, assemble, and apply knowledge.

✔ Identify elements of the interface layer: clients, server, gateways, and the platform.

✔ Decide on the collaborative platform: Web or Notes?

✔ Identify and understand components of the collaborative intelligence layer: artificial intelligence, data warehouses, genetic algorithms, neural networks, expert reasoning systems, rule bases, and case-based reasoning.

✔ Optimize knowledge object molecularity; balance cost versus value-added.

✔ Balance push-based and pull-based knowledge delivery.

✔ Identify the right mix of components for searching, indexing, and retrieval.

✔ Create knowledge tags and attributes: domain, form, type, product/service, time, and location tags.

KNOWLEDGE IS THE SMALL PART OF IGNORANCE THAT WE ARRANGE AND CLASSIFY

—AMBROSE BIERCE

Accepting knowledge as the primary strategic asset is a decisive recognition that underlies the success of many a thriving firm. Coke, Microsoft, Philips, and Buckman are only recent examples of this recognition. Successful companies have long recognized the need for effective and efficient creation, location, capturing, and sharing of their knowledge and the need to bring that knowledge to bear upon their problems and opportunities.[1] Idle knowledge is often useless knowledge. A little knowledge that is locatable and usable in making one critical decision is perhaps of much more significance than gigabytes of data that are not being used.

In this chapter, we implement step 3 of the 10-step roadmap by way of the seven-layer knowledge management architecture and its underlying infrastructural elements. Most technology needed to manage knowledge already exists, so we begin to look at technological pieces that make up these layers and analyze various components that can be deployed to transform existing infrastructure into one that supports KM. Our discussion of the seven-layer architecture spans more than one chapter: You'll become familiar with the illustration in the next few chapters.

The first layer in the architecture is the interface between the user and the system. We examine the elements and components to best manage this portal. We identify various knowledge sources to integrate into the KM system; this subject leads us to the third layer, where knowledge sources are used. Hence, we defer discussion of the access and authentication layer.

The third layer, the collaborative layer, prescribes the architectural elements of data storage, and we discuss implementation of its components: artificial intelligence, data warehousing, genetic algorithms, etc. We evaluate the merits of the Web or Notes as a platform for your company at the collaborative layer. We then discuss methods for searching and retrieving information from this layer. Finally, we retrofit information technology components on Nonaka's SECI (socialization-externalization-combination-internalization) model.

Recognizing this, in this chapter I will introduce the seven-layer knowledge management architecture and its underlying infrastructural elements. Most technology needed forknowledge management already exists. What is needed is the effective integration of this technology supported by organizational enablers that can make it deliver business results. I will describe technological pieces that make up each layer, focusing on those that are lesser used or oblivious. I will discuss various components that help develop existing infrastructure into requisite *infostructure* that is required for effective knowledge management. I will help you identify various knowledge source feeds to integrate into the knowledge management system. I will work through the process of helping you select IT components to find, create, assemble, and apply knowledge, and to identify elements of the interface layer such as clients, server, gateways, and the platform. I will help you take your own company into account when we try to reason through the choice of the preferred collaborative platform to arrive at the decision whether the Web or Notes is better suited in your instance. We will take your company into account and try to identify and understand components of the collaborative intelligence layer including artificial intelligence, data warehouses, genetic algorithms, neural networks, expert reasoning systems, rule bases, and case-based reasoning. I will describe techniques that you can use to optimize knowledge-object molecularity. I will help you identify the right mix of components for searching, indexing, and retrieval and will help you create knowledge domain, form, type, product/service, time, and location tags and attributes. I will also describe how you can create profiling mechanisms for push- and pull-based knowledge delivery while balancing cost versus value-added for each additional enabling component. Finally, I will retrofit the aforementioned information technology components on Nonaka's SECI model: a technique that you can then use to validate the comprehensiveness of your own knowledge management system's component set.

TECHNOLOGY COMPONENTS
OF THE KM ARCHITECTURE

Before we delve into actually using the seven-layer architecture for developing a knowledge management system, we examine the technology pieces that constitute the seven layers. The seven layers of the knowledge management system architecture that we use in the following chapters to help you build your knowledge management system are illustrated in Figure 7-1.

TWO PRIMARY ENABLERS: STORAGE AND COMMUNICATIONS

The combination of technologies upon which a knowledge management system rests is tricky to define. The focus of technology should primarily be on enhancing two broad areas:

- Storage and retrieval
- Communications

Technology for managing information has often taken a limited view of regarding only explicable, captured information as information that needs to go into an information system; there have only been a few, moderately successful attempts to take information technology further than that. While technologies that we will examine in the next section are limited to some extent by this constricted view of what comprises information, they capture and distribute structured knowledge and enhance the broad area of storage and retrieval. Communications is another domain where IT provides incalculable opportunity in terms of mobilizing tacit knowledge.

Initial thoughts about communication networks often tend to be restrictive and bound by conventional thinking about their use. Businesses have been using such networks to create links across distributed databases for decades now, but the application of networks in knowledge management goes beyond that limited domain. The primary strengths that a communications network brings to a knowledge management system is that of transfer and collaboration. Just like the telephone provides a channel for informal communication among peers,

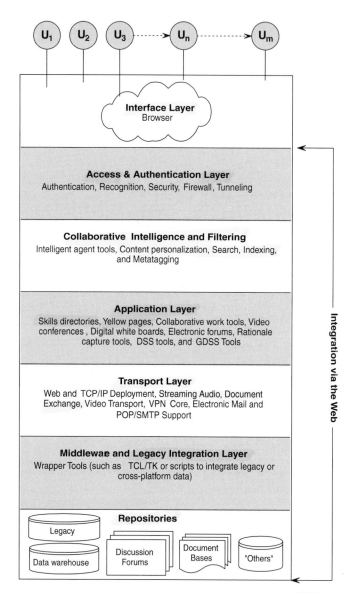

Figure 7-1 The seven layers of the knowledge management system architecture.

networks provide richer channels for informal communication among peers distributed globally. For example, video conferencing (when done over a high bandwidth channel), provides a rich medium of visual and aural communication through the Internet, and electronic mail has already changed the way we communicate within and beyond our organizations.

CASE IN POINT: BRITISH PETROLEUM

While communications technology does provide for transfer and exchange of structured and formalized knowledge, it also provides an outlet for knowledge that cannot or has not yet been structured yet can be immediately applied. British Petroleum (BP) provides a picture-perfect example of the usefulness of video conferencing. BP experts in Italy used it to fix a problem in an oil rig in Latin America. While flying experts would have taken days, video conferencing allowed them to look at the problematic site remotely and diagnose the problem. Even though video conferencing cannot capture structured knowledge or distribute it, it facilitates the real-time transfer of contextual information—in this case, the condition of the oil rig—to enable application of distributed skills that exist in an organization. The video clip that might appear to be a simple piece of information to one person could be turned into applicable knowledge by specialists who can add context, experience, and interpretation to it.

SELECTING TECHNOLOGY

Select your technology components with the objectives clearly defined beforehand. Table 7-1 provides a technology selection map[2] that can help guide the technology selection process while keeping the actual need in focus. The processes that a knowledge management system should support are listed in Table 7-1.

Table 7-1 Knowledge Processes and Technology Enablers

Knowledge Objective	Technology Enablers
Find knowledge	Knowledge-bases in consulting firms; search and retrieval tools that scan both formal and informal sources of knowledge; employee skills yellow pages.
Create new knowledge	Collaborative decision-making processes; DSS tools; rationale capture tools; Notes databases; decision repositories; externalization tools.
Package and assemble knowledge	Customized publishing tools; information refinery tools; push technology; customized discussion groups.
Apply knowledge	Search, retrieval, and storage tools to help organize and classify both formal and informal knowledge.
Reuse and revalidate knowledge	Customer support knowledge bases; consulting firm discussion databases; past project record databases and communities of practice.

As companies and work groups work their way, in sequence or in parallel, through one or more of the processes listed in Table 7-1, inputs are transformed into knowledge that is applied to create new products and services as shown in Figure 7-2.

Process Support

As we discuss in depth in the following chapter, you must identify the areas of focus for your knowledge management tools from among the areas outlined below:

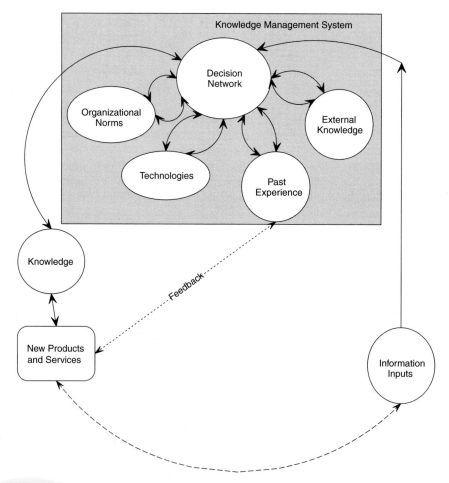

Figure 7-2 The incremental development cycle of a KM system shows how knowledge improves as a company transforms information inputs into new products, services and decisions over time.

WHERE DO WE BEGIN?

Organizations that want to go beyond the unagreeable perfect definition of "what" precisely and comprehensively needs to be managed, captured, explicated, applied, and used, need to put boundaries on their knowledge management initiatives. Focus on what works, not on perfection. Focus on directions that will have near-term payoffs, and then move to those that look promising in the long term. In making the choice of technologies to develop, you will have to view knowledge as comprising of two dimensions: an object dimension and a process dimension.* Knowledge can be viewed as both a "thing" to be stored, manipulated, and used as well as a process of simultaneously knowing and acting; in other words, applying expertise, as Michael Zack describes it.[3]

As companies have started to reorganize work around teams, adopted lean structures where employees are empowered and middle managers eliminated, the original storehouses of informal knowledge that rested in the middle management have begun to disappear. Time is perhaps the biggest influencer of all—decisions need to be made accurately and they need to be made fast. Knowledge of what is already known helps improve these decisions.

And again, globalization has taken its toll. While the size of our global gross domestic product (GDP) has doubled from under 25 percent to over 50 percent in under 20 years, that share is now intensively contested. It is no longer just a question of knowing what your competitor in Richmond, Virginia, is doing; it's a question of knowing what your competitor in Penang, Malaysia, doing and what your Richmond, Virginia, competitor is doing in Bangalore, India. Complexity and not information is now the problem. Excess of information, not the lack of it, is the threat.

Companies need to center work around their ability to learn how to learn *and unlearn*, not just learn something new. Core competencies, as Dorothy Leonard-Barton warns,[4] can too easily become core rigidities. Company structures that are not defined by geographical boundaries place severe and even more challenging demands on the success of a knowledge management system. While casual and localized informal networks sufficed earlier, geographical distributed firms need deliberately created ones. Although networks can probably never replace the *water coolers*,[5] they surely can compensate for their lack. Thanks to the world's largest free network, the Internet, using information technology to create such deliberate networks for knowledge sharing is not a far-out idea anymore.

---

*This is consistent with the view of many other researchers who have suggested that knowledge about processes is an often ignored but significant category. See, for example, Michael Zack, An Architecture for Managing Explicated Knowledge, *Sloan Management Review* (forthcoming).

- Knowledge creation and acquisition through interaction, recording failures, and successes
  - Within teams—A large amount of knowledge resides in people's minds and e-mail, but rarely organized in a fashion that allows retransmission and sharing with others later on.[6] Design your policies, practices, and organizational structures to remove barriers and encourage knowledge creation.
  - Between teams.
  - Between individual knowledge workers.
  - Between organizations.
- Knowledge transformation
  - From different vocabularies.
  - From tacit to explicated/codifiable knowledge.
- Identification and removal of hurdles to best practice and skills transfer[7]
  - Within groups.
  - Within companies across multiple locations.
  - Across cultures.
  - Across companies.
- Rapid delivery to the right person
  - Support for knowledge application, distribution, and shared problem solving
  - Support for creative discussion.
  - Organization of knowledge.
    - Indexing.
    - Screening.
    - Classification.
  - Filtering.
  - Mining.
  - Aggregating.
  - Synthesizing.
  - Linking.
    - Cataloging.
    - Interconnecting external and internal sources.
- Distribution of knowledge
  - Packaging.
    - Databases.
    - Discussion lists.
    - Notes databases.

- Rationale capture.
- Push delivery.
- Collaborative filtering and collating.
- Delivery
  - Networks, Web, intranets.
  - Subscription services.
  - FAX collated delivery solutions.
  - E-mail.
- Storage
  - On media (distributed or centralized).
  - Custom CD-ROM runs.
  - Pointers to informal knowledge.
  - Pointers to knowledge resources and expertise (people, employee skills directories).
- Importing and absorbing technological knowledge from outside the firm
  - Via strategic alliances.
  - Via partner firms.
  - From competitors.
- Interaction, combination, and sense making (mostly through tools that capture context along with the knowledge element; also through good graphical user interfaces for the technology back end).
  - A company that strongly builds on its potential ability to combine all relevant knowledge throughout the organization in its end products or services is bound to have a more competitive position in both the short and long run.[8]
  - Technology enablement to support collaboration, content creation and management, content/context linkage, navigation and retrieval, and content distribution. Integrate knowledge systems with business applications. Software packages can support many types of collaboration as well as content access, creation and distribution, and content value addition based on the history of content access and use.
  - Services to facilitate and coach communities of interest, perform research, administer content and technology, and build awareness and skills around knowledge access and use.
- Communities of interest and networks of people that share common objectives and interests, to create and maintain knowledge content, improve processes, and to serve as a mechanism for the exchange and development of tacit knowledge.
- What-if analysis.
  - Explicating and recording assumptions that people from different functional backgrounds make in their decision processes.
  - Recording values, norms, and beliefs in the right decision context.

Cost Versus Value-Added Technology

Technology tools for building a knowledge management system broadly fall into two expansive categories. The *must-have* tools and the *should-have* tools. Very often, the should-have tools add a substantial resource burden to a knowledge management system. In a perfect world, both these types should be made an integral part of a knowledge management system. However, with the financial and resource constraints that most companies operate under, the ideal is often far from feasible. The key, at least in the beginning, lies in driving out resources and costs that are not adding value as perceived by the *key stakeholders* in the company.[9]

THE SEVEN-LAYER KM SYSTEM ARCHITECTURE

Let us gain a passing acquaintance with the seven-layer knowledge management system architecture before we examine infrastructural components that comprise it. Figure 7-1 shows the seven layers in the KM system architecture.

A knowledge management system interfaces with its users U_1 through U_n (and offers scalability to handle even more users as denoted by U_m) at the interface layer.

FOUNDATION FOR THE INTERFACE LAYER

The interface layer is the topmost layer in the knowledge management system architecture. This is, for the most part, the only layer with which end users directly interact. The effectiveness of this layer is a dominant determinant of the usability of a knowledge management system. Let us first examine the requirements for the collaborative platform that such a layer must be based on.

SELECTION CRITERIA FOR THE COLLABORATIVE PLATFORM

For effective collaboration across the enterprise and the smooth sharing of structured knowledge, the collaborative knowledge management platform must satisfy the following set of basic needs.

1. *Efficient protocols:* The network protocols used should not clog up bandwidth of the network and should allow secure and fast sharing of content across far-flung locations, including mobile clients and traveling machines.

2. *Portable operation:* Companies often have various platforms and operating system environments in use by different departments. The collaborative platform must be able to operate in a *portable* manner across all these platforms. The Web with the use of the HTTP protocol remains unbeaten in this respect. The browser is the most suitable uni-

versal client through which end users can run applications and access repositories without having to switch familiar platforms or operating environments. Since there are very few competing browsers (the count ends at two) and applications (for the most part) run consistently in either browser, a contiguous look and feel across KM applications can be maintained. Major companies like Microsoft are moving toward the use of rich HTML as the default file format for the storage of their office suite documents,[a] which makes the option of the Web even more attractive. We talk more about the Web in the next sections.

3. *Consistent and easy-to-use client interfaces:* Do not assume that users are technology experts; many of them might come from highly nontechnical domains, departments, and backgrounds. Ease of use therefore becomes an imperative. The Web provides unrestricted opportunity for tweaking the interface to make it extremely easy to use.

4. *Scalability:* As the number of users grows, the collaborative platform should be able to scale up without degradation in performance. In Figure 7-2, this growth is represented by an increase in the number of users from n to m. Both Lotus Notes and the Web provide high levels of scalability. However, the cost of extensive scalability would, arguably, be lower in the case of an intranet based on Web protocols.

5. *Legacy integration:* A large chunk of operational data in more seasoned (been around forever) companies often lies in mainframe databases. Therefore, the collaborative platform that you decide to use must be able to integrate this data into the final interface. The Web-based intranet is again the best choice for this. A wide array of tools and scripting languages such as TCL/TK (Tool Command Language/Tool Kit) are available to accomplish such integration. They can create *wrappers* that allow data from legacy systems to be accessed from Web browsers irrespective of their platform.

6. *Security:* Collaborative platforms such as Lotus Notes already have the security tools and features built into them. However, doing the same for a Web-based intranet requires additional expenditure in the acquisition of such tools. However, as an enterprise becomes increasingly distributed, virtual private networks (VPNs) become a feasible networking option. Not only is the security aspect well covered in such configurations; they also minimize the longer-term costs[10] by tightly integrating the virtual network tunnels with the existing Intranet. Table 7-2 provides a side-by-side comparison of these two options and the characteristics that recommend their adoption as a primary collaborative environment.

7. *Integration with existing systems:* While legacy integration is important, it is also essential that a collaborative knowledge-sharing platform integrate well with existing systems and applications. The Web, again, beats most proprietary standards in this regard.

8. *Flexibility:* The lack of the end user's ability to filter out irrelevant content is perhaps the root cause for the information overload that most companies are facing. The choice of platform should allow for a reasonable degree of customization and flexibility in terms of what the user sees and needs to see. Lotus Notes is, by default, highly customizable

---

[a]Microsoft's Office 2000 suite, for example, can store documents in .DOC or .HTML formats without losing any content richness or formatting.

in this regard, and such capability needs to be built, usually from ground up in the case of intranets.

9. *Structure:* Lotus Notes provides a high degree of structure in terms of the ways the content can be organized. Intranets can effectively make use of tools such as GrapeVine to filter, categorize, and arrange explicated and well-(semi)structured content.

THE WEB OR NOTES?

In the preceding section, we compared the Web and Notes in passing. Let's look at the issues involved in this choice in more detail. In the recent past, firms tended to rely on external repositories of knowledge such as market intelligence databases for bringing in new knowledge with which they could run the company and make decisions. However, with the increased penetration of digital work using personal computers, work done by employees is already in a form ready for electronic manipulation. Companies are therefore creating internal repositories of knowledge bases of market knowledge, customer relationship management knowledge, profile knowledge, product development traceability knowledge, and collaborative knowledge repositories.

While it is easier for raw inputs such as spreadsheets, meeting notes, design documents, etc., to be converted into a storage-friendly format, another problem arises: Companies have not been able to standardize on specific platforms and operating systems in a perfect manner. Some employees work on UNIX machines, some on Macintoshes, some on Linux platforms, and most others use Windows systems as their primary work environments. Some companies also use incompatible networks across organizational units. When companies try to integrate whatever structured content exists throughout their organizational rungs, this effort poses a serious challenge.

Lotus Development Corporation, a subsidiary of IBM, has long touted its Notes system as a perfect collaborative solution. While the value of such a system cannot be undersold, even with Lotus's recent Web integration efforts, there are better alternatives, such as the Web, as a basis for a collaborative environment.

Although solutions like Notes require less up-front development time because of their more comprehensive out-of-the-box attributes and have capabilities like replication, security, controls, and development tools tightly integrated with them, the Web-based intranet might require a higher investment in the development stages. Tools like Lotus Domino can allow Notes databases to be shared over the Web; the Web provides a universal platform for the integration of structured knowledge across any existing platform or a combination of platforms. Many companies that embraced Notes early on probably believed that *a good plan today is better than a perfect plan tomorrow.*[11]

Increasingly high levels of integration of multimedia capabilities into Web browsers along with guaranteed backward compatibility allow easier representation of informal content than is possible using proprietary technology such as Notes. Since tens of thousands of companies are developing Web-based applications as compared to essentially one company (and associated developers) developing for Notes, it is more likely that cost-effective, innovative

Table 7-2 Comparison of Key Characteristics of Lotus Notes and the Web Protocol–based intranets as Primary Knowledge-Sharing Platforms

Characteristic	Notes	TCP/IP Intranets	Comments
Architecture	Proprietary	Open/evolving	The World Wide Web (www.w3.org) consortium is placing an increased focus on developing the Web as a powerful collaborative platform.
Security	High	Low by default	Can be enhanced with a variety of security tools.
Authentication	Strong	Stronger if used in a Windows 2000 type environment	Windows 2000 (the successor to Windows NT 4.0) provides strong authentication and security features for use in distributed environments such as those built around Web servers and wide-area networks.
Direct (initial) cost	Moderate to high	Close to none	The Internet is basically free. The only direct cost is that of a service provider, which most companies already have. You still do need someone to build the application, or you can buy it from someone.
Development cost	High	Low	You can use existing Web development skills within the company to build an intranet with a minimal number of inexpensive tools.
Technological maturity	High	Low	Web protocols are still evolving. However, most popular browsers support plug-ins to add newer capabilities to the client software.
Employee training cost	High	Low	Employees are often familiar with the Internet and the Web browser interface.
Initial investment	High	Low	Indicative only of the upfront costs.
Legacy integration	Low	High	*Wrappers* can be written to allow access to legacy data through a Web browser.
Cross-platform integration	Low	High	HTTP acts as the universal protocol that brings together content across all platforms that might be in use in your company.
Deployment time	Fast	Slower	While Notes deployment and customization is not always fast, it is usually faster than deploying an intranet with similar functionality.
Out-of-the-box solution	Yes	No/sometimes	Software vendors can customize generic intranets for quicker deployment.

tools will first emerge for Web-based knowledge management systems. There is also a significant level of competition in the market for Web-based tools, which favorably shifts the balance toward this base in terms of price competitiveness.

WORDS OF CAUTION

Commercial factors can be quantified by defining scenarios and probabilities. In choosing a technology standard, for example, the assumption is that the chosen technology succeeds in the market. The alternative scenario is that it loses the standards battle. An example would be the choice of Lotus Notes over Microsoft Exchange and Internet Information Server (IIS). Quantifying the alternative scenario (failure) involves calculating the cost of converting to the successful standard that you did not adopt in the first place.

Once a company has identified all relevant costs and benefits, the next step in the analysis is to evaluate their impacts. Hard impacts are easily quantified, but you cannot stop at those. Soft impacts must be quantified or *guesstimated* to see their magnitude and to understand the forces that drive, impact, and influence them. Putting these into the actual financial budget might provide a good business case that most knowledge management projects need whenever they are close to the CFO's trash can!

THE VITAL INTEGRATOR: THE WORLD WIDE WEB

Besides the reasons for choosing the Web over other proprietary technologies as a collaborative platform that we discussed above, several more are worth noting. A few essential technology components, which lie at the transport layer level, needed for this integration are discussed below.

Client Software

To provide intranet access and collaborative work support for employees, you need to install a Web client on each PC, workstation, or mobile computer. If you plan to use the Windows environment to run such a client, you will need to configure it in a way that allows it to access the Internet through a TCP/IP stack with Windows sockets. Support, in the form of plug-in applications, will be needed to view video feeds or audio through the connection. Similar functionality, usually available by default on most Web browsers, is also needed for non-Windows operating systems such as MacOS. If Microsoft's Windows environment is used as the primary operating platform, most of socket-level linking is accomplished automatically by the operating system.

Server Software

To use the Web as your company's knowledge management portal, you will need to deploy a Web server. Although this server space could be rented from an ISP on a time-priced basis, it is preferable to eventually move it in-house because security is often a driving concern.

Moving such operations in-house, however, often translates to increased costs. Companies such as Buckman Labs have successfully used services provided by CompuServe to run their knowledge management efforts for several years. The best, if not the most inexpensive, strategy will be to base such a server on a Windows platform and run IIS on it (see Chapters 10 and 11).

Server Hardware

Companies have traditionally run servers on UNIX machines. With the advent of low-cost yet very powerful PCs, this balance has started shifting toward Windows-based machines such as Windows NT and Windows 2000-based servers (although Linux is a notable contender). A single-processor PC with a 500-MHz processor and 256-MByte RAM was the minimum, low-end configuration recommended in late 1999. If significant traffic is expected, consider running Windows NT or 2000 along with Microsoft's IIS on a multiple-processor machine with a significant amount of RAM. If a choice is available, choose the *Wintel* [b] platform over any others for the sake of customer support warranted by a large user base and a sustainable upgrade path.

Gateways

To extend access from the intranet and collaborative environment within the company to the Internet and beyond, you must install a company-wide gateway to the Internet. A dedicated server is the best choice for a gateway. Installing such a gateway (which might already be in place in your company) brings up security and accessibility issues that need to be seriously considered and addressed.

A connection for the knowledge management network for mobile employees and teleworkers can be established by means of a modem and registering those employees as valid users with an Internet service provider; you need not go the extra mile by installing dial up lines. [c] Dial-up lines tend to be more expensive in the long run, both to operate and maintain, especially if your employees travel extensively.

GroupWare Versus Web Client Interface?

Even if your company is currently using GroupWare-based collaborative tools, it might be a good idea to gradually move toward a generic Web-based structure such as an intranet. Products such as Notes already provide a fair level of Web connectivity, but the underlying core is still proprietary. Such proprietary systems might be good to begin with, but such focused dependence does not bode well for an open knowledge management system in the long term. The Web is the unquestionable choice for that matter.

---

[b]The term *Wintel* is used informally to describe an Intel microprocessor based system running Windows. This term encompasses other Intel microprocessor clones including those manufactured by AMD (notably its K6-3 and K7 processors) and Cyrix (which went out of business as a division of National Semiconductors in May 1999 and was bought out by Via Technologies in June 1999).

[c]The ISP option can be easily pursued by smaller companies that do not have the financial muscle to support dial-up modem banks. Companies like AltaVista (www.altavista.com) and NetZero (www.netzero.com) offer advertising-supported free Internet access throughout the United States; this can be used if content is not bandwidth intensive.

COLLABORATIVE INTELLIGENCE AND FILTERING LAYER

Effectiveness of interactive networks such as knowledge management systems is not only dependent on technical ability and reliability, that is, the infrastructure, but also on conversational robustness. This has been referred to as *infostructure:*[12] the extent to which the system provides a language structure and resources that people use to make sense of events taking place within the network. The infrastructure underlying the intelligence and filtering layer supports the necessary transition from infrastructure to infostructure. The aspect of taking infostructure into consideration along with the infrastructure is a crucial determinant of whether users will actually appreciate your system in preference over other sources and use it; the lack of this is the killer antidote for any KM system.[d]

For a capitalist company or for-profit business, it is important to avoid the "philosopher's trap" by getting entangled in the bottomless issues that lie at the heart of knowledge management. Instead, use clear models or building blocks that define key concepts and provide direction for analysis, action, and, most importantly, for results. Develop practical working definitions and move on. The focus, at least in the beginning, needs to be on solutions that can find, summarize, interpret, and analyze large volumes of data and contextualize information efficiently and effectively. The listing below exemplifies sources and types of feeds that a marketing knowledge management system needs.[e]

Source	Examples
Customer knowledge processes	1. Feedback from customers.
	2. Knowledge of new product development projects in customer companies.
	3. Potential needs of customers; possibly new needs.
	4. Level of customer dissatisfaction.

[d]Research has shown that potential users react with concerns regarding their difficulty to "digest the system." The key point to keep in mind while designing the KM system is that the system should not be designed in a manner that overwhelms the users. Feature richness is good—but users should be able to disable and totally remove from sight any features that they do not use or need. In IT terms, that would translate to customizability.

[e]Based on an adaptation from Li and Calantone, The Impact of Market Knowledge Competence on New Product Development: Conceptualization & Empirical Examination, *Journal of Marketing,* vol. 62 (October 1998), 13–29.

Source	Examples
Marketing—research/development connections	1. The level to which the market data is used by your company's development teams. 2. The level to which marketing departments actually use insights provided by the development staff. 3. The extent to which your new service/product development efforts jointly involve ideas from both these parties. 4. Evaluation of one party's products (e.g., marketing plan evaluation by development staff), and vice versa.
Competitor knowledge processes	1. How well are competitor information sources integrated within your internal information systems (e.g. online bookstores that allow buyers to compare prices for their selections with their competitor's prices in real time)? 2. Is the analysis of competitor information systematic and thorough throughout throughout the development process for new services and products? 3. Do you use customer evaluations of your competitors' products as a benchmark for your own products or services? 4. Do you regularly examine the IT support that your competitors use?
Market performance	1. How does your product perform in comparison to other competing products? 2. How do customers rate your service in comparison to your competitor's services? —In terms of quality. —In terms of value. 3. How well are information sources about the product markets in general integrated with your planning and development support systems? Your intranet?
Technology change	1. Rate of obsolesce of your product/service/methodology? 2. Is your market's underlying technology rapidly evolving or mature? How does this figure into your decisions? How do you know it is even considered when key decisions are made? 3. Are sources of this information linked to the information systems used within your company? How well?

INFRASTRUCTURAL ELEMENTS OF COLLABORATIVE INTELLIGENCE

The collaborative filtering and intelligence layer of the knowledge management system builds on several possible combinations and permutations of technologies: artificial intelligence tools, intelligent data warehouses, genetic algorithm tools, neural networks, expert systems, case-based reasoning (CBR) applications, rule bases, and intelligent agents. To understand which of these technologies fit with your own knowledge management system and how they can be integrated, it is essential to understand their role in the context of knowledge management.

Driving Decisions With Data

While lack of data was a problem in the 1970s, excess of data is the problem now. We have been a data-rich and a knowledge-poor society. We might have all the necessary raw data, even cleanse it in data warehouses, but rarely do we convert it into knowledge that makes the difference. Data warehouses take only one step—they bring together data from disparate sources and at least in part, organize it.

Figure 7-3 illustrates a typical data warehouse running in conjunction with an online analytical processing (OLAP) system. As the figure shows, a data warehouse is of little use unless the data is converted to meaningful information and applied when needed. Even if this data is used everytime a relevant decision is made, it still represents only a fraction of the knowledge assets that the firm has and does not account for expertise that has not been explicated in databases and files.

Data-driven decision support is only one aspect of assisting decision making with what is known, more specifically, what is known explicitly. Data representations such as hypercube data models[f] in multiple dimensions do help immensely in supporting decision making with concrete data from the past.

Artificial Intelligence

While knowledge management is a fairly recent term, companies have been trying to capture and manipulate knowledge with computers since the 1970s. Artificial intelligence promised a lot but delivered little. What was once a crying concern among socialists and humanists is now close to a joke. Although some spin-offs of artificial intelligence have indeed been truly useful—expert systems, case-based reasoning systems, neural networks, and intelligent agents—their application domains are pretty narrow. The dream of the intelligent machine that would replace the human brain is long dead. However, that endeavor has left us with some technologies that have indeed penetrated businesses for good.

Expert systems have been particularly strongly affected victims of excessive hype and overly high expectations.[13] MIT media lab professor Marvin Minsky predicted in 1970:

---

[f]A simple way of thinking about a hypercube model is as a system that lets you slice and dice existing data along various dimensions. An excellent discussion of this appears in Dhar, V. and R. Stein, *Intelligent Decision Support Methods: The Science of Knowledge Work,* Prentice Hall, Upper Saddle River, NJ (1997).

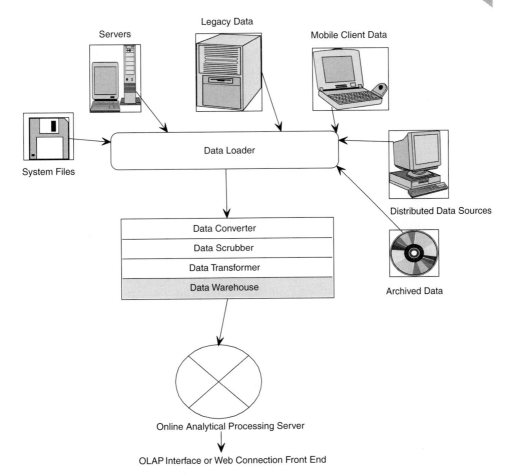

Figure 7-3 The data warehouse represents only a very small portion of the data assets that a firm has.

"In from three to eight years we will have a machine with the general intelligence of an average human being. It will be able to read Shakespeare, grease a car, play office politics, tell a joke, have a fight. At that point this machine will begin to educate itself, and in a few months its intelligence will be at the level of a genius. After that, its power will be incalculable.*

Thirty-odd years later, expert systems have not lived up to those expectations. They have not revolutionized or rationalized the whole business environment, but they have left us with

---

*Quoted by T. Rozak, The Virtual Duck and the Endangered Nightingale, *Digital Media,* June (1995), 68–78.

one profound understanding: Human knowledge is often too complex to fully comprehend. It is with that caution that you need to approach the idea of a knowledge management system and the knowledge management initiative. It will not suddenly make your company the biggest money-maker in the industry. At best, it will help your company compete better and maybe contribute to its long-term survival. Let's restrain our hopes. Doing better than we hope to can only be a pleasant surprise!

Data Warehouses

While we do not want to get overly involved in discussing data warehouses, let us examine how a data warehouse falls into place in the scheme of things in a knowledge management initiative. Many companies often have multiple databases existing throughout their hierarchy. A data warehouse becomes the big unifier of all these databases. A data warehouse becomes especially useful when you need to look at several different databases at once, combine their content, make it possible to run queries simultaneously across all of them, and reduce data clutter that can otherwise fast overwhelm decision makers.

Since data warehouses combine and aggregate data from multiple sources and scrub the data in the process, they do improve the quality of data that actually gets used. Another gain is in performance: Data warehouses often result in a in performance gain of several orders of magnitude even for standard database queries. However, for this gain, data warehouses lose the ability to deliver data in real time. Consequently, time-critical decisions being made on data coming out of such systems might be using data that is several hours old. Unless time-dependent decisions as critical as stock market purchases are being made, this tradeoff is usually acceptable because the data is already corrected for garbled content, missing values, and nonsense characters. In other words, this data is of much higher quality than the sources that feed it.

The key characteristics of a data warehouse and its relative fit are summarized in Table 7-3.

Genetic Algorithm Tools

Genetic algorithms are an interesting development. Like neural networks, this technology has its roots in biology and is based on Charles Darwin's theory of natural selection—extended from animals to data. Genetic algorithms were developed in the early 1970s by John Holland, who tried to apply Darwin's *survival of the fittest* theory to computer programs and data. The programs and data sets that solve a problem survive and those that do not, die. Heuristic techniques and rules of thumb cannot guarantee optimal solutions, so users have to settle for nearly optimal solutions. In Herbert Simon's words we would call this a *satisficing*[g] solution rather than a satisfying solution.

A genetic algorithm experiments with new and novel solutions to problems. If an experimental solution is not successful, it is assigned a low rank and discarded. If it solves a problem, such as an optimization problem, it is ranked high and retained for *genetic refinement*.

---

[g]Nobel Laureate Herbert Simon introduced the concept of satisficing solutions to describe solutions that are good enough in view of constraints and the relative worth of doing any better. See Simon, Herbert, *The Sciences of the Artificial,* 2nd edition, MIT Press, Cambridge, MA (1981).

Table 7-3 Characteristics and Relative Fit of a Data Warehouse in the KM Infrastructure

Characteristic	Level	Downside
Response time	Low	Data might not be real time.
Scalability with growing needs	Medium	Depends on initial design optimization.
Flexibility of use	High	None.
Ease of use	High	Needs a good front end and interface for use.
Retrieval of data	Medium	The user needs to navigate through the interface and find the relevant data that helps make a decision.
Processing overhead	High	Not a relevant concern if the size is not too large. Parallel processing on x86 architecture and NT platforms makes it very viable. Cost might not be a major concern.
Accuracy	High	Depends on the quality* of data scrubbing. Accuracy is higher than the sources since "bad" data has been cleansed out.

*Quality is occasionally described as "goodness" of scrubbing and cleansing.

The good parts of this solution are kept, and the less useful parts are simply discarded. Genetic algorithms can be used very effectively in making decisions where the amount of data to be taken into account is very large and there are disconitinuities in available data.

If you are trying to solve a problem or make a decision where standard rules of thumb fail to work or are impossible to use, trying genetic-algorithm-based solutions is a good choice. Chapter 16 provides additional details on several products that use genetic algorithm techniques for solving business problems.

Very often, a genetic algorithm can simplify the amount of work required to solve a complex, decision-related problem in comparison to techniques such as rule-based methods or case-based reasoning. Genetic algorithms (GAs) form populations of solutions: GAs therefore try a number of solutions at the same time. In essence, genetic algorithms enable a decision maker to say "I do not know how to build a good solution, but I will know it when I see it!"[14]

Table 7-4 summarizes the fit of genetic algorithm tools within the knowledge management technological framework.

Neural Networks

Neural networks, much like genetic algorithms, have their roots in biology. The Merriam-Webster Dictionary (www.m-w.com) defines a neural network as a networked computing architecture in which a number of processors are interconnected in a manner sugges-

Table 7-4 The relative fit of GA-based tools in the KM technological framework

Characteristic	Downsides for Knowledge Management
Medium to high accuracy of solutions	Limited and relatively specialized applications.
High response speed/fast problem solving	May deteriorate as the problem increases in complexity.
Limited scalability	Computing resources often fall short of a complex GA-based solution. Some tools are available for Windows NT and Windows 2000 platforms and take advantage of the multi-processor capability that NT brings to the low-cost, high-performance x86 microprocessor family.
High levels of embeddability	Tools based on genetic algorithms tend to be highly dependent on software and the nature of the problem. While this specialization probably improves the performance of the tool, it also severely constrains its usability in other problem domains.
Development speed of typical solutions based on genetic algorithms is fairly high*	Solutions tend to be fairly specialized and have a narrow application domain
Low to medium ease of use	A majority of popular commercial tools available are for non-Windows platforms that are typically not used in most business environments.

*Several commercial tools are available to assist with such expedition.

tive of the connections between neurons in a human brain and that can learn by a process of trial and error. A neural network tool becomes especially useful when you are trying to solve a problem or make a decision based on very limited inputs from domain experts.

In contrast, *fuzzy logic* systems, for example, need to be trained by domain specialists or experts—often too expensive or unfeasible. There might be experts available and accessible, but their opinions might differ, or none of them might have a comprehensive understanding of the problem. Even if you do get experts, they might have a problems explicating their decision-making process in sufficient detail. Several companies have invested millions of dollars in expert systems but to little avail—simply because the experts were unable to *exactly* state what they knew and how they knew it. This will bring us back to the basic problems of explicating tacit knowledge, but we will steer clear of that for the moment. Neural networks overcome many problems that have plagued fuzzy logic systems.

A neural network becomes immensely promising when you have the data but lack experts to make judgments about it. A neural network can identify patterns within such data without the need for a specialist or expert. A basic neural network is illustrated in Figure 7-4. The top layer, called the input layer, receives data from external sources. The internal processing layer, which is hidden from the outside, is where all processing takes place. The lowest layer is the output layer, which transmits the outputs or guesses to the user. The internal layer has already learned from solving earlier problems and tries to apply those "lessons" to the new datasets that are fed into the neural network. In real applications, the neural networks are far more complex than the simple example described in Figure 7-4 and, in effect, more promising.

There is a wide variety of tools based on neural network technology, some of which are discussed in Chapter 16. While theories on which neural networks are built might suggest that such nets can deal with "dirty" data, reality is quite different. If you decide to use a neural network as a part of your explicative knowledge management system, be prepared to spend a considerable amount of time training the neural network, cleaning up data, and preprocessing so that the neural net can better comprehend data that is fed to it. As problems becomes increasingly complex, the ability of neural networks to find proper solutions degrades.[15] The key characteristics of neutral networks are summarized in Table 7-5.

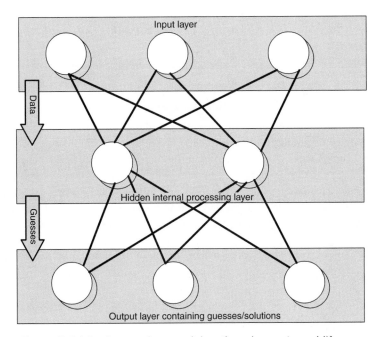

Figure 7-4 A basic neural network has three layers. In real-life applications, these nets grow immensely complex.

Table 7-5 Key Characteristics of Neural Networks and Their Fit in the KM System Architecture

Characteristic	Downsides for KM Applications
High accuracy	Requires thorough training and preprocessing of data. Accuracy degrades as size and complexity increase beyond a certain level (depending on the type of problem being solved).
High response speed	Degrades as the net becomes increasingly complex.
High tolerance for "bad" data and noise contained within the input data	Requires preprocessing of data for the network to comprehend it. This requirement alone takes up a majority of the time spent building a neural network.
Mediocre flexibility	The neural network needs to be retrained with relevant data if it is to be used for a new application.
Low processing resource requirement	Requirements for processing power are lower than for most other types of data-based decision support systems. Commonplace desktop computing resources often suffice. These resources need to be boosted if larger amounts of data are fed or if the network size is scaled up.
Limited scalability	Data is needed; complexity of the problem might constrict scalability.
Limited need for domain experts or recorded expertise	Relevant data is needed. It also needs to be preprocessed.

Expert Reasoning and Rule-Based Systems

The accounting profession has, for decades, accomplished tasks on the basis of rules—ranging from simple to complex. Take a hypothetical example of what your tax accountant goes through when she has to deal with the IRS each April 15: If a person's annual income is $120,000, then his tax rate is 30 percent with a minimum deductible amount, and so forth. Similarly, engineering departments have often followed rules for design and development. However, problems in business that tend to involve higher levels of creativity and innovative off-the-block thinking might not seem to fit well into such problem-solving and analysis schemes.

Rules can be represented in very simple terms after they have been broken down. A generic example is the following:

```
IF
   {some condition is met}
THEN
   {do this}
ELSE
   {do something else}
```

A more complex, nested version of this would look like

```
IF
   ({some condition is met}
AND
   {this condition is also met})
OR
   {this other condition is met}
THEN
   {do this}
ELSE
   (do something else)
```

After some values are plugged in, a rule might look like this:

```
IF
   (retail price of generic PC is at least 25% lesser than a
name brand PC)
AND
   (warranty period is the same)
AND
   (processing power is at least 30% higher than the compara-
ble name brand unit)
THEN
   ( it will sell)
ELSE
   ((it will not sell)
AND
   (the retail price or configuration will have to be read-
justed)
```

Interpreting this rule is fairly straightforward. Assume that I am Xiao Wang, a generic computer parts importer who sells generic personal computers while competing against the more expensive name-brand machines that are sold in other stores. My pricing decisions are based on a model represented in a simple rule refined over time. The rule, as stated above, simply says that to be able to sell profitably, the prices of my generic, no-brand PCs need to be at least 25 percent lower and configurations 30 percent faster than comparable name-brand machines.

Such rules applied in business, often existing as rules of thumb, can be easily embedded into systems to help make decisions better, more accurately, and faster. Their value becomes even more uncontestable once they are integrated into a larger grouping of tools that will constitute the technology enablers for your company's knowledge management program. While the examples above are unrealistically simple, actual rules tend to be far more complex and do very well once they are hard-coded into systems (by hard coding I do not mean unchangeably coded). While all automata can be used to make sense of information that can be run through these techniques, it frees your employees to spend their brain power on other knowledge tasks, such as socialization, that these techniques cannot address.

Although rule-based systems look neat, their application is rather restricted. They work well only when the following five conditions are simultaneously satisfied:

1. You know what the variables in your problem are.

2. You can express them in hard terms (such as numbers, dollars, speeds, etc.).

3. The rule to apply actually covers most, if not all, variables that are encountered.

4. The rules that collectively apply do not overlap; for example, you cannot have two different rules in the above example that determine the price independently.

5. Your rules have been validated to some extent. In other words, you have more reason than creative thought to have come up with these rules.

Rule-based systems are diametric opposites of genetic algorithm systems. In genetic algorithms, you can specify universal conditions under which solutions are considered good, but you cannot apply expert knowledge on how to solve the problem. In rule-based systems, you can bring in expert knowledge, but you cannot specify any universal conditions that denote a good solution.

Table 7-6 Rule-Based Systems and Their Relative Fit in the KM Infrastructure

Characteristic	Downsides of Using in a KM System
High dependence on domain experts and specialists	Extensive inputs from domain specialists are needed. Very often, expert knowledge is explicated only to a limited extent, since much of it is tacit. First cuts on elicitation of this knowledge range from poor to acceptable and rarely ever rise to the level of perfection.
Higher speed of development	Rule-based systems can be developed at a fast pace only if knowledge can be elicited from experts in a thorough manner. This often takes up the largest chunk of development time.
Low levels of scalability	As problems being addressed become complex or evolve over time, rule bases need to be refined. If rules change over time, experts often need to be brought in again to revalidate the rules in use.
Slow response speeds	If the datasets grow large, rules grow more intermingled and complicated. This can often pose a serious challenge to the computing power in use. As problems get complicated, a multitude of rules need to be matched, which again degrades the response speed.
Low to medium flexibility	While small bases are quite flexible, as the problem becomes more complicated or involves new variables, the inflexibility of the system becomes an apparent disadvantage.

An example of such a situation is credit rating systems. In the rating of credit worthiness of a person, rules allow application of specific expert elicited dictum, but no criteria can universally suggest whether the person is creditworthy or not. Similarly for auto insurance, rule-based systems can apply the universally accepted (for the insurance industry) and empirically validated rules that risks are higher among males who are single and under age 25; however, no universal condition determines the riskiness of an applicant.

Rule-based systems can be expensive to develop because much of the development time and resources are spent eliciting knowledge from an expert. However, much of the knowledge is tacit, and as you would guess, not all of it is explicated.

Case-Based Reasoning

Case-based reasoning is a promising candidate for the knowledge management infrastructure. This approach allows companies to take advantage of previous problems or cases and related attempts to solve them. When faced with a problem, a case-based reasoning system searches its case base (i.e., a collection of previous cases) for past cases with attributes that match the current case in hand. Figure 7-5 illustrates in simple terms, the inner workings of a case-based reasoning system.

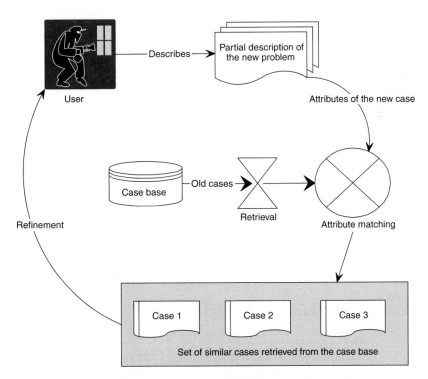

Figure 7-5 The basic idea behind case-based reasoning.

You, as the user, define a new problem that you are trying to solve on the basis of some attributes. These attributes might have varying degrees of importance. You can assign a weight to each attribute, based on your earlier experience or knowledge of the domain. Based on this set of attributes, a search engine searches through all the cases in the case base. Cases that are closest matches to the case at hand are then retrieved. These cases can be used to further refine the search to retrieve even closer matches.

The consulting industry has been successfully using this approach for consulting assignments. Using past knowledge gained from projects, consultants often, with a bit of justified exaggeration, reduce the task to a simple match and cut-and-paste job. Solving the problem by analogy makes the process of arriving at the solution faster, better, and easier than it would have been had the consultant started from scratch. The distinguishing characteristic of case-based reasoning that makes it a very good fit for a knowledge management system is the fact that concepts are stored as real images and the context of past decisions is retained to a satisfactory extent. This helps overcome one of the biggest problems—losing context of solutions when they are reached and recorded.

Case-based reasoning also works very well with other decision-support technologies discussed earlier, allowing sufficient room for integration of case-based reasoning with several other components within a larger KM system. Case-based reasoning tools work especially well when the choice is between basing a decision on *some* data and no data at all. However new or however crude a case-based reasoning system is, it will always give *some* solution. As new cases are added, the case-based reasoning becomes increasingly powerful and accurate.

On the downside, a case-based reasoning system needs thorough initial planning. You must include all possible attributes that you might even remotely anticipate the need for later. If you add attributes later on, older cases that have those attributes will not show up in the search-and-retrieval process unless those attributes are explicitly added to old cases as well.

If you decide to build a new case-based reasoning system, it is often a wise idea to add new cases as they occur rather than trying to add past cases through post hoc reconstruction (much like software documentation that does little good if written after the fact). Adding past cases can be a laborious and expensive process and is often the root cause of errors if not done rigorously. Table 7-7 provides the characteristics that determine case-based reasoning's fit in your knowledge management infrastructural decisions.

Companies have successfully applied case-based reasoning to tasks such as planning, scheduling, design, and legal deliberation. However, the best success stories of case-based reasoning lie in the areas of managing customer support knowledge at telephone help desks run by software companies. One can also envision the application of case-based reasoning to search for knowledge across a knowledge management system. The logic would be as follows: "If Sam accessed sources A, M, and Z to solve a scheduling problem for our product in category S, then what knowledge sources would I need to access to solve a problem defined by attributes A1 and A2 in product category H?"

Video Conferencing

Video conferencing enables people to exchange both full-motion video and audio across a distributed network. Although video conferencing technology has existed for several years,

Table 7-7 Characteristics of Case-Based Reasoning in Knowledge Management

Characteristic	Downside of Using Case-Based Reasoning in a Knowledge Management System
High level of independence from specialists and domain experts	An expert must fine-tune the attribute matching and retrieval criteria.
High accuracy of solutions	Accuracy is not high to begin with. It improves as more cases are added to the case base.
Higher response times	As more cases are added to the case base, the performance of a case-based reasoning system can degrade. Attribute definition and indexing need substantial forethought to prevent serious problems due to growing case density.
High levels of scalability	Case-based reasoning systems offer a high level of scalability and lend themselves to work in distributed environments, such as across enterprise networks, rather easily. However, the attributes are not easily scalable, and all possible future attributes should be pre-defined at the outset, when possible.
Unaffected by noise	The retrieval cases will not be affected by the presence of "garbage" or noise in the input case attributes as long as the case base is populated with a sufficient number of cases.
Low ability to handle complexity	As the number of attributes increases, case-based reasoning begins to show weaknesses. First, all attributes in use now might not have been defined in older cases. Second, the interactions between multiple attributes cannot be judged accurately even if the case base is well populated with cases.

most of the available solutions needed dedicated networks. Video conferencing requires high bandwidth on the network, since each frame contains about as much data as an equivalent still picture file. Typically, 30 to 80 frames of video need to be delivered every second to deliver reasonable quality video. Lackluster bandwidth availability prevents these frames from refreshing several times every second: The refresh rate can be slowed down so much that video content delivery might begin to resemble a series of independent delayed static pictures following each other. Although video conferencing can, at best, be frustrating if you try it over a dial-up connection, faster connections such as a T1 or ADSL line allow for usable-quality, real-time conferencing through the Internet and without the expense of a non-PC conferencing system. Many newer commercial video cameras (such as Logitech's Quickcam VC) are optimized for video conferencing over low bandwidth networks.

Push or Pull?

A push approach to knowledge delivery actively sends relevant actionable information to the recipient. A pull approach, on the other hand, requires that the recipient pull out the needed information from the repository. This is an important choice that needs the right balance (or possible adoption of both), since neither approach can serve all users' needs equally well. The important point here is that the users should be able to choose between these two delivery methods.

Summary: Technological Fit

A critical differentiator among the tools discussed so far is the level of knowledge needed to successfully use and apply a particular technology or tool. Some tools require a high level of domain knowledge from the user, whereas others assume that the end user is a relatively passive observer in the process. The second dimension is the amount of time that is needed to find a solution with a knowledge management tool in the specific business application domain of interest. Selection of these tools can be guided by the dimensions of these tools, as illustrated in Figure 7-6.

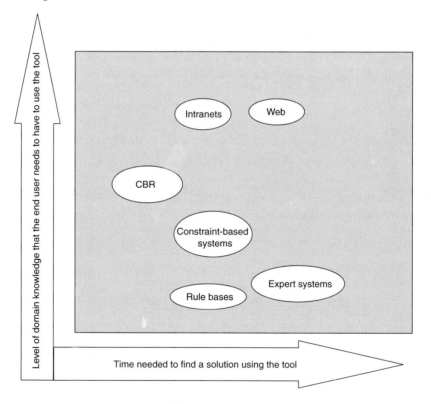

Based on an adaptation from Thomas Davenport and Lawrence Prusak, Working Knowledge: How Organizations Manage What They Know, Harvard Business School Press, Boston, (1998), page 130. Their dimensions have been extended to include additional tools here.

Figure 7-6 The technological fit of various knowledge-based reasoning tools along two dimensions.

Table 7-8 Levels of Increasing Granularity in a KM System Represent the Depth of Detail that a KM System Deals With

Knowledge Object	Example of Such an Object in a Clinical (Diagnostic) Knowledge Management System
Knowledge domain	Internal medicine.
Knowledge region	Neurology.
Knowledge section	Brain diseases; tumors.
Knowledge segment	Diagnosis of brain tumors and cancerous growth.
Knowledge element	General diagnostic strategies.
Knowledge fragment	If the symptom reported by the patient is continual headaches, then consider the possibility of a brain tumor.
Knowledge atom	Excessive and continual headaches is a symptom.

LEVEL OF KNOWLEDGE GRANULARITY IN OBJECTS

Since a knowledge management system is intended as a mechanism for securing corporate knowledge, it needs to be populated with knowledge objects. However, these knowledge objects can be specified at different levels of detail. For example, tasks in past projects can be recorded at different levels of detail. A key failure point in the design of a knowledge management system is not deciding at the start on the right level of detail. Let's take a look at a knowledge management system in a diagnostic clinic.[h] The knowledge elements or objects can be represented at different levels of detail, as shown in Table 7-8.

Too high a level of granularity will result in the loss of knowledge richness and context; too low a level will cause unnecessary drain on network, storage, and human resources, raise the cost, and reduce the value of the object.

Now, let us reframe this example using business data. Let us consider the use of a knowledge management system to support customers who buy an AS/400 computer system that your company sells. Such a domain of knowledge could be represented as shown in Table 7-9. The key lies in selecting the right level of molecularity of knowledge that will be stored in your knowledge management system: the level that strikes an optimum balance between the two opposite extremes of too much detail and too little detail, both of which can render knowledge only marginally useful.

---

[h]This example is chosen for its ease of comprehensibility and similarity to Wiig's discussion of urology knowledge in Wiig, Karl *Knowledge Management Foundations—Thinking About Thinking—How People and Organizations Create, Represent and Use Knowledge,* Schema Press, Arlington, Texas (1993).

Table 7-9 Customer Support and Knowledge Levels: An Example

Knowledge Object	Example of Such an Object in a Business Knowledge Management System
Knowledge domain	Customer support for home computers.
Knowledge region	Hardware.
Knowledge section	Memory diagnostics.
Knowledge segment	Diagnosis of memory-related problems using general diagnostic strategies.
Knowledge element	Memory diagnostic strategies based on symptoms; collect all symptoms and eliminate all possibilities until the only one left is a memory failure/hardware fault.
Knowledge fragment	If the symptom reported by the customer is system lockups and continual beeping, consider the possibility of a memory problem.
Knowledge atom	Frequent lockups; blue-screen-related beeping; failure to boot up are all symptoms.

INFRASTRUCTURAL ELEMENTS FOR SEARCHING, INDEXING, AND RETRIEVAL

Indexing and retrieval capabilities of a knowledge management system determine the ease with which a user can find relevant knowledge on the system. Four types of navigation strategies can be deployed in varying combinations: meta searching, hierarchical searching, attribute searching, and content searching.

Meta Searching

Unlike the categories that follow, an approach based on meta categories allows the user to determine the focus of the search. This idea is conceptually similar to the purpose served by the *browse* functionality provided by the hierarchical search capability in a knowledge management system. The main purpose of a meta search function is to minimize the time spent in locating a general category for a piece of potential knowledge within a repository.

This concept is remarkably well illustrated by Figure 7-7. If the user types in a keyword *programming,* what exactly does *the user* mean? If this simple keyword returns subcategories as shown in Figure 7-7, the user can potentially avoid the trap of going in the wrong direction altogether. He can focus on what the word *programming* means in specific context of his task and continue the search process in a more focused manner, using the other strategies we discuss. Meta searching provides a clearer view of the bigger picture as well as context clarification.

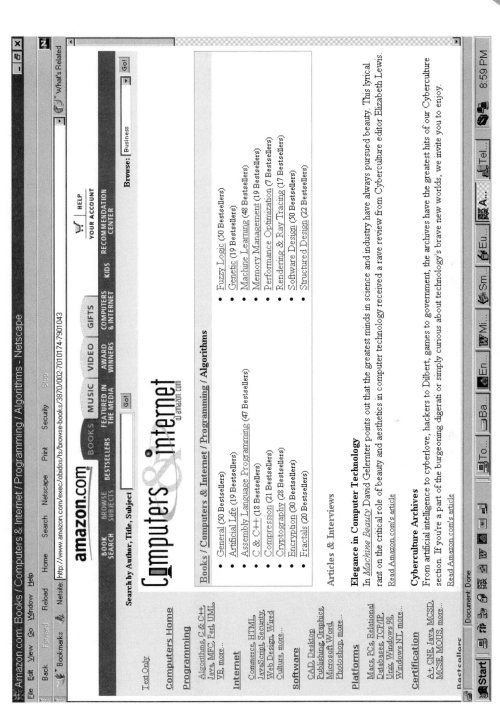

Figure 7-7 An illustration of meta-categorical searching.

Hierarchical Searching

If the user has successfully identified the broad categories, as illustrated in Figure 7-7, she can then continue to dig deeper into the repository without running the risk of going in a totally irrelevant or wrong direction. A hierarchical search strategy organizes knowledge items in a fixed hierarchy. The user can follow or traverse links within such a structure to efficiently locate the right knowledge element in a timely manner. The idea of using hyperlinks similar to those used in Web pages is a good example of such a navigation and search technique. This method is therefore apt for use in intranets, since they support hyperlinking by default.

Attribute Searching

Searching by attributes uses a value input by the user. This attribute value is matched against closely related values attached to documents and pointers such as skills databases. Those that closely match are returned as the final search results. Most commercial search engines that can be added to intranets, such as Verity and Infoseek, provide a direct solution for the implementation of such a search method within a knowledge management system.

Content Searching

Content searching is the least efficient of the search strategies discussed here. The user enters an arbitrary search term, keyword, or text string. All items that match are returned with a relevance score. It is necessary that items with the highest scores (strongest match) are reported on the top of the results that are returned by such a search. (The meta search technique is simply a more focused version of this technique that matches broad categories rather than individual knowledge elements.) Score assignment is based on the frequency of matches within each knowledge element such as a document or Website. Commercial tools such as GrapeVine allow users to record their judgment of relevance, thus cumulatively refining searches over time. Most Web crawlers and spiders[i] deployed by commercial Web search engines such as Yahoo, Hotbot, and Excite use this technique.

Combining Search Strategies

To enable effective searching, use all or several of these search and retrieval strategies in parallel. Using a single search technique can pose severe limitations on the quality of the search. For example, attribute searching can work well only with textual knowledge items. However, this technique will not work too well for extracting informal knowledge items such as sketches, audio files, video clips, or pointers to experts. However, the meta search technique might serve that purpose well if the informal knowledge content is properly tagged. In the commercial implementations of such techniques, the Excite search engine (www.excite.com) uses a combination that delivers results based on both meta and content-searching algorithms. Figure 7-8 shows how the upper portion of the results screen reports results from a meta

---

[i] *Web crawlers* and *spiders* are descriptive terms used to represent mobile intelligent software agents that "crawl" through one Web server after another to collect information that is then stored at the search engine portal site and returned in response to queries initiated by users.

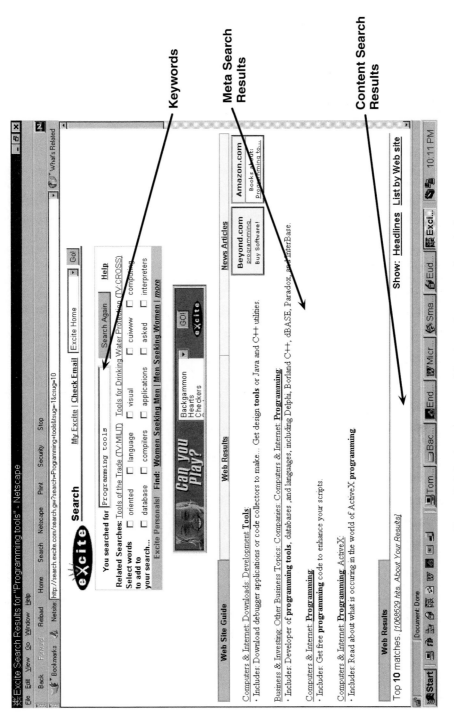

Figure 7-8 Excite uses a combination of two search techniques.

search, while the remaining set is based on a content search. Implementing all these techniques simultaneously is not challenging, since commercial search tools such as Infoseek can be licensed for use on intranets for a small fee.

TAGGING KNOWLEDGE ELEMENTS WITH ATTRIBUTES

Since searching works primarily on the basis of textual string matching, it is important that content—both formal and informal—be tagged with a proper set of attributes. More advanced tools are available for pattern matching in drawings, photographs, etc., but these are not always a feasible option for two reasons. First, these tools are still in their initial stages of development and work within highly specialized categories of informal data (rather than information or knowledge). Second, these tools are more expensive and complicated to implement when compared to traditional, commercially available search tool solutions. Consequently, a company must define its own set of attributes to tag knowledge content with. Although many of these attributes can be common to a company and its partners, the need for such clear-cut definition cannot be overemphasized. A basic set of tagging attributes[16] is listed in Table 7-10; the attributes are described below.

Table 7-10 Tagging Attributes for Knowledge Content in a KM System

Attribute Type	Tagging Attribute
A	Activities
D	Domain
F	Form
T	Type
P	Products and services
I	Time
L	Location

Tagging attributes are identified on the basis of extensive research on knowledge usage reported in Heijst, Spek, et al., The Lessons Learned Cycle in Information Technology for Knowledge Management, in Borghoff, U. and R. Pareschi *Information Technology for Knowledge Management,* Springer Verlag, Berlin (1998), 17–34.

Activities Attribute

The activities attribute refers to the organizational activities to which the given knowledge element is related. The values of this attribute must be defined up front, and individual values need not be mutually exclusive. This means that the same knowledge item could possibly fall under two or more activity categories. For example, a knowledge element related to burn-in testing of the computers that your company produces could fall under the following possible categories: testing, quality control, finishing, fault tolerance analysis, MTBF (mean time between failures) determination, etc.

Therefore, your company must have an explicit model of the activities and processes that are carried on during the course of "running the business." This might not be a perfect model to begin with. Begin with your best shot and incrementally improve the activity attribute value set.

Domain Attribute

The domain attribute tags the knowledge item to its subject matter. This attribute is the primary attribute that drives the meta search process. Your company has most likely already identified the broad domains of expertise and skill areas that constitute it. Be wary of the trap of trying to define such domains at too micro a level. Domains need to be defined at an aggregate level, as illustrated in Table 7-8.

Principles of knowledge engineering (a branch of computer science, not management information systems, that is often erroneously confused with knowledge management) cannot be applied here, since those are more concerned with modeling knowledge at the level of concepts and relations, which is too micro for our purpose here. If your company does not have such domains defined, you need to explicitly determine what your employees *think* their domains are and account for vocabulary mismatches to avoid overlapping domain names. This is a process best accomplished by trial and error; sequential application of guidelines of any sort will be of little or no avail.

Form Attribute

The form attribute defines the physical representation of the knowledge element. This attribute is tricky to define. You can begin with a basic set of values such as:

- Paper
- Electronic
- Formal (file, word document, spreadsheet, etc.)
- Informal (multimedia, sound, videotape, etc.)
- Collective
- Tacit or mental knowledge
- Pointer (to a person who has solved a problem of that nature before, etc.)

If information is available in other forms in your company, then add them to this basic "starter" list. The pointer attribute value is similar to the concept of employee skills databases, where you might perform a search on "Web-database integration experts," and detailed contact information for all employees matching that attribute set will show up in the results. This is especially useful when your company's offices are geographically distributed or employee counts are high. For example, a search for a given attribute might help a consultant in Atlanta find a find a knowledgeable fellow consultant in the firm's New Delhi office.

Type Attribute

The type attribute is more relevant to formalized knowledge that is captured in electronic or textual form such as a document or a report. It specifies what type of a *document* that knowledge element is. Such values can be standardized across multiple companies, such as your company and its suppliers. Suggested starting values for this attribute, which can be later extended to account for tacit knowledge types, are:

- Procedure
- Guidelines
- Protocol
- Manual
- Reference
- Time line
- Worst practice report
- Best practice report
- Note
- Memo
- Failure report
- Success report
- Press release/report
- Competitive intelligence report

Beginning with these values, you can add other relevant types applicable to your company. This checklist also appears in Appendix A in a fill-in form.

Products and Services Attribute

The products and services attribute specifies the product or service to which the knowledge element relates. This list should be kept specific and nonoverlapping. A consulting company, for example, might have, among others, the following attribute values:

- Strategic consulting

- Implementation consulting
- e-commerce consulting

Time Attribute

The time attribute is useful for time-stamping events and knowledge elements. time-stamping is done automatically for files, but that time-stamp marks the creation of that object, which might have a value different from the actual creation of that knowledge object. Consequently, creation or use of an explicated knowledge object must be specified. Not all knowledge objects can be assigned a value for this attribute, so assign a value to this attribute where possible. The time attribute can also be useful for narrowing retrieval processes.

Location Attribute

Use the location attribute to specify the location of pointers that track people within and outside the company. Not all knowledge elements will have a value assigned to this attribute, but it can be used to narrow searches by location. For example, a search procedure for an employee with certain skills could be restricted to Japan, or at a finer level, Tokyo. Be careful not to use too micro level classifications for this attribute tag. Make sure that the attribute usage and its values are actually significantly relevant. If the relevance or need for this attribute is moderate to low, you might save your company much time and money by simply dropping this off your list of attribute tags to be used.

PUSH/PULL REVISITED

After attributes and tags for knowledge elements are assigned, delivery based on *push* technology becomes remarkably viable. The term *push delivery* should not be confused with Web-based active-push services such as Netscape Netcaster or Pointcast running through browsers or active desktops. Push technology for knowledge management systems should provide employees a variety of options for both retrieval and delivery. For example, employees could be given an option to select relevant tags of interest to them. Using collaborative filtering, the most appropriate set of content can be automatically assembled into a *customized package* for delivery through an intranet Web page, facsimile, or e-mail.

If some employees do not prefer push delivery, they should be provided an option to pull content on demand, such as through a search conducted via a Web browser or desktop client interface.

A pull-based mechanism for knowledge retrieval can aid decision making throughout problem-solving processes surrounding delivery of new products and services. Experiential knowledge can help you answer questions like:

1. Have we faced this problem before?
2. What was done?

3. Did it work?

4. What solutions were considered but rejected?

5. If a fundamental assumption that formed the basis of an earlier decision were to change, what would happen?

6. What criteria formed the basis of the last decision?

7. Who has worked on related projects in the past?

8. Where can we find them now?

9. What were the assumptions at that time?

10. How have they changed?

In any case, using the Web as the primary push or pull delivery mechanism will help your company leverage and fully utilize your mixed (and possibly incompatible) hardware and platform set in use throughout the company, across multiple locations, and in real time. We explore the detailed implementation aspects of collaborative filtering in Chapters 10 and 11.

CIGNA AND KNOWLEDGE MANAGEMENT

At CIGNA Property & Casualty, a Philadelphia-based insurance company, the aim was to create an upward value spiral for know-how to be shared throughout the company. Information and knowledge contributed by employees are processed by "knowledge editors"—usually experienced underwriters—and distributed throughout the organization. CIGNA also uses knowledge management to discover and maintain profitable niches and is using the skills and experience of people as building blocks for its success. CIGNA now recognizes that it is not the quantity of knowledge that is important; rather, the quality of that knowledge is the key determinant of profitable underwriting. Every company has a gazzilion bytes of information in its databases; the key to profitable underwriting isn't giving access to every bit of information; it's how you determine which information is relevant.

SUMMARY

Collaboration support can expedite problem solving and task accomplishment in current situations. Using the approach initiated in this chapter can lead, in the most optimistic case, to one or more of these potential benefits:

- The process-centered view and the product-centered view of KM are effectively integrated to make well-reasoned and more accurate decisions.

- Higher-paid workers spend less time looking for information needed to make decisions.

- The decision-making process is streamlined and expedited.

- Tacit knowledge is leveraged and put into action.

- Tacit knowledge begins to be externalized.

- Ad hoc teams are built with a proper blend of skills regardless of geographic distribution of employees.

- Experiential knowledge is leveraged in making new decisions.

- Suboptimal product or service quality is avoided by smooth flow of actionable information and knowledge throughout the company.

- External knowledge is applied in a relevant and timely manner.

- Costly errors resulting from repeated mistakes are avoided.

- Valuable knowledge does not become a victim of information glut.

- All relevant knowledge is integrated into the existing work environment.

- Work processes and outputs are systematically organized.

- Knowledge continues to evolve, grow, and remain relevant.

- Active sharing, creation, distribution, and sharing of knowledge becomes a reality.

LESSONS LEARNED

Most technology needed for knowledge management already exists. The critical part is determining the best mix of available tools and integrating them in your project's knowledge management architecture. Keep in mind the lessons about these infrastructural components while determining this mix:

- *Choose IT components to find, create, assemble, and apply knowledge.* Since content comes from a variety of sources both within and outside your company, the optimal choice of components must let you create, assemble, find, and apply knowledge in a cost-effective and timely manner.

- *Pick one: Web or Notes.* Customized implementations of proprietary technology might seem to be easier to implement than Web-based intranets with equivalent functionality; using open standards such as intranets holds more long-term promise both in terms of cost containment and incremental development. Choosing the Web option over other options can potentially lead to tighter integration of commercially available complements such as CBR systems and push delivery mechanisms.

RETROFITTING THE SECI MODEL

Now that you have a grasp on the technology and human components needed to implement a knowledge management strategy in your company, let's see how they all fit into Nonaka's SECI model.[17] Figure 7-9 illustrates this fit.

The interaction of knowledge at enterprise-wide (company) levels is indicated by C; at group or task team level, by G; and at individual level, by I. The corresponding technology enablers are exemplified in each quadrant. Knowledge management is done according to the SECI model through a cycle of socialization, externalization, combination, and internalization of knowledge. Figure 7-9 illustrates how each of these phases is supported by technology that we discussed in this chapter. Note that some of the components overlap across phases of knowledge creation. This implies that the benefits of one technology element is manifested in multiple knowledge creation phases.

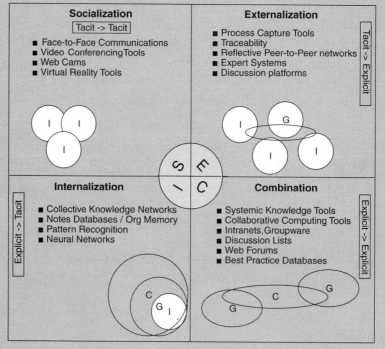

Socialization

Tacit -> Tacit

- Face-to-Face Communications
- Video ConferencingTools
- Web Cams
- Virtual Reality Tools

Externalization

- Process Capture Tools
- Traceability
- Reflective Peer-to-Peer networks
- Expert Systems
- Discussion platforms

Tacit -> Explicit

Internalization

Explicit -> Tacit

- Collective Knowledge Networks
- Notes Databases / Org Memory
- Pattern Recognition
- Neural Networks

Combination

- Systemic Knowledge Tools
- Collaborative Computing Tools
- Intranets, Groupware
- Discussion Lists
- Web Forums
- Best Practice Databases

Explicit -> Explicit

Legend

C: Company's Knowledge
G: Group or Team Knowledge
I: Individual Employee's Knowledge

Figure 7-9 Nonaka's SECI model and the places where IT support fits in.

- *Identify and understand components of the collaborative intelligence layer.* Artificial intelligence, data warehouses, genetic algorithms, neural networks, expert reasoning systems, rule bases, and case-based reasoning are some of the technologies that provide intelligence to the knowledge management system. Understand how these tools and technologies work and when their use is appropriate.

- *Optimize knowledge object granularity.* Granularity of knowledge (represented in terms of knowledge objects or elements that are specified in descending order as knowledge domains, regions, sections, segments, elements, fragments, and atoms) objects refers to the level of detail in which they are stored in the knowledge management system. Avoid overpopulating your company's knowledge repositories. At the same time, too little detail might make content useless or unactionable. The key lies in striking the right balance between too much and too little detail.

- *Create knowledge tags and attributes.* Domain, form, type, product/service, time, and location tags automatically classify content along several dimensions. Using standardized tags allows for uniformity in retrieval and storage of content. Defining such tags up front also helps you determine the right mix of components for searching, indexing, and retrieval.

The fourth step, auditing, discussed in the next chapter takes into account the knowledge assets that exist within your company; let's figure out next how you can *know what you know.*

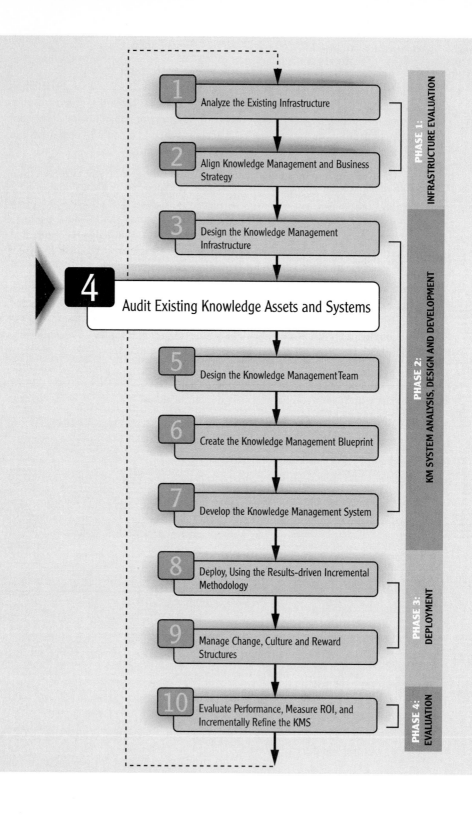

1   Analyze the Existing Infrastructure

2   Align Knowledge Management and Business Strategy

3   Design the Knowledge Management Infrastructure

4   Audit Existing Knowledge Assets and Systems

5   Design the Knowledge Management Team

6   Create the Knowledge Management Blueprint

7   Develop the Knowledge Management System

8   Deploy, Using the Results-driven Incremental Methodology

9   Manage Change, Culture and Reward Structures

10   Evaluate Performance, Measure ROI, and Incrementally Refine the KMS

PHASE 1: INFRASTRUCTURE EVALUATION

PHASE 2: KM SYSTEM ANALYSIS, DESIGN AND DEVELOPMENT

PHASE 3: DEPLOYMENT

PHASE 4: EVALUATION

CHAPTER 8

KNOWLEDGE AUDIT AND ANALYSIS

IN THIS CHAPTER

✔ Understand the purpose of a knowledge audit.

✔ Use Bohn's Stages of Knowledge Growth framework to measure knowledge.

✔ Identify, evaluate, and rate critical process knowledge.

✔ Select an audit method.

✔ Congregate a preliminary knowledge audit team.

✔ Audit and analyze your company's existing knowledge.

✔ Identify your company's k-spot.

✔ Choose a strategic position for your knowledge management system.

A GREAT DEAL OF INTELLIGENCE CAN BE INVESTED IN IGNORANCE
WHEN THE NEED FOR ILLUSION IS DEEP
—SAUL BELLOW

Douglas Adam's *Hitchhiker's Guide to the Galaxy* has a short conversation between the Hitchhiker and his computer. The computer says, "I've checked it very thoroughly and that's quite definitely the answer. I think the problem, to be quite honest with you, is that you've never actually known what the problem is." Nothing sums up the current state of knowledge management better than this conversation. Companies are realizing that managing their knowledge is the definite answer to *almost all* of their problems, but little do they act to discover where exactly the problem lies!

With exactly that in mind, we will take a look at how we can define the exact problem and its roots. The knowledge audit and analysis process, the fourth step in the 10-step knowledge management roadmap, is the key. You must begin knowledge management by taking responsibility for and appraising what knowledge already exists. In this chapter, we discuss the purpose of a knowledge audit and see how Bohn's Stages of Knowledge Growth framework can be used to measure knowledge. We select an audit method to identify, evaluate, and rate critical process knowledge, using a preliminary knowledge audit team. By identifying the k-spot that your knowledge management project best fits in, we can then appropriately position and scope the knowledge management initiative. Until you know what knowledge and knowledge processes surround your business, any knowledge management effort is bound to go off course.

HINDSIGHT + INSIGHT = FORESIGHT

Experience is the greatest teacher of all. Just like nothing but actually receiving an electric shock can convince you that it's not a wise idea to go around touching electrical outlets, nothing teaches companies not to repeat mistakes and do things in certain ways better than having actually done them.

In the knowledge management audit, you must look at all the intangible assets and knowledge assets that exist in your company: its rituals, processes, structure, communities, and people. Then you must document their existence, explicate their current state, and maybe put a dollar figure on what their value might be. Your company, with only a limited dollar figure to spend on knowledge management, would be better off investing in areas that hold the most potential for future growth and strategic advantage. In the *ideal* world this audit should never end; it should be a continuous process. However, in the real world, even if the process is continuous, it will be continuous in discrete steps or clumps, which means that you have to have a clear idea of what you are up to, and know when and where to stop.

WHY AUDIT KNOWLEDGE?

Knowledge of knowledge assets is critical to the proper planning of a knowledge management system and is a rich source of information about where the strengths of your company lie. The knowledge audit provides value when your company is doing one or more of the following:

- Devising a knowledge-based strategy
- Architecting a knowledge management blueprint or roadmap
- Planning to build a knowledge management system
- Planning research and development
- Seeking to leverage its "people assets"
- Seeking to leverage what it already knows
- Trying to figure a way out of corporate ebbing such as competitive failure, earning shortfalls, or financial overruns
- Attempting to assess the value of the enterprise as a whole
- Seeking to provide a focus for company-wide learning and education
- Striving to strengthen its own competitive weaknesses
- Facing competition from knowledge-intensive competitors that are far ahead on the learning curve
- Looking for direction for planning a market entry or exit strategy

In essence, this audit develops better knowledge of the direction in which your knowledge management strategy and investments must be focused. Figure 8-1 shows the basic steps involved in the audit process. We discuss each of them later in this chapter.

MEASURING KNOWLEDGE GROWTH

Very often, companies do not know where they stand in terms of the knowledge that they possess for accomplishing work processes. Bohn's framework, adapted from and primarily built upon academic research literature,[1] provides an excellent starting point for figuring out where you stand, relatively, in terms of your firm's knowledge. This framework applies strictly to the type of knowledge used to produce goods and services. But, even with this limitation, it does cover almost all types of industries that are interested in knowledge management, from consulting (production of services based on knowledge) to software (production of information products based on knowledge), to hard-goods production (physical goods) and publishing (services and production). In its most basic form, the growth of such knowledge in a firm can be described according to the stages illustrated in Table 8-1.

On these lines, as we move from the lowest stages of knowledge—stage 1 (or zero, discussed later) toward the stages of perfect knowledge, like stage 8, the way things are *normally* done in a company change. Take a look and compare how your company ranks along this scale. This should give you a fair idea of how strong the need for knowledge management in your firm possibly is. Table 8-2 shows where worker characteristics, suitability for automation, process types, and skill levels fall along each level along this continuum of stages.

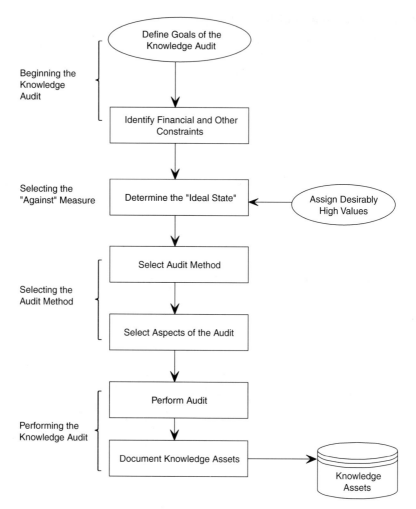

Figure 8-1 The series of steps involved in the knowledge audit and analysis process.

Integrating these two framework variations and applying that integration specifically to knowledge measurement, we get Table 8-3, which provides the final frame of reference against which you can measure the intellectual dimensions of the following:

- Your company's initial standing
- Your competitor's standing (you do not need inside financial information)
- Your company's progress along this scale
- Steps and directions to move your company up on this scale

Table 8-1 Bohn's Stages of Knowledge Growth

Stage	Name	Comment	Typical Form of Knowledge
1	Complete ignorance	Nothing known.	Does not exist anywhere.
2	Awareness	Resembles pure art.	Knowledge is primarily tacit.
3	Measure	It's pretechnological.	Knowledge is primarily written.
4	Control of the mean	A scientific method is feasible.	Written and embodied in hardware.
5	Process capability	A local recipe exists	Hardware and operating manuals.
6	Process characterization	Tradeoffs to reduce costs are known.	Empirical equations (quantitative).
7	Know why	Takes on the form of science.	Procedures, methodologies, scientific formulas, and algorithms.
8	Complete knowledge	Nirvana.	Never happens; but you can always hope for it!

Table 8-2 Ranking Characteristics of Knowledge Work and Processes Along Each Stage and the Effects of Each Stage on Them*

Stage of Knowledge	1	2	3	4	5	6	7	8
Nature of production	Expertise based				Procedure based			
Role of workers	Everything			Problem solving			Learning and improving	
Location of knowledge	Tacit			Written and oral			In databases or software	
Nature of problem solving	Trial and error			Scientific method			Table lookup	
Natural organization type	Organic			Mechanistic			Learning	
Suitability for automation	None					High		
Ease of transfer	Low					High		
Feasible product variety	High			Low			High	
Quality control	Sorting			Statistical process control			Feed forward	

*Since the distinction between adjacent stages in Bohn's stages is subtle, the breakdown of processes, as done in the table, is subject to minor debates. However, all classifications are within an approximate stage range.

You can use this framework to precisely map, evaluate, and compare the levels of knowledge existing in your company. The level of knowledge that a process has reached determines how a process could be possibly automated and controlled and how the primary tasks of the knowledge workers and other aspects of knowledge management can be planned to deliver maximum results. At the higher stages, knowledge can be used to make predictive inferences, as my "coffee" example describes in a following section. It can also make causal associations and prescriptive decisions that often tend to be tricky otherwise.

Table 8-3 Stages of Knowledge Growth: Where Does Your Company Stand?

Stage	Knowledge Stage	Knowledge Characteristic	Location of Knowledge	Work Processes	Learning Method
0	Total Ignorance	Cannot tell the good state from the bad	Undefined.	Undefined.	Undefined.
1	Pure Art	Pure art	In the expert's head; so tacit that it cannot even be articulated.	Rely on trial and error.	Keep repeating processes. Hope for some pattern(s) to emerge.
2	Awareness	List of possibly relevant variables exists	In the expert's head (tacit); however, the expert can express it in words, diagrams, etc., although in a very limited way.	Experts can dictate conditions for processes to work well. Some degree of randomness still exists; start with methods that might have worked in earlier problems.	Experts, instead of all other people, keep repeating processes. Hope for some pattern(s) to emerge.
3	Measure	Pretechnological	You are able to decide which variables are more important by noting their correlation with desirable outputs.	Patterns begin to emerge; experts will, however, differ in their opinions on why successful processes were successful.	Same as above. You can be more creative and tweak processes to see changes.
4	Control of the mean	Scientific method feasible	Written and embodied in hardware/software to some extent.	Some parts of the knowledge underlying the process can be explicated, codified, and written down. However, a "recipe" is yet to emerge.	Keep good records of what was done, what happened, and the final outcomes.

Table 8-3 Stages of Knowledge Growth: Where Does Your Company Stand? (cont.)

Stage	Knowledge Stage	Knowledge Characteristic	Location of Knowledge	Work Processes	Learning Method
5	Process capability	Local repeatable recipe	A local recipe based on experience is developed; it often works, but not always; the notion of following a procedure to obtain desirable results begins to emerge. The recipe might or might not be formally written down in its entirety.	A semi-reliable recipe emerges. Some steps in the recipe might still be random or inconsistent. Work processes are tackled using this somewhat repeatable (partially explicated recipe).	Use the records kept in the preceding stages and determine statistic patterns that work.
6	Process characterization	Tradeoffs to reduce costs; a well-developed recipe along with a limited knowledge of how contingencies are to be handled now exists.	Knowledge is well documented in the recipe; a methodology is developed; it almost always works; applying the process is almost a mechanical task of applying the recipe.	Very mechanized; highly automated; uses a time-proven methodology.	Use the proven methodology; continuous application of the methodology (recipe) will allow weaknesses and problems in the recipe to emerge.
7	Know why	Science; automation is possible; a formal or informal quantitative model is developed.	Most of the relevant knowledge is documented; most of tacit knowledge is converted to explicit; almost all knowledge can be codified and built into computer software; strong knowledge of how contingencies can be dealt with now exists.	Codifed in computer software and process manuals.	More of the above; this is as good as it gets!

Table 8-3 Stages of Knowledge Growth: Where Does Your Company Stand? (cont.)

Stage	Knowledge Stage	Knowledge Characteristic	Location of Knowledge	Work Processes	Learning Method
8	Complete knowledge	Nirvana	Rarely possible.	No need for knowledge management or knowledge managers. Knowledge management becomes a natural part of the firm or group; it is done perfectly; unlikely to ever be achieved.	This stage might never be reached; you will never know when you are here; occasional variations resulting in the inability to apply processes from the preceding stage push it back to stage 7.

Based on Bohn, Roger. E. Measuring and Managing Technological Knowledge, *Sloan Management Review*, vol. 36, Fall (1994), 61–73. Bohn provides an excellent discussion on measuring technological knowledge in this 1994 piece. My book extends this discussion to using it to measure knowledge in conventional knowledge or skill intensive processes.

THE ROAD FROM ART TO SCIENCE

Progression of a company from one that is highly dependent on the tacit knowledge of a few individuals to one in which both explicit and tacit knowledge are shared and easily accessible can be best described as a progression from art (highly subjective and dependent on the doer's tacit knowledge) to science (repeatable and robust methodology capable of handling variations). At the higher stages, such as stages 6 and 7, a company gets a better handle on what should be done if the process has some unavoidable variation that is not documented. Causal prediction might take the form of statements such as "When the client asks for a detailed activity report from the consultant, he is considering canceling the contract for lack of proper billing documentation." It might be causal association such as "When software crashes in the middle of a multiple-document task, it means that the memory buffer is getting too small." Most companies are at stage 2 or 3. To be effectively managing knowledge, a company must progress to stage 5, 6, or 7. Stage 8, although desirable, should be counted out for four reasons:

- Not even a single example of a company that has reached it exists.
- It is extremely difficult to reach.
- You cannot be sure when you have reached it.
- Your company does not need you after it reaches this stage!

MAKING COFFEE: A KNOWLEDGE-BASED EXAMPLE

Like many other overcaffeinnated knowledge workers, I nominate Starbucks Coffee as my favorite coffeeshop.[a] The reason is that their coffee tastes almost the same in any of their locations throughout the United States. As Mrs. Field did for cookies, Burger King did for burgers, and Dunkin Donuts did for doughnuts, Starbucks managed to perfect a recipe for making good coffee by developing a methodology (if you can even call it that) for the coffee-brewing business. Each new employee is trained and taught this procedure before he begins to work in the store. The result is consistently good, fresh, and strong coffee, the taste of which seems even more consistent than the coffee I make in my own coffeemaker at home! If we apply this scenario and retrofit it to the eight stages of knowledge growth, we could categorize it either at stage 6 or 7. In a metaphor for understanding the eight stages of process knowledge growth, let's see how the process of making coffee develops over different stages.

Stage 0: Total Ignorance

You do not know the difference between good and bad coffee. Good coffee is the coffee that regular customers will like, and bad coffee is the type that will make those customers never return.

Stage 1: You Can Tell Good From Bad Coffee

You know when coffee is good once you have tasted it. When you taste the same type of coffee again, you can compare it with the "good" (optimal value of "goodness") coffee you've had earlier.

Stage 2: You Have Created a List of Variables

You begin to figure out that the *goodness* of coffee (process output quality) is related to the following variables:

- Strength
- Temperature (not too hot and not cold) when delivered to the customer
- Bitterness due to strength
- Viscosity (increases as coffee sits for a few hours)
- And some other taste variables that you cannot name

You also realize that there are certain background controls such as:

- Amount of coffee added
- Temperature setting on the coffee percolator
- How long you let it sit after it has percolated

---

[a]This section was inspired by a Venti-sized cup of strong Starbucks coffee that the author was drinking while writing this chapter!

- Weight of coffee/volume of water (coffee per cup)
- Order in which you added coffee and water (immaterial!)
- Fineness to which coffee beans were ground
- Elapsed time since coffee beans were roasted
- Elapsed time since coffee beans were ground (coffee beans oxygenate if exposed to air for a prolonged period of time)
- Other control variables

Stage 3: You Can Determine the Significance of Variables

At this stage you can tell which variables in the list that you compiled above are important, marginally important, and unimportant.

You can now tell that:

- Too bitter = bad.
- Too "unbitter" = bad.
- "Unstrong" = bad.
- Too strong to drink = bad.
- Using beans ground yesterday morning and left exposed to air = bad.
- Coffee percolated more than 15 minutes ago = bad (the reason why Starbucks drains percolated but unsold coffee every 10 minutes).
- Hot coffee = good (100 degrees < serving temperature > 80 degrees).
- Unroasted coffee = bad.
- Coffee roasted > 24 hours back = bad.
- Coffee ground < 2 hours back = very good.
- Order of ingredients = immaterial.

Stage 4: You Can Now Measure Variables

As you move up the stages and progress to stage 4, you can now *measure:*

- Weight to coffee to be added
- Volume of water to be added
- Initial temperature settings on the percolator
- Percolation temperature
- Percolation time
- Post-percolation temperature
- Temperature at the time the coffee is served
- Elapsed time since coffee beans were roasted

- Elapsed time since coffee beans were ground

However, you cannot measure the more qualitative factors such as bitterness or strength. This is a good example of how some factors can now be measured and have moved up to a higher stage; however, some processes are still at the lower stages. You might eventually find that these difficult-to-measure factors could be correlated with other factors that are measurable, such as the ratio of water to coffee grounds.

Stage 5: Repeatable Methodology or Recipe

You develop a recipe or methodology to make what is *typically* considered good coffee. You can now follow certain steps with a reasonable expectation that the resulting coffee will be acceptably good most of the time. You know the components of this recipe or methodology in terms of:

- Temperature settings
- Timing
- Length of time you can let coffee *sit* after percolation
- Amount of ground coffee per cup of coffee

Stage 6: Repeatable Methodology + Localized Adaptability

Stage 6 is a slight improvement over stage 5. You can now adapt the recipe in a way that compensates for different types or flavors of coffee. You know that Colombian coffee need not be used in amounts measuring close to Italian Supreme or the Starbucks house brand. So you have a methodology and a limited degree of adaptability to compensate for variations within the time-proven recipe approach that you are using.

Stage 7: A Formal or Informal Model

You now have a formula approach to carrying out your process. You might have a specific formula saying that good coffee is made when (0.56 x weight of coffee + 0.12 x volume of water) = 1.414, or something like that![b] The model need not be quantitative. It could be qualitative, partially empirical, or semiformal. But, at the very least, it specifies the exact relationship between the significant variables.

In a similar vein, a consulting company might develop a model for strategic consulting analysis; a product designer might develop a model for product acceptance in typical markets; etc. Rarely does a business run as predictably and smoothly as employees in Starbucks make their coffee! But there are excellent examples that exhibit that rarity. Skandia and Monsanto are two such businesses.

---

[b]I just made those numbers up! Often, inspiration is stimulated by strong coffee! However, on a serious note, the point is just to illustrate that you can have a quantitative model to show the relationship among the dominant variables.

Stage 8: Perfect Knowledge

This is the final frontier that we can never hope to reach, principally because we can never know when we are there. There might still be loopholes in processes that need plugging, or there might be changes in the environment that need compensation, and so forth. And these relegate us to stages 7 or below, every time we think that we have reached stage 8. To come close to this stage, we need to be able to predict and compensate for the effect of disruptions and know what to measure in *advance*. This is why you need to build "unlearning" capabilities into your knowledge management system. In spite of all my love for coffee, a more accurate statement would be: Perfect coffee is something I have never had. If I ever did have it, I would never know. All I know is what good coffee tastes like! That about sums my coffee-based reasoning (not to be confused with CBR) for why we can never come up to stage 8 and stay there.

THE KNOWLEDGE AUDIT TEAM

To perform knowledge audit and analysis, you need to select a multidisciplinary group of people, truly representative of your company. Using IT staff is not an option, since they are likely to miss critical viewpoints and aspects in the final outcome. The audit team, in its totality, as shown in Figure 8-2, needs representatives from *at least* the following functional areas.

- *Corporate strategist:* Sets goals, determines optimal performance levels, brings the big picture perspective into the analysis.

- *Senior management, company visionary, long-term planner, or evangelist:* Brings long-term KM vision, aligned with the business strategy of the corporate strategists.

- *Financier:* Brings the ability to value and attach a fair-dollar figure to knowledge assets.

- *Human resource manager:* Brings good understanding of employee skills and skills distribution within the organization.

- *Marketer:* Provides a fair picture of actual market performance of the firm and the possible implications of its knowledge assets on the marketability of the firm's products and services at new price-service function points.

- *IS/IT expert:* Brings in knowledge, skills, and expertise for mobilizing the technology implementation aspects of your knowledge management strategy. Also has intimate knowledge of existing infrastructure.

- *Knowledge manager, CKO, or knowledge analyst:* The middle role that integrates inputs from all other participants on the knowledge audit team in a consensual, unbiased, and fair manner. The analyst contributes a reasonably accurate market valuation of proprietary technology and processes based on perspectives elicited from other team members. The analyst can be drawn from any functional area and must

Analyzing Knowledge in Legal Services: An Example

Legal services run the range described in Table 8-3. Preparing a simple will, for example, can be done with a $19.95 software program sold in most office supply stores in the United States. With your answers to specific questions, the program prepares a simple, legally acceptable will. This typifies legal service that has reached stage 7 in terms of its underlying process knowledge.

Preparing taxes with tax software, for people who have a single employer and no other sources of income, for example, can be done without the need for a tax accountant and with a $10 software program. This is another example of knowledge at stage 6 or 7, representative of a rather mechanical and highly automated procedure. The whole purpose of knowledge management is to let us actually do things as simply, perfectly, accurately, and surely as we do our taxes by using software. Wishful thinking.

Consider taxes for people with multiple citizenships, taxes for people who might have changed state residency, or taxes for people with exceptionally high income. These situations still need an approach distant from an automated methodology. So these are at stages 3 and below.

Knowledge in Criminal Law: An Example

Consider criminal law. Trial strategy, use of evidence, historical data, etc., that are involved in such cases are still at stages 3 or below. This profession requires experienced and skilled lawyers who need to use their tacit skills, experience, and judgment at each moment. People working on these tasks have both skills and tacit knowledge that they use to carry out the tasks, but they are rarely able to explain in sufficient detail how they do them.

However, some processes within these tasks can be pushed up to the higher stages. In criminal law, knowledge management can be used to bring up profiles of past, similar cases to automate at least the argumentative defense that could be used in a court of law. So, certain processes can be moved up to the higher stages of knowledge.

Knowledge Management in Consulting: An Example

Strategic consulting companies like McKinsey and the Boston Consulting Group (BCG) can, and often do, operate at stages 2 and 3. New consultants (often, fresh MBAs) might be at stage 0, where they cannot even tell the difference between a good consulting project outcome and a bad one. As firms begin to proceduralize strategy projects and to execute them according to methodologies developed over time, these processes move to stages 5 and 6. BCG's well-known two-by-two grid describing cash cows, dogs, stars, and question marks is such an attempt to move from the lower pure-art stages to more procedural stages where divestiture decisions are reduced to two main variables: market share and rate of growth. However, BCG's recognition that there might be other variables that are also (probably) important indicates an awareness that some of their knowledge is at the lower stages even though much of their analysis operates at the higher stages of knowledge.

have a good understanding of both the business and business implications of each stream of knowledge assets that the firm owns.

Figure 8-2 illustrates the minimal team. Since the team is interdisciplinary in nature, it is reasonable to expect some degree of discord and lack of agreement. However, as these differences are resolved, the different backgrounds and strengths of participants will turn out to be the biggest strength of the audit team. It is a learning process, where each functional representative must eventually learn to be tolerant and willing to understand the reason for differences of opinion.

PLANNING A KNOWLEDGE AUDIT

Once the knowledge audit team has been formed, members must agree on the motives and reasons for the audit. This is the hardest part and is often highly subjective and firm specific. Once the rationale is explicitly written down, the team must identify the optimum level of performance and the highest, reasonably achievable levels of performance that each component of the knowledge assets *should* operate at. For example, the marketing department might say that it seeks to lower customer product return rates to 2 percent of all goods sold. Similarly, in a consulting company, the team might agree that it must be able to realize 98 percent customer retention or deliver all consulting deliverable within 60 days from the start of a project, for all consulting projects and engagements under $20,000.

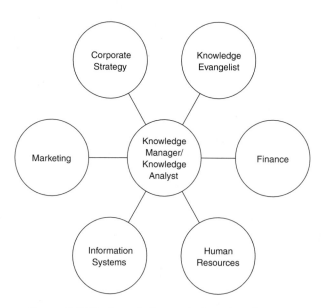

Figure 8-2 The knowledge analysis and audit team.

CONDUCTING THE KNOWLEDGE AUDIT

Building on the process model described in Figure 8-1, let us go through the actual audit and analysis. The knowledge audit consists of a sequence of six steps as described below.

1. *Define the goals.* The knowledge management audit team agrees upon the reasons for the audit, decides on the goals, and identifies the key financial, organizational, privacy-related, and strategic constraints that influence it. Define *specific* goals that both the audit process and knowledge management are targeting.

2. *Determine the ideal state.* This need not be all encompassing during the initial stages of the audit process. Begin with a few key variables that are equivocally considered critical and that can scope your knowledge management project.

3. *Select the audit method.* You will actually use a company specific instantiation of the generic method to perform the audit. So it should account for employee know-how, reputation and market good will, and organizational culture as they apply to your company.

4. *Perform the knowledge audit and document existing knowledge assets.* This provides an internal benchmark to evaluate the effects of knowledge management initiatives after they have been put in place.

5. *Track knowledge growth over time.* Progression from the initial stage (when the knowledge audit process is performed for the very first time) to later stages allows for easy comparison with the *ideal* state.

6. *Determine your company's strategic position within the technology framework.* As cells in the strategic technology framework (shown later in Figure 8-7) are populated *after* the audit, you can decide on the direction in which knowledge management and technology support should focus and where support is least needed.

DEFINING THE GOALS

The first step in the knowledge audit process is to define the goals of the knowledge audit process and the constraints surrounding them. In a wishful-thinking corporate world, we would like to have all the resources that we want, but in reality the situation is often very different. Goals need to be very specific because they provide the basis for many of the decisions that follow (see Figure 8-3).

Although organizing and managing the firm's knowledge in its entirety might be a worthy thought, the resources needed for that ambition might well be matched only by companies with *very* deep pockets. Besides, it's futile to begin on the knowledge management road without knowing what brought you there in the first place. When you think about goals, think of specific ones like:

•   We need to increase profits by 40 percent by next year.

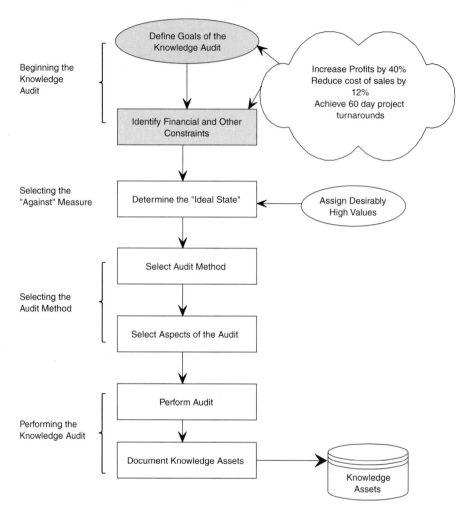

Figure 8-3 The knowledge audit process begins with goal and constraint definition.

- We need to reduce cost of sales by 12 percent before the end of the fiscal year.
- We want to improve customer retention by 4 percent within 18 months.
- We want to increase project turnaround speed by 14 days on the average over the next 3 years.

You can rarely be too specific in explicitly defining such goals. You might have found goals such as "increase sales by next year" or "reduce cost of sales by 12 percent," missing in the above examples. They are excluded because without a very well explicated goal, you can never be sure when to start and when to stop measuring. This means that you cannot have a reasonably safe idea whether the approach devised by your team is *really* working. Goals need not always be defined in terms of increased financial or performance measures. Other examples of less quantitatively oriented yet very specific goals are:

- Prepare a company for an initial public offering.[2]
- Prepare to develop a knowledge management strategy.
- Validate the current business strategy/model.
- Validate assets for investors.
- Assess a requirement for additional investment.
- Assess the market for certain (where certain is clearly defined) product types.

A knowledge management audit is *never* an all-or-nothing exercise. While taking a very comprehensive knowledge audit might seem like a long-term, expensive, and daunting task, you often do better by breaking it up into more solvable and realizable pruned-down pieces. This pruning is best done automatically, as I describe next.

Constraint-Based Pruning

Automatic pruning refers to the next stage after goal identification, that is, constraint recognition. For example, if our big question is "How do we increase profits?" knowing the constraints will help prune it down. If you know that you need to show an increase in profits within six months, you have taken yet another step in narrowing the focus of your efforts. You might also know that a division of your company, say, HR consulting, is not making any money. You might also know that the senior management has put a hold on any new hires. You might also know that you have almost 90 percent of the customers in the market. Putting these together automatically prunes the goals and the original question. It now becomes "How do we increase profits within six months without hiring any new people or trying to get new customers?"

DETERMINING THE IDEAL STATE

Determining what your company considers an *ideal state* is the second stage of the knowledge audit. In this stage, you and your knowledge audit team must reach a consensus on what you consider the best state that you could only wish for, and more reasonably, albeit with great difficulty, reach. This is the best case scenario against which you will judge your entire knowledge management initiative later on (see Figure 8-4).

Knowledge of what the best value of your knowledge assets should be, is essential to allow you to measure the results of your knowledge management efforts against a relevant and stationary benchmark. As Figure 8-5 shows, an optimum target point is needed to measure performance in any given area. Optimums also allow for easy comparability of performance of multiple competitors and are especially useful for evaluating knowledge processes.

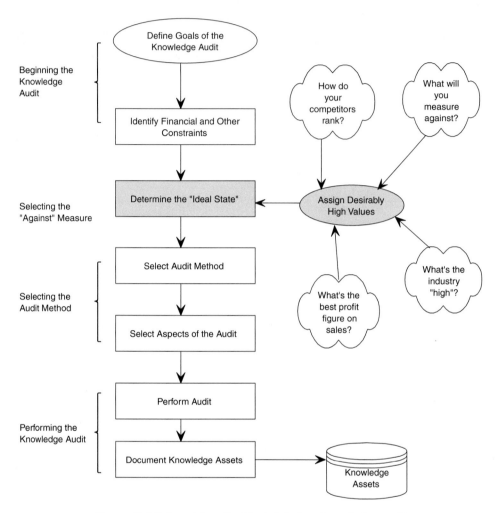

Figure 8-4 Determining the ideal state in a knowledge audit.

The first point in the figure, indicated by the first quarter in which the knowledge management effort was initiated, indicates where the company began. The graph indicates customer response speed as a parameter, and the last value on the chart indicates the target value. This target value might be the company's self-set goal or a goal based on a competitor's performance. For example, you might decide that your company needs to beat its competitors by a 10 percent margin on this front. The graph then traces how your company is progressing on this front over (different) ensuing quarters.

Customer response speed illustrated here is only an example. Knowledge management systems usually start out to tackle much more complex and compound issues. However, since there is no acceptable unit for measuring knowledge on any front, it's best to measure all para-

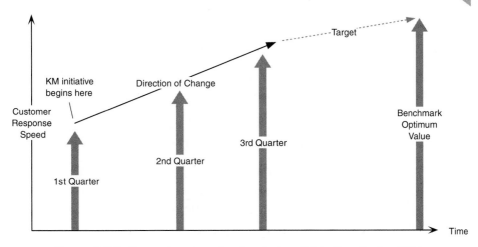

Figure 8-5 Optimum benchmark values help validate the effects of KM.

meters in their original units and maybe devise a composite measure. (More specifics on measurement and metrics follow in Chapter 14.) All these measures can help you assess the performance—good or bad—of your knowledge management investments.

It's usually a good idea to assign high values to all these aspects. Process performance need not be compared to some arbitrary figure: It could be based on a function (such as 110 percent of the industry average) derived from industry averages, competitor figures, or market predictions. Lacking any such bases, you could always shoot for the *perfect figure,* such as no customer returns or 100 percent conversion of research outcomes to marketed products, etc. Though optimism is a good thing, be cautious of overly depending on such an approach: It can be far from realistic if perfect figures are used as a basis for comparison. Table 8-4 gives a few examples of such measures.

Table 8-4 Measuring Knowledge Assets Against Optimum Values

Knowledge Asset	Aspect	Current Firm Values	Optimum Values
Trademark	Value in dollars	$4 million	$25 million
Patents→products	% converted	40%	90%
Know-how	IT architecture design; how many consultants actually know how to do it?	5 employees	40 employees
Repeat business	% of existing customer base	96%	100%

SELECTING THE AUDIT METHOD

The method you use for auditing your company's or group's knowledge determines the degree to which you will accurately gauge the current (pre-KM) state of that aspect or knowledge dimension (see Figure 8-6). This assessment is what helps you decide on the processes that need reinforcement and the processes that need capitalization.

For example, you might realize that there just isn't enough conversation and sharing of ideas going on in a specific department in your company. You might decide to augment this shortcoming with a Web-based message board and physical common space. In short, the choice of technologies (and accompanying cultural reinforcements) you focus on will largely be determined and influenced by this step in the knowledge audit process.

Perhaps the most useful resource at this stage will be the knowledge management assessment tool provided in Appendix A, which enables you to select the aspects that rank on the top of your company's list.[c]

The audit method that you decide to use must account for at *least* the following three critical intangible assets:

- Employee know-how
- Reputation (including good will or value attached to your company brand)
- Organizational culture

Reputation and culture can be thought of as diffused tacit knowledge, so it follows that knowledge and know-how, in some form or another, account for the bulk of the value of the firm.[3] You must also determine the nature, strength, and sustainability of the current competitive advantage that the firm derives in terms of product and service delivery system features that it employs.[4] It helps to think in terms of the issues of protection, maintenance, enhancement, and leverage of these intangible assets.

DOCUMENTING KNOWLEDGE ASSETS

It is essential to document the knowledge-based assets that your company has in a consistent framework. The framework makes it easier to compare with previously measured values and with corresponding values for your competitors. Such a framework typically takes the form of the capability framework described in Table 8-5.

---

[c]Customer surveys, interviews with clients, analysis of sales data, cost of sales, market reputation measures, analysis of competitor data, analysis of cash flows, analysis of knowledge flow bottlenecks, Delphi studies, and focus groups can provide a lot more insights into the actual state of your company's knowledge assets than pure guesswork can. Market pull for your products and services, return on investments in IT and knowledge/discussion databases, employee skills, sharing of best practices across the enterprise, and core competencies are other feasible indicators.

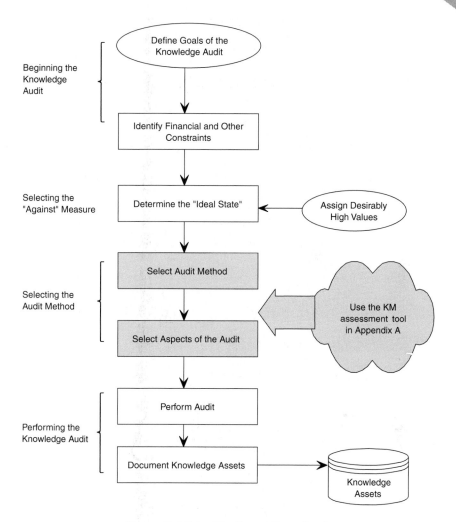

Figure 8-6 Selecting the audit method.

Each unit of knowledge analysis and each diagnostic question can be answered in terms of Table 8-6, which allows you to measure "tacitness" of each knowledge element. The answer that closely matches the description identifies the stage of knowledge along the scale described in Table 8-3. The lower the value on this scale, the more important it might become to support that dimension of knowledge with a knowledge management system, for example, to convert it into a form that can be more readily applied in a more explicit form.

Once you go through this iteration, you can add it to a base starting-value set against which you will be able to compare developments and improvements over time, after a knowl-

SAMPLE DIAGNOSTIC QUESTIONS

Asking questions like the ones listed below can help you identify important knowledge assets:

1. Do you consider your business to be knowledge intensive?
2. Do you consider your business to be information intensive?
3. Would it be possible to actually use knowledge, skills, competencies, and best practices in your company in a better way than you see them being used?
4. What types of knowledge do you think are critical to your business competitiveness?
5. What would you rate as the top three in answers to question 3?
6. What benefits do you think your company could realize if it improved the ways in which it organizes and reuses existing skills and experience?
7. Where, on the scale defined in Table 8-3, do you think your organization falls *as a whole?*
8. Where, on the scale defined in Table 8-3, do you think your organization falls in terms of its key processes that drive your business?
9. Would you be able to claim that your company deals with processes rather than functions? This means that your company or department is process not function centered.
10. How would you characterize your company's structure and organization?
11. Could you say that authority is decentralized to the business unit level?
12. Would you agree that most business units in your company have a great deal of freedom to act and have a bottom-line responsibility for their own actions?
13. Are functional disciplines in your company team-based rather than job-based?

edge management program is implemented. Declining values will indicate a failure to improve processes, and climbing values indicate successful knowledge management directions.

ANALYZING THE POPULATED CAPABILITY QUADRANTS

At the end of this audit process, you will have populated the capability framework (Table 8-5) with answers and ratings derived from diagnostic questions that you pose to your audit team. Some cells will have a lot of 1's and 2's (indicating highly tacit knowledge and a lack of explicated methodology that the entire firm can directly apply) while others will be populated with more 5's and 6's (indicating high capability maturity and the existence of a recipe).

14. Is composition of teams in your company governed by creating the right mix of competencies needed for the work process or project at hand?

15. Does your company depend on the knowledge and competence surrounding its people, processes, and technology infrastructure?

16. What emphasis does your company actually place on these people, processes, and technological enablers?

17. What type of culture do you have in your company? Is it an open, trusting, and sharing culture?

18. Does your company's culture reflect internal competitiveness?

19. Can knowledge of multiple team members or stakeholders be added to create synergy and cohesion?

20. What does your company reward—team performance or individual performance?

21. Has your company identified the processes that are needed to achieve long-term business objectives and corporate goals? (You need to know the goals first.)

22. If you were to state one single reason why knowledge management could never work in your company, what would that be?

23. Does your senior management focus on financial performance alone or both financial performance and future growth planning?

24. Are your employees responsible for creating additional value in processes? Does it count in their compensation arrangements?

25. Would you regard your company's management style as reactive or proactive?

These questions help you identify knowledge-related areas and their relative mapping on the framework described in Table 8-5. For a comprehensive analysis, use the set of tools provided in Appendix A.

An easy way to determine the quadrant that your own company's knowledge management system needs to support might be to add the numbers in each of the four quadrants and analyze the ones with the weakest scores. However, you must avoid this easy way out, as it can be highly error prone. Since the number of diagnostics in each quadrant is not standardized and the significance of each question (as perceived by a number of stakeholders) will vary from one company to another, direct results cannot be calculated. However, these numbers (representing Bohn's scores) will help your audit team decide and weigh each of these quadrants on a composite–score basis. The populated cells of the framework can, therefore, help you determine the quadrants (representing four types of capabilities) that need the strengthening support of knowledge management most and those that are already healthy.

Table 8-5 The Capability Framework for Positioning Knowledge Related Assets

Regulatory Capability	Positional Capability
• Patents	• Path-dependent capabilities
• Trademarks	• Reputation
• Registered designs	• Value chain configuration
• Trade secrets	• Distribution networks
• Licenses	• Installed base
• Proprietary technology	• Customer base
• Methodologies	• Market share
• Databases	• Liquidity
	• Product reputation
	• Service reputation
	• Service product (such as consulting outcomes) reputation

Functional Capability	Cultural Capability
• Lead times	• Tradition or corporate culture of being the best (Apple?)
• Accessibility of past knowledge	• Tradition of sharing
• Innovative capabilities	• The tradition of co-opetition
• Individual and team skills	• The tradition of co-operation
• Distributor know-how	• Perception of quality standards
• Employee skills	• Ability of employees to work in teams
	• Capability to respond to market challenges
	• Innovation
	• Entrepreneurial and intrapreneurial drive in employees
	• Employee initiative and motivation

Based on an expanded adaptation from R. Hall and P. Andriani (1998), Analyzing Intangible Resources and Managing Knowledge in a Supply Chain Context, *European Management Journal,* vol. 16, no. 6 (1998), 685–697.

Table 8-6 Diagnostic Questions to Evaluate Each Unit of Knowledge Analysis on Bohn's Scale

Stage	Description/Diagnostic
0	We don't even know the good from the bad in terms of outcomes! (You probably don't need this book then; nothing is going to help!)
1	We have no knowledge; each time we have to make a decision, it is by trial and error.
2	We have only tacit knowledge which is in the form of personal knowledge held by person _____ and _____.
3	We have tacit knowledge; we have converted it into heuristics and rules of thumb;* they often work.
4	Knowledge (some) exists in explicated form, but no one really uses it.
5	Knowledge exists in explicated form. We use it but need tacit knowledge possessed by person _____ to be able to apply it in some circumstances; but unless things are really different from normal, we can do without the tacit component. Whenever we use this explicit knowledge, we validate it or contribute back to it.
6	Knowledge exists in explicated form. We use it but need tacit knowledge possessed by person _____ to be able to apply it in some circumstances; but unless things are really different from normal, we can do without the tacit component. Whenever we use this explicit knowledge, we validate it or contribute back to it.
7	Tried and tested models now exist. We can simulate conditions; do what-if analysis in complex circumstances; modify behavior accordingly; it always works. Tacit content of the sum total of knowledge is very low. We validate existing knowledge whenever we use it. Our company has a strong "unlearning" capability. Our culture truly promotes knowledge sharing and synergy. We do not think that we have left any stone unturned in leveraging our company's knowledge. Employee walkouts do not hurt us in any significant way.
8	Difficult to characterize.

*For example, it often, *but not always,* is true that your car's battery is discharged if you left the headlights on for a few hours and now it does not start.

TRACKING KNOWLEDGE GROWTH OVER TIME

As you keep a score of these aspects surrounding knowledge, you can recognize changes over time by asking diagnostic questions (see Appendix A). Examples of such diagnostic questions include:

1. How is the *stock* of this knowledge resource increasing?
2. Is it increasing? If so, how do we know that it is?
3. How can we ensure that the stock (of knowledge) continues to increase?
4. Are we making the best use of this knowledge resource?
5. Do all employees recognize the value of this resource?
6. How durable is this knowledge asset? Will it decline over a period of time? How easily can others (competition) identify and copy this resource?
7. Can the competition easily nurture and grow this knowledge?
8. Is there any aspect that our competition has leveraged, but we have not?
9. Can we imitate it? Need we?
10. Can this knowledge "walk out of the door"?
11. How is it changing *over time?*
12. Will our company need it after x (define x) years?

CHOOSING YOUR COMPANY'S K-SPOTS

It is the sum total of the decisions made on the front lines that decide the future well-being of your company.[5] The knowledge audit provides a clearer picture of the k-spots or the knowledge niches on which a company must focus its knowledge management efforts. Choosing these knowledge spots or areas of focus provides the best unbiased view of the technology investment needed to drive potent knowledge management in your company.

STRATEGIC POSITIONING WITHIN THE TECHNOLOGY FRAMEWORK

Mapping knowledge in each of the areas that you chose in the earlier stages of the knowledge audit, as described in Figure 8-7, provides excellent insight into the way knowledge management and business strategy can be kept in perfect synchronization. This insight can help in determining the strategic position and competitive advantage possessed by the firm in terms of the explicit and tacit knowledge contained within the firm-in people's heads, databases, resident experience, electronic discussions—and knowledge management systems

The results of the audit can then help you decide how you want to position knowledge management to provide the maximum value while balancing competitive advantage possessed by your firm. Four positioning choices are described next.

THE FOUR POSITIONING CHOICES

Once you map each knowledge element or asset on the framework described in Figure 8-7, you can tell whether it is a strength or weakness. The shaded areas indicate a high competitive advantage: areas where your knowledge is already well managed but can possibly be improved. Similarly, the shaded areas in Figure 8-8 represent the two quadrants where knowledge management holds the most promise for producing ground-breaking results. Knowledge that falls outside these shaded areas represents those areas where the support of a knowledge management system and an effective knowledge management strategy is most needed. Strategic positions A through D (see Figure 8-7) are described below.

Figure 8-7 Determining the strategic k-spot using the results of the knowledge audit.
Based on an adaptation from R. Hall and P. Andriani, Analyzing Intangible Resources and Managing Knowledge in a Supply Chain Context. European Management Journal Vol. 16, no. 6 (1988), 685–697.

Strategic Position A

Strategic position A indicates that your company is internally safe but externally vulnerable on this front. The level of explicated knowledge is high, and tacit content is low. Your competitors do not have much more knowledge than you have available and ready to apply. This is perhaps the best-case scenario for knowledge management.[d] Very few companies actually fall in this quadrant. We researched several companies that have had a fair degree of success in their knowledge management efforts, and our initial findings indicate that companies that are actually pursuing knowledge management effectively, fall in Quadrant A.[6] However, in that quadrant your company is externally vulnerable because almost all the knowledge you have is well explicated and codified. If your competitors manage to obtain any portion of this readily applicable and explicitly codified knowledge, they could use it to their advantage and against you in their own business. In such a case, your focus should be more on security measures rather than on knowledge management.

Strategic Position B

Position B indicates that your company has managed to explicate *some* portion of its knowledge; however, this is a relatively small percentage of what your competitors have managed to explicate. In this position, tacit content of knowledge in your company is rather high. This is an excellent scenario for an efficacious knowledge management initiative using a well-funded knowledge management system. Technology can be a major, if not the only, savior for your firm's competitive advantage. Even though your company might be externally safe, a key employee leaving your company and joining a competitor might reverse the entire balance.

Strategic Position C

This position is a fundamentally weak position, where your company has no strategic advantage whatsoever. Probably a lot more issues besides knowledge management need to be addressed.[7]

Strategic Position D

Most companies considering knowledge management fall into this quadrant. These companies are presently successful but need to manage knowledge in such a manner that their temporary advantage is converted into a longer-term, sustainable competitive advantage. These companies have much to gain from an investment in knowledge management systems,[8] technology, and infrastructure. Such companies include consulting companies, where the founders of the firm have a bulk of the firm's total knowledge. In such cases, the tacit portion of knowledge is very high in relation to the portion that has been formalized, captured, and explicated (or externalized).

---

[d]This holds especially true for companies that have a strong leaning toward codification. See M. Hansen, N. Nohria, and T. Tierney, What Is Your Strategy for Managing Knowledge? *Harvard Business Review,* March–April (1999), 106–116.

WHO ACTUALLY SEES THE ROAD AHEAD?

An outstanding example of a company that falls in this quadrant, often a topic of passionate debate both in business school classrooms and Web chatrooms, is Microsoft. Bill Gates, its founder, has provided the driving "bigger-picture" vision to the company since its inception. Microsoft has been trying to both distribute and explicate *his* knowledge by bringing complementary and intellectually able stakeholders such as Nathan Myvrhold into the company and documenting decisions more excruciatingly than ever before. The same has reportedly been going on at lower levels throughout the company as well.

Companies falling into strategic positions B and D are the best cases for knowledge management. The areas of your firm's knowledge that fall in these zones, as shown in Figure 8-8, are the ones on which you must focus your knowledge management strategy.

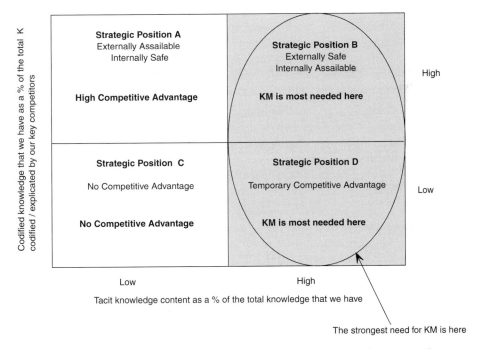

Figure 8-8 Areas that your knowledge management system needs to strengthen.

LESSONS LEARNED

The knowledge audit process, the fourth step in the 10-step knowledge management roadmap, begins with a clear understanding of its purpose, its short-term and long-term goals, and the identification of its constraints. Knowledge of knowledge assets is critical to the proper planning of a knowledge management system and is a rich source of information about where the strengths of your company lie. Keep in mind the following points while auditing your company's knowledge assets:

- *Hindsight + insight = foresight.* Extrapolation from the past cannot, by itself, predict the future course of events such as project success. However, if hindsight is combined with insight into past processes, the combination can provide a robust, partial-indicator for the future. Keep this in view when you are trying to decide on processes that are considered critical (which is a highly subjective judgment) by your company.

- *Apply the six-step knowledge audit process.* The six-step knowledge audit process includes the following: defining the goals, selecting the audit method, determining the ideal state, performing the knowledge audit, documenting existing knowledge assets, and determining your company's strategic position within the technology framework.

- *Think of coffee, processes, and knowledge management together.* The coffee-brewing example, in spite of my warnings against using examples as guiding principles, effectively demonstrates how processes move from being highly tacit to highly methodological. If you cannot decide what stage your processes are at, try matching them to this example.

- *Bohn's Stages of Knowledge Growth framework is only a preliminary measure for knowledge.* To effectively manage its knowledge, your company must progress to stage 5, 6, or 7. Be wary of using this framework as your primary knowledge management metric—quality function deployment and balanced scorecards (described in Chapter 14) are better suited to that task. Stage 8 on the process knowledge competence framework is a mirage.

- *The knowledge audit team must be cross-functional.* The audit team must include participants from at least the following five areas: corporate strategy, marketing, information systems, human resources, and finance. Make sure that you have someone from senior management on board along with a knowledge champion (you?). The knowledge analyst, who plays the integrative part, should be able elicit both extant and missing knowledge and also analyze the possible categories in which each piece of knowledge or stream of knowledge fits best.

- *Identify, evaluate, and rate critical process knowledge.* Look at all the intangible assets and knowledge assets that exist in your company including its rituals, processes, structure, communities, and people.

- *Use a consistent framework for documenting knowledge audit results.* Document the results of the audit in the consistent capability framework to allow for comparison over time. Focus on the cells with low scores *and* those that represent critically weak areas.

- *Select your company's k-spots carefully.* The knowledge audit provides a clearer picture of the k-spots or the knowledge niches on which a company must focus its knowledge management efforts. You can identify promising processes that stand to gain the most through knowledge management. The most promising opportunities for knowledge management are indicated by strategic positions B and D in the strategic capability framework.

A preliminary audit provides a good point both for identifying areas and processes that can benefit from knowledge management most and for deciding on the structure of the implementation team. Chapter 14 discusses knowledge metrics that can directly link knowledge management design to business strategy. You might want to glance at the measures there, and at the toolkit in Appendix A before you proceed to the next chapter, in which, as the fifth step on our 10-step roadmap, we will analyze a strategy for building the knowledge management team that will actually develop and implement your company's knowledge management system.

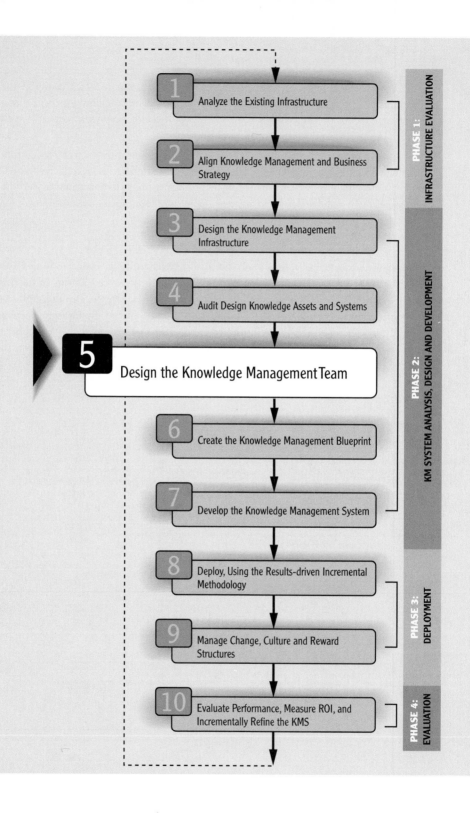

1 Analyze the Existing Infrastructure

2 Align Knowledge Management and Business Strategy

PHASE 1: INFRASTRUCTURE EVALUATION

3 Design the Knowledge Management Infrastructure

4 Audit Design Knowledge Assets and Systems

5 Design the Knowledge Management Team

6 Create the Knowledge Management Blueprint

7 Develop the Knowledge Management System

PHASE 2: KM SYSTEM ANALYSIS, DESIGN AND DEVELOPMENT

8 Deploy, Using the Results-driven Incremental Methodology

9 Manage Change, Culture and Reward Structures

PHASE 3: DEPLOYMENT

10 Evaluate Performance, Measure ROI, and Incrementally Refine the KMS

PHASE 4: EVALUATION

CHAPTER 9

DESIGNING THE KM TEAM

GOOD JUDGMENT COMES FROM EXPERIENCE, AND EXPERIENCE
OFTEN COMES FROM BAD JUDGMENT.
—RITA MAE BROWN

Teams in IT projects have traditionally involved two parties: end users and IT staff. However, for a knowledge management system, teams need to be more comprehensive to be effective. A knowledge management system is built on expertise, knowledge, understanding, skills, and insights brought into the project by a variety of stakeholders who might have little in common from a functional standpoint. The quality of the collaborative relationship between these stakeholders determines the ultimate success of the system. Having the world's best knowledge management system still does not guarantee successful management of knowledge: That success comes from KM's implementation and cultural embodiment by both the knowledge workers and the employees who will ultimately use it. This relationship is complex and often highly problematic;[1] Therefore, selecting the right blend of team members to lead the knowledge management project is a critical step.

The fifth step on the KM roadmap involves design of the knowledge management team that will build, implement, focus, and deploy the KM system. In this chapter, we identify sources of internal and external expertise needed, prioritize stakeholder needs, evaluate member selection criteria, and examine team life span and sizing issues. We identify characteristics of the KM project leader to determine mechanisms to streamline internal dynamics and maximize users' participation. Next, we identify tasks for the KM team and fit them to the risk evaluation matrix to circumvent common points of failure.

SOURCES OF EXPERTISE

Companies implementing knowledge management must draw their expertise from several different sources:

- Internal, centralized IT departments
- Team-based local experts
- External vendors, contractors, partners, and consultants
- End users and front-line staff

Although we cannot undermine the importance of IT staff who will actually build a system, the most important part of this team member set is the set of local team-based expert(s). The burden of balancing counteracting requirements falls on the shoulders of the knowledge management team (see Figure 9-1). As we discussed in the Chapter 8, drawing participants from a variety of functional groups within and outside your company is essential. If done properly, this approach will become the strength of your knowledge management team and a major contributor to the success of such an endeavor.

Local Experts and Intradepartmental Gurus

Active end-user involvement throughout the knowledge management project is critical to its success. In most companies, there are the early adopters of technology—the so-called gurus within your company. These are the people who come in early or stay late to play with new tools that become available. Even though many of these folks tend to be nontechnologists,

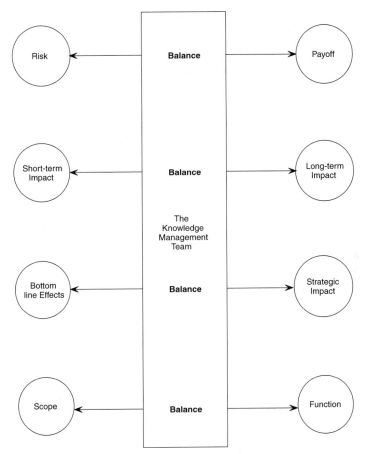

Figure 9-1 The KM team must strike the right balance.

they are the best people to gauge the possible usefulness of each feature that your system has. These local experts are often the first to notice the limitations of existing systems, and to think of possible upgrades and changes to meet the evolving needs of their group. Examples of such workers include marketing people who realize that existing technology could possibly be used to deliver the latest sales figures and data needed by traveling salespeople in remote locations.

INTERNAL IT DEPARTMENTS

Relying solely on local experts, of course, has its limitations. Even though local experts might possess a fairly high degree of technical knowledge besides knowledge of their own job, they might lack an understanding of the interdependencies between complex systems, networks, and technology that pure technologists like the IT staff might be able to bring in. While the local experts will bring in the business case and ideas, it is IT staff who will bring in knowledge of:

WHAT MATTERS MOST

Platinum Technology exemplifies these ideas. The company decided that their knowledge management effort was a critical factor in empowering its sales staff, so its main focus was providing its sales force with all the information that they could use when trying to sell a product or service to a potential customer. The system includes feeds from all internal sources within the company, data from partners and past customers, and their responses to the company's products. In addition, electronic sources of data relating to competitors' products are actively integrated into the system. The result is a concise summary of all relevant information that the salesperson can *act* on while trying to close a sale—therefore, knowledge.

- Infrastructural capabilities and limitations
- Connectivity and compatibility among the team-based systems and the overall organizational technology infrastructure
- Standardization issues across different platforms, applications, and tools
- Technicalities underlying the adaptation of these tools by various knowledge worker groups within the company

When you are selecting team members from the internal IT department within your company, it is critical that you select personnel with credibility in the eventual user group. This helps ensure that the *relevant* set of stakeholder needs are adequately represented. With increased emphasis on customer service, it is easy for internal customers to outsource their development services to external consultants. Therefore, delegates selected from the IT department must have a more expansive view of who the customer is. This must include the internal customer at the same level of significance as they would view an external customer or buyer. Technical skills, of course, are a priority in making these decisions.

NONLOCAL EXPERTS AND EXTRADEPARTMENTAL GURUS

Nonlocal experts and extradepartmental proponents promote team laterality. *Laterality* refers to the ability to cut across functional boundaries and relate to people from different areas.[2] People who exhibit this characteristic are best suited to be on a knowledge management team. Such members can:

- Act as a bridge and as interpreters between people from different backgrounds, skill areas, and specializations

- Learn faster than the average person in your company and are not defensive about their lack of understanding or knowledge in areas other than their own
- Bring value to the overall team synergy as they tend to be confident but not egoistically constrained
- Learn the basic lingo and understand the frameworks that their collaborators refer to
- Have the ability to deal creatively and rationally with the problems that the aforementioned differences can, and often do, lead to

Groups of such people have also been referred to as *communities of practice;* they are characterized by:

- Multifunctional groups that incorporate diverse viewpoints, training, ages, and roles
- Enacting a common purpose by engaging in real work, building things, solving problems, delivering service, and using real tools
- Developing intellectual property, knowledge, firm culture, internal language, and new skills
- Making lasting changes in the people and the competency that they embody

CONSULTANTS

Even though most of the technical, design, and soft skills needed for the knowledge management project might be available in-house, there might be some areas that are no one's strength within the company. These shortcomings can often be overcome by bringing in external consultants. Internal participants might have slight cultural differences owing to their differing departmental and functional affiliations, but they are still tied together by a common frame of reference built around the overall company culture, dominant values, and image. However, external consultants do not always fit into this frame of reference. Because external participants often lack this common frame of reference, it is essential that other binding mechanisms, such as their personal characteristics, be strongly matched with those of internal team members.

Nevertheless, this lack of shared culture can often be turned from a liability into an asset. These external participants *can* bring a balanced, unbiased outsider perspective into the entire design process.

In such cases, trust becomes another significant issue. Given the nature of the consulting business, it should come as no surprise if the consultant is developing exactly the same type of system for your competitor a few months down the road. Selecting a consultant should therefore be partially based on the extent to which the person (or consulting company) is willing to transfer existing skills to your company's employees. Some of the other issues that must be considered while selecting a consultant include:

- The consultant's reputation for integrity
- The consultant's history that demonstrates the ability to maintain confidentiality about past projects
- Whether the consultant has worked successfully for your own company on earlier projects
- Whether the consultant (or consulting company) is working on a similar project for a competitor
- Whether your internal team trusts and has confidence in the consulting company

In any case, highly specialized and capable consultants are often hard to find. Since knowledge management projects are strategically oriented, the level of confidentiality must be backed up with specific, legal nondisclosure agreements. Where highly confidential material is involved, it might be a better idea to have an employee trained in the deficient area rather than bringing in a consultant. An option that is always open, budgets permitting, is to lure a consultant from the consulting position to a permanent job within your company. However, corporate budgets can often restrict this option.

KM stakeholders should typify the group that they represent. For example, the person representing your company's human resources department should be one who is typical (where the meaning of *typical* is highly subjective) of the HR department, and has had a sufficient level of experience within your own company.[a]

As Figure 9-2 shows, the human resources and project sponsors or senior management provide overall stability to the knowledge management project team.

MANAGERS

The status and influence of senior managers would make one assume that they are the least likely group to be left out of the development process. However, several studies have shown that this exclusion is not only possible but one that also frequently does happen. As teams become too deeply engrossed in the user/developer relationship, senior managers tend to be left out of the loop. As we have been discussing throughout this book, managers should be kept active in the knowledge management project; and without their active involvement the entire project may end up on shaky ground.

---

[a]Recent research points out that a good number of projects fail because the users (and in turn the HR department) do not play a significant enough role in the development process. See Bush, A., A. Tiwana, and M. Keil, Assessing User Risk Perceptions in Software Development Projects, in *The Proceedings of Southern Association of Information Systems SAIS-99,* Atlanta, Georgia, April 21–24 (1999). The roles of various participants are summarized in Table 9-1.

Table 9-1 Structuring the Knowledge Management Team

Focus	Shareholder Group	Role in the Knowledge Management Project	Characteristics Strongly Desired
Teams	User teams Finance Marketing Other functional areas with which the knowledge management initiative is concerned	• Provide functional expertise. • Provide business expertise in their specific area. • Participate in the process design stage. • Help in the implementation stages of the system.	• Must understand work processes in their area. • Must have good interpersonal and team skills. • Must have a certain degree of credibility within other participating groups. • Must be willing to see from other functional viewpoints.
Technology	IT experts/information systems Internal IT staff External consultants	• Provide technology expertise. • Participate in the actual implementation and design. • Represent the internal and internally proficient technologists. • Actually write the code. • Bring in a perspective on functional capabilities and limitations of existing systems.	• Must understand technology in depth. • Must have good interpersonal skills. • Must have strong team skills. • Must be willing to understand the perspectives brought in by other team members and actually incorporate them into the design. • Must be willing to learn. • Must be credible. • Must have an expansive customer orientation.

Table 9-1 Structuring the Knowledge Management Team (cont.)

Focus	Shareholder Group	Role in the Knowledge Management Project	Characteristics Strongly Desired
Organizational	Senior management/sponsors/ knowledge champion(s)/CKO	• Support the legitimacy of the project. • Bring in vision that correlates with the overall company-wide vision. • Serve on steering committees (if needed). • Commit the resources needed.	• Understand the management and strategic processes. • Must be credible. • Must have a strong leadership position that almost everyone on the team accepts. • Must have a clear idea of the bigger picture of where knowledge leveraging should take the company. • Must "eat their own dog food," that is, they must themselves believe what they say. • Need to be thoroughly convinced of the worth of the project.

TEAM COMPOSITION AND SELECTION CRITERIA

As with most other technologically driven enterprise-wide teams, functional diversity in knowledge management teams should be taken as a given characteristic. Teams need to be designed for effectiveness. While there is no straightforward formula for designing a good knowledge management team, the team's design has much to do with the nature of the project itself. Functional diversity can lead to only two possible outcomes, depending on how it's handled. The first, and very common, outcome is destructive conflict and tension. The second, more desirable, outcome is characterized by synergy, creativity, and innovation. This happens only when laterality among team members is high and there is sufficient room to accommodate different backgrounds, values, skills, perspectives, and assumptions that the members bring into the team. Table 9-2 summarizes the major team design considerations.

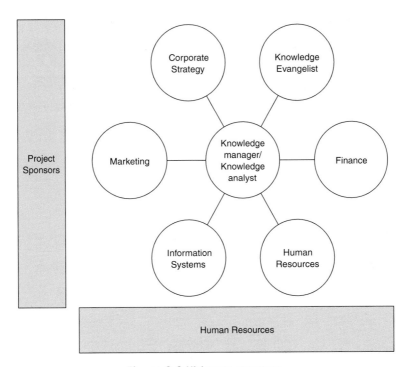

Figure 9-2 KM team structure.

TEMPORARY VERSUS PERMANENT TEAM MEMBERS

Knowledge management is not like a typical business restructuring or technology introduction project. Those projects are temporary and depend on temporary teams, whereas a knowledge management project needs at least a small portion of the group to be permanent. A knowledge management project is not over once a knowledge management system is implemented; it must go on and continually improve and change with changing external and internal environments. While some members might be needed on the team only during the initial stages, others are not as temporary. I use the term *core team* to refer to this permanent, essential group. Team members can be dedicated to the project either full time or part time. The size of the core team must be kept to the smallest size possible—the smallest member count that can actually do the work. Temporary team members often belong to specific user groups. The core team should consist of only the following participants:

- Knowledge champion or a senior manager.
- IT staff.

Table 9-2 Designing the Knowledge Management Project Team

Team Design Element	Characteristics of the Knowledge Management Team Members Selected	Notes
Defining the knowledge management project leader's role	The leader of the team: • Must be credible. • Must have a sufficient level of authority and resource capability. • Should not change; must be stable. • Must know how to facilitate, consult, and resolve conflicts. • Must take charge of the conventional project management, scheduling, and coordination duties. • Must have direct reporting capability to upper management or should be drawn from within upper middle management. • Must manage the life cycle of the team, as well as selection of the core team members. • Must encourage structured decision making. • Must be experienced in both complex projects and in various roles within the company.	These criteria can be also used for selecting the project leader.
Defining the team composition and selection criteria for team members	Knowledge management project team members must be drawn from different functional areas and departments of the firm. As expected, they will have different areas of specialization and backgrounds. The following common characteristics must be shared by members selected for the team: • Must have specialized expertise. • Must have had sufficient experience within the company or working with the company as an external consultant. • Must have the required competencies that truly represent the concerns of the department or functional area that the team member represents. • Might work full time or part time on this project. • Might be a member of the core team or the temporary startup team. • Must demonstrate laterality. • Must believe in the project and must have a clear vision for what improved knowledge flows can and should do for this unit or department.	All groups that will be affected by the knowledge management project and, conversely, all groups that are expected to use and contribute to this knowledge and knowledge management efforts must be adequately and accurately represented in the team.

- User delegates representing the core business area that is going to depend on the knowledge management system. This could be engineering staff in case the knowledge management system is built to support research and development; it could be marketing if the KM system is for sales force enablement, etc.

The remaining participants, in most cases, should be involved in the startup phases of the project and can be called in later for further input as and when needed.

TEAM LIFE SPAN AND SIZING ISSUES

There are two schools of thought on the future of knowledge management: One school believes that knowledge management will continue to depend on people to manage knowledge throughout the lifetime of the organization; the second and more convincing school believes that knowledge management is a *self-eliminating* field. This means that as a company begins to accept knowledge management practices, they should, over several years, become so second nature to employees as the company evolves that eventually there should be no need for a knowledge manager or CKO to manage knowledge. Knowledge workers themselves should be able to handle all KM tasks once KM becomes embedded in the company culture and in work practices.

One would argue why the knowledge management team would, in the first place, do their job so well that it would eliminate their very need! That is a hard question to answer. Though there is a lot of ongoing research to find an answer to this question, there is little other than very strong financial and promotional incentives that can help here. For that matter, team members on the knowledge management team should be promised strong rewards and promotions should the knowledge management initiative truly succeed. A team that sets out to work with the fear of losing their job by performing too well is bound to be undermotivated, if not unmotivated.

THE KNOWLEDGE MANAGEMENT PROJECT LEADER

The KM project team leader's role, by its very nature, is different from one occasioned by a typical organizational change or technology implementation project. The leader does not direct: Instead, she facilitates. The KM project leader might or not be the same person as the CKO (or equivalent). Unlike conventional project management, knowledge management projects need leadership that helps create a supportive, unobtrusive, and focused environment within which team members can concentrate on their primary substantive tasks with minimal distraction. The project leader must take on the conventional load of tracking progress, budgets, workloads, and schedules. The KM project leader serves as the visionary for the entire project by helping members on the team understand the project's mission and align their efforts with the project's overall goals and objectives. A project leader must resolve internal dynamics, serve as a translator, and take charge of task delegation, as the following sections describe.

INTERNAL DYNAMICS

The project leader must facilitate the internal functioning of the knowledge management team by helping members objectively resolve differences, using structured decision-making techniques. While conflict is undesirable on a large scale, a basic level of conflict is essential and inevitable in teams as diverse as knowledge management teams tend to be. Many of the differences that emerge are due to the differing needs and concerns of the stakeholder groups involved. The project leader plays an essential part here by helping team members understand why even trivially straightforward issues and differences seem to be so difficult to resolve. In their facilitating role, project leaders can pose the key questions, clarify differences and their underlying assumptions, and then give members of the knowledge management team sufficient room to actually resolve these differences.

TRANSLATION AND DELEGATION

The project leader also needs to be able to act as a translator in the startup stages of the project when the user teams and the IT participants fail to understand each other's viewpoints because of vocabulary differences. What might comprise a good design in the opinion of a technologist might not qualify as a good design in the opinion of a marketing manager, for example. Therefore, the project leader must not try to push or pull the team toward specific directions, design solutions, or technology choices. Instead, he must facilitate effective and well-moderated brainstorming within the group. Besides this role, the project leader must brief senior management on the progress and milestones in the project.

To determine the actual issues of concern and to identify the actual knowledge flow problems that exist within the company, the project leader should encourage participants to actually collect relevant data from their own departments through meetings, surveys, interviews, and focus groups. These communications can ensure that the direction the team is moving in is not unduly influenced by the ill-placed opinion of specific stakeholders and instead reflects the actual concerns that their department might have.

USER PARTICIPATION

It is the project manager's role to ensure that the knowledge management project is going in a direction that builds toward a system that users *actually need*. While the actual requirements might have been elicited in the knowledge audit described in Chapter 8, maintaining the link between the users and the knowledge management group ensures that changing conditions are kept in view. One of the most effective ways of verifying this linkage is to show a preliminary version of the knowledge management system to actual users.

Prototypes: A Stitch in Time Saves Nine

Systems developers have long realized the value of prototypes. A prototype provides both the developers, in this case the knowledge management team, and the users with an idea of how the system in its final form will function.

By using such a prototype, even if it is incomplete, users can see the possibilities of the knowledge management system under construction, and this improved understanding of the final product can lead to, or trigger, highly desirable refinement of its features, interface, functionality, and design. Tweaking the system's design based on user feedback in the prototype stages can save your company much headache and unnecessary rework-related expenses at a later date. Other ways the project manager can link to the final user are illustrated in Figure 9-3.

THE KM TEAM'S PROJECT SPACE

One of the first tasks that the knowledge management team needs to undertake is that of understanding the project's strategic intent, organizational context, technological constraints, monetary limitations, and short-term as well as long-term goals. Members of your knowledge management team should be able to provide adequate answers to these questions collectively:

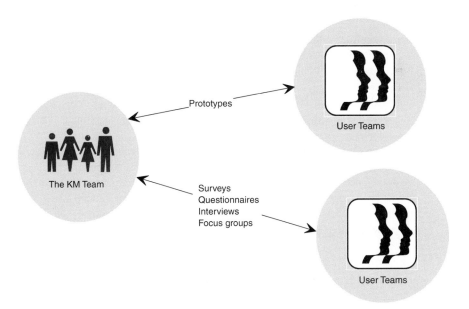

Figure 9-3 Prototyping and other methods of linking the user and the knowledge management project.

1. What is the company's strategic goal?

2. What is the company's performance goal? Knowing where the company stands before the project provides a healthy basis for answering this question in specific terms.

3. Where does the knowledge management team fit in the organizational hierarchy?

4. Does the knowledge management project fit vertically or horizontally in the value chain?

5. What are the financial constraints?

6. What are the technical limitations in terms of existing platforms, company-wide network standards, etc.?

7. What are the critical missing elements in terms of skills, people, and knowledge that are still missing in the team? Can consultants help? If so, which ones and how?

8. What is the time frame within which the project must be delivered?

9. What are the immediate payoffs? If there are none, when will the payoffs begin to show up? If that is not viable either, how will the value of the project be demonstrated and tested? The discussion on metrics in Chapter 14 can assist in this evaluation.

10. What level of commitment does the team have from the senior management and from the users? If it's poor, what can be done about it? Are there representatives from both these camps on the knowledge management team?

11. What are the cultural blockades that should be expected? Does the company culture actually fit with the knowledge-sharing attitude that is needed to make a knowledge management system work? If not, what changes in reward structure are necessary? Who has the authority to make such changes? Are they willing to make them?

12. Has any competitor or noncompeting firm implemented a project like this? What do we know about it? If it was successful, is there some way to get a key participant to switch jobs? Should we call that transfer of experiential knowledge?

Judging the *true* value of the project is a critical issue. If the project costs more than the long-term value that it adds to the firm, it's probably not worth the investment. Therefore, exploring these initial questions is critical before the next step can be taken. If there are no direct answers, surrogate measures might be adopted. If your knowledge management team cannot collectively answer these questions, revisit its structure and constituents. For example, if the primary objective of the knowledge management project is to improve product quality by managing past and current knowledge about product quality problems, it might be valuable to question quality quantitatively. How much quality and at what cost? Can the customers tell the difference? Will they be willing to pay, say, 7 percent more for the same product if higher quality is guaranteed?

MANAGING STAKEHOLDER EXPECTATIONS

The second task, after the knowledge management team has decided on an initial set of objectives for the knowledge management initiative, is to formally present this work to various stakeholder groups. The biggest advantage of such an interaction is that it can help the team compare the project's objective with stakeholder expectations and perceptions. Resolving differences at this point is a more efficient approach than trying to fix basic design assumptions and errors after the fact—when the project is ready for implementation.

TEAM CONSTITUTION VALIDITY: SUMMARIZING THE PROCESS

Figure 9-4 summarizes the initial process that the knowledge management team must go through before the initial design effort is organized well enough to proceed to the next stage. Examine this process flowchart and determine if your team, as constituted, is collectively able to elicit these requirements and design goals for the knowledge management system.

POINTS OF FAILURE

Let's take a quick look at the key points of failure in systems-oriented KM projects. Perhaps the most important study of project risks is by some colleagues, who examined software project risks in several international companies.[3] In the United States alone, almost $60 billion was spent in cost overruns and another $80 billion in canceled projects in 1995 alone. Although other, more recent figures abound, this is perhaps one of the most rigorous studies done in this area, and the figures proposed here are depressing! An informal study of a group of 2,600 CEOs, CIO, and technology managers by the *Cambridge Information Network* in 1999 revealed that approximately 90 percent of IT projects exceed their budgets and over 20 percent exceed their budgets by more than 100 percent.[b]

THE BREAKPOINT: BUY-IN FAILURE

Lack of an active role of the top management has been identified as the primary reason why many projects fail; and the second reason is failure of the users to buy in to the project. If you decide to invest in a knowledge management project, and either your top management remains unconvinced of the value of the idea or the users you are building it for fail to see why they need the system, you are venturing in murky waters.

---

[b]Figures reported by *Cambridge Information Network*. See results of an Informationweek survey and another CIN survey at www.cin.ctp.com/production/ThinkTank/ROI/roi1.html.

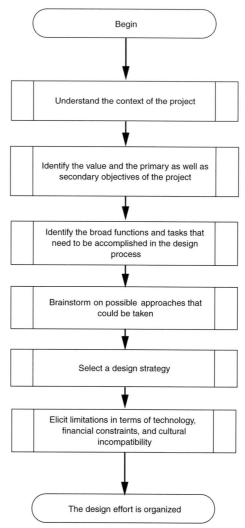

Figure 9-4 The initial stages of the knowledge
management project team work
involve precursory organization of
the design effort.

CATEGORIZING RISKS

Figure 9-5 illustrates the four categories in which knowledge management project risks can be classified. This framework describes four quadrants on which project risk can be classified: the level of risk (high/low) and the level of control that a project manager has on each cate-

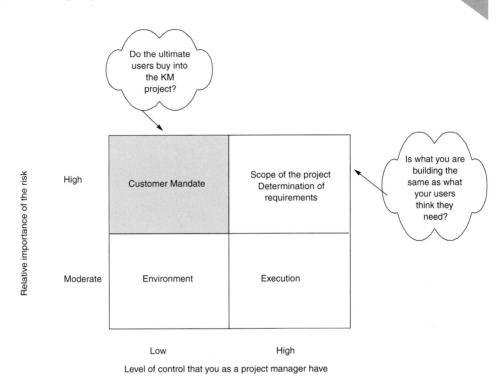

Figure 9-5 Categorizing risks in building the knowledge management system proactively.

gory. Customer mandate, the shaded quadrant, is a high-risk area over which you have little control.

Customer mandate refers to the level of buy-in from the ultimate users, who in effect are your system's customers. Unless they buy in to the whole notion of the knowledge management system that you are building or planning to build, they will have neither the inclination to use it nor support it.

Similarly, initial commitment from the top management is a necessary but insufficient condition for your project's success. This support must be ongoing and active throughout the project. The problem with many of the companies that we have studied often falls into one of these two areas. Once a project has been initiated, the project leader must gauge the level of commitment from both senior management and the end-user community to avoid being caught in a situation where support for the project suddenly evaporates.[4]

CONTROLLING AND BALANCING REQUIREMENTS

As shown in Figure 9-5, there are some areas where you, as the knowledge champion or knowledge management project manager, have significant control. However, there are some areas in which you have little or no control. Not having control over an area does not, by any stretch of imagination, mean that it will not contribute to the potential failure of your project! Customer or end-user buy-in and the environment in which the knowledge management system will be used are two such factors. The only thing you can do about customer buy-in problems is to try selling the project harder, and gauge end-user needs more appropriately; the operating environment is a wholly different story. That is where the cultural aspects of a knowledge management system and the people around it (discussed in Chapter 13) come into play. While all these risks must be thought of together rather than independently, a strong focus must be on the risks over which you have little control.

SOLVING USER BUY-IN PROBLEMS

End-user buy-in problems can be tackled effectively by including representatives from the actual would-be end-user community in the knowledge management team.[5] The scope and requirements of the project can be more in line with what the actual would-be users need, and once they are on your side, you have a few more in your group of KM advocates when it comes to facing senior management. Similarly, management (which eventually ensures a stream of funding for your project) must be actively involved for two reasons:

- To ensure that senior managers *actually* buy into the project
- To ensure that the "bigger-picture" that the management has in mind is well accommodated and incorporated into your design and infrastructural architecture

Some of these risks cannot be controlled by the KM project champion, leader, or team, but you certainly can influence them. Knowledge management initiatives can be trickier than their notoriously political cousin, data warehousing.

LESSONS LEARNED

The fifth step on the knowledge management roadmap involves designing and building an effective knowledge management team. The ultimate goal, after the knowledge management enabling technology and culture are in place, is to encourage every employee to become a manager of knowledge.[6] Employees shouldn't have to think twice before they contribute, use, validate, update, or apply knowledge explicated within and outside the firm. Keep the following lessons in mind while designing a knowledge management team:

- *Identify a few key core stakeholders.* A knowledge management project most go on and continually improve and change with changing external and internal environments. Select a group of people representing IT, management, and the end-user group that will form a core part of your team on a relatively long term basis. Other team members can serve temporarily.

- *Identify sources of requisite expertise.* Sources of expertise representing all divisions or departments that will use the knowledge management system are best drawn from those organizational units. Managerial participants with sufficient knowledge of the company and a clear big picture provide strategic direction for the project.

- *Select a visionary and experienced project leader.* The knowledge management project leader helps members of the team understand the project's mission and align their efforts with the company's overall goals and objectives. The project leader must facilitate the internal functioning of the knowledge management team by helping members objectively resolve differences.

- *Identify critical failure points.* There are some high-risk areas where the knowledge champion has little control: those involving end-user and management support. Make sure that you include representatives from these stakeholder groups to minimize buy-in problems and poor management support in the later stages. Users might necessitate "dangling a convincing carrot" to motivate them to actively participate.

- *Avoid external consultants if possible.* Be warned that due to the nature of the consulting business, your competitor might have a system similar to yours a few months down the road. It might be worth the extra time to train one of your own employees in organizationally lacking skills and legally protecting details of your KM system with nondisclosure agreements.

- *Balance the knowledge management team's managerial and technological structure.* Knowledge management is not solely a technical project, so the project team needs to balance both managerial and technical participants.

In the next chapter, we discuss the design and implementation of the technology infrastructure and architecture for KM.

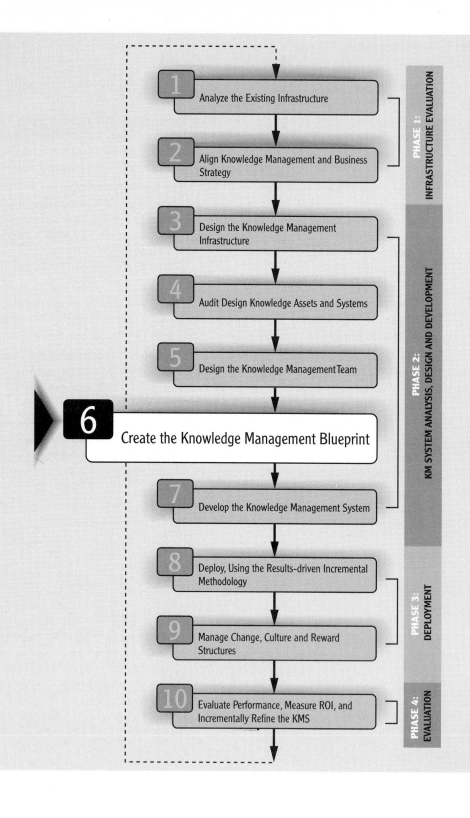

1. Analyze the Existing Infrastructure

2. Align Knowledge Management and Business Strategy

PHASE 1: INFRASTRUCTURE EVALUATION

3. Design the Knowledge Management Infrastructure

4. Audit Design Knowledge Assets and Systems

5. Design the Knowledge Management Team

6. Create the Knowledge Management Blueprint

7. Develop the Knowledge Management System

PHASE 2: KM SYSTEM ANALYSIS, DESIGN AND DEVELOPMENT

8. Deploy, Using the Results-driven Incremental Methodology

9. Manage Change, Culture and Reward Structures

PHASE 3: DEPLOYMENT

10. Evaluate Performance, Measure ROI, and Incrementally Refine the KMS

PHASE 4: EVALUATION

CHAPTER 10

CREATING THE KM SYSTEM BLUEPRINT

HE THAT WOULD PERFECT HIS WORK MUST FIRST SHARPEN HIS TOOLS.

—CONFUCIUS

To remain sustainably competitive, companies must effectively and efficiently create, locate, capture, share their organization's knowledge, and bring that knowledge to bear on new problems and opportunities in a timely manner. Many companies have become so complex that their knowledge is fragmented, extremely difficult to locate and share and therefore inconsistent, redundant, and ignored throughout the decisions that propel the company.[1] This is where a stable knowledge management blueprint fits in perfectly.

To be able to effectively leverage this asset, the knowledge management team identified in Chapter 9 needs to build upon a knowledge management blueprint that provides a roadmap for building and incrementally improving a knowledge management system. This chapter describes step 6 of the 10-step knowledge management roadmap: creating the knowledge management blueprint.

We work toward building a knowledge management architecture, understanding its seven layers specifically in the context of your company, and determining how it can be optimized for performance and scalability as well as high levels of interoperability. We take a closer look at the tradeoffs involved in deciding to build or buy most of the system so that you can make a well-informed choice taking your own company into account. We will also decide upon the components that are needed right from the start.

Knowledge management repository life-cycle management, user interface (UI) considerations, and problem scoping are also described. Finally, we discuss practical design considerations to *future-proof* your knowledge management system.

The best place to begin is by taking account of the explicated knowledge assets that already exist in your company. Declarative, causal, and procedural knowledge broadly falls into this category of explicated knowledge.[2] While explicit knowledge comprises only a minuscule segment of the firm's total knowledge assets, a good knowledge management blueprint also provides for the explication of invaluable tacit knowledge that exists in the minds of its employees. Although tacit knowledge develops naturally as a byproduct of action, it is more easily exchanged, combined, distributed, and managed if it is converted to explicit knowledge. It is toward this end that the knowledge management architecture plays a pivotal role.

ANALYZING LOST OPPORTUNITIES

While prioritizing the explication of knowledge, companies can easily fall into the trap of attempting to explicate knowledge that is not explicable, and failing to explicate knowledge that *should* have been converted from tacit to explicit. Figure 10-1 shows the mistakes that companies often make in deciding on these tradeoffs.

The shaded gray box that represents appropriately leveraged knowledge indicates the correct positioning of a knowledge management system and knowledge management strategy. To give a fitting example, proponents of expert systems believed that it was possible to build a system that could replace human judgment. While this might be possible in theory, it is too often far removed from reality. With unlimited time and money, very few things in this world

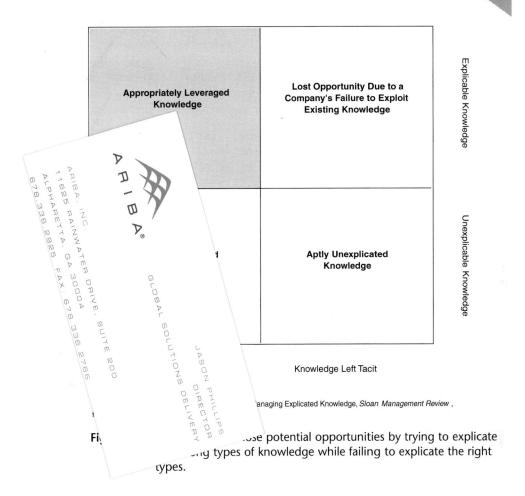

Appropriately Leveraged Knowledge	**Lost Opportunity Due to a Company's Failure to Exploit Existing Knowledge**
	Aptly Unexplicated Knowledge

Explicable Knowledge

Unexplicable Knowledge

Knowledge Left Tacit

...anaging Explicated Knowledge, *Sloan Management Review* ,

Fi...   ...se potential opportunities by trying to explicate
...ng types of knowledge while failing to explicate the right
types.

are impossible.[a] The question that opponents of expert systems have always posed is whether expert systems are worth it. Knowledge management takes a more cautionary position and does not propose that a system will solve your company's knowledge problems by itself. What will, however, is a system that serves as nothing but an enabler (in most cases) for knowledge sharing and that links people, processes, culture, and values of the organization as a whole.

As Figure 10-1 illustrates, knowledge that could have been explicated, shared, distributed, and applied, but was never articulated, represents a lost opportunity due to the failure

---

[a]The CYC project conducted at Microelectronics and Computer Corporation (MCC) in Austin, Texas, was one such attempt that cost millions and took over 10 years before it was realized that this project was too difficult, its goals too lofty, and its benefits too expensive to even try. See www.cyc.com for details on this project. Also see a discussion on CYC later in this chapter.

to leverage this asset. Expert systems often border the unsafe territory of to trying to articulate knowledge that cannot be explicated with the given resource constraints. Resource constraints that are the most deterministic in the process include time, people, and money. Knowledge workers have often seen management take the familiar "add more people" approach to salvage a failing project or effort. As one would expect, this does not work as well in a knowledge-centered work environment as it once did in a mechanistically industrial economy.

THE KNOWLEDGE MANAGEMENT ARCHITECTURE

Information technology is a great enabler for sharing, application, validation, and distribution of knowledge—primarily explicit knowledge. Its weaknesses become apparent when companies try to use the same techniques and systems to leverage tacit knowledge. As I have stressed, the fundamental challenge, given constraints on available resources, is that of determining which knowledge should be made explicit and which is best left tacit. Striking the right balance and arranging priorities in the right order are critical for competitive performance. It would be safe to assume that there is little that IT can do to support tacit knowledge in any way, shape, or form. It provides a channel for the exchange of such tacit knowledge. For the most part, this channel is not rich enough to truly transfer tacit knowledge. However, it can expedite the conversion processes that explicate tacit knowledge from heads to disks!

With that in mind, the knowledge management architecture should be seen as an enabler for knowledge management and not a complete solution: a means and not an end in itself. As we analyze knowledge management architecture design, try to relate it to your own company and see which elements seem to fit your case best.

COMPONENTS OF A KNOWLEDGE MANAGEMENT SYSTEM

A knowledge management system, in its initial stages, can be broken into several subcomponents:

1. *Repositories:* Repositories hold explicated formal and informal knowledge and the rules associated with them for accumulation, refining, managing, validating, maintaining, annotating (adding context), and distributing content.

2. *Collaborative platforms:* Collaborative platforms support distributed work and incorporate pointers, skills databases, expert locators, and informal communications channels.

3. *Networks:* Networks support communications and conversation. These might include hard networks such as your company's leased lines, your intranet, your extranets, and soft networks such as shared spaces, industry-wide firm collaborations, trade nets,

industry forums, and exchanges (both live and teleconferenced). We do not discuss networks in depth here because we started with the assumption that your company already has network infrastructure in place.

4. *Culture:* Cultural enablers to encourage sharing and use of the above. This topic is covered in Chapter 13.

THE KNOWLEDGE REPOSITORY

An information repository differs from a knowledge repository in the sense that the context of the knowledge object needs to be stored along with the content itself. A knowledge platform may consist of several repositories, each with a structure that is appropriate for the particular type of knowledge or content that is stored. Such repositories may be logically linked to form a cohesive consolidated repository. The content of each will provide the context for interpreting the content of other repositories. For example, there might be multiple Lotus Notes databases containing content pertinent to sales, best practices, marketing, etc. However, they can be logically viewed in an integrated manner to provide a composite picture of what is contained within them along with the associated context. Figure 10-2 illustrates how this association is possible.

Repositories such as these should record the following elements of knowledge content:

- *Declarative knowledge* such as significant and meaningful concepts, categories, definitions, and assumptions
- *Procedural knowledge* such as processes, sequences of events and activities, and actions
- *Causal knowledge* such as rationale for decisions, rationale for rejected decisions or alternatives, eventual outcomes of activities, and associated informal pieces
- *Context* of the decision circumstances, assumptions, results of those assumptions, and informal knowledge such as video clips, annotations, notes, and conversations

Subsequent users who access these pieces should be able to add to or modify content. Products such as GrapeVine allow follow-up users to make comments on the usefulness and applicability of incoming external information, for example, content that is distributed on a company intranet.

Well-integrated knowledge repositories do not require the user to know in which repository the knowledge resides. In other words, transparency, as perceived by the user, is highly desirable and very much possible. Other companies actually allow the creators or authors of a knowledge content unit to tag an expiration date to the content. This ensures that content that is no longer valid or content that expires after a certain date is automatically relegated to an *expired* status. If you are making critical decisions based on available information, knowing what is old, outdated, incorrect, or invalid can help you avoid potentially expensive mistakes. Therefore, such tools partially automate maintenance and validation of explicated knowledge within the knowledge management system.

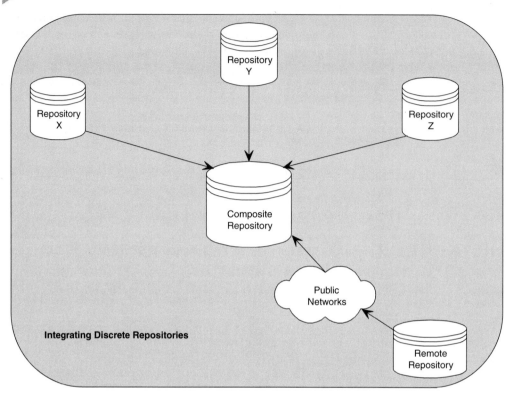

Figure 10-2 Building a composite knowledge repository by integrating multiple knowledge repositories.

The Evils of Integrative Repositories

While integrative repositories might seem like a good idea to begin with, they can be the victims of their own success. As users begin to add content to multiple repositories, and if there is no clear-cut validation or expiration mechanism, a situation similar to an information overload problem can begin to emerge.

A good example is Arthur Andersen Consulting group's KnowledgeSpace™. With the extensive use of the Lotus Notes–based repositories, the extant content has grown into almost 3,000 repositories of Notes discussion databases. If this were one integrated repository, maintenance of these could have been managed better and more efficiently. However, centralized administration is not a viable option for a knowledge management system, since content needs to be added and revalidated by the people who actually use it, not by a central "knowledge administrator." There are plenty of other examples of such problems that arise when companies fail to manage the explicated repository life cycle.

Managing content in repositories should not be limited to adding new content, but throwing out, if you will, old content. Obsolete content must be regularly deleted, less relevant content must be archived. What is left must be "defragmented" to eliminate redundancies, combine similar contributions, generalize content for smoother reuse, and possibly restructure classification mechanisms and tag handles. Companies that want their knowledge management system to succeed must proactively maintain their knowledge repositories instead of waiting for signs of noticeable decline in quality. Reactivity is of little help if invalid or outright obsolete content influences a critical, irreversible decision.

While centralizing the storage is a viable possibility and perhaps the way to go if you are building such a repository from scratch, you must ensure that the power of content and context management ultimately lies in the hands of its users, not the centralized technology maintenance staff. This would also necessitate a capable, high-bandwidth communications network connecting the entire enterprise in a reliable manner.

If you already have some repositories to begin with or if the platforms in use are too diverse to physically integrate cost effectively, you might simply rely on a Web-based front end to integrate existing repositories while building new ones on a centralized base.

Content Centers

When you are trying to integrate multiple repositories into one central repository, pay close attention to content centers that are typically good candidates for integration. Examples of such content centers include:

- Production department
- Customer services
- Market intelligence and competitive planning
- Employee resources and the human resources department
- Administrative department
- Sales and marketing
- Finance
- Business partners and suppliers

A wide variety of relevant information is publicly available in electronic form. A sample checklist for competitive knowledge, provided below, is an example of a good starting point. Such checklists can be useful for making sure that existing and available sources are tapped into.

1. What are others saying about your competition?
    - *Public:* case studies, articles, newspapers, consultants, employee search firms, and consumer groups
    - *Trade and professional organizations:* trade publications, industry news, customers, users, vendors, suppliers, and professional organizations
    - *Investors and government agencies:* securities analysts, industry data, government agencies and litigation information sources

2. What is your competition saying about themselves?

    • *Public:* advertising, promotional material, articles, employment advertisements and press releases

    • *Trade and professional organizations:* licenses, manuals, patents, and trade shows

    • *Investors:* Annual reports, stock issues, and annual meetings

Open and Distributed

The use of open systems ensures that employees can obtain information they need from any place and at any time. Adherence to industry standards ranging from HTML, XML, TCP/IP protocols, and ODBC means that you can implement the knowledge management system quickly, and easily extend and customize it in the future. As content might be distributed across multiple platforms, devices, servers, and locations, the ability of the knowledge management system to build upon this characteristic is crucial.

XML (extended markup language), notably, will play a dominant role that will eventually supersede HTML, for two reasons: (1) XML's extensive tagging features can reduce the load on back end servers, and on the network itself, (2) XML can interoperate easily with middleware servers.[3]

Knowledge Aggregation and Mining

As anyone who has used a search engine on the Internet can tell you, simple keyword searches often result in a meaninglessly large number of *hits.* To save users from this boo, a well-designed knowledge management system should include a mechanism to appropriately cluster search results in different prespecified content categories as specified in the knowledge map discussed in Chapter 7. The user can drill down into a relevant category without having to learn the subtleties of complex query languages and syntaxes. If clustering is deployed, it should be done using multiple methods. One such method could be content categories; others could be source, date, author, department, and other company-specific taxonomies.

Although information retrieval tools and relevancy rankings still fall short of the requirements, a number of commercial tools based on pattern recognition, agent-based retrieval, and thesauri *almost* make the mark. For example, if a user is looking for "knowledge management consulting," the system should be able to figure out what he *means* rather than report all keyword hits. When using the term *knowledge management consulting,* the user could potentially be looking for information on consultants, knowledge management in consulting practices, reports by consulting companies, or knowledge and management consulting, among others. A simple but effective approach for a knowledge management system, for example, could be to respond with all of these possible choices and ask the user which of those options she *means.* The user should have the ultimate choice of method. Similarly, knowledge mining and Web farming techniques can be deployed, as discussed in Chapters 5 and 7.

From Skills Databases to Knowledge Directories

Companies such as Microsoft have traditionally relied on skills databases to locate subject matter experts both within and outside their organizational bounds. While such a mechanism is useful, it needs to be kept up to date. For this extra bit of effort required of users and for a lack of incentive to put that effort in, skills databases in most companies have been notoriously unsuccessful. A knowledge directory takes the concept underlying skills databases one step further by linking people to their skills, experiences, know-how, insights, and contributions to discussions and debates within the knowledge management system. Such a knowledge directory can infer what an employee knows, based on the knowledge that he shares and contributes. This automation also overcomes the overreliance on manual updates to keep skills databases current and arguably helps match employees with their interests and not just past work experience.

Automated Categorization

As we discussed in Chapter 7, each contribution of knowledge should contain relevant meta data or tags that associate it with the broad category under which it falls. Categorization need not be a manual procedure and often can be accomplished, in part, by knowing the nature of the contribution, such as its context, source, and originator. GrapeVine (www.grapevine.com) is an excellent commercial tool that can help with such categorization. With the availability of context, some meta data can be tagged automatically.

Personalized Content Filtering and Push Delivery

Personalized content filtering refers to the process of categorizing items by their content: images, video, sound, text, etc. A user profile defines the content *types* that are relevant to each user. Different tools use different techniques to create such profiles. The tools range from a simple registration process (where a user check marks areas of interest) through the entire spectrum to determine profiling information by clustering bookmarks (which raises some privacy concerns) or browsing habits. These profiles can then be automatically updated through automatic refinement and derivation by statistical learning algorithms that many commercial packages use. Marimba, Netscape, BackWeb, and Pointcast offer products in this area.

The limitation of such tools is that most of them need high bandwidth that remote connections, such as dial-up telephone lines, lack. Broadband access might change this scenario to one more viable for the deployment of content push technologies. Much can be learned from Amazon.com (as well as CDNow.com) and the way it keeps track of its customers' interests based on past purchases. Like anything else, the effectiveness of this mechanism depends on the level of accuracy with which the underlying assumptions work. Amazon.com, for example, assumes that you are buying books that you are interested in (which is often the case!). When you visit that site again, it recommends new books that are of a similar nature or fall within a broad category as your previous purchases. When you browse books, the site often makes recommendations like *"Since you are interested in X you might also be interested in Y"* or *"Other people who bought books by XYZ also bought books by DEF."*

A similar method can be emulated in the design of knowledge management systems. Users who look for information on a certain topic can, for example, automatically have that topic added to their profiles.

Another excellent implementation that has a lot to teach is the Reveal™ search service (uncweb.carl.org/reveal/) provided by UnCover Corporation. Although this site is primarily of interest to academics and researchers, its design has a number of useful tips for KM system push delivery design in general. Subscribers can specify up to 25 searches for an annual fee. The service then automatically searches through new issues of 17,000 different journals and reports matches to the user periodically by sending an e-mail message. A similar idea could be used in a knowledge management system to report new relevant additions to the company's explicated repository. Variations from delivery time frames and criteria can be easily implemented. Each user can then receive pointers to new content added both to the explicated knowledge repository and to the more tacit sources such as new employee skills and discussions.

THE COLLABORATIVE PLATFORM

The collaborative platform, along with the communications network services and hardware, provides the pipeline to enable the flow of explicated knowledge, its context, and the medium for conversations. Besides this, the collaborative platform provides a surrogate channel for defining, storing, moving, and linking digital objects, such as conversation threads that correspond to knowledge units. The collaborative platform enables the content of the knowledge management system with a high degree of flexibility so that it is rendered meaningful, useful, and applicable across the many possible contexts of use (and abuse). Most importantly, the collaborative platform empowers the user. The user can either search for content—the pull approach to content delivery—or subscribe to content, that is, have content pushed to her.

Collaborative Filtering

Sharing of knowledge through peer recommendations is a widely used mechanism for distributing information.[b] Collaborative filtering can be built into a knowledge management system by deploying one of two possible mechanisms:

1. *Active filtering:* Users manually define filters and pointers to interesting content and share them across their work group.

2. *Automated filtering:* Statistical algorithms make recommendations based on correlations between the user's personal preferences and content ratings. Content ratings can either be generated automatically (such as those produced by measuring the average time all readers spent on reading the item) or by manually assigning an average rating (aggregated across multiple readers).

Firefly, GroupLens, GrapeVine, and Tapestry are some better-known examples of such collaborative filtering tools.

---

[b]*CIO* magazine (www.cio.com), for example, prints an extra "FYI flap" to encourage readers to pass on special supplements to its magazine to colleagues and friends. Readers can make a note (annotation) or cite page numbers (pointers) that they would recommend to their colleagues.

Community-Centered Collaborative Filtering

Automated collaborative filtering might seem to be a reasonable approach, but it will not provide the expected benefits or gain a sufficiently high level of commitment from its users if it ignores the community that it is built for. Separation of automated filtering from personal relationships limits its usefulness to a greater degree than one might expect.[4] The network of existing social relationships between employees can be a valuable basis for improving the collaborative filtering process. While anonymity of contributors is essential, anonymous reviews tend to carry less weight than signed ones do. This is especially true in collaborative communities where people know colleagues by name and reputation.[5] Reputation, trust, and reciprocity come into the picture of collaborative process enhancers when contributions are (optionally) signed.

Meta Knowledge

Meta knowledge implies *knowing what you know.* When a request for information is sent to a computer-based repository or database, the system has no way of determining whether the information is known or present in its memory. For example, if a traditional database is confronted with a request for information on two customers, only one of which exists in the database, the system will have to exhaustively search through all records before it can determine whether a record on the missing customer exists in the database. In the same vein, when a company is faced with an incoming glut of information, confusion often surrounds the determination of the presence or absence of that information. In other words, there is little that the company can do to figure out whether that information represents something truly new or unknown.

New information can often result in strategic redirection of work processes. However, if a company cannot determine this redirection fast enough, as is often the case, it might be too late to act or make relevant changes to work processes.

Creation of meta knowledge is often extremely context dependent and requires the use of pattern recognition or analogical reasoning. Being able to extract meta knowledge from knowledge is a necessary characteristic of an effective knowledge management system.

Accommodating Multiple Degrees of Context

The effective use of IT tools requires that an organization share an interpretive context.[6] The higher the degree to which such a similar background, experience and context is shared by people working together, the more effective is the use of such technology enablers. If this were the requirement for effective sharing of knowledge through such a knowledge management system, then most companies should have a reason to panic. Most companies build upon cross-functional teams—people with differing backgrounds, areas of expertise, organizational affiliations, and culture to solve problems, make decisions, and develop new products and services. In work groups where context is not well shared, knowledge tends to be primarily tacit in nature. Therefore, the significance of rich communications channels and a high degree of interactivity cannot be overemphasized. If loose social bonding exists between potential users of the system, ensure that rich communications (video conferencing, voice, multimedia support, and informal channels) are built into your knowledge management system as an integrated feature, not as a separate add-on component. In other words, make sure that it is a design feature and not merely an afterthought.

Technology Choices

When choosing a technology or a vendor, it is vital to consider whether that technology or that vendor will be around for the entire life of the system. Many other questions come up as well:

- Will the vendor's technology capture enough of the market to ensure that ancillary products and services remain available?
- Can the technology deliver the consistency that the application requires?
- Can the technology provide the quality that the market and your customers demand?

Companies have, time and again, floundered in making good decisions when the basis of those decisions, especially technology choice decisions, was solely existing market leadership of those choices. Even the IBM slogan "Nobody gets fired for choosing IBM," begins to fade here. IBM is good at most things it does, but does that always mean that buying your company's PCs from IBM was the best decision? Netscape invented the modern-day browser, but does that mean that ensuring 100% compatibility with Netscape HTML standards is the best choice? The best-in-its-class technologies do no good if the provider loses the standards battle against a competitor, especially when standards differ significantly.

The Web, though evolving, seems to be a technology that promises to be around for a while. HTML will most likely be superseded by backward compatible successors. As we saw in Chapter 7, the Web provides the capability required to build a collaborative platform on which a rich multimedia repository for explicit knowledge and an informal communications channel for *conversation making*[c] can be firmly established. A Web-based collaborative platform can provide a high degree of customizability by assigning labels, categories, and tags to links to each unit of knowledge as it is added to the system. Such a structure provides flexibility in the use of links and indices that reflect the structure of contextual knowledge and the content of factual knowledge artifacts of the organization (or organizational unit), displayed as flexible subsets collated through dynamically generated views.[d]

DESIGNING INTEGRATIVE AND INTERACTIVE KNOWLEDGE APPLICATIONS

At a high level, a knowledge management application set can be viewed from two angles of functionality. The first view is the *integrative* view and the second is the *interactive* view. Both these viewpoints must be satisfied *simultaneously* to provide a requisite broad set of knowledge processing and management capabilities.

---

[c]The term *conservation making* was coined by Choo Wei in 1996.

[d]Dynamically collated views of content can be generated through Web pages generated on the fly, for example, and viewed through a Web browser.

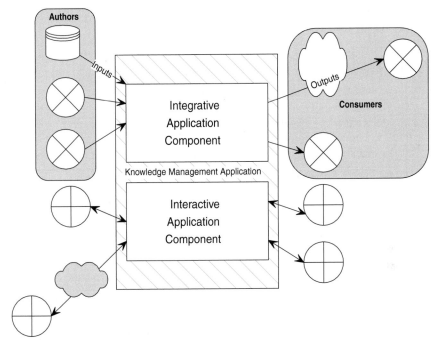

Figure 10-3 A knowledge management application needs both integrative and interactive capabilities to provide the richness of media required for effective knowledge processing.

The integrative ability, as illustrated in Figure 10-3, supports the collation of distributed knowledge repositories containing explicated or explicitly captured content. The difference between explicated and explicitly captured content is a subtle yet important one. Explicated content is content that has been codified or formalized for storage in conventional repositories such as databases. Examples include project timelines, presentation overheads, memos, and code documentation. Explicitly captured content could include a recording of a manager's talk or a product designer's vision of a product. This type of content might have been recorded in a system, but its context might not have been recorded[7] or might be subject to multiple, incompatible interpretations.

Support for interactivity is required to allow the integration and possible capture, analysis or even explication of tacit knowledge of the system's users (who are sometimes called knowledge authors).

We next discuss the integrative and interactive components, then we fit them into place in the overall architecture on which we are basing our blueprint.

INTEGRATIVE APPLICATION SUPPORT

The integrative component of a knowledge management system helps users in critically evaluating, interpreting, and adapting knowledge to new contexts, domains, and applications. Integrative applications, as Figure 10-3 shows, support sequential flow of explicated knowledge in and out of the repository. The integrative application component provides a shared medium for knowledge exchange where members of the user community (e.g., company employees and partners) share, see, and contribute their knowledge, task experiences, and views. The authors and consumers, therefore, directly interact with this application rather than with each other.[e] As Figure 10-3 clarifies, this component focuses on the explicit knowledge that can be put into and stored within the repository and not on the tacit knowledge that the authors and consumers possess. The authors are often also the consumers of knowledge, and their positions are often interchangeable, depending on their current activity and direction of knowledge flows they are engaged in. Integrative functionality in a knowledge management system provides the key centripetal force that pulls together all explicated knowledge assets that a company has.

Knowledge Flow Models: Centripetality and Centrifugality

Let us compare that model to the concepts underlying electronic publishing. Electronic publishing follows a *centrifugal* model unlike KM's *centripetal* model. This conceptual difference is illustrated in Figure 10-4. In electronic publishing,[8] consumers rarely fall into the same community of practice or work group as the authors. Content, in that case, tends to be relatively stable, and further additions to it are made solely by the knowledge authors. The consumer accepts the content on an as-is basis and, in some cases, might be allowed and able to provide feedback to the knowledge author(s). In this sense, intranets have traditionally been closer to electronic publishing than knowledge management. Companies have posted reports, files, memos, and directories to intranets in a way that is quite similar to electronic content publishing.[f]

THE INTERACTIVE APPLICATION COMPONENT

The integrative components of a knowledge management system primarily support codified and explicitly captured knowledge. However, as we have seen in earlier chapters, the tacit component must be effectively supported if effective knowledge transfer and sharing are to take place and the explicated content is to retain its proper context.

The interactive component therefore focuses on enabling interaction among people and providing a basic channel for sharing tacit knowledge. In such a component, building or

---

[e]This is not to say that direct interactions are unnecessary or insignificant.

[f]Examples of electric content publishing include electronic versions of magazines (www.zdnet.com, www.ntmag.com, www.fortune.com) and newspapers (www.ajc.com, www.nytimes.com, www.sanjosemercurynews.com, www.mercurycenter.com etc.), besides company intranets.

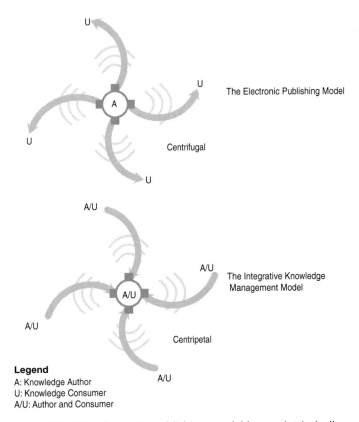

The Electronic Publishing Model

Centrifugal

The Integrative Knowledge
Management Model

Centripetal

Legend
A: Knowledge Author
U: Knowledge Consumer
A/U: Author and Consumer

Figure 10-4 The electronic publishing model has an intrinsically
centrifugal design where knowledge consumers,
denoted by U, view knowledge created by the
author(s), represented by A. The knowledge management integrative approach is, in contrast, centripetal.

enhancing the repository is not the primary focus. Development of content within the repository is a (secondary) byproduct of the collaborative work that it enables.[g]

Such applications can vary from relatively structured to totally unstructured depending
on the levels of expertise and similarities between the authors and consumers (acting interchangeably). Toward the more structured types of deployments are Web-based forums and
specialized discussion groups. Such forums consist of the same group of participants compris-

---

[g]Researchers such as Michael Zack, Nonaka, and Tom Davenport have referred to this as distributed
learning.

ing the set of content authors who are also the consumers (see Figure 10-5). Moving toward the somewhat totally unstructured type application deployments are video conferencing tools and like technologies. Technology elements such as electronic whiteboards fall some where in between. Forums, including live text/video-based ones, are the most complex types of applications because of their high level of interactivity and their inherent characteristic of spanning the entire tacit and explicit knowledge processing cycle.

As interaction complexity rises, your challenge is to make the interactive knowledge management components of a system more social, cognitive, and behavioral, and less technical in focus. We must, therefore, create a flexible knowledge management system blueprint and customize it to make room for future changes.

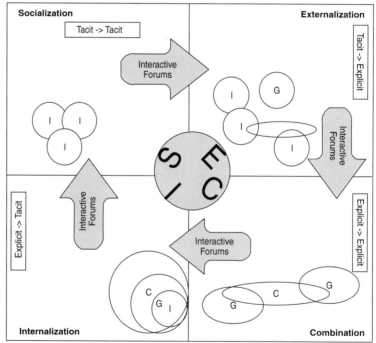

Legend

C: Company's Knowledge
G: Group or Team Knowledge
I: Individual Employee's Knowledge
Based on Nonaka Reinmoeller, et al. (1998). The ART of Knowledge: Systems to Capitalize on Market Knowledge, *European Management Journal* 16(6), 673-684.

Figure 10-5 Rich media forums that run through high-bandwidth networks often tend to be the most complex knowledge interaction applications, since they span the entire knowledge cycle.

THE FIT INTO OVERALL ARCHITECTURE

To see how the integrative and interactive components fit into our architecture, let us review the seven layers (see Figure 10-6) before looking deeper.

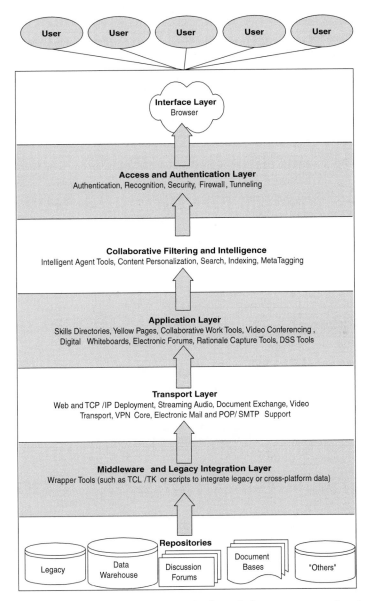

Figure 10-6 The seven layers in the knowledge management system architecture.

The knowledge management architecture consists of seven layers as shown in Figure 10-6. Each layer is described in detail in Chapters 11 and 12, and we are already acquainted with the first and third layers (see Chapter 7). For now, let's examine how this architecture meets the requirements set forth in the preceding sections of this chapter.

Figure 10-7 shows the generic system architecture. The knowledge management system deployment initiative assumes that you already have a corporate network in place. The knowledge management applications will go one layer above this existing architecture. The shaded components in Figure 10-7 indicate the components of the system architecture that must be modified to build a knowledge management system.

The middleware architecture is modified to incorporate applications that otherwise might not *talk* to each other, into a tightly integrated system. The repository architecture includes all existing databases.

Figure 10-8 shows how the dimensions of the overall system architecture can be viewed for modification.

As the integrative component of a knowledge management system comes into play, the overall effect on the existing system components is visible in the level of integration that is provided. In this case, the clients can be located anywhere and can connect to the enterprise through a universally initiated network connection (see Figure 10-9). The effects of the interactive components are further reaching.

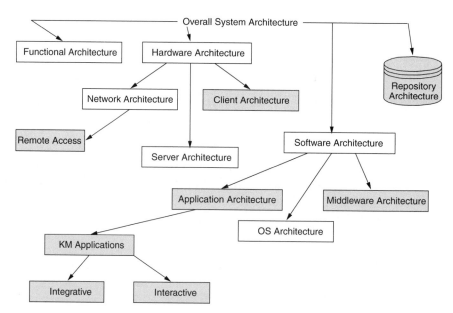

Figure 10-7 Architectural components (shown shaded) to be modified or expanded to integrate the KM system with the existing architecture.

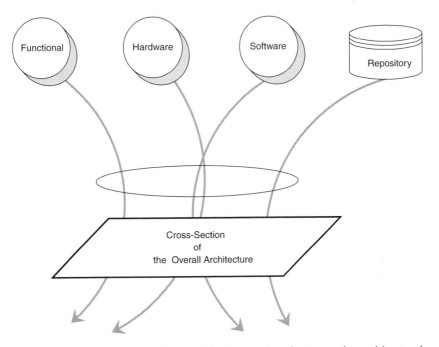

Figure 10-8 A cross-sectional view of the interactions between the architectural components.

BUILD OR BUY?

If you run a for-profit business, in most likelihood, you have both time and resource constraints under which you are expected to run the show. While building a knowledge management system can often be the best, albeit more expensive, way to go, customizing an off-the-shelf system is usually a faster alternative. When you begin development, your choices are:

- To build a system in-house, using team members from the internal IT department and the end-user community of knowledge workers for whom the system is being built
- To add external consultants to strengthen the weaker expertise areas for the option described above
- To develop the system from scratch (not recommended)
- To buy an off-the-shelf, shrink-wrapped solution such as Lotus Notes and customize its installation

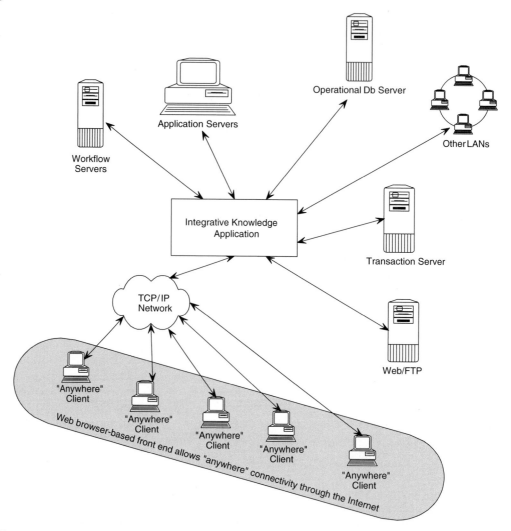

Figure 10-9 The composite enterprise as viewed after the integrative knowledge management applications are introduced.

- To buy an off-the-shelf solution sold by a consulting group and modify it to meet your needs
- To buy and combine an off-the-shelf set of applications and customize it to fit your needs
- To build in part, and buy in part
- A combination of the above approaches

Customization, for example, as is the case with most ERP packages such as SAP R/3, can go deeper than the front end. In addition, many commercial applications discussed in Chapter 16 and on the companion CD allow a reasonable degree of configuration flexibility.

Your decision will be influenced by the time, resources, and money at your disposal. The size of the end-user group will also influence the make-or-buy decision. If you are a small company with under a hundred employees, financial considerations might force you to take the off-the-shelf option. However, if there is serious support for the project right from the beginning or if you are a larger company, you should consider doing at least a part of the development in-house and plugging in the rest of the components. With powerful Web development tools that are now available, the development of the intranet-based front end need not be a pain. Table 10-1 compares the options that are available.

INTEROPERABILITY CONSIDERATIONS

When you are selecting the components on which you will build the knowledge management system, pay requisite attention to the interoperability between them. Some of the standards to keep an eye on include:

- *Electronic mail:* SMTP, X.400 Post Office Protocol (POP) server support.
- *Video conferencing:* H.323 and H.324 standards.
- *Documents:* RTF (Rich Text Format) is the lowest common denominator format that needs to be supported. Many companies have standardized on a single office suite such as Microsoft Office or Lotus SmartSuite. For Web-based, read-only documents, portable document format (PDF) is usually a safe bet. A number of word processors, notably Office 2000, are standardizing on rich HTML formats, which of course, can be read on any platform through any browser client.
- *Data access:* SQL and ODBC support is highly desirable.
- *Internet:* HTTP and FTP support is a requisite, and is rarely omitted. XML functionality is worthy of consideration.
- *Audio:* Wave file and audio streaming support enable wide distribution of digitized audio.

PERFORMANCE AND SCALABILITY

Scalability refers to the ability of the knowledge management system to support an increasing number of users and a higher load of transactions. It is essential that a system be scalable well beyond the original level if the number of users is expected to grow as system use becomes more prevalent. This is especially true if you decide to build a knowledge management system from off-the-shelf components. A system that performs well within a work group of limited size might not perform well when it is extended to an enterprise-wide level. An obvious but

Table 10-1 Making the Build-or-Buy Decision

Option	Upfront Cost	Quality of Solution	Time to develop	Flexibility	Customizability	Notes
Customized in-house development	High	Depends	High	High	High	Quality can vary. Depends on the expertise available within the company.
Customized in-house development with consulting support	High	Depends; better than above	Medium	High	High	Quality can vary. The skills of the consultant can influence the project. Costs will be higher. There is a risk that the same consultant may develop a similar system for a competitor. Contractual agreements are needed to prevent this.
Customized solution provided by a consulting company	Medium	Average	Low	Medium	Medium	Your competitors might already have the same systems!
Development by the end users themselves	Usually low	Usually low	Depends	High	High	Not recommended.
Standard off-the-shelf and out-of-the-box solution	Low	High	Zero	Low	Low	The only time investment required is the installation time.
Customized off-the-shelf solution	Medium	High	Low	Medium to low	Medium	This should be among your first set of choices.
Off-the-shelf components integrated through an intranet	Low	High	Low	Extremely High	Extremely high	This should be your first choice!

frequently ignored issue, scalability can make the knowledge management system a victim of its own success if it comes in as an afterthought.

Scalability also affects performance of the system at later stages. Keep the following set of key performance-related factors in mind when you are deciding on the design of a knowledge management system:

1. *Plan and account for additional time delays as usage grows.* Time delays for retrieval of information from a message or transaction database must be kept to a minimum. As the number of users grows, failure on this front might result in unacceptable delays in responses to even the simplest queries.

2. *Keep repository update times in perspective.* Time for updates and inserts of new records into the database or repository must be kept to a minimum.

3. *Keep time delays for navigating between different parts of the interface to a minimum.* For example, it should *not* take a minute for dialog boxes to reappear when a user switches from a messaging application to a bulletin board application. Two to three seconds, as a rule of thumb, is a longest acceptable delay for localized applications. This delay should not be significantly higher when a slower connection such as a dial-up networking channel is used.

USER INTERFACE DESIGN CONSIDERATIONS

Several design features of the user interface need to be considered. Without an effective user interface, even the best knowledge management system is bound to fail.

- *Functionality:* The idea behind a user interface is to allow users to accomplish their tasks quickly, effectively, *and without frustration* over the system's usability. The system needs to take the end user's needs and requirements into consideration. A terrible example of a highly redundant interface is that of Netscape's popular browser. It uses both graphical icons and text to identify buttons (this setting can be changed); however, the icons are not very easily recognizable by themselves, nor are they exceptionally intuitive.

   Make sparing use of graphical icons if they do not add to the usability of the system. If possible, let the users pick their icons. If you do use icons, make sure that they are big and bold so that users with high screen resolutions can easily identify them.[h]

- *Consistency:* Systems that have a consistent interface are often considered easier to use. A good example is Microsoft Office 2000 and its predecessor, Office 97. The

---

[h]Many users, including me, prefer very high screen resolutions. Icons are not easily distinguishable at resolutions beyond 1,024 x 768 pixels.

word processor, spreadsheet, database, and presentation tool in this software suite use a consistent set of menus and buttons that have the same meaning across the entire tool set. Similarly, there should be consistency across all parts of the knowledge management system in the way(s) in which information is presented, accessed, and used.

- *Visual clarity:* Users need to be able to easily find information that they need. Present all information that relates to the user's task on one screen if possible and hide unrelated information or controls by default. Have sufficient white space on the screen and use lowercase text for textually dense portions of the interface. This not only makes the text easier to read but also decreases search time. Serif fonts look good on paper, but they are more difficult to read on a screen. Use a nonserif font if you use a small point size for screen text. Use hyperlinks to provide further information on a text string to avoid excessive cluttering on a screen. Avoid excessive jargon or abbreviations that can change meaning from one user to another.

- *Navigation and control:* The way in which information is structured has a clear impact on its accessibility. A site map can be *very* useful with a browser-based front end. If there are multiple tools within the knowledge management system, the user should be able to tell which tool she is using at a given moment. Avoid using multiple modes of operation, and have one shared interface to all underlying applications such as messaging, document repository navigation, and discussion forums. Audible cues can be helpful as long as they are not overused or distracting.

- *Relevancy:* Display only the information relevant to the user's task. This might be a tricky scheme to implement, since there will be as many preferences as there are users, so allow users to customize their interface to a certain degree.

- *Feedback:* The system's users should receive feedback from the system so that they know what the system is doing and what is expected (from either the system or the user) next. Audible cues and alerts can be very useful here. Avoid using excessive dialog boxes that require the user to click on an OK button incessantly. Interactive intelligent agents can be useful feedback enablers, but they come with their own threats. Excessive feedback mechanisms using interactive agents similar to those introduced in Microsoft Word 97 might only irritate users and restrict their ability to use the system. Lotus SmartSuite and the Mac OS are good examples of systems where feedback mechanisms are useful and unobtrusive. Figure 10-10 shows an example of the implementation of one such feedback mechanism.

A NETWORK VIEW OF THE KM ARCHITECTURE

You should also take the time to consider the knowledge management system from a network design perspective. The term *network* should not be confused with the idiosyncratic communications network in the generic sense. An alternative view of the knowledge management system architecture described in Figure 10-6 is provided in Figure 10-11.

Figure 10-10 Context-specific feedback and help in pop-up balloons are considered unobtrusive by many users. The example shown here is from Lotus SmartSuite.

The network constitutes both the technological network and the underlying social and organizational network in which the technology operates. As Figure 10-11 shows, the entire knowledge management system can be viewed as a networked whole, comprising data sources, information exchange enabling networks, knowledge flow channels, static and mobile intelligent agents, and integrative technologies that bind them all together.

Nevertheless, the technical aspects of the knowledge network design should be kept in focus. Optimize network usage by paying close attention to the implementation of technologies that support compression (for large files, teleconferencing and voice), byte-level differential updating (for document and content versioning/updates), and multithreaded communications (for discussion groups and Web forums). However, those are still just the technical aspects of the design.

Although this view can be used for planning the underlying network requirements, it is too simplistic to base your company's knowledge management architecture on. However, the presence of collaborative tools in almost every element of this knowledge network hierarchy reinforces the importance of enabling rich collaboration through the system, whereby users can add contextual information to the artifacts and elements in the KM system. Examples of such features include the ability to add notes, markings, annotations, and marginal notes on documents, and the ability to track and maintain multiple versions of documents as they are

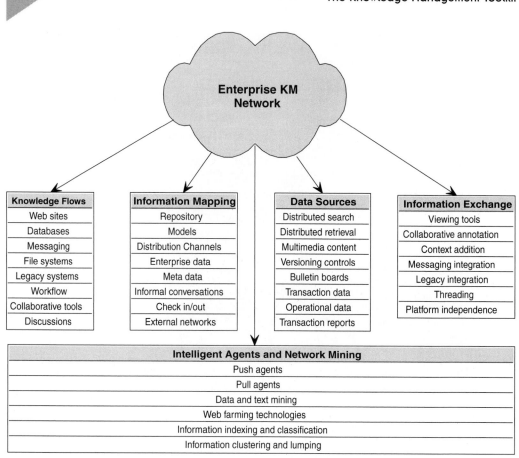

Figure 10-11 A network-oriented view of the knowledge management system.

collaboratively exchanged. As business needs evolve, the components within this network might change, but the overall structure of the network should remain relatively stable; it is an indicator of the stability of the infrastructure itself.

If we classified the knowledge management system within the hierarchy of the IT infrastructure, as suggested by Peter Weill and Marianne Broadbent,[9] it should broadly fall under the category of shared IT applications and services, as shown in Figure 10-12. These are applications and infrastructural elements that remain relatively stable over time even as the deployed applications evolve.

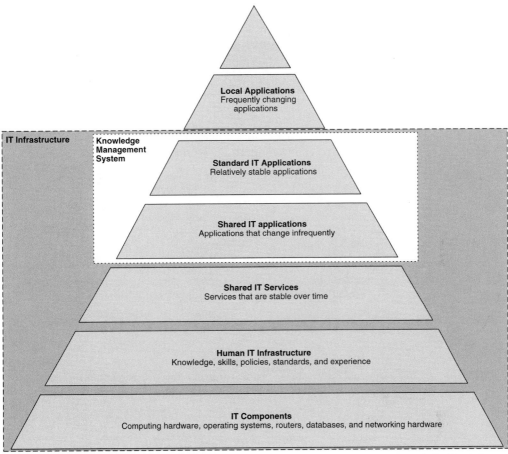

Based on an adapted extension of the infrastructure design suggested by Peter Weill and Marianne Broadbent in Leveraging the New Infrastructure: How Market Leaders Capitalize on Information Technology Harvard Business School Press, Boston, Massachusetts, (1998), page 86.

Figure 10-12 The knowledge management system falls in the infrastructural portion of the information technology architecture.

FUTURE-PROOFING THE KNOWLEDGE MANAGEMENT SYSTEM

Collaborative knowledge management systems should be able to grow and adapt to changing business needs. Keep the following tips in mind while making the key design decisions on your company's knowledge management system.

BUILDING CYC: HAL'S LEGACY OR A SHATTERED DREAM?

Cycorp, Inc., based in Austin, Texas, is the leading supplier of formalized common sense tools. Its CYC software has been under development since 1984 by AI pioneer Doug Lenat. The CYC product family comprises an immense multicontextual knowledge base, an efficient inference engine, a set of interface tools, and a number of special-purpose application modules running on UNIX, Windows NT, and other platforms. The knowledge base is built upon a core of over one million hand-entered assertions or rules designed to capture a large portion of what we normally consider consensus knowledge about the world.

The project originally began with MCC's ambition to create an artificial intelligence tool with general knowledge at the level of an average human being. The idea was to create a program, CYC, with common sense. The team would "prime the knowledge pump" by handcrafting and spoon-feeding CYC with a couple of million important facts and rules of thumb. The goal was to give CYC enough knowledge by 1995 to enable it to learn more by means of natural language conversations and reading, and by 2000, to have it learning on its own by automated-discovery methods guided by minitheories of the real world. After millions of dollars and over 10 years of work by dozens of Ph.D.'s, the CYC project only brought us to the realization that even creating common sense (not intelligence) equaling that of an average human being was close to impossible. Things that you and I simply "know" are things that CYC had to be taught through complex rules—millions of them. For example, CYC had to be taught that:

- Once people die, they stop buying things.
- Trees are usually outdoors.
- Glasses containing liquids should be carried right side up.

Details on what is considered one of the most ambitious project ever carried out by the artificial intelligence community can be found on the spin-off company's Website at www.cyc.com; it's worth a look. Although the dream of AI has not been realized, CYC has found some interesting applications in the business world. The moral: Tacit knowledge is occasionally best left tacit. Don't get too caught up trying to convert all tacit knowledge into explicit knowledge: It's neither possible nor feasible—even with unlimited resources, time and money (as CYC demonstrates). Your blueprint should therefore reflect the scope of the knowledge management system that you are trying to build.

1. *The intranet is king.* One thing companies can count on is that technology will change.[10] What might be state of the art today might be outdated long before you recoup your investment. The standards underlying Internet-based systems inherently have a high degree of modularity and extensibility. Use the Internet/intranet approach where feasible. That way your knowledge management system will still be in business if the vendor that supplies the proprietary technology you use goes out of business. This approach also allows smooth integration with outside systems that might not be using the same software as you.

2. *Business drivers:* Commercial knowledge is very close in concept to what the French call *bricolage:*[i] the provisional construction of a messy array of rules, tools, heuristics, and guidelines that produce according to the expertise and sensitivity of the *craftsman,* not the empirical accuracy of the rules, tools, and guidelines. This notion implies that the people who use a knowledge management system are the ones who create value out of it, or collusively decide to let it die. Focusing on the properties of technology independent of its identified needs is a recipe for failure.[11] Technology design must be driven by business objectives, problems, and opportunities. In other words, keep the design of your knowledge management system *mission focused.*[j]

3. *Separation of push:* Implement push technology as a layer *above* the basic knowledge management infrastructure. This approach will keep your system maintainable if a certain push standard goes out of favor.

4. *RDI and OO methodology:* Use object-oriented techniques for components that you decide to build in-house. First, doing so allows a certain degree of flexibility that might be needed to adapt the system to changes in business structure and processes. Second, the techniques enable reuse of some of the components and processes in other implementations. In addition to OO, use a results-driven—incremental deployment process to expand the knowledge management system. Chapter 12 describes the RDI methodology.

5. *Common standards:* Stick to standards that have the highest level of industry support. Using a vanilla intranet-based design is a better choice than using a proprietary technology such as Lotus Notes. This practice also keeps costs down in the long run. It also enables better integration of work tools and prevents the creation of useless *islands of information and technology.*[k]

---

[i] This association was introduced by Marc Demarest in Understanding Knowledge Management, *Long Range Planning,* vol. 30, no. 3 (1997), 374–384.

[j] A study of 31 different KM projects identified a link to industry performance or value as a critical success factor. See Thomas Davenport, David DeLong, and Michael Beers, Successful Knowledge Management Projects, *Sloan Management Review,* vol. 39, no. 2 (1998), 43–57.

[k] Adherence to standards has sparked off many industry disasters. Apple's LISA and more recently its NEXT platforms died an early death due to the high cost and lack of a commonly acceptable standard (NEXT was significantly different from both Windows and MacOS). This standards war is also extensively witnessed in the hand-held computing model with PalmOS (which is, arguably, superior) and Windows CE (which integrates well with the ubiquitous Windows platform and is supported by Microsoft) vying for the dominant piece of the cake.

6. *Users:* Keep your users on the forefront. Make sure that users are not only actively involved in the future refinements of the system, but also in the initial design and prototyping stages. Failure to gain their buy-in can potentially lead to the lack of acceptance and subsequent failure of your entire endeavor. Users do not exist in vacuum but in relatively stable communities. Leverage the bindings of users within the community (e.g., see Figures 10-13 and 10-14).

7. *Intuitive:* Make the knowledge management system intuitive to use. If you have ever tried to reprogram your number header on a personal fax machine and had no clue where to begin, you can empathize for the users who *could* feel the same way when a

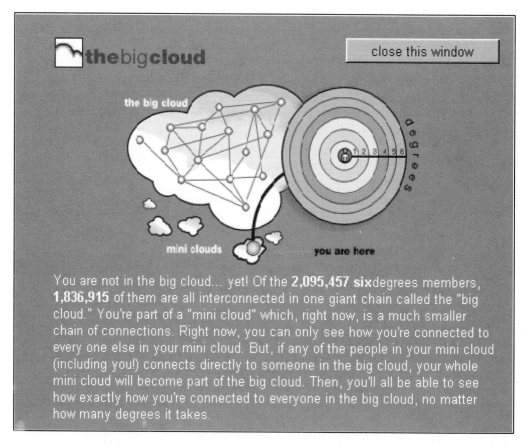

Figure 10-13 The cloudlike structure of the six degrees community denotes the different levels at which relationships between members within a community emerge (see www.sixde-grees.com).

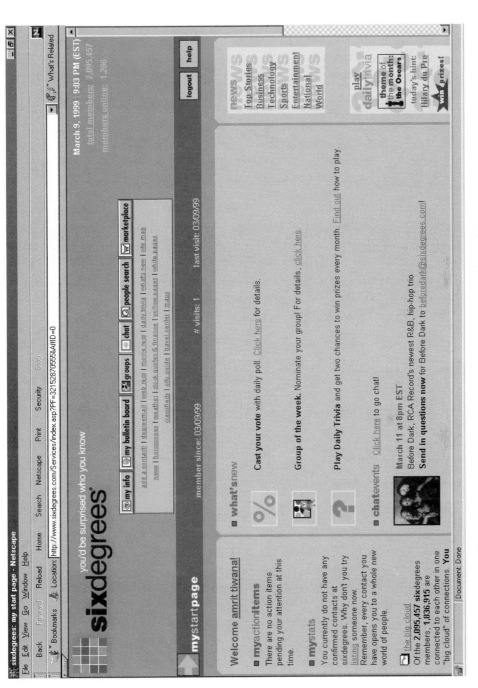

Figure 10-14 Six Degrees is a good example of a community built around relationships of collaborative filtering and members' recommendations.

system is not intuitive to use. You can find good examples of intuitive interface design from successful programs and Websites. I also highly recommend Patrick Lynch and Sarah Horton's excellent book on designing intuitive Web-based front ends, *Web Style Guide: Basic Design Principles for Creating Web Sites* (Yale University Press, 1999).

8. *Metrics and performance:* Measure performance and actively incorporate feedback that you get from your users.

9. *Legacy integration:* Bias your technology choices in favor of software components that integrate well with your company's legacy systems. Even the most difficult integration processes can be accomplished with commercially available tools such as KQML (knowledge query markup language) and similar scripting languages.

LESSONS LEARNED

A knowledge management system built without a well-defined architecture will lead only to chaos at later stages. Make sure that the architecture is clearly defined, since this part of the infrastructure can be very expensive to fix at a later stage. Keep in mind these points:

- *Understand the architectural components of the knowledge management system.* Pay close attention to integrative repositories, content centers, knowledge aggregation and mining tools, the collaborative platform, knowledge directories, the user interface options, push delivery mechanisms, and integrative elements.

- *Design for both interactive and integrative content aggregation.* Both these needs must be met simultaneously.

- *Optimize for performance, scalability, and flexibility.* Make sure that your KM system works as well for 600 people as it does for 60. Play close attention to short delays in processing transactions—these will amplify by orders of magnitude as you begin to scale the system upward.

- *Plan for interoperability.* Plan for high levels of interoperability with existing protocols and implementations.

- *Decide whether to build or buy.* One option is not necessarily better than the other; examine the pros and cons of each option.

- *Pay attention to the user interface and its design.* The user interface provides an excellent opportunity for ensuring buy-in by the user community. A user interface that is built in synchrony with the user community help creates a perception that the knowledge management system is an asset, and not a liability that needs to be side-stepped

- *Position and scope the knowledge management system.* In some cases, it is not only difficult, but also foolhardy to try explicating tacit knowledge that your employees possess. Scope the system to support only those categories of knowledge that have the potential for maximizing opportunity and returns. Include the network viewpoint in your assessment.

- *Future-proof your knowledge management system.* Take substantive steps to ensure that your knowledge management system does not become obsolete as technologies or business environments evolve. If the system is well future proofed, changes should affect only the content in your knowledge management system, not its structure or design.

Now, with our blueprint for your knowledge management system, let us proceed to the seventh step in the knowledge management road map: developing the actual system.

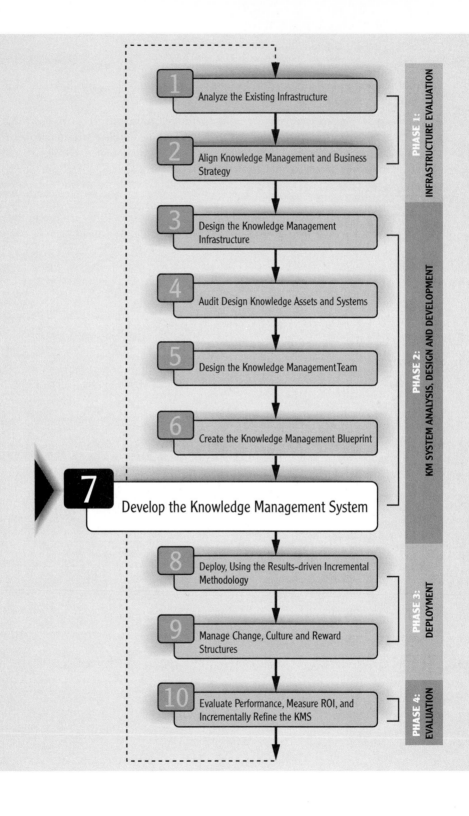

1   Analyze the Existing Infrastructure

2   Align Knowledge Management and Business Strategy

3   Design the Knowledge Management Infrastructure

4   Audit Design Knowledge Assets and Systems

5   Design the Knowledge Management Team

6   Create the Knowledge Management Blueprint

7   Develop the Knowledge Management System

8   Deploy, Using the Results-driven Incremental Methodology

9   Manage Change, Culture and Reward Structures

10   Evaluate Performance, Measure ROI, and Incrementally Refine the KMS

PHASE 1: INFRASTRUCTURE EVALUATION

PHASE 2: KM SYSTEM ANALYSIS, DESIGN AND DEVELOPMENT

PHASE 3: DEPLOYMENT

PHASE 4: EVALUATION

CHAPTER 11
DEVELOPING THE KM SYSTEM

IN THIS CHAPTER

✔ Define the capabilities of each layer of the KM system architecture in the context of your company.

✔ Create platform independence, leverage the Intranet, enable universal authorship, and optimize video.

✔ Develop the access and authentication layer: Secure data, control access, and distribute control.

✔ Develop the collaborative filtering and intelligence layer.

✔ Develop and integrate the application layer with the intelligence layer and the transport layer.

✔ Leverage the extant transport layer.

✔ Develop the middleware and legacy integration layers

✔ Integrate and enhance the repository layer.

✔ Shift from a client/server to agent computing orientation.

NOW, IF ESTIMATES MADE BEFORE THE BATTLE INDICATE VICTORY, IT IS BECAUSE CAREFUL CALCULATIONS SHOW THAT YOUR CONDITIONS ARE MORE FAVORABLE THAN THOSE OF YOUR ENEMY; IF THEY INDICATE DEFEAT, IT IS BECAUSE CAREFUL CALCULATIONS SHOW THAT FAVORABLE CONDITIONS FOR BATTLE ARE FEWER. WITH MORE CAREFUL CALCULATIONS, ONE CAN WIN; WITH LESS, ONE CANNOT. HOW MUCH LESS CHANCE OF VICTORY HAS ONE WHO MAKES NO CALCULATIONS AT ALL!
—SUN TZU IN *THE ART OF WAR*

Once you have created a blueprint for your knowledge management system, the next step, step 7, is that of actually putting together a working version of the system. Development of the system begins by defining the seven layers of the knowledge management architecture. Of the many possible interface choices, leveraging the existing intranet is the most feasible and effective approach. So, in this chapter, we see how to convert the intranet to the front end for your knowledge management system.

We look at the layers from these points of view:

- Interface layer—incorporating platform independence, optimizing content, and enabling universal authorship
- Access and authentication layer—providing a firewall for internal content
- Collaboration layer—providing opportunity to build industry-standard document systems (and Web-friendly document standards such as DMA and WebDMA); shifting from client/server to agent/computing architecture
- Application, transport, and repository layers—forming a nodding acquaintance with these three layers
- Middleware and legacy integration layers—connecting the KM system to both true legacy data and recent legacy data repositories and databases

We also see how to take advantage of the hardware built around these standards.

THE BUILDING BLOCKS: SEVEN LAYERS

Let's go back to the knowledge management system architecture introduced in Chapter 10 and see how the seven layers are actually built (see Figure 11-1, reprinted for convenience). The seven layers within the knowledge management system architecture provide a guideline for the choice of technology components that enable effective sharing of knowledge across a distributed enterprise. What we have analyzed up to now is the functionality provided by each of these layers. Let us now see how a knowledge management system can be actually built along each layer.

1. Interface layer
2. Access and authentication layer
3. Collaborative filtering and intelligence layer
4. Application layer
5. Transport layer

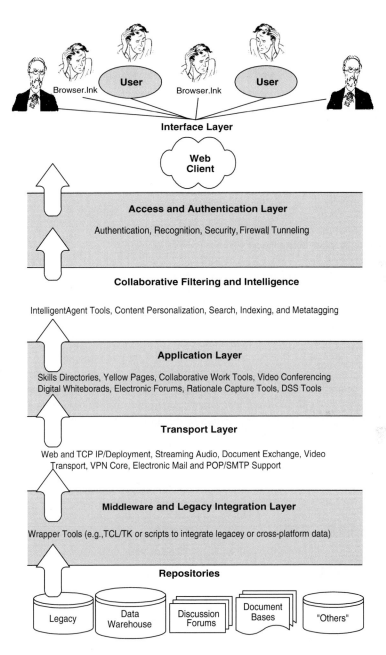

Figure 11-1 The seven layers of the knowledge management system architecture.

6. Middleware and legacy integration layer
7. Repository layer

THE INTERFACE LAYER

The top layer moves information in and out of the knowledge management system. When this information is relevant, timely, and actionable, it represents knowledge. The top layer, the interface layer, connects to the people who use this IT infrastructure to create, explicate, use, retrieve, and share knowledge.

CHANNELS FOR TACIT AND EXPLICIT KNOWLEDGE

The interface layer is the primary point of contact between the users and KM system content. Technology best supports explicit knowledge; we considered how the inclusion of informal communications channels and a rich medium was critical to the success of a knowledge management system. The interface layer must provide a channel for tacit as well as explicit knowledge flow.

The essential step in tacit knowledge transfer between people is the conversion of tacit knowledge to information and back to tacit knowledge, as Figure 11-2 illustrates.

Whether this transfer happens through formal processes such as knowledge capture in databases or through informal mechanisms such as conversations, this intermediate step is almost always involved. The implication of this intermediacy is that knowledge *can* be trans-

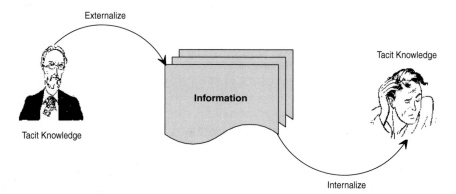

Figure 11-2 Knowledge transfer involves information as an intermediate state.

ferred through something as complex as an intranet or a discussion database, or through something as straightforward and commonplace as a telephone, fax, or a face-to-face conversation.[a] Technology is not a precursor to knowledge exchange but an enabler in situations that do not allow for face-to-face transfer of knowledge.

CONTEXTUAL EXPRESSION AT THE INTERFACE

The artificial intelligence (AI) community spent years trying to figure out ways to encapsulate knowledge in a repository. Alan Turing once remarked, "I do not want to create a machine with extraordinary intelligence, just average will do." The efforts of the AI research community met with failure but were not in vain: All the effort that the AI community expended over the past 40 years has brought us to the realization that human intelligence and knowledge cannot be fully codified. With that in mind, let's realize that a knowledge management system should not seek to eliminate the need for direct human interaction. There is a lot of context (such as the tone of conversation or facial expressions) that cannot be represented well in any type of knowledge base or repository.

Electronic mail, a component of communications technology that most of us overly rely on, provides a good case in point: How many of your e-mail messages have some recipient misunderstood or misinterpreted because of your inability to add context or tone? As we saw in Chapter 5, technology helps knowledge management primarily in two respects: storage and communication. While storage includes databases, repositories etc., it does not limit communications technology to the connections between such databases. The catch phrase is *rich communications*—communications that can allow people to converse almost as becomingly as they would if they were talking face to face. What does that bring to mind? Video conferencing, chat, live audio applications, the telephone, its Internet spin-offs, and other informal interaction mechanisms.

As Figure 11-3 shows, tacit knowledge can be transferred by purely explicit mechanisms through possible explication, by purely informal mechanisms such as conversations, or by technological enablers such as such as CrossPads, electronic whiteboards. etc. that fall somewhere in between these two extremes.

The interface layer is the layer at which users of the knowledge management system interact with the system. The interface layer provides a universal mechanism for accessing all the layers below it. By choosing the HTTP standard underlying the Web, users can access data formats independently of the platform on which data resides. A typical organization has Windows PCs, Macintoshes, Linux, and UNIX machines that store content that is appropriate to the respective platforms. Trying to integrate all this existing content on one single plat-

---

[a]Even transfer of knowledge through apprenticeship requires subtle transfer of information along with its context.

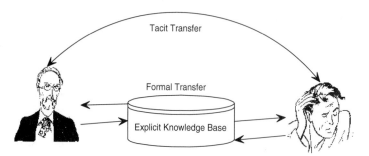

Figure 11-3 Transfer of knowledge can be through informal or formal channels.

SEMIFORMAL KNOWLEDGE TRANSFER MECHANISMS

While we are on the topic of informal communications technology, let us not ignore the potential that some recent, though little noticed innovations promise us. An example of one such technology is the CrossPad (www.cross-pcg.com) digital notepad made by the Cross Pen Computing Group. While users can jot down meeting notes just the same way they normally do—on a regular legal pad, CrossPad digitizes everything that was written on the pad (such as informal sketches, notes, drawings, etc.) and stores it in its RAM. This content can then be transferred to a PC and further to any conventional word processor. CrossPad is an excellent example of a technology that allows you to capture relatively informal data in a very unobtrusive and transparent manner that makes perfect sense to the writer and, in context, to others.

form would not only be prohibitively expensive but would also require changing—often forcing—users to change the environment[b] in which they work. Besides, legacy data that exists on such platforms is extremely difficult to move because of the (often) proprietary mechanisms used to store it.

Using a Web browser as the final interface allows these islands of information to be connected at an external level. Legacy data on UNIX machines can, for example, be read, written, and edited through a Web browser, using scripting languages such as TCL/TK and KQML to create *wrappers*.

---

[b]*Environment* here refers to the computing platform and the associated software tools that users run on it.

PLATFORM INDEPENDENCE

The use of a Web browser as a client also enables universal access the relevant portion of the KM system from any location or computer terminal connected to the Web. While using an application through a Web browser can be painstakingly slow if the application itself is accessed through a slow dial-up connection, most companies considering knowledge management are expected to have high-speed networks already in place. Similarly, increasing penetration of broadband access into homes makes this problem marginally relevant for remote access.

Content can further be optimized to move through low bandwidth networks by the use of cache memory (which is already a part of most popular browsers) on the client and server side, by minimizing the depth/resolution of graphics, and by using mobile applications written in Java. However, a slow network will impede smooth functioning of the system if multimedia content such as images, video, and sound are routinely transmitted over such networks.

LEARNING FROM INTRANETS

All basic ideas underlying the design of an intranet front end apply well to this layer. You can create the interface itself using a GUI Web design tool such as Microsoft FrontPage or a similar Web graphics editor. An evaluation version of Microsoft FrontPage 2000 is included on the companion CD-ROM. Perhaps one of the best resources for effective Web interface design is the *Web Style Guide* by Patrick Lynch and Sarah Horton.[1]

To be useful and successful, an intranet site must organize information and assemble it in a consistent, logical, and systematic manner. With respect to a knowledge management system, an intranet front end must allow users to get to the information that they need in a painless and fast manner. What you definitely do not want is users lingering over their browsers in frustration. Frustration usually results from the inability to find exactly the information that is needed (and information that probably exists), in real time. This failure relegates that information back to its default status of information that simply exists, rather than elevating it to the status of usable knowledge.[c]

OPTIMIZING VIDEO CONTENT

Many browser plug-ins counter the speed limitations of networks by incorporating a feature called *fast start*. This technique applies to video clips that are stored as a part of aggregated content. For most video content that is involved in a knowledge-sharing application, video qual-

---

[c]Lynch and Horton report that Sun Microsystems' intranets, for example, have a consistent navigation menu. Some guesstimates suggest that this alone saves Sun up to $10 million in terms of employee time and increased productivity.

ity is not the primary concern; the concern is the system's ability to deliver video content in real time in the face of network bottlenecks and speed limitations.

Plan to use mechanisms that can be used to reduce this bottleneck. Mechanisms such as *fast start* in QuickTime, for example, allow a video clip to start playing before the clip is fully downloaded. The catch is that a clip plays in real time only if the data rate that the network connection can handle either equals or exceeds the movie's data rate. Many HTML editors enable an *autoplay* function through an HTML tag by default to start playing a clip as soon as it is accessed. This might not be a desirable setting in most intranets; disable it to provide additional control to the end user who wants to bypass the video clip to get to some other piece of linearly arranged information.

The essential point to keep in mind while configuring a server for video delivery is to optimize the video clip file itself for existing network bandwidth. Calculate the data rate considering using the worst-case scenario with a sufficient number of users simultaneously connected to the available channel.

For example, if a typical channel available on an office network has a bandwidth of 100 Mbps and 15 users are connected to that channel, it will be unwise to estimate that streaming video content needs to be optimized for a channel capacity of 100 Mbps. On the other hand, it is unlikely that all users will be sharing an equivalent portion of the available bandwidth at a given time. The correct answer for the channel capacity needed for optimizing video content and resolution lies somewhere in between.

A safe assumption to make as a starting point would be to optimize content for 60 percent of the available bandwidth, then realign it based on actual usage patterns. In any case, it is better to underestimate available bandwidth than shoot yourself in the foot by overestimating it.

Universal Authorship

Another benefit of using a Web-based front end is that users working on different platforms can add content to the overall repository in HTML format, which is the same across all platforms. Therefore, a report created and posted in HTML format by a salesperson using an Apple computer can be read by someone using a Windows PC.

A Walkthrough: Urban Motors

An intranet, as you know by now, is the best choice for a knowledge management system's front end. Even though all work in a knowledge management system is done on the back end, the only part that the average user interacts with is the front end. We use an example provided by IntraNetics (a live version of this example is included on the companion CD). We go through the structure and design of an intranet-based front end for a hypothetical company called Urban Motors. All conventional ideas underlying the good design of intranets apply to such a front end. Since this information is discussed in extensive detail in other books,[2] we do not go into specifics of intranet design per se in this section.

The Opening Page

Functionality, not graphic-laden attractiveness, is the catchword. As Figure 11-4 shows, Urban Motors decided to use a corporate image that allows the users to immediately identify the opening page that they call their "Welcome Page."

A list of favorite applications that an employee can customize appears on the upper left corner. At the bottom left, a visually intuitive set of folders links the user to other areas of the system. A search box on the opening page allows users to search for content on the Web. In an ideal system, the user should be able to choose among the Web and the intranet from the accompanying drop-down box. The Urban Motors deployment lets users search the Web for general content, pictures, or sounds.

It would be useful to limit this search capability to the intranet alone (and not the Web), at least in the beginning.

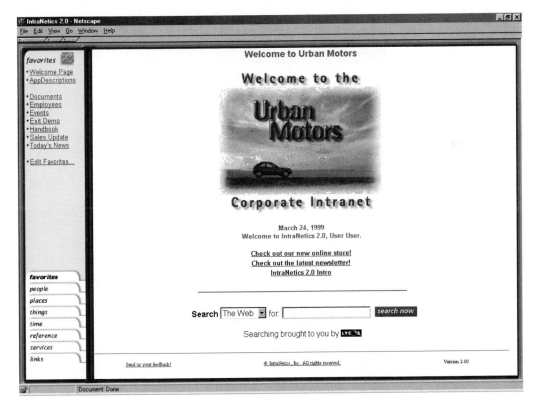

Figure 11-4 The opening page for a sample intranet-based KM system front end.

Search Mechanisms

Figure 11-5 shows the results of a search within the picture category using the search term *knowledge management*. As the results show, intranets searching the Web in general tend to deliver less value because the results of the search are very similar to those delivered by the search engine. The value of such search mechanisms lies in their ability to search the intranet in the same way. Since different users prefer different mechanisms and engines, limit the breadth of such searches to the intranet and its back-end repositories. As searches are done on better tagged content, the value of the "hits" of such a search will be much higher if they are limited to the intranet or extranet.

A variety of commercially packaged search engines for intranet deployment are available at a low cost. For KM system deployments, Verity's engine (www.verity.com) seems to be the best option; other strong contenders include Autonomy's knowledge server (www.autonomy.com), Business Miner (www.businessobjects.com), AltaVista (www.altavista.com), and My Eureka! (www.infoadvan.com).

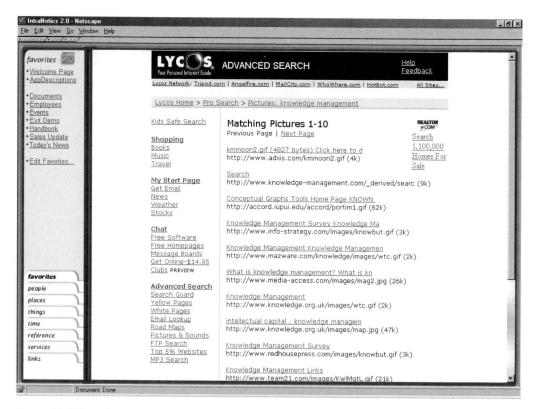

Figure 11-5 Searching the Web through an intranet delivers less value and more information overload.

People and Pointers

One of the "folders" on the opening page leads to Urban Motors' contacts database. The contact list is extracted from a database that stores the data. As Figure 11-6 shows, contacts can fall into several categories. These categories must encompass both internal and external contacts. When a user enters the people page, the left frame changes to the subclasses within the contact list. Figure 11-6 shows people within functional categories. An alternative way to show the same information is to categorize people by their skills or past projects.

Similarly, such contacts can be listed by their relative place in the organizational hierarchy. Figure 11-7 shows contacts listed by their relationship with the company displayed in a browser window. Every employee must be able to add information to the contact database, but that requires a very high level of trust.

To be on the safe side, allow addition of contextual data to contacts but do not allow alterations to the data itself (except by a few authorized people). In addition, use filters to specify that customers are unable to see internal comments (such as those exchanged by employees on, say, the financial standing of a potential customer).

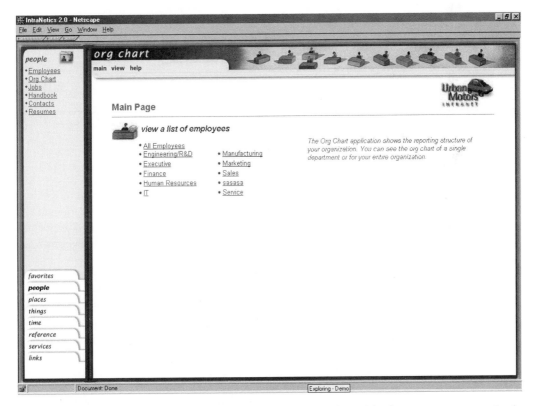

Figure 11-6 The contacts listing shows people both within and outside the company categorized by their functional departments.

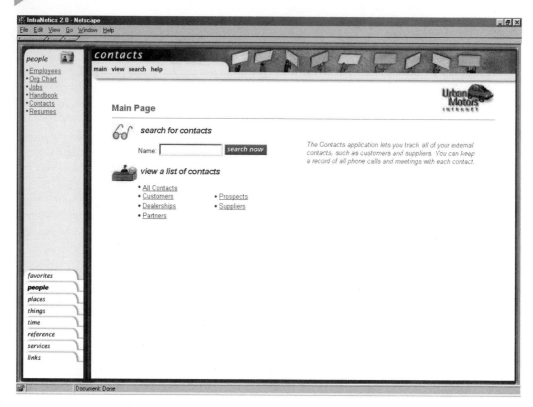

Figure 11-7 Contacts based on organizational relationships.

Figure 11-8 shows a listing of contacts extracted in real time from a database. Hyperlinks provide the ability to view additional details on each contact listed. Although each contact has an e-mail address and telephone number listed, additional criteria such as past projects and areas of expertise (which might differ from functional classification) might be worth considering for inclusion.

Furthermore, the same information must be viewable in different clusters and categories. Figure 11-9 shows a bare-bones implementation of this concept where the same list can be viewed from multiple perspectives. You can add to such categories depending on how such information is actually used and can be used within your company and by your partners.

For listings to serve as an effective knowledge pointer, they must include skills and past projects. In addition, employees must be able to add contextual information to such a database. The few employees with editing capabilities can remove anything malicious or offensive. Contextual information is essential in adding value to a bare-bones contacts listing. Every employee must be able to edit his or her own information. Without this capability, the burden of maintenance will fall on the IT support department, defeating the purpose of making this a useful and constantly updated set of skill pointers.

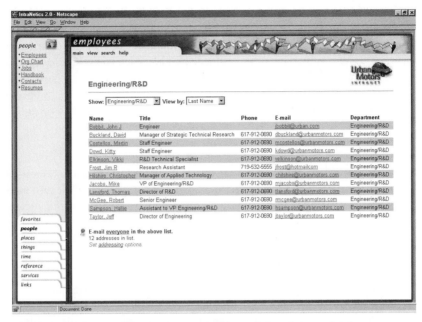

Figure 11-8 Listing of contacts extracted in real time from a database.

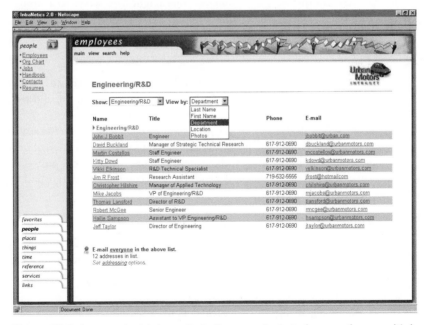

Figure 11-9 A contacts database that allows contacts to be seen from multiple categorical viewpoints.

Meta tags—specified automatically or manually—can associate each employee with different skill categories. At later stages, you can add text mining tools to search through the content and content structure to determine additional categories or classification typologies under which a given employee can be classified. This approach allows such categories to go beyond those formally defined or those related purely to work tasks and assigned roles.[d]

Such categories might not have been formally defined and might be unrelated to work but can be indispensable in finding employees interested in ad hoc assignments that might come up or in projects for which no formally identified expertise exists in the company.

Thesauri

A good electronic thesaurus can be indispensable for automatically cross-referencing related concepts described in searches performed by other employees. While such mechanisms would be of limited value in a small company, they become exponentially useful under two conditions:

1. The company is geographically scattered or entirely virtual.
2. The company's employee count is high (over 200).

One consulting company was able to use such a mechanism for identifying a potential candidate for heading a startup office in Bombay, India, based on his personal references to India (not Bombay) in discussion group postings that a thesaurus could correlate with his interests. This was certainly a better approach to identifying potential candidates based on their interests (in this case, travel interests that might have served as a strong motivation for that employee) rather than by random assignment, or doing what is done more frequently for matching people and assignments—guesswork!

Places

Urban Motors uses another link from the opening page that leads users to virtual places such as the company store, online supplies stores, training partners, and travel services (see Figure 11-10).

The choice of places that you would want to include on such a collation of services depends on your company, policies, commonplace processes, and internal structure. In many cases, you might not even want such a category. The "easy," generic answer that we teach in all business schools: It depends! It depends on your company's situation and knowledge management system usage context.

Documents

Another folder from the main page links users to internal documents, external reports, expense filing forms, etc. Urban Motors decided to put these elements under a broad "things"

---

[d]For example, by being able to see that an employee mentioned amateur radio on his personal (not company) Web page (that such a system could link to either visibly or behind the scenes), a text mining tool can classify such an employee among the set of employees knowledgeable in the area of radio communications.

Figure 11-10 Services and stores are one possible broad category.

category. In all the noise about tacit knowledge, you must make sure that you do not fail to appropriately leverage explicated knowledge that already exists in the form of documents, both digital and on paper.

There are several alternative ways to organize the same material. When a user clicks on the "things" category, she is shown a new frame menu that allows her to reach other subparts of that category. Among the most important one here is the category storing documents. Such documents might be internal reports, past project records, or general informational documents.

If a large number of internal documents are produced in your company, it is a wise idea to further classify them. In either case, meta tag all documents to enable efficient identification through multiple and nonoverlapping searches.

The document search interface used by Urban Motors is very simple. On the opening screen, as shown in Figure 11-11, the user can choose between options to browse or search for documents.

As more categories of documents begin to emerge, they must be incorporated into the search mechanism to allow users to do precise searches.

Figure 11-11 A document repository should allow the user to choose between search and browse retrieval.

Figure 11-12 shows how the results of a typical search can be clustered along multiple dimensions or views. Although the sample application shows a limited number of views that are almost standard across all applications, these choices will vary depending on your user groups and specific industry.

Figure 11-13 illustrates a starter set of search views where the user can select documents by type and see the clusters by which they are arranged.

Licenses

When you are integrating all content into one consistent interface, it is worthwhile to integrate both file server and application server content into the same interface. Figure 11-14 shows how Urban Motors did this.

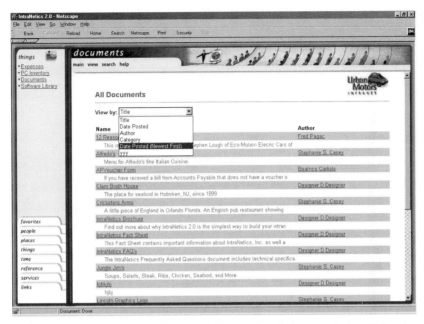

Figure 11-12 Different views let users view retrieved documents in overlapping clusters.

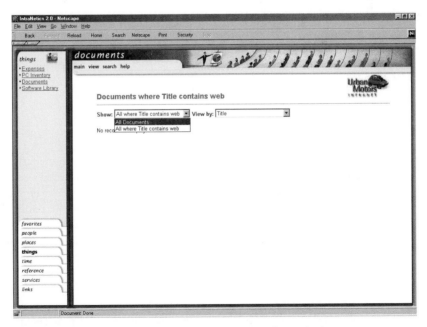

Figure 11-13 This illustration shows a starter set of search views.

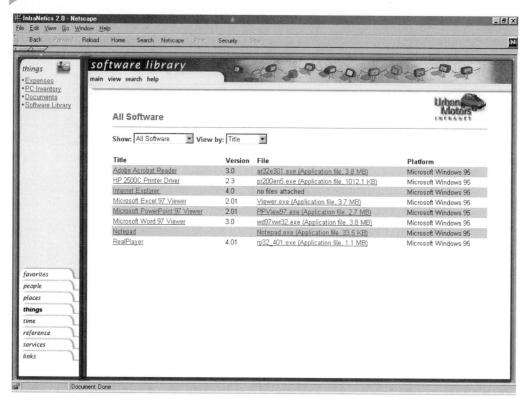

Figure 11-14 Integration of applications and files at the front end.

DOCUMENT MANAGEMENT THROUGH THE INTERFACE LAYER

A lot of what happens in a knowledge management system is at the back end. Nevertheless, without proper mechanisms to tap into the back-end repositories through the front end (the intranet), it is unlikely that those applications will be used efficiently. Two standards, DMA and WebDAV, are about the only widely accepted standards for document management.

When you are selecting this component of your KM system, make sure that you select one that complies with these standards to ensure that the system will be supported even if the vendor goes out of business. Moreover, an accepted standard means that you have fallback support from peer firms, should technical implementation hurdles crop up.

Applying DMA Standards

The Association for Information Management (AIIM) has proposed a document management standard called the DMA specification. This standard provides an opportunity to strengthen the back end of our knowledge management system.

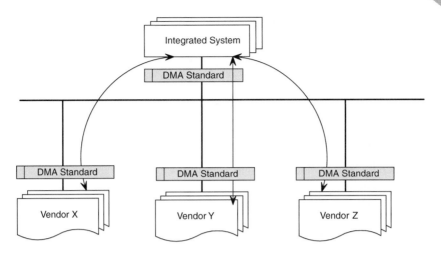

Figure 11-15 DMA compliant systems from multiple vendors can integrate smoothly.

The Document Management Alliance (DMA) standard is a document management standard proposed by AIIM. Electronic document management systems (DMSs)—commercial off-the-shelf software packages—are primary candidates for using this standard, but knowledge management systems can also benefit from it.[3] The DMA standard provides a common, standardized base for interoperability across a multitude of compliant applications. Without such interoperability, companies are often forced to purchase both the information management base platform and applications from a single vendor. Figure 11-15 shows how DMA-compliant systems interact.

What is imperative is interoperability across multiple applications. Without this interoperability, companies are forced to purchase both the information management base platform and applications from a single vendor. The DMA standard provides a common, standardized base for interoperability across a multitude of compliant applications (see http://www.aiim.org/industry/standards/index.html for details on the DMA standard and compliant products).

The DMA standard, as described by AIIM, provides a rich set of standardized features and capabilities:

- A mechanism for automatically locating repositories
- Capability to map common attributes across repositories, even when those attributes have different names on different repositories
- Support for content versioning

---

[e]Some key differences between database and document management systems are in order. DBMSs store structured data; however, DMSs store, retrieve, and manage unstructured data such as files, text, spreadsheets, images, sound clips, multimedia, and compound documents.

- Support for location-independent folders
- Ability to browse across DMSs using Internet browsers
- Ability to manage multiple renditions of a document
- Automatic discovery of document classes, properties, and search operators
- Ability to search across multiple repositories simultaneously, and merge the search results
- Full international support (including extended characters)

Due to the growing support for this standard, you can expect most leading document management tools to be compliant to this standard. A single DMA-compliant application program can interact with any DMA-compliant system to do the following:

- Store and retrieve documents in multiple formats using DMA *renditions*
- Control the evolution of documents through DMA's versioning model
- Organize documents in folders using DMA's *containment* model
- Search for documents and folders across multiple systems in a single DMA query
- Discover systems and documents through DMA's dynamic self-describing object model
- Gain access to an organization's intranet by using DMA as a universal Web gateway on the Web server

The strength of the DMA standard comes from its ability to integrate multiple repositories through the Web. This standard is specified in the ODMA (Open Document Management) API (Application Programming Interface) characteristics. An extension of the original DMA standard to allow such interaction through the Web is illustrated in Figure 11-16.

COMPLEMENTING DMA WITH WEBDAV

Web-Distributed Authoring and Versioning (WebDAV) is an extended standard for document management that allows authoring of documents (not just word processor documents) in a distributed manner through the Web. Instead of relying on a single proprietary client interface, this standard allows the user to work through a generic[f] Web browser. Through extensions to the Web's HTTP protocol, a document (created in HTML, e.g.) can be created with one tool, such as FrontPage 2000 and then edited with another, such as DreamWeaver or Netscape Composer. Users can *check out* a Web page for editing or can track versions of a page as they can with any document management tool.

---

[f]Generic Web browsers refer to one of the two popular browsers—Netscape Navigator and Internet Explorer. The term *generic* is used to describe the types of functionality natively supported by both of them.

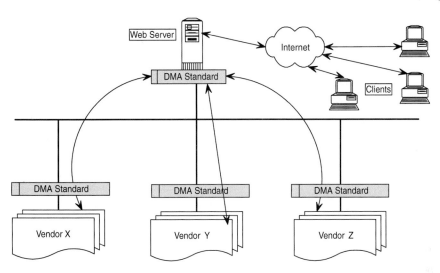

Figure 11-16 The ODMA standard.

DMA and WebDAV are complementary standards and do not seek to replace each other! WebDAV, as illustrated in Figure 11-17, creates interoperability between the tools used to create and edit Web pages and documents.[3] DMA, on the complementary side, allows Web servers to interoperate with a multitude of document repositories that, until DMA, were unable to work together.

Events

Urban Motors also lists events related to the company on its intranet. Such events can be conferences, trade meetings, social events, or sales drives. The types of events are limited only by the nature of your company and your employees' interests. Figure 11-18 shows the events section on the intranet.

Figure 11-19 shows how Urban Motors lets users view events in time frames such as a week, a month, or a year. Similarly, the types of events, as shown in the drop-down box, can be easily customized if a tool such as an IntraNetics is used to build the intranet front end for the knowledge management system.

Hyperlinks from each event listing lead the users to additional details on the event as shown in Figure 11-20.

As Urban Motors did, you can also easily customize the event categories to a limited extent if an out-of-the-box customizable intranet solution is used to create the front end for your knowledge management system.

Reference

Many companies have realized substantial cost savings by moving their operational manuals, procedures, forms, etc., to an electronic environment. Urban Motors has a subsec-

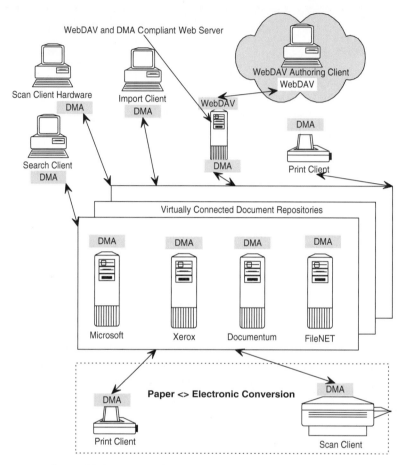

Figure 11-17 How WebDAV and DMA work in conjunction.

tion (see Figure 11-21) in the reference component of the interface where users can access internal and company-specific discussion groups, externally collected information and news, newsletters, press releases, industry updates, competitive data, and other general news in an organized and consistent manner.

Services and Links

In addition to other *folders,* Urban Motors decided to use a *services and links* category for pointing users to services such as FedEx and similar delivery services that the company uses (see Figure 11-22).

By opening such sites within an intranet browser frame, users can consistently navigate and reach relevant external services. The types and categories of such services will vary from one company to another, and in some cases they might be integrated within other categories.

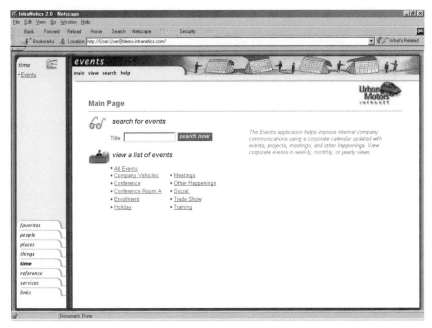

Figure 11-18 Events listings can be categorized by types, dates, or nature.

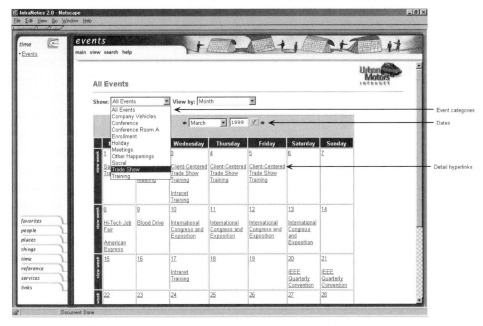

Figure 11-19 Different views and categories of events are displayed within the events frame.

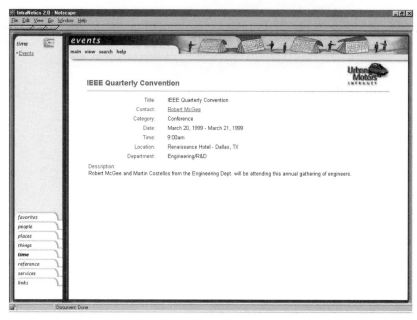

Figure 11-20 Additional details on each event can be viewed through hyperlinks associated with the listing.

Figure 11-21 The news and reference section as displayed on an Urban Motors intranet browser client.

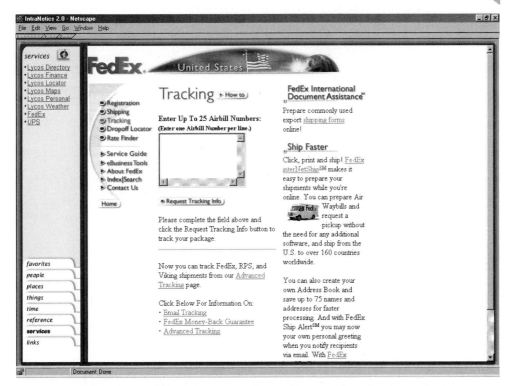

Figure 11-22 The services link on the Urban Motors browser client lets internal users access services such as FedEx tracking.

Customizability

Demonstrating customizability in its basic form, Urban Motors allows users to select from a restricted set of options to customize their favorites list (see Figure 11-23). In a real-world application, such customizability must be tightly integrated with collaborative filtering tools that are used as a part of the knowledge management system.

Although tools such as Microsoft FrontPage 2000 can be used to create such front ends for knowledge management systems, they are rarely out-of-the-box solutions. If you start with a solution such as IntraNetics, you can always use FrontPage to edit and build the site further. Many out-of-the-box intranet front ends do provide a high degree of customizability and tight integration with other applications throughout the network or the enterprise-wide extranet. From purely a cost standpoint, an out-of-the-box solution is often the most cost effective way. A comprehensive out-of-the-box solution such as IntraNetics intranet can support up to 500 users and costs only about $5,000.[g] A basic version of IntraNetics that supports 50 users costs about one-third as much. Such tools also integrate well with popular databases and electronic mail clients.

---

[g]A smaller version that supports 50 users and works with Microsoft BackOffice costs $1,495.

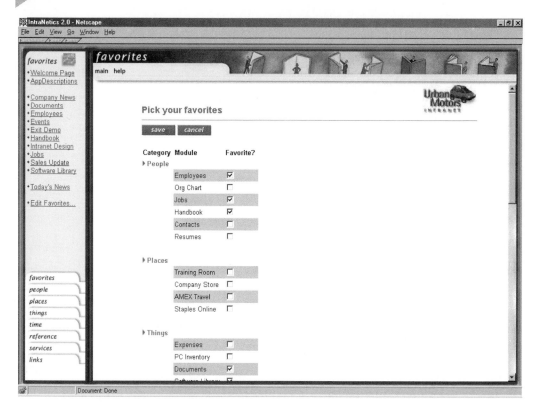

Figure 11-23 Bare-bones out-of-the-box customizability is a limited, though good, starting point.

THE ACCESS AND AUTHENTICATION LAYER

The layer immediately below the interface layer is the access and authentication layer. This is the layer that authenticates valid users. Security and restricted access for the remaining layers are maintained at this level. The strength of security provided by this layer has increased largely because of the penetration of intranets into many companies and vulnerabilities thus arising.

Companies are increasingly adopting intranets and extranets to connect workers both within and beyond their organizational boundaries. Intranets and extranets are hybrid information systems built on open Internet protocols such as HTTP and TCP/IP and related Web technologies. They enable business partners to efficiently share resources to accomplish common goals such as information exchange, collaboration, invoicing, electronic funds transfer, supply chain management, document exchange, and communication. The architecture of extranets is derived from and often integrates both intranets and corporate Websites.

Extranets not only provide the privacy and security of intranets (which are designed exclusively for internal usage) but also permit restricted access for external users via Internet connections or VPNs. The majority of extranet development uses the Internet as an access mechanism owing to its low (close to zero) usage cost. Technologies are interchangeable because they use standard Internet protocols.[h] This means the extranet is platform independent and not bound by proprietary protocols or technologies. Tools and services that use open protocols can be introduced with relative ease as features and functionality necessitate change. Since an extranet uses the Internet, data that moves across it goes over the open and exposed information superhighway. Security then becomes a primary concern. Although I will not go into depth on security implementation, I will point you to my book on Web security.[4]

Some of the issues that must be addressed are:

1. *Access privileges:* Assign rights to permit different levels of access to data such as read-only, write, edit, and delete capabilities.

2. *Firewalls:* Construct a firewall between the extranet and Internet. Thoroughly test the firewall by mock attacks.

3. *Backups:* Create backups, staging areas, and mirror sites. Duplicate information so that if disaster strikes, such as hardware failures, security violations, or undetected viruses, the network along with its data can be quickly reconstructed. Online backup services are extremely cost effective and offer unprecedented safety. An example of one such service is @Backup (www.backup.com).

VIRTUAL PRIVATE NETWORKS

The Internet is, in many respects, similar to the interstate highway system, just as some interstates require the payment of a toll for entry, the Internet requires an online Internet provider service for access. However, the ride itself is free.

Penetration of the Internet in most business networks provides multitudinous opportunities to eliminate the expense and gain the speed of high-speed private lines by means of VPN technology. VPNs eliminate the need for fixed point-to-point communication lines. Instead they operate within a public network, such as the Internet, but with security that is as strong as that of more expensive leased private lines. Various mechanisms allow this operation; most rely on tunneling that works by running one protocol inside another, in effect creating a private tunnel. By running the network protocol inside the Internet TCP/IP protocol, proprietary protocol networks connect and communicate over the Internet. A protocol for such activities is PPTP, or *point-to-point tunneling protocol,* an extension of the Internet point-to-point protocol (PPP) used in conventional Internet communications. Windows NT 4.0 and Windows 2000 provide native support for the PPTP protocol.

---

[h]A note of caution: Not all browsers fully support Internet standards as defined by the World Wide Web Consortium. Microsoft's Internet Explorer 5.0—which deploys proprietary extensions for improved interoperability with Microsoft's other Web products—is one such product.

Standards and Protocols for Expansive Networks

Many of the cost savings of extranets come from their reliance on nonproprietary solutions for cross-platform, Internet-based applications. Some of the standards that have been put forth and endorsed by companies such as Microsoft, Netscape, Digital, Novell, and Sun Microsystems include the following:

- *LDAP:* Lightweight directory access protocol is a format to store contact and network resource information, register Web clients and application servers, and store certificates in a directory. The Internet Engineering Task Force (IETF) guides LDAP.
- *PPTP:* Point-to-point tunneling protocol is an extension of the Internet point-to-point protocol used in everyday Internet communications. PPTP permits network protocols to be encrypted inside the Internet TCP/IP protocol so that proprietary protocol networks can connect and communicate over the Internet.
- *S/MIME:* Secure Mime is a standard that lets users send secure e-mail messages by using certificate-based encryption and authentication. S/MIME is one part of the RSA Labs Public Key Cryptographic Standard framework. X.509 Certificates is a specification for electronic credentials used for strong authentication and encryption. These certificates provide a secure container of validated and digitally signed information. Operation of digital certificates can be limited to within an intranet, or between enterprises with public certificates issued by the company and a certification authority such as VeriSign. Digital certificates eliminate login and password procedures and can have access privileges and permissions coded into them.
- *vCARD:* Virtual Card is a format for storing and presenting contact or registration information. It was proposed to the IETF as a standard and is implemented in many Windows products.
- *Signed Objects:* Signed Objects is a format for automating trusted software and document distribution defined by the JavaSoft Java Archive specification.

Biometrics and Other Forms of Authentication

Biometrics, voice recognition, and fingerprint recognition are promising technologies that will allow users of a company or enterprise-wide network to get into the system in a rather transparent manner. Swipe cards and one-time login mechanisms are commercially available, and Windows 2000 provides support for these mechanisms at a native level.

For companies that already have an adequate network in place, the access and authentication layer of a knowledge management system does not require extensive work. Most of the components needed here will either already be in place or can easily and inexpensively be put in by the computing support staff.

THE COLLABORATIVE FILTERING AND INTELLIGENCE LAYER

The collaborative filtering and intelligence layer is the one that constitutes intelligence within a knowledge management system. The process of adding tags and meta tags to knowledge elements (units of actionable information), either through automated mechanisms or manual procedures, is done at this level. Intelligent agents are perhaps the best thing to happen to artificial intelligence in terms of viable applications to the Web. Collaborative filtering and business intelligence tools are built into this layer and, as we see later, they build very heavily on agent technology.

FROM STATIC TO DYNAMIC STRUCTURES

Figure 11-24 shows how information in conventional intranets is structured. Each document is connected to other documents through hyperlinks. These links are statically contained in each document and refer to other documents, video files, sound files, etc., by URLs. Activating a hyperlink means jumping from one document to another.

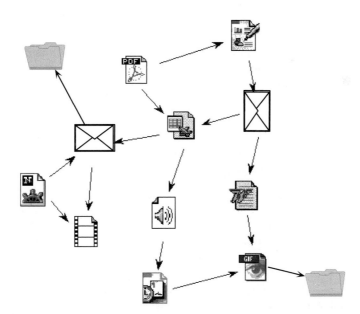

Figure 11-24 The classic hyperlink based model used to structure information on the Web.

This approach has contributed enormously to the growth of the Web but has created other problems at the same time:

- *Navigational encumbrances:* Navigating large hypertext documents is difficult. As the number of documents and their hyperlinks grows, users find it increasingly hard to get an overview of available information, to find the information they are looking for.

- *Extensive collaborative authoring:* Intranet sites almost always require collaboration from a multitude of authors. Problems grounded in link consistency come up here. When you delete a document, the links in other documents pointing to the document just deleted break. This often results in the infamous *Error 404* message.

  Another problem is that of orphan links—a document becomes unreachable when the last link pointing to it is removed. These problems compound in a multiple-author environment because the actions of one author (deleting a link or a document) can lead to problems with another author's documents without the other author(s) ever knowing of the existence of the problem. The basic Web model is, therefore, unable to support a mechanism that is well suited for collaborative work.

- *Difficulty in generating complex views:* The simple URL-based navigation mechanism used by hypertext makes it impossible to combine individual documents to self-contained information components that can be reused in different contexts in slightly different ways, known as customizable views.

Various commercial tools use the concept of abstract structural elements called *containers.* A container contains a number of other elements, which could be documents or other containers.

We included a limited version of Hyperwave, one of these tools, on the companion CD-ROM. So let's use Hyperwave to exemplify features of this layer. There are a number of predefined container classes in Hyperwave:

- *Collection:* This class refers to collections of content.

- *Sequence:* This class is a predefined container class that focuses on content sequence.

- *MultiCluster:* A container class with multiple clusters.

- *AlternativeCluster:* Another predefined container class that deals with clusters.

Hyperwave can run on the top of the classic file mechanism that most users are familiar with. For further details, explore the documentation in the Hyperwave Folder on the companion CD.

Virtual Folders

Tools such as Hyperwave Information Server allow for the creation of virtual folders on an end user's desktop. Figure 11-25 shows such a virtual set of folders, which appear as the Hyperwave neighborhood on the user's Explorer window.

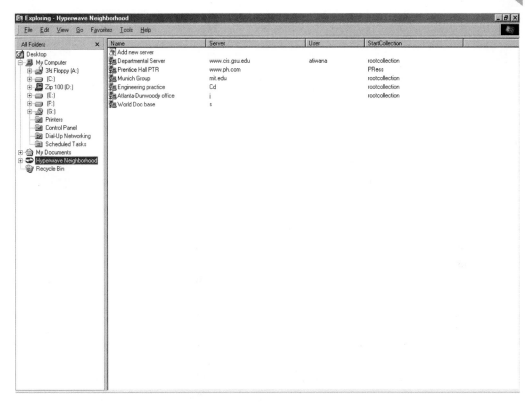

Figure 11-25 Hyperwave virtual folders show up as the Hyperwave neighborhood on the user's desktop.

Using such a mechanism, users can reach the same information element in multiple ways:

1. *By navigating:* Users can point and click by following hyperlinks.

2. *By searching meta data:* Users can search meta tags associated with files and digital content.

3. *By searching content:* Users can search, using keywords that are matched against content within documents.

4. *By subscription:* Users can subscribe to predefined channels; or through the use of intelligent agents, they can receive notifications about new documents that match prespecified criteria.

This concept is also based on the presumption that users will not add content to the corporate repositories if it is too complex for them to do so. The goal is to make it possible to

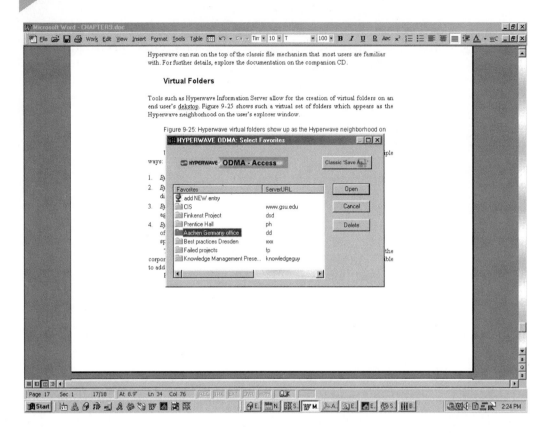

Figure 11-26 Tight integration with existing windows applications allows users to save to the Hyperwave neighborhood.

add to the repository with little or no effort on the part of the user. Without such functionality, this work runs the risk of being *perceived* as useless at code checkin/checkout procedures that most programmers have to unwillingly follow.[i]

For this reason, the user can publish directly from a Windows application. Figure 11-26 shows how Hyperwave allows me to save a working copy of this Microsoft Word chapter directly to the Hyperwave neighborhood.

---

[i]Being perceived as useless does not imply that it actually is useless. Writing software documentation is another good example. Programmers rarely gain from writing up detailed documentation for their code. Very often it is written post hoc, that is, after coding has been completed. This ties in strongly with my idea that knowledge sharing requires clearly visible benefits to the contributor. Some obscure "corporate good" can rarely, if ever, motivate people to share their knowledge.

Automatic Full Text Indexing

The collaborative filtering layer is responsible for indexing content in a manner that permits fast retrieval through multiple search mechanisms. In Hyperwave, 200 default document types are automatically indexed as soon as they are saved to the corporate repository.

Automatic Meta Tagging

Meta tags can be automatically added to documents and other content using software tools that are readily available. Some tools allow the knowledge management team to add meta tags beyond those that the vendor might have already specified, but most do not. Hyperwave attaches the following meta tags to each document:

1. Who published the document?
2. When was it last modified?
3. Who reviewed it?
4. Who approved it?
5. What is the size of the document?

This is still a very restricted set of meta tags. See the discussion on meta tagging in Chapter 7 to determine whether or not the default set of meta tags provided by a vendor's tool will satisfy the requirements of your application.

Virtual folders in Hyperwave can be extended by addition of more servers to the existing set. Figure 11-27 illustrates the wizard that allows such additions.

Security settings and authentication mechanisms can be specified within this wizard as shown in Figure 11-28.

In addition, friendly names can be assigned to such machines as they are added, as Figure 11-29 shows.

FROM CLIENT/SERVER TO AGENT/COMPUTING

Agents, based on an old metaphor in the field of artificial intelligence, have suddenly become a part of mainstream computing because of their suitability for open environments such as the Web. Agents can be thought of as active objects with their properties tailored to environments such as the Web and intranets.[5] Agent properties relevant to knowledge management include the ability of agents to perceive, reason, and act in the environments within which they operate. Second, some agents have an ability to learn from past mistakes at an explicit level: something very much in line with what a knowledge management system is intended to help with. Since information cannot be understood without the context of its creation or the processes that lead to its consumption, the ability of agents to learn from past failures and bring the learning to bear upon future actions is a very relevant set of characteristics.

Agents can be broadly classified into three categories: agents that are static in the client, agents that are static in the server, and agents that are mobile. The primary types of agents that have direct implications for knowledge management systems are mobile agents. Such agents

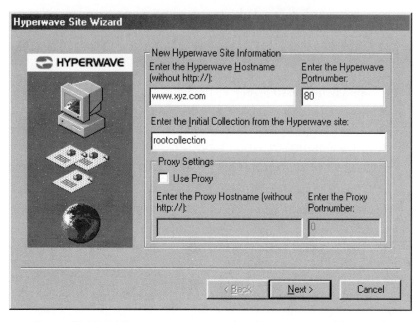

Figure 11-27 Adding more servers to the Hyperwave neighborhood.

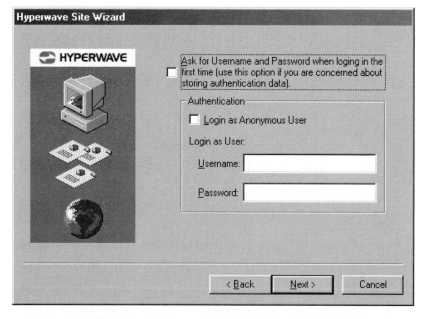

Figure 11-28 Authentication and security settings for new additions.

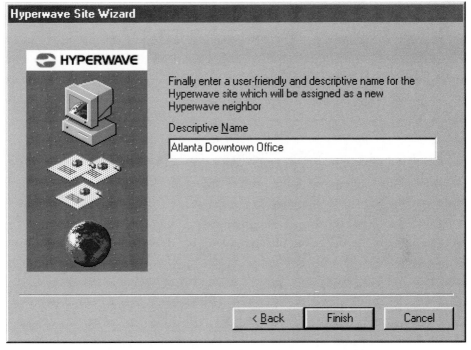

Figure 11-29 Assigning friendly names to new machines.

can move from one server to another to find the information that they need. Most current agent deployments are coded in Java. Many of the commercial tools mentioned in this book and included on the companion CD already use agents in the background. Besides these tools, IBM Japan also freely distributes an intelligent agent programming language called ASDK 1.03 (Aglets Software Development Kit). ASDK is available for download at http://www.trl.ibm.co.jp/aglets/ free of charge. IBM, however, charges for the most current version of this kit.

The concept of agent mobility grows out of three preceding technologies:[6]

- Process migration
- Remote evaluation
- Mobile objects

Of all possible options, Java is the language best suited for implementing mobile agents because it allows the conversion of an agent into a form suitable for electronic transmission and its subsequent reconstruction on the receiving end.

Figure 11-30 shows a comparison between traditional client/server architecture and agent/computing models of network operations. As shown, in the client/server setup, the network load primarily exists between the client and the server (indicated by more interaction

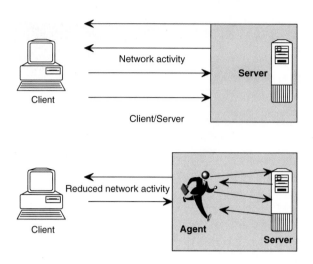

Figure 11-30 Client/server versus agent/computing models.

lines between the client and the server). On the other hand, in the agent/computing model, this load is shifted to the space between the agent and the server. The overall load on the network, therefore, is dramatically reduced.

Benefits of Agent Mobility

While the area of intelligent agents is still being investigated by researchers, a few characteristics of mobile agents show a lot of promise in terms of their application to knowledge management systems. Mobility is an orthogonal property: Not all agents are mobile. Agents that cannot move are often referred to as *stationary agents.* Stationary agents execute only on the system on which they are initially invoked. All communications and interactions with other systems are done with a communications protocol such as *remote procedure calling* (RPC).

In sharp contrast, a mobile agent is not bound to the system on which it is executed. Such an agent is free to move around the network across multiple hosts. Even though it is created in one execution environment, it can transport its *state*[j] and code with it to the next host within the network where it continues code execution.[7]

Mobile Agents for Knowledge Management

Pattie Maes and her colleagues have identified seven benefits of agent mobility as they apply to network transactions.[8] We can extend six of their descriptions to a knowledge management perspective:

---

[j]*State* refers to an agent's attribute values that tell it what to do next when it resumes execution at its destination node.

1. *Mobile agents reduce network load:* Distributed systems on which a knowledge management system is based often rely on communication protocols that involve multiple interactions between computers within a network, to accomplish a given task. Mobile agents let systems cut down on the number of such interactions and, as a result, reduce the load on the network by a considerable amount. Even if you already have a very fast network in place, the bandwidth freed up by such agents can be used to move bandwidth-intensive content, such as sound and video, over the same network. Mobile agents move the computation to the data rather than the data to the place of computation. When large volumes of data are present on remote hosts, mobile agents process data locally on the remote host and transfer the results to the local client.

2. *Real-time operations:* Bill Gates, in his new book, *Business at the Speed of Thought,* says that the need for the times is to do business at the speed of thought; actions must be taken right when they need to be taken. Mobile agents leave little to be desired in helping perform transnetwork operations almost in real time. They can be dispatched from a central host and execute at the destination, thereby overcoming the effects of network latency and transit time that otherwise make real-time operations impossible.

3. *Protocol encapsulation:* Mobile agents can encapsulate various protocols and build a channel for communication between two machines that ordinarily cannot create a mutually interpretable protocol for data exchange. This is a significant enabler for legacy system and data integration.

4. *Asynchronous and autonomous execution:* We saw the need to be able to connect mobile workers and tools such as PDAs, digital notepads, and palmtops to network nodes. Very often, such wireless connections depend on cellular phone lines, which can be very expensive to operate on a continual basis. Mobile agents can execute independently of both the process and the device that created them. This implies that a PDA user could send out an agent to look for specific information and then disconnect from a network. The agent can then autonomously perform its search task and reconnect to the PDA user to report back what it found. Therefore, the need for continuous connectivity is minimized.

5. *Seamless integration and heterogeneity:* Networks are usually heterogeneous because of the different and often incompatible hardware and software that runs on such hardware. Since mobile agents are generally computer and transport-layer independent and depend only on their execution environment, they can seamlessly integrate devices across such heterogeneous networks.

6. *Mobile agents are fault tolerant:* If a network node such as a server is going down, agents can be warned in good time about an impending nodal crash. They can then continue their operations on another host and save time as well as *their* effort. Although this concept is rather new and is not used in any of the products that this book discusses, we can expect to soon see applications based on this method.

Agents and Push Models for Knowledge Delivery

Mobile agents embody the Internet push model. Agents can disseminate news, bulletins, warnings, notifications, and automatic software and content updates. This makes mobile agents especially useful for delivery of knowledge in accordance with the push delivery model. Collaborative filtering tools such a GrapeVine include such agents, as do tools like Hyperwave.

The strength that mobile agents bring to such knowledge-centered applications lies in their *asynchrony*. An agent can monitor information at the source without being dependent on the system from which it originates. Agents can also be dispatched to wait for information matching certain prespecified criteria to become available. Several commercially available tools, some of which are, in a limited form, included on the companion CD, use this feature to their advantage. A user can therefore dispatch an agent using such software, and the agent can either report the results on a periodic basis or report if and when it finds something relevant.

LOOKING FOR IKUJIRO NONAKA WITH MOBILE AGENTS

An example of such an application is CARL UnCover's *Reveal* service. My own ongoing research is based on a stream of research introduced by a Japanese scholar, Ikujiro Nonaka. Since Dr. Nonaka is based in Japan (and divides his time between Japan and Berkeley, California), he publishes in a variety of research-oriented journals in the United States, Japan, and Europe. Considering the fact that there are 17,000 major journals in existence worldwide, it would be impossible to keep track of what he is publishing. Besides, there might be research papers that he has coauthored with other researchers. Mobile agents solve my problem in a perfect manner.

Using CARL UnCover Web (http://uncweb.carl.org:80/reveal/) I can specify a number of loosely structured searches. Agents are assigned to each search. At any given time, I can have up to 25 sets of agents working for me. An agent waits to come across an instance of the search term *Ikujiro Nonaka* all week. If it comes across a match, it reports back to me by sending me an e-mail. It also tells me what the e-mail is about (adds context, without which the information might have no meaning for me).

THE APPLICATION LAYER

The application layer is the next layer. Applications such as skills directories, yellow pages, collaborative tools (often the back ends of Web-based collaborative tools), video conferencing software and hardware (and integration with the rest of the system), and conventional decision support tools are placed at this level. Since Figure 11-1 shows that the Web front end comes above this level, numerous tools at this level might have a common Web front end integrated with them. Discussion webs and forums for group problem solving and deliberation also exist at this level, even though the actual interface might be a plain

Here is an e-mail reporting a match:

```
From: uncover@csi.carl.org
Date: Wed, 17 Mar 1999 14:10:26 -0700 (MST)
To: atiwana@acm.org
Subject: Reveal Alert: Nonaka
Your Reveal search strategy:
N Nonaka
which was matched against new articles, retrieved 2 articles this week.
JT Prometheus : the journal of issues in technology
DA DEC 01 1998 v 16 n 4
PG 421
AU Nonaka, Ikujiro
AU Ray, Tim
AU Umemoto, Katsuhiro
TI Japanese Organizational Knowledge Creation in Anglo-American
Environments.
SI 0810-9028(19981201)16:4L.421:JOKC;1-
AV Article availability and price:
$ 17.00 Total = 10.00 Service + 7.00 Copyright
>> Profile # 350xxxx UnCover #: 251,108,203,082
Thank you for using REVEAL.
```

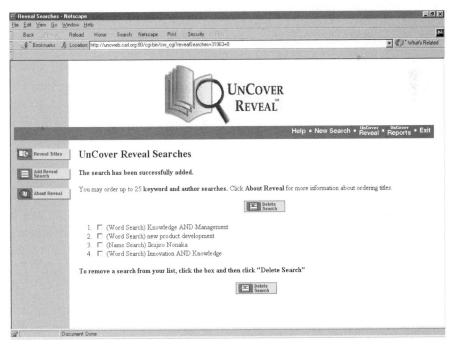

Figure 11-31 Agent-based intelligent retrieval from complex databases.

Web browser. Actual applications that constitute this layer are specific to the functions and processes supported by the knowledge management system, as discussed in Chapters 7 and 10.

THE TRANSPORT LAYER

Assuming that your company at least has a network in place, the transport layer already exists. This includes at least the following components to support a knowledge management system:

- TCP/IP connectivity throughout the organization.
- An up-and-running Web server.
- A POP3/ SMTP or MAIL server.
- A virtual private network such as a PPTP-based VPN running on Windows 2000 (formerly Windows NT). This is also needed to support remote communications, access, and connectivity.
- Support for streaming audio and video on the central server(s).

THE MIDDLEWARE AND LEGACY INTEGRATION LAYER

Let us assume that you have decided to use a Windows NT 4.0 or Windows 2000 Professional environment for your knowledge management system. When you attempt to standardize on one such platform for reasons such as cost of training, maintenance, or acquisition, you must make sure that both the data and the critical applications existing on incompatible platforms (such as UNIX) still remain usable. The term *legacy systems* is often used in the context of mainframes, but for the purpose of building a knowledge management system we need a broader and more accurate definition incorporating both mainframe systems and other contemporary, retired, custom systems.

The legacy integration layer provides such connections between legacy data and existing and new systems. The middleware layer, similarly, provides connectivity between old and new data formats, often through a Web front end. Although this problem is well documented in the area of systems integration and legacy integration, it needs to be addressed within the context of a knowledge management system. A number of companies have used technologies similar to TCL/TK scripts to integrate data sources such as those on mainframes that were otherwise hard to integrate. Similarly, knowledge query markup language (KQML) allows the application of ideas underlying intelligent agents to enable legacy and incompatible-data integration.

THE REPOSITORIES LAYER

This bottom layer in the knowledge management system architecture is the repository layer. This layer consists of operational databases, discussion databases, Web forum archives, legacy data, digital or digitized document archives, and object repositories. Islands of data, often standalone and distributed, exist in this layer. As we move up the layers in this architecture, these repositories are integrated and combined with contextual information and tacit knowledge. In all likelihood, this layer already exists in your organization if you are thinking of putting together a KM system. The use of widely accepted standards such as DMA and WebDAV provides a high degree of uniformity to explicit content. Such compliance makes documents more amenable for Web-based interface access because of the fewer number of distinct formats that the system has to be capable of handling through the interface layer.

LESSONS LEARNED

The seventh step in the 10-step knowledge management roadmap involves actually building the system. Keep the following highlights of what we discussed in this chapter in view:

- *The seven-layer knowledge management system architecture.* Understand exactly what purpose each layer serves. A poorly performing layer can marginalize the performance of the entire system and can be an expensive bottleneck to fix at a later date. Several components of this architecture already exist in your company. Analyze which portions of this architecture need to be developed from the ground up, which need to be built further upon existing components, and which are already in place in their entirety.

- *The interface layer is what users actually see.* The interface layer is the topmost layer in the knowledge management system architecture. Remember that this layer can be easily built with an intranet development tool and then customized. The interface layer must create platform independence, leverage the intranet, and enable universal authorship. Since a large proportion of content enters and leaves the knowledge management system through this layer, it must be optimized to handle unconventional traffic such as audio and real-time video. Two different browsers can deliver content layouts in two different ways or visual formats, so make sure that you support at least Internet Explorer and Netscape Navigator.

- *Secure content using the access and authentication layer.* If you have a company-wide network, then you already have most security mechanisms in place. Make sure that you extend these mechanisms to secure knowledge management system content, and raw data; restrict access only to authorized users and distribute control.

- *KM system intelligence lies in the collaborative filtering and intelligence layer.* The collaborative filtering and intelligence layer can help advance the system from a client/server to agent/computing orientation. A number of commercially available tools can be used to build this layer without too much groundwork. Intelligent agents can significantly drive this layer. Deploying such agents rarely requires programming from scratch. Be careful about vendor claims while selecting components of this layer, and use qualifying criteria discussed in this chapter to make an informed choice.

- *Integrate applications with the intelligence layer and transport layer.*

- *Leverage the extant transport layer.* The transport layer is built on existing network infrastructure. If you already have a 100-Mbps network in place, you can leave this layer untouched. Remote access through direct connections and dial-up lines must be able to handle rich communications traffic from traveling users and occasional home-office workers.

- *Think beyond the mainframe legacy.* Develop the middleware and legacy integration layer to connect mainframe legacy data, incompatible platforms, inconsistent data formats, and retired systems. In some respects, DMA and WebDAV standards provide a high degree of uniformity to explicit content and documents and make them more amenable for Web-based interface access.

- *Integrate and enhance the repository layer.* Often, repositories need to be supplemented with new ones to be able to handle various types of content, such as discussions in discussion databases.

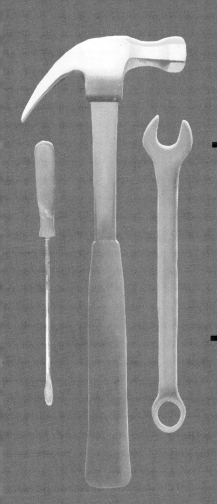

PART IIC
THE THIRD PHASE: KMS DEPLOYMENT

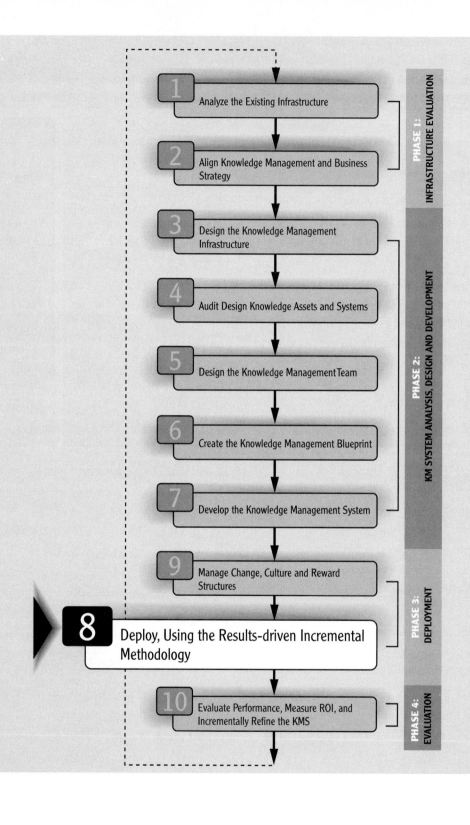

Chapter 12
Prototyping and Deployment

TRY A THING YOU HAVEN'T DONE THREE TIMES. ONCE, TO GET OVER THE FEAR OF DOING IT. TWICE, TO LEARN HOW TO DO IT. AND A THIRD TIME, TO FIGURE OUT WHETHER YOU LIKE IT OR NOT
—VIRGIL THOMSON.

The eighth step in the knowledge management implementation road map, the deployment stage, is the point where not even the best of intentions and technology for a knowledge management system can not keep the whole effort from crashing down to the ground. The biggest mistake that companies often make is that they assume that the intrinsic value of an innovation such as a knowledge management system will lead to its enthusiastic adoption and use. This assumption is too often shot to pieces.[a]

In this chapter, we examine how you decide about the need for a pilot KM deployment, how you select the right pilot project, and how you identify and isolate its likely failure points. We talk about results-driven incrementalism (RDI): how to use it to deploy a pilot KM system project; how to create and maximize release payoffs; and how to avoid RDI pitfalls.

MOVING FROM FIREFIGHTING TO SYSTEMS DEPLOYMENT?

Besides training costs, companies almost never budget for nontechnology costs related to deployment and implementation of knowledge management systems. Implementation of a system then resembles ad hoc firefighting more than something that seems like it has a plan![1] Deployment of a knowledge management system and strategy is the point where the off-road activities of team, knowledge management, and technology design need to effectively merge with the existing work processes within the company. In other words, it's time to take your KM system for a test drive.

Deploying any new system is usually a learning experience. The knowledge management team can learn from the users' perceptions about the system, study its functionality, the suitability of the chosen interface, and discover often unanticipated changes that can be and *need* to be made. Since there is so much to learn by actually putting the knowledge management system *out there,* it's always safer to field-test the design with a scaled-down version of the system early on in the process of development. But first, the field test.

PROTOTYPING

When you are in the midst of building a system, don't wait to finish the product before you put it into a pilot deployment. If all you have at the beginning is the interface, run it by a few users. The comments you might get at that stage could save your team much of the agony of reworking the final pilot version. Iteratively improving a system with incremental prototypes lets the users see, touch, and feel a system even before a system is completed. This is especial-

---

[a]The most recent example of one such technology is the data warehouse. Companies that have tried their hands at this technology have miserably failed in over half of the implementations, even after having made over an average of $1 million worth of investments in each such project.

ly true when the purpose of the system is not to automate user tasks but to allow them to perform new ones.[2] By being able to concretize the abstract details that you might have been giving to your potential users, you stand a chance to give your system a thorough test run even before it's ready.

Prototypes are perhaps the most underused form of *rejection insurance* that a development team can ever purchase. And the best part is that it's almost always free![b]

PILOT DEPLOYMENTS

A pilot implementation of the knowledge management system on a small scale can lead to insights that might prove to be invaluable *before* the full-blown system is implemented at an enterprise-wide level. For example, users in a particular group like marketing might feel that the user-friendly interface that your team designed is not exactly all that user friendly. Knowing this ahead of time can provide a sufficient time buffer for appropriate changes.

When such changes are made, they are best implemented in *chunks*,[3] that is, a set of technology modules that functionally fit together and can be implemented *as a whole*. The change implemented within such a chunk should be large enough to enable potential users to accomplish a task in a measurably improved way.

A pilot test reveals significant, and often fundamental, design flaws early on in the deployment process. At that stage, it is still possible to rework the problematic aspects of the design to meet the needs of the users and suit their preferences without major expense or significant rework.

Selecting a Pilot Project

The pilot project is an important step that helps companies in evaluating both the technology and in learning how it creates or contributes to actual business value. Unfortunately, many companies make the mistake of selecting the wrong project as a pilot project.

To maximize the potential impact of the knowledge management project right from the pilot stage, pick the pilot project with care. Once you have chosen the best possible pilot case for knowledge management, you are better able to judge whether similar projects on an enterprisewide scale will have a potent enough impact to justify their cost.

Find a project that the team agrees will have significant potential impact. Knowledge-intensive projects that run on a very tight time schedule are often the best place to begin. At the same time, be careful not to force the technology on a stream of work that constitutes the lifeblood of your company's income. Make sure that the team members that you choose for the pilot KM project are those people in your company who truly buy into the value of knowledge management for the business processes that they are considering. User mandate coupled with managerial mandate is often a critical part of the whole game.[4] If the users for whom are

---

[b]Even though some managers realize this, they are reluctant to expose imperfections in their work and give the often-used excuse, "It's not ready yet."

BEYOND JAVA

Without sufficient feedback, even the most basic assumptions about your users can fall apart and lead to chaotic failure or rejection of the entire system.* An example of such a failure was obvious on the design of a Java-enabled Website that was implemented at a major southern university. The design team never quite involved any of the 30,000 regular users (mostly students and faculty) in the design process where the interface was completely revamped to work with Java-based menus. Fancy technology and novel design do not always meet the needs of users. In this case, the new interface, while much flashier than the original version, was painstakingly slow when users tried to access it through slow dial-up connections from home, as they often did, resulting in mass dissent and resentment over the usability of the new interface. The end result was that the design team had to re-create a non-Java version of the same system as well. Nevertheless, here again, the only way to go to the non-Java version of the site was to go through the Java version and click on the "Non Java version" hyperlink!

---

*Rejection need not always be formal. If a system is designed without taking the *actual* user needs into account, users will simply try to avoid using it or find workarounds.

building the system do not believe that such an infrastructure will truly help them, that is probably the wrong project to hand-pick. Follow these tips for evaluating potential projects and their viability as pilot projects:[5]

1. Avoid trivial projects.
2. Stay away from your company's lifeblood.
3. Favor projects with widespread visibility and noticeable effects.
4. Select a problem that the chosen piece of technology fits well with.
5. Select a project that will last long enough to build necessary synergy within the team and the user community.
6. Set tangible deadlines and metrics for success.
7. Select a process-intensive project that can be highly impacted by the use of a knowledge management system.

Here is an example of such a project in a consulting company. Consider a system to support bidding for potential clients. A pilot for that case is a system that allows a consultant to pull up information (related to, and information from past projects) to bid for a consulting project. Such a project is not overly critical if it fails outright. If it does not work, it will still mean that the consultant can continue to bid the way he would have normally done it. Since

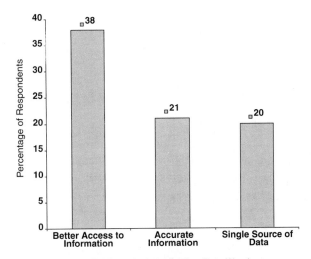

Reasons for Investing in a Data Warehouse

Figure 12-1 Reasons for investing in a data warehouse.

such a project is time critical, it will greatly enhance the process if it works. At the same time, such a project will have very visible and tangible outcomes if the knowledge management system helps the work group manage and access existing knowledge efficiently and effectively. While this example applies to a consulting firm, projects in the same vein can be easily identified in most other types of businesses as well. A similar pilot project, for example, can also be implemented in an engineering or contracting firm.

Lessons From Data Warehouses

Data warehouses are the political cousins of knowledge management systems. There is probably a lot to learn from other firms' experiences with data warehousing. Data warehouses, necessarily, are expensive undertakings. At the end of 1999, there were over a thousand vendors specializing in data warehouse solutions, software, and hardware. A typical project cost over $1 million, yet the failure rates exceeded 50 percent.[c]

Most companies pursued investments in data warehouses to improve the quality of information within the organization,[6] and to improve access to it (see Figure 12-1). Many companies start with small versions of a data warehouse (akin to pilot projects), usually centered on an application or a data set. Such a *data mart* is often an independent *proof-of-concept* system that can be built in a short time frame, at a lower cost (than the entire data warehouse), and can possibly generate a high payoff. Similarly, pilot projects for knowledge management systems can provide such a proof of concept and simultaneously allow you to figure out every *goof of concept,* early on!

---

[c]Figures based on estimates by Watson, H., and B. Haley, Data Warehousing: A Framework and Survey of Practices, *Journal of Data Warehousing,* vol. 2, no. 1 (1997), 10–17.

The danger of implementing and experimenting with such a pilot is that its success can lead to rapid proliferation of data marts that are independent of one another. Creating silos of information often comes with demanding integration problems at later stages. Similarly, knowledge management system pilots, if successful, can rapidly lead to the rise of small independent and specialized knowledge management systems (which are not even knowledge management systems in the true sense) that can rapidly create disconnected silos of knowledge.

While data warehouses do not lend their intangible payoffs for measurement without pain, knowledge management can use a few proven metrics. The key barrier to further development shows up expectedly as management (often) expects to see a return on investment (ROI) analysis on the initial funding proposal itself.[7] While the usual benefits such as time savings, better decisions, improved processes, and support for strategic business needs can always be listed, some quantitative hard-dollar figures are often asked for.[8]

LESSONS FROM WAL-MART

Wal-Mart is an excellent example of a company that has structured its work processes around its data warehouse. It collects data from its 2,800 stores in real time to be able to continually maintain its 24-terabyte warehouse. By using such massive amounts of data, it has successfully streamlined its logistics and reduced overheads that allow it to stay healthy while its competitors have been busy closing down their stores or going out of business. The big lesson from Wal-Mart is about transparency. Most employees are perhaps not even aware that every time they scan a product at the checkout counter or on the shelf, they are updating data that is fed to the central data warehouse. Wal-Mart's employees do not have to do an extra thing to contribute to the set of inputs that feed the main system. UPS' Web-based package tracking system is another close example. A knowledge management system that is truly not considered a pain by its users needs to come close to this level of transparency.

PRE-RDI DEPLOYMENT METHODS

The incremental approach to systems development and deployment, illustrated in Figure 12-2, assumes that functions required of a system, such as a knowledge management system, cannot be known completely in the initial stages. This approach suggests that developers implement a part of the system and increment it rapidly, as new requirements surface. This way, the entire system can be implemented in increments, and changes can be made along the way.

The *waterfall model*, the parent of the incremental model for systems development, was the mainstay of the systems development methodologies for years but has recently fallen out

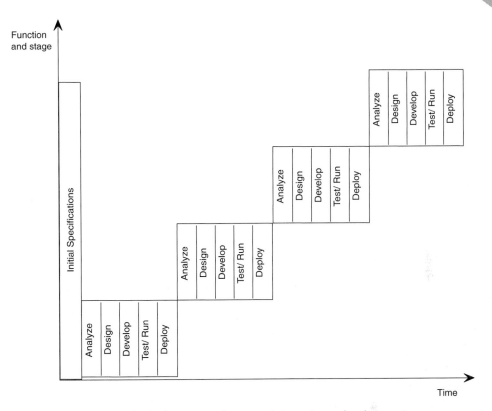

Figure 12-2 The incremental approach to systems development.

of favor. It is called the waterfall model because of the shape of the sequential activities that constitute it. The critical points of failure are shaded in gray in Figure 12-3. The requirements determination phase, as shown in Figure 12-3, is the point within the waterfall methodology where many projects start out on the wrong foot. The waterfall method allows little scope for the last phase, the postdeployment review, which was added to the original model at a later stage. In addition, as "clients" often express opinions or preferences much later in the process, not all requirements are captured in the initial phases. Without stable requirements, development activities in parallel can, at best, be poor.

The waterfall model is a bad approach to take for implementing complex systems. It not only allows but also encourages implementers to focus on the technology itself, rather than on the changes needed at a company level to actually derive business value from the new functionality that it provides.

If the feedback and learning loop is incorporated into this model and the project is broken down into discrete phases that build upon one another, it gives us the incremental approach model as shown in Figure 12-2. However, for their lack of flexibility and their relative inability to track complex relationships, these two methods provide little

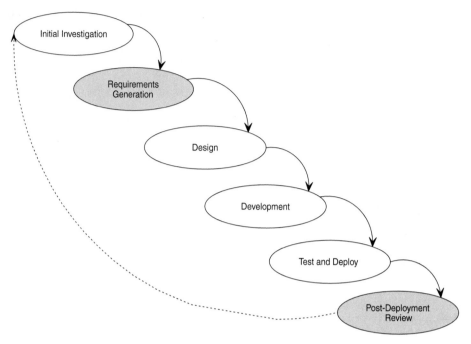

Figure 12-3 The waterfall methodology.

support for managing a relatively complex project like a knowledge management system. An alternative approach is the *spiral model* approach, also called the *learning loop* approach, discussed next.

THE INFORMATION PACKAGING METHODOLOGY

The learning loop or spiral model approach to system deployment is often called the information packaging methodology (IPM). The basic processes involved in the IPM approach are shown in Figure 12-4. The first stage involves architecture and system planning. Design and analysis follow this. Next, the actual technology implementation is done. Finally, the system is deployed and evaluated against user reactions and formal alignment metrics such as balanced scorecards or quality function deployment (QFD). Measurement of the level of strategic alignment level connects phases 1 and 4. This connection distinguishes this methodology from conventional systems development by bringing in the softer (strategic and human issues) factors influencing systems success. The spiral represents the infinite loop between stages 4 and 1 that leads to iterative and incremental improvements in *chunks*.

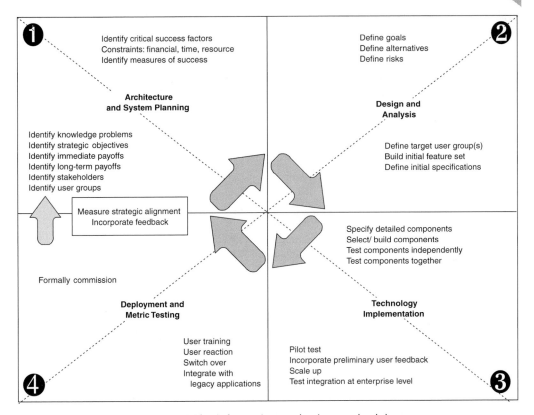

Figure 12-4 The information packaging methodology

An alternative way that the information packaging spiral methodology can be represented is shown in Figure 12-5.[d]

I wish I could honestly claim that the information packaging methodology can be scaled up to an enterprise level, especially in complex projects such as KM system development that can be very expensive and very instrumental to the firm. But the fact still remains that even this methodology has its limitations when it comes to large-scale systems such as KM systems.

---

[d]A different version of this was originally suggested by the Patricia Seybold Group in 1994, and an adapted version was presented in Mankin, Don, Susan Cohen, and Tora Bikson, *Teams and Technology*, Harvard Business School Press, Boston (1996).

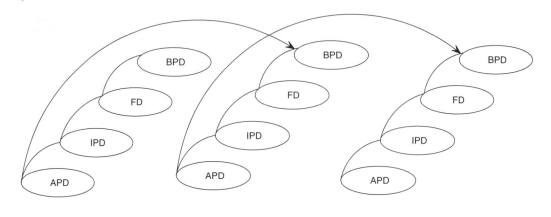

BPD   Business Process Design
FD   Functional Design
IPD Interface Prototype Design
APD   Application Prototype Design

Figure 12-5 A spiral representation of the information packaging methodology.

THE BIG-BANG APPROACH TO DEPLOYMENT

One of the common misnotions associated with software projects is, in part, the root of frequent adoption of the wrong—"big bang"—approach to systems deployment: *Delivery equals implementation.* That is, develop the software system in its entirety and implement everything at once, after the code is compiled. This approach is in stark contrast to the incremental approach that any complex and encompassing project, such as a knowledge management system, requires.

In the past, software packages seemed to contain more rigid assumptions about organizational structures, processes, and norms. Advanced software is no longer brought in to automate some process that is done manually; it is brought in to make a fundamental shift in the ways in which work is done and policies are run.

Project teams that use the traditional model for systems development have relied on the big-bang finish, where a lengthy period of disconnected effort results in a supposedly working product, as characterized in Figure 12-6.

As Figure 12-6 shows, the deployment team's targets or milestones A, B, and C pass but no benefits are realized by the company until the end of target deadline C. Here, the system goes "live" and the entire set of benefits is realized simultaneously. While developers always hope that those benefits are truly realized, if something was messed up by the time the team reached target A, it remained so through all successive stages, and successive work was done on a faulty foundation. If something could have been tweaked at stage A to simplify work at stages B and C, it was impossible with the traditional model.

AN ANALOGY OF RELAY RACES AND RUGBY

Ikujiro Nonaka, the Japanese scholar and father of knowledge management, says that he is amused by the way software and other new products are developed. He uses a metaphor from sports and urges businesses to "stop running relay races and take up rugby.*

In a relay race, the baton is passed from one player when she reaches the next. A relay race assumes that the path is straight ahead and clear; most often this assumption is fundamentally flawed. Most systems development methods are linear and similar to a relay race: One step is completed and the next one is taken up, and the relay race continues. With the pace of change in the surrounding business environment that most companies live with, why would you even waste your energy trying to convince *anyone* that markets, financial conditions, opportunities, and products that companies are built around, cannot or do not inordinately change every few months?

Contrast that with rugby. It is more representative of today's business environment. The player with the ball carries it around, moves forward, backward, sideways, and is always looking for an opportunity to pass the ball to a teammate—a hidden opportunity that he does not know will come.

*Nonaka Ikujiro, Managing Innovation Self-Renewing Process, *Journal of Business Venturing,* vol. 4, (1989), 299–315. A comparison of Japanese "ba" and the American business environment appears in Nonaka Ikujiro, Tim Ray, and Katsuhiro Umemoto, Japanese Organizational Knowledge Creation in Anglo-American Environments, *Prometheus: The Journal of Issues in Technology,* vol. 16, no. 4 (1998), 421.

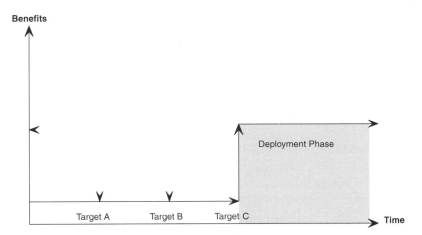

Figure 12-6 The traditional development model relies on the idea of the big-bang deliverable.

THE DEATH OF TURNKEY SOFTWARE

While *paradigm shift* and *transformation* are a common part of the business world lingo, they seem to be abused for everything irrelevant and rarely used for anything truly relevant. A critical place where these words truly apply but are rarely used is prevalent software implementation methodologies. Turnkey software deployment, for one, is long dead. There is no serious software than can be installed, turned on, and used without any organizational alternation or managed change, anymore. You cannot turn a key and make software work. Even single-user programs like Microsoft Word need tweaking before you feel comfortable using them for *productive* work!

Software deployment has taken on the nature of sometimes evolutionary, sometimes revolutionary, technological process innovation. Even when parts of your knowledge management system are purchased off the shelf, you should not assume that the difficulties of writing the system code have already been packaged up or eliminated by the vendor! Installing, configuring, and customizing some of the complex commercial software systems have complexity levels that come close to custom development associated with them. While this shift from project factors to processes might be the only possible approach that can be applied in situations that do not allow technology pieces to be subdivided into independent modules, divisibility is often the norm in complex applications.

ENTERPRISE INTEGRATION: BOON OR BANE?

Just as the demise of the typewriter changed the focus of our work from dealing with a physical machine to dealing with a software program, the penetration of computers in work-related activities has had exactly the same effect on work processes. The problem lies in the expansive flexibility of software. While this has arguably reduced up-front costs of putting a system in place, there are newer problems that come as a part of the package.

Baan and Peoplesoft, for example, are massive and expensive enterprise-level packages but still cost a fraction of what something similar would cost to develop in-house. This flexibility is a boon because it offers intensively amplified benefits and abundance of functionality. But this boon is also the primary bane. The excessive flexibility means that you have to tweak it to work for *your* company, and this necessity changes a software introduction initiative into an organizational change initiative. The one out of several thousand possible configurations that you choose to use must complement the processes, policies, culture, structure, and metrics specific to your company.

THE RESULTS DRIVEN INCREMENTAL METHODOLOGY

Implementation of complex pieces of technology such as a knowledge management system need a new approach that can overcome the limitations posed by all deployment strategies discussed earlier. *Results-driven incrementalism*[9] (RDI) is the most promising methodology for such use. The RDI methodology specifies that the project be broken up into a series of short, fast-paced development cycles coupled with intensive implementation cycles, each of which delivers a *measurable* business benefit. The benefits curve for such a technique is illustrated in Figure 12-7. Benefits are realized as each discrete stage is completed (benefits are shown in the gray area under the curve) as opposed to cumulatively at the end of several stages.

The most obvious benefit of the RDI approach is that business benefits of the knowledge management system can be realized much sooner compared to a more traditional *big-bang* approach. Implementers using this methodology report that the method increases not only the speed of the achievement of some tangible business benefit, it also increases the overall level of benefits. In addition, it dramatically reduces the overall time required to implement the project. Since every step taken is a concrete one and points of failure are rectified right after that step, it is more likely that the project will *actually* get completed.

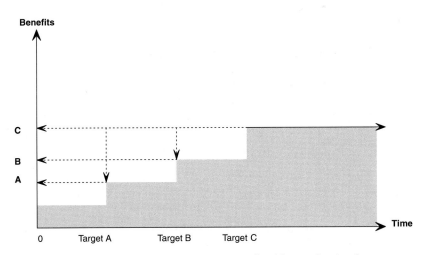

Figure 12-7 Benefits of each RDI stage are realized immediately after completion of each release.

Steps Involved in the RDI Methodology

The steps in the RDI methodology are based on five ideas underlying it:

1. *Objective-driven decision support:* Use targeted business results and end objectives to drive decision making at each point throughout the deployment process. For example, each phase of knowledge management system implementation has its desired results (the *whys*) and projected outcomes (the *so whats*) clearly answered before it is initiated.

2. *Incremental but independent results:* "Divide the implementation into a series of nonoverlapping increments, each of which enables measurable business benefits and improvements, even if no further increments are implemented."[e]

3. *Software and organizational measures clearly laid out at each stage:* Each increment must implement *everything* required to produce the desired subset of results. This means that software functionality must be accompanied by the necessary changes in policies, processes, and measures that are needed to make it work. For example, if one step includes the deployment of a discussions database, it must be accompanied by changes that motivate employees to use it, look for information on it, and contribute to it.

   The deployment plan should also include appropriate rewards that encourage employees to integrate it into existing work processes. In a collaborative environment such as a university, this would mean that participation in such discussions should or could count toward participation measures for student grades. In a software company, it might be counted toward peer-peer assistance. In a consulting company, it might count toward aggregated measures of overall participative problem solving by individual consultants.

4. *Intensive implementation schedules:* Each increment must be planned in a way that it can be implemented within a short time frame. Depending on the overall complexity of the knowledge management project, the time for completion of each incremental feature should range from two weeks to three months.

5. *Results-driven follow-ups:* Results of each increment must be the basis for adjusting and fine-tuning potential flaws in subsequent increments.

Business Releases

Incremental segments of an implementation using the RDI methodology are called its *business releases.* The notion of a release comes from the software industry where the software developer takes several iterations to get the final, polished version of the product to the customer (often over a period of several years). In the meantime, as the new and improved version is being devel-

---

[e]This idea is based on the experience of Fichman and Moses with several companies that have tried this technique.

oped, the customer can get an intermediate release and realize some of the final set of benefits and functionality that are expected. Each release constitutes a software-based system and accompanying organizational measures to make it work. The performance of each release is judged against a few *key performance indicators* (KPIs), which guide the next release.

Business releases must be short, and unlike software releases, must not overlap. Long segments defeat the entire purpose of deploying the RDI methodology by working against the goal of providing isolated, independent, and cumulative episodes of functionality and learning.[f] Each business release should address at least the following questions:

- What is the targeted business result?
- What is the *exact* software functionality required to achieve these results?
- How will the results be measured?
- What complementary changes are needed in terms of:
  - Policies?
  - Measures and metrics?
  - Structure?
  - Employee incentives?
  - Procedures?

Without specific answers to these questions, it is too easy to fall into the old trap of nonindependent increments that do not deliver actual business benefits. Table 12-1 offers a sample set of questions and answers for a discussions database implementation in a consulting firm.

As you will notice, metrics in this sample business release are largely subjective. Although quantitative metrics are often desirable, it is hard to make accurate judgments about those figures. In such cases, make sure that you have at least clearly defined the basis for defining success. If you can make (nonrandomly generated) estimates of benefits in quantitative terms, add them to the business release. For example, if you can estimate or accurately "guesstimate" that you expect to reduce the average cost per contract by 12 percent or by $7,000, by all means, add it to the information above. However, if you cannot accurately determine these numbers within a reasonable margin of error, it's best not to guess to avoid causing a perception of failure when the release has actually succeeded in delivering expected benefits.

The Traps in Selecting the Release Sequence

The important consideration in the use of RDI methodology is the sequence in which business releases are taken up. The ideal sequence should promote multiple objectives for knowledge management deployment.[10]

---

[f]If segments are long, RDI methodology begins to resemble the *big-bang* notion of all-at-once delivery of tools.

Table 12-1 A Sample Business Release for a Consulting Company Based on the RDI Methodology

Incremental Business Release	Details
Business release number	23454-11.
Start date	05-11-2000.
Due date	05-28-2000.
Release manager	Leigh Jones.
Targeted business result	Improve partners' use of records and code from past ERP implementation in Malaysia to slash costs of new ERP projects in Singapore.
Software functionality	An intranet connected to the Singapore office. Access to design documentation on the Malaysia document server must be available. Hyperwave information server and a VPN must be used to enable low-cost access without a dedicated line. The software must support Mac and Windows users. The link must be secured with SSL (available in Hyperwave). Use 128-bit encyrption provided by software that is not subject to export restrictions from the United States.
Preliminary metrics and success measures	An improvement in the speed of execution of contracts. Lower cost per contract. Reduced travel expenses on the Singapore-Penang route.
Policy changes	Incorporate the following into partner appraisals: Use of the new system to access information Timely filing of project data Cost reduction: travel and project averages
Accessibility	Provide each partner a laptop with a wireless LAN link; alternatively provide each partner a Palm VII PDA, a wireless connection, a direct access account, and an analog modem.
Other measures and notes	To be added.

1. *Expected success:* Focus the initial releases on those areas that are most favorable to success. A flopped business release 1.0 is unlikely to retain management support and funding.

2. *Cumulative:* Begin with an area where learning is most cumulative. This could be something as explicit as the interface or something as hidden as the mechanism for data access. Whatever areas you select, make your choice such that the lessons learned in the initial releases are those that can potentially impact the knowledge management project the most. Using such incremental and cumulative business releases divides both learning and deployment into discrete and more manageable segments.

3. *Highest payoff:* Take up the releases that have the possibility of the maximum payoff early on in the process and those with marginal payoffs toward the end. That way, you will know whether the biggest benefits of knowledge management can be realized with the approach you adopted. At the same time, the stream of funding you need to keep a knowledge management project moving will also remain steady!

4. *Balance of the above:* The three tips above are countersupportive. For example, a business release with the highest expectation of success might not be the one with the highest payoffs. Similarly, one with the highest payoff might not be one that produces cumulative learning. The trick lies in balancing the above three at an optimal point. Determining an optimal point where the payoffs are maximized and the risks minimized is subjective and often depends on your particular situation.

Process Divisibility and RDI Releases

The RDI methodology works best if the technology component of knowledge management itself is divisible, as is usually the case. This means that results and benefits that have accumulated still remain, even if subsequent segments are never implemented. Unlike other traditional approaches to systems deployment, neither the cause nor its benefits are lost if the knowledge management project is scrapped at a later stage.

Divisibility can be viewed from two possible perspectives. The first perspective divides the technology in such a manner that successive increments involve the same software modules but at a deeper level of detail. The alternative is to break the technology deployment into pieces, each of which is implemented at the deepest level of detail in the first round itself. The second approach is more feasible for building a knowledge management system. This prevents the usual excuse that the benefits could not be realized because the implementation process was not completed.

The RDI methodology provides a technique that allows for refinement of the current stock of deployment and process knowledge by ongoing releases.[g] The RDI methodology

---

[g]Anil Khurana, of Boston University, has suggested that such learning is important when a firm is dealing with an extremely complex production process. Deploying a knowledge management system is an extremely complex process, since it involves both technology and its cultural acceptance within the firm. See Khurana, Anil, Managing Complex Production Processes, *Sloan Management Review,* Winter (1999), 85–97.

beats all older techniques by allowing the actual targeted users to become the critical link between the knowledge management system development team and the end users that constitute the actual set of knowledge workers.

RDI's ROLE IN TOOL AND TASK REINVENTION

New technologies are almost never perfect when they are initially introduced.[11] User's efforts to apply technologies to their work processes and tasks reveal problems and contingencies that were not apparent before introduction. These problems in turn require adaptation of the technologies already in use.[12] Reinvention of the tools, interfaces, and task environment such as the design or aesthetic fit of the knowledge management system often goes hand in hand with reinvention of the job itself ("using" the knowledge management system). It would be ideal if the design of the knowledge management system were such that the interface was very similar to the one that existed earlier and the whole process of using the knowledge management system was almost transparent to the user. However, this is rarely possible.

On one hand, you will have a set of technophobic users to deal with. Such users will fear the introduction of a new technology that changes the way they have always worked. On the other hand are the technoliterate users who run the risk of getting so caught up in exploring the features of the new system that they neglect the tasks that they actually need to accomplish using the system. This implies that both these categories of users should be kept in mind while designing the system. The interface itself should be user customizable to a fairly high degree. Appropriate reward structures based on the level of use of the new knowledge management system for accomplishing their tasks, shared by both these categories of users, will prevent problems with either group.

Cross-Functional Synergy

Synergy refers to the ability of the system to produce a result that is greater than the sum of individual components. In this case, synergy refers to the ability of the knowledge management system to allow different groups of users, representing different functional departments, to produce results exceeding those that they would produce working without the support of such a system. Synergy has often been called the *Holy Grail* of business strategy.[13] A successful knowledge management deployment should bring in synergy between knowledge workers from different functional areas and departments. This goal is often pursued but rarely achieved. By bringing the work, documents, pointers, results, people, data, and other artifacts on one common collaborative platform, knowledge management promises to enable such synergy. However, due to the multiplicity of functional areas that are expected to structure their work around a common system, it is critical that the viewpoints that form the basis for improvement, both before and after implementation, are not solely those of one group or department. Sharing resources is a necessary condition for creating synergy, but it is rarely sufficient.[14]

Functional Complexity

As cross-functional and cross-institutional complexities of collaboration are unleashed with the use of a knowledge management system, the processes of dealing with this type of complexity must be addressed from both the knowledge management team's perspective and the end user's viewpoint. The critical set of complexities that you need to be concerned about while designing a KM strategy result from the changed face of interaction between people who exchange knowledge to perform their tasks, and their inability to decompose tasks and decisions into smaller chunks or segments. The various levels of complexity[15] that must be figured into the design of a knowledge management system include:

1. *Logistical complexity:* Resulting from a high volume of transactions, projects, categories, and tasks that a typical knowledge worker needs to deal with.

2. *Technological complexity:* This is rooted in the inherent nature of the systems and technologies that the user needs to interact with both at a product and service level and at a process level. While some of these, like interaction complexity, are decomposable, others are not.

3. *Organizational complexity:* This results from the meshing and collation of multiple organizations and departments into one workgroup. It may come from the new procedures that employees are expected to adhere to, changed structures of interaction (e.g., an employee needs to report to a team member in another firm but is appraised by her boss locally), and similar factors.

4. *Environmental complexity:* This comes from the pace of change in markets, regions, and industries that drives adaptation of knowledge and its frequent invalidation (that knowledge you know no longer holds true).

Avoiding Overengineering

Overengineering refers to the act of implementing system functions that may never be used, or adding details that are unnecessary for deriving the desired business results. The RDI methodology prevents the common tendency to overengineer technology solutions and maintains implementation focus and momentum. This substantially reduces the risk of failure and expedites the realization of business benefits. Although many managers may preach incrementalism in systems deployment, they rarely practice it. The reasons are twofold:

1. Incrementalism and structured methodologies are viewed as being noncomplementary

2. The benefits of incrementalism are perceived to be so marginal that it *seems* like it is not worth the effort.[16]

Developing Clear Communication Processes

Develop a clear communication process that explains the expectations and reasoning behind the introduction and integration of the knowledge management system with business processes. This communication leaves no surprises for the users and makes it easier for them to accept a culture where continuous change is a normal part of work life.

Human Barriers in Technology Design

Some technology vendors would wrongly have you believe that technology can capture all tacit knowledge in a database (see, e.g., the stand that Lotus partially takes in its 1998 strategic white paper. *Lotus, IBM, and Knowledge Management* available online at www.lotus.com). Not all tacit knowledge can be captured in a database, but a significant proportion of pointers to it can be. However, without an incentive that makes it a part of the natural way in which a person works, it is unlikely that even such pointers will be added to the system.

The key lies in offsetting such human barriers by a combination of appropriate design of technology and complementary incentives. If you asked your employees to keep their skills up to date in a skills database, that task will probably slide down to the bottom of their list of priorities. An immediate reward for an employee can compensate for an immediate effort that can result in a long-term reward for the firm. Linking long-term goals to long-term rewards rarely works.

One Infinite Loop

Apple Computer Inc.'s address is an interesting one: One Infinite Loop, Cupertino, California. This address also captures the essence of what represents the completion of a knowledge management system implementation in the true sense. However tempting it might be to say that the knowledge management system implementation is complete after step 10 in the knowledge management road map, we know better. To keep a knowledge management system kicking and alive, it needs iterative improvements as the business environment and accompanying processes evolve over time.

LESSONS LEARNED

Step 8, the deployment stage, is the point where the knowledge management rubber actually meets the road. Keep the following key points about the deployment stage in mind:

1. *Select and test-fire the knowledge management system using a pilot deployment.* Select a pilot project that is representative, and that will help identify and isolate failure points in the final deployment stages. Select a project that has high visibility and has tangible outcomes. Prevent independent or specialized knowledge "silos" from arising.

2. *Use prototypes to involve end users.* Iteratively improving a system with incremental prototypes lets the system's potential users see, touch, and feel a system even before a system is completed. Many flawed assumptions in the system's design can be corrected inexpensively at this stage.

3. *Focus on results-driven incrementalism of the RDI methodology.* Use the RDI methodology to deploy the system. Convert factors to processes. Eliminate information packaging methodology, SDLC orientation, and traditional big-bang methodological variants. The RDI methodology lets your team capitalize on insights provided by preceding incre-

ments. The methodology works best if the technology component of knowledge management itself is divisible

4. *Create effective business releases.* Create cumulative results-driven business releases. Select and initialize releases with the highest payoffs first. Well-crafted business releases will help you identify and avoid the traps inherent in the RDI methodology.

5. *Budget for nontechnology costs in RDI business releases.* Besides training costs and work processes integration, budget for costs related to deployment and implementation of your knowledge management system.

6. *Develop a clear communication process with users.* Develop a clear communication process that explains the expectations and reasoning behind the introduction and integration of the knowledge management system with business processes.

7. *Strive for iterative perfection.* A healthy knowledge management system needs iterative improvements as the business environment and accompanying processes evolve over time. The deployment process should not come to a halt once step 10 of the knowledge management "methodology" is completed.

Next, let's meet the people who are essential to the long-term success of a knowledge management system and see what's needed to ensure their unequivocal support and the eventual success of the knowledge management system.

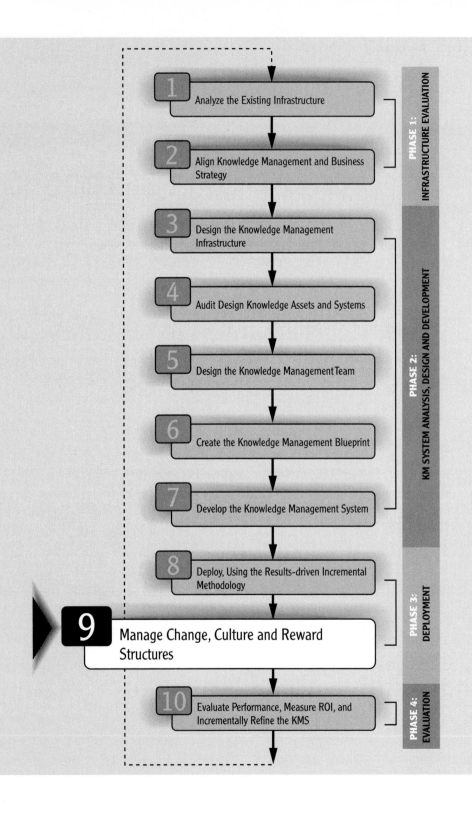

CHAPTER 13
THE CKO AND REWARD STRUCTURES

IN THIS CHAPTER

✔ Understand what exactly is a CKO's role.

✔ Understand how a CKO is related to the CIO, CFO, and CEO.

✔ Decide whether your company needs to have an "actual" CKO at all.

✔ Understand the successful CKO's technological and organizational functions.

✔ Plan for knowledge management success using the CKO as an agent for selling foresight.

✔ Manage and implement cultural change and process triggers to make knowledge management succeed.

✔ Implement reward structures to complement successful knowledge management.

THERE IS ONLY ONE WAY UNDER HIGH HEAVEN TO GET ANYBODY TO DO ANYTHING. AND THAT IS BY MAKING THE OTHER PERSON WANT TO DO IT.
—DALE CARNEGIE

Knowledge sharing cannot be mandated. The whole notion of sharing what an employee knows is diametrically opposite to the way in which reward structures in most companies work. Why would anyone want to share his knowledge if that knowledge is what provides his job security?

Successful knowledge management takes more than just technology; it takes cultural change and a change in the reward structures that drive work in most companies. *You have to gain the hearts and the minds of the workers. They are not like troops; they are more like volunteers.*[1]

This chapter discusses the leadership roles of people involved in a knowledge management team. Until now, we have focused on the key participants in the knowledge management team. However, knowledge management needs a champion to succeed, a leader who will take charge of running the show *after* implementation. So we look at what Nonaka calls *knowledge activists*[2] and discuss the emerging role of the *chief knowledge officer* (CKO). After examining the technological and organizational roles of the CKO , we evaluate whether your knowledge management project needs a CKO in the first place. Finally, we turn to change management processes, new reward structures, and process enablers that can be put in place to complement the knowledge management system.

A recent study of leading CKOs across the United States and Europe provides some new insights into this role and the characteristics of a typical successful CKO (see Figure 13-1). Whether you use this to appoint your company's CKO or gauge your own role, there will be something useful to take away from this chapter. Enthusiasm and active contribution by its proponents are, after all, the key determinants of a successful knowledge management system.

FROM THE CIO TO THE CKO

CIOs have distinct responsibilities: IT strategy, development of systems, connectivity, IT support, and general IT management. The CIO need not always be entreprenurially oriented to be successful, but the same is not true for the CKO. The CIO can rarely be both the CIO and the CKO; the characteristics underlying the CKO's role are different.

THE CKO TITLE: SUBSTANCE OR LIP SERVICE

After a flood of companies jumped ahead in the race and appointed CKOs, many Fortune 1000 companies are showing a decline in terms of CKO appointments. There is no need for an explicitly separate position such as a CKO. A CKO can be the same as a CEO or a senior manager, as many companies have successfully demonstrated. Knowledge management should be self-destroying if it is truly successful. That would represent its becoming such an integral part of management and problem-solving tasks that it is no longer treated as a separate "overhead."

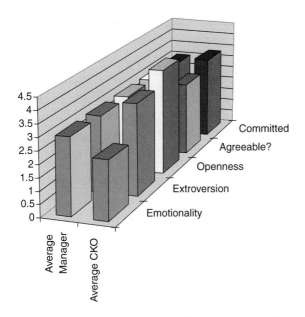

Based on aggregated data from Daintry Duffy, Knowledge Champions: What Does it Take to Be a Successful CKO?
CIO Enterprise, November 15th 1998), 66-71 and Earl and Scott, What is a Chief Knowledge Officer, *Sloan Management Review,* Winter (1999), 29-38.

Figure 13-1 How does a typical CKO compare to an average manager?

CKOs come in many guises and with many titles:

- Director of intellectual capital (e.g., Skandia)
- Director of knowledge management
- Director of organizational learning
- Director of best practices management
- Knowledge or competence evangelist
- Director of sales enablement (e.g., Platinum)
- In some cases, best practices manager, CEO, or strategic knowledge manager

But the key role that this individual plays is still the same: to make the knowledge management system and processes an integral part of regular, daily work. While there is often a CIO where there is a CKO, the reverse is not always true.[3]

KNOWLEDGE MANAGEMENT LEADERSHIP ROLES

A common weakness in knowledge management programs is that the information technology component is often overemphasized at the expense of well-articulated knowledge management roles and responsibilities.[4] Traditional roles, Michael Zack cautions us, do not address either knowledge management or the cross-functional, cross-firm processes that underlie creation, sharing, application, and distribution of knowledge. These processes for managing, defragmenting, and scrubbing knowledge, which can be managed by people other than the formally appointed CKO, include the following tasks:

- *Championing:* Actively promoting the KM project, its adoption, and use.

- *Educating users:* Users not only need to know about the use and value of knowledge management; they also need to be shown what's in it for *them.* That is, corporate knowledge objectives should be tied to personal rewards such as compensation and promotion.

- *Educating the management team:* Management support is critical for the long-term success of any strategic KM system, and showing managers the value of KM is a necessary precursor to successful management of knowledge.

- *Measuring the impact of knowledge management:* Metrics, the hardest part of KM, are also the most convincing of all talking points. (Chapter 14 examines metrics in depth.)

- *Mapping existing knowledge:* Knowledge management must begin with what already exists. Don't try to build new knowledge repositories before you've inventoried the critical parts of explicit and tacit knowledge that already exist.

- *Defragmenting scattered knowledge:* Knowledge might be scattered. Linking this extant knowledge is, for the most part, a technology-based problem.

- *Creating the technology channels:* Technology channels are the sociotechnical networks that help move knowledge around the organization in an efficient manner. Technology channels and their choice are largely determined by the CKO's understanding of what would work, user perceptions of what they need, and organizational work culture.

- *Integrating business processes with the technology enablers:* Knowledge management systems must be built to support business processes. A high-level manager (CKO or equivalent) is usually in the best position to identify business processes that most affect the bottom line.

The CKO's Job Description

As one CKO put it, *"Most CKOs are on a vertical learning curve about managing knowledge."*[a] The CKO focuses on correcting the knowledge flow and eliminate related deficiencies and inefficiencies that exist within the company. The CKO job description looks like this:

---

[a]A comment from one of the 20 CKOs studied in Earl, Michael, and Ian Scott, What is a Chief Knowledge Officer, *Sloan Management Review,* Winter (1999), 29–38.

1. *Optimizing process design for knowledge management:* Design processes for creating new knowledge, distribute existing knowledge, and apply or reuse what is already known.

2. *Creating channels:* Create channels for leveraging untapped knowledge and competencies within the firm. This also implies leveraging the latent value of hidden knowledge for the good of business development—a commonly observed deficiency in CKOs researched.

3. *Integrating knowledge management:* Embody knowledge management in the routine tasks and activities of the firm's employees.

4. *Breaking barriers and eliminating impediments:* Break down technical, cultural, and workflow barriers in communication and knowledge exchange processes. The CKO must also break internal funding barriers by making a strong case for KM investments.

5. *Watching the learning loop:* Ensure that the firm is learning from its past mistakes and failures. While this problem might seem to be ridiculous on first thought, companies in the United States alone spend close to $10 billion on repeating mistakes and solving problems that do not need to be solved again.[5]

6. *Creating financial and competitive value:* Create value out of both the knowledge assets and the knowledge management system. Value need not be solely financial.

7. *Supporting IT and eliminating knowledge flow gaps:* Support the above tasks with IT; bridge knowledge flow gaps.

The CKO as Organizational Glue

Not listed in the CKO's job description is a major challenge—convincing two distinct groups about the value of knowledge management. The first group is management, and the second group is the knowledge workers who will actually use knowledge management as a part of their work. Management needs to be convinced that KM will have a financial payback and will not turn into a financial black hole; employees need to be convinced that KM will not be yet another pain in the neck, akin to project charts, fill-in grids, time sheets, or code checkin/checkout procedures. Persuasive arguments required to convince these two groups can often conflict.

The CKO serves the purpose of *organizational glue* that brings these groups together. Figure 13-2 shows some of the people in the management and user community that a CKO needs to unite. On one side, there are the champions who believe in knowledge management and are willing to stand behind it even if it takes *a leap of faith.* The CKO might fall into this group.

Then, there is a core group with whom a CKO needs to collaborate. These are the knowledge collaborators who often include IT staff, intranet zealots, human resources managers, and occasionally, department (typically technical) heads. Only rarely do collaborators come from outside the organization. External consultants who have jumped on the knowledge management bandwagon rarely know as much as you might know about managing your own firm's knowledge.

Aside from knowledge champions, corporate sponsors, and adherents, there are the knowledge cynics who do not agree on the value of knowledge management. While having

WHO'S REALLY LEARNING AT KM CONFERENCES?

Research studies have found that most CKOs find knowledge management conferences to be a waste of their time. The reason is quite clear: So little is known about knowledge management in these early stages of development that such conferences become excellent *knowledge extraction* (as opposed to knowledge sharing) opportunities for attendees, especially consultants. And remember, conferences can be a good source of examples, but examples should not be mistaken for successful strategies that your company could adopt.

a few cynics is perhaps a good thing, too many can hinder the knowledge management initiative. Without bringing all these stakeholders together on common ground, a CKO cannot even begin to put knowledge management policies and processes in place.

Initiatives and the CKO

A study of 20 CKOs in the United States and Europe revealed that most CKOs believed that the best place to begin knowledge management was by taking charge of explicit knowledge. This was easier for most sponsors and champions to agree upon and understand; the benefits are often more visible. Intranets are perhaps the

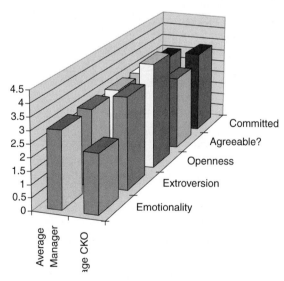

Figure 13-2 The CKO is the organizational glue that binds five distinct groups to knowledge management.

SELLING FORESIGHT IS LIKE TRADING OXYGEN

Selling foresight to senior management and potential users of a knowledge management system is like selling oxygen, suggests, George Von Krogh,* of University of St. Gallen in Switzerland. Rightly so. The customer, who might be the sponsor, the employee, the knowledge worker, the end user, or the collaborator, cannot really see *what* she is buying. You, the seller, in this case, need instruments that are well calibrated to show that you have delivered what you promised in exchange for the money, effort, funding, or resource that was given to you.†
The internal working of those instruments has to be well understood both by you and the person(s) to whom you are selling the idea of knowledge management.

Besides being understood, the use of metrics and values must also be agreed upon.**

---

*See Lorange, Peter, *Implementing Strategic Processes: Change, Learning, and Cooperation*, Blackwell Business, Oxford, Cambridge (1993), and also see Von Krogh, George, and Johan Roos, *Managing Knowledge: Perspectives on Cooperation and Competition*, Sage Publications, Thousand Oaks, CA (1996).

†This is akin to selling oxygen: something that people need but cannot see. The only way of knowing that you got the oxygen that you paid for is to see it on a well-calibrated meter attached to the oxygen cylinder.

**As a senior consultant at the Boston Consulting Group notes that, metrics are, in fact, the hardest part of knowledge management, after its technical implementation and cultural acceptance. Some early proponents adopted purely financial metrics out of sheer frustration from the lack of any other measures.

---

first piece of technology that such initiatives are likely to put into place (if one does not exist yet). The second thing that most CKOs identified was video conferencing. This is one of the best channels for tacit knowledge sharing. Having sponsors buy into this initiative is an easier task, owing to its intensively technological nature, than is buy-in for most other tacit knowledge sharing channels and enablers.

The initiatives that a CKO must take fall into four broad categories as shown in Figure 13-3.

The primary task of a CKO is to enable, not control, knowledge management. Management initiatives relating to both tacit and explicit knowledge can be subclassified into two groups of tasks for a CKO: the organizational and the technical responsibilities.

On the technological front, a CKO needs to build channels for distribution of explicit knowledge and for sharing of tacit knowledge. Note that converting all tacit knowledge into codified form is not one of the priorities mentioned.

On the organizational front, these tasks include the following:

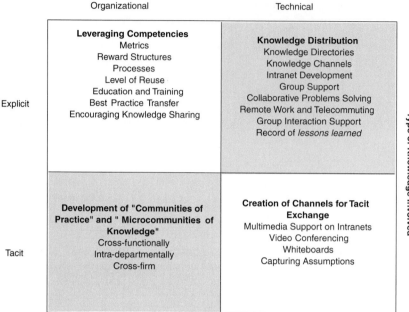

Figure 13-3 Four categories of initiatives for which the CKO or equivalent is often responsible.

1. *Identifying knowledge gaps:* Identify knowledge gaps that exist in critical work processes, and assess ways and tools to bridge such gaps.

2. *Creating a culture of knowledge sharing:* Change corporate culture from that of defensive knowledge hoarding to a knowledge sharing one. The basic assumptions that most companies have developed in the Western Hemisphere are based on the well-proven notion that retaining knowledge and keeping it to yourself works rather well for maintaining job security, respect among peers, and compensation-related rewards. Breaking organizations out of this mold requires strong incentives and the elimination of related risks. These incentives must provide a compelling response to workers who ask the question "Why should I ever share the very knowledge that provides me my job security?"

3. *Creating appropriate metrics:* Create metrics for knowledge work (see Chapter 14), and reward schemes for individuals who share their knowledge.

4. *Developing communities of practice:* Communities of practice must extend across the department(s), throughout the firm, and across collaborating firms, customer sites, allies, and partners.

5. *Diffusing best practices:* Enable sharing and transfer of best practices across the board.

6. *Training:* Educate knowledge workers about the value of knowledge management, and then train them to use the KM system and related protocols. This includes showing knowledge workers how to ask better and smarter questions of their knowledge resources and repositories.

7. *Structuring processes:* Not only should processes be structured, but the CKO should promote better understanding of the types of knowledge created and used by them.

8. *Removing knowledge sharing barriers:* Remove technical and sociocultural barriers to knowledge sharing, transfer, use, and distribution.

9. *Aligning local knowledge:* Align local knowledge creation activities in individual departments and teams with the long-term strategic knowledge vision of the firm.

10. *Creating process triggers:* Improve the level of reuse of existing knowledge by creating *process triggers*[6] and context for reuse. Examples of process triggers could include questions such as:

    • Why is the customer retention level so low for product X?

    • Why does the customer want to buy a competing product (at a higher price) after having tried ours?

    • Why is the customer not satisfied with our product?

    • Why do our products fail to drive out competition?

    • Why is our pricing strategy not working?

    • Why does it take us six months to launch a product that took four months to develop?

11. *Making knowledge management a part and parcel of routine work:* Some theorists have suggested that a successful CKO is one who integrates knowledge management so tightly with the company's ways and processes that he eliminates his own job. This also means that the expectations from a CKO and his future role in the company must be clearly articulated.

Similarly, the technological initiatives that a CKO is responsible for include the following:

1. *Building directories:* Create enterprisewide skills and knowledge directories.

2. *Creating channels:* Create channels for exchange of documents and other codified forms of explicated knowledge.

3. *Extending the intranet:* Develop the intranet and include rich multimedia support within it.

4. *Supporting group work:* Support group and collaborative work through collaborative technology tools and new policies that promote such work.

5. *Providing tools for collaborative problem solving:* Develop and implement tools for collaborative problem solving.

6. *Supporting remote work:* Provide support for distributed work, remote access, telepresence, and telecommuting.

7. *Building repositories:* Build repositories to store "lessons learned." These can begin with simple Notes databases and later be expanded to relational databases tightly integrated with the intranet front end.

8. *Infusing external knowledge:* Enable infusion of external task-specific, domain-specific, and competitive knowledge to provide a more stable competitive stand for the firm.

9. *Enabling tacit knowledge transfer:* Improve knowledge sharing using tools such as video conferencing, whiteboards, mind maps, etc.

10. *Introducing cross-functional tools:* Introduce tools for capturing and exposing assumptions of teams whose members often come from different functional backgrounds.

THE SUCCESSFUL CKO

Since the CKO often works closely with the technology staff, she must have a fairly good understanding of the technology that she intends to deploy as a part of the knowledge management system. Credible discussions with technology partners are unlikely to happen if a CKO is not even sure what an intranet is!

On the other hand, the CKO also needs the skills of an effective manager and an entrepreneur. A CKO needs to understand the workings of the company inside out to be able to comprehend its vital processes. In a way, a CKO must be successful as a *merchant of foresight.*[7] The job involves radical redesign of performance measurement metrics and employee compensation systems to effectively encourage employees to share what they know. If a CKO is unsuccessful on this front, the only possible outcome is enterprise-wide knowledge hoarding.

These two qualities go hand in hand for a typical CKO whose primary responsibility is to be able to create and see the *big picture* and, at the same time, translate it into tasks and concrete deliverables. A CKO will have a zero net effect if she does not clearly understand the business model of the firm and the types of knowledge that are relevant and have the potential for adding value to the business.

HISTORY

The CKO needs to have the breadth of understanding of a CEO and the technological understanding level approximating that of a CIO. It comes as no surprise that many CKOs come with a wide variety of experiences in one or more companies, and many have, in the past, served as CIOs. A formal technical background is not the norm; many CKOs have come from a diverse array of departments such as human resources, internal consulting, finance, marketing, new product development, and even academia.

Another study of 52 CKOs in the United States revealed that the background of the average successful CKO resembles that of a traditional Japanese manager.[8] Unlike most U.S. managers who tend to switch jobs and companies but stay in the same functional area of spe-

CHEVRON'S CASE

Chevron used several tactics to gain support for the CKO's role at both the managerial level and the user level.* These include:

1. *Tying knowledge management initiatives to the knowledge vision:* Chevron uses something equivalent to *The Chevron Way*—an integrated value statement that endorses the management and transfer of knowledge and best practices.

2. *Telling success stories of the knowledge management initiatives at each top management meeting:* This keeps the knowledge management program highly visible.

3. *Removing barriers to knowledge sharing:* The not-invented-here syndrome and the lack of motivation to find new ideas to improve processes were two barriers that had to go. Chevron opened communication channels between executives, managers, employees, customers, and suppliers.

4. *Applying and demonstrating:* All stakeholder groups had a chance to see the benefits of such practices and systems.

*Reported in O'Dell, Carla, and C.J. Grayson, If Only We Knew What We Know: Identification and Transfer of Internal Best Practices, *California Management Review,* vol. 40, no. 3 (1998), 154–173.

cialization, CKOs tend to stay with the same company through different roles. Most CKOs are hired internally simply because there is a stronger likelihood that such a person would have a deeper knowledge of the given firm and a clearer understanding of the big picture.

While a past history of success can get a CKO started on his job, delivering results is the only keeper of that job in the long term. As some CKOs put it, "It is essential to have a strong track record in a variety of roles. Management will buy into your ideas of revamping the way the business works only if they also know that you've been there and done that."[b] Based on CKO data collected in an international study by Earl and Scott, Figure 11-1 shows the typical personality traits found in successful CKOs and their comparison against those of average middle managers. Because of the challenging role of the CKO, 25 percent of the CKOs interviewed in a *CIO* magazine survey quit their jobs for lack of management commitment to the knowledge management project and joined other companies in similar positions. Remember,

[b]Quoted in a sample response reported in Earl, Michael, and Ian Scott, What Is a Chief Knowledge Officer, *Sloan Management Review,* Winter (1999), 29–38.

a formally appointed CKO is not always necessary for a knowledge management project so long as someone is galvanizing and coordinating the knowledge management initiative well (especially in smaller companies where a senior manager or CEO can handle the task).

REWARD STRUCTURES TO ENSURE KNOWLEDGE MANAGEMENT SUCCESS

Employees who will actually use the knowledge management system must have their expectations clearly laid out. Each employee must know why her opinion and contribution to the knowledge management system, as a whole, counts. Trust and cooperation are critical factors in the smooth integration of a knowledge management system into the firm's employee base and as a cultural whole. If a knowledge-related role is assigned and results expected, the CKO must ensure that employees are given the time to contribute to it *as a part* of their job.[9]

It's the CKO's responsibility to motivate employees to use and add value to the knowledge management system and, in turn, the firm. Many companies have successfully established this link. At Buckman Labs, for example, incentive, evaluation, and promotion systems are designed to recognize those who do the best job of knowledge sharing and to penalize those who don't. Similarly, Chaparral Steel has successfully changed its pay structure to reward accumulation of skills, in addition to performance.

Pfizer has developed *competency models* for its treasury executives that call for more than basic financial skills. Knowledge building and knowledge sharing are considered critical for management as the company has successfully created knowledge linkages across the organization. For this reason the contribution to such linkages is strongly linked to employee compensation packages.

This discussion also implies that technology *by itself* is not the complete solution. If a technology focus becomes the bloodstream of the knowledge management strategy, little, if anything, will be accomplished. The solution does not lie in trying to index everything or in storing it in a database; it lies in focusing on the critical knowledge management activities that (initially) add immediate value to the firm.[c]

LESSONS LEARNED

We examined the need for a leadership role for the continued success of the knowledge management system and the knowledge management strategy. As the ninth step in the 10-step road map, we discussed how change management must occur and how reward structures must be modified to help the knowledge management system succeed.

---

[c]Immediate value can be both in the short term and in the long term.

Some lessons that you should take away with you include:

- *You might or might not need a CKO.* A separate person serving as the CKO *might* be justified in large-size companies, but it is not always a requirement. The ideal CKO always encompasses the definition of the role, and not the person with that title: It can be an existing senior manager, the CEO, or occasionally, even the CIO. The CKO should have a fairly good understanding of the company's business model and driving technology enablers. Plan for knowledge management success using the CKO as an agent for selling foresight, and select one who can actually make a convincing case for knowledge management in front of knowledge skeptics.

- *Understand exactly a chief knowledge officer's role.* The CKO serves as organizational glue that binds key stakeholders in a company. Understand how a CKO is related to the CIO, CFO, and CEO, and choose a leader who qualifies. Remember that most successful CKOs come from within the organization and rarely, if ever, from outside.

- *Knowledge management is only about 30 percent technical.* The hardest part comes after the KM system is built. That part involves the cultural changes needed in the company's work processes to make knowledge management acceptable as a way of work life for both your company's knowledge workers and managers. These challenges dwarf those faced by data warehouses and electronic commerce systems.

- *Knowledge management needs strong reward structures.* Knowledge sharing cannot be mandated; it can only be encouraged by complementary reward structures that encourage knowledge sharing and use.

The success of knowledge management in any company, big or small, depends on how well the knowledge champion, whatever you decide to call her, brings all stakeholders—management, employees, partners, and sponsors—to agree on beliefs and expectations. A knowledge management project *sold* to this stakeholder group is almost half-successful even before the first line of code is written, or an initial strategic change made.

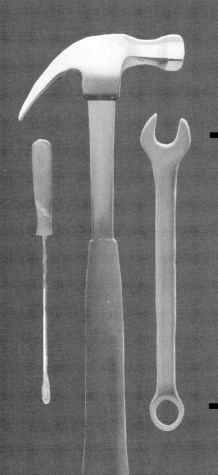

PART IID
THE FINAL PHASE
AND BEYOND:
MEASURING ROI
AND PERFORMANCE

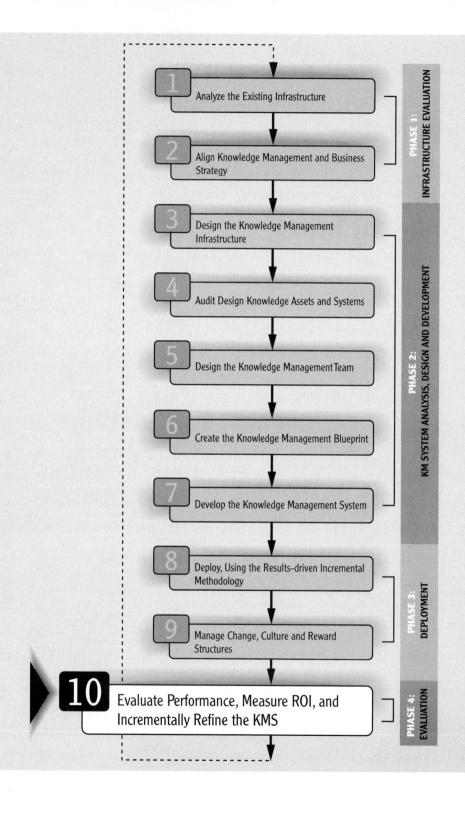

CHAPTER 14

METRICS FOR KNOWLEDGE WORK

IN THIS CHAPTER

✔ Calculate return on investment for knowledge management investments.

✔ Evaluate benchmarking as a comparative knowledge metric.

✔ Evaluate knowledge management ROI by using the balanced scorecard (BSC) method.

✔ Use quality function deployment for creating strategic knowledge metrics.

✔ Identify what *not* to measure.

✔ Understand alternative metrics such as the Skandia Navigator and the FASB approach.

✔ Classify and evaluate processes using the APQC process classification framework.

✔ Review and select software tools for tracking complex metrics, QFDs and BSCs.

VAGUELY RIGHT IS BETTER THAN PRECISELY WRONG
—L. LODISH[1]

Having deployed the knowledge management system and put a knowledge management strategy in place, how do you measure and evaluate its business impact? I have researched several companies that have been successful in implementing knowledge management but have yet to come across one that has a strong measurement program in place. Some companies, for example, Dow Chemical, Skandia, Canon, and Buckman Laboratories, have begun to measure their intellectual capital, with the belief that growth on this front is often a good indicator of future financial health, and that decline is an early warning signal that cannot be ignored.

So, with this in mind, in this chapter (the tenth step of the KM road map) we bypass traditional measurements (such as ROI and Tobin's *q)* and avoid pitfalls to explore three ways of measuring: financial and competitive RoKI-benchmarking, QFDs, and the balanced scorecard. We select an appropriate set of metrics and arrive at a lean but powerful composite. The indicators, tools, and guidelines that are discussed here can help shape both your company's knowledge management system design and its knowledge management strategy.

We also see how to classify and evaluate processes with the APQC process classification framework, and we identify software tools for tracking complex metrics, QFDs, and BSCs.

Finally, through case studies, we see how successful companies approached metrics, what errors they made, and what we can learn from both their mistakes and successes.

TRADITIONAL METRICS

Let's dispose of two metrics that, perhaps useful in their place, do not transfer to a meaningful role in knowledge management metrics: financial ROI and total cost of ownership (TCO).

FINANCIAL ROI AND TOBIN'S Q

Albert Einstein, very thought provokingly, reminds us that *what can be measured is not always important and what is important cannot always be measured.* It does not take an Einstein to conclude that the value of knowledge management cannot be fully measured in terms of financial return on investment.

A relatively old measure that has been in use for many years within business and academic circles is Tobin's *q.* This metric essentially measures the ratio between the firm's market valuation and the cost of replacing its physical assets. While Tobin's *q* provides a snapshot of the firm's state of intellectual health at a given point in time, it provides no direction for knowledge management strategy development. It does not tell you what you are doing wrong or what to focus on. What is needed is a more dynamic view of knowledge performance that can help a firm trace both the growth and decline of its knowledge assets and the reasons underlying such changes. Traditional metrics like Tobin's *q* do not tell a firm how it can create further value, prevent imitation or substitution,[2] and leverage its knowledge assets to gain a sustainable competitive advantage.

Nevertheless, when it comes to measuring returns on investment in knowledge management, two conventional approaches are in common use: putting a dollar figure on intellectual assets, and determining the dollar amounts saved or earned by using existing knowledge.

TOTAL COST OF OWNERSHIP

Current methods of measuring and evaluating information technology investments do little justice to information technology itself. How, then, can we expect those methods to be able to give us a clear picture of how our knowledge investments—which stretch far beyond pure technology alone—are faring? Our interviews and studies show that companies do not always demand solid business cases for IT investments but have trouble handling decisions based on *soft* gains and benefits. Maturity of judgment becomes a distinctive inhibiting factor that prevents them from making decisions where limited quantitative data exists.

Many companies have responded by falling back on a *total cost of ownership* approach, which is much touted by Microsoft's release of Windows 2000. This methodology identifies and measures components of IT expense beyond the initial cost of implementation. While TCO can be a useful tool to reduce ongoing costs by improving IT management practices, it does not provide a sound foothold for decision making. TCO does not cut it as a sufficient knowledge metric for several reasons:

- It leaves out significant cost categories, such as complexity costs.
- It ignores benefits beyond pure costing.
- It neglects strategic factors.
- It provides little or no basis for comparison with other departments and other companies, such as competing firms operating in the same markets.
- Lifecycle costs are difficult to gauge.

Applying TCO blindly can lead to bad and highly impolitic decisions. For example, the decision to switch vendors to get the lowest prices does not capture the implicit cost of supporting multiple vendors, the cost of dealing with compatibility issues, or the benefits of high-volume purchasing. Total cost of ownership (or a similar measure fails) to do justice, comprehensively or completely, to the decisions made.

LEARNING MORE FROM THE TELEPHONE

Just as a telephone is hard to cost-justify and evaluate, knowledge management is something firms often find difficult to cost-justify in the face of other needed investments, but is something they want to and should have. Even though middle managers feel the need for a strong knowledge management initiative, convincing senior management to shell out the couple of million dollars for an initiative with intangible results can be a hard sell. However, there are ways and means to measure the short-term gains to demonstrate the need for, and the extent

Two Ways to Measure—The Case of KEMA and Platinum

Companies have approached knowledge measures from different perspectives. What is commonly seen is a combination of the following:

Cost-based approach
      Did it reduce costs?
      Did we accomplish more by spending the same?
Market-value-based approach
      Did it improve our market leadership?
      Did it bring more stability to the company?
      Did we increase our market share?
      Did our company stock rise in value?
Effect-on-income approach
      What effect did it have on expense reduction?
      What effect did it have on customer retention?
      What effect did it have on repeat business?
      What effect did it have on profit margins?
      What effect did it have on the bottom line?

One way to measure the performance of knowledge investments is to put a dollar value on the company's intellectual assets. In doing this, one might examine the firm's patents, proprietary technologies, or products. When we talk about products, we also need to take into account processes. Very often, a company gains an edge because it can perform certain tasks in a better, cost-effective, or quality-enhancing way. Many companies, such as the Swedish financial services group Skandia, have calculated a dollar value for intellectual capital to claim that previously immeasurable productivity gains were overlooked by "old economy" accountants. The Dutch engineering business KEMA calculated that its employees are worth more than the profits they make from installing and fixing power supplies. In 1994, KEMA put a price tag of 700 million Dutch guilders (US$400 million) on

of the longer-term *guesstimations* of value added by knowledge management to the firm's bottom line and competitive standing.

The Metric Is the Limitation

A recurring problem in knowledge management is the problem posed by a lack of standard metrics for measuring the impact of KM. Two of the most widely cited research projects relating to knowledge management and organizational learning are the case descriptions provided by DeGeus[3]

the intellectual prowess of its 1,200 employees, calculated as a sum of training fees, experience within the company, and the value of university degrees. In 1994, however, KEMA's profits had amounted to just 19.8 million Dutch guilders (US$12 million), representing a rather poor return on the company's knowledge "investment."

When the company realized the actual value, it was rather concerned at the poor return on its knowledge-based investments. This made the future work for the company's management clear—to make more money out of the knowledge assets that it had.

Separate work was done on three fronts: strategic knowledge management (understanding what kinds of intelligence the company would like), operational knowledge management (defining processes to help staff learn), and the valuation of knowledge as an asset.

The second type to measurement mechanism looks at how much money the firm saves or makes if it relies on using knowledge that exists both inside and outside the firm. For example, does using knowledge help the company get newer versions of its products out on the shelves faster? Does it reduce costs? Similarly, processes can be measured on the basis of how much they add to productivity, speed, additional revenues, and customer satisfaction. Yet another way might be to measure cost savings associated with putting a given piece of information online, as opposed to circulating it on paper.

Platinum Technology has successfully used this approach. Platinum rationalized the expense involved in initiating a knowledge management program in terms of the dollar figures that it saved in FedEx expenses in the very first year. Instead of using some elusive measure to justify the value of knowledge management to senior management, Platinum's knowledge management champions used something very visible and clearly defined (FedEx savings) to measure cost savings that resulted from using the knowledge management system. The actual benefits, as would be anyone's guess, were much higher than just these cost savings.

Soon, it will become clear why such measurements do not faithfully reflect the value added by management of a firm's knowledge. There is no perfect way to determine just how much knowledge and its effective management contributed to the outcomes.

at Shell Corporation and by Ray Stata[4] at Analog Devices. DeGeus' approach at Shell used scenarios in the strategic planning cycle that encouraged managers to revisit and challenge commonly accepted assumptions. The underlying belief was that learning would not take place unless managers exposed the hidden and embedded assumptions with which they approached new problems.[a]

---

[a]This finding is very much in line with some of the research done by some of my own colleagues. For example, see the research work done by Balasubramaniam Ramesh at the J. Mack Robinson College of Business at Georgia State University, Atlanta, and at the Naval Postgraduate School, Monterey, California.

Similarly, Stata found that focusing on activities, such as improving response time to external changes and utilizing planning and quality improvement as learning tools rather than purely administrative tools, could accelerate learning.

Chaparral Steel, a large U.S. steel producer, similarly found that there was a lot to gain by emphasizing problem solving, constantly integrating internal and external knowledge into daily work-related activities of employees,[5] and allowing the time and resources needed to make this integration happen. In addition, a good reward structure helped further.

COMMON PITFALLS IN CHOOSING METRICS

No metric is better than one that is *absolutely wrong*. A choice of a wrong metric can have more ill effects than positive ones. Metrics, when applied to knowledge work, or in general, are vulnerable to seven common pitfalls.

USING TOO MANY METRICS

A few robust metrics are better than a number of marginally significant ones. A good rule of thumb is about 20 metrics. They need to focus on the past, present, and future *simultaneously* to be able to relate past performance, present processes, and future results. The common problem that many measurement programs become victims of is that of putting too much emphasis on the past. Knowing the past is good, but it rarely is sufficient to give you a concrete idea about where your present efforts are leading your company. As John Naisbitt put it, *"We are drowning in a sea of information and starving for knowledge."* Make sure you do not add any further to that glut of information by introducing more metrics than can be effectively, accurately, and efficiently tracked. Forget quantity; focus instead on linking measures to strategic capabilities, competitive positioning, customer expectations, and financial indicators.[6]

As Josh Billings once said, "Knowledge is like money, the more he gets, the more he craves."[b] Nothing perhaps captures the essence of manager's rush to add more metrics once "they" figure out that they have found something that affects their company's bottom line. In this rush, many finally end up with more metrics than they can simultaneously keep track of.

Robert Kaplan and David Norton have an interesting discussion between a pilot and a passenger on the opening page of their book.[7] The pilot says that he needs to work on airspeed, so he *ignores* the altitude and fuel gauge altogether. "It is not what I am focusing on," he says. Amused at their own interesting analogy, they think that you would not want to fly in his plane, ever! Isn't this very close to what companies do when they focus on a single metric such as the bottom line or market share? On the other hand, some go to the opposite

---

[b]The original source of this quote is disputed. Found on www.amorphismsgalore.com, March 18, 1999.

extreme and try to track too many of them at the same time. This is where *lean* metrics fit in. Lean metrics are the *few but essential* metrics that can be simultaneously tracked.

Some metrics might seem reasonable, but when they are put into action, they result in counterproductive consequences. A good lean metric must be precise, tied to overall value (not just profits), applicable, and designed to motivate extranormal effort from employees.

DELAYED AND RISKY REWARD TIES

Rewards that are tied to metrics with a relatively longer term focus should be robust and structured in a manner that allows employees to reap short-term benefits by successfully achieving them. Job mobility is a fact of life. Delayed rewards will only bias employees to work toward metrics that deliver short-term payoffs to *them*. To keep the *long view*, select metrics that can be measured today but impact future outcomes. Alternatively, the long-term gains of the firm should be tied closely to the compensation of the employees (stock options are a good example).

CHOOSING METRICS THAT ARE HARD TO CONTROL

Companies often make the grave mistake of implementing metrics that are beyond the control of their employees. Phrases such as "Build a $2 billion browser market by 2001," "Let every hand in America hold a Palmtop by the dawn of the next millennium," or "Put a NetPC on every desktop" are visionary ideas but almost impossible to control or achieve even through systematic efforts. There are exceptions of course: Microsoft's Internet strategy and Netscape's browser business are a few of those. But these are exceptions rather than examples of what can be normally[c] achieved. Similarly for knowledge management systems, you cannot have metrics that cannot be controlled. Statements such as "Build the largest knowledge repository of Website design solutions" look good on paper, and that's about it.

CHOOSING METRICS THAT ARE HARD TO FOCUS ON

Performance of a company is not solely based on internally generated ideas. 3M and Xerox are leaders in innovation. But the difference is that 3M has actually commercialized more ideas than Xerox. The result has been that Bill Gates and Steve Jobs built entire industries on a few ideas that Xerox created (in its Palo Alto Research Center, PARC) but never used.

The goals of the metrics you decide to use for managing knowledge should be crystal clear; *external knowledge* should be very tightly integrated into any knowledge management strategy. Metrics need to reward not just internal ideas but *all* ideas that can be actually used.

---

[c]And let us not forget that Microsoft had a cash surplus of $9 billion, and Netscape had a truly innovative idea backed by enormous amounts of venture capital.

If you think that the PalmPilot family of Palm PCs are surprisingly successful products coming out of 3COM's bag of tricks, remember that the product was externally acquired from US Robotics (which had previously bought out Palm Computing, the commercial originator of the device). The key idea is that the metrics that you select must encourage decisions that also move your company in the same direction as its long-term goals. This concept is illustrated in Figure 14-1.

CHOOSING METRICS THAT EMPHASIZE HARD RESULTS AND NEGLECT THE "SOFT STUFF"

Many companies emphasize hard (often financial) results while neglecting or totally ignoring soft ones. A national survey[8] of U.S. organizations revealed that about 60 percent of the organizations studied never officially set any soft goals related to managing people, suppliers, customers, and innovation even when the hard goals were clearly laid out. In spite of all the windy rhetoric about loving customers, empowerment, and learning, not many executives are willing to put measures where their mouths are.[d] It is dangerous for top management to focus on hard results and expect lower-level managers to take care of the rest. Financial success, for example,

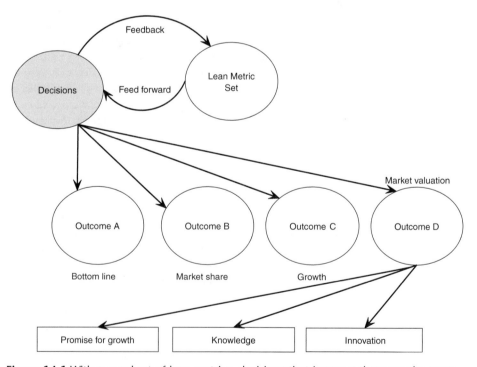

Figure 14-1 With a good set of lean metrics, decisions that improve them are the same decisions that improve the company's desired long-term outcomes.

as many research studies have shown, is highly dependent on "soft" employee attitudes and behavior. Make sure that your hard and soft measures go hand in hand and are well balanced.

CHOOSING METRICS THAT ARE TOO REAR-VIEW ORIENTED

Too often, measurement is not used to anticipate the future but to record the past.[9] One way to avoid this trap is to ask yourself this question: Do we have metrics that can serve as early warning signals for future problems and signal future opportunities?

MEASURING THE WRONG THINGS

Companies can run into troubled waters when they decide to measure things that are precisely wrong. This is very different from the notion that a few good measures today are better than a perfect one tomorrow. One lousy metric tomorrow is better than a wrong one today. If that happens, tomorrow might never come![e]

Wrong metrics can often prove more damaging than helpful. Not all metrics, such as calls answered per hour or sales pitches per week, that can be measured easily and cleanly are necessarily good. Similarly, for knowledge work, measuring aspects such as time spent reading knowledge reports or intranet screens are poor metrics. I could as well be sipping coffee (God forbid vodka!) while playing Quake II on my laptop while my desktop is connected to the knowledge management system at work! A poor metric would still create a perception of productivity. The number of contributions by employees to a knowledge repository is an equally worthless measure. Employees then try to maximize the *number* of contributions, and then the value of those contributions takes a second place.[f] There is something to be learned from McKinsey; McKinsey places value on the number of times its consultants' contributions are accessed by other consultants.

All the Right Things Not Measured

The other side of the coin is not measuring all the right things. Without getting into the complexities of agency-agent conflict theory, a manager or employee will tend to maximize

---

[d]William Schienmann and his colleagues point to the serious gulf between what should be measured and what actually is measured. See Schienmann, William, and John Lingle. Seven Greatest Myths of Measurement, *IEEE Engineering Management Review,* Spring (1998), 114–116.

[e] "…tomorrow might never come," from a song by Janis Joplin, in *The Best of Janis Joplin,* Warner Music.

[f]When I tried to judge the level of contribution of my students (forum members) in one of my classes based on the number of contributions, I ran into a similar problem. Members tried to push up the count of their contributions rather than focus on their relative worth. I tried a more successful approach later on: I counted the number of follow-up comments that their contributions raised and the number of times they responded to other people's posts. Such an policy was arguably more conducive to conversations and problem solving.

RIGHT ANSWERS TO WRONG QUESTIONS

An interesting example* comes from a services firm that wanted to improve customer satisfaction with their telephone customer support center. Reasonably enough, the firm's managers decided to use the following metrics. On first thought, all of these seemed to make perfect sense:

Number of rings until the phone was answered
Average waiting time till a representative came on line
Number of calls answered per hour per representative
Number of times a customer was put on hold
Percentage of each hour that an average representative spent talking to a customer

All of them seemed easy to measure accurately and with little human effort. Very soon the firm improved on all of these measures, but customers were highly dissatisfied. When the researchers probed a little deeper, they realized how the choice of metrics had created an *exactly opposite* effect of what the firm had expected. Representatives were rushing their customers through their queries, were hanging up on them, were giving them the most convenient answers, were refusing to transfer them to more knowledgeable staff, and had become driven by exactly what was being measured—a lot of calls per hour without long holding times!

As Figure 14-2 illustrates, these metrics did not produce an effect that was intended, since the ones that mattered most (customer satisfaction and accurate answers) were never measured. Perhaps they were more difficult to measure, and automated telephone monitoring equipment could not be used for the purpose. If such wrong metrics had not been chosen, customer satisfaction levels would not have taken a downward nose dive as they did.

---

*This example is actually a collection of anecdotes across multiple firms that J. Hauser and G. Katz reported in Metrics: You Are What You Measure! *European Management Journal,* vol. 16, no. 5 (1998), 517–528, encountered in the course of a consulting project for their research paper.

the metrics that are actually measured. If a manager is told that a high market share for a product indicates brand value, he will try to maximize the market share of that product, even though quality (not measured) might be equally important. John Hauser and Gerald Katz explain this concept,[10] which is further illustrated in Figure 14-2.

Let A, B, C, Y, and Z be some arbitrary metrics. If all five of these are important, but only three of these, A, B, and X, are actually measured, employees will focus only on those and simply ignore Y and Z, however important they might be. Managers and employees who maximize A, B, and X will be rewarded for their performance even if Y and Z go to the dogs. Soon

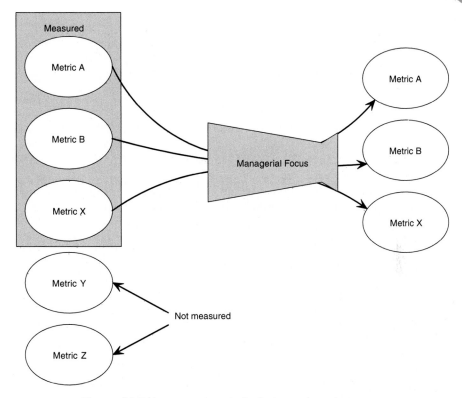

Figure 14-2 You cannot control what you do not measure

the entire company or department is focused on improving the metrics that are actually measured, as they alone provide an indication of the quality of their work. If A, B, and X lead to productive results, then the metrics are *considered* effective. If they fail to produce good results, they are considered ineffective. Hauser and Katz suggest that the chosen metrics gain tremendous inertia and that employees who have painfully learned to maximize the chosen metrics fear to change course. The problem begins right there.

Knowledge sharing and creation often tend to be akin to metric Y—ignored and little rewarded. Knowledge-intensive companies, on the other hand, have included knowledge sharing and creation in their repertoire of critical metrics. Every employee's compensation is, in part, determined by the amount of knowledge that the employee adds and the frequency with which other employees refer back to that contribution.[g] Choosing the right metrics is therefore critical both to evaluate the performance of your knowledge management strategy and to make it work in the first place.

---

[g]Davenport and Prusak also suggest that employees need to be given unbridled time to share knowledge and exchange ideas *as a part* of their jobs. If the time spent doing this is not one of your selected and appropriately rewarded metrics, knowledge creation and sharing are unlikely to happen.

THREE WAYS TO MEASURE

We met Roger Bohn's *Stages of Knowledge Growth* framework in the preceding chapters. Thanks to its simplicity and ease of use, it provides a more readily usable method for the measurement of process and technological knowledge. However, the biggest strength of this framework is also its primary weakness. The Stages of Knowledge technique is good at providing a 15,000-foot view and a clear *bigger picture,* but it does not let you examine processes and improvements at a lower level. While we began with that model, we will need to progress to some technique that is better suited for a microlevel analysis.

In the following sections, we examine three possible approaches to measuring knowledge work and the efficacy of the knowledge management system.[h] The first is a straightforward benchmarking methodology; this can be a good starting point, but in the long term, this technique loses value and flexibility. The second technique is the House of Quality.[11] That competes with the third technique: the *balanced scorecard* approach. The advantage of the House of Quality (QFD) methodology is that it has been widely used and a number of low cost software tools can partially automate its application.

BENCHMARKING

Robert Camp aptly describes benchmarking as the *"search for industrywide best practices that lead to superior performance."*[12] In plain English, this simply means that benchmarking is an undertaking of companies that aim to emulate the ways things are done best, anywhere within or outside their firm, industry, or sector. Many large firms have adopted benchmarking as a significant, systematic technique for measuring the company's performance toward its strategic goals. This concept was popularized by Carla O'Dell[13] and her colleagues at the American Productivity and Quality Center (www.apqc.org). One argument for benchmarking is that there are existing best practices within different parts of the same company. So we should begin by identifying those skills and capabilities within our own organizations before we look outside. Companies repeatedly end up solving the same problems that have already been solved in other offices or locations of the same company; they expend time and money building solutions to issues that have already been addressed: *If only we knew what we know!*[14] Texas Instruments, Harris Corporation, AMP, UNISYS, and Rank Xerox have tried this approach and reaped substantial benefits and cost savings.

The benefits of benchmarking are not limited just to process improvement or reuse; they extend far beyond and promote both the growth and acceptance of a learning culture throughout the organization. Benchmarking efforts can often provide insights into areas such as:

---

[h]There are other possible, although lesser-structured approaches that might be considered besides the three approaches that I discuss in this chapter.

- Overall productivity of knowledge investments
- Service quality
- Customer satisfaction and the operational level of customer service
- Time to market in relation to other competitors
- Costs, profits, and margins
- Distribution
- Relationships and relationship management

The Wise Learn Many Things from Their Enemies[i]

Even though the term *benchmarking* probably did not exist when Aristophanes made the above quote in 414 B.C., he said something very profound about it! By benchmarking your own business against your competitor's, you get information on how to tweak your company's performance goals to stay competitive in relation to your competitors. Arthur Andersen, an international consulting firm, perhaps took the first strike at the intimidating problem of measuring knowledge work. Andersen developed a tool[15] in association with APQC called the Knowledge Management Assessment Tool (KMAT); it contained a series of questions on a scale. Answers to these questions could then be compared to the industry-specific and cross-industry averages of the responses. This process is, in essence, benchmarking.

By using such a relative measure, all companies stand to gain. By knowing where they stand on the intellectual forefront in relation to their competition, companies can focus on improving processes and process knowledge in areas where their scores are below average. Benchmarking, like any other business process, is most likely to produce a payback when strategic business objectives and goals drive it.[16]

Benchmark Targets

Table 14-1 summarizes possible targets against which you can benchmark your company's knowledge management initiatives. You can identify other relevant targets from your own company, from rival firms, from nonrival firms, or from averages representing your industry or sector. Each has its own benefits and downsides, and the choice, finally, is one of subjective judgment and weighted costs.

Stephen Drew proposed the original version of the target set that this table is built upon.[17] He also suggested that a possible target was international firms. I disagree with this stand and have not included that as a potential target, since the preceding options, by themselves, encompass international firms. Rarely do American firms compete solely with domestic rivals.

There are companies that represent *the ideal firm* within each industry. Lacking any other options, this is usually the best place to begin. These firms have performance levels that other

---

[i]Aristophanes: *Birds,* 414 B.C. as cited at http://www.aphorismsgalore.com/. Little did Aristophanes guess at that time, about 2,400 years ago, that his ideas would be so applicable to knowledgement management!

Table 14-1 What Do You Benchmark Against?

Benchmark Target	Upsides	Downsides
Other units within your company	This breaks down internal barriers to communication and conversation between various divisions and offices of your company; targets are easily accessible.	Internal policies might come into play; the measures are not indicative of what is considered superior performance in your industry.
Competing firms	Your company is measured against its direct competition; you get a fair understanding of the knowledge assets of your competitors as an aggregate; partners can easily be identified.	Legalities can make this very difficult; if a trusted third party such as a consulting firm is brought in, additional costs are imposed.
Industry	All of the above; this also lets you gauge your company's standing in the overall market	This can be very expensive; privacy issues begin to surface.
Cross-industry	You might be able to gain valuable insights from noncompeting firms and apply them to your own company.	All of the above; this does not let you gauge your company's standing in relation to your competitors; the sample population is not truly representative of your own industry or sector; it is often difficult to persuade companies to participate in such an effort; the cost of such an effort is rarely worth it.

firms aspire to achieve. In the software industry, arguably, every firm aspires to be a Microsoft. In terms of customer loyalty, every firm aspires to be an Apple Computer. Other examples, including some provided by Stephen Drew,[18] of such role models are listed in Table 14-2.

Although benchmarking can be a good starting point, you need to be aware of its limitations. Benchmarking, by itself, cannot be used as a strategy for knowledge management. The best that it can do is provide a relative set of measures that can help gauge what your efforts are leading to. Many companies, including Xerox, have successfully used it in their *10-step* program; however, it is not a sufficient metric for knowledge work in and of itself.

THE BENCHMARKING PROCESS

On the lines of Xerox's benchmarking program, M.J. Spendolini[19] has suggested a five-step procedure for benchmarking efforts. An adapted version of this process, applied to knowledge work, is shown in Figure 14-3.

Table 14-2 Prevalent Role Models in the Benchmarking Process

Performance Areas	Commonly Accepted Role Models
Speed of product development	Netscape Corporation
Knowledge management integration	Buckman Labs
Knowledge management technology implementation	Platinum Technology
Software development and marketing	Microsoft Corporation
Innovation and new product development	3M
Customer loyalty	Apple Computer
Brand management	Disney
JIT manufacturing	Toyota
Logistics and enterprise-wide IT leverage	Wal-Mart
Knowledge management measurement efficacy	Skandia
Mail order	Dell, L.L. Bean, Lands End, Gateway
Franchising	McDonald's
Quality management	Motorola
Product line recognition	O'Reilly publishers
Strategic planning	General Electric
Cost-based competition through logistics and market demand volume	E-machines Inc., Airtran, Southwest Airlines, Apollo Printers

The benchmarking process can be used for *self-comparison* as well. That is, you can use the benchmark to obtain an initial benchmark value before you implement a knowledge management system or program. You can then, at a later stage, run the same benchmark to see if anything improved from last time. For example, you might want to see if your knowledge sharing network and customer support repository have a positive effect on the average level of customer satisfaction. You can benchmark the level of customer satisfaction both before and after the new system is implemented and see if any changes occurred. Be cautioned, however, that this is a slippery road: If you select the wrong benchmark, you will end up focusing on the wrong set of processes.

Benchmark Lessons

If you consider your company's knowledge management system as a competitive resource, then build into the four things that benchmarking teaches:

1. *Make it valuable.* Focus on including knowledge that is most valuable and then expand the coverage to less valuable knowledge. The key phrase is "valuable knowledge with rel-

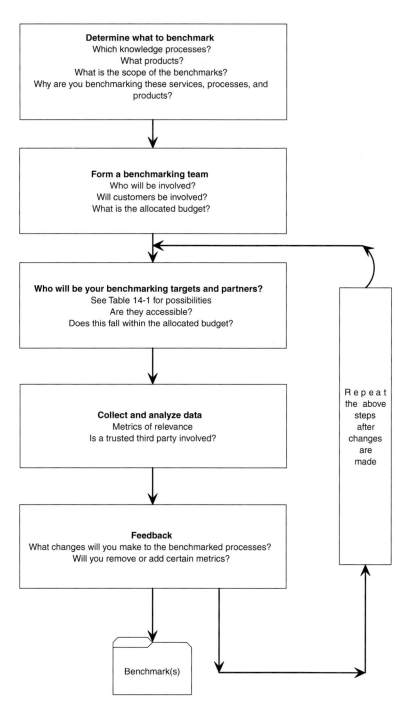

Figure 14-3 The benchmarking process adapted to knowledge work.

atively short term payoffs." However, be careful not to ignore the long-term payoffs and investments. Let the types of knowledge (such as customer support knowledge, design knowledge, and competitive bid-related knowledge) that have immediate outcomes be the starting point, and then expand the benchmark's coverage to other less compelling or semisignificant areas. Benchmarking will, at the very least, provide information about the areas where you lag behind your competition. Focus on those areas *first.*

Anecdotal evidence suggests that managers do not buy into ideas that strain finances of a company without short-term payoffs for too long. Even though a comprehensive knowledge management strategy might be at work in the background, show your senior management some short-term outcomes.

2. *Make it rare.* Focus on the areas of knowledge that give you an edge over competition. Through benchmarking studies, you can easily figure out the areas in which your competition is not strong. If any of those areas are a possible source of competitive advantage, by all means, support them!

    Gateway, for example, is known for its customer service. If you have a problem with a computer you bought from them, you know that you will probably find a knowledgeable customer support representative on the other end. Almost all PC manufacturers have some kind of customer support, but Gateway decided to strengthen this over anything else. Most Gateway's customers tend to be repeat buyers simply because of their excellent customer service. Gateway also uses a customer knowledge repository to be able to track all previous problems that a customer might have had in the past.

    Some companies build a competitive advantage by taking one of the given metrics to a level that is rare and that customers value. NEC has built on this rarity as well. NEC's printer division provides an overnight replacement warranty for all its laser printers for two years from the date of purchase. By being able to track customer information through a sophisticated knowledge retrieval system, NEC provides overnight replacements after asking little more than one question (the printer's serial number) on the phone.[20]

3. *Make it hard to copy.* Customer data is an excellent example of a resource that is very hard to copy. Benchmarking can help you figure out the resources that you have and your competition does not. If you focus on resources that can be copied, it will, at best, buy you a temporary competitive advantage. However, if you focus on knowledge areas in which your employees possess skills, you can make it immensely difficult for your competition to copy those without luring away your employees. Consulting companies have known this for a long time, and it's about time you thought of applying the same idea to the knowledge assets within your own company.

4. *Make it hard to substitute.* Whatever categories of knowledge that you focus on, make sure that straightforward substitutes do not exist. Companies that thought they had gained an edge by outsourcing a part of their manufacturing operations to firms in Third World countries did not take long to realize that everyone else could do the same. And they did.

    Knowledge relating to skills, reputation, and experience cannot be easily substituted with close equivalents. Make sure you focus on such areas when you begin.

Benchmarking is unlikely to reveal such areas unless a high level of job diversity exists in the employee pool that is involved in the effort.[j]

Benchmarking practices often reveal anecdotal evidence and impressions about competition. It's dangerous to rely on such impressions[21] because they cannot be generalized in any way. Benchmarking is most useful when you know what your expectations and objectives are and the process itself is closely tied to your firm's strategic knowledge drivers.

HOUSE OF QUALITY AND QUALITY FUNCTION DEPLOYMENT

The House of Quality[k] approach was developed by Hauser and Clausing in an original paper that appeared in the *Harvard Business Review*.[22] This methodology has been successfully adapted to link customer needs to business processes and internal decisions.

House of Quality Metrics Matrix

Figure 14-4 shows the basic House of Quality metrics matrix. We begin by listing the desirable outcomes on the left wall of the house. As the *quality function deployment* (QFD) method incorporates an increasing number of these desired outcomes, the *outcomes* wall of the *house* begins to build up.

Be careful to select outcomes that are that observable without much delay and can be seen clearly. Being able to see outcomes clearly does not imply that they must be easily measurable quantitatively. Outcomes can be high level or low level. Examples of such target outcomes include:

• Improve knowledge sharing to a level where 20 percent of an average employee's work is based on existing knowledge.

• Speed up problem solving by a factor of 5 percent over the next six months.

• Improve quality such that the rate of failure of product X decreases by 15 percent within the next 12 months.

• Generate more conversations among employees in our Atlanta and Barbados offices (a relatively vague but measurable outcome).

• Increase customer satisfaction levels by 50 percent (as measured by our surveys).

• Create a comprehensive knowledge repository on our Winblows 2004 (fictitious product) operating system for use by support representatives within three years, etc.

---

[j]This is in line with the Ikujiro Nonaka's idea that employees might not be aware of factors contributing to their success because these factors are often deeply embedded in their practices. Diversity in the population implies that participants starting at the upper-management level and going right down to the lay worker are involved.

[k]The use of this technique is commonly referred to as quality function deployment (QFD).

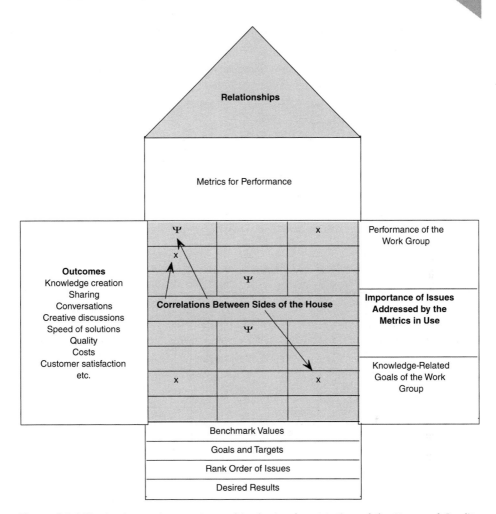

Figure 14-4 The basic metrics matrix used in the implementation of the House of Quality methodology

Although these should not exactly be your own goals, the point is that even though some of the objectives might be high level, the outcomes are observable. On the other hand, an objective like "create new knowledge" or "dominate the South American coffee markets" (where the coffee market is a vague definition, domination is not articulated, and the extent of what is considered South American is unclear) is too vague. You'll never know when you get there, and when you get there you'll never know that you are already there!

To attach relative priorities to each of these objectives, we attach weights to each of them. These weights form the right-hand wall of the house and indicate the importance of the issues in question. See Figure 14-5, for an example.

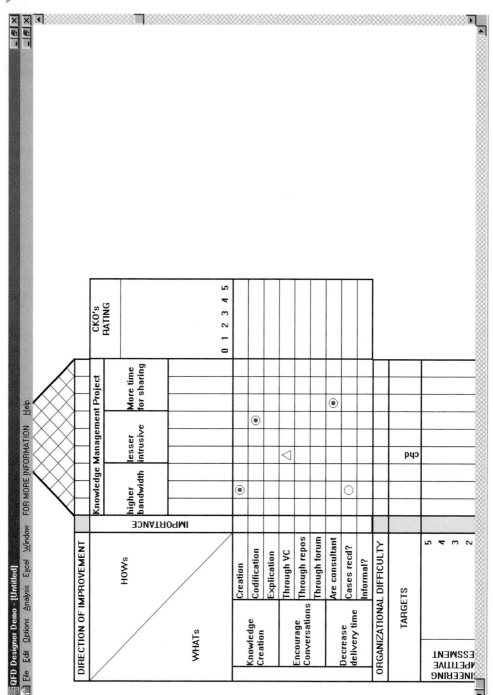

Figure 14-5 An example of the House of Quality approach applied to a knowledge management project

The selected objectives are grouped and listed on the left-hand side of the house matrix. The relative weights are assigned to each of these objectives on a scale of 1 to 5. Some other tools let you attach weights on a percentage scale of 0 to 100, as originally proposed in the House of Quality approach. A simple 5-point scale is easier to track than a 100-point scale, which only makes some decisions and weight assignments both arbitrary and confusing.

Appropriate performance metrics can then be listed and clustered on the top of the matrix (the ceiling). The matrix itself indicates the levels of correlation between the metrics and the performance outcomes. Figure 14-5, for example, uses three different symbols to represent these levels of correlation (high, medium, and low). Alternatively, a numerical value can be used. The decisions and metrics that also improve the outcome are said to have a high level of correlation. The interrelationships between all these parameters are represented on the roof of the house. By looking at the correlations within the body of the matrix, we can accurately focus on those areas of knowledge management that are most likely to affect overall company performance and help us move toward preset goals.

Software Tools for QFD Analysis

A variety of software tools can help automate the QFD analysis process. One of the more popular tools is QFD Designer (by Qualisoft Corporation) shown in Figure 14-6 and Figure 14-7. Software tools allow real-time evaluation of the percentage of fills along different dimensions (see Figure 14-8).

Skandia's Intellectual Capital (IC) annual report also provides indicators of some other parameters that can be added to the House of Quality outcomes for analysis of knowledge management effectiveness. Some ideas, including some found in Skandia's annual IC report, for such parameters are the following:

- Competence development expenses per employee in dollars
- Employee satisfaction
- Marketing expense per customer
- Time spent on systematic packaging of know-how for future use, after a project is completed
- Research and development expense to overhead expense ratios
- Training expenses per employee
- Payback on development activities
- Average development time per new product
- Average expense per dollar earned (e.g., in consulting)
- Renewal expense per existing customer
- Level of customer attrition
- Expense of business development (new customers) per dollar spent on overheads
- Training expenses per customer per year in dollars
- Information-gathering expenses per existing customer

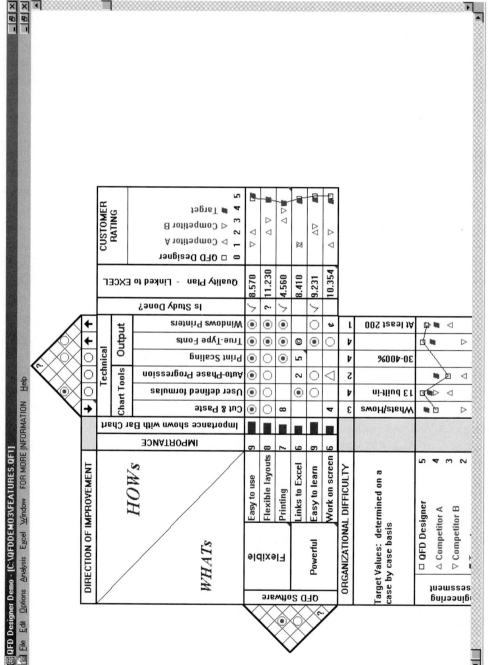

Figure 14-6 The QFD Designer allows users to automate House of Quality analysis.

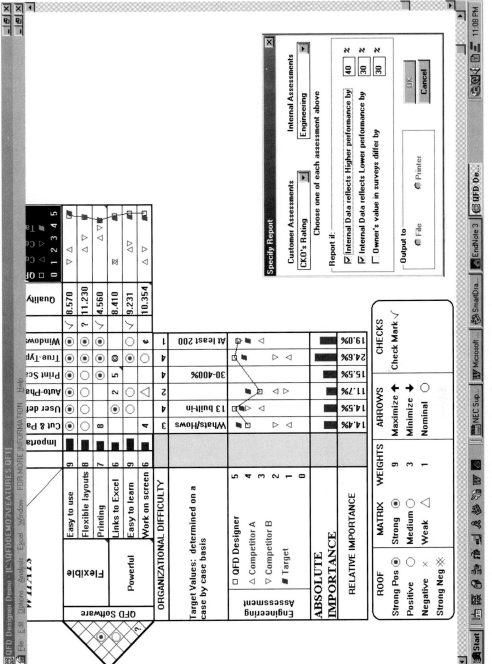

Figure 14-7 QFD Designer allows users to automatically generate reports based on internal and external assessments.

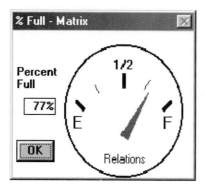

Figure 14-8 The percentage fill on the roof and the sides of the QFD matrix can be easily assessed.

- Total competitive intelligence expense per year
- Expense (dollars) of distribution of new sales material and data
- Time spent per unsuccessful business bid
- Total number of patents held
- Number of patents pending
- Average time of approval for pending patents
- Employee attrition rate
- Dollar figure value of losses per employee lost
- Dollar figure value of losses per employee *lost* to a competing firm
- Expense of reinventing solutions per year
- Success ratio of new products and/or services
- Number of ideas implemented from the "suggestion box"
- Total production capacity or internal production capacity (this can be applied both to production and service firms)
- Capacity utilization
- Delivery time deviation rate

THE BALANCED SCORECARD TECHNIQUE

The third approach that is a viable method for measuring knowledge-centric performance of your organization is the *balanced scorecard* approach. Kaplan and Norton originally proposed the balanced scorecard in their landmark article published in the *Harvard Business Review*. The balanced scorecard provides a technique to "maintain a balance between long-term and short-term objectives, financial and nonfinancial measures, lagging and leading indicators, and between internal and external perspectives." The basic scorecard for translating vision and strategy into actual goals is shown in Figure 14-9.

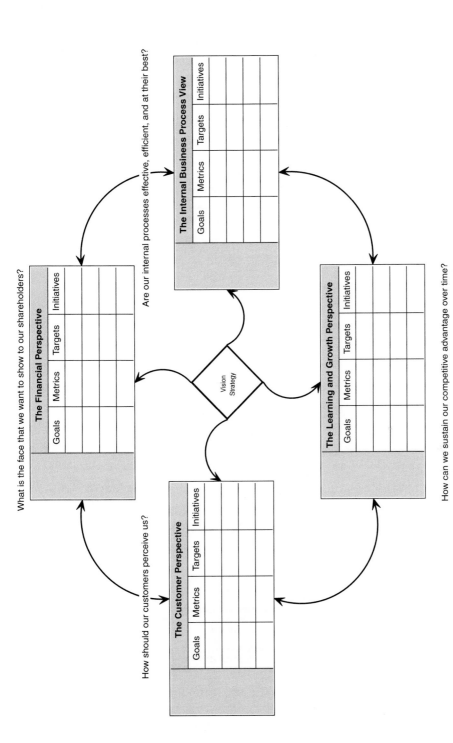

What is the face that we want to show to our shareholders?

Are our internal processes effective, efficient, and at their best?

How should our customers perceive us?

How can we sustain our competitive advantage over time?

The Financial Perspective

Goals	Metrics	Targets	Initiatives

The Internal Business Process View

Goals	Metrics	Targets	Initiatives

The Customer Perspective

Goals	Metrics	Targets	Initiatives

The Learning and Growth Perspective

Goals	Metrics	Targets	Initiatives

Vision
Strategy

Figure 14-9 The balanced scorecard is a useful tool for translating strategy and vision into actual goals and targets.

The balanced scorecard can also be used to evaluate the impact of the knowledge management system on four complementary criteria. The four processes involved in using the balanced scorecard approach for managing knowledge are described in Figure 14-10. These processes specifically put in the context of knowledge management, involve the following steps:

1. *Translate the knowledge management vision.* As Figure 14-10 describes, this is the first process in the balanced scorecard strategy. At this stage, managers need to reach consensus as to why knowledge is being managed or needs to be managed. What are the firm's visions for the knowledge management investment? The vision needs to be translated into concrete goals and objectives before any actions can be measured. The beauty of the balanced scorecard is that it can be used to create short-term, specific goals for individual employees, all of which feed to the organizational vision.

   While we are on the subject of vision, let me make it very clear that this vision rarely comes by copying the mission statement! Mission statements often carry too much fluff or are at too high a level to be actually useful. They need to be brought down to the

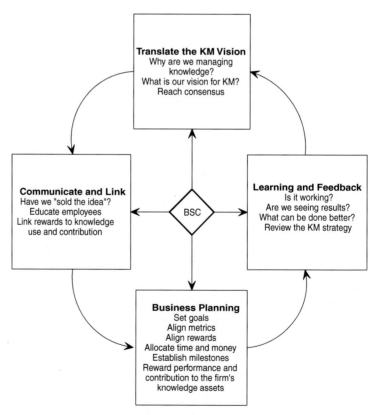

Figure 14-10 The knowledge management balanced scorecard.

level where two people can agree on what it says after reading the same document; and that is rarely the case with mission statements that most companies have. That's probably the reason why most mission statements are updated only when the next year's annual reports are due.[1]

2.   *Communicate and link.* This lets you measure as you go along your objective of selling the idea to your company's employees. You can gauge how well your employees are being trained to use the system as a part of their work. You can also measure how well you have linked rewards to both the effective use and contribution of knowledge. Here, the KM champion must communicate the strategy along the entire rung of employees and *demonstrate* the links between individual employee goals, and the departmental/organizational goals in terms of leveraging knowledge.

3.   *Do a reality check.* This part of the balanced scorecard strategy determines how well your chosen metrics, explicated goals, targets, and allocated resources align with the initial ideas you had in mind for the knowledge management system.

4.   *Incorporate learning and feedback.* The balanced scorecard lets you evaluate the goals, metrics, and targets that you have chosen for your knowledge management system and then analyze how well they are actually working.

In summary, the balanced scorecard approach lets you track the current health of the knowledge management strategy that you have chosen for your company.

By replacing the original four perspectives with measures successfully used by Skandia, a knowledge-based version of the balanced scorecard can be obtained. The underlying implementation and use would be akin to the conventional balanced scorecard method, but the measures provided will be those relating to knowledge management. This way, the financial, customer-related, process-capability-related, and employee-performance-related gains coming from the knowledge management system can be simultaneously tracked.

The actual implementation and use of the balanced scorecard approach is beyond the intended scope of this chapter. Now, you have a starting point for applying the balanced scorecard to knowledge management. For implementation level details, I recommend reading *The Balanced Scorecard* (Harvard Business School Press, 1996) by Kaplan and Norton.

As Kaplan and Norton state, a balanced scorecard need not just have four dimensions. It can have five, six, or seven. The only concern of going beyond seven is that you have too much to keep track of and a lot of it isn't even critical. KPMG, for example, uses five different dimensions for its scorecards (see Table 14-3).

Although these choices seem reasonable, I recommend that you initially try using the dimensions similar to those suggested in Figure 14-11, which are based on Skandia's Navigator and which the company has used very effectively. The choice of dimensions is not set in stone. As long as you are sure about what you are measuring and why you are measuring it, that variable has a justifiable place on the balanced scorecard that your company adopts.

---

[1]As Kaplan and Norton have suggested, statements such as "The number one supplier," "best in class," and "empowered organization" should be kept far away from the balanced scorecard!

Table 14-3 KPMG's Choice of Dimensions for its Balanced Scorecard

Balanced Scorecard Dimensions	Questions
Client orientation	What do I want to achieve with my existing clients?
Market orientation	What am I going to do to decrease existing client turnover and find new clients? What am I going to do to strengthen my position in the business?
People orientation	What am I going to do to enable the team that I am managing to function better and to help my employees gain stronger competencies?
Result orientation	How can I attain better results with the same inputs? How can I increase the added value of my teams and myself?
Personal effectiveness	What am I going to do in the coming year to improve weak points and strengthen strong points?
Professionalism	How do I keep abreast of the newest developments? How do I collaborate with my peers more extensively?

Advantages of KM Balanced Scorecards

The balanced scorecard has some characteristics that the other approaches discussed in this chapter do not have. These characteristics make it especially useful as a knowledge metric.

- Ability to provide a snapshot of the intellectual health of your firm at any point in time.
- Built-in cause-and-effect relationships that can help you guide your knowledge management strategy.
- Sufficient (neither too many nor too few) number of performance drivers and metrics.
- Capability to communicate the knowledge management strategy throughout the firm.
- Capability to link individual goals with the overall knowledge strategy of the firm. This implies that each employee can *do his own* and continue to contribute toward the goals of the knowledge management system and strategy without even realizing it!
- A direct, and often missing, link between long-term knowledge and competence goals of the firm and its annual budget.
- Translation of the lofty visions of a firm into more doable, realistic, manageable, and specific performance goals.
- Logical integration into the overall strategy of your business, and still make sense.
- Objective measurement of the contribution of knowledge to the more intangible sources of competitive advantage, such as customer satisfaction and employee skills and competencies.

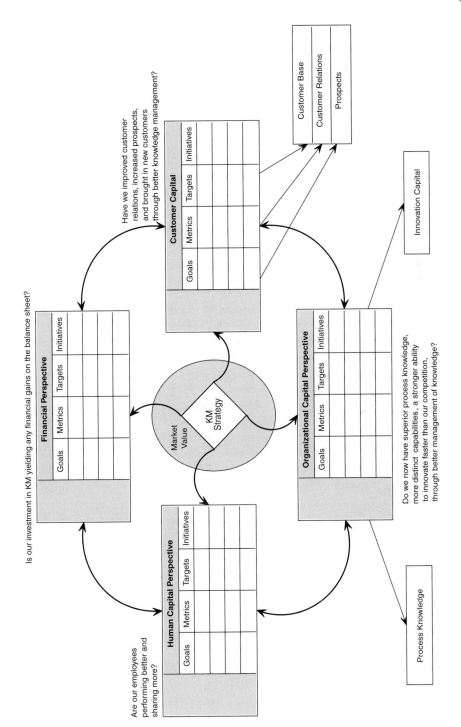

FIGURE 14-11 Relating the balanced scorecard to knowledge management outcomes—a variant of Skandia's classification scheme.

- Direct link to financial measures and your knowledge management system's effect on the company bottom line.

Limitations of KM Balanced Scorecards

On the downside, a well-designed balanced scorecard is more difficult to develop than a similar QFD/HoQ (House of Quality) model. It is rarely possible to directly adopt another firm's balanced scorecard because subtle differences exist even between *very* similar firms. However, there are some software tools that can make the initial ride lesser bumpy, such as the balanced scorecard tool, Gentia Balanced Scorecard, sold by Gentia Inc. (http://www.gentia.com).

CLASSIFYING AND EVALUATING PROCESSES

This section touches on a very useful taxonomy that can help you classify, sort, and organize processes by their category. Understanding and classifying processes helps firms effectively manage these processes as well as the knowledge that drives them. The sales process, for example, might have very little to do with the sales department in some high-technology companies where primary customer interaction is with the engineering staff. What can be readily used here is a taxonomy of processes that has been developed by the American Productivity and Quality Center (APQC) benchmarking clearinghouse.

The process classification framework (PCF) was originally developed as a collaborative effort across 80 organizations and envisioned as a *taxonomy* of business processes in 1991. A primary issue with the PCF continues to be the enablement of process benchmarking across industry boundaries. The utility of this process taxonomy is not just limited to benchmarking. It can be used to better structure the clustering of processes and functionalities within your own company. The biggest strength of this framework comes from the fact that it was built by the joint effort of almost 100 U.S. organizations, many of which had an international presence.

The APQC *process classification framework* (see Table 14-4) serves as a high-level, generic enterprise model that encourages businesses and other organizations to see their activities from a cross-industry process-oriented viewpoint rather than from a narrow, functionalist viewpoint. The process classification framework supplies a generic view of business processes often found in multiple industries and sectors—manufacturing and service companies, health care, government, education, and others, thereby allowing companies to compare their processes meaningfully to other, different organizations.

The process classification framework represents major processes and subprocesses, not functions, through its structure and vocabulary. The framework does not list all processes found within any specific organization. Likewise, not every process listed in the framework is present in every organization.

Table 14-4 The APQC Process Classification Framework

The APQC Process Classification Framework

1.0   UNDERSTAND MARKETS AND CUSTOMERS

    1.1   Determine customer needs and wants

           1.1.1   Conduct qualitative assessments

                  1.1.1.1   Conduct customer interviews

                  1.1.1.2   Conduct focus groups

           1.1.2   Conduct quantitative assessments

                  1.1.2.1   Develop and implement surveys

           1.1.3   Predict customer purchasing behavior

    1.2   Measure customer satisfaction

           1.2.1   Monitor satisfaction with products and services

           1.2.2   Monitor satisfaction with complaint resolution

           1.2.3   Monitor satisfaction with communication

    1.3   Monitor changes in market or customer expectations

           1.3.1   Determine weaknesses of product/service offerings

           1.3.2   Identify new innovations that are meeting customer needs

           1.3.3   Determine customer reactions to competitive offerings

2.0   DEVELOP VISION AND STRATEGY

    2.1   Monitor the external environment

           2.1.1   Analyze and understand competition

           2.1.2   Identify economic trends

           2.1.3   Identify political and regulatory issues

           2.1.4   Assess new technology innovations

           2.1.5   Understand demographics

           2.1.6   Identify social and cultural changes

           2.1.7   Understand ecological concerns

    2.2   Define the business concept and organizational strategy

           2.2.1   Select relevant markets

           2.2.2   Develop long-term vision

           2.2.3   Formulate business unit strategy

           2.2.4   Develop overall mission statement

    2.3   Design the organizational structure and relationships between organizational units

    2.4   Develop and set organizational goals

Table 14-4 The APQC Process Classification Framework (cont.)

The APQC Process Classification Framework

3.0   DESIGN PRODUCTS AND SERVICES

3.1   Develop new product/service concept and plans

    3.1.1   Translate customer wants and needs into product and/or service requirements

    3.1.2   Plan and deploy quality targets

    3.1.3   Plan and deploy cost targets

    3.1.4   Develop product life cycle and development timing targets

    3.1.5   Develop and integrate leading technology into product/service concept

3.2   Design, build, and evaluate prototype products and services

    3.2.1   Develop product/service specifications

    3.2.2   Conduct concurrent engineering

    3.2.3   Implement value engineering

    3.2.4   Document design specifications

    3.2.5   Develop prototypes

    3.2.6   Apply for patents

3.3   Refine existing products/services

    3.3.1   Develop product/service enhancements

    3.3.2   Eliminate quality/reliability problems

    3.3.3   Eliminate outdated products/services

3.4   Test effectiveness of new or revised products or services

3.5   Prepare for production

    3.5.1   Develop and test prototype production process

    3.5.2   Design and obtain necessary materials and equipment

    3.5.3   Install and verify process or methodology

3.6   Manage the product/service development process

4.0   MARKET AND SELL

4.1   Market products or services to relevant customer segments

    4.1.1   Develop pricing strategy

    4.1.2   Develop advertising strategy

    4.1.3   Develop marketing messages to communicate benefits

    4.1.4   Estimate advertising resource and capital requirements

    4.1.5   Identify specific target customers and their needs

Table 14-4 The APQC Process Classification Framework (cont.)

The APQC Process Classification Framework

		4.1.6	Develop sales forecast
		4.1.7	Sell products and services
		4.1.8	Negotiate terms
	4.2	Process customer orders	
		4.2.1	Accept orders from customers
		4.2.2	Enter orders into production and delivery process

5.0	**PRODUCE AND DELIVER FOR MANUFACTURING**		
	5.1	Plan for and acquire necessary resources	
		5.1.1	Select and certify suppliers
		5.1.2	Purchase capital goods
		5.1.3	Purchase materials and supplies
		5.1.4	Acquire appropriate technology
	5.2	Convert resources or inputs into products	
		5.2.1	Develop and adjust production delivery process (for existing process)
		5.2.2	Schedule production
		5.2.3	Move materials and resources
		5.2.4	Make product
		5.2.5	Package product
		5.2.6	Warehouse or store product
		5.2.7	Stage products for delivery
	5.3	Deliver products	
		5.3.1	Arrange product shipment
		5.3.2	Deliver products to customers
		5.3.3	Install product
		5.3.4	Confirm specific service requirements for individual customers
		5.3.5	Identify and schedule resources to meet service requirements
		5.3.6	Provide the service to specific customers
	5.4	Manage production and delivery process	
		5.4.1	Document and monitor order status
		5.4.2	Manage inventories
		5.4.3	Assure product quality
		5.4.4	Schedule and perform maintenance
		5.4.5	Monitor environmental constraints

Table 14-4 The APQC Process Classification Framework (cont.)

The APQC Process Classification Framework

6.0 PRODUCE AND DELIVER FOR SERVICE ORIENTED ORGANIZATIONS

   6.1   Plan for and acquire necessary resources

       6.1.1   Select and certify suppliers

       6.1.2   Purchase materials and supplies

       6.1.3   Acquire appropriate technology

   6.2   Develop human resource skills

       6.2.1   Define skill requirements

       6.2.2   Identify and implement training

       6.2.3   Monitor and manage skill development

   6.3   Deliver service to the customer

       6.3.1   Confirm specific service requirements for individual customer

       6.3.2   Identify and schedule resources to meet service requirements

       6.3.3   Provide the service to specific customers

   6.4   Ensure quality of service

7.0 INVOICE AND SERVICE CUSTOMERS

   7.1   Bill the customer

       7.1.1   Develop, deliver, and maintain customer billing

       7.1.2   Invoice the customer

       7.1.3   Respond to billing inquiries

   7.2   Provide after-sales service

       7.2.1   Provide post-sales service

       7.2.2   Handle warranties and claims

   7.3   Respond to customer inquiries

       7.3.1   Respond to information requests

       7.3.2   Manage customer complaints

8.0 DEVELOP AND MANAGE HUMAN RESOURCES

   8.1   Create and manage human resource strategies

       8.1.1   Identify organizational strategic demands

       8.1.2   Determine human resource costs

       8.1.3   Define human resource requirements

       8.1.4   Define human resource's organizational role

   8.2   Cascade strategy to work level

       8.2.1   Analyze, design, or redesign work

Table 14-4 The APQC Process Classification Framework (cont.)

The APQC Process Classification Framework

	8.2.2	Define and align work outputs and metrics
	8.2.3	Define work competencies
8.3		Manage deployment of personnel
	8.3.1	Plan and forecast workforce requirements
	8.3.2	Develop succession and career plans
	8.3.3	Recruit, select, and hire employees
	8.3.4	Create and deploy teams
	8.3.5	Relocate employees
	8.3.6	Restructure and rightsize workforce
	8.3.7	Manage employee retirement
	8.3.8	Provide outplacement support
8.4		Develop and train employees
	8.4.1	Align employee and organizational development needs
	8.4.2	Develop and manage training programs
	8.4.3	Develop and manage employee orientation programs
	8.4.4	Develop functional/process competencies
	8.4.5	Develop management/leadership competencies
	8.4.6	Develop team competencies
8.5		Manage employee performance, reward, and recognition
	8.5.1	Define performance measures
	8.5.2	Develop performance management approaches and feedback
	8.5.3	Manage team performance
	8.5.4	Evaluate work for market value and internal equity
	8.5.5	Develop and manage base and variable compensation
	8.5.6	Manage reward and recognition programs
8.6		Ensure employee well-being and satisfaction
	8.6.1	Manage employee satisfaction
	8.6.2	Develop work and family support systems
	8.6.3	Manage and administer employee benefits
	8.6.4	Manage workplace health and safety
	8.6.5	Manage internal communications
	8.6.6	Manage and support workforce diversity
8.7		Ensure employee involvement
8.8		Manage labor-management relationships
	8.8.1	Manage collective bargaining process

Table 14-4 The APQC Process Classification Framework (cont.)

The APQC Process Classification Framework

		8.8.2	Manage labor-management partnerships
	8.9		Develop Human Resource Information Systems (HRIS)

9.0   MANAGE INFORMATION RESOURCES

9.1   Plan for information resource management

    9.1.1   Derive requirements from business strategies

    9.1.2   Define enterprise system architectures

    9.1.3   Plan and forecast information technologies & methodologies

    9.1.4   Establish enterprise data standards

    9.1.5   Establish quality standards and controls

9.2   Develop and deploy enterprise support systems

    9.2.1   Conduct specific needs assessments

    9.2.2   Select information technologies

    9.2.3   Define data life cycles

    9.2.4   Develop enterprise support systems

    9.2.5   Test, evaluate, and deploy enterprise support systems

9.3   Implement systems security and controls

    9.3.1   Establish systems security strategies and levels

    9.3.2   Test, evaluate, and deploy systems security and controls

9.4   Manage information storage & retrieval

    9.4.1   Establish information repositories (databases)

    9.4.2   Acquire and collect information

    9.4.3   Store information

    9.4.4   Modify and update information

    9.4.5   Enable retrieval of information

    9.4.6   Delete information

9.5   Manage facilities and network operations

    9.5.1   Manage centralized facilities

    9.5.2   Manage distributed facilities

    9.5.3   Manage network operations

9.6   Manage information services

    9.6.1   Manage libraries and information centers

    9.6.2   Manage business records and documents

9.7   Facilitate information sharing and communication

    9.7.1   Manage external communications systems

Table 14-4 The APQC Process Classification Framework (cont.)

The APQC Process Classification Framework

		9.7.2	Manage internal communications systems
		9.7.3	Prepare and distribute publications
	9.8	Evaluate and audit information quality	

10.0   MANAGE FINANCIAL AND PHYSICAL RESOURCES

10.1	Manage financial resources	
	10.1.1	Develop budgets
	10.1.2	Manage resource allocation
	10.1.3	Design capital structure
	10.1.4	Manage cash flow
	10.1.5	Manage financial risk
10.2	Process finance and accounting transactions	
	10.2.1	Process accounts payable
	10.2.2	Process payroll
	10.2.3	Process accounts receivable, credit, and collections
	10.2.4	Close the books
	10.2.5	Process benefits and retiree information
	10.2.6	Manage travel and entertainment expenses
10.3	Report information	
	10.3.1	Provide external financial information
	10.3.2	Provide internal financial information
10.4	Conduct internal audits	
10.5	Manage the tax function	
	10.5.1	Ensure tax compliance
	10.5.2	Plan tax strategy
	10.5.3	Employ effective technology
	10.5.4	Manage tax controversies
	10.5.5	Communicate tax issues to management
	10.5.6	Manage tax administration
10.6	Manage physical resources	
	10.6.1	Manage capital planning
	10.6.2	Acquire and redeploy fixed assets
	10.6.3	Manage facilities
	10.6.4	Manage physical risk

Table 14-4 The APQC Process Classification Framework (cont.)

The APQC Process Classification Framework

11.0   EXECUTE ENVIRONMENTAL MANAGEMENT PROGRAM

  11.1 Formulate environmental management strategy

  11.2 Ensure compliance with regulations

  11.3 Train and educate employees

  11.4 Implement pollution prevention program

  11.5 Manage remediation efforts

  11.6 Implement emergency response programs

  11.7 Manage government agency and public relations

  11.8 Manage acquisition/divestiture environmental issues

  11.9 Develop and manage environmental information system

  11.10 Monitor environmental management program

12.0   MANAGE EXTERNAL RELATIONSHIPS

  12.1 Communicate with shareholders

  12.2 Manage government relationships

  12.3 Build lender relationships

  12.4 Develop public relations program

  12.5 Interface with board of directors

  12.6 Develop community relations

  12.7 Manage legal and ethical issues

13.0   MANAGE IMPROVEMENT AND CHANGE

  13.1 Measure organizational performance

    13.1.1 Create measurement systems

    13.1.2 Measure product and service quality

    13.1.3 Measure cost of quality

    13.1.4 Measure costs

    13.1.5 Measure cycle time

    13.1.6 Measure productivity

  13.2 Conduct quality assessments

    13.2.1 Conduct quality assessments based on external criteria

    13.2.2 Conduct quality assessments based on internal criteria

  13.3 Benchmark performance

    13.3.1 Develop benchmarking capabilities

    13.3.2 Conduct process benchmarking

Table 14-4 The APQC Process Classification Framework (cont.)

The APQC Process Classification Framework

	13.3.3	Conduct competitive benchmarking
13.4	Improve processes and systems	
	13.4.1	Create commitment for improvement
	13.4.2	Implement continuous process improvement
	13.4.3	Reengineer business processes and systems
	13.4.4	Manage transition to change
13.5	Implement TQM	
	13.5.1	Create commitment for TQM
	13.5.2	Design and implement TQM systems
	13.5.3	Manage TQM life cycle

*For more details, contact APQC International Benchmarking Clearinghouse, Information Services Dept., 123 North Post Oak Lane, 3rd Floor, Houston, Texas 77024, http://www.apqc.org.

Reproduced with permission from the Houston-based American Productivity and Quality Center.

ALTERNATIVE METRICS

Besides the three methods that we discussed in this chapter, there are two other specific ways to evaluate returns on knowledge investments (RoKI): the Skandia method and the FASB method. Since none of these are mainstream nor do they lend themselves to easy adaptation by most organizations because of vagueness and company specificity (especially in the case of Skandia's method) involved, they are mentioned here only for completeness.

THE SKANDIA METHOD

The method used by the Swedish insurance company Skandia is one of the pioneering attempts at measuring knowledge. Skandia still refuses to call it knowledge and calls it "intellectual capital" instead. Skandia uses a number of ratios in which the company not only looks back at the past, but also looks at the present and to the future. The objections to this method include the notion that such ratios are easy to influence, and each company can decide for itself which ratios to use and which not to. Skandia makes its Intellectual Capital reports, which are an addendum to its annual financial report, publicly available over the Web (see www.skandia.se). The IC addendum to the annual report makes very interesting reading and provides insights into the manner in which the pioneering company approached knowledge management metrics.

THE FASB METHOD

The other method that has been developed in the United States by the Financial Accounting Standards Board (FASB) is the FASB knowledge measurement method, which aims to find an answer to the question of how companies can and should report their knowledge. The proposed method is based on the notion that there should be a division between financial capital and intellectual capital in a company's annual report. If this actually becomes a guideline, companies will be legally required to present and evaluate their knowledge assets in a standard format in their annual reports. That will produce an unprecedented amount of valuable information for the company's shareholders and other interested parties.

LESSONS LEARNED

There are no perfect metrics for knowledge work, but this chapter provides you with a good starting point. Of the six approaches mentioned here, the balanced scorecard and the QFD/House of Quality approach seem to be the most promising. To be able to truly understand them and apply them well, read the original book and the *Harvard Business Review* articles (see the bibliography for details) by the inventors. Measuring the performance of your knowledge management system and its contribution to your company's financial and competence bottom line is absolutely critical. After all, measuring where KM is taking you, and demonstrating it well, might be critical for the next round of funding that the project must receive from your CFO.

Keep the following tips in mind while devising knowledge management metrics for your company:

- *Metrics define knowledge management success.* Robust metrics help measure the business impact of knowledge management. Well-chosen metrics serve as the indicators, tools, and guidelines that can help shape both your company's knowledge management system design and its knowledge management strategy. Knowledge work and knowledge management system performance must be one of your core metrics if any knowledge management initiative is to succeed. A few robust metrics with immediate reward ties for knowledge workers are better than many weak ones that cannot be controlled. Focus on knowledge that is valuable, rare, hard to copy, and hard to substitute when you are trying to decide on metric variables. Reward both internal and external knowledge integration through metrics that can be measured today with impact on future outcomes.

- *Benchmarking is a starter, not a strategic metric.* Benchmarking is a good comparative tool that lets you judge how high you stand in comparison to other firms both within and outside your industry. Beyond that, it provides little to guide knowledge management at a microstrategic firm level. Select an appropriate company as a role model before you begin the process externally. Remember that benchmarks do tell you what to do next, but not *how* to do it.

- *QFDs relate high-level goals to discrete actions.* QFDs let you link goals, relationships, perceived significance, and outcomes for each strategic step that you take with your knowledge management system. QFDs integrate inputs from all stakeholders and provide explicit direction for enhancing your company's knowledge management strategy. QFDs can be automated to a fairly high degree with readily available software. You can translate high-level goals to specific tasks, and these tasks can further be decomposed into measurable and manageable actions.

- *The balanced scorecard links strategy, technology, competitiveness, and knowledge management.* The KM BSC method helps you translate the knowledge management vision into action, communicate the KM strategy bottom up, validate your choice of metrics, and analyze results of knowledge management in the long run. It will provide a robust direct link between knowledge management, the system, your company's clients, markets, people, results, and profitability.

- *Do not ignore the soft stuff.* Metrics must take both hard and soft results into account to present a true picture of your firm's intellectual health.

- *Metrics in the rearview mirror appear more significant than they are.* Ask yourself: Do we have metrics that can serve as early warning signals for future problems and those that signal future opportunities?

Understand this chapter well to make sure that this round was not the last one!

In the next chapter, we take a closer look at the cases of some companies representing a diversity of industries. All of them have one thing in common: They are immensely successful both from a competitive standpoint and a financial one because they realized the value of knowledge management and appropriately put their idle knowledge to work, and work hard.

CHAPTER 15
CASE STUDIES

IF A MAN EMPTIES HIS PURSE INTO HIS HEAD, NO MAN CAN TAKE IT AWAY FROM HIM. AN INVESTMENT IN KNOWLEDGE ALWAYS PAYS THE BEST INTEREST
—BENJAMIN FRANKLIN

Edward Deming once commented, "Learning is not compulsory...neither is survival." Deming made that comment when businesses operated in an asset-based environment, not a knowledge-based environment, as they do today. In this chapter we will take a closer look at some companies that have had the distinction of being enthusiastic early adopters of knowledge management. Their outcomes have had mixed results—some have fallen flat while others have provided their organizations with an unprecedented competitive advantage. There is a lot to learn from these early pioneers who dared to make that leap of faith in the face of unsupportive accounting analysis. When the accountants said, "But it does not show up on the balance sheet," they replied, "How does it matter if there *is* no balance sheet in two years?!" Every case in this chapter proves how true Deming's words still are.

SOME BACKGROUND

A research project across 93 knowledge management applications and 83 different firms (conducted by Teltech Resource Network Corporation, www.teltech.com) shows knowledge management projects in these companies represented differing real-life expectations.[a] Some were focused on increasing revenues in the short run, but most were not focused on short-term objectives, as Table 15-1 reveals.

This trend is also illustrated in Figure 15-1. Although half the companies surveyed fell back on knowledge management as a possible lifesaver for falling revenues, the other half embraced it from a growth and quality improvement perspective.

Out of the 93 projects examined in this survey, a few that had the highest level of impact on the company were those that focused on leveraging expertise, sharing knowledge and best practices, and improving collaboration in team-based work. Table 15-2 shows the exact breakdowns.

Table 15-1 The Drivers of Knowledge Management Investments in 83 Different Firms

| Strategic Focus | Strategic Focus and Knowledge Managment Objectives | | | | |
	Increased Revenue	Cost Containment	Improved Customer Service	Quality	Improved Internal Processes
Percentage of companies surveyed	45	35	10	6	4

Source: Teltech Resource Network Corp., September 1998.

[a]See the report in Hildebrand, Carol, Making KM Pay Off, *CIO Enterprise* (1999), 64–66.

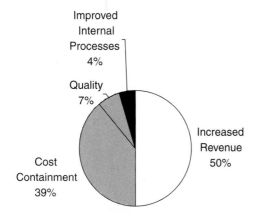

Figure 15-1 Knowledge management and its strategic drivers—the tale of 83 companies.

PROCESS DISTRIBUTION IN HIGH-PERFORMANCE KM PROJECTS

High-performing knowledge management projects have focused on activities involving delivery and production of services, customer support, competitive intelligence and external knowledge integration, project management in virtual teams, sales enablement, and intellectual asset management.

This should give you an idea about the approximate areas on which you must focus your knowledge management investments. Table 15-3 shows the distribution of high-impact knowledge management applications by the process areas on which they initially focused.

The common failure point in a knowledge management system in over 50 percent of the cases examined here was found to be the lack of commitment or resources for managing the system once it was implemented. Managing content is an important activity even though content is added by its users. Change management programs explicitly supported 74 percent of the high-impact projects.

Table 15-2 What Do High Performers Do?

High-Impact Application Objectives	Percentage of Cases Found
Leverage best practices	45
Improve collaboration	25
Leverage expertise	15
Enterprise-wide integration	5
Accelerate product/service development	5
Integrate external Information	5

Source: Teltech Resource Network Corp., September 1998, and Hildebrand, Carol, Making KM Pay Off, *CIO Enterprise* (1999), 64–66. The study involved 93 knowledge management projects in 83 different companies.

Table 15-3 Where Do High Impact Knowledge Management Projects Begin?

Process Focus	Percentage of Cases*
Product and service development	25
Delivery of products and services	30
Customer service	15
Competitive intelligence and strategic planning	10
IC management and patent portfolio management	5
Project management	5
Sales enablement	5
Enterprise-wide focus	5

*The percentage of cases is relative to the total number of high-impact knowledge management projects identified within the group of 93 projects analyzed. Source of data: Hildebrand, Carol, *Making KM Pay Off*, *CIO Enterprise* (1999), 64–66.

KNOWLEDGE MANAGEMENT IN THE AEROSPACE INDUSTRY: THE CASE OF ROLLS ROYCE

Rolls Royce was founded in 1906. In addition to making expensive cars, Rolls Royce is also a market leader in the long-haul aircraft engines market. As of 1999, Rolls Royce was serving about 300 commercial airlines where its competitive stance was the total cost of ownership.

THE PROBLEM

The problem with Rolls Royce was that everything that was done to maintain engines was time sensitive. However, 20 million pages of paper documenting a variety of aspects of aircraft engine parts (as shown in Table 15-4) were produced by the company. Each engine model had over 20 variants. Each variant needed to be serviced differently. About a 100 airlines with which Rolls Royce had active relationships were based in other countries. Even with several gigabytes of data in the company's mainframes, it was often difficult to get to the right piece of information in time. The consequences were not just limited to productivity and the financial health of the company, but also linked to safety of the aircraft that company employees worked on.

PROBLEM SCOPE

Rolls Royce decided to scope the problem down to the critical issues that had immediate paybacks for the firm. They decided that the key players to be considered would be limited to:

Table 15-4 Rolls Royce and Referential Sources of Knowledge

Aircraft	Referential Knowledge
Trent 700	Engine maintenance manuals
Trent 800	Illustrated catalogs of parts
RB 211-524	Supply diagrams
RB 211-535	Service bulletins
	Time limits manuals
	Standard practices
	Overhaul manuals
	Maintenance manuals
Tay	
IAE V2500-A1A5	
IAE V2500-D5	

Source: Data based on a presentation by Rolls Royce's Bob Cole at Delphi's knowledge management empower, October 1998, Chicago, IL.

- Airlines
- Airframe manufacturers
- Engine and engine part manufacturers
- Component manufacturers

It was also decided that the scope of the initial knowledge management project would be restricted to enabling different levels of reuse: mechanisms that would allow workers to find, use, reuse, and reintegrate knowledge related to servicing long-haul commercial engines.

Such scoping is essential to place reasonable limits on the expectations from a knowledge management system. Scoping helps firms figure out if the targets of their knowledge management investments are the ones that need immediate attention, both in terms of business sense and strategic urgency.

KNOWLEDGE MANAGEMENT PROJECT GOALS

Rolls Royce was very good at laying out realistic and achievable goals up front. The initial set of goals specified for the KM system were classified in two broad categories:

- *Customer-oriented goals*: These were goals that would accrue benefits for the customer.

  1. Reducing equipment downtime for maintenance
  2. Doing it right the first time

3. Improving maintenance quality

4. Improving maintenance scheduling

5. Reducing data handling as well as access and search costs

- *Internal goals:* These were the benefits in terms of improved internal efficiency that were expected from the Rolls Royce knowledge management system. The knowledge management team hoped that the new system would help the company in the following ways:

   1. Improve customer data access across multiple platforms

   2. Deliver applications that required little or no training

   3. Reduce publishing costs, ensure security, and comply with ATA (Air Transport Association) specifications

MEASUREMENT

Lacking any other mechanisms for measurement, Rolls Royce measured its return on investment by using surrogate financial measures. Most of these figures were translated into dollar figures as shown below:

- Paper costs savings of $3 million
- Customer productivity savings worth $1 million
- 5 percent improvement in maintenance time
- Unmeasured savings in data processing costs

Out of all the technical features and development path options mentioned in Chapters 7 and 11, this system resembled an improved version of an intranet. It had user-specific table of contents, a customizable interface, the ability to add annotations; provided dynamic updates; and delivered automatic notifications. Content authoring in this system (called Enigma) was done with SGML (Standard Generalized Markup Language) and a primitive Word interface rather than a Web browser.

KNOWLEDGE MANAGEMENT IN SALES AND MARKETING: THE CASE OF PLATINUM TECHNOLOGY

Platinum Technology Inc., based in Oakbrook Terrace, Illinois, is a company on the fast track. With close to $800 million in revenues in 1997 alone, Platinum has been on an acquisition warpath since 1994. Between 1994 and 1998, the company bought out 70 other companies.

This series of acquisitions resulted in a 500 percent growth in its portfolio of product offerings. Platinum has almost 7,000 employees and has seen a sixfold growth in its sales force head count since 1995. These employees are distributed across Platinum's 120 offices worldwide.

Platinum realized early on that managing the company's knowledge assets was a critical enabler that would allow it to sustain this growth. With strong commitment from senior management, Platinum has been exploring the use of knowledge management in the following areas of operation:

- Sales and marketing
- New product development
- Contracting and outsourcing
- Customer and partner interaction knowledge management
- Consulting
- Education

In the sales and marketing division alone, an employee has a number of potential sources that she can tap into for information needed to make a sale or to pursue a prospective customer. These include:[b]

- Over 100 Lotus Notes databases
- Two custom developed applications
- 35 intranet sites
- Thousands of networked disk drives
- Printed documentation
- Discussion forums

THE PROBLEM

Platinum's marketing and sales department was faced not with information paucity but with information overload and redundancy. Even if an employee making a sales call could retrieve information that she needed, she would come across multiple versions of it in different locations. There was no telling what content was current and applicable. To overcome these challenges, Platinum's marketing and sales department took its first steps toward building a comprehensive knowledge management system.

---

[b]The statistical information in this section is based on 1998 conversations with and a presentation by Glenn Shimkus, Director of Sales Enablement, Platinum Technology, Inc., at KM Empower '98 conference. Platinum Technology was bought out by Computer Associates (CA) in 1998.

The System

The knowledge management system that Platinum built was called *Jaguar*. Jaguar began with two components: an intranet-based system that contained detailed documents and information and Jaguar Direct, a machine-resident bullet style nugget information repository. The system was built on Documentum's EDMS software and E@asy software from WisdomWare (www.wisdomware.com) for capturing context and tacit forms of knowledge. The driving Web servers were based in the United States, Singapore, and Europe and were supplemented with fortnightly updated Notes databases replicated on 65 servers worldwide. Since the system was meant to support sales and marketing staff, it provided the following information:

1. Platinum's products
2. Current pricing
3. Competitive information,
4. Enterprise-wide information including that about other divisions of the company
5. Worldwide sales calendars
6. Information on Platinum's partners
7. Details on mergers and acquisitions that were relevant to the company
8. References to documents and manuals
9. Subscription service that allowed users to subscribe to content of interest

Development Stages

Platinum started at the point where it was easy to get a stable start: managing explicit knowledge. Only later did the company proceed to manage tacit forms of knowledge. The system made extensive use of icons to represent different types of content, and each content element had meta data attached to it. Easily recognizable icons were used to identify information that was newer than two weeks and information that had changed in the preceding seven days. As a knowledge management team member put it, "We are a very visual society so we made excessive use of icons. Ridiculous? Yes! But effective? Yes!"

Throughout the development process, the knowledge management team asked the actual sales staff (the users) about what seemed to work and what did not. Based on their feedback, the system's developers promptly incorporated relevant suggestions and features. The company's knowledge champion says that over 50 percent of the enhancements came from end-user suggestions. As a result, about 40 percent of the company's sales force personnel use the system daily. With such an exceptionally high level of usage, Platinum found that banner advertisements within the site were the most effective way of making company-wide announcements.

At a later stage, the system introduced push content delivery. Users could select content areas that were of interest to them. As new content came in, users could either opt to receive it in an e-mail message or go to a personalized page on the site (akin to my.yahoo.com) and follow hyperlinks pointing them to new and relevant information as it became available. General updates were automatically sent every Sunday. The company hopes that by analyzing usage statistics on Jaguar, it can predict sales activity ahead of time. To ensure that content is relevant and up to date, e-mails are sent to contributors by the system one week before an expiration date (which is predetermined). If they do not review their contribution, it gets archived. Since the additional burden of validating and reviewing their own contributions was placed on employees, Platinum made sure that they were given extra time to spend on that task.[c]

The initial version of the system was implemented within four months of its initial approval. The system was so successful that it became the second most widely used application in the company, next only to e-mail.

MEASUREMENT

Lacking any other formal mechanisms for demonstrating a return on investment for their knowledge management investments, Platinum *demonstrated* the success of its system entirely in terms of financial benefits. Benefits quantified in terms of their effect on the company's bottom line are easier to sell to senior management. The knowledge management team quantified benefits in the following terms:

- The system paid for itself in 1.5 months.
- The knowledge management system resulted in cost savings of about $6 million in its very first year.
- Sales force productivity increased by a then current run rate of 6 percent.
- The system reduced international FedEx shipments by 15 percent (primarily resulting from the savings resulting from not having to produce and distribute Lotus Notes and database CD-ROM updates to several dozen offices worldwide, every few weeks).

The knowledge management team further estimated that Jaguar saved an average sales and marketing person about two hours every week, created a *bottom-up pull* of knowledge, and contributed to the competitive stand of the firm as a whole. Although the aforementioned benefits delivered a lot more value to the company, the knowledge management team initially quantified these benefits only in terms of FedEx savings that resulted from the introduction of this system. By choosing such a metric, the KM team was able to successfully demonstrate the tangible benefits (which exceeded the cost) of the system (even although one might argue that they were pessimistically underestimated).

---

[c]This is in line with our earlier observation that you cannot force employees to go out of their way to contribute their part to content maintenance, without giving them the time leeway to do so.

KM IN CUSTOMER SUPPORT: THE CASE OF NORTEL

Nortel Corporation sells a suite of design and manufacturing applications in the United States and Europe. The Global Support Group (GSG) provides support to both European customers and United States. There are groups of support personnel in both the United States and Europe. Nortel is required to provide 24-hour support, seven days a week, with limited budgets and restricted head counts of workers.

ISSUES

Nortel was facing problems providing support to its customers primarily because there was no suitable mechanism that allowed a support representative to check if anyone in the support organization had encountered a certain problem before.[d] This meant that the teams in different offices did not share any of their knowledge related to problem solving and ended up reinventing solutions time and again. Nortel identified several knowledge-related problems that its support group faced:

- Unclear definition of roles and responsibilities of personnel
- Lack of a formal process and guiding documentation
- Informal service-level agreements
- Inconsistent measures of customer satisfaction
- Lack of formal training for support staff
- No centralized collection or repository of predefined solutions
- Excessive rework and reinvention of solutions (no formal mechanism for capturing problems and solutions existed)
- European and U.S. offices operating as groups of teams rather than as a single distributed team
- Lack of knowledge sharing between teams based in the two continents

THE THREE PHASES OF ORGANIZING KNOWLEDGE

The support group knowledge management team at Nortel decided to manage knowledge more effectively, hoping to help the support group perform better, given budget and head-count constraints. They decided to tackle the whole process of managing knowledge in three discrete steps:

---

[d]Identified by Gordon Podolski, Director, Nortel, in a presentation on *Strategic Tools for the Deregulated Marketplace* at McCormick Place, Chicago, IL, October 1998.

1. *Phase 1:* Capturing knowledge and processes that were being used by their American and European support offices

2. *Phase 2:* Consolidating these processes to provide an environment for cooperative trans-Pacific problem solving

3. *Phase 3:* Implementing integrated systems to enable collaborative knowledge-intensive processes

Nortel began by bringing in an external consultant who interviewed support staff both in Europe and the United States. After receiving positive feedback from these interviewees, the knowledge management team concluded that it had the support of prospective end users. To gain acceptance, the external consultant(s) presented their understanding of the process to key stakeholders and support staff. Following this, feedback from employees was incorporated into the process descriptions that the consulting company had written. The processes identified were then classified into different areas of process ownership. Roles were assigned to each area on the basis of training provided to support employees.

Nortel support staff members were then trained in terms of the new, integrated processes that were synthesized. As a final step, Nortel implemented an integrated progress tracking system that allowed team members to track progress on solving a problem as teams across the globe worked on it. The final step in terms of support technology was the implementation of a centralized database where all problems and their outcomes were recorded.

Although the implementation done by Nortel seems to be less sophisticated in comparison to some other companies' knowledge management systems, its results were delivered exactly where they were needed most. Remember that esoteric notions of organizational good cannot drive knowledge management until it is helping the company solve critical process problems and eliminating knowledge-related problems that are threatening to bring the company down. Nortel expended more effort on the people side than it did on the technology side: a perfect way to begin when the processes themselves are not clearly understood or explicitly defined. The lesson here is that the problem should define knowledge management technology; technology should not define the problem (or solution). The effort paid strong dividends: Nortel is a leading provider in its markets and enjoys high levels of customer loyalty.

KM IN THE SEMICONDUCTOR INDUSTRY: GASONICS INTERNATIONAL

GaSonics is a company operating out of North America, Europe, Asia, and the Pacific Rim with annual revenues in the range of $120 million. GaSonics produces processing systems for fabrication of semiconductor wafers. Companies manufacturing electronic chips for use in electronic equipment use systems such as the ones that GaSonics produces.

GaSonics systems have, for a long time, enjoyed a reputation for high reliability and low systems downtime when compared to industry averages. The company depends on its customers for feedback, and it extensively uses this feedback to improve both its existing systems and services. Faced with extremely low margins like other competitors operating in the industry, GaSonics realized that it needed to reduce operating costs and improve internal efficiencies. Since the whole process of designing and building wafer processing equipment is knowledge intensive, GaSonics decided that the answer lay in streamlining its use of internal knowledge.

The Starting Point: Technical Publications

The technical publications department writes, typesets, updates, provides, and supports technical manuals, literature, and other information that support GaSonics' products. The company found that its technical publications department was an increasingly major cost center for four reasons:

1. As equipment sold by GaSonics was expensive, typically over $100,000 apiece, downtime costs for customers resulted in thousands of dollars worth of loss every time the system went down. Hence, the technical publications department at GaSonics needed to provide an increasingly high number of customers customized versions of their publications. This, in effect, is similar to mass customization.

2. Updates were frequently required.

3. Customers demanded electronic versions of product manuals.

4. The cost of archiving old documentation was increasing at an abnormal rate.

GaSonics realized that its technical publications department was the most logical place to begin its knowledge management initiative. Since the goals of the business unit and the technical publications department were highly congruent, improving one, the company hoped, would improve the other. Table 15-5 shows the two sets of objectives.

THE GOAL: THREE MONTHS TO TARGET

GaSonics planned for a knowledge management system that could be operational within three months. The challenges that came up included:

- The need to replace legacy data and paper-based information with consistent and accurate electronic data equivalents
- The ability of customers to customize product and service documentation electronically
- Integration with other enterprise systems
- Justification of costs involved in doing the above

GaSonics reduced paper-related costs by 50 percent immediately. Besides this obvious financial benefit, the company reduced training costs, used technicians instead of engineers for providing support, and improved the quality of solutions provided by making maintenance efforts work right the first time more frequently than it had done in the past.

Table 15-5 Technical Publications Department and Business Goals at GaSonics

Technical Publications Department Goals	Business Unit Goals
Speed up delivery of technical documentation	Reduce training and support costs
Improve usability of documentation and application manuals	Increase equipment uptime Reduce training and support costs
Improve content and currency of publications	Increase equipment uptime Increase service revenues Reduce training and support costs Improve customer service through better feedback mechanisms
Link publications to other enterprise resources	Improve customer service
Make technical literature, documentation, and publications easily accessible	Improve product and service offerings Improve customer service

KM PILOT CASE: MONSANTO NUTRITION AND CONSUMER PRODUCTS

Monsanto, a Chicago-based company with over 2,000 employees, is the owner of leading brands of nutrition products such as NutraSweet and Equal. The employee base consists of sales, marketing, research, manufacturing, and administrative personnel. Monsanto began its knowledge management efforts with a small community of analysts consisting of marketing and business strategy analysts. This effort served as a pilot project for the large scale deployment of its knowledge sharing network based on Plumtree knowledge server. As John Ferrari, the process and technology manager at Monsanto aptly puts it, "You do not want to focus too much time and energy into solving technology problems; focus on process issues and use off-the-shelf customizable applications where possible."

By using a pilot deployment, Monsanto identified the areas in which expected problems of deploying a large-scale, organization-wide knowledge management system were concentrated. The pilot implementation led it to believe that about 75 percent of the issues were people, process, and culture. Technology, the easy part, was the remaining 25 percent.

KM TO BUILD ECONOMIES OF REUSE: THE CASE OF TEXAS INSTRUMENTS

Texas Instruments, the semiconductor firm that is credited with commercialization of the integrated circuit (also known as an electronic chip), began its knowledge management initiatives centered on its technical literature and documentation. As one would expect, TI has overwhelming amounts of data relating to its semiconductor products. This data needs to be managed, updated, and effectively distributed. For example:[e]

- TI has about 3,100 data sheets relating to its semiconductor products. Each of these averages about 12 pages in length.
- TI produces and maintains about 50 user guides, each of which averages 250 pages.
- TI supports its products with 400 application notes, each of which is between 2 to 100 pages in length.
- TI maintains 14 gigabytes of SGML files and 12 gigabytes of meta data.
- TI revises about 90,000 pages of documentation every year.
- TI has about 100 technical writers, 5 illustrators, and 10 team leaders who collectively manage this process.

Texas Instruments decided to change these work processes so that they would be better aligned with the ways in which documentation staff worked on these documents and technical literature. The focus was on creating content in a manner that allowed ease of *reuse* and enabled production of multiple outputs from a single input or data source. By tagging all content, TI hoped to be able to manage context along with associated data. TI uses the notion of a fundamental shift to describe this process migration: from document thinking to object thinking.

To make this shift happen, the knowledge management team actually converted all paper documents to an electronic form. The expense of the conversion process (which cost in the range of $12 per page) was justified on the basis of the following:

- *Cost containment:* Reusing portions of existing documents resulted in cost savings of up to 70 percent of the cost of new documents.
- *Value added:* By adding nontextual information to documents (such as code, models, executable files, and demo files), additional context was added to knowledge that was well explicated and codified.

---

[e]These figures are based on a presentation by Jeff Barton, Information Architect at Texas Instruments, given at the Empower '98 conference in Chicago, IL.

- *Reduced labor cost:* It took fewer people to do the same job, so savings in employee compensation were a direct outcome.

The important lesson to take from this highly specialized initiative that primarily focused on managing already codified knowledge is that a good place to begin knowledge management is with content that is already there. Creating meta data for that content is the next logical step. But Jeff Barton of Texas Instruments warns that creating such meta data can be the most expensive part of the process!

LESSONS LEARNED

We looked at cases analyzing knowledge management projects in some of the most innovative pioneers in knowledge management. We examined the strategic drivers for knowledge management in various companies and found that most early adopters of knowledge management have put these programs into place primarily as a vehicle for increasing revenues and cost containment. The common thread running through most of these cases was an intent to leverage best practices, improve collaboration, profit from knowledge, strengthen organizational competence, widen competitive gaps, and leverage expertise.

Clearly identify the business objectives that drive knowledge management. All these companies have demonstrated their ability to show tangible, even if small, returns on their knowledge management investments. Otherwise, it is all too easy to lose focus of what the project is supposed to actually accomplish.

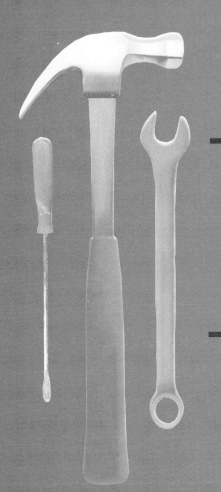

PART III
SIDE ROADS:
APPENDICES

APPENDIX A

THE KNOWLEDGE MANAGEMENT ASSESSMENT KIT

This appendix brings together lists, questions, evaluation formats, diagnostics instruments, and techniques to help you get started on the knowledge management road. For convenience, these processes are assembled as electronic software-based forms on the companion CD-ROM. Each user-editable (fill-in PDF and Microsoft Word) form can be customized and filled out with details specific to your knowledge management project and then printed.

You follow the phases of the now-familiar 10 steps, beginning with an inventory of existing physical assets and going to the more difficult task of inventorying existing knowledge. Use this tool to gauge the pre-implementation rankings on the specified criteria[a] and to track improvement after the introduction of a knowledge management system and knowledge management strategy.

---

[a]While there have been attempts to create a universal benchmark for knowledge work, such as American Productivity and Quality Center and Andersen Consulting's knowledge management assessment tool, such benchmarks cannot be used to guide knowledge management implementation in the long term due to the differences between industries and differences within any given industry. The diagnostics in this appendix provide a method for judging knowledge management benefits within the same company over time. Two time frames, for example, could be before and after the introduction of a knowledge management system.

As with most projects, preplanning and thorough grounding in the subject are essential to success. And they take the most time and effort. So take time and whatever effort is needed to work through the forms provided in this Knowledge Management Assessment Kit (KMAK). Edit, circulate, send out for review by colleagues, and revise. Then go through that cycle again. By the end of this process, you'll find that you have agreeable answers to questions that will come up at various stages on the 10-step roadmap.

The result of this kit is your own, populated roadmap, which serves as a guide to, as well as a checklist for, an effective, valuable, efficient knowledge management system; we provide an example that was built from the preceding chapters.

THE 10-STEP POPULATED ROADMAP

Figure A-1 provides a populated version of the roadmap that we built upon in the preceding chapters. Each step is detailed with the key tasks involved.

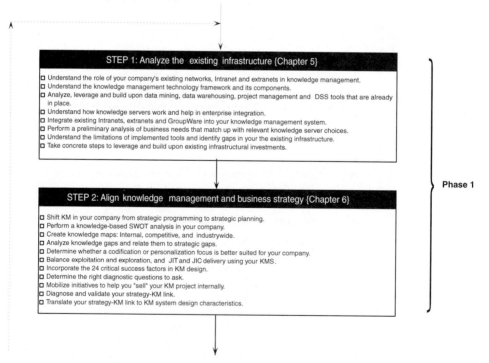

Figure A-1 The populated version of the 10-step knowledge management roadmap.

STEP 3: Design the knowledge management infrastructure {Chapter 7}

- ☐ Comprehend various components of the knowledge 'infostructure'.
- ☐ Identify knowledge management source feeds to integrate.
- ☐ Choose IT components to find, create, assemble, and apply knowledge.
- ☐ Identify elements of the interface layer: Clients, server, gateways, and the platform.
- ☐ Decide on the collaborative platform: Web or Notes?
- ☐ Identify and understand components of the collaborative intelligence layer: artificial intelligence, data warehouses, genetic algorithms, neural networks, expert reasoning systems, rule bases and case-based reasoning.
- ☐ Optimize knowledge object granularity.
- ☐ Balance cost versus value-added for each enabling component; push and pull based knowledge delivery.
- ☐ Identify the right mix of components for searching, indexing, and retrieval.
- ☐ Create knowledge tags and attributes: Domain, form, type, product/service, time, and location tags.
- ☐ Create profiling mechanisms for knowledge delivery.
- ☐ Retrofit IT on the SECI knowledge management model.

STEP 4: Audit existing knowledge assets and systems {Chapter 8}

- ☐ Understand the purpose of a knowledge audit.
- ☐ Use Bohn's Stages of Knowledge Growth framework to measure knowledge.
- ☐ Identify, evaluate and rate critical process knowledge.
- ☐ Select an audit method.
- ☐ Assemble a preliminary knowledge audit team.
- ☐ Audit and analyze your company's existing knowledge.
- ☐ Identify your company's K-spot.
- ☐ Choose a strategic position for your knowledge management system.

STEP 5: Design the knowledge management team {Chapter 9}

- ☐ Identify key stakeholders: IT, management, and end users.
- ☐ Identify sources of requisite expertise.
- ☐ Identify critical points of failure: requirements, control, management buy-in, and end user buy-in.
- ☐ Structure the knowledge management team: organizationally, strategically, and technologically.
- ☐ Balance technical and managerial expertise.
- ☐ Manage stakeholder expectations.
- ☐ Resolve team sizing issues.

STEP 6: Create the knowledge management blueprint {Chapter 10}

- ☐ Develop the knowledge management architecture.
- ☐ Understand the seven layers of the knowledge management system.
- ☐ Understand and select the components: Integrative repositories, content centers, knowledge aggregation and mining tools, the collaborative platform, knowledge directories, the user interface options, push delivery mechanisms and integrative elements.
- ☐ Design for high levels of interoperability.
- ☐ Optimize for performance and scalability .
- ☐ Understand repository life-cycle management.
- ☐ Incorporate requisite user interface considerations.
- ☐ Position and scope the knowledge management system.
- ☐ Make the build-or-buy decision and understand the trade-offs.
- ☐ Future-proof the knowledge management system.

STEP 7: Develop the knowledge management system {Chapter 11}

- ☐ Define the capabilities of each layer of the seven-layer KMS architecture in the context of your company.
- ☐ Develop the interface layer. Create platform independence, leverage the Intranet, enable universal authorship.
- ☐ Develop the access and authentication layer: secure data, control access, and distribute control.
- ☐ Develop the collaborative filtering and intelligence layer.
- ☐ Develop and integrate the application layer with the intelligence layer and the transport layer.
- ☐ Leverage the extant transport layer.
- ☐ Develop the middleware and legacy integration layer to connect mainframe legacy data, incompatible platforms, inconsistent data formats, and retired systems.
- ☐ Integrate and enhance the repository layer.
- ☐ Apply DMA and WebDAV standards to explicit content and documents.
- ☐ Advance the system from a client/server to agent computing orientation.

Phase 2

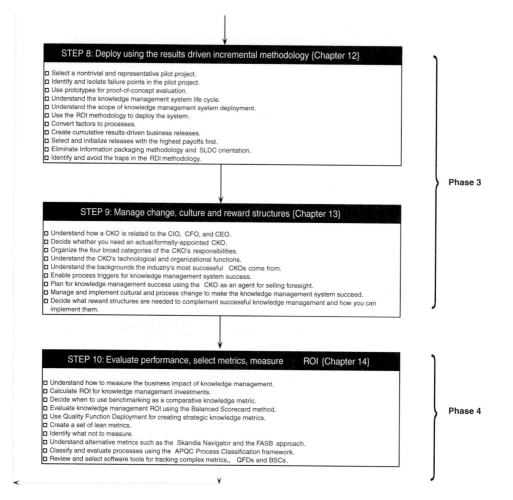

STEP 8: Deploy using the results driven incremental methodology {Chapter 12}

- ☐ Select a nontrivial and representative pilot project.
- ☐ Identify and isolate failure points in the pilot project.
- ☐ Use prototypes for proof-of-concept evaluation.
- ☐ Understand the knowledge management system life cycle.
- ☐ Understand the scope of knowledge management system deployment.
- ☐ Use the RDI methodology to deploy the system.
- ☐ Convert factors to processes.
- ☐ Create cumulative results-driven business releases.
- ☐ Select and initialize releases with the highest payoffs first.
- ☐ Eliminate Information packaging methodology and SLDC orientation.
- ☐ Identify and avoid the traps in the RDI methodology.

STEP 9: Manage change, culture and reward structures {Chapter 13}

- ☐ Understand how a CKO is related to the CIO, CFO, and CEO.
- ☐ Decide whether you need an actual/formally-appointed CKO.
- ☐ Organize the four broad categories of the CKO's responsibilities.
- ☐ Understand the CKO's technological and organizational functions.
- ☐ Understand the backgrounds the industry's most successful CKOs come from.
- ☐ Enable process triggers for knowledge management system success.
- ☐ Plan for knowledge management success using the CKO as an agent for selling foresight.
- ☐ Manage and implement cultural and process change to make the knowledge management system succeed.
- ☐ Decide what reward structures are needed to complement successful knowledge management and how you can implement them.

STEP 10: Evaluate performance, select metrics, measure   ROI {Chapter 14}

- ☐ Understand how to measure the business impact of knowledge management.
- ☐ Calculate ROI for knowledge management investments.
- ☐ Decide when to use benchmarking as a comparative knowledge metric.
- ☐ Evaluate knowledge management ROI using the Balanced Scorecard method.
- ☐ Use Quality Function Deployment for creating strategic knowledge metrics.
- ☐ Create a set of lean metrics.
- ☐ Identify what not to measure.
- ☐ Understand alternative metrics such as the Skandia Navigator and the FASB approach.
- ☐ Classify and evaluate processes using the APQC Process Classification framework.
- ☐ Review and select software tools for tracking complex metrics,, QFDs and BSCs.

Phase 3

Phase 4

PHASE 1: INFRASTRUCTURAL EVALUATION

The following forms help you evaluate your company's existing infrastructure, and then identify what the missing pieces are. Use Form 1 (FORM1.PDF on the companion CD-ROM provides additional space for adding comments and selecting responses) to inventory existing infrastructure and Form 2 (FORM2.PDF on the CD-ROM) to identify KM enablers. (Figure A-2 provides an edited version of Form 1 on the CD-ROM. Similar versions exist for all other forms.)

Form 1 Infrastructural diagnostics

Inventory Question	Your Company Yes/No	Comments
Does your company have a local-area/wide-area computer network?		
What is the bandwidth of this network in Mbps (typical values range from 10 Mbps to 100 Mbps)?		
Does your company network support remote access?		
Does it support remote dial-up access? If not, does it allow remote connectivity through an ISP's network?		
Does your company currently use an intranet?		
Does your company currently use an extranet?		
Does your company use video conferencing?		
Does your company use any specific decision support systems?		
Is your company standardized on a single computing platform such as Windows or Mac? If not, what are the different platforms used by your company's employees?		
Does your company currently use GroupWare or collaborative platforms such as Lotus Notes?		
Does your company extensively use mobile computing solutions such as PalmPilots? If your company does not officially use such solutions, do your employees use these in high numbers?		
Does your company currently deploy something like a skills database? If so, are your employees satisfied with its (a) currency and (b) quality?		
Does your company currently use document management solutions? If yes, can you list the primary reason why? (This is a seemingly straightforward question but one that is the most difficult to answer accurately.)		
Does your company currently use a project management tool for tracking projects and assignments? Examples of such tools include MS Project.		
Does your company acquire software through site licenses?		

Form 2 Knowledge processes and technology enablers: Which are already in your company?

Knowledge Objective	Technology Enablers	What Currently Exists in Your Company?
Find knowledge	Knowledge bases in consulting firms; search and retrieval tools that scan both formal and informal sources of knowledge; employee skills yellow pages.	
Create new knowledge	Capture of collaborative decision-making processes; DSS tools; rationale capture tools; Notes databases; decision repositories; externalization tools.	
Package and assemble knowledge	Customized publishing tools; information refinery tools; push technology; customized discussion groups.	
Apply knowledge	Search, retrieval, and storage tools to help organize and classify both formal and informal knowledge.	
Reuse and revalidation of knowledge	Customer support knowledge bases; consulting firm discussion databases; past project record databases and communities of practice.	

ANALYZING KNOWLEDGE MANAGEMENT AND YOUR BUSINESS STRATEGY

The next set of forms help you analyze critical linkages between knowledge management and your company's business strategy.

Your Business and Your Competition

Try to answer the strategic diagnostic questions in Form 3 (FORM3.PDF on the CD) in the context of your own company. If the current project is department specific or location specific, consider only that segment of your company that this project might directly affect.

Next, use Form 4 (FORM4.PDF) to create a comprehensive knowledge map for your competitors and your own company. By placing each company on a single knowledge map, you can identify relative strengths and weaknesses and consequently identify areas of knowledge that will strengthen your own company's position.

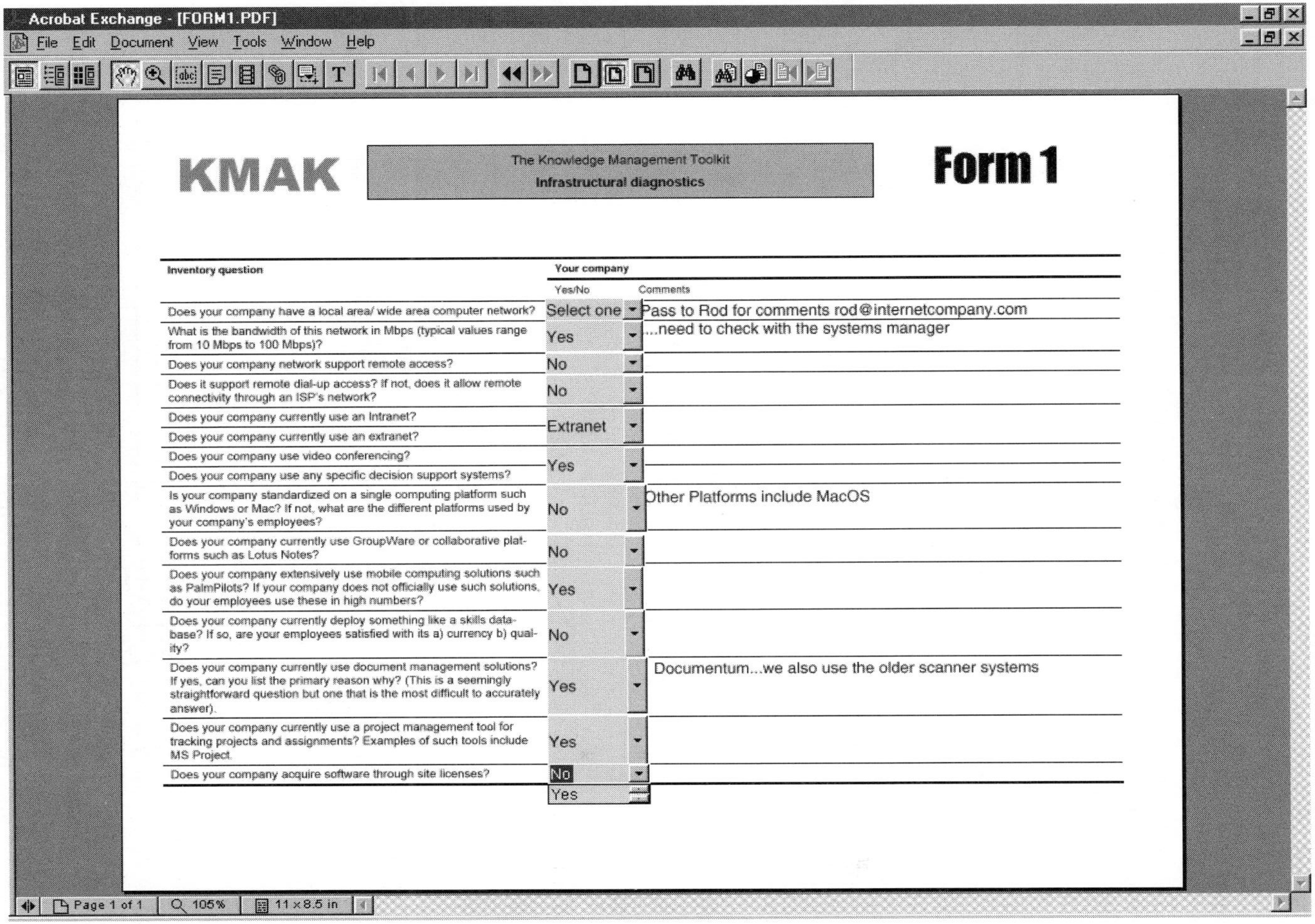

Acrobat Exchange - [FORM1.PDF]

File Edit Document View Tools Window Help

KMAK

The Knowledge Management Toolkit
Infrastructural diagnostics

Form 1

Inventory question	Your company	
	Yes/No	Comments
Does your company have a local area/ wide area computer network?	Select one	Pass to Rod for comments rod@internetcompany.com
What is the bandwidth of this network in Mbps (typical values range from 10 Mbps to 100 Mbps)?	Yes	....need to check with the systems manager
Does your company network support remote access?	No	
Does it support remote dial-up access? If not, does it allow remote connectivity through an ISP's network?	No	
Does your company currently use an Intranet?	Extranet	
Does your company currently use an extranet?		
Does your company use video conferencing?	Yes	
Does your company use any specific decision support systems?		
Is your company standardized on a single computing platform such as Windows or Mac? If not, what are the different platforms used by your company's employees?	No	Other Platforms include MacOS
Does your company currently use GroupWare or collaborative platforms such as Lotus Notes?	No	
Does your company extensively use mobile computing solutions such as PalmPilots? If your company does not officially use such solutions, do your employees use these in high numbers?	Yes	
Does your company currently deploy something like a skills database? If so, are your employees satisfied with its a) currency b) quality?	No	
Does your company currently use document management solutions? If yes, can you list the primary reason why? (This is a seemingly straightforward question but one that is the most difficult to accurately answer).	Yes	Documentum...we also use the older scanner systems
Does your company currently use a project management tool for tracking projects and assignments? Examples of such tools include MS Project.	Yes	
Does your company acquire software through site licenses?	No	
	Yes	

Page 1 of 1   105%   11 x 8.5 in

Figure A-2 An editable version of Form1 on the CD-ROM.

Form 3 Initial strategic diagnostics

Strategic Questions	Rating	Notes
How high would you rate your company's reliance on past data patterns for future decision making?	① ② ③ ④ ⑤	
Where does your company rank in terms of its possession of core knowledge required in your industry relative to other industry players?	① ② ③ ④ ⑤	
Where does your company rank in terms of its possession of advanced knowledge required in your industry?	① ② ③ ④ ⑤	
Where does your company rank in terms of its possession of innovative knowledge required in your industry? Does this knowledge let your company change the rules of the game and compete in the same markets without any visible competitive threat?	① ② ③ ④ ⑤	

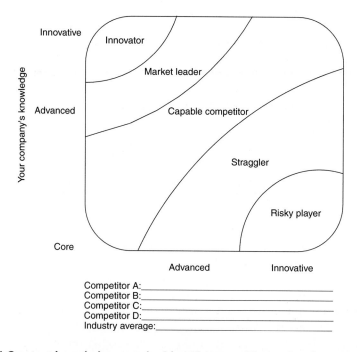

Competitor A:_____
Competitor B:_____
Competitor C:_____
Competitor D:_____
Industry average:_____

Form 4 Create a knowledge map by identifying positions of each competitor (use the editable version of this on the CD).

INITIAL ASSESSMENT OF KM AND YOUR BUSINESS

One of the first tasks that the knowledge management team needs to work on is that of understanding the project's strategic intent, organizational context, technological constraints, financial considerations, and short-term and long-term goals. These diagnostics will help you place the strategic orientation of your company and the knowledge management project in a mutually beneficial position. Use Form 5 on the CD to answer these questions.

Form 5 Evaluating your project's strategic intent, organizational context, technological constraints, financial considerations, and short-term and long-term goals

STRATEGIC INTENT

What is the time frame within which the project must be delivered. Focus on the initial phases of the knowledge management project and keep the complete knowledge management system and strategy in view at the same time.

Does your company leverage supplier and partner knowledge to strengthen its competitive standing? Do they have any say in how your firm manages its intellectual assets (such as patents, customer databases, expertise, etc.)?

Can you identify changes in the basis of competitive advantage that your company enjoys? When these begin to change for any reasons do you think your company is capable of redirecting its learning efforts to create new competencies and knowledge that help it retain its standing as a strong competitor in the market place?

Does your company's management understand what, if anything, differentiates your products and services from competition?

ORGANIZATIONAL CONTEXT

Where does the knowledge management team fit in the organizational hierarchy? Does it fit vertically or horizontally in the value chain?

Do your company's employees understand your firm's core competitive strengths? Are they encouraged to do so? Are they given the time to do so?

What level of commitment does the team have from the senior management and from the users? If it's poor, what can be done about it?

What are the cultural blockades that should be expected? Does the company culture actually fit with the knowledge-sharing attitude that is needed to make a knowledge management system work? If not, what changes in reward structure are necessary? Who has the authority to make such changes? Are they willing to make them?

Has any competitor or noncompeting firm implemented a project like this (such as the project you are considering)? What do we know about it? If it was successful, is there some way to get a key participant to switch jobs? Should we call that transfer of experiential knowledge!

Form 5 Evaluating your project's strategic intent, organizational context, technological constraints, financial considerations, and short-term and long-term goals (cont.)

TECHNOLOGICAL CONSTRAINTS

What are the technical limitations in terms of existing platforms, company-wide and enterprise-wide network standards, etc.?

FINANCIAL CONSIDERATIONS

What are the internal financial constraints?

What are the formal budgetary limitations?

What are the payoff demonstration requirements imposed by senior management?

What are the critical missing elements in terms of skills, people, and knowledge that are still missing in the team? Can consultants help? If so, which ones and how?

What are the immediate payoffs? If there are none, when will the payoffs begin to show up? If that is not viable either, how will be value of the project be demonstrated and tested?

Does your company understand the revenue and competitiveness related benefits that its knowledge assets hold for the future?

SHORT-TERM AND LONG-TERM GOALS

What is the company's strategic goal in the long term?

What is the company's performance goal in the short term and the long term? Note that "long term" could be as long as 15 years for a typical plastics manufacturer and the same "long term" could be a year for a software company that goes through three different versions of a product in a given year.

Building further upon the 24 lessons learned in Chapter 6, answer the following questions (Form 6, the 24-point evaluation) specifically in the context of your own company.

1. What are the logical business processes that knowledge management can provide logical extensions for?

2. Is your company more focused on its products or services than on the processes that go into building them?

3. What are the selling points that will help convince your senior management of the business value of managing knowledge of these processes?

4. What are the selling points that will help convince your company's employees of the business value of managing knowledge of these processes?

5. In what terms can you demonstrate short-term benefits (primarily financial) of knowledge management in your company?

6. In what terms can you demonstrate long-term benefits (primarily competitive) of knowledge management in your company?

Next, use Form 7 (FORM7.PDF on the CD-ROM) to generate initial knowledge diagnostics. The CD-ROM version provides additional space for comments. There is no objective way, such as a raw score, to interpret these diagnostics. Instead, they will help you answer questions raised in the initial design stages of your knowledge management system. Tally your responses with several colleagues. The results of this form must then be subjectively interpreted in the context of your organization.

Form 7 Initial organizational, process, culture, and infrastructure dependency knowledge diagnostics

Initial Diagnostic Question	Your company (use CD-ROM Form 7)
OVERALL	
Do you consider your business to be knowledge intensive?	
Do you consider your business to be information intensive?	
What types of knowledge do you think are critical to your business competitiveness?	
What would you rate as the top three in the above list?	
Where, on the Bohn scale (in Chapter 6), do you believe your organization falls as a whole?	
Where do the key processes that drive your business rank on this scale?	
Would you be able to claim that your company deals with processes rather than functions? This means, it's process centric not function centric.	
Has your company identified the processes that are needed to achieve long-term business objectives and corporate goals?	
If you were to state one single reason why knowledge management could never work in your company, what would that be?	
Do you consider your company's competitive advantage to be grounded in its intellectual property assets—patents, methodologies, formulas, etc.?	
ORGANIZATIONAL	
What benefits do you think your company could realize if it improved the ways it organizes and reuses existing skills and experience?	
Is composition of teams in your company governed by creating the right mix of competencies needed for the task or project at hand?	

Form 7 Initial organizational, process, culture, and infrastructure dependency knowledge diagnostics (cont.)

Initial Diagnostic Question	Your company (use CD-ROM Form 7)
How do you characterize your company structure and organization?	
Could you say that authority is decentralized to the business unit level?	
Are functional disciplines in your company team based rather than job based?	
Does your senior management focus on financial performance alone? Financial performance and future growth planning?	
Would you regard your company's management style as reactive or proactive?	

INTELLECTUAL AND CULTURAL

Would it be possible to actually use knowledge, skills, competencies, and best practices in your company in a better way than you see them being used at this point in time?

Would you agree that the business units in your company have a great deal of freedom to act and have bottom-line responsibility for their actions?

Does your company depend on the knowledge and competence surrounding its:

People?

Processes?

Technology infrastructure?

What emphasis does your company actually place on these?

What type of culture do you have in your company? It is a sharing culture?

Does your company's culture reflect internal competitiveness?

Can knowledge of multiple team members or stakeholders be added to create synergy and cohesion?

When your firm encounters a new problem can you quickly identify and mobilize the people who can solve it?

What does your company reward—team performance or individual performance?

Are your employees responsible for creating additional value in processes? Does it count in their compensation arrangements?

Form 7 Initial organizational, process, culture, and infrastructure dependency knowledge diagnostics (cont.)

Initial Diagnostic Question	Your company (use CD-ROM Form 7)
Do you consider your company's competitive advantage to be grounded in its human centric assets—skills, competencies, etc.?	
Is out-of-the-box thinking encouraged?	
Is out-of-the-box thinking rewarded?	
Does your company encourage socialization across unrelated knowledge worker groups?	
Does your company use professional discussion groups such as Web-based forums?	

INFRASTRUCTURAL—HARDWARE, SOFTWARE, DBS

Does your company have data communication networks?	
Does your company have knowledge base and repositories such as customer support logs?	
Does your company have and support telecommuting? Mobile clients?	
Does your company have an intranet?	

Choosing a KM Focus

The questions in Form 8 (FORM8.PDF on the CD-ROM) determine whether your company needs to adopt a personalization or codification strategy[b] for knowledge management. Refer to the question in the *middle column* and decide where you would place your company or department. If you are planning a knowledge management system for departmental use, answer these questions with that in mind. If the knowledge management system plan is for the entire company, think of these questions at an enterprise level. Depending on whether you chose the left or the right column as an appropriate answer, tally the scores on either side.

Don't make the overall decision solely on the basis of scores. Each of the diagnostic questions in the middle column will have varying degrees of importance for different businesses. Place everything in the context of *your* business. Remember that these two strategies are not mutually exclusive. You can, and should, have both strategies as active knowledge man-

---

[b]For details on the two strategies, see Chapter 6.

Form 8 Does your business fit the codification or the personalization knowledge management strategy?

Codification	Weight	Business Strategy Question	Weigth	Personalization
Providing high-quality, reliable, fast, and cost-effective services.		What type of business do you think your company is in? _____ _____ _____		Providing creative, rigorous, and highly customized services and products.
You reuse portions of old documents to create new ones. You use existing products to create new ones. You know that every time you have to deliver something new to a customer, you need not begin from scratch.		How much old material such as past project data, existing documents, and archived projects do you reuse as a part of new projects? _____ _____ _____		Every problem has a high chance of being a "one off" and unique problem. Although cumulative learning is involved, highly creative solutions are often called for.
Price-based competition.		What is the costing model used for your company's products and services? _____ _____ _____		Expertise-based pricing; high prices are not detrimental to your business; price-based competition barely (if at all) exists.
Very low profit margins; overall revenues need to be maximized to increase net profits.		What are your firm's typical profit margins? _____ _____ _____ Your industry's? _____ _____ _____ _____ _____		Very high profit margins.

Form 8 Does your business fit the codification or the personalization knowledge management strategy?(cont.)

Codification	Weight	Business Strategy Question	Weigth	Personalization
IT is a primary enabler; the objective is to connect people distributed across the enterprise with codified knowledge (such as reports, documentation, code, etc.) that is in some reusable form.		How best can you describe the role that IT plays in your company's work processes? _____ _____ _____ _____ _____ _____ _____ _____ _____ _____ _____		Storage and retrieval are not the primary applications of IT; IT is considered a great enabler for communications; applications such as e-mail and video conferencing are considered the most useful applications; conversations, socialization, and exchange of tacit knowledge are considered to be the primary use of IT.
Employees are rewarded for using and contributing to databases such as Notes discussion databases.		What is your reward structure like? _____ _____ _____ _____ _____		Employees are rewarded for directly sharing their knowledge with colleagues and for assisting colleagues in other locations or offices with their problems.
Employees refer to a document or best practices database that stores, distributes, and collects codified knowledge.		How is knowledge exchanged and transferred? _____ _____ _____ _____ _____		Knowledge is transferred person to person; intrafirm networking is encouraged to enable sharing of tacit knowledge, insight, experience, and intuition.

Form 8 Does your business fit the codification or the personalization knowledge management strategy? (cont.)

Codification	Weight	Business Strategy Question	Weigth	Personalization
Economies of scale lie in the effective ruse of existing knowledge and experience and applying them to solve new problems and complete new projects.		Where do your company's economies of scale lie? _____ _____ _____ _____ _____		Economies rest in the sum total of expertise available within the company; experts in various areas of specialization are considered indispensable.
Large teams; most members are junior-level employees; a few project managers lead them.		What are your typical team structure demographics? _____ _____ _____ _____		Junior employees are not an inordinate proportion of a typical team's total membership.
Andersen Consulting, The Gartner Group, Delphi Consulting, ZDNET, Delta Airlines, and Oracle.		What company's services do your company's services resemble? _____ _____ _____ _____ _____		Boston Consulting Group, McKinsey and Company, Rand Corporation.
Pizza Hut, Dell Computer, Gateway, Microsoft, SAP, People Soft, Baan, America Online, Bell South, Air Touch Cellular, Lotus, SAS Institute, IBM, Hewlett-Packard, Intranetics and 3COM.		What company's products do your company's products resemble?		A custom car or bicycle manufacturer, Boeing, a contract research firm, and a private investigator.
TOTAL WEIGHT				

agement strategies, but focus primarily on one. Assign weights on a scale of 1 to 5 to each on the personalization side and the codification side. Next, tally the weights to evaluate your project's primary focus (the one with higher weightage). Recent research shows that companies that have given equal weights to both have failed miserably at both and succeeded at neither!

If you think your business needs a codification strategy, the primary focus of the knowledge management system must be technical. Databases and repositories will be the primary focus of investments in such a case. If your company is focused on personalization, content, storage and retrieval must only be a secondary focus. Besides necessary social enablers, IT support must focus on conversations, video conferencing, discussion forums, and tacit knowledge transfer mechanisms. Communications network bandwidth expectations and enterprise-wide and remote connectivity requirements are higher in the latter case.

Identifying and Assessing Key Resources

Next, we identify and analyze key resources of your company and their relationships with knowledge management. List the top five resources that you consider to be a source of competitive advantage for your company in Form 9 (FORM9.PDF on the CD-ROM). For each of these, answer the diagnostic questions that follow using Form 10 (use the electronic version, FORM10.PDF, on the companion CD-ROM five times). This will help you pinpoint the knowledge-based resources that you consider quintessential to your company.

Next, we need to evaluate where you are with respect to each resource at this point in time. Go through the table below and analyze the level at which you can classify each of your knowledge assets, as identified above. Use Form 11 (FORM11.PDF on the CD-ROM) to create a comprehensive analysis sheet for each knowledge resource.

Form 9 Top five sources of your company's competitive advantage

Resource	Description
Knowledge/competitive advantage resource 1	
Knowledge/competitive advantage resource 2	
Knowledge/competitive advantage resource 3	
Knowledge/competitive advantage resource 4	
Knowledge/competitive advantage resource 5	

Form 10 Knowledge resource analysis

Resource number (circle one) 1 2 3 4 5 Resource description:	Comments Yes	No
Example: Our ability to solve customer configuration problems with a below (industry) average hold time.		
How is the stock of this knowledge resource increasing?		
Is it decreasing?		
How can we ensure that the stock continues to increase?		
Are we making the best use of this knowledge resource?		
Do all employees recognize the value of this resource?		
How durable is this knowledge asset?		
Will it decline over a period of time? Example of this can include the skills of employees in a technology bound to be obsolete after a certain period of time, such as skills tied to a specific version of a programming language.		
How easily can others (competition) identify and copy this resource?		
Can the competition easily nurture and grow this knowledge without copying it?		
Is there any aspect that our competition has leveraged, but we have not?		
Can be imitate it? Need we?		
Can this knowledge "walk out the door"?		
How is it changing over time?		
Will our company need it after X (decide what the value of X, in months or years is) years?		

Assessing Core Processes

Next, fill out a value that you think best describes the level of core processes that your company is involved in, in the rightmost column in Form 12 (FORM12.PDF on the CD-ROM).

Form 11 Current standing of our top five knowledge resources

Stage	Resource 1	Resource 2	Resource 3	Resource 4	Resource 5	Description/Diagnostice
0						We don't even know the good from the bad in terms of outcomes.
1						We have no knowledge; each time we have to make a decision, it's by trial and error.
2						We have only tacit knowledge, which is in the form of personal knowledge held by person _____ and _____.
3						We have tacit knowledge; we have converted it into heuristics and rules of thumb; it often works (but need not always be true).
4						Some knowledge exists in explicated form, but no one really uses it.
5						Knowledge exists in explicated form. We use it but need tacit knowledge possessed by person _____ to be able to apply it well.
6						Knowledge exists in explicated form. We use it but need tacit knowledge possessed by person _____ to be able to apply it in some circumstances; but unless things are really different from "normal" we can do without the tacit component. When ever we use this explicit knowledge, we validate it or contribute back to it (examples would include consultants using Lotus Notes databases for "quick and dirty" consulting jobs).
7						Tried and tested models now exist; We can stimulate conditions; do what-if analysis in complex circumstances; we can modify behavior accordingly; it always works. Tacit content of the sum total of knowledge is very low. We validate existing knowledge when ever we use it. Our company has a strong "unlearning" capability. Our culture truly promotes knowledge sharing and synergy. We do not think we have left any stone unturned in leveraging our company's knowledge. Employee walkouts do not hurt us in any significant way.
8						Difficult to characterize.

Form 12 Ranking characteristics of knowledge work processes along each stage and the effects of each stage on them*

Your Company	Characteristic to Be Evaluated	Stage of Knowledge							
		1	2	3	4	5	6	7	8
	Nature of production	Expertise Based			Procedure Based				
	Role of workers	Everything			Problem solving			Learning and improving	
	Location of knowledge	Tacit			Written and oral			In databases or software	
	Nature of problem solving	Trial and error			Scientific method			Table look-up	
	Natural organization type	Organic			Mechanistic			Learning	
	Suitability for automation	None						High	
	Ease of transfer	Low						High	
	Feasible product variety	High			Low			High	
	Quality control	Sorting			Statistical process control			Feed forward	

*Since the distinction between adjacent stages in Bohn's stages is subtle, the breakdown of processes done in the table above is subject to minor debates. However, all classifications are within an approximate stage. Remember that there are no clearcut boundaries between adjacent stages.

Process capability of your company can be viewed from four angles: regulatory, positional, functional, and cultural. Process capability is critical to knowledge management and knowledge management, strategy building as knowledge management is process centered. Where does your company stand with respect to its competitors along the following dimensions? Write in the positions of two (or more) of your competitors and your own company in Form 13 (FORM13.PDF on the CD-ROM).

Form 13 Fitting the capability framework for knowledge-related assets

Dimension	Your Company	Competitor 1	Competitor 2
REGULATORY CAPABILITY			

Patents

Trademarks

Registered designs

Trade secrets

Licenses

Proprietary technology

Methodologies

Databases

POSITIONAL CAPABILITY

Path-dependent capabilities

Reputation

Value chain configuration

Distribution networks

Installed base

Customer base

Market share

Liquidity

Product reputation

Service reputation

Service produce (such as
consulting outcomes reputation)

FUNCTIONAL CAPABILITY

Lead times

Accessibility of past knowledge

Innovative capabilities

Individual and team skills

Distributor know-how

Employee skills

Form 13 Fitting the capability framework for knowledge-related assets

Dimension	Your Company	Competitor 1	Competitor 2
CULTURAL CAPABILITY			
Tradition of being the *best*			
Tradition of sharing			
Tradition of coopetition			
Tradition of risk sharing			
Perception of quality standards			
Ability of employees to work in teams			
Capability to respond to market challenges			
Innovation			
Entrepreneurial and intrapreneurial drive in employees			
Employee initiative and motivation			

PHASE 2: ANALYSIS, DESIGN, AND DEVELOPMENT

The following set of forms will help you assess analysis, design, and development of your knowledge management system.

TAGS AND ATTRIBUTES

If you were to select a limited number of tags or identifiers for classifying content in your company's planned knowledge management system, which ones would you add to the default list in Form 14 (FORM14.PDF on the CD-ROM)?

Limit the added attributes to no more than 21 (a semiflexible rule of thumb); they should not overlap those already listed.

Identifying Activities Attributes

Define the values of the activities attribute up front; individual values contained in this set need not be mutually exclusive. Your company must have an explicit model of the activities and processes that are carried on during the course of running the business. This might not be a perfect model to begin with. Begin with your best shot, and incrementally improve the activity attribute value set. Add activity attributes specific to your company in Form 15 (FORM15.PDF on the CD-ROM).

Form 14 Tagging attributes for knowledge content in a knowledge management system

Default Attribute Set		Add Additional Attributes Here			
Attribute Type	Tagging Attribute	Attribute Type	Tagging Attribute	Attribute Type	Tagging Attribute
A	Activities				
D	Domain				
F	Form				
T	Type				
P	Products and services				
I	Time				
L	Location				

Form 15 The activities attribute set

Activity Attributes	Definition
DEFAULT SET	
Testing	
Quality control	
Evaluation	
Fault tolerance analysis	
MTBF (mean time between failures) determination, etc.	
ADDITIONAL ATTRIBUTES	

Identifying Domain Attributes

The domain attribute tags the knowledge item to its subject matter. This attribute is the primary attribute that drives the meta search process. Your company, most likely, already has identified the broad domains of expertise and skill areas. Domains need to be defined at an aggregate level, not a microscopic level. If your company does not have such domains defined, you need to explicate what your employees think their domains are and fix vocabulary mismatches to avoid overlapping domain names. This process is best accomplished by trial and error, and a sequential application of guidelines of any sort will be of little or no avail. Add domain attributes specific to your company in Form 16 (FORM16.PDF on the CD-ROM).

Form 16 Domain attributes

Domain attribute	Details
Domain attribute 1	
Domain attribute 2	
Domain attribute 3	
Domain attribute 4	

Form Attribute

The form attribute defines the physical representation of the knowledge element. This is a tricky attribute to define. You can begin with a basic set of values such as those described in Form 17 (FORM17.PDF on the CD-ROM).

If information is available in other forms in your company, add them to this basic list. The pointer attribute value is similar to the concept of employee skills databases, where you might do a search on "e-commerce experts," and detailed contact information for all employees matching that attribute will show up in the results. This is especially useful when company offices are geographically distributed or when employee counts in your company are high.

Type Attribute

This attribute is more relevant to formalized knowledge that is captured in electronic or textual form such as a document or report. It specifies what type of a *document* object that knowledge element is. Such values can be standardized across multiple companies, such as your company and its suppliers, etc. Suggested starting values for this attribute are listed in Form 18. Beginning with the default types specified, add additional types (and their descriptions) that your company uses. Also circulate this form in your department to accommodate an exhaustive list.

Form 17 Form attributes

Form Attributes	Physical Counterpart
Paper	
Electronic	
Formal (file, word document, spreadsheet, etc.)	
Informal (multimedia, sound, videotape, etc.)	
Collective	
Tacit or mentally held knowledge	
Pointer (to a person who has solved a problem of that nature before, etc.)	

COMPANY-SPECIFIC FORM ATTRIBUTES

Products and Services Attribute

This attribute specifies the product or service that the knowledge element relates to. This list should be kept specific and nonoverlapping. A consulting company, for example, might have, among others, the following attribute values:

- Strategic consulting
- Implementation consulting
- E-commerce consulting, etc.

Use Form 19 to create a list of product and service attributes.

Form 18 Type attributes

Default Types		Company-Specific Types	
Type Attributes*	Description	Type Attributes	Description
Procedure			
Guidelines			
Protocol			
Manual			
Reference			
Timeline			
Worst practice report			
Best practice report			
Note			
Memo			
Failure report			
Success report			
Press report			
Competitive intelligence report			

*Beginning with the values in the first column, add relevant *Types* as applicable to your company.

Time Attribute

The time attribute is useful for time-stamping events and knowledge elements. This is done automatically for files, but that time stamp is for the creation of that object, which might have a very different value from the actual creation of that knowledge object. Therefore, either the creation or use of an explicated knowledge object must be specified. Not all knowledge objects can be assigned a value for this attribute. So assign a value to this attribute where possible. It can be useful for narrowing retrieval processes.

Location Attribute

The location attribute can be used to specify location of the pointers specified to track people within and outside the company. Not all knowledge elements will have a value assigned to this attribute, but, like the time attribute, this attribute can be used to narrow searches by location. Be careful not to use too low level classification here. Make sure that the attribute usage and its values actually have a significant relevance. If the relevance or need for this attribute is moderate to low, you might save your company much time and money by simply dropping this off your list of attribute tags to be used.

Form 19 Products and services attribute

Product Attribute	Description	Service Attribute	Description

DEPLOYMENT

RDI Methodology Checklists

Form 20 (FORM20.PDF on the CD-ROM) provides a checklist for knowledge management system deployment. Using the RDI methodology, deployment must be partitioned into business releases, as described in Form 21 (FORM20.PDF on the CD-ROM).

Releases

Create your set of business releases for the whole project using the template provided in Form 21 and use the checklist in Form 22 for gauging its precision and adequacy.

Schedule all your business releases in a tabular format as shown in Form 23 (the CD-ROM version, FORM23.PDF has more room in the columns as well as more rows).

PUTTING IT ALL TOGETHER

Use the data collected through these steps to fill in the specifics of steps 1 through 10 as described by the populated knowledge management roadmap.

Finally, use the blank road map in Form 24 to create your own customized version of the 10-step knowledge management roadmap. This will help you ensure that your knowledge management system is strategically integrated with actual business processes relevant to your company.

Form 20 The RDI methodology checklist

Key Guideline	Yes	No	Notes
Is the knowledge management system providing objective-driven decision support?			Use targeted business results and end objectives to drive decision making at each point throughout the deployment process.
Do you have incremental but independent results?			Divide the implementation into a series of nonoverlapping increments, each of which enables measurable business benefits and improvements even if no further increments are implemented
Have you established software and organizational measures at each stage?			Each increment must implement everything required to produce the desired subset of results. The deployment process should also include appropriate rewards for the relevant set of employees integrating it into work processes.
Is your implementation schedule time intensive?			Each increment must be planned in a way that it can be implemented within a short time frame. Depending on the overall complexity of the knowledge management project, the time for completion of each incremental feature should range from two weeks to three months.
Do you have results-driven follow-ups in place?			Results of each increment must be used as a basic for adjusting and fine-tuning potential flaws in subsequent increments.

Form 21 The RDI methodology business release template

Incremental Business Release	Details
Business release number	
Start date	
Due date	
Release manager	
Targeted business result	
Software functionality	
Preliminary metrics	
Policy changes	
Accessibility	
Other measures and notes	

Form 22 Checklist for business release preparation

Guiding Factors for Initial Business Releases	Yes	No	Comments	Notes
Is the release focused on expected success?				Focus the initial releases on those areas that are most favorable to success. A flopped first business release is unlikely to retain management support.
Are your business releases cumulative?				Begin with an area where learning is most cumulative. Whatever area you select, make your choice such that the lessons learned in the initial releases are those that can impact the knowledge management project the most.
Have you addressed releases with the highest payoffs first?				Take up the releases that have the possibility of the maximum payoff early on in the process and those with marginal payoffs toward the end.
Did you balance the above?				The trick lies in balancing the above three at an optimal point. Determining an optimal point where the payoffs are maximized and the risks minimized is a very subjective judgment and often depends on your company's and project's particular situation.

Form 23 Combining business releases to guide the deployment strategy for a knowledge management system

Business Release Number	Key Performance Indicators	Description	Starting Date	Due Date	Software Functionaliity	Organizational Changes
1						
2						
3						
4						
5						
6						
7						

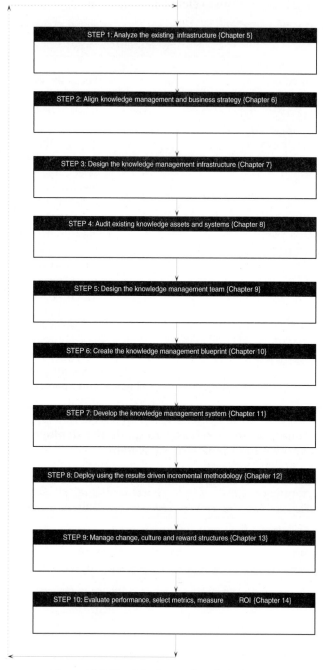

Figure A-3 The blank populated roadmap

Appendix B

Alternative Schemes for Structuring the KM System Front End

Web-based front ends for knowledge management systems, such as intranets, need not be arranged in hierarchical structures as they have traditionally been arranged. This appendix provides examples of several alternative arrangement schemes both for site content and maps. Each style is followed by an example and a location URL that you can investigate further.

ALTERNATIVE STRUCTURES

The key point is that there are many other ways of organizing content when you are creating a Web-based front end for your knowledge management system, so do not just limit your choices without taking a look at these alternatives. The structures are presented in the order of popularity of use and perceived usefulness.

ALPHABETICAL

The alphabetical approach is illustrated in Figure B-1. As shown, everything on the site and the system is arranged alphabetically. This scheme does not work well if content is not referred to consistently by everyone. It is a bad idea when cross-functional teams are involved in your company, and a good one when everyone shares the same vocabulary. The sample site can be found at http://www.molndal.se/bibl/subject.htm.

ALPHANUMERIC

The alphanumeric style (see Figure B-2) is very similar to the alphabetical structure, except that content under each alphabetical category is arranged by the numeric code. This works only when you can have some kind of numeric codes assigned to *each* content item. This style seems to have very low applicability to knowledge management design. The sample site can be found at http://www.dvjb.kvl.dk/dvjbfag/umnet02.htm.

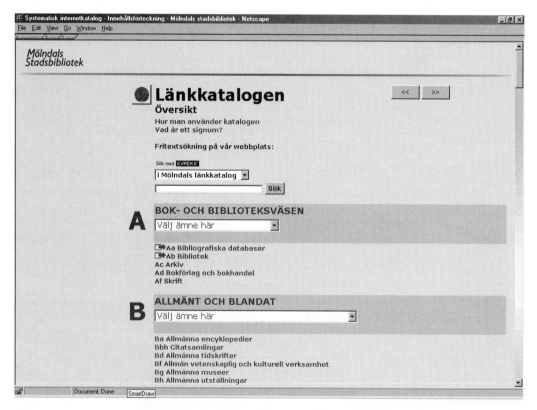

Figure B-1 Alphabetically arranged site structure.

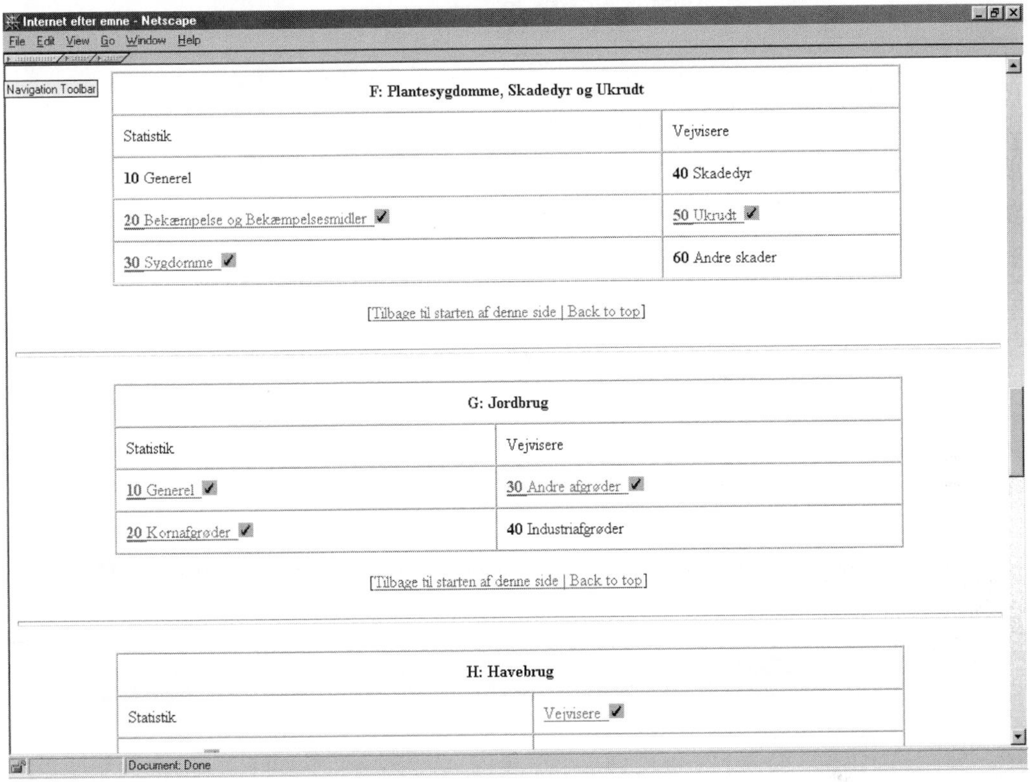

Figure B-2 Alphanumeric site structure.

DEWEY DECIMAL CODES

Dewey Decimal Coding (DDC) is a classification scheme used in libraries. If your content can be neatly categorized in such categories, this might be an option to consider. Figure B-3 illustrates ADAM. ADAM helps you find the relevant information by providing a searchable online catalogue describing Internet resources such as Websites or electronic mailing lists, in much the same way as a library catalogue describes bibliographic resources such as books and journals. This site can be found at http://adam.ac.uk/adam/index.html.

Another example (Figure B-4) can be found on the Web at http://bized.ac.uk/roads /htdocs/subjectlisting/Default/numlist.html.

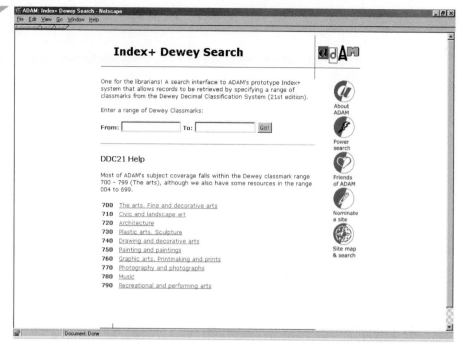

Figure B-3 A site using the DDC classification scheme.

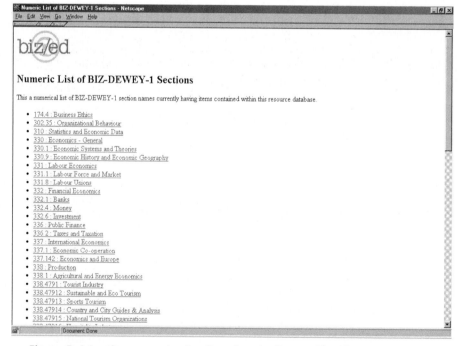

Figure B-4 Another example of a site using the Dewey Classification Codes to structure, classify, and arrange content.

CLASSIFICATION SCHEMES FOR PUBLIC LIBRARIES

A number of library classification schemes exist. One such site based on public library classification schemes is the Finnish site *Suomalaisia linkkejä alanmukaisesti järjestettynä*. This site (shown in Figure B-5) can be found at http://www.kirjasto.sci.fi/lindex.htm.

UNIVERSAL DECIMAL CLASSIFICATION

Yet another mechanism to organize and structure content, as seen through the system front end, is the Universal Decimal Classification scheme. A sample site, the NISS Directory of Networked Resources (Figure B-6) uses this scheme. As you might guess, this is appropriate only for content that is highly structured. Rarely do companies—even those that follow a deep structured codification strategy for knowledge management—have content so highly structured. This site can be found at http://www.niss.ac.uk/subject/index.html.

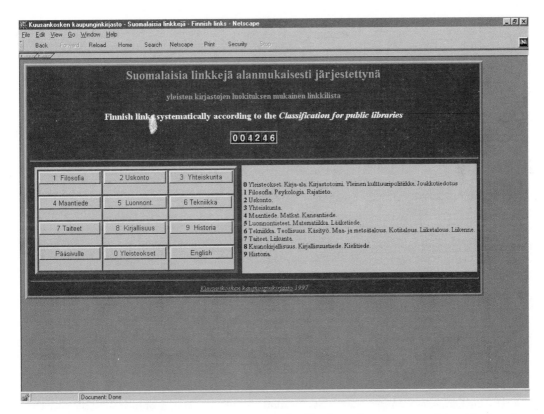

Figure B-5 A Finnish site that uses a public library classification scheme to organize content and drive its structure.

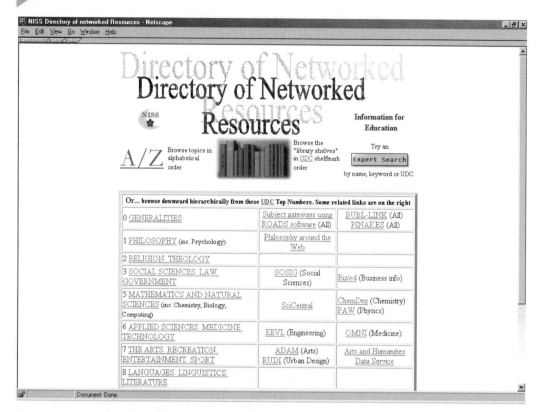

Figure B-6 The NISS Directory of Networked Resources uses Universal Decimal Classification to drive its structure.

ACM COMPUTING CLASSIFICATION SYSTEM

The Computing Research Repository (CoRR) (Figure B-7), which is sponsored by ACM, the Los Alamos e-Print archive, and NCSTRL (Networked Computer Science Technical Reference Library), uses the ACM computing classification system for driving its structure. This method might be useful for organizing content and driving structure for highly organized explicated documents and artifacts that exist in electronic form. The site can be found on the Web at http://xxx.lanl.gov/archive/cs/intro.html

THE LIBRARY OF CONGRESS CLASSIFICATION SCHEME

A promising method for classification and categorization of general content is that based on the Library of Congress (LOC) classification scheme. An example of such a site is Cyberstacks at Iowa State University. This site, shown in Figure B-8, can be found on the Web at http://www.public.iastate.edu/~CYBERSTACKS/narrow.htm.

- **AR - Architecture** - William Waite
- **AI - Artificial Intelligence** - Erik Sandewall
- **CC - Computational Complexity** - Lane Hemaspaandra
- **CG - Computational Geometry** - Joe O'Rourke
- **CE - Computational Science, Engineering, and Finance** - Ron Boisvert
- **CL - Computation and Language** (*subsumes cmp-lg*) - Stuart Shieber
- **CV - Computer Vision and Pattern Recognition** - Gio Wiederhold and Oscar Firschein
- **CY - Computers and Society** - Lorrie Cranor
- **CR - Cryptography and Security** - Mihir Bellare
- **DB - Databases** - Jim Gray
- **DS - Data Structures and Algorithms** - David Karger
- **DL - Digital Libraries** - Michael Lesk
- **DM - Discrete Mathematics** - Joe O'Rourke
- **DC - Distributed Computing** - Tushar Chandra
- **GL - General Literature** - Joe Halpern
- **GR - Graphics** - Alain Fournier
- **HC - Human-Computer Interaction** - Terry Winograd
- **IR - Information Retrieval** - Bruce Croft
- **LG - Learning** - Tom Dieterrich
- **LO - Logic in Computer Science** - Gopalan Nadathur
- **MS - Mathematical Software** - Ron Boisvert
- **MA - Multiagent Systems** - Michael Huhns and Jose Vidal
- **MM - Multimedia** - Richard Muntz
- **NI - Networking and Internet Architecture** - Scott Shenker
- **NE - Neural and Evolutionary Computation** - Jordan Pollack
- **NA - Numerical Analysis** - Ron Boisvert
- **OS - Operating Systems** - William Waite
- **OH - Other** - Joe Halpern
- **PF - Performance** - Richard Muntz
- **PL - Programming Languages** - Nadathur Gopalan
- **RO - Robotics** - Bruce Donald
- **SE - Software Engineering** - Peter Wegner
- **SC - Symbolic Computation** - Rich Zippel

CoRR was opened on Sept. 15, 1998. Send any comments to cs-admin@xxx.lanl.gov

Figure B-7 The Computing Research Repository: An example of a site structured on the ACM computing classification system.

Figure B-8 The Library of Congress Classification Scheme drives the structure of Cyberstacks at Iowa State University.

PREDICAST REVISED EVENT CODES

Bay Networks, Inc., used this set of codes for figuring out ways in which people looked for information. Since one artifact can fall under multiple categories, clustering schemes need to be consistent. This scheme is based on the *Predicast Revised Event Code and Event Name List*, a reader's guide to business press. Detailed information can be found in the awfully expensive book (over $600) *Predicasts Basebook*, available in many libraries.

CAN THESE REALLY BE USED?

The schemes described above are excellent for highly structured content. They could be used if content within your system is highly structured and can be fitted into a limited number of categories. If this is not the case, which is most likely to be true, you must not try using such a scheme.

However, if some of the content in your system could (due to the nature of your business) neatly fit into one of the above categories, you can use category codes (such as LOC or ACM codes) to assign meta tags to content. These tags can be used to retrieve and find content based on standardized codes even when they are not explicitly used. It is unlikely that *any* knowledge management system can manage with such a limited set of classification categories, but these could be used (or combined) to transparently add one more level of tagging to your knowledge management system's content—both formal and informal.

Two very worthwhile books on the topic of organizing sites that I would highly recommend are:

1. Lynch, Patrick, and Sarah Horton, *Web Style Guide: Basic Design Principles for Creating Web Sites,* Yale University Press, Yale (1999).
2. Rosenfeld, Louis, and Peter Morville, *Information Architecture for the World Wide Web,* O'Reilly, Cambridge; Sebastopol (1998).

These books talk about the Web in general, but most ideas are directly applicable to a knowledge management system if you decide to use an intranet front end.

APPENDIX C
SOFTWARE TOOLS

COMPUTERS MAKE IT EASIER TO DO A LOT OF THINGS, BUT MOST
OF THE THINGS THEY MAKE IT EASIER TO DO DON'T NEED TO BE DONE.
—ANDY ROONEY

This appendix reviews some software tools that are relevant to the creation of a knowledge management system. Some tools can fit into multiple categories and can be used in several knowledge management system layers. For this reason, tools are listed alphabetically, and the multitude of uses are described under individual listings. Many of the tools reviewed here are also included on the companion CD-ROM (indicated by)

SOFTWARE TOOLS

acCRAWL

acCrawl is a component that returns links and information about the links from a local HTML document or an active Web page. Information about the link, including its title, URL, locality, relative depth level, and parent document, is returned as an event fires for each link encounter. acCrawl also supports recursive crawling in linked documents to search out additional links.

The programmer can set the number of levels to crawl or set the component to crawl all levels. Since extensive link information is returned, users can map or otherwise monitor sites. A time-limited version of this tool is included on the companion CD-ROM. For further details and pricing information, visit the product's information page at www.actools.com.

acSGML

acSGML is a component that programmatically reads and writes SGML documents. For reading SGML documents, acSGML parses an SGML file into individual tags and text, then fires events for each item to make it easy for programmers to find the data they are interested in. In addition, "smart" logic fires individual events of each columnar data element for columnar data found in the SGML <TABLE> </TABLE> tag set. A limited version of this tool is included on the companion CD-ROM. Further details can be found at www.actools.com.

ALPHA STOCKVUE 99

AlphaCONNECT StockVue 99 (Figure C-1) automatically tracks stocks and mutual funds via the Internet. This tool is a great example of a mechanism for integrating readily available external information (such as competitor information) and "feeding" it to an integrated knowledge management system. With StockVue 99, you can access the latest quotes, company news, and SEC filings on stocks and mutual funds directly from the Internet. StockVue automatically exports the retrieved financial data directly into Quicken (including Quicken 99), Microsoft Word, or Excel for easier performance charting and better investment management. StockVue also automatically updates portfolios and calculates current values from

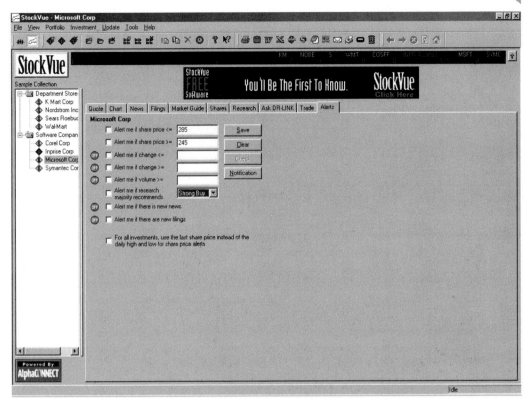

Figure C-1 AlphaCONNECT's StockVue.

once a day to every 15 minutes. StockVue 99, a full, no-restrictions version of which is included on the companion CD-ROM, includes AlphaCONNECT BusinessVue.

A feature worth mentioning in this tool is its ability to exchange information with mobile computing devices including the PalmPilot and Windows CE family of hand-held PCs (HPCs). StockVue 99 can also maintain a historical "calendar," where you can easily identify stock milestones, including news, filings, and 52-week highs and lows. It further allows you to trade stocks with your favorite online broker without exiting StockVue 99 using a special deep-linking feature. You can also receive notification via e-mail, fax, or pager when a stock reaches a specified level or volume when the company issues news or SEC filings.

More than anything else, this tool demonstrates excellent software design and tight functional integration with existing devices such as your PalmPilot and pager. This tool can serve as a guideline for creating tools that can take external information—which is often readily available in electronic format—and convert it into actionable information, that is, knowledge. For further details, explore the unrestricted/full version on the companion CD-ROM or visit AlphaCONNECT's home page at www.alphaconnect.com.

ASCENT

Ascent develops custom database mining software, using a spectrum of techniques developed in artificial intelligence and allied fields. These techniques include decision tree construction, neural-net training, genetic evolution, clustering, derived-attribute discovery, and visualization, with the characteristics of the application always driving the technique-selection process. Ascent also develops the sophisticated infrastructure needed to support database mining applications, with a special expertise in database system management, database conditioning, client/server computing, knowledge engineering, and the construction of regularity-exposing graphical user interface. Ascent's database mining and visualization are very expensive, typically in the range of $75,000 and up. For further information, visit Ascent's Web site at www.ascent.com.

BRAINFOREST PROFESSIONAL FOR PALMPILOT PDAS

BrainForest Professional (Figure C-2) for your hand-held PDA and your desktop is an action item, checklist manager, idea keeper, and project planner for mobile users. For knowledge management systems that support mobile users, this application can be used as a component for linking personal digital assistants, desktops, and shared systems. BrainForest displays information on a hand-held device or desktop computer using an intuitive trees, branches, and leaves analogy, similar to the Outline function in Microsoft Word.

   BrainForest groups related ideas, action items, checklists, to-dos, Internet URLs, electronic mail addresses, etc., together. Users can keep track of teams and projects, recurring items, due dates, and priorities. BrainForest is sold in two versions: a mobile PDA-only version and an extended version (Figure C-3) that includes a desktop client. For further information, visit Aportis' Website at www.aportis.com.

BUSINESSVUE 2.0

BusinessVue (Figure C-4) is a corporate intelligence software that is also included in AlphaCONNECT's StockVue 99 program. This program allows you to retrieve corporate profiles via Market Guide, query the DR-LINK™ database, and get access to thousands of news stories, link to Dun & Bradstreet for business-to-business credit information on companies worldwide, get stock quotes and news articles from PC Quote, gain access to analyst recommendations with Zack's Investment Research, and research SEC filings with Edgar Online. You can also configure it to automatically send important information to key contacts via e-mail, pager, or fax and export information to leading business applications like Excel and ACT!

   BusinessVue an excellent example of intelligent filtering technology used to gather corporate intelligence from the Internet. A full version of this tool is included on the companion CD-ROM. Further details can be found on AlphaCONNECT's home page at www.alphaconnect.com.

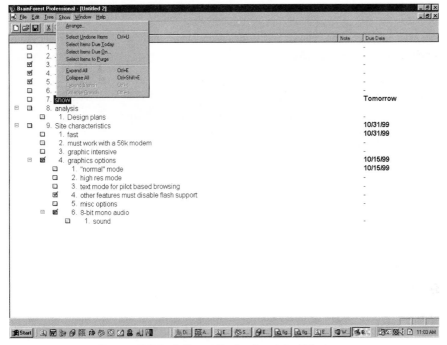

Figure C-2 BrainForest Professional for Windows.

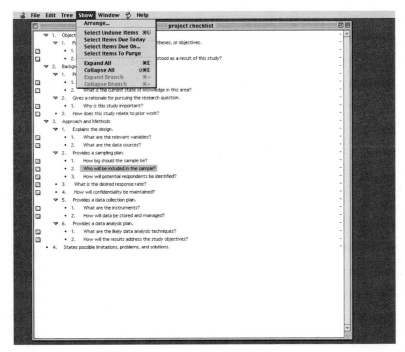

Figure C-3 BrainForest Professional for Macintosh.

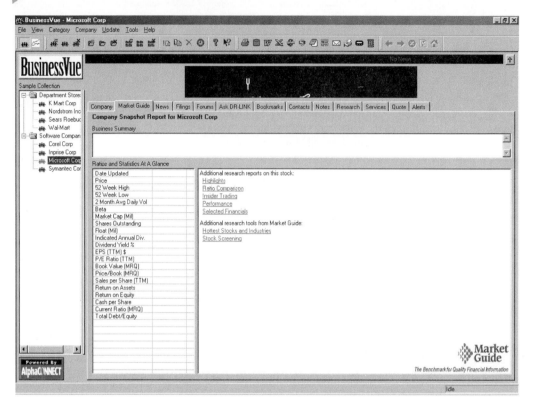

Figure C-4 BusinessVue 2.0.

CBR Content Navigator

Inference Corporation's CBR Content Navigator provides "conversation-based access to multiple sources of knowledge." Access to the knowledge can be via the Web, CD-ROM, or call center representative. CBR knowledge management technology captures the diagnostic process of solving problems and allows a knowledge base to be built. Users can then type in descriptions of queries in everyday language. An intelligent analysis of this query provides the parameters to define a search of the knowledge base by means of case-based retrieval techniques. The search results are used to generate a set of questions to diagnose customer problems and recommend solutions. More information on this product can be found at www.inference.com.

CONCEPT EXPLORER

Concept Explorer is a family of visual, knowledge-based tools for searching Web content. Users can visually explore relationships between search terms to build effective search queries without needing to understand the details of search engine query syntax. The program analyzes sample ASCII documents or HTML Web pages and identifies semantic relationships among the most useful words and phrases to represent their subject matter. The result is a web of connections between key concepts, which is stored in a knowledge base. A graphical visualizer enables users to explore this knowledge base and build queries that can improve the accuracy of standard search engines. For further details, visit Knowledge Discovery Systems on the Web at http://www.kdsystems.com/.

DATAWARE KNOWLEDGE MANAGEMENT SUITE

The DataWare knowledge management suite unifies access to disparate corporate knowledge repositories such as document management systems, RDBMS, GroupWare applications, electronic mail systems, and external news feeds. It seamlessly integrates material from all of these sources into a central information repository while allowing users to continue working in familiar formats. The suite uses natural language querying, an ANSI-compliant thesaurus, concept-clustered results, and relevance ranking to facilitate linking between related materials and, on request, notifies users of updates or changes to specific topics of interest. For further details, visit DataWare Technologies on the Web at www.dataware.com.

DELTAMINER

MIS-AG's DeltaMiner integrates new search techniques and business intelligence methodologies into an OLAP front end that embraces the concept of *active information management*. MIS suggests that such an approach can maximize returns from tremendous amounts of little-used data collected in data marts assembled by many companies.

Finding useful information using traditional "passive" search techniques can be slow and cumbersome, and usually leaves a large amount of important trends and variance sources hidden, especially when they lie outside of the normally examined controlling paths. By integrating standard OLAP analysis techniques, this tool makes it possible to pivot and cross-tabulate data for analyzing OLAP hypercubes. DeltaMiner automatically seeks the views that will be most meaningful, thereby increasing analysis efficiency. DeltaMiner further highlights the most significant exceptions by reorganizing cross-tabulations to magnify the 10 best or 10 worst results from the given data set. This tool also provides extensive graphic visualization features that help users graphically interpret significant exceptions.

DeltaMiner also automates ranking and portfolio analysis techniques and automatically suggests classifications for data sets. Further, by employing chain analysis techniques, this tool lets users ask new and more relevant questions of their data. All these techniques can be cross-linked to create powerful analysis chains. This analysis path is visually recorded in an analysis tree, as MIS describes it. Via a data-driven drill down that does not follow any preset paths, DeltaMiner guides you rapidly to the main causes of exceptions in your data.

A feature that makes this tool an excellent candidate for an expansive knowledge management system is its open database connectivity. DeltaMiner can directly be connected to various data sources including MIS ALEA, TM/1, Microsoft OLAP Service, and Oracle Express.

For further information, test-run the trial version of this tool on the companion CD-ROM or visit MIS AG on the Web at www.mis.de.

EMAIL FERRET

Email Ferret (Figure C-5) is a small utility for finding electronic mail addresses of people on the Web. Unlike most e-mail directories, it runs as a client on your desktop rather than in a browser. Email Ferret seeks out e-mail addresses by simultaneously querying multiple Web-based e-mail directories. Addresses can then be added to an electronic address book, copied, or mailed to, using a standard electronic mail client.

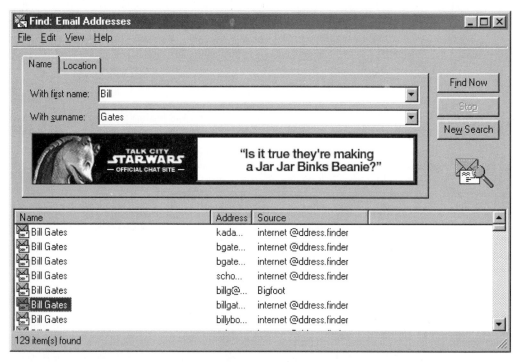

Figure C-5 Email Ferret uses multiple Web-based directory services to retrieve contact information.

Like most other FerretSoft utilities, this tool automatically updates itself every time it is run (it automatically checks the FerretSoft configuration server for any updates). Updates and new search engine configurations are extremely small, and the entire update process is fast and unnoticeable.

An unrestricted freeware version of Email Ferret is included on the companion CD-ROM. For more information, visit FerretSoft's home page at http://www.ferretsoft.com.

EMPLOYEE APPRAISER 4.0

In Chapter 13 we discussed the importance of change management and cultural incentives needed to make knowledge management succeed. This also includes the task of appropriately judging performance and knowledge contributions of individual employees. Employee Appraiser 4.0 (Figure C-6) includes hundreds of professionally written phrases and paragraphs that you use to get started. When you've got the right combinations of paragraphs that you want, you can choose the Writing Tuner buttons and adjust tone or intensity.

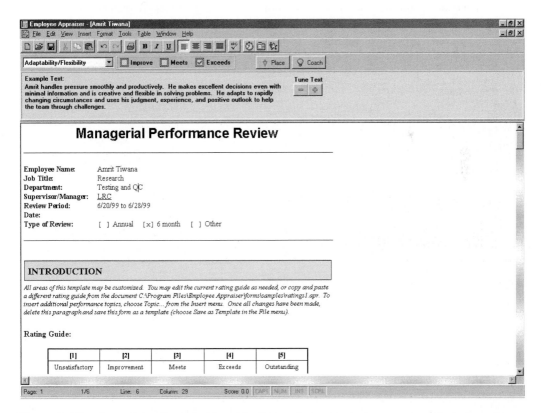

Figure C-6 Employee Appraiser provides objective performance reviews, such as those based on employees' knowledge contributions.

Forms in Microsoft Word, Corel WordPerfect, Lotus Word Pro, and other programs can be imported into Employee Appraiser. A word-scanning glossary feature checks for inappropriate or illegal language.

The Employee Folder helps managers track performance against objectives all year. When it comes time to write the review, Employee Appraiser shows you the key events and lets you easily put them into the appraisal form. Using this feature ensures that appropriate credit is given to each employee and that evaluations are truly evaluations rather than last-minute perceptions. A trial version of this tool is included on the companion CD-ROM. For further information visit Austin Hayne's Website at http://www.austin-hayne.com.

FILE, PHONE, AND NEWS FERRETS

File Ferret (Figure C-7), Phone Ferret, and New Ferret are three additional utilities from FerretSoft.

File Ferret searches both Web-based file databases and the Archie protocol databases for Shareware, public domain software, and other files. Retrieved files can then be downloaded by built-in file transfer protocol (FTP) support.

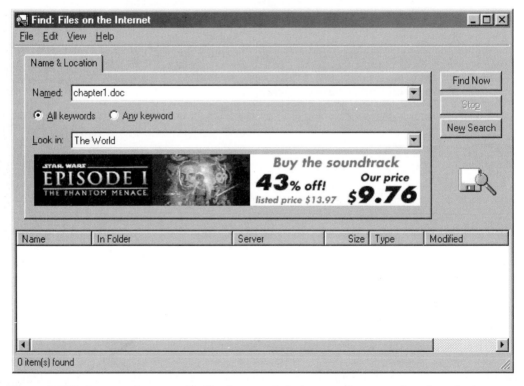

Figure C-7 File Ferret retrieves specific files from a relatively expansive network such as the Internet.

Phone Ferret retrieves information from white pages and locates United States telephone numbers by searching the most popular phone number directories. For users with dialer software installed, numbers can be directly dialed from the search results.

News Ferret searches multiple newsgroups to locate Usenet articles, automatically joining multipart messages, and decoding binary attachments. The articles can then be retrieved and displayed, or saved for later review. Search results can be sorted according to different criteria such as source, etc.

Unrestricted freeware versions of these three products Ferret are included on the companion CD-ROM. For more information, visit FerretSoft's home page at http://www.ferretsoft.com.

G2 WebMiner

G2 WebMiner enables applications created with G2 to access and reason about data available over the Internet to provide intelligent decision support solutions. It can be used to mine data from an organization's Internet Website or intranet, perform rule-based analysis, and then make intelligent decisions. For further details, visit Gensym Corporation's Web site at www.gensym.com.

HyperKnowledge

HyperKnowledge is a knowledge modeling tool. It assists in tasks such as knowledge capture, process design, team building, training and education, and information systems definition. One repository of knowledge can be exploited in multiple ways. HyperKnowledge models provide a means of prototyping business logic, since they can be executed as they are being built. The HyperKnowledge approach is to regard all knowledge as knowledge of processes. Specifically, knowledge is represented in terms of the what, how, and why of processes. A HyperKnowledge model consists of reuseable components of knowledge, and because it inherently contains all the processes from which any concept is made, an appropriate component or class structure can be automatically derived. When used for information systems design, the model can be exported into an information systems development environment using the industry standards. For further details, visit HyperKnowledge on the Web at www.hyperknowledge.com, or send e-mail to sales@hyperknowledge.com.

Hyperwave

Hyperwave Information Server (Figure C-8) is a flexible and feature-rich platform that can provide your portal solution "out of the box," or can be easily customized to meet specific needs. Built upon the Hyperwave Information Server, Hyperwave Information Portal provides a secure and single point of integration, access, and navigation through the myriad enterprise systems and information sources facing workers in today's "middle office." The middle office is where organizations' unstructured data resides, where the front office and the back office collide, where negotiation, product differentiation, and competitive advantage thrive

The Hyperwave Information Portal provides a searchable repository that aggregates key information sources by automatically and dynamically creating and maintaining hyperlinks to your organization's unstructured data including documents, e-mail, PowerPoint presentations, videos, images, etc., as well as giving access to structured data. User access is directly from a browser. Browser-based access provides ease of use for users and administrators alike plus the integrity of accurately hyperlinked information.

Displaying information in a familiar and easy-to-navigate hierarchical structure, the system seamlessly integrates access to information stored in a variety of native formats. Users can be set up to receive e-mail notifications of new or changed information so they are always up to date with the information that's most relevant to them.

Fully automated hyperlink generation and management coupled with sophisticated document management capabilities ensure information context, consistency, and accessibility.

Extensive security and personalization mechanisms are built into Hyperwave. For further details, see the limited version of Hyperwave on the companion CD, or visit Hyperwave on the Web at www.hyperwave.com.

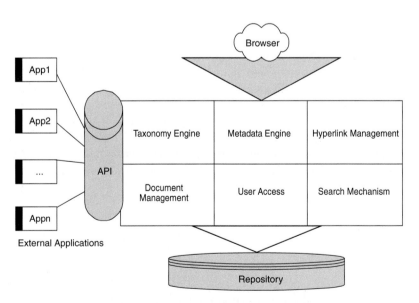

Figure C-8 How Hyperwave is structured.

Info Ferret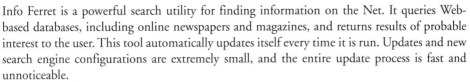

Info Ferret is a powerful search utility for finding information on the Net. It queries Web-based databases, including online newspapers and magazines, and returns results of probable interest to the user. This tool automatically updates itself every time it is run. Updates and new search engine configurations are extremely small, and the entire update process is fast and unnoticeable.

A full version of Info Ferret is included on the companion CD-ROM. For more information, visit FerretSoft's home page at http://www.ferretsoft.com.

Inspiration Professional

Inspiration Professional (Figure C-9) is a powerful visual thinking tool that helps clarify and organize ideas and information. Inspiration's Diagram view makes it easy to brainstorm, plan, and explain the interrelationships between processes, variables, and events. A powerful feature that makes Inspiration stand out against competing products is its ability to convert visual diagrams and mind maps to outlines (using tightly integrated Diagram and Outline views) readable by any word processor. It can create concept maps, process flows, knowledge maps, and flowcharts. Inspiration also comes with an extensive set of symbols (over 500), templates (and example files) specifically suited for diagramming, outlining, flowcharting, knowledge mapping, brainstorming, and multimedia design. For more information, visit Inspiration Software's Website at www.inspiration.com.

Intranetics

Intranetics 2.0 is a suite of 20 intranet applications and is a highly recommended route for basing your knowledge management system's front end using an intranet. Each application can be customized to meet your specific business needs. Intranetics is created for businesses and departments with up to 500 users. The software also provides a flexible application framework that allows you to easily integrate existing or custom applications. Through its secure extranet capabilities, your customers, business partners, and remote offices can have access to specific applications with either password-protected or anonymous access. A key strength of this suite comes from its ability to integrate existing applications currently in use within your company.

Intranetics 2.0 security provisions build on those provided by the network operating system and Web server, greatly easing administration requirements. Intranetics 2.0 allows companies to define their own security scheme and set levels of access for individual users, including access to specific applications and information fields within an application. Intranetics 2.0 works with a Web server and so is integrated into the server's own security mechanisms.

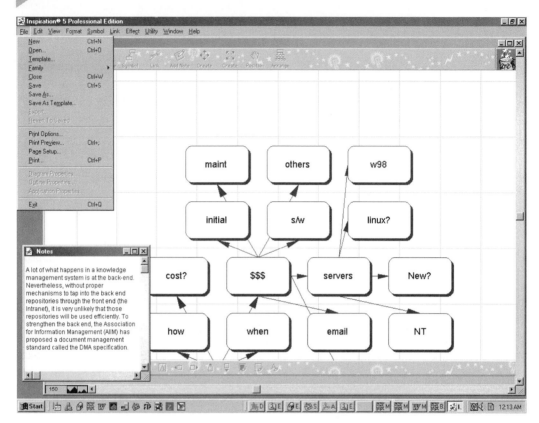

Figure C-9 Inspiration Professional dynamically maintains links between diagrammatic representations and textual outlines.

Two versions of Intranetics are currently available: the standard version and the Microsoft BackOffice Small Business Server version. The standard edition, which costs under $5,000, can support up to 500 users. The smaller version costs $1,495 and is optimized for Microsoft BackOffice Small Business Server. This version is capable of supporting up to 50 users. Both versions support most 4.0 version browsers. The company also offers reasonably priced technical support programs. Intranetics is more highly recommended than any other competing tools in its target market because it offers good value and powerful functionality. For detailed information, run the time-limited version of Intranetics 2.0 on the companion CD-ROM, or visit the company's home page at http://www.intranetics.com/.

KA² KNOWLEDGE AGENTS

Knowledge agents gather, filter, and disseminate information from external and internal sources (such as electronic mail, GroupWare, databases, document management systems, intranets, business intelligence applications, and external news feeds) and automatically profile and distribute it against individual requirements. They are designed to provide a centralized corporate knowledge base that acts as the main storage repository and broker for the corporate memory.

Knowledge agents includes a full text search engine capable of indexing more than 200 file formats. Using automatic profiling and knowledge mapping technology, the system constantly queries the knowledge base and responds the instant a relevant piece of material is identified. This technology is based on what is described as a *vocabulary of interest,* which is compiled for each individual, group, or organization. For more details, visit AppliedNet Ltd. on the Web at www.appliednet.co.uk.

KEYFLOW

KeyFlow is a dynamic workflow management tool that enables users to easily visualize and automate existing business processes, monitor their progress, and modify them in real time to improve efficiency and respond rapidly to changing business needs.

With KeyFlow, documents can be automatically circulated through a business process according to predetermined criteria, ensuring that established policies and procedures are observed. KeyFlow allows knowledge workers to apply their knowledge of the business to design efficient business processes that can be used by anyone within a department or across the enterprise.

KeyFlow integrates seamlessly into the Microsoft Exchange environment, taking advantage of client user interface, standard active messaging, user addressing, and public folder and replication facilities. KeyFlow's graphical user interface allows users to select the steps needed to build a business process and to link several steps to create a workflow map. KeyFlow also provides a full suite of controls, such as voting, and conditional prerequisites that enable you to automate business processes. For a demonstration, see the files included on the companion CD-ROM. For further information, visit KeyFile Corporation's product site at http://www.keyflow.com.

KNOWLEDGESEEKER

KnowledgeSEEKER is a data mining software tool that employs a unique cross-referencing process that enables businesses to draw conclusions from varied and disparate databases. The application of KnowledgeSEEKER can be tailored to suit the specific needs of any number of different business tasks, from customer profiling and segmentation to fraud detection and risk analysis. The conclusions that can be drawn from the data are often surprising, since the software works independent of any user bias, putting less importance on pre-conceived ideas.

Angoss, the developer, claims that KnowledgeSEEKER is faster and easier to use and interpret than both traditional statistical models and new technologies such as neural networks. Analysis results are rapidly displayed in the form of a clear and interactive decision tree, or for more advanced users, as Prolog source code. Both the sensitivity of the correlation finding and the volume of the information displayed are easily user defined. For further details, visit Angoss International's Website at www.angoss.com.

MARKETFIRST

MarketFirst, although developed for electronic commerce marketing applications, can be a powerful tool to build into a knowledge management system design. A simple drag-and-drop interface utilizes a flowchart metaphor based on business rules, audience segmentation. The feature of most interest in KM applications is its automatic profiling and segmentation capability. MarketFirst's extensible database features automatic incremental profiling, a capability that allows you to easily customize profile attributes and extend the database to reflect specific needs. Workgroup collaboration through e-mail messaging is enabled by its support for popular e-mail servers. All MarketFirst reports can be published for review to a corporate intranet or Internet Website and viewed through a Web browser. For more information, visit MarketFirst's Website at www.marketfirst.com.

MICROSOFT FRONTPAGE 2000

The Microsoft FrontPage 2000 Website creation and management tool is very well integrated with Microsoft Office 2000. A relatively low cost tool, FrontPage can be a very good intranet front-end development tool. The multiple views in FrontPage 2000 (Figure C-10) allow you to see all the files in your Web, run reports to find slow pages and older files, set up your site's navigational structure, and keep track of Web tasks. For example, you can create and edit Web pages in Page View, use Folders View to see all the content on your Web, then set up how your pages link to one another in Navigation View. FrontPage 2000 features extensive summary report capabilities and can help you identify changed or broken links. When you are considering remote access through dial-up connections, its "Find Slow Pages" option lets you locate pages that take too long to load based on the modem speed you've specified.

You can create Websites in a folder on your hard disk without installing a Web server. This makes getting started with FrontPage 2000 as simple as getting started with Microsoft Office. FrontPage also supports nested sub-Webs and document check-in/check-out capabilities. Flexible security in FrontPage 2000 allows you to turn a folder in your Web into a sub-Web, complete with unique permissions by group or user. FrontPage also supports collaborative development that, in effect, almost duplicates a light version of its project management

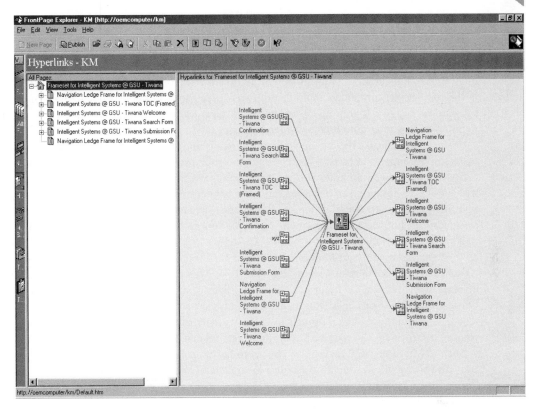

Figure C-10 The hyperlink view is one of many possible ways of viewing complex relationships and linkages between Web pages on a FrontPage-based intranet.

tool. This feature can be very useful if multiple people are involved in the development of your knowledge management system front end.

The only downside of this tool is that it inserts a lot of Microsoft-specific HTML that can make manual editing both confusing and tedious. This additional code inserted into Web pages also bloats their file sizes. If your Web server supports FrontPage extensions (on UNIX or NT), its FrontPage components can simplify the task of building interactive pages. This tool is strongly recommended *if* your servers support FrontPage extensions and if you use Microsoft Office 2000 as your company's official work suite. However, if you need extensive manual editing for your Web pages, other good alternatives (which lack the ease of use and integration with MS Office), such as Macromedia DreamWeaver, are worth considering. A time-bombed version of Microsoft FrontPage 2000 is included on the companion CD. Further information, templates, and sample sites can be found at www.microsoft.com/frontpage/.

MICROSOFT PROJECT

Microsoft Project is a popular project management tool that can help you plan and track your projects effectively and identify and respond to conflicts *before* they happen. It allows scheduling and tracking of project information by hour, day, week, or month. Collaborative features in this tool let you consolidate multiple projects to view cross-project dependencies and multiple-project (up to 1,000 projects) reports. MS Project features custom time-period tracking to pinpoint how long team members spend on each task, each day.

It further allows efficient time allocation using multiple critical paths that allow you to identify groups of tasks that could jeopardize your project's completion date. Through extensive cross-project linking, you can track changes and links between separate projects with new placeholder tasks that represent dependencies on other project plans. Through tight integration with e-mail systems and browsers (which makes it an attractive choice for integrating in knowledge management systems), you can assign tasks and then get status updates from team members.

Integration with your local intranet means that you can post project information and Gantt charts to your intranet, where they can be viewed easily in a Web browser by those involved with the project. It further allows for sharing information across other Microsoft Office applications such as Microsoft Excel spreadsheets and the Microsoft PowerPoint presentation graphics program. Through its full open database connectivity (ODBC) support, you can directly save and retrieve Microsoft Project 98 data from ODBC-compliant databases, such as Microsoft SQL Server and Oracle, to facilitate enterprise-level analysis, reporting, and data integration. For further details and templates, visit the Microsoft site at http://www.microsoft.com/office/project/.

MIND MANAGER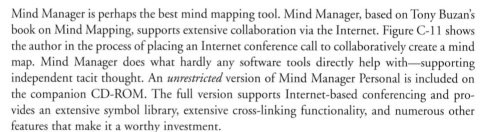

Mind Manager is perhaps the best mind mapping tool. Mind Manager, based on Tony Buzan's book on Mind Mapping, supports extensive collaboration via the Internet. Figure C-11 shows the author in the process of placing an Internet conference call to collaboratively create a mind map. Mind Manager does what hardly any software tools directly help with—supporting independent tacit thought. An *unrestricted* version of Mind Manager Personal is included on the companion CD-ROM. The full version supports Internet-based conferencing and provides an extensive symbol library, extensive cross-linking functionality, and numerous other features that make it a worthy investment.

Although Mindjet, the developer, claims that it is an organization tool, that statement underestimates its true value for knowledge management applications. Try the version on the companion CD-ROM for a hands-on evaluation. For further information, sample mind maps, user guides, and extensive links to mind mapping concept sites, visit Mindject LLC on the Web at www.mindman.com.

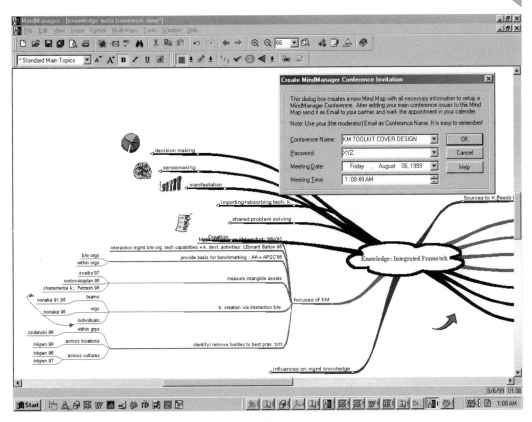

Figure C-11 A mind map for a book, collaboratively created with Mind Manager.

MIS ALEA

MIS Alea, developed by MIS AG of Germany and distributed by its subsidiaries in the United States and several other countries, allows easy multidimensional analysis of data and brings in capabilities far beyond those possible by using conventional multilevel database queries. In effect, complex queries and relationships can be analyzed using existing data in databases and data warehouses.

MIS Alea lets you define the relationships that you are interested in and make comparisons instantaneously by building hierarchies to view data from the highest level to the lowest. Thanks to the excellent drag-and-drop support provided by this tool, creating hierarchies and new relationships is as simple as dragging and dropping the elements of your model under each other.

Expandability and scalability are key. If your company, for example, opens another market or launches a new product, MIS Alea allows you to add these elements by using a dimension editor feature and without rebuilding your tables or database. Such updates are immediately reflected in every aspect of your model.

For further information, test-run the trial version of this tool on the companion CD-ROM, or visit MIS AG on the Web at www.mis.de.

MIS INTERFACEBUILDER

The MIS InterfaceBuilder is a powerful development tool for the construction, maintenance, and refinement of professional planning and information systems. Applications created with MIS InterfaceBuilder are made available to a wide circle of users through MIS Interface Viewer.

The critical stages of development and prototyping can be carried out by skilled users; quick results are guaranteed by involving people with expert knowledge, thus avoiding unnecessary friction.[a] This development tool integrates seamlessly into existing Excel installations, so the designer can often build on existing know-how especially in the sensitive areas of formats and layouts.

The "assistants" and "wizards" in MIS InterfaceBuilder support the links between reports and the MIS Solutions OLAP-Base. This support enables features such as drop-down lists, check boxes, and scrolling to be integrated easily, and helps users to gain quick access later.

The large number of ready-to-use standard functions often enables the developer to create complex functionalities, using what the company describes as *point and click* programming. Drill-down sensitivities, QDBC-Drill-Through, signals, printing piles, comment sheet functions, and user-specific system behavior are examples of the many standard functions available on demand.

The extensive graphics capabilities of Excel can be used in conjunction with OLAP data and control elements of the Builder. Typical EIS (Enterprise Information System) tools such as drill-down or signal functions can be added to expand the functionality of reports.

Its universal alias administrator makes it possible to use a variety of aliases, so, for instance, a product could be offered under a product number or under a name in a selection of languages. For further information, test-run the trial version of this tool on the companion CD-ROM (use the following trial code: 03ED4005-111), or visit MIS AG on the Web at www.mis.de.

---

[a]In a different but related concept, long lead time, described by Zack as *knowledge friction,* typical of knowledge management projects, can be further minimized through strategic external joint ventures used as means of getting access to relevant knowledge.

OPENTEXT LIVELINK

Livelink 8 (Figure C-12), developed by Opentext Corporation, is a Web-based application that provides a comprehensive, off-the-shelf collaborative platform for organizations. Aptly, Opentext claims that "Livelink enables companies to speed their metabolism and bubble up vital corporate information across functional, organizational and geographic boundaries." Livelink is easy to implement, use, and maintain. Livelink server enables companies to scale up content sharing to enterprise-wide levels through extensive use of dynamic hyperlinks. This product also provides an Intranet solution that seamlessly integrates with many products and existing technologies.

Hundreds of Global 2000 companies such as AT&T, ISO, OSRAM, Oracle, Swiss Bank Corporation, and Union Bank of Switzerland use Livelink as their mission-critical collaborative application. For further information, see the demo on the companion CD-ROM, or visit Opentext Corporation on the Web at http://www.opentext.com/livelink/.

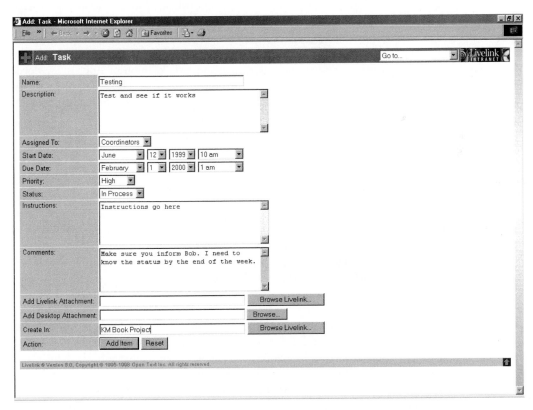

Figure C-12 A sample Intranet based on Opentext Livelink.

PALMPILOT APORTISDOC

AportisDoc is an unofficial industry standard for displaying and interchanging electronic text across enterprise systems on 3Com Palm computing devices. The program itself lets you read, search through, and annotate Palm .Doc documents in an efficient, compressed form, enabling users to carry more documents that are larger. This program also supports teleprompting and book marking of portions of large documents. Thousands of electronic books and useful materials are available today in AportisDoc format, including reference works, weather reports, HTML codes, the Bible, postal and country codes, bus and subway schedules, travel guides, and sports schedules (see www.memoware.com and www.macduff.net for thousands of free documents).

More significantly, documents of any nature (say, reference information internal to your company) can be made accessible to your employees in this format. This means that some of the essential reference information that is made available to your employees through your company's intranet can then be made available to these users even when they do not have access to the Web in order to get to the intranet.

AportisDoc is distributed in three editions, AportisDoc Mobile Edition, AportisDoc Professional, and the free AportisDoc Reader. Besides including all of the functionality of the AportisDoc Mobile Edition, AportisDoc Professional includes the "Make AportisDoc" drag-and-drop desktop applications for Windows 95/98/NT and Macintosh users, and desktop-based readers. AportisDoc Professional offers drag-and-drop creation of AportisDoc documents from Microsoft Word, TEXT, HTML, and other documents. The version included on the CD is a 30-day version. Registration costs $30. For further details, see the companion CD-ROM, or visit Aportis on the Web at www.aportis.com.

PALMPILOT BRAINFOREST MOBILE EDITION

BrainForest is a desktop-to-PalmOS linked tool for visualizing textual information. BrainForest displays information on a hand-held computing device such as a PalmPilot or desktop computer using an intuitive trees analogy. It groups related ideas, action items, check-lists, to-dos, Internet URLs, e-mail addresses, etc., together.

Items can be rearranged via simple dragging of an item from one location to another. Trees may be copied and pasted, shown or hidden. On an enterprise-wide shared knowledge management system, it can be used to keep track of teams and projects, recurring items, due dates, and priorities, so that projects can be kept under control.

BrainForest is distributed in two editions, BrainForest Mobile Edition and BrainForest Professional. BrainForest Mobile Edition software included on the companion CD-ROM does not expire, operates without limitations, has simple import and export capabilities, but requires payment ($30) after 30 days of use. BrainForest and AportisDoc are useful tools worth considering if your employees use PalmPilots extensively. Wireless connectivity of the Palm VII, built-in TCP/IP support that allows users to reach intranets and easily available, inexpensive customization tools make the PalmPilots a viable alternative to on-the-field, connected knowledge workers. For further details, see the companion CD-ROM, or visit Aportis on the Web at www.aportis.com.

PALMPILOT DATEBK3

PalmPilot Datebk3 is a replacement shell for PalmOS devices that allows users to create graphically oriented visual displays of information about scheduling and project management activities (see Figures C-13 and C-14). Using the PalmPilot-to-Web connectivity supported by many commercially available group scheduling and activity management software tools, this application can create a potent weapon in the efficiency-oriented arsenal.

This Web-Palm linkage not only creates an excellent link to the rest of the enterprise but also arguably smooths the introduction of a knowledge management system with a "sweet reward," that is, Palm computers for employees.

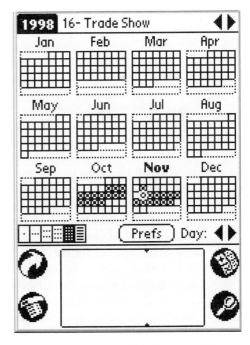

Figure C-13 Datebk3 enhances collaborative scheduling processes using hand-held computing devices such as PalmOS Palm PCs.

Figure C-14 Datebk3 replaces built-in PalmOS
applications.

Performance Now

Performance Now Enterprise Edition is based on the thesis that good, solid performance management is the key to retaining and developing the most valuable knowledge asset in your company: its people. Performance Now, developed by KnowledgePoint Inc., is a total performance management solution for organizations of all sizes.

The tool supplies the framework for implementing a comprehensive performance management system that aligns employee focus with corporate objectives. It includes support for providing valuable day-to-day feedback, for writing meaningful performance reviews, and providing effective coaching to knowledge workers.

Such a tool can be extremely helpful in objectively tying employee compensation to their contribution to your company's knowledge assets. It also streamlines the process and puts HR in control while giving managers powerful tools to track performance, provide valuable feedback, and write the kind of employee reviews that help maximize potential.

Performance Now Enterprise Edition is made up of four core modules (Figure C-15). The Form Designer and Application Administrator supply powerful tools for designing, implementing, and monitoring your performance management system. The Performance Manager and Performance Appraiser give managers valuable tools and just-in-time training to help them better manage and develop their people. The result is an integrated approach to performance management that results in consistency and focus throughout your company. Figure C-16 illustrates a typical goal and the weight associated with it.

Additional modules allow you to further customize Performance Now, modify competencies, and customize the associated review text and coaching ideas. Other modules can add industry-specific competency information to create versions for manufacturing, health care, finance, and state and local government. A restricted version of this tool can be found on the companion CD-ROM, and further information can be obtained from KnowledgePoint's Website at http://www.performancenow.com/.

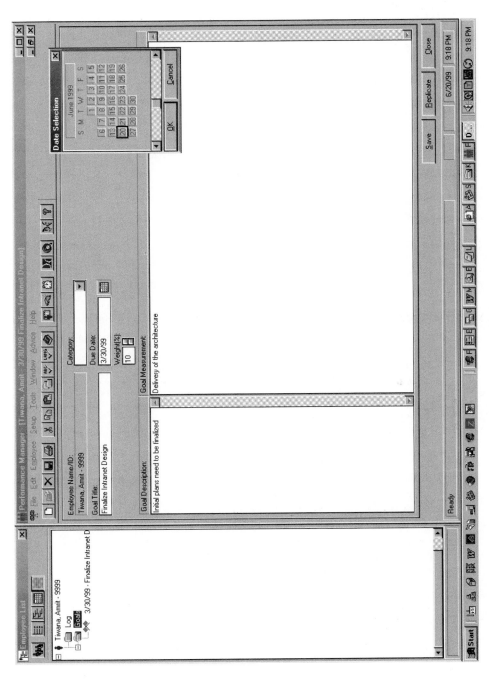

Figure C-15 Performance Now lets managers link individual employee goals and metrics.

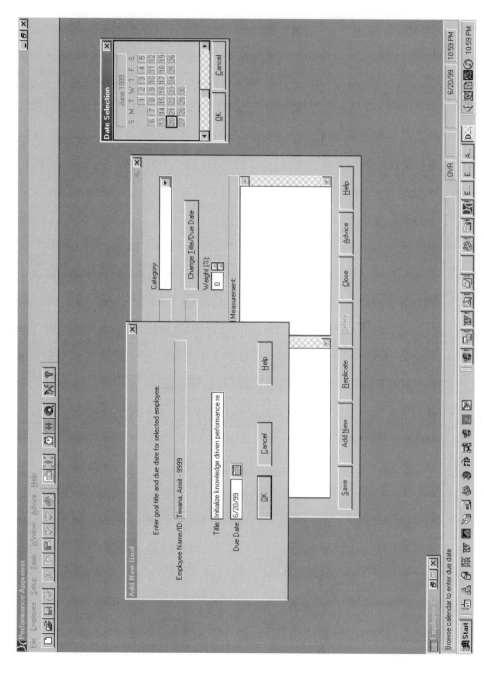

Figure C-16 Managers can associate weights to each contribution such as knowledge sharing, development, use, and contribution.

PERSPECTA

Perspecta allows users to query databases using conceptual navigation without needing to understand the schema and idiosyncrasies of the underlying databases. It provides users with the right queries for a given context and set of interests and suggests alternatives as the dialog progresses. It is equivalent to providing each of your users with a trained expert librarian who intimately understands the form and content of your information. Perspecta uses knowledge-based, statistical, and linguistic techniques to integrate database meta data into an overall conceptual network. This is done by using a Concept Editor to build a Concept Database—a collection of linked concepts and relationships that define the domain of the database. More information can be found on Perspecta's Website at www.perspecta.com.

PROFILER

Profiler is an intelligent employee-screening package that enables employers to select job applicants who are like their company's proven performers. If enough data is collected, information on current employees can help determine which applicants for the same job would, or would not, meet the criteria for that job. Evaluating these complex patterns within large amounts of data is a very difficult job for a person, but quite easy for the computer when given the task.

Profiler brings complex pattern recognition technology down to the user's level, allowing the HR manager to determine what is important to measure in an employee and what is important to screen for in an applicant. Be forewarned: Using such profiling might be illegal in some countries. Further information can be found on American Heuristics Corporation's site at http://www.heuristics.com.

REMOTE CONTROL TOOLBAR

The Remote Control Toolbar is a complement to the FerretSoft family of utilities. It launches with your browser and resides in the system tray so installed Ferrets can quickly and easily be initialized and put to work. A freeware version of this add-on is included on the companion CD-ROM. Visit FerretSoft's home page at http://www.ferretsoft.com for updates.

RETRIEVALWARE

RetrievalWare and its associated products constitute a set of tools for building text-based knowledge retrieval solutions. RetrievalWare uses Semantic Networks and adaptive pattern recognition processing (APRP) technologies to do "fuzzy" searching for producing accurate matches even if queries or terms in the documents are misspelled or the documents have been poorly scanned. It also employs an embedded, full semantic dictionary—available in English, French, Spanish, and German—of more than 400,000 word meanings, 50,000 language idioms, and 1.6 million word associations. This dictionary is used to expand queries and produce results based on word meanings, related words, and concept analysis. For further details, visit Excalibur, Inc. on the Web at www.excalib.com.

SEMIOMAP

SemioMap performs text mining rather than data mining. Instead of exploring relationships within structured data, it explores relationships within text, a form of unstructured data. It does this by building concept maps of large, dynamic text collections, using sophisticated linguistic semiotic analysis to identify the linkages of concepts in different documents.

SemioMap uses "lexical extraction" software that automatically extracts the concepts from a text collection. The list of concepts, the lexicon, is used to identify clusters of related concepts within the documents. The SemioMap lexical extractor is based on research in "linguistic semiotics" (hence the product name). It extracts phrases instead of keywords from text and tracks the co-occurrences of extracted phrases. The extractor can be customized to improve its performance in different environments.

SMARTDRAW

SmartDraw (Figure C-17) is an excellent graphics tool that can be used to create process diagrams and models. Its extensive set of graphics libraries include UML and process modeling. SmartDraw sells in two versions: standard and professional. These retail for $49 and $99, respectively. This is an extremely good value and with extensive integration with Microsoft Office, it is perhaps one of the best choices in its category of tools for Windows-based collaborative enterprises. As an aside, all figures in this book were prepared with SmartDraw.

A 30-day version is included on the companion CD-ROM. For further information, visit SmartDraw on the Web at www.smartdraw.com.

SOLUTIONSERIES

SolutionSeries is "problem resolution" software for capturing, diagnosing, solving, and distributing resolutions to problems. Users can describe problems in natural language. Knowledge in external documents and third-party knowledge bases can also be used. A "solution" is a collection of statements that describe a problem in terms of its cause, symptoms, and fix. Primus, the developer, describes its search method as *associative problem-solving* technology. A customizable dictionary is used to recognize synonyms. For further details, visit Primus, Inc. at www.primus.com.

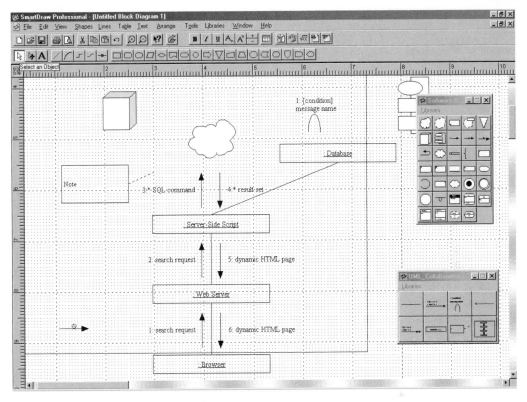

Figure C-17 SmartDraw is a powerful diagramming tool with thousands of customizable symbol libraries such as those used to model processes.

THOUGHTFLOW

ThoughtFlow is a goal-oriented collaboration framework. It can assist in tasks such as goal setting, strategic planning, problem solving, decision making, and performance management. It provides a method of organizing information and sharing knowledge during such tasks. ThoughtFlow has a "goal-oriented language definition" framework that gives users a shared verbal and visual language about the domain under discussion. Key issues and the connections between them are shown visually, and knowledge elements are made explicit and indexed, allowing context-specific retrieval. Further details can be found at Vidya Technologies' home page at www.vidyainc.com.

Web-Enabled ART* Enterprise

ART*Enterprise is the development tool for building high-performance Web-enabled intelligent applications. The product builds on a combination of artificial intelligence (AI) techniques for representing and automating knowledge, with a highly scalable inference engine. ART*Enterprise provides a rich environment for rapid prototyping, object-oriented programming, and quick development of intelligent applications using CBR and pattern matching rules. Further details can be found on Brightware's home page at www.brightware.com.

Web Ferret

Web Ferret is a desktop-based, meta search Web client utility for finding Web pages on the Net. This tool automatically updates itself every time it is run. Updates and new search engine configurations are extremely small and the entire update process is fast and unnoticeable.

This utility and its other counterparts, such as e-mail Ferret and Info Ferret, make extensive use of the multithreading capabilities of Windows95, Windows 98, and Windows NT to query multiple databases or search engines simultaneously. Query results are made available immediately and can be acted upon by a simple double-click on the result of interest. This opens up the user's default browser or tool associated with the URL, while the query can continue in the background.

A full version of Web Ferret is included on the companion CD-ROM. For more information, visit FerretSoft's home page at http://www.ferretsoft.com.

Appendix D
Resources on the Web

This section provides pointers to sources of further information on the Web, concerning KM practices, tools, consultants, resources, etc. A description of the world's intellectually richest companies appears toward the end. These companies can serve as good examples of specific knowledge management capabilities in which they demonstrate strength.

KNOWLEDGE MANAGEMENT: WEB POINTERS

Site	Notes	URL
Brightware	Developer of ART* Enterprise software.	http://www.brightware.com
Active Software	Specializes in enterprise application integration.	http://www.activesw.com/
Alpha Micro	Home page of Alpha Microsystems, a company that develops several enterprise knowledge tools and software enablers.	http://www.alphamicro.com/
AlphaCONNECT	Provides free and trial versions of AlphaCONNECT's software tools.	http://www.alphaconnect.com/freesoft.asp
Analysis-by-design, Inc.	Canadian information resource that calls itself the "watchdog of knowledge management."	http://www.analysis-by-design.on.ca/
Aspen Technology	Develops manufacturing intelligence software and integrated manufacturing process management tools.	http://www.aspentech.com/
Austin Hayne	Performance measurement tool vendor. An Austin Hayne's trial version can be found on the companion CD.	http://www.austin-hayne.com/
BackWeb Technologies	Home page of BackWeb, a knowledge management tools developer.	http://www.backweb.com/
Balanced Scorecard	Balanced scorecard information resource.	http://www.balancedscorecard.com/
Best Manufacturing Practices	Contains a wealth of information resources pertaining to best practices in manufacturing.	http://www.bmpcoe.org/
The BMA Group	Consulting firm based in Australia. Specializes in balanced scorecard implementation, performance measurement, business intelligence, and analytic applications, OLAP software, and market and customer analysis.	http://www.bma.com.au/

Site	Notes	URL
Brio Technology	Company that provides software tools for knowledge management.	http://www.brio.com/
BT Labs	British Telecom's knowledge management projects. These projects are fairly technical and include the frequently mentioned tool: Jasper.	http://www.labs.bt.com
Buckman Labs	Home page of Buckman Labs, a chemical company that is considered to be a pioneer in knowledge management and its applications.	http://www.buckman.com/eng/home.html
Cognos Corporation	Develops software and components for developing knowledge management systems.	http://www.cognos.com
Corporate Renaissance Group	Consulting company specializing in technology-bottom-line analysis.	http://www.crgroup.com/
CorVu	Company that specializes in the balanced scorecard methodology and provides tools for business intelligence.	http://www.corvu.com/
Cross Pen Computing	Manufacturer of the Cross-Pad.	http://www.cross-pcg.com/
David Skyrme	British knowledge management consultant.	http://www.skyrme.com/
Deja News	Newsgroup meta search engine.	http://www.dejanews.com/
Dimensional Insights	Develops a complete line of data visualization, analysis, and reporting software tools.	http://www.dimins.com/
Distributed Knowledge Management Systems	Collection of white papers	http://www.dkms.com/
Enrich	Site built around the theme of "Enriching Representations of Work to Support Organizational Learning."	http://kmi.open.ac.uk/projects/enrich/
Ernst and Young	Hosts Ernst and Young Consulting's business innovation journal.	http://www.businessinnovation.ey.com/journal/loader.html
Entovation	Consulting and training company whose site contains a number of readable articles and tidbits	http://www.entovation.com/

Site	Notes	URL
	relating to knowledge management on its site.	
MIT Center for Organizational Learning	MIT's "learning organizations" research site and discussion forum.	http://learning.mit.edu
FerretSoft Computing, LLC.	Develops the Ferret series of search tools. Most of these tools are in the public domain, and a few of them can be found on the companion CD.	http://www.ferretsoft.com/netferret/index.html
FileNet Corporation	Developer of integrated document management (IDM) software for corporate and government organizations.	http://www.filnet.com
Fortune	*Fortune* magazine's Home page. *Fortune* frequently publishes articles on knowledge management and intellectual capital.	http://www.pathfinder.com/fortune/
Gentia	Consulting firm that specializes in the balanced scorecard methodology.	http://www.gentia.com
GrapeVine	Develops and sells enterprise collaboration software.	http://www.grapevine.com/
Hyper Corp.	Small section of this site is dedicated to knowledge management.	http://www.hypercorp.com/km/
Hyper Knowledge	Knowledge management consulting firm.	http://www.hyperknowledge.com/
Hyperion	Provides services for automating the balanced scorecard methodology in your company.	http://www.hyperion.com
Hyperwave	Developer of hyperwave information server and similar knowledge sharing products. A limited version of Hyperwave can be found on the companion CD.	http://www.hyperwave.com/
IBM	IBM's knowledge management–related site.	http://ibmpnyx1.palisades.ihost.com/ikm/ikmhome.html
Image Ware	Offers advanced 3D surface modeling and verification technology for the automotive, aerospace, consumer products, and	http://www.iware.com/

Site	Notes	URL
	entertainment industries. Such software can be useful for data visualization and multimedia enablement.	
Inference Corporation	Business intelligence software developer.	http://www.inference.com/
Instinctive Technology	Developer of the software tool, e-Room. The site provides an online demonstration.	http://www.instinctive.com/
Intellectual Capital	Home site of the U.K.-based company, Intellectual Capital, referenced by many earlier knowledge management works.	http://www.intcap.com/
Intelligenesis	Internet intelligence tool developer. The Website provides online demonstration of some of the company's products.	http://www.intelligenesis.net/
Intelligent Enterprise	*Intelligent Enterprise* magazine.	http://www.intelligententerprise.com/
international Quality & Productivity Center	Provides training materials and educational services on quality and productivity.	http://www.iqpc.com./
Intranetics	Home site of Intranetics Corporation. The companion CD-ROM also has a limited version of their intranet toolkit. The site also contains an online demo intranet.	http://www.intranetics.com/
KMI	Knowledge Management Institute.	http://kmi.open.ac.uk/ksg.html
KMI and Organizational Knowledge	Dedicated to organizational knowledge creation and management.	http://kmi.open.ac.uk/org-knowledge/
KMI Knowledge Web	Area on the KMI site dedicated to knowledge management.	http://kmi.open.ac.uk/knowledgeweb/
Knowledge 2000	Knowledge management discussion forum.	http://www.geocites.com/~knowledge2000/index.html
Knowledge Associates	Knowledge management consulting firm. This site provides a lot of resources and topical	http://www.knowledgeassociates.com/

Site	Notes	URL
	information on the subject of knowledge management.	
Knowledge Management Café	Discussion area run by Hyperwave Corporation.	http://www.kmcafe.com./
Knowledge Management in the Chemical Industry	Internal knowledge management strategies in the chemicals industry. Informational page from a conference held in 1998. This site provides a lot of useful pointers to companies currently involved in knowledge management initiatives.	http://www.firstconf.com/c42/day2.html
Knowledge Management Magazine	Another free knowledge management publication. An online subscription form is available on the Website.	http://www.kmmag.com/
Knowledge Management Network	Pointers and links to the topic of knowledge management.	http://kmn.cibit.nl/web/kmn/index.html
Knowledge Management World	Home page of *Knowledge Management World* magazine. This magazine is offered free to qualified subscribers. The site provides links to several knowledge management solution/component providers.	http://www.kmworld.com/
Knowledge Nurture	Perhaps one of the best knowledge management sites in existence. Unlike the vendor pitches that overpower many other sites, this site, sponsored by Buckman Labs, is truly a resource devoid of sales pitches. The site provides excellent links to resources, presentations, discussion forums, etc. Some of the major pieces of academic literature, including some papers by Nonaka and Drucker, are also summarized here.	http://www.knowledge-nurture.com/
Knowledge Point	Developer of several popular human resource management tools (such as People Manager).	http://www.knowledgepoint.com/welcome.html

Site	Notes	URL
Knowledge World	Information site. This site contains a useful white paper on the organization's EC^2 methodology.	http://www.ec2.edu/cke/tools.htm1
Knowledgies	Knowledge management consulting company. The Website has numerous resources on knowledge management.	http://www.knowledgies.com/
KPMG Netherlands	KPMG's Dutch operations. This is the home of the concept behind value-based knowledge management and other softer aspects of knowledge management initiatives	http://kpmg.interact.nl/
Marimba	Provides the management infrastructure for intranet, extranet, and Internet business applications.	http://www.marimba.com/
Mathworks	Develops and sells mathematical, statistical, and pattern analysis software by the same name.	http://www.mathworks.com/
Metamor Worldwide SPR Inc	IT solutions provider with an entire division dedicated to enterprise-wide integration. This site also provides detailed information on the company's products and services.	http://www.metamor.com/
Micro Strategy	Develops and sells DSS tools. The Website provides online demonstrations and information.	http://www.strategy.com/products/index.htm
MIT Center for Organizational Learning	Resource-filled site with discussions and conversations on organizational learning. OL is a concept that knowledge management heavily builds on.	http://learning.mit.edu/
MIT Media Lab	MIT's media lab has a rich collection of projects dedicated to intelligent agent technology.	http://agents.www.media.mit.edu/groups/agents/projects
Mosaix, Inc.	Division of Lucent Technologies, this company provides customer relationship management solutions.	http://www.mosaix.com/
NASA	Quality function deployment from the perspective of competitive advantage	http://mijuno.larc.nasa.gov/dfc/qfd.html

Site	Notes	URL
Object Knowledge	Knowledge management consulting firm that also conducts knowledge management and intranet training seminars throughout the United States.	http://www.objectknowledge.com/
Opentext	Canadian developer. Opentext is the producer of the Opentext Livelink Intranet solution on the companion CD. A demo can also be found online.	http://www.opentext.com/ http://www.opentext.com/demo/
Optika	Knowledge management tool developer.	http://www.optika.com/
Orbital Software	Developer of knowledge management support tools such as the Orbital Knowledge Server.	http://www.orbitalsw.com/
Orbital Software	Knowledge management solution/component developer.	http://www.orbitalsw.com/
Orexis Inc.	Knowledge management consulting firm.	http://www.orexis.com/
Primus Software	Specializes in customer relationship management and problem resolution tracking software tools.	http://www.primus.com/
Process Edge	Process management consulting company with a wealth of white papers on its site	http://www.processedge.com/
P-Tech, Inc.	Information management tools developer.	http://www.ptechinc.com/
Quality One	Quality management tools and services.	http://www.quality-one.com/
Quality Software Guide	Guide to quality analysis software.	http://www.qsoftguide.com/
Scorecard, Germany	German site (in English) that provides information on the balanced scorecard strategy and its technological enablers.	http://www.scorecard.de/
Global Web Interactive Network	Excellent global online community that offers feeds to internal networks and knowledge management systems; content and discussions here will be of particular interest to innovative businesses.	http://www.gwin.net

Site	Notes	URL
Six Degrees	Online community that demonstrates key ideas behind close referential electronic communities.	http://www.sixdegrees.com/
Skandia	Sweden's home page. Skandia was one of the first companies to report its knowledge assets on its financial balance sheet.	http://www.skandia.se/group/index.htm
Sovereign Hill Software	InQuiry support and documentation.	http://www.sovereign-hill.com/
SPSS Software	Sells statistical analysis and data mining software tools. The Website has an entire section dedicated to data mining.	http://www.spss.com/
Team Building, Inc.	Team building consulting and training firm.	http://www.teambuildinginc.com/
Teltech Corporation	Information services and consulting company that specializes in research and content management.	http://www.teltech.com/
Thinking Tools, Inc.	Develops and markets interactive simulation software as products combine interactive multimedia interfaces with agent-based adaptive simulation technology.	http://www.thinkingtools.com/
Tom Stewart's Home Page	Author of the 1997 best-selling book *Intellectual Capital*.	http://members.aol.com/thosstew/
University of California, Business Initiatives and Performance Partnership	Knowledge resources for new business ventures.	http://www.ucop.edu/ucophome/businit/
University of North Texas	Center for the Study of Work Teams. Contains papers, links, and resources.	http://www.workteams.unt.edu/
Verge Software	Verge develops software tools such as Verge Insight and enterprise-wide knowledge sharing applications.	http://www.vergesoftware.com/
WatchDog	Online service that tracks technological developments in the knowledge management industry.	http://www.analysis-by-design.on.ca/rd/Watchdog/body.htm

Site	Notes	URL
Waterworks, Lotus Development Corporation	Details on Lotus Waterworks and Lotus Notes.	http://waterworks.lotus.com/
Wisdom Ware	Developer of Wisdom Ware software.	http://www.wisdomware.com/
Xplor	Provides training sessions and seminars on knowledge management and related topics.	http://www.xplor.org/
Zigon Performance group	Provides an excellent set of pointers to sites containing information about performance measures. Perhaps this is one of the most comprehensive set of links on the subject.	http://www.zigonperf.com/ Links.htm

INTELLECTUALLY RICH COMPANIES

Intellectually rich companies provide a lot of insight into how successful knowledge management and knowledge leverage strategies work in different industries. A point to note here: Companies that have the most intellectual assets are not necessarily the ones with the most intellectual capital. The difference is subtle, and the companies that have managed to leverage their knowledge-based assets and intellectual assets are the ones that top the list in terms of market value. Table C-1 shows the top 10 patent recipients for 1998, and Table C-2 shows the companies that actually had the highest market valuation during the same time frame.

Table D-1 The top 10 recipients of U.S. patents, 1998

Rank	Company	Patents
1	IBM	2,682
2	Canon	1,934
3	NEC	1,632
4	Motorola	1,428
5	Sony	1,321
6	Samsung Electronics	1,306
7	Fujitsu	1,205
8	Toshiba	1,194
9	Eastman Kodak	1,125
10	Mitsubishi	1,120

Source: IFI Plenum, 1999.

Table D-2 US top nine stocks ranked by market value

Company	Value (in billions)
GE	$239.5
Coca-Cola	164.8
Microsoft	156.5
Exxon	150.3
Merck	126.5
Intel	114.4
Philip Morris	109.8
Procter & Gamble	107.1
IBM	101.3

Source: Forbes, vol. 162, no. 3, August 10 (1998), 122, ISSN: 0015-6914.
Also, see Standard & Poor's Compustat.

Table D-3 Companies obtaining the most U.S. patents

Rank	Company	Country	Number of patents
1	IBM	U.S.	1,742
2	Canon	Japan	1,381
3	NEC	Japan	1,101
4	Motorola	U.S.	1,065
5	Mitsubishi	Japan	925
6	Hitachi	Japan	922
7	Fujitsu	Japan	909
8	Toshiba	Japan	891
9	Sony	Japan	867
10	Eastman Kodak	U.S.	795
11	Lucent Technologies	U.S.	770
12	Matsushita Electrical	Japan	756
13	General Electric	U.S.	665
14	Texas Instruments	U.S.	610
15	Xerox	U.S.	607
16	Samsung Electronics	Korea	585
17	Philips	Holland	556
18	Minnesota Mining & Manufacturing (3M)	U.S.	549
19	Hewlett-Packard	U.S.	532
20	Nikon	Japan	479

Compiled from statistics reported in the Tablebase database and Euromoney Publications PLC.
Figures are from 1997.

Table D-4 Most admired knowledge enterprises based on eight key knowledge performance attributes

Knowledge Performance Attribute	Top Performers
Overall quality of knowledge management programs	1. Xerox 2. Ernst and Young 3. Monsanto
Top management support for knowledge management	1. Buckman 2. Hewlett-Packard 3. British Petroleum
Contribution of knowledge to innovation	1. Lucent Technologies 2. 3M 3. Nokia
Maximizing intellectual assets	1. Intel 2. Lucent Technologies 3. Monsanto
Effectiveness of knowledge sharing	1. Ernst and Young 2. Xerox 3. Intel
Culture of continuous learning and knowledge creation	1. Lucent Technologies 2. 3M 3. Nokia
Creating customer value and loyalty through knowledge management	1. Lucent Technologies 2. Arthur Andersen 3. Ernst and Young
Contribution to shareholder value	1. Microsoft 2. Intel 3. Lucent Technologies

Companies are listed in the order of their rankings. Data was collected through interviews with Fortune Global 500 company senior managers and reported at the Knowledge Management '98 conference in London. Industry-specific rankings can be found at www.knowledgebusiness.com/mostad.htm.

ENDNOTES
AND BIBLIOGRAPHIC
REFERENCES

ENDNOTES

CHAPTER 1

1. Drucker, P., *Management Challenges for the 21st Century*, Harper Business, New York (1999).

2. Andriesz, Mike, Managing Knowledge, *The Scotsman*, Glasgow, Scotland, June 1 (1999), 13.

3. Hoare, Stephen, It's True: Knowledge Is Power, *The Times*, London, May 24 (1999).

4. Leow, Jason, Know What? Your Firm Needs a CKO, *The Strait Times*, Singapore, May 15 (1999), 53.

5. Tan, Audrey, Knowledge Sharing in Civil Service Moderate: Survey, *Business Times*, Singapore, May 13 (1999).

6. Klasson, Kirk, Managing Knowledge for Advantage: Content and Collaboration Technologies, *The Cambridge Information Network Journal*, vol. 1, no. 1 (1999), 33–41.

7. Hewson, David, It's Not What You Know… , *Sunday Times*, London, April 25 (1999).

8. Johnston, Stuart, and Beth Davis, Smart Moves, *Informationweek*, May 31 (1999), 18–19.

9. Davenport, Thomas, H., and Laurence Prusak, *Working Knowledge: How Organizations Manage What They Know*, Harvard Business School Press, Boston (1998), 5.

10. Paul Quintas, Open University Professor of Knowledge Management quoted in Open Eye: Head Back to the Business Cafe, *The Independent,* London, February 4 (1999), OE9.

11. Davenport and Prusak, *Working Knowledge.*

12. See Blair, Jim, Knowledge Management: The Era of Shared Ideas, *Forbes*, September 22 (1997).

13. See Hansen, M., N. Nohria, and T. Tierney, What's Your Strategy for Managing Knowledge? *Harvard Business Review,* March–April (1999), 106–116.

14. Drucker, *Management Challenges for the 21st Century,* 74.

15. Abramson, Gary, The Thrill of the Hunt, *CIO Enterprise,* January 15 (1999), 35–42.

16. Davenport, Thomas, From Data to Knowledge, *CIO*, April 1 (1999), 26–28.

17. Dhurana, Anil, Managing Complex Production Processes, *Sloan Management Review,* Winter (1999), 85–97.

18. Drucker, Peter, *The Post Capitalist Society,* First edition, Harper Business Press, New York, (1993).

19. Moore, Connie, KM Meets BP, *CIO,* November 15, (1998), 64–68.

20. For a detailed account of how Bay Networks ended up saving $10 a year through knowledge management, see Peter Fabris, *You Think Tomaytoes, I Think Tomahtoes, CIO,* April 1 (1999), 46–52.

21. Dempsey, Michael, Buzzword Has Already Made a Lot of Enemies: The Role of the Chief Knowledge Officer, *Financial Times,* London April 28 (1999), 2.

22. Krochmal, Mo, Tech Guru: People Are Key to Knowledge Management, *The New York Times,* New York, June 9 (1999), quoting Laurence Prusak, executive director of knowledge management at IBM.

23. Zack, Michael H., Developing a Knowledge Strategy, *California Management Review,* vol. 41, no. 3, Spring (1999), 125–145.

24. Drucker, *Management Challenges for the 21st Century,* 20.

25. Small Firms in Tune With Knowledge Management, *The Irish Times,* Dublin, April 23 (1999), 61.

26. Schwartz, Mathew, Wherefore Art Thou, CKO? May 20 (1999), *Cambridge Information Network Think Tank on Knowledge Management,* URL: http://www.cin.ctp.com.

27. Klasson, Kirk, *Managing Knowledge for Advantage: Content and Collaboration Technologies, The Cambridge Information Network Journal,* vol. 1, no. 1 (1999), 33–41.

28. Hewson, It's Not What You Know… .

29. Unlike business process reengineering, knowledge management is about supporting critical processes such as business decisions with the *right* knowledge at the right time. Also see Drucker, *Management Challenges for the 21st Century,* 33.

30. Iansiti, Marco, and Alan MacCormack, Developing Products on Internet Time, *Harvard Business Review,* September–October (1977), 108–117.

31. White, David, Human Resources: Why Managers Really Believe Knowledge Is Power, *The Guardian,* London, April 10 (1999), 47.

32. Lotus Challenges Microsoft in Knowledge Management Software Market, *Businessworld,* Philippines, February 16 (1999).

33. Duffy, D., Knowledge Champions: What Does It Take to Be a Successful CKO? *CIO Enterprise,* November 15 (1998), 66–71.

34. Moore, KM Meets BP.

35. This characterization is inspired by Shapiro, C., and H. Varian, *Information Rules: A Strategic Guide to the Network Economy,* Harvard Business School Press, Boston (1999).

CHAPTER 2

1. Ford can be found on the Web at http://www.ford.com.

2. Information about Texas Instrument's PDA, Avigo, can be found on the Web at www.ti.com/avigo/.

3. Sharp can be found on the Web. For the SE-500 PDA mentioned here, see http://www.sharp-usa.com/se500/.

4. Figures based on Fortune's Fortune 500 list are available at http://cgi.pathfinder.com/cgi-bin/fortune/fortune500/.

5. Data based on figures provided by the Ford Motor Company as described in a presentation given by Leifer et al. at Stanford Center for Design and Manufacturing Research, Palo Alto, CA, March 1990.

6. These are exact quotes from the Stanford presentation report.

7. See Tom Davenport, Sirikka Jarvenpaa, and Michael Beers, Improving Knowledge Work Processes, *Sloan Management Review,* Summer (1996), 53–65, and Davenport, Thomas, David DeLong, and Michael Beers, Successful Knowledge Management Projects, *Sloan Management Review,* vol. 39, no. 2 (1998), 43–57.

8. KPMG, The Power of Knowledge, *KPMG Whitepaper* (1998).

9. See Ramesh, Bala, and Vasant Dhar, Supporting Systems Development Using Knowledge Captured During Requirements Engineering, *IEEE Transactions on Software Engineering* (1992), and also see Ramesh, Balasubramanian, and Kishore Sengupta, Multimedia in a Design Rationale Decision Support System, *Decision Support Systems,* no. 15 (1995), 181–196.

10. Dhar, Vasant, and Roger Stein, *Seven Methods for Transforming Corporate Data into Business Intelligence,* Prentice Hall, Upper Saddle River, NJ (1997).

11. KPMG *Knowledge Management Survey Report,* KPMG (1998).

12. Davenport, Thomas, David DeLong, and Michael Beers, Successful Knowledge Management Projects, *Sloan Management Review*, vol. 39 no. 2 (1998), 43–57.

13. Song, Michael, and Mitzi Montoya-Weiss, Critical Development Activities for Really New Versus Incremental Products, *Journal of Product Innovation Management*, no. 15 (1998), 124–135.

14. Ramesh and Tiwana, Supporting Collaborative Process Knowledge Management, in New Product Development Teams, *Decision Support Systems*, forthcoming.

15. Grudin, J., Evaluating Opportunities for Design Capture, in M. Carroll (Ed.), *Design Rationale: Concepts, Techniques & Use*, Lawrence Erlbaum Associates, Mahwah, NJ (1996).

16. A very thorough description of this concept was first proposed in Markides, article on Strategic Innovation. See Markides, Constantinos, Strategic Innovation in Established Companies, *Sloan Management Review*, vol. 39, no. 3 (1998).

17. The use of the term *team liquidity* is widely reported in research literature; it was also suggested by my colleague, Bala Ramesh and used in our research on new product development reported in our research paper: Ramesh, B., and A. Tiwana, Supporting Collaborative Process Knowledge Management in New Product Development Teams, in *Decision Support Systems*, forthcoming. The consequences of such liquidity are discussed further in this paper.

18. See Iansiti, Marco, and Alan MacCormack, Developing Products on Internet Time, *Harvard Business Review*, September–October (1997), 108–117, for an interesting account of Netscape and its strategy for dealing with compressed time frames.

19. Teece, David, Research Directions for Knowledge Management, *California Management Review*, vol. 40, no. 3 (1998), 289–292.

20. An in-depth treatise can be found in Porter, Michael E. *Competitive Advantage: Creating and Sustaining Superior Performance*, Free Press, New York (1985).

21. See Asea Brown Boveri's Website at www.abb.com.

22. Quinn, James Brian, Philip Anderson, and Sydney Finkelstein, Managing Professional Intellect: Making the Most of the Best, *Harvard Business Review* March–April (1996), 71–80.

23. Drucker, P., *Management Challenges for the 21st Century*, Harper Business, New York (1999).

24. Zack also illustrates this point with a case study of Lincoln Re, the insurance company in Zack, Michael H, Developing a Knowledge Strategy, *California Management Review*, vol. 41, no. 3, Spring (1999), 125–145.

25. See a discussion of 3M in Eisenhardt, K., and S. Brown, Time Pacing: Competing in Markets That Won't Stand Still, *Harvard Business Review*, March–April (1998) 59–69.

26. See Nonaka, Ikujiro, and Hiro Takeuchi, *The Knowledge-Creating Company: How Japanese Companies Create the Dynamics of Innovation*, Oxford University Press, New York (1995), for a detailed description.

CHAPTER 3

1. Davenport, Thomas H., and Laurence Prusak, *Working Knowledge: How Organizations Manage What They Know,* Harvard Business School Press, Boston (1998).

2. Quinn, James Brian, *Intelligence Enterprise: A Knowledge and Service-based Paradigm for Industry,* Free Press, New York (1992).

3. Dhar, Vasant, and Roger Stein, *Seven Methods for Transforming Corporate Data Into Business Intelligence,* Prentice Hall, Upper Saddle River, NJ (1997).

4. See Davenport, T., S. Jarvenpaa, and M. Beers, Improving Knowledge Work Processes, *Sloan Management Review,* Summer (1996), 53–65, and Davenport, Thomas H., *Process Innovation: Reengineering Work Through Information Technology,* Harvard Business School Press, Boston (1993).

5. Ramesh, Balasubramanian, and Kishore Sengupta, Multimedia in a Design Rationale Decision Support System, *Decision Support Systems,* no. 15 (1995), 181–196.

6. Nonaka, Ikujiro, The Knowledge Creating Company, *Harvard Business Review,* November–December (1991), 2–9; Nonaka, Ikujiro, and Noboru Konno, The Concept of "Ba": Building a Foundation for Knowledge Creation, *California Management Review,* vol. 40, no. 3 (1998), 40–55.

7. Albert, Steven, and Keith Bradley, *Managing Knowledge: Experts, Agencies and Organizations,* Cambridge University Press, Cambridge, England (1997).

8. Davenport, Thomas, David DeLong, and Michael Beers. Successful Knowledge Management Projects, *Sloan Management Review,* vol. 39, no. 2 (1998), 43–57.

9. Ikujiro, The Knowledge Creating Company.

10. Davenport, and Prusak, *Working Knowledge; How Organizations Manage What They Know,* Harvard Business School Press, Boston, (1998) and Davenport, Jarvenpaa, and Beers, Improving Knowledge Work Processes.

11. See Dhar and Stein, *Seven Methods for Transforming Corporate Data Into Business Intelligence.* Prentice Hall: Upper Saddle River, NJ (1997).

12. Eureka, William E., and Nancy E. Ryan, *Quality Up, Costs Down: A Manager's Guide to Taguchi Methods and QFD,* ASI Press, Burr Ridge, Ill. (1995), and also see Fahey, Liam, and Laurence Prusak, The Eleven Deadliest Sins of Knowledge Management, *California Management Review,* vol. 40, no. 3 (1998), 265–276.

13. Grochow, Jerrold M., *Information Overload: Creating Value With the New Information Systems Technology,* Yourdon Press, Upper Saddle River, NJ (1997).

14. See Ramesh, B., and A. Tiwana, Supporting Collaborative Process Knowledge Management in New Product Development Teams, in *Decision Support Systems* (forthcoming).

15. A noteworthy retrospective commentary of this appears in Simon's own words in Simon, Herbert, A., Bounded Rationality and Organizational Learning, *Organization Science,* vol. 2, no. 1 (1991), 125–134.

16. The concept of an informated organization is further described by Bob Travie in Information Aspects of New Organizational Designs: Exploring the Non-Traditional Organization, *Journal of the American Society for Information Science,* vol. 49, no. 13 November (1998), 1224–1244.

17. Quinn, James Brian, Philip Anderson, and Sydney Finkelstein, Managing Professional Intellect: Making the Most of the Best, *Harvard Business Review* (1996), 71–80.

18. This is an extension of the classification scheme originally proposed by ibid.

19. For a detailed analysis of how Netscape built earlier versions of its Web browser, see Iansiti, Marco, and Alan MacCormack, Developing Products on Internet Time, *Harvard Business Review,* September–October (1997), 108–117. Netscape was bought out by America Online in 1998 for approximately $4 billion in a three-way arrangement between Netscape, America Online, and Sun Microsystems.

20. This observation, in the context of knowledge management was recently noted by Teece, David, Research Directions for Knowledge Management, *California Management Review,* vol. 40, no. 3 (1998), 289–292.

21. Ruggles, Rudy, The State of Notion: Knowledge Management in Practice, *California Management Review,* Spring (1998), 80–89.

22. Larsson, R., B. Lars, K. Henriksson, N. and J. Sparks, The Inter-Organizational Learning Dilemma: Collective Knowledge Development in Strategic Alliances, *Organization Science,* vol. 9, no. 3 (1998), 285–305.

23. Nevis E., A. DiBella, and J. Gould, Understanding Organizations as Learning Systems, Sloan Management Review, vol. 36, no. 2 (1995), 73–85.

CHAPTER 5

1. See, for example, a discussion by Marianne Broadbent and Peter Weill in *Leveraging the New Infrastructure: How Market Leaders Capitalize on Information Technology,* Harvard Business School Press, Boston (1998).

2. Found on the Internet. Source unknown. www.aphorismsgalore.com.

3. Davenport, Thomas, and Laurence Prusak, *Working Knowledge: How Organizations Manage What They Know,* Harvard Business School Press, Boston (1998).

4. This focus has been validated by the findings of a research study spanning several companies, as reported in Davenport, Thomas, David DeLong, and Michael Beers, Successful Knowledge Management Projects, *Sloan Management Review,* vol. 39, no. 2 (1998), 43–57.

5. A discussion on several emerging knowledge management technologies can be found in a collection of research papers published as Borghoff, Uwe, and Remo Pareschi, *Information Technology for Knowledge Management,* Springer Verlag, New York (1998).

6. See Davenport, T., S. Jarvenpaa, and M. Beers, Improving Knowledge Work Processes, *Sloan Management Review,* Summer (1996), 53–65. For an analysis of mistakes that companies often make, see Fahey, Liam, and Laurence Prusak, The Eleven Deadliest Sins of Knowledge Management, *California Management Review,* vol. 40, no. 3 (1998), 265–276.

7. See Davenport and Prusak, *Working Knowledge.* For an appreciation of the nature of knowledge management technological enablers, see Borghoff and Pareschi, *Information Technology for Knowledge Management.*

8. See Nonaka's view on the human side in Nonaka, Ikujiro, Managing Innovation Self-Renewing Process, *Journal of Business Venturing,* vol. 4 (1989) 299–315. Also see Nonaka, Ikujiro, and Noboru Konno. The Concept of "Ba": Building a Foundation for Knowledge Creation, *California Management Review,* vol. 40, no. 3 (1998), 40–55.

9. Gonzalez, J., *The 21st Century Intranet,* Prentice Hall, Upper Saddle River, New Jersey (1998).

10. Thomas Davenport and his colleagues stress this notion. See Davenport, DeLong, and Beers, Successful Knowledge Management Projects, for an excellent summary of successful KM adopters who began in this manner.

11. Ginsburg, M. and S. Duliba, Enterprise Level GroupWare Choices: Evaluating Lotus Notes and Intranet Based Solutions, *Computer Supported Collaborative Work: The Journal of Collaborative Computing,* no. 6 (1997), 201–225.

12. Davenport and Prusak, *Working Knowledge.*

13. Ramesh, B., and A. Tiwana, Supporting Collaborative Process Knowledge Management in New Product Development Teams, in *Decision Support Systems* (forthcoming).

14. Zack, Michael, An Architecture for Managing Explicated Knowledge, in *Sloan Management Review* (forthcoming).

15. Ramesh and Tiwana, Supporting Collaborative Process Knowledge Management in New Product Development Teams.

16. Coleman, David, *GroupWare: Collaborative Strategies for Corporate LANs and Intranets,* Prentice Hall PTR, Upper Saddle River, NJ (1997).

17. Davenport and Prusak, *Working Knowledge.*

18. More information on Microsoft Project can be found online at www.microsoft.com/msproject/ and on the companion CD-ROM.

19. See www.cross-pcg.com for more details on the Crosspad.

20. Andrew Inkpen, for example, has demonstrated the need for trust in international joint ventures (a complex, knowledge sharing process) in a research study published as Inkpen, Andrew, Creating Knowledge Through Collaboration, *California Management Review,* vol. 39, no. 1 (1996), 123–140.

21. See www.excalibur.com for further details.

22. Tiwana, A., and B. Ramesh, *Identifying Knowledge Flow Problems and IT Support Candidates for Process Knowledge Repositories in Product Development Groups,* in The Proceedings of SAIS-99, Atlanta, GA, April 21–24 (1999).

23. A thorough analysis of this point appears in Thomas Davenport and Lawrence Prusak's, *Information Ecology: Mastering the Information and Knowledge Environment,* Oxford University Press, New York (1997).

CHAPTER 6

1. See, for example, Davenport, T., S. Jarvenpaa, and M. Beers, Improving Knowledge Work Processes, *Sloan Management Review,* Summer (1996), 53–65.

2. Zack, Michael H., Developing a Knowledge Strategy, *California Management Review,* vol. 41, no. 3, Spring (1999), 125–145.

3. Michael Zack observes that 31 different knowledge management projects reported in Davenport et al.'s *Sloan Management Review* study did not even take strategy into account as a key motivating factor driving KM.

4. Mintzberg, Henry, The Fall and Rise of Strategic Planning, *Harvard Business Review,* January–February (1994), 107–114.

5. Beinhocker, Eric, Robust Adaptive Strategies, *Sloan Management Review,* Spring (1999), 95–106. This paper also contains an excellent discussion of the concept of path dependence as applied to strategy formulation.

6. Cohen, W., and D. Leventhal, Absorptive Capacity: A New Perspective on Learning and Innovation, *Administrative Science Quarterly,* vol. 35 (1990), 128–152.

7. This concept was introduced in Hansen, M., N. Nohria, and T. Tierney, What's Your Strategy for Managing Knowledge? *Harvard Business Review,* March–April (1999), 106–116. This is a "must-read" article.

8. This point is well noted, yet little elaborated by Hansen et al.

9. Zack further indicates that every strategic position is linked to some often-unique set of knowledge resources and capabilities.

10. The idea of using these three categories for creating a knowledge map was first suggested by Michael Zack.

11. Zack, Michael H., Developing a Knowledge Strategy, *California Management Review,* vol. 41, no. 3, Spring (1999), 125–145.

12. Also see Kim, W. Chan, and Renée Mauborgne, Strategy, Value Innovation, and the Knowledge Economy, *Sloan Management Review,* Spring (1999), 41–54.

13. Kim et al. excellently characterize that companies spend too much time by fixating on daily competitive moves rather than creating growth opportunities through their knowledge.

14. Kim, C. and R. Mauborgne, Strategy, Value Innovation, and the Knowledge Economy, *Sloan Management Review,* Spring (1999), 41–54.

15. Fahey, Liam, and Laurence Prusak, The Eleven Deadliest Sins of Knowledge Management, *California Management Review,* vol. 40, no. 3 (1998), 265–276.

16. This point is stressed by both Nonaka and Davenport camps. See, for example, Nonaka, Ikujiro, and Hiro Takeuchi, *The Knowledge-Creating Company: How Japanese Companies Create the Dynamics of Innovation,* Oxford University Press, New York (1995), and Davenport, Thomas H., and Laurence Prusak, *Working Knowledge: How Organizations Manage What They Know,* Harvard Business School Press, Boston (1998).

17. Skandia can be found on the Web at www.skandia.se.

18. See our discussion in Ramesh, B., and A. Tiwana, Supporting Collaborative Process Knowledge Management in New Product Development Teams, in *Decision Support Systems* (forthcoming), for further elaboration and a case study involving a hand-held computing device manufacturer.

19. Nonaka, Ikujiro, The Knowledge Creating Company, *Harvard Business Review,* November–December (1991), 2–9.

20. This was found by Fahey and Prusak, Eleven Deadliest Sins of Knowledge Management.

21. An interesting aside is discussed by Fisher and his colleagues in Fisher, G., A. Lemke, R. McCall, and A. March, Making Argumentation Serve Design, *Human Computer Interaction,* vol. 6 (1991), 383–420. Also see Fisher, G., A. Lemke, R. McCall, J. Ostwald, B. Reeves, and F. Shipman, Supporting Indirect Collaborative Design With Integrated Knowledge Based Design Environments, *Human Computer Interaction,* vol. 7 (1992), 281–314.

22. Jungwoo Lee, now a research professor at University of Nevada, did a doctoral dissertation on this. Jungwoo Lee and Duane Truex, two researchers at the J. Mack Robinson College of Business, Georgia State University, Atlanta, have found that our leap of faith in OO methodologies is occasionally misplaced and groundless.

23. See Leonard-Barton, Dorothy, and Sylvia Sensiper, The Role of Tacit Knowledge in Group Innovation, *California Management Review,* vol. 40, no. 3 (1998), 112–131.

24. KPMG, *Knowledge Management Research Report* (1998) and (1999). Full versions of these reports are available from KPMG Netherlands.

25. See Davenport et al., Improving Knowledge Work Processes, and Davenport and Prusak, *Working Knowledge.*

26. Fahey and Prusak, Eleven Deadliest Sins of Knowledge Management.

27. Davenport and Prusak give an excellent description of the movement from inadequate data to excessive data with the emergence of electronic data processing in the late 1970s in *Working Knowledge.* For a historical account of the problems that plagued EDP in 1970s, see Jones, Malcolm M., and Ephraim R. McLean, Management Problems in

Large-Scale Software Development Projects, *Industrial Management Review,* vol. 11 (Spring 1970), 1–15.

28. See Hildebrand, Carol, Making KM Pay Off, *CIO Enterprise,* February 15 (1999) 64–66.

CHAPTER 7

1. See Zack, Michael, An Architecture for Managing Explicated Knowledge, *Sloan Management Review* (forthcoming).

2. See Davenport, T., S. Jarvenpaa, and M. Beers, Improving Knowledge Work Processes, *Sloan Management Review,* Summer (1996), 53–65.

3. Marc Meyer and Michael Zack of the Northeastern University Business School have published an excellent paper: Meyer, Marc and Zack, Michael, The Design & Development of Information Products, *Sloan Management Review,* vol. 37, no. 3 (1996), 43–59.

4. Also see Leonard-Barton, D., and S. Sensiper, The Role of Tacit Knowledge in Group Innovation, *California Management Review,* vol. 40, no. 3 (1998), 112–131.

5. Davenport, Thomas, and Laurence Prusak, *Working Knowledge: How Organizations Manage What They Know,* Harvard Business School Press, Boston (1998).

6. Powell, Betty, Learning From Collaboration, *Sloan Management Review,* vol. 30 (Spring 1998), 228–239.

7. Also see Inkpen, Andrew, Creating Knowledge Through Collaboration, *California Management Review,,* vol. 31, no. 1 (1996), 123–140. Inkpen, A., and A. Dinur, Knowledge Management Processes and International Joint Ventures, *Organization Science,* vol. 9, no. 4 (1998), 454–469. Also see Jassawalla, A. R., and H. C. Sashittal, An Examination of Collaboration in High Technology New Product Development Process, *Journal of Product Innovation Management,* vol. 15 (1998), 237–254, for detailed analysis of collaborative work in high-technology NPD processes.

8. See Borghoff, U., and R. Pareschi, *Information Technology for Knowledge Management,* Springer Verlag, Berlin (1998), 19, for an analysis of how this concept relates to corporate memory.

9. See Whitehill, M., Knowledge Based Strategy to Deliver Sustained Competitive Advantage, *Long Range Planning,* vol. 30, no. 4 (1997), 621–627, for a detailed analysis of this point.

10. See Ginsburg, M., and L. Duliba, Enterprise Level GroupWare Choices: Evaluating Lotus Notes and Intranet Based Solutions, *Computer Supported Collaborative Work: The Journal of Collaborative Computing,* vol. 6 (1997), 201–225, for a detailed treatment of this point.

11. To quote B. Patman, www.aphorimsgalore.com, Sept. 1999.

12. Also see Claudio Ciborra and Gerardo's GroupWare and Team Work in New Product Development: The Case of Consumer Goods Multinationals, in *GroupWare and Teamwork,* Wiley, New York (1996), 121–137.

13. Noted in Davenport and Prusak, *Working Knowledge.*

14. Dhar, V., and R. Stein, *Intelligent Decision Support Methods: The Science of Knowledge Work,* Prentice Hall, Upper Saddle River, NJ (1997), describes the actual technical details of GAs in very lay terms.

15. For a comprehensive technological treatment of neural networks, see Anderson, J. A., and E. Rosenfeld, *Talking Nets: An Oral History of Neural Networks,* MIT Press, Cambridge (1998); Arbib, M., *The Metaphorical Brain 2: Neural Networks and Beyond,* Wiley, New York (1989); applications in the domain of financial planning are discussed in Beltratti, A., and S. Margarita, *Neural Networks for Economic and Financial Modeling,* International Thomson Computer Press Boston (1996); Levine, D. S., and M. Aparicio, *Neural Networks for Knowledge Representation and Inference,* Lawrence Erlbaum Associates, Hillsdale, NJ (1994).

16. These attributes are identified on the basis of extensive research on knowledge usage and reported in Heijst, Spek, et al., The Lessons Learned Cycle, in *Information Technology for Knowledge Management,* U. Borghoff and R. Pareschi, Berlin, Springer Verlag (1988), 17–34.

17. The ART (action-reflex-trigger) concept along with the SECI model were proposed in Nonaka, I., and S. Reinmoeller, The ART of Knowledge: Systems to Capitalize on Market Knowledge, *European Management Journal,* vol. 16, no. 6 (1998), 673–684.

Chapter 8

1. See Bohn, R. E., Measuring and Managing Technological Knowledge, *Sloan Management Review,* vol. 36, Fall (1994), 61–73. Also see my paper, Ramesh, R., and A. Tiwana, Supporting Collaborative Process Knowledge Management in New Product Development in *Decision Support Systems* (forthcoming), for an extension and application to collaborative knowledge management in new product development teams.

2. An IPO is often considered the final objective (also called "exit strategy" in venture capital circles) of successful technological startups, and historical data indicates that thousands of entrepreneurs have made fortunes through the IPO. The trend has since caught on in other parts of the world, notably Great Britain, where FreeServe PLC., an ISP, achieved a market valuation of $3.3 billion on the first day of trading in July 1999. An IPO might be called flotation, initial stock offering, or "going public" in other parts of the world.

3. See Hall, R., and P. Andriani, Analyzing Intangible Resources and Managing Knowledge in a Supply Chain Context, *European Management Journal,* vol. 16, no. 6 (1998), 685–697, for a first-hand account of intangible asset management.

4. Many researchers have suggested that Michael Porter's well-respected and widely used models of strategic planning begin to fall apart when knowledge assets are taken into account. See Porter's work on sustainable competitiveness in Montgomery, Cynthia A., and Michael E. Porter, *Strategy: Seeking and Securing Competitive Advantage,* Harvard Business School Press, Boston (1991). For a critical assessment of its weaknesses, see Zack, Michael H., Developing a Knowledge Strategy, *California Management Review,* vol. 41, no. 3, Spring (1999), 125–145.

5. In business, as in war, front-line decisions can have critical impact on performance. See Novins, Armstrong, Choosing Your Spots for Knowledge, *Ernst and Young Journal,* (1998), 45–52, for a further discussion on this.

6. For example, see Ramesh and Tiwana, Supporting Collaborative Process Knowledge Management in New Product Development Teams.

7. Mintzberg, Henry, James Brian Quinn, and John Voyer, *The Strategy Process,* Prentice Hall, Englewood Cliffs, NJ (1995), provide an outline of some of the other strategic issues that might be important in such a situation.

8. Albert, Steven, and Keith Bradley, *Managing Knowledge: Experts, Agencies and Organizations,* Cambridge University Press, New York (1997).

CHAPTER 9

1. See Mankin, Donald, Susan Cohen, and Tora Bikson, *Teams and Technology: Fulfilling the Promise of the New Organization,* Harvard Business School Press, Boston (1996).

2. First suggested by ibid.

3. This study encompassed the United States, Finland and Hong Kong. See Keil, Mark P. Cule, K. Lyytinen, and R. Schmidt, A Framework for Identifying Software Project Risks, *Communications of the ACM,* vol. 41, no. 11 (1998), 76–83.

4. Ibid.

5. This is an accepted strategy, suggested by Mankin et al., *Teams and Technology.*

6. See Davenport, Thomas H., and Laurence Prusak, *Working Knowledge: How Organizations Manage What They Know,* Harvard Business School Press, Boston (1998).

CHAPTER 10

1. See Zack, Michael, An Architecture for Managing Explicated Knowledge, *Sloan Management Review* (forthcoming).

2. Court, A. W., The Relationship Between Information & Personal Knowledge in New Product Development, *International Journal of Information Management,* vol. 17, no. 2 (1997), 123–138.

3. Lawton, George, Unifying Knowledge with XML, *Knowledge Management,* August (1999), 38–45, provides a list of companies using XML for knowledge management.

4. See, for example, an argument on page 40 by Natalie Glance and her colleagues in Borghoff, Uwe, and Remo Pareschi, *Information Technology for Knowledge Management,* Springer, New York (1998).

5. Borghoff et al., *Information Technology for Knowledge Management.*

6. Michael Zack cautioned that this must be reflected in the design of any such system in his Sloan Paper. See Zack, An Architecture for Managing Explicated Knowledge.

7. Such as positions taken by team members on issues and their arguments for those positions. Extensive research on this has been done by Ramesh, Balasubramaniam at the J. Mack Robinson College of Business. See, for example, Balasubramaniam, Ramesh, and Kishore, Sengupta, Multimedia in a Design Rationale Decision Support System, *Decision Support Systems,* vol. 15 (1995), 181–196. Follow-up work can be found in Ramesh, B., and Tiwana, A., Supporting Collaborative Process Knowledge Management in New Product Development Teams, *Decision Support Systems* (forthcoming).

8. See, for example, Zack, M., Electronic Publishing: A Product Architecture Perspective, *Information & Management* vol. 31 (1996), 75–86.

9. See Weill, Peter, and Marianne Broadbent, *Leveraging the New Infrastructure: How Market Leaders Capitalize on Information Technology,* Harvard Business School Press, Boston (1998), 86.

10. Mankin, Don, Susan Cohen, and Tora Bikson, *Teams and Technology,* Harvard Business School Press, Boston, Massachusetts (1996).

11. Ibid.

CHAPTER 11

1. See Lynch, Patrick, and Sakah Horton, *Web Style Guide: Basic Design Principles for Creating Web Sites,* Yale University Press (1999). An online version of this book is also available at http://info.med.yale.edu/caim/manual/contents.html.

2. See, for example, Gonzalez, J., *The 21st Century Intranet,* Prentice Hall, Upper Saddle River, NJ (1998); for a more general overview, see Hendee, William R., and Wells, *The Perception of Visual Information,* Springer-Verlag, New York (1993). Another excellent discussion on structuring content for a Web-based environment appears in Rosenfeld, Louis, and Peter Morville, *Information Architecture for the World Wide Web,* O'Reilly Publishers, Cambridge (1998).

3. Adapted from a presentation by Jean Heminway of AIIM/DMA at AIIM '99 conference held in April 1999 in Atlanta, Georgia.

4. Tiwana, A., *Web Security,* Butterworth Heinemann/Digital Press, Boston (1999).

5. Jain, A., M. Aparico, and M. Singh, Agents for Process Coherence in Virtual Enterprises, *Communications of the ACM,* vol. 42, no. 3 (1999), 62–69.

6. Wong, David, P. Noemi, and D. Moore, Java-Based Mobile Agents, *Communications of the ACM,* vol. 42, no. 3 (1999), 92–102

7. See a discussion on mobility by Oshima Lange on page 88 in Maes, P., R. Guttman, and A. Moukas, Agents That Buy and Sell, *Communications of the ACM,* vol. 42, no. 3 (1999), 81–91.

8. These benefits were originally proposed for electronic commerce enabling networks, but I have extended their applicability to knowledge management systems. See the original paper, Maes et al., Agents That Buy and Sell, for the initial discussion on electronic commerce applications. Pattie Maes is familiarly referred to as the *mother of all agents,* for her role in bringing agent computing to the mainstream with the founding of Firefly, a company that pioneered agent applications on the Web.

CHAPTER 12

1. Mankin, Donald, Susan Cohen, and Tora Bikson, *Teams and Technology: Fulfilling the Promise of the New Organization,* Harvard Business School Press, Boston (1996).

2. This is very much the case with knowledge management systems. For an in-depth analysis in the generic context of team-built systems, see the discussion in ibid.

3. This idea is also put forth by ibid. Also see the discussion in Ciborra, Claudio, *Teams, Markets, and Systems: Business Innovation and Information Technology,* Cambridge University Press, New York (1993), in the general context of business impact of technology.

4. See further elicitation of this point in Keil, Mark, P. Cule, K. Lyytinen, and R. A Schmidt, Framework for Identifying Software Project Risks, *Communications of the ACM,* vol. 41, no. 11 (1998), 76–83.

5. Based on an extension of a list of suggestions in Grochow, Jerrold M., *Information Overload Creating Value With the New Information Systems Technology,* Yourdon Press, Upper Saddle River, NJ (1997), and also in Oki Goldberg, B., D. Nichols, and D. Terry, Using Collaborative Filtering to Weave an Information Tapestry, *Communications of the ACM,* vol. 35, no. 12 (1992), 61–70.

6. See, for example, a survey of 121 U.S. firms with investments in data warehousing, reported in Watson, H., and B. Haley, Data Warehousing: A Framework and Survey of Practices, *Journal of Data Warehousing,* vol. 12, no. 1 (1997), 10–17.

7. Ibid.

8. Watson, H., and B. Haley, Managerial Considerations, *Communications of the ACM,* vol. 41, no. 9 (1998), 32–37.

9. The entire RDI methodology is described in Fichman, R., and S. Moses, An Incremental Process for Software Implementation, *Sloan Management Review,* Winter (1999), 39–52. Since it was introduced in the beginning of 1999, it is one of the newest techniques on the block. However, it has been used to successfully deploy massive projects in multiple instances.

10. Scott Moses of i2 Technologies suggested the original selection criteria.

11. A detailed analysis of this point has been carried out by Orlikowski, Wanda, CASE Tools as Organizational Change: Investigating Incremental and Radical Changes in Systems Development, *MIS Quarterly,* vol. 17, no. 3 (1993), 309–340; also see Tyre, Marcie, and Wanda J. Orlikowski, Windows of Opportunity: Temporal Patterns of Technological Adaptation in Organizations, *Organization Science,* vol. 5, no. 1 (1994), 98–118.

12. Orlikowski, Wanda J., Learning From Notes: Organizational Issues in Groupware Implementation, *The Information Society,* vol. 9, no. 3 (1993), 237–250.

13. For an extended discussion on the idea of synergy being the Holy Grail of business strategy, see Gruca, T., D. Nath, and A. Mehra, Exploiting Synergy for Competitive Advantage, *Long Range Planning,* vol. 30, no. 4 (1997), 605–611.

14. See an example from the transportation industry provided in ibid., for further details and a different perspective.

15. For an excellent discussion on process complexity that this section is theoretically built further on, see Khurana, Anil, Managing Complex Production Processes, *Sloan Management Review,* Winter (1999), 86.

16. This observation was made by Fichman and Moses after their extended experience with incremental deployment. Another factor that can cause the RDI methodology to fail involves the inability to *sign on* a critical mass of users. Ibid., 47.

CHAPTER 13

1. Anonymous.

2. Nonaka, Ikujiro, and Noboru, Konno, The Concept of "Ba": Building a Foundation for Knowledge Creation, *California Management Review,* vol. 40, no. 3 (1998), 40–55.

3. Earl, M., and I. Scott, What Is a Chief Knowledge Officer, *Sloan Management Review,* Winter (1999), 29–38.

4. Zack, Michael, An Architecture for Managing Explicated Knowledge, *Sloan Management Review* (forthcoming).

5. This estimate is based on research from organizational learning. Similar figures reported in software-based reuse research and estimates by consulting groups widely vary.

6. Von Krogh, G., I. Nonaka, and K. Ichijo, Develop Knowledge Activists! *European Management Journal,* vol. 15, no. 5 (1997), 475–483.

7. Ibid., 477.

8. Duffy, D., Knowledge Champions: What Does It Take to Be a Successful CKO? *CIO Enterprise,* November 15 (1998), 66–71,.

9. Davenport, Thomas H., and Laurence Prusak, *Working Knowledge: How Organizations Manage What They Know,* Harvard Business School Press, Boston (1998).

CHAPTER 14

1. Originally from Vaguely Right Approach to Sales Force Automation, *Harvard Business Review,* vol. 52, 119–124. As quoted by J. M. Keynes, *Forbes* online edition, January 25, (1999). Used by permission.

2. See, for example, Barney, J., Types of Competition and the Theory of Strategy: Towards an Integrative Framework, *Academy of Management Review* (1991), 791–800.

3. DeGues, A., Planning as Learning, *Harvard Business Review,* March–April (1988), 70–74.

4. Stata, Ray, Organizational Learning—the Key to Management Innovation, *Sloan Management Review,* Spring (1989), 63–73.

5. See Leonard-Barton, Dorothy, and Sylvia Sensiper, The Role of Tacit Knowledge in Group Innovation, *California Management Review,* vol. 40, no. 3 (1998), 112–131, and her Harvard Business School book *Wellsprings of Knowledge* (1995).

6. See Schienmann, William, and John Lingle, Seven Greatest Myths of Measurement, *IEEE Engineering Management Review,* Spring (1998), 114–116.

7. Kaplan, R., and D. Norton, *Translating Strategy Into Action: The Balanced Scorecard,* Harvard Business School Press, Boston (1996).

8. See Schienmann and Lingle, Seven Greatest Myths of Measurement. Their results are, however, not reported in this paper.

9. Ibid.

10. See Hauser, J., and G. Katz, Metrics: You Are What You Measure! *European Management Journal,* vol. 16, no. 5 (1998), 517–528.

11. Hauser and Clausing popularized this technique in their 1988 *Harvard Business Review* article. Further details can be found in the following writings: Bickness, Barbara A., and Kris D. Bicknell, *The Road Map to Repeatable Success Using QFD to Implement Change,* CRC Press, Boca Raton, FL (1995); Bossert, James L., *QFD, A Practitioner's Approach,* ASQC Quality Press, Milwaukee, WI (1990); Cohen, Lou, *Quality Function Deployment: How to Make QFD Work for You,* Addison-Wesley, Reading, MA (1995); Daetz, Doug, William Barnard, and Rick Norman, *Customer Integration: The Quality Function Deployment (QFD) Leader's Guide for Decision Making,* Wiley, New York (1995). For customer driven design using QFDs, see Terninko, John, *Step-by-Step QFD: Customer-Driven Product Design,* St. Lucie Press, Boca Raton, FL (1997); Zairi,

Mohamed, *Quality Function Deployment: A Modern Competitive Tool,* Technical Communications, Letchworth, Hertfordshire, England (1993).

12. Camp, R., *Benchmarking: The Search for Best Practices That Lead to Superior Performance,* ASQC Quality Press, Milwaukee, WI (1989).

13. For an excellent discussion on benchmarking, see O'Dell, Carla S., APQC International Benchmarking Clearinghouse, and American Productivity & Quality Center, *Knowledge Management: Consortium Benchmarking Study: Final Report,* American Productivity & Quality Center, Houston, TX (1996). Details of this report are available online at www.apqc.org.

14. O'Dell, Carla, and C. Grayson, If Only We Knew What We Know: Identification and Transfer of Internal Best Practices, *California Management Review,* vol. 40, no. 3 (1998), 154–173. Carla O'Dell has also authored an excellent book by the same name.

15. Andersen's Website can be found at www.arthurandersen.com.

16. See the results of an APQC study of 111 participants reported in O'Dell.

17. See Drew, S., From Knowledge to Action: The Impact of Benchmarking on Organizational Performance, *Long Range Planning,* vol. 30, no. 3 (1997), 427–441.

18. See, for example, ibid., p. 429.

19. See M.J. Spendolini, *The Benchmarking Book,* AMACOM, New York (1992).

20. My own experience with NEC bears this out. When I encountered a problem with my one-and-a-half-year-old NEC laser printer, after a little more than one question I was told that my replacement printer was on the way and would be in the next day. With such excellent customer service, it would be anyone's guess which laser printer I will buy next time I am in the market for one.

21. A managerial prescription proposed in a study of five international firms as reported in Drew, From Knowledge to Action.

22. J. Hauser and L. Clausing, The House of Quality, *Harvard Business Review,* vol. 3 (1988), 63–73.

23. See Kaplan, R., and D. Norton, *Translating Strategy Into Action: The Balance Scorecard,* Harvard Business School Press, Boston, MA (1996), for a detailed discussion.

BIBLIOGRAPHIC REFERENCES AND FURTHER READING

Abelson, R.P., Black, J.B., and Galambos, J.A., *Knowledge Structures,* Lawrence Erlbaum Associates, Hillsdale, N.J. (1986).

Abramson, G., The Thrill of the Hunt, *CIO Enterprise,* January 15 (1999), 35–42.

Abramson, G., Wiring the Corporate Brain: Knowledge Management, *CIO,* vol. 12, no. 11 (1999), 30.

Adler, P.S., When Knowledge Is the Critical Resource, Knowledge Management Is the Critical Task, *IEEE Transactions On Engineering Management,* vol. 36, no. 2 (1989), 87–94.

Adler, P.S., *Technology and the Future of Work,* Oxford University Press, New York (1992).

Ahn, M.J., and Falloon, W.D., *Strategic Risk Management: How Global Corporations Manage Financial Risk for Competitive Advantage,* Probus Publications Company, Chicago (1991).

Alavi, M., An Assessment of the Prototyping Approach to Information Systems Development, *Communications of the ACM,* 27, June (1984), 556–563.

Alavi, M., KPMG Peat Marwick: One Giat Brain, *Harvard Business Review Case,* Case # 9-397-108, July (1997).

Alavi, M., and Joachimsthaler, E.A., Revisiting DSS Implementation Research: A Meta-Analysis of the Literature and Suggestions for Researchers, *MIS Quarterly,* vol. 16, no. 1 (1992), 95–116.

Albert, S., and Bradley, K., *Managing Knowledge: Experts, Agencies and Organizations,* Cambridge University Press, Cambridge [England], (1997).

Allee, V., 12 Principles of Knowledge Management, *Training & Development,* vol. 51, no. 11 (1997), 71–74.

Allee, V., *The Knowledge Evolution: Expanding Organizational Intelligence,* Butterworth-Heinemann, Boston, Massachusetts (1997).

Alvesson, M., *Management of Knowledge-Intensive Companies,* Walter de Gruyter, Berlin (1995).

Amidon, D.M., *Innovation Strategy for the Knowledge Economy: The Ken Awakening,* Butterworth-Heinemann, Boston (1997).

Andersen, A., Knowledge Services, Knowledge Consulting Services Brochure Arthur Andersen Consulting (1996).

Anderson, R.D., Gallini, N.T., and Canada, Industry Canada, *Competition Policy and Intellectual Property Rights in the Knowledge-Based Economy,* University of Calgary Press, Calgary (1998).

Andrews, K.R., *The Concept of Corporate Strategy,* Dow-Jones Irwin, Homewood, IL (1971).

Andriesz, M., Managing Knowledge, *The Scotsman,* June 1 (1999), 13.

Anonymous, Creating a Successful Knowledge Management System, *The Journal of Business Strategy,* vol. 20, no. 2 (1999), 23.

Anonymous, From Idea to Business—How Siemens Bridges the Innovation Gap, *Research Technology Management,* vol. 42, no. 3 (1999), 26.

Anonymous, The Human Side, *Research Technology Management,* vol. 42, no. 3 (1999), 56.

Anonymous, Leading the Technology Development Process, *Research Technology Management,* vol. 42, no. 3 (1999), 49.

Anonymous, Lotus Challenges Microsoft in Knowledge Management Software Market, *Businessworld,* February 16 (1999).

Anonymous, Managing Complex Networks—Key to 21st Century Innovation Success, *Research Technology Management,* vol. 42, no. 3 (1999), 13.

Anonymous, Open Eye: Head Back to the Business Cafe, *The Independent,* February 4 (1999), OE9.

Anonymous, Small Firms in Tune With Knowledge Management, *The Irish Times,* April 23 (1999), 61.

Anonymous, Two Heads Are Better Than One if Your Company Spans the Globe, *The Academy of Management Executive,* vol. 13, no. 2 (1999), 89.

Apostolou, D., and Mentzas, G., Managing Corporate Knowledge: A Comparative Analysis of Experiences in Consulting Firms, Basel, Switzerland (1998).

Appelhans, W., Globe, A., and Laugero, G., *Managing Knowledge: A Practical Web-Based Approach,* Addison-Wesley, Reading, MA (1999).

Argyris, C., Skilled Incompetence, *Harvard Business Review,* September-October (1986), 74–79.

Argyris, C., *Knowledge for Action: A Guide to Overcoming Barriers to Organizational Change,* Jossey-Bass, San Francisco (1993).

Armistead, C., Pritchard, J.-P, and Machin, S., Strategic Business Process Management for Organisational Effectiveness, *Long Range Planning,* vol. 32, no. 1 (1999), 96–105.

Ashby, W.R., Requisite Variety and Its Implications for the Control of Complex Systems, In G. Klir (Ed.), *Facets of Systems Science,* Plenum Press, New York (1991), 405–417.

Aune, B., *Knowledge of the External World,* Routledge, New York (1991).

Badaracco, J., *The Knowledge Link: How Firms Compete Through Strategic Alliances,* Harvard Business School Press, Boston (1991).

Baerentsen, K.B., and Slavensky, H., A Contribution to the Design Process, *Communications of the ACM,* vol. 42, no. 5 (1999), 72–79.

Baets, W.R.J., *Organization Learning and Knowledge Technologies in a Dynamic Environment,* Kluwer Academic Press, Boston (1998).

Bair, J., Knowledge Management: The Era of Shared Ideas, *Forbes,* September 22 (1997), 28.

Balakrishnan, S., and Koza, M.P., Information Asymmetry, Adverse Selection and Joint-Ventures, *Journal of Economic Behavior & Organization,* vol. 20, no. 1 (1993), 99–117.

Banker, R.D., Kauffman, R.J., and Mahmood, M.A., *Strategic Information Technology Management: Perspectives on Organizational Growth and Competitive Advantage,* Idea Group Pub., Harrisburg, PA (1993).

Barquín, R.C., and Edelstein, H., *Planning and Designing the Data Warehouse,* Prentice Hall, Upper Saddle River, NJ (1997).

Baskerville, R., and Stage, J., Controlling Prototype Development Through Risk Analysis, *MIS Quarterly,* December (1996), 481–504.

Baudin, C., Sivard, C., and Zweben, M., Recovering Rationale for Design Changes: A Knowledge-Based Approach, Los Angeles (1990).

Beinhocker, E., Robust Adaptive Strategies, *Sloan Management Review,* Spring (1999), 95–106.

Belanger, F., and Collins, R., Distributed Work Arrangements: A Research Framework, *The Information Society,* vol. 14 (1998), 137–152.

Benaroch, M., and Kauffman, R.J., A Case for Using Real Options Pricing Analysis to Evaluate Information Technology Project Investments, *Information Systems Research,* vol. 10, no. 1 (1999), 70.

Betz, F., *Managing Technological Innovation: Competitive Advantage From Change,* Wiley, New York (1998).

Bharadwaj, A., and Konsynski, B., Capturing the Intangibles, *Informationweek,* September 22 (1997), 71–75.

Bhargava, H., Krishnan, R., and Whinston, A., On Integrating Collaboration and Decision Technologies, *Journal of Organizational Computing,* vol. 3, no. 4 (1994), 297–317.

Bicknell, B.A., and Bicknell, K.D., *The Road Map to Repeatable Success Using QFD to Implement Change,* CRC Press, Boca Raton, FL (1995).

Blose, L., and Shieh, J., Tobin's Q-ratio and Market Reaction to Capital Investment Announcements, *The Financial Review,* vol. 32, no. 3 (1997), 449–476.

Bohn, R. E., Measuring and Managing Technological Knowledge, *Sloan Management Review,* vol. 36, Fall (1994), 61–73.

Borghoff, U., and Pareschi, R., *Information Technology for Knowledge Management,* Springer, New York (1998).

Bossert, J.L., *QFD: A Practitioner's Approach,* ASQC Quality Press, Milwaukee (1990).

Bradski, G., Carpenter, G.A., Grossberg, S., Boston University Center for Adaptive Systems, and Boston University Dept. of Cognitive and Neural Systems, *Store Working Memory Networks for Storage and Recall of Arbitrary Temporal Sequences Technical Report CAS/CNS; TR-92-028,* Boston University (1992).

Brenner, W., Zarnekow, R., and Wittig, H., *Intelligent Software Agents: Foundations and Applications,* Springer Verlag, Berlin (1998).

Brown, J. and Dugid, P., Organizing Knowledge, *California Management Review,* vol. 40, no. 3 (1998), 90–111.

Buber, M., and Friedman, M.S., *The Knowledge of Man: Selected Essays,* Harper & Row, New York (1965).

Buckles, B.P., and Petry, F., *Genetic Algorithms,* IEEE Computer Society Press, Los Alamitos, CA (1992).

Bui, T., and Lee, J., An Agent-Based Framework for Building Decision Support Systems, *Decision Support Systems,* vol. 25, no. 3 (1999), 225.

Burrell, G., and Morgan, G., *Sociological Paradigms and Organizational Analysis,* Heinemann, Portsmouth, NH (1979).

Buur, J., and Bagger, K., Replacing Usability Testing With User Dialogue, *Communications of the ACM,* vol. 42, no. 5 (1999), 63–69.

Callon, J.D., *Competitive Advantage Through Information Technology,* McGraw-Hill, New York (1996).

Camp, R., *Benchmarking: The Search for Best Practices That Lead to Superior Performance,* ASQC Quality Press, Milwaukee (1989).

Carley, K., Organizational Learning and Personnel Turnover, *Organization Science,* vol. 3, no. 1 (1992), 20–46.

Chatzoglou, P.D., Use of Methodologies: An Empirical Analysis of Their Impact on the Economics of the Development Process, *European Journal of Information Systems,* vol. 6, no. 4 (1997), 256–270.

Chesley, J.A., and Wenger, M.S., Transforming an Organization: Using Models to Foster a Strategic Conversation, *California Management Review,* vol. 41, no. 3 (1999).

Choo, C., *The Knowing Organization,* Cambridge University Press, New York (1998).

Chow, C., Teknika, O., and Williamson, J., The Balanced Scorecard: A Potent Tool for Energizing and Focusing Healthcare Organization Management, *Journal of Healthcare Management,* vol. 43, no. 3 (1998), 263–280.

Chow, C.W., Haddad, K.M., and Williamson, J.E., Applying the Balanced Scorecard to Small Companies, *Management Accounting,* vol. 79, August (1977), 21–27.

Ciborra, C., *Teams, Markets, and Systems: Business Innovation and Information Technology,* Cambridge University Press, New York (1993).

Clark, K.B., and Fujimoto, T., *Product Development Performance: Strategy, Organization, and Management in the World Auto Industry,* Harvard Business School Press, Boston (1991).

Cohen, L., *Quality Function Deployment: How to Make QFD Work for You,* Addison-Wesley, Reading, MA (1995).

Cohen, M.D., and Sproull, L., *Organizational Learning,* Sage Publications, Thousand Oaks, CA (1996).

Cohen, S.S., and Fields, G., Social Capital and Capital Gains in Silicon Valley, *California Management Review,* vol. 41, no. 2 (1999), 108.

Cohen, W., and Leventhal, D., Absorptive Capacity: A New Perspective on Learning and Innovation, *Administrative Science Quarterly,* vol. 35 (1990), 128–152.

Comerford, R., Pocket Computers Ignite OS Battle, *IEEE Spectrum,* May (1998), 43–48.

Connell, J., and Shafer, L., *Structured Rapid Prototyping: An Evolutionary Approach to Software Development,* Prentice Hall, Englewood Cliffs, NJ (1989).

Cool, K.O., Dierickx, I., and Szulanski, G., Diffusion of Innovations Within Organizations: Electronic Switching in the Bell System, 1971–1982, *Organization Science,* vol. 8, no. 5 (1997), 543.

Crossan, M.M., Lane Henry, W., and White, R.E., An Organizational Learning Framework: From Intuition to Institution, *The Academy of Management Review,* vol. 24, no. 3 (1999), 522–537.

Daetz, D., Barnard, W., and Norman, R., *Customer Integration: The Quality Function Deployment (QFD) Leader's Guide for Decision Making,* Wiley, New York (1995).

Daft, R.L., and Lengel, R.H., Information Richness: A New Approach to Managerial Behavior and Organizational Design. In L. L. Cummings and B. M. Staw (Eds.), *Research in Organizational Behavior,* 6, JAI Press, Greenwich, CT (1984), 191–233.

Daft, R.L., and Lewin, A.Y., Where Are the Theories for the "New" Organizational Forms? An Editorial Essay, *Organization Science,* vol. 4 November (1993), i–vi.

Danjoh, K., Thinking Globally: Product Development, Registration, and Marketing in the New Millennium, *Drug Information Journal,* vol. 33, no. 1 (1999), 327.

Darke, P., Shanks, G., and Broadbent, M., Successfully Completing Case Study Research: Combining Rigor, Relevance and Pragmatism, *Information Systems Journal,* vol. 8, no. 4 (1998), 273–289.

Davenport, Jarvenpaa, and Beers, Improving Knowledge Work Processes, *Sloan Management Review,* Summer (1996), 53–65.

Davenport, T., From Data to Knowledge, *CIO,* April 1 (1999), 26–28.

Davenport, T., DeLong, D., and Beers, M., Successful Knowledge Management Projects, *Sloan Management Review,* vol. 39, no. 2 (1998), 43–57.

Davenport, T., Jarvenpaa, S., and Beers, M., Improving Knowledge Work Processes, *Sloan Management Review,* Summer (1996), 53–65.

Davenport, T.H., *Process Innovation: Reengineering Work Through Information Technology,* Harvard Business School Press, Boston (1993).

Davenport, T.H., Saving IT's Soul: Human-Centered Information Management, *Harvard Business Review,* March–April (1994), 119–131.

Davenport, T.H., and Prusak, L., *Information Ecology: Mastering the Information and Knowledge Environment,* Oxford University Press, New York (1997).

DeGeus, A., Planning as Learning, *Harvard Business Review,* March–April (1988), 70–74.

DeLone, W., and McLean, E., Information Systems Success: The Quest for the Dependent Variable, *Information Systems Research,* vol. 3, no. 1 (1992), 60–95.

Demarest, M., Understanding Knowledge Management, *Long Range Planning,* vol. 30, no. 3 (1997), 374–384.

Dempsey, M., Buzzword Has Already Made a Lot of Enemies: The Role of the Chief Knowledge Officer, *Financial Times,* April 28 (1999), 2.

DeSanctis, G., and Gallupe, R., A Foundation for the Study of Group Decision Support Systems, *Management Science,* vol. 33 (1987), 589–609.

DeSanctis, G., and Poole, M.S., Capturing the Complexity in Advanced Technology Use, *Organization Science,* vol. 5, no. 2 (1994), 121–147.

Dewan, S., and Min, C., The Substitution of Information Technology for Other Factors of Production: A Firm Level Analysis, *Management Science,* vol. 43, December (1977), 1660–1675.

Dhar, V., and Stein, R., *Seven Methods for Transforming Corporate Data Into Business Intelligence,* Prentice Hall, Upper Saddle River, NJ (1997).

Dillon, P.M., *Data Mining: Transforming Business Data into Competitive Advantage and Intellectual Capital,* Information Management Forum Publications, Atlanta (1998).

DiRomualdo, A., and Gurbaxami, V., Strategic Intent for IT Outsourcing, *Sloan Management Review,* vol. 39, no. 4 (1998), 67–80.

Drew, S., From Knowledge to Action: The Impact of Benchmarking on Organizational Performance, *Long Range Planning,* vol. 30, no. 3 (1997), 427–441.

Drew, S., Strategy at the Leading Edge—Building Knowledge Management Into Strategy: Making Sense of a New Perspective, *Long Range Planning,* vol. 32, no. 1 (1999), 130.

Drucker, P., *Post Capitalist Society,* Harper Business Press, New York (1993).

Drucker, P., *Management Challenges for the 21st Century,* Harper Business, New York (1999).

Drucker, P.F., Knowledge-Worker Productivity: The Biggest Challenge, *California Management Review,* vol. 41, no. 2 (1999), 79–85.

Drummond, H., *Escalation in Decision-Making: The Tragedy of Taurus,* Oxford University Press, Oxford (1996).

Dubin, R., Theory Building in Applied Areas. In *Handbook of Industrial and Organizational Psychology,* Rand McNally College Publishing Co., Chicago (1976), 17–26.

Duffy, D., Knowledge Champions: What Does It Take to Be a Successful CKO? *CIO Enterprise,* November 15 (1998), 66–71.

Earl, M., and Scott, I., What Is a Chief Knowledge Officer, *Sloan Management Review,* Winter (1999), 29–38.

Edberg, D., Creating a Balanced Measurement Program, *Information Systems Management,* Spring (1997), 32–40.

Eisenhardt, K., and Brown, S., Time Pacing: Competing in Markets That Won't Stand Still, *Harvard Business Review,* March–April (1998), 59–69.

Epstein, M., and Manzoni, J.-F., The Balanced Scorecard and Tableau de Bord: Translating Strategy into Action, *Management Accounting,* vol. 79, August (1977), 28–36.

Ewusi-Mensah, K., Critical Issues in Abandoned Information Systems Development Projects, *Communications of the ACM,* vol. 40, no. 9 (1997), 74–80.

Fabris, P., You Think Tomatoes, I Think Tomahtoes, *CIO,* April 1 (1999), 46–52.

Fahey, L., and Prusak, L., The Eleven Deadliest Sins of Knowledge Management, *California Management Review,* vol. 40, no. 3 (1998), 265–276.

Fielding, Whitehad, and Anderson, Web Based Development of Complex Information Products, *Communications of the ACM,* vol. 41, no. 8 (1998), 84–92.

Filbeck, G., Gorman, R., and Preece, D., Fortune's Most Admired Firms: An Investor's Perspective, *Studies in Economics and Finance,* vol. 18, no. 1 (1997), 74–93.

Fisher, G., Lemke, A., McCall, R., and March, A., Making Argumentation Serve Design, *Human Computer Interaction,* vol. 6 (1991), 393–420.

Fisher, M., Ramdas, K., and Ulrich, K., Component Sharing in the Management of Product Variety: A Study of Automotive Braking Systems, *Management Science,* vol. 45, no. 3 (1999), 297.

Frame, J.D., *Managing Projects in Organizations: How to Make the Best Use of Time, Techniques, and People,* Jossey-Bass, San Francisco (1987).

Frappaolo, C., Defining Knowledge Management: Four Basic Functions, *Computerworld,* vol. 32, no. 8 (1998), 80.

Fruin, W.M., *Knowledge Works: Managing Intellectual Capital at Toshiba,* Oxford University Press, New York (1997).

Gable, G.G., Integrating Case Study and Survey Research Methods: An Example in Information Systems, *European Journal of Information Systems,* vol. 3, no. 2 (1994), 112–126.

Galbraith, J.R., and Lawler, E.E., *Organizing for the Future: The New Logic for Managing Complex Organizations,* Jossey-Bass, San Francisco (1993).

Galegher, J., Kraut, R.E., and Egido, C., *Intellectual Teamwork: Social and Technological Foundations of Cooperative Work,* Lawrence Erlbaum Associates Inc., Hillsdale, NJ (1990).

Ganssle, J.G., Navigating Through New Development Environments, *Embedded Systems Programming,* vol. 12, no. 5 (1992), 22.

Gardner, J., Strengthening the Focus on Users' Working Practices, *Communications of the ACM,* vol. 42, no. 5 (1999), 79.

Gardner, S., Building the Data Warehouse, *Communications of the ACM,* vol. 41, no. 9 (1998), 52–60.

Garrity, E.J., and Sanders, G.L., *Information Systems Success Measurement,* Idea Group Publishing, Hershey, PA (1998).

Gibson, D.V., and RGK Foundation, *Technology Companies and Global Markets: Programs, Policies, and Strategies to Accelerate Innovation and Entrepreneurship,* Rowman & Littlefield, Savage, MD (1991).

Ginet, C., *Knowledge, Perception, and Memory,* D. Reidel Publishing Company, Dordrecht, Holland (1975).

Glaister, K.W., and Falshaw, J.R., Strategic Planning: Still Going Strong? *Long Range Planning,* vol. 32, no. 1 (1999), 107.

Glazer, R., Measuring the Knower: Towards a Theory of Knowledge Equity, *California Management Review,* vol. 40, no. 3 (1998), 175–194.

Glinow, V., Young, M., and Mohrman, S.A., *Managing Complexity in High Technology Organizations,* Oxford University Press, New York (1990).

Goldberg, D., Oki, B., Nichols, D., and Terry, D., Using Collaborative Filtering to Weave an Information Tapestry, *Communications of the ACM,* vol. 35, no. 12 (1992), 61–70.

Gonzalez, J., *The 21st Century Intranet,* Prentice Hall, Upper Saddle River, NJ (1998).

Gregerman, I.B., *Knowledge Worker Productivity,* Amacom, New York (1981).

Greif, I., Desktop Agents in Group Enabled Products, *Communications of the ACM,* vol. 37, no. 7 (1994), 100–105.

Griffith, T.L., Technology Features as Triggers of Sensemaking, *The Academy of Management Review,* vol. 24, no. 3 (1999), 472–493.

Grochow, J.M., *Information Overload: Creating Value With the New Information Systems Technology,* Yourdon Press, Upper Saddle River, NJ (1997).

Gross, S.E., *Compensation for Teams: How to Design and Implement Team-Based Reward Programs,* Amacom, New York (1995).

Gruca, T., Nath, D., and Mehra, A., Exploiting Synergy for Competitive Advantage, *Long Range Planning,* vol. 30, no. 4 (1997), 605–611.

Grudin, J., Evaluating Opportunities for Design Capture. In M. Carroll (Ed.), *Design Rationale: Concepts, Techniques & Use,* Lawrence Erlbaum Associates, Mahwah, NJ (1996), 43–57.

Hearer, D., and Rosenkranz, H.J., Mayer's Interdisciplinary Research Philosophy, *Advanced Materials,* vol. 11, no. 7 (1999), 515.

Hackbarth, G., and Grover, V., The Knowledge Repository: Organizational Memory Information Systems, *Information Systems Management,* vol. 16, no. 3 (1999), 21.

Handfield, R., and Melnyk, S., The Scientific Theory Building Process: A Primer Using the Case of TQM, *Journal of Operations Management,* vol. 16, no. 4 (1998), 321–339.

Hansen, M., Nohria, N., and Tierney, T., What's Your Strategy for Managing Knowledge? *Harvard Business Review,* March–April (1999), 106–116.

Harris, L.C., Initiating Planning: The Problem of Entrenched Cultural Values, *Long Range Planning,* vol. 32, no. 1 (1999), 117.

Harvard Business Review on Knowledge Management: Collection of Past Papers, Harvard Business School Press, Boston (1998).

Hauser and Clausing, The House of Quality, *Harvard Business Review,* vol. 3 (1988), 63–73.

Hauser, J., and Gerald, K., Metrics: You Are What You Measure! *European Management Journal,* vol. 16, no. 5 (1998), 517–528.

Hedlund, G., A Model of Knowledge Management and the N-form Corporation, *Strategic Management Journal,* vol. 15, Summer Special Issue (1994), 73–90.

Heertje, A., and Perlman, M., *Evolving Technology and Market Structure: Studies in Schumpeterian Economics,* University of Michigan Press, Ann Arbor (1990).

Heijst, J., Spek, V., and Kruizinga, L. The Lessons Learned Cycle. In U. Borghoff and R. Pareschi (Eds.), *Information Technology for Knowledge Management,* Springer Verlag, Berlin (1998), 17–34.

Hewson, D., It's Not What You Know…, *Sunday Times,* April 25 (1999). 2.

Hidding, G.J., Reinventing Methodology: Who Reads It and Why, *Communications of the ACM,* vol. 40, no. 11 (1997), 102–109.

Hildebrand, C., Making KM Pay Off, *CIO Enterprise,* February 15th (1999), 64–66.

Hirsh, H., *Incremental Version-Space Merging: A General Framework for Concept Learning,* Kluwer Academic Publishers, Boston (1999).

Hoare, S., It's True: Knowledge Is Power, *The Times,* May 24 (1999), L-3.

Hoecklin, L. A., *Managing Cultural Differences: Strategies for Competitive Advantage,* Addison-Wesley, Wokingham, England (1995).

Holland, C.P., and Lockett, A.G., Mixed Mode Network Structures: The Strategic Use of Electronic Communication by Organizations, *Organization Science,* vol. 8, no. 5 (1997), 475.

Holsapple, C.W., and Whinston, A.B., *The Information Jungle: A Quasi-Novel Approach to Managing Corporate Knowledge,* Dow Jones-Irwin, Homewood, IL (1988).

Howard, G.S., Bodnovich, T., Janicki, T., and Liegle, J., The Efficacy of Matching Information Systems Development Methodologies With Application Characteristics—An Empirical Study, *The Journal of Systems and Software,* vol. 45, no. 3 (1999), 177–195.

Hyde, A.C., The Balanced Scorecard—Moving Above the Bottom Line, *Public Manager,* vol. 27, Fall (1998), 57–59.

Hyun, Y., The New Product Development Capabilities of the Korean Auto Industry: Hyundai Motor Company, *International Journal of Vehicle Design,* vol. 21, no. 1 (1999), 8.

Iansiti, M., and MacCormack, A., Developing Products on Internet Time, *Harvard Business Review,* September–October (1997), 108–117.

Inkpen, A., Creating Knowledge Through Collaboration, *California Management Review,* vol. 39, no. 1 (1996), 123–140.

Inkpen, A., and Dinur, A., Knowledge Management Processes & International Joint Ventures, *Organization Science,* vol. 9, no. 4 (1998), 454–469.

Inmon, W.H., Zachman, J.A., and Geiger, J.G., *Data Stores, Data Warehousing, and the Zachman Framework: Managing Enterprise Knowledge,* McGraw-Hill, New York (1997).

Isakowitz, T., Kamis, A., and Koufaris, M., Reconciling Top-Down and Bottom-Up Design Approaches in RMM, Atlanta (1997), 190–199.

Ives, B., and Jarvenpaa, S., Writing the Stateless Corporation: Empowering the Drivers and Overcoming the Barriers, *SIM Network,* vol. 6, no. 5 (1991), 5–8.

Jain, A., Aparico, M., and Singh, M., Agents for Process Coherence in Virtual Enterprises, *Communications of the ACM,* vol. 42, no. 3 (1999), 62–69.

Janson, M.A., Woo, C.C., and Smith, L.D., Information Systems Development and Communicative Action Theory, *Information and Management,* vol. 25, no. 2 (1993), 59–72.

Jassawalla, A.R., and Sashittal, H.C., An Examination of Collaboration in High Technology New Product Development Process, *Journal of Product Innovation Management,* vol. 15 (1998), 237–254.

Jin, L., DePledge, G., Tiwana, A., and Straub, D., Outsourcing. In J. G. Webster (Ed.), *Wiley Encyclopedia of Electrical and Electronics Engineering,* vol. 15, John Wiley & Sons, New York (1999), 455–463.

Johanessen, J.A., Olsen, B., and Olaisen, J., Aspects of Innovation Theory-Based on Knowledge-Management, *International Journal of Information Management,* vol. 19, no. 2 (1999), 121–134.

Johnston, S., and Davis, B., Smart Moves, *Informationweek,* May 31 (1999), 18–19.

Jones, M.R., Post-industrial and Post-Fordist Perspectives on Information Systems, *European Journal of Information Systems,* vol. 1, no. 3 (1991), 171–182.

Kautz, H., Selman, B., and Shah, M., Referral Web: Combining Social Networks and Collaborative Filtering, *Communications of the ACM,* vol. 40, no. 3 (1997), 63–65.

Keeney, R.L., The Value of Internet Commerce to the Customer, *Management Science,* vol. 45, no. 4 (1999), 533.

Keil, M., Cule, Lyytinen, and Schmidt, A Framework for Identifying Software Project Risks, *Communications of the ACM,* vol. 41, no. 11 (1998), 76–83.

Kendall, J.E., and Kendall, K.E., Metaphors and Their Meaning for Information Systems Development, *European Journal of Information Systems,* vol. 3, no. 1 (1994), 37–47.

Kessler, E.H., and Chakrabarti, A.K., Speeding Up the Pace of New Product Development, *The Journal of Product Innovation Management,* vol. 16, no. 3 (1999), 231.

Khaslavsky, J., and Shedroff, N., Understanding the Seductive Experience, *Communications of the ACM,* vol. 42, no. 5 (1999), 45.

Khurana, A., Managing Complex Production Processes, *Sloan Management Review,* Winter (1999), 85–97.

Kim, W.C., and Mauborgne, R., Strategy, Value Innovation, and the Knowledge Economy, *Sloan Management Review,* Spring (1999), 41–54.

King, P., and Tester, J., The Landscape of Persuasive Technologies, *Communications of the ACM,* vol. 42, no. 5 (1999), 31.

Kirsch, L.J., The Management of Complex Tasks in Organizations: Controlling the Systems Development Process, *Organization Science,* vol. 7, no. 1 (1996), 1–21.

Klempa, M.J., and Britt, J.A., Managing Information Technology: An Integrative Information Technology Acquisition/Diffusion Contingency Model. In M. Khosrowpour (Ed.), *Emerging Information Technologies for Competitive Advantage and Economic Development, 1992 IRMA Conference Proceedings,* Idea Group Publishing, Charleston, SC (1992), 343–356.

Kollock, P., An Eye for an Eye Leaves Everyone Blind: Cooperation and Accounting Systems., *American Sociological Review,* vol. 58, no. 6 (1993), 768–786.

Konstan, J., Miller, B., Maltz, D., Herlocker, J., Gordon, L., and Riedl, J., Recommen-sys: Applying Collaborative Filtering to Usenet News, *Communications of the ACM,* vol. 40, no. 3 (1997), 77–87.

Koppius, Dimensions of Intangible Goods, *32nd Hawaii International Conference on System Sciences,* vol. 32 (1999).

Koput, K.W., A Chaotic Model of Innovative Search: Some Answers, Many Questions, *Organization Science,* vol. 8, no. 5 (1997).

Kraemer, K., and Pinsonneault, A., Technology and Groups: Assessment of the Empirical Research. In J. Galegher, R., Kraut, and C. Egido (Eds.), *Intellectual Teamwork,* Lawrence Erlbaum and Associates, Hillsdale, NJ (1990), 375–405.

Krochmal, M., Tech Guru: People Are Key to Knowledge Management, *The New York Times,* June 9 (1999).

Kuhn, T., Second Thoughts on Paradigms. In *The Essential Tension: Selected Studies in Scientific Tradition and Change,* University of Chicago Press, Chicago, IL (1977), 292–319.

Kuhn, T.S., *The Structure of Scientific Revolutions,* University of Chicago Press, Chicago (1970).

Kuwada, K., Strategic Learning: The Continuous Side of Discontinuous Strategic Change, *Organization Science,* vol. 9, no. 6 (1998).

Lai, V.S., and Mahapatra, R.K., Exploring the Research in Information Technology Implementation, *Information & Management,* vol. 32, no. 4 (1997), 187–201.

Lawton, G., Unifying Knowledge With XML, *Knowledge Management,* May (1999), 38–45.

Lazere, C., Balancing the Balanced Scorecard, *CFO,* 14, February (1998), 34.

Lee, A.S., Falsifiability and the Nolan Stage Hypothesis, Information and Decision Sciences Workshop, University of Minnesota, Minneapolis, MN (1989).

Lee, H., and Lee, J., Analyzing Business Domain: A Methodology and Repository System, Hawaii (1997), HICSS-30 Conference Proceedings on CD-ROM, unnumbered.

Lee, J., Sybil, A Qualitative Decision Management System. In Whinston and Shellard (Eds.), *Artificial Intelligence at MIT: Expanding Frontiers,* MIT Press, Cambridge, MA (1990).

Lee, J., Design Rationale Capture & Use, *AI Magazine,* vol. 14 (1993).

Leonard-Barton, D., and Sensiper, S., The Role of Tacit Knowledge in Group Innovation, *California Management Review,* vol. 40, no. 3 (1998), 112–131.

Leow, J., Know What? Your Firm Needs a CKO, *The Straits Times,* May 15 (1999), 53.

Lev, B., The Old Rules No Longer Apply, *Forbes,* April 7 (1997), 1–4.

Lewellen, W.G., and Badrinath, S.G., On the Measurement of Tobin's Q, *Journal of Financial Economics,* vol. 44, no. 1 (1997), 77–122.

Li, L., and Calantone, S. The Impact of Market Knowledge Competence on New Product Development: Conceptualization & Empirical Examination, *Journal of Marketing,* vol. 62, October (1998), 13–29.

Liebowitz, J., and Wilcox, L.C., *Knowledge Management and Its Integrative Elements,* CRC Press, Boca Raton, FL (1997).

Lloyd, P., and Whitehead, R., *Transforming Organizations Through GroupWare: Lotus Notes in Action,* Springer-Verlag, London (1996).

Lotus, *Pointers,* 1998, December 21 (1993), www.Lotus.com, 1–12.

Lotus, *Lotus, IBM and Knowledge Management: A Strategic White Paper,* August (1998).

Lynch, P., and Horton, S., *Web Style Guide: Basic Design Principles for Creating Web Sties,* Yale University Press, New Haven, CT (1999).

Lynn Gary, S., Abel, K.D., and Wright, R.C., Key Factors in Increasing Speed to Market and Improving New Product Success Rates, *Industrial Marketing Management,* vol. 28, no. 4 (1999), 319.

Maes, P., Guttman, R., and Moukas, A., Agents That Buy and Sell, *Communications of the ACM,* vol. 42, no. 3 (1999), 81–91.

Malone, T., and Crowston, K. What Is Coordination Theory & How Can It Help Design Cooperative Work Systems? *Proceedings of the Conference in Computer Supported Cooperative Work* (1990), 357–370.

Malone, T., Yates, J., and Benjamin, R., Electronic Markets and Electronic Hierarchies, *Communications of the ACM,* vol. 30, no. 6 (1987), 484–497.

Malone, T., Grant, K., Turbak, F., Brobst, S., and Cohen, M., Intelligent Information-Sharing Systems, *Communications of the ACM,* vol. 30, no. 5 (1987), 390–402.

March, J.G., Exploration and Exploitation in Organizational Learning, *Organization Science,* vol. 2, no. 1 (1991), 71–87.

March, J.G., *The Pursuit of Organizational Intelligence,* Blackwell, Malden, MA (1999).

March, S., and Smith, G., Design and Natural Science Research on Information Technology, *Decision Support Systems,* vol. 15, no. 4 (1995), 251–266.

Markides, C., Strategic Innovation in Established Companies, *Sloan Management Review,* vol. 39, no. 3 (1998), 23–37.

Markus, L., and Robey, D., Information Technology and Organizational Change: Causal Structure in Theory and Research, *Management Science,* vol. 34 (1988), 583–598.

Markus, M.L., and Keil, M., If We Build It, They Will Come: Designing Information Systems That Users Want to Use, *Sloan Management Review,* vol. 35, no. 4 (1994), 11–25.

Martinsons, M., Davison, R., and Tse, D., The Balanced Scorecard: A Foundation for the Strategic Management of Information Systems, *Decision Support Systems,* March (1999).

McKee, D., An Organizational Learning Approach to Product Innovation, *Journal of Product Innovation Management*, vol. 9 (1992), 232–245.

Meyer, M., Terzakian, P., and Utterback, J., Metrics for Managing Research and Development in the Context of the Product Family, *Management Science*, vol. 43, no. 1 (1997), 88–125.

Meyer, M., and Zack, M., The Design & Development of Information Products, *Sloan Management Review*, vol. 37, no. 3 (1996), 43–59.

Miller, B., Satellites Free the Mobile Phone, *IEEE Spectrum*, March (1998), 26–35.

Mintzberg, H., The Fall and Rise of Strategic Planning, *Harvard Business Review*, January–February (1994), 107–114.

Mintzberg, H., and Lampel, J., Reflecting on the Strategy Process, *Sloan Management Review*, vol. 40, Spring (1999), 21–30.

Mintzberg, H., Quinn, J.B., and Voyer, J., *The Strategy Process*, Prentice Hall, Englewood Cliffs, NJ (1995).

Montgomery, C.A., and Porter, M.E., *Strategy: Seeking and Securing Competitive Advantage*, Harvard Business School Press, Boston (1991).

Moore, C., KM Meets BP, *CIO*, November 15 (1998), 64–68.

Morell, J., Metrics and Models for the Evaluation of Supply Chain Integration, *EDI Forum*, vol. 10, no. 1 (1997).

Morik, K., *Knowledge Representation and Organization in Machine Learning*, Springer-Verlag, Berlin (1989).

Mudge, A., Knowledge Management: Do We Know That We Know? *Communication World*, vol. 16, no. 5 (1999), 25.

Mukerjee, A., Lapre, M., and Wassenhove, L., Knowledge Driven Quality Improvement, *Management Science*, vol. 44, no. 11 (1998), 35–49.

Müller, J.P., *The Design of Intelligent Agents: A Layered Approach*, Springer, Berlin (1996).

Muller, M.J., and Czerwinski, M., Organizing Usability Work to Fit the Full Product Range, *Communications of the ACM*, vol. 42, no. 5 (1999), 87.

Mullin, R., Knowledge Management: A Cultural Evolution, *Journal of Business Strategy*, vol. 17, no. 5 (1996), 56–59.

Mullins, J.W., Forlani, D., and Walker, Jr., O.C., Effects of Organizational and Decision-Maker Factors on New Product Risk Taking, *The Journal of Product Innovation Management*, vol. 16, no. 3 (1999), 282.

Mullins, S., New Product Development in Rapidly Changing Markets: An Exploratory Study, *Journal of Product Innovation Management*, vol. 15 (1998), 224–236.

Nayyar, P.R., Stock Market Reactions to Related Diversification Moves by Service Firms Seeking Benefits From Information Asymmetry and Economies of Scope, *Strategic Management Journal*, vol. 14, no. 8 (1993), 569–591.

Nelson and Cooprider, The Contribution of Shared Knowledge to IS Group Performance, *MIS Quarterly,* December (1996), 409–429.

Newman, M., and Sabherwal, R., Determinants of Commitment to Information Systems Development: A Longitudinal Investigation, *MIS Quarterly,* vol. 20, no. 1 (1996), 23–54.

Nobeoka, K., Organizational Coordination for Project Interdependency in New Product Development, *Kobe Economic & Business Review,* vol. 42 (1997), 1–97.

Nonaka, I., Reinmoeller, J., and Senoo, K., The Art of Knowledge: Systems to Capitalize on Market Knowledge, *European Management Journal,* vol. 16, no. 6 (1998), 673–684.

Nonaka, I., Managing Innovation Self-Renewing Process, vol. 4 (1989), 299–315.

Nonaka, I., The Knowledge Creating Company, *Harvard Business Review,* November–December (1991), 2–9.

Nonaka, I., and Konno, N., The Concept of "Ba": Building a Foundation for Knowledge Creation, *California Management Review,* vol. 40, no. 3 (1998), 40–55.

Nonaka, I., Ray, T., and Umemoto, K., Japanese Organizational Knowledge Creation in Anglo-American Environments, *Prometheus: The Journal of Issues in Technology,* vol. 16, no. 4 (1998), 421.

Nonaka, I., and Takeuchi, H., *The Knowledge-Creating Company: How Japanese Companies Create the Dynamics of Innovation,* Oxford University Press, New York (1995).

Nunamaker, J., Applegate, L., and Konsynsky, B., Facilitating Group Creativity: Experience With a Group Decision Support System, *Journal of Management Information Systems,* vol. 3, no. 4 (1987), 6–19.

Nwana, H., and Nduma, D., A Brief Introduction to Software Agent Technology. In K. Jennings and J. Wooldridge (Eds.), *Agent Technology: Foundations, Applications & Markets,* Springer, Berlin (1998), 29–47.

O'Dell, C.S., *Knowledge Management: Consortium Benchmarking Study: Final Report,* American Productivity & Quality Center, Houston (1996).

Oomens, M.J.H., and van den Bosch, F.A.J., Strategic Issue Management in Major European-Based Companies, *Long Range Planning,* vol. 32 no. 1 (1999), 49.

Orlikowski, W.J., Division Among the Ranks: The Social Implications of CASE Tools for System Developers, 16th International Conference on Information Systems (ICIS), Proceedings (1989), 199–210.

Orlikowski, W.J., Integrated Information Environment or Matrix of Control? The Contradictory Implications of Information Technology, *Accounting, Management, & Information Technology,* vol. 1, no. 1 (1991), 9–42.

Orlikowski, W.J., The Duality of Technology: Rethinking the Concept of Technology in Organizations, *Organization Science,* vol. 3, August (1992), 398–427.

Orlikowski, W.J., Learning From Notes: Organizational Issues in GroupWare Implementation, *The Information Society,* vol. 9, no. 2 (1993), 237–250.

Orlikowski, W.J., Improving Organizational Transformation Over Time: A Situated Change Perspective, *Information Systems Research, Special Issue on Information Technology and Organizational Transformation,* vol. 7 no. 1 (1996), 63–92.

Orlikowski, W.J., and Baroudi, J.J., Studying Information Technology in Organizations: Research Approaches and Assumptions, *Information Systems Research,* vol. 2, March (1991), 1–28.

Orlikowski, W.J., and Robey, D., Information Technology and the Structuring of Organizations, *Information Systems Research,* vol. 2, June (1991), 143–169.

Orlikowski, W.J., and Yates, J., Genre Repertoire: The Structuring of Communicative Practices in Organizations, *Administrative Science Quarterly,* vol. 39 (1994), 541–574.

Orlikowski, W., and Debra, C., Technological Frames: Making Sense of Information Technology in Organizations, *ACM Transactions on Information Systems,* vol. 12, no. 2 (1994), 174–207.

Pare, G., and Dube, L., Ad Hoc Virtual Teams: A Multi-Disciplinary Framework and Research Agenda, *Ecole des Hautes Etudes Commerciales* Working Paper 98–04, June (1998).

Partridge, M., and Perren, L., Winning Ways With a Balanced Scorecard, *Accountancy,* vol. 120 August (1977), 50–51.

Peha, J.M., Lessons From Haiti's Internet Development, *Communications of the ACM,* vol. 42, no. 6 (1999), 67–72.

Pentland, B.T., The Learning Curve and the Forgetting Curve: The Importance of Time and Timing in the Implementation of New Technology, Paper presented at Academy of Management Meeting (1989).

Perrow, C., *Normal Accidents: Living With High-Risk Technologies,* Basic Books, New York (1984).

Pfeffer, J., and Veiga, J.F., Putting People First for Organizational Success, *The Academy of Management Executive,* vol. 13, no. 2 (1999), 37.

Polley, D., Turbulence in Organizations: New Metaphors for Organizational Research, *Organization Science,* vol. 8, no. 5 (1997), 445.

Porter, M., How Information Gives You Competitive Advantage, *Harvard Business Review* July–August (1985), 149–160.

Porter, M.E., *Competitive Advantage: Creating and Sustaining Superior Performance,* Free Press, New York (1985).

Powell, W., Learning From Collaboration, *Sloan Management Review,* vol. 40, no. 3, Spring (1998), 228–239.

Powell, B., *Knowledge of Actions,* Humanities Press, New York (1967).

Prattipati, S.N., and Mensah, M.O., Information Systems Variables and Management Productivity, *Information & Management,* vol. 33. no. 1 (1997), 33–43.

Prusak, L., *Knowledge in Organizations,* Butterworth-Heinemann, Boston (1997).

Prusak, L., Laurence Prusak Shares Thoughts on Success and Knowledge Management, *Information Outlook,* vol. 3, no. 5 (1999), 31.

Quinn, J.B., *Intelligent Enterprise: A Knowledge and Service Based Paradigm for Industry,* Free Press, New York (1992).

Quinn, J.B., Anderson, P., and Finkelstein, S., Managing Professional Intellect: Making the Most of the Best, *Harvard Business Review,* March–April (1996), 71–80.

Quinn, J.B., Baruch, J.J., and Zien, K.A., *Innovation Explosion: Using Intellect and Software to Revolutionize Growth Strategies,* Free Press, New York (1997).

Quintas, P., Lefrere, P., and Jones, G., Knowledge Management: A Strategic Agenda, *Long Range Planning,* vol. 30, no. 3 (1997), 385–391.

Ramesh, B., and Dhar, V., Supporting Systems Developing Using Knowledge Captured During Requirements Engineering, *IEEE Transactions on Software Engineering,* vol. 16, no. 2 (1992), 498–511.

Ramesh, B., and Sengupta, K., Multimedia in a Design Rationale Decision Support System, *Decision Support Systems* vol. 15 (1995), 181–196.

Ramesh, B., and Tiwana, A., Supporting Collaborative Process Knowledge Management in New Product Development Teams, *Decision Support Systems* (1999), 38.

Rao, V., and Goldman-Segal, R., Capturing Stories in Organizational Memory Systems: The Role of Multimedia, Hawaii International Conference on System Sciences, IEEE Press, January (1995), 333–341.

Reisman, A., *Management Science Knowledge: Its Creation, Generalization, and Consolidation,* Quorum Books, Westport, CT (1992).

Rheingold, H., *The Virtual Community: Homesteading on the Electronic Frontier,* Addison-Wesley, New York (1993).

Riecken, D., Intelligent Agents, *Communications of the ACM,* July (1994), 18–21.

Robertson, D., and Ulrich, K., Planning for Product Platforms, *Sloan Management Review,* Summer (1998), 19–31.

Robey, D., and Newman, M., Sequential Pattern and Information Systems Development: An Application of a Social Process Model, *ACM Transactions on Information Systems,* vol. 14 (1996), 30–63.

Robey, D., Smith, L.A., and Vijayasarathy, L.R., Perception of Conflict and Success in Information Systems Development Projects, *Journal of Management Information Systems,* vol. 10, no. 1 (1993), 123–139.

Robey, D., Wishart, N.A., and Rodriguez-Diaz, A.G., Merging the Metaphors for Organizational Improvement: Business Process Reengineering as a Component of Organizational Learning, *Accounting, Management & Information Technology,* vol. 5, no. 1 (1995), 23–39.

Robillard, J., The Role of Knowledge in Software Development, *Communications of the ACM,* vol. 42, no. 1 (1999), 87–92.

Rogers, P.R., Miller, A., and Judge, W.Q., Using Information-Processing Theory to Understanding Planning/Performance Relationships in the Context of Strategy, *Strategic Management Journal*, vol. 20, no. 6 (1999), 567.

Roos, G., and Roos, J., Measuring Your Company's Intellectual Performance, *Long Range Planning*, vol. 30, no. 3 (1997), 413–426.

Rosenfeld, L., and Morville, P., *Information Architecture for the World Wide Web*, O'Reilly, Cambridge (1998).

Rossett, A., Knowledge Management Meets Analysis, *Training & Development*, vol. 53, no. 5 (1999), 62.

Ruggles, R.L., *Knowledge Management Tools*, Butterworth-Heinemann, Boston (1997).

Rusbult, C., and Farrell, D., A Longitudinal Test of the Investment Model: The Impact on Job Satisfaction, Job Commitment, and Turnover of Variations in Rewards, Costs, Alternatives, and Investments, *Journal of Applied Psychology*, vol. 63, no. 3 (1983), 429–438.

Saarinen, T., System Development Methodology and Project Success, *Information & Management*, vol. 19 (1990), 183–193.

Sanchez, R., and Heene, A., *Strategic Learning and Knowledge Management*, Wiley, Chichester, England (1997).

Sarvary, M., Knowledge Management and Competition in the Consulting Industry, *California Management Review*, vol. 41, no. 2 (1999), 95.

Satzinger, J.W., Garfield, M.J., and Nagasundaram, M., The Creative Process: The Effects of Group Memory on Individual Idea Generation, *Journal of Management Information Systems*, vol. 15, no. 4 (1999), 143.

Savage, C.M., *Fifth Generation Management: Co-creating Through Virtual Enterprising, Dynamic Teaming, and Knowledge Networking*, Butterworth-Heinemann, Boston (1996).

Schein, E., On Dialogue, Culture and Organizational Learning, *Organizational Dynamics*, Autumn (1993), 23–29.

Schwartz, M., Wherefore Art Thou, CKO? May 20 (1999).

Senge, P.M., *The Fifth Discipline: The Art and Practice Of the Learning Organization*, Doubleday Currency, New York (1990).

Shapiro, C., and Varian, H., Versioning: The Smart Way to Sell Information, *Harvard Business Review*, November–December (1998), 16–114.

Shapiro, C., and Varian, H., *Information Rules: A Strategic Guide to the Network Economy*, Harvard Business School Press, Boston (1999).

Sharma, A., Central Dilemmas of Managing Innovation in Large Firms, *California Management Review*, vol. 41, no. 3 (1999), 147.

Shepherd, D.A., Venture Capitalists' Assessment of New Venture Survival, *Management Science*, vol. 45, no. 5 (1999), 621.

Shilito, M.L., *Advanced QFD: Linking Technology to Market and Company Needs,* Wiley, New York (1994).

Shön, D., *The Reflective Practitioner: How Professionals Think in Action,* Basic, New York (1983).

Shukla, M., *Competing Through Knowledge: Building a Learning Organization,* Sage India Private, Thousand Oaks, CA (1997).

Silk, S., Automating the Balanced Scorecard, *Management Accounting,* vol. 79, May (1998), 38–42+.

Sillince, J.A.A., and Mouakket, S., Varieties of Political Process During Systems Development, *Information Systems Research,* vol. 8, no. 4 (1997), 368–397.

Simon, H., *The Sciences of the Artificial,* MIT Press, Cambridge, MA (1981).

Simon, H.A., *The New Science of Management Decisions,* Harper and Row, New York (1960).

Simon, H.A., Bounded Rationality and Organizational Learning, *Organization Science,* vol. 2, no. 1 (1991), 125–134.

Simonin, B.L., Ambiguity and the Process of Knowledge Transfer in Strategic Alliances, *Strategic Management Journal,* vol. 20, no. 7 (1999), 595–609.

Sivaramakrishnan, K., Information Asymmetry, Participation, and Long-Term Contracts, *Management Science,* vol. 40, no. 10 October (1994), 1228–1244.

Smith, P.G., From Experience: Reaping Benefit From Speed to Market, *The Journal of Product Innovation Management,* vol. 16, no. 3 (1999), 222.

Song, M., and Montoya-Weiss, M., Critical Development Activities for Really New Versus Incremental Products, *Journal of Product Innovation Management,* vol. 15 (1998), 124–135.

Steeb, R., and Johnson, S., A Computer-Based Interactive System for Group Decision Making, *IEEE Transactions on Communications,* vol. 11 (1981), 544–552.

Stein, D.G., and Rosen, J.J., *Learning and Memory,* Macmillan, New York (1974).

Stein, E., and Zwass, V., Actualizing Organizational Memory With Information Systems, *Information Systems Research,* vol. 6, no. 2 (1995), 85–117.

Stewart, T.A., *Intellectual Capital: The New Wealth of Organizations,* Doubleday Currency, New York (1997).

Straub, D.W., and Trower, J.K., The Importance of User Involvement in Successful Systems: A Meta-Analytical Reappraisal, Working Paper 89-01, MIS Research Center, University of Minnesota (1988).

Straub, D.W., and Trower, J.K., The Role of User Involvement in Successful Systems: A Meta-Analysis of the User Involvement Literature (1995).

Sull, D.N., Why Good Companies Go Bad? *Harvard Business Review,* vol. 77, no. 4 (1999), 42.

Sveiby, K., *The New Organizational Wealth,* Berrett-Koehler Publishers Inc., San Francisco, (1995).

Swanson, E.B., and Ramiller, N.C., The Organizing Vision in Information Systems Innovation, *Organization Science,* vol. 8, no. 5 (1997), 458.

Talukdar, S.N., Collaboration Rules for Autonomous Software Agents, *Decision Support System,* vol. 24, no. 3 (1999), 269.

Tan, A., Knowledge Sharing in Civil Service Moderate: Survey, *Business Times,* May 13 (1999), 2.

Taylor, B., The Darwinian Shakeout in Financial Services, *Long Range Planning,* vol. 32, no. 1 (1999), 58–69.

Taylor, J.G., *The Promise of Neural Networks,* Springer-Verlag, London (1993).

Teece, D., Research Directions for Knowledge Management, *California Management Review,* vol. 40, no. 3 (1998), 289–292.

Teigland, R.E., Fey, C., and Birkinshaw, J., Knowledge Dissemination in Global R&D Operations: Case Studies in Three Multinationals in the High Technology Electronics Industry, Stockhold School of Economics (1998).

Terninko, J., *Step-by-Step QFD,* St. Lucie Press, Boca Raton, FL (1997).

Terwiesch, C., and Loch, C.H., Measuring the Effectiveness of Overlapping Development Activities, *Management Science,* vol. 45, no. 4 (1999), 455.

Thompson, M., The Economic Impact of E-commerce, *The Industry Standard,* April 26 (1999).

Tiwana, A., Choice of IT Infrastructural Components for Strategic Explication of Knowledge, Informs, Philadelphia (1999).

Tiwana, A., The Contribution of Process Knowledge Management on Efficacy of Collaboration Within Information Product Development Teams, SAIS–99, Atlanta (1999).

Tiwana, A., Methodological Directions on Preparing Data-Warehouses for Data, Text and Knowledge Mining, Kuwait City, Kuwait (forthcoming).

Tiwana, A., *Web Security,* Butterworth Heinemann/Digital Press, Boston (1999).

Tiwana, A., and Ramesh, B., Identifying Knowledge Flow Problems and IT Support Candidates for Process Knowledge Repositories in Product Development Groups, SAIS–99, Atlanta (1999).

Tiwana, A., and Raven, A., Extending the Product Platform Architecture Approach to Enhance Knowledge Transfer in Information Product Development, SAIS–99, Atlanta (1999).

Toulmin, S., *The Uses of Arguments,* Cambridge, Cambridge, U.K. (1958).

Toulmin, S., Rieke, R., and Janik, A., *An Introduction to Reasoning,* Macmillan, New York (1984).

Townsend, A., DeMarie, S., and Hendrickson, A., Virtual Teams: Technology and the Workplace of the Future, *Academy of Management Executive,* vol. 12, no. 3 (1998), 17–23.

Truex, D.P., Baskerville, R., and Klein, H.K., Growing Systems in an Emergent Organization, *Communications of the ACM,* August (1999).

Turoff, M., Virtuality, *Communications of the ACM,* vol. 40, no. 9 (1997), 38–43.

Turoff, M., and Hilt, S., Computer Support for Group Versus Individual Decisions, *IEEE Transactions on Communications,* vol. 30, no. 1 (1982), 82–90.

Tyre, M.J., and Orlikowski, W.J., Exploiting Opportunities for Technological Improvement in Organizations, *Sloan Management Review,* vol. 35, no. 1 (1993), 13–26.

Tyre, M.J., and Orlikowski, W.J., Windows of Opportunity: Temporal Patterns of Technological Adaptation in Organizations, *Organization Science,* vol. 5, no. 1 (1994), 98–118.

Ungson, G., and Trudel, J., The Emerging Knowledge-Based Economy, *IEEE Spectrum,* May (1999), 60–65.

Vallance, E., Sleeping With the Enemy or Learning From Each Other? Sharing Ethical Experiences Between the Public and Private Sectors, *Long Range Planning,* vol. 32, no. 2 (1999), 199–207.

Van Buren, M.E., A Yardstick for Knowledge Management, *Training & Development,* vol. 53, no. 5 (1999), 71.

Vedder, R.G., Vanecek, M.T., and Cappel, J.J., CEO and CIO Perspectives on Competitive Intelligence, *Communications of the ACM,* vol. 42, no. 8 (1999), 108–114.

Venkatraman, N., The Concept of Fit in Strategy Research: Toward Verbal & Statistical Correspondence, *Academy of Management Review,* vol. 14, no. 3 (1989), 423–444.

Von Krogh, G., and Roos, J., *Managing Knowledge: Perspectives on Cooperation and Competition,* Sage Publications, London; Thousand Oaks, CA (1996).

Von-Glinow, M.A., and Mohrman, S.A., *Managing Complexity in High Technology Organizations,* Oxford University Press, New York (1990).

VonKrogh, G., Nonaka, I, and Ichijo, K., Develop Knowledge Activists! *European Management Journal,* vol. 15, no. 5 (1997), 475–483.

Vredenburg, K., Increasing Ease of Use, *Communications of the ACM,* vol. 42, no. 5 (1999), 67.

Wah, L., Making Knowledge Stick, *Management Review,* vol. 88, no. 5 (1999), 24.

Wallham, S., The Importance of Measuring Intangible Assets: Public Policy Implications. In N. Imparato (Ed.), *Capital for Our Time,* Hoover Institution Press, Stanford, CA (1999), 131–191.

Walsh, J., and Ungson, G., Organizational Memory, *Academy of Management Review,* vol. 16, no. 1 (1991), 57–91.

Wand, Y., Monarchi, D.E., Parsons, J., and Woo, C.C., Theoretical Foundations for Conceptual Modeling in Information Systems Development, *Decision Support Systems,* vol. 15, no. 4 (1995), 285–304.

Watson, H., and Haley, B., Managerial Considerations, *Communications of the ACM,* vol. 41, no. 9 (1998), 32–37.

Watson, H., and Haley, B., Data Warehousing: A Framework and Survey of Practices, *Journal of Data Warehousing,* vol. 2, no. 1 (1997), 10–17.

Webber, A., What's So New About the Economy, *Harvard Business Review,* January–February (1993), 4–11.

Wenger, E., *Communities of Practice: Learning, Meaning, and Identity,* Cambridge University Press, New York (1998).

White, D., Human Resources: Why Managers Really Believe Knowledge Is Power, *The Guardian,* April 10 (1999), 47.

Whitehill, M., Knowledge-Based Strategy to Deliver Sustained Competitive Advantage, *Long Range Planning,* vol. 30, no. 4 (1997), 621–627.

Whittaker, D.H., *Managing Innovation: A Study of British and Japanese Factories,* Cambridge University Press, Cambridge, England (1990).

Wiig, K., *Knowledge Management Foundations—Thinking About Thinking—How People and Organizations Create, Represent and Use Knowledge,* Schema Press, Arlington, TX (1993).

Wilson, A.L., Ramamurthy, K., and Nystrom, P.C., A Multi-Attribute Measure for Innovation Adoption: The Context of Imaging Technology, *IEEE Transactions on Engineering Management,* vol. 46, no. 3 (1999), 311–329.

Winslow, C.D., and Bramer, W.L., *FutureWork: Putting Knowledge to Work in the Knowledge Economy,* Free Press, New York (1994).

Wright, D.J., International Technology Transfer With an Information Asymmetry and Endogenous Research and Development, *Journal of International Economics,* vol. 35, no. 1 August (1993), 47–67.

Xiao, Powell, and Dodgson, The Impact of Information Technology on Information Asymmetry, *European Journal of Information Systems,* vol. 7 (1998), 77–89.

Yates, J., Orlikowski, W.J., and Okamura, K., Constituting Genre Repertoires: Deliberate and Emergent Patterns of Electronic Media Use, Academy of Management (1995), 353–357.

Yoffie, D.B., and Cusumano, M.A., Building a Company on Internet Time: Lessons From Netscape, *California Management Review,* vol. 41, no. 3 (1999).

Zack, M., Electronic Publishing: A Product Architecture Perspective, *Information & Management,* vol. 31 (1996), 75–86.

Zack, M., *Knowledge and Strategy,* Butterworth-Heinemann, Boston (1999).

Zack, M., Managing Codified Knowledge, *Sloan Management Review,* vol. 40, no. 4 (1999), 45–51.

Zack, M.H., Developing a Knowledge Strategy, *California Management Review,* vol. 41, Spring (1999), 125–145.

Zahra, S., The Changing Rules of Global Competitiveness in the 21st Century, *Academy of Management Executive,* vol. 13, no. 1 (1999), 36–42.

Zeleny, M., Management Support Systems: Towards Integrated Knowledge Management. In *Human Systems Management,* North-Holland, Amsterdam (1987), 59–70.

Zmud, R.W., An Examination of "Push-Pull" Theory Applied to Process Innovation in Knowledge Work, *MISQ,* vol. 30, no. 6 (1984), 727–738.

Zohar, D., *Rewiring the Corporate Brain: Using the New Science to Rethink How We Structure and Lead Organizations,* Berrett-Koehler Publishers, San Francisco (1997).

GLOSSARY

This section describes common terms that have been used throughout the book relating to knowledge, knowledge management, collaborative work, strategy, methodologies, organizational learning, networks, and process management. Other terms, such as *collaborative filtering*, which is explained at depth where it occurs, are not included here.

agricultural economy   Traditionally, a land and labor-intensive economy primarily aimed at the production of food.

analytical applications   Analytical applications help analyze information. These include fishbone diagrams, cash cow analysis using BCG grids, mind maps, critical path analysis tools, decision trees, force-field analysis, Strengths, Weaknesses, Opportunities, system thinking tools, etc.

artificial intelligence   The use of human models for cognition and perception to create computer systems to solve human-like problems.

browser   A program that allows users to access documents on the World Wide Web (WWW), typically using the HTTP protocol. Browsers can be either text or graphic. They read HTML and interpret the code into what we see as Web pages. The two popular browsers in use are Microsoft's Internet Explorer and America Online's Netscape Navigator. Browsers are often used as the primary front-end interface for knowledge management systems that rely on intranet technology.

business process reengineering   BPR focuses on detecting the core processes that make up the business and then reassemble them more efficiently in a way that is free of functional divides and that reduces complexity by reengineering operational and customer-directed activities into processes.

business value orientation   Determines where a company principally derives value from.

chief knowledge officer (CKO)   Along with other senior management members, the chief knowledge officer is responsible for creating the vision of what is possible and designing the framework for realizing the results.

communication processes   Information technology and cultural processes that enable people to share information in an efficient and effective manner. Remember that the term *process* does not describe just the technical process underlying message delivery, but the whole act of communicating. If I were to describe it as a purely technical process, I would be straying too far away from knowledge management, where the human/ cultural side is as important, if not more, than the technological side.

communities of practice   Groups of virtual or local members with similar specializations.

content directors   Executive management levels that design, set, and execute strategies on issues for which they provide focus regarding the process of knowledge sharing.

content organizers   The organizational unit (usually the corporate office of a company) that coordinates, controls, and communicates knowledge by combining and connecting strategy to operations.

control processes   Control processes enable a company to create and maintain stability within business performance and legal and financial systems.

coordination processes   Coordination processes are activities that link strategic and operational processes in an efficient, effective, financially acceptable, timely, and value-adding manner.

core competencies   A company's unique combination of available knowledge capabilities that represent its key strength. Core competencies reflect key strengths of companies to such an extent that they allow the company to sustain its competitive advantage in order to add value to customers. Core competencies are often considered semipermanent in nature, that is, sustainable over a period of time.

corporate processes   Corporate processes are coordination, control, and communication processes that allow companies to link strategic processes to operational processes, and vice versa.

customer capital   The value of an organization's relationships with its customers.

data   Raw transactional representations and outputs without inherent meaning.

data mining   A technique to analyze data in very large databases with the goal of revealing trends and patterns.

expertise   The ability to take information and apply it to a particular situation.

firewall   Device that protects a private network from the public domain. A computer that monitors traffic between an Internet site and the Internet. It's designed to prevent unauthorized people from tampering with a computer system thereby increasing security.

functional alignment   Remembering that companies are not in the business of building knowledge but in the business of creating value, functional disciplines are increasingly redesigned to become more business and process oriented. By ensuring functional alignment, functional expertise has a clearer and more direct impact on strategic and operational performance.

genetic computing   Genetic computing uses DNA strings to perform computations. Its four basic materials—adenine, guanine, thymine, and cytosine—are combined to form strings of information. A closely related concept is that of genetic algorithms. The strength of this emerging technique for arriving at the best fitting solutions comes from the notion of Darwin's theory of natural selection: A test tube of one billion DNA strings has a capacity of one billion parallel computations per second.

hard networks   Hard networks distribute data and information by connecting computers through a variety of information technology systems (network computing).

human capital   The knowledge, skills, and competencies of people in an organization.

integrated knowledge environment   Information technology that supports the flow of knowledge throughout the enterprise.

intellectual capital   Intangibles such as information, knowledge, and skills that can be leveraged by an organization to produce an asset of equal or greater importance than land, labor, and capital.

knowledge repository   A collection of information or knowledge stored in *any* type of database or its offshoot that is of interest to the company and made accessible to a broad population. Also a collection of information or knowledge, usually centered on specific issues of interest to the company and accessible through technologies such as intranets and browsers.

knowledge   A fluid mix of framed experience, values, contextual information, expert insight, and grounded intuition that provides an environment and framework for evaluating and incorporating new experiences and information. It originates and is applied in the minds of knowers. In organizations, it often becomes embedded not only in documents or repositories but also in organizational routines, processes, practices, and norms. See Chapters 2 and 3. Also management of organizational knowledge for creating business value and generating a competitive advantage.

knowledge segment   Everything a company's professionals and systems know about a specific domain.

k-spots   These represent the knowledge niches on which a company must focus its knowledge management efforts. Based on how the audit process populates the strategic capability framework (see Chapter 8), you can identify promising processes that stand to gain the most through knowledge management.

lessons learned and best practices   Databases in which examples of previous experiences are stored, the reasons why they worked best or failed miserably, and the lessons that were learned from them.

operational processes   Logically grouped support activities that, together, form a core operational process.

performance appraisal   Performance appraisal provides an overall evaluation of how well a team or an individual is doing in the eyes of its members as well as its customers. For an example of a tool used to support performance appraisal, see the companion CD-ROM.

process organization   A process organization is characterized by its horizontal flow of information and communication and its decentralized authority over decisions. This viewpoint led to Business Process Reengineering (BPR), and then to process knowledge management.

process team   A group of professionals responsible for a company's operational, corporate, and/or strategic processes.

RDI methodology   A results-driven incremental methodology suited for complex projects such as knowledge management system deployment. The key idea is that each phase incrementally builds upon a learning experience gained from the preceding phase.

reflecting   The act of playing back and thinking about the lessons learned each day. This is also called action replay or rationale reconstruction in some software engineering circles.

sensing   The ability to observe and perceive without passing judgment.

smart networks   Smart networks combine hard and soft networks, as described elsewhere in this glossary. This results in effective linking of smart business strategies to every employee throughout the company. Smart organizations are entirely process and team based and use knowledge as their primary asset and are characterized by such smart networks.

soft networks   The process of establishing a community of practice and collating a number of people who can be called upon when such expertise is required.

strategic holding   A corporate office acts as a strategic holding when its core purpose is not to direct operational processes but to prepare, design, and implement a long-term business strategy.

strategic knowledge management   Links the building of a company's knowledge to a business strategy. See Chapter 12 for details on how QFD type approaches make this possible. Also see Chapter 6 for details on creating this link through knowledge maps.

structural capital   The processes, structures, and systems that a firm owns less its people. Skandia reported its structural capital in its 1996 annual report intellectual asset supplement. A simple way to think of it is in terms of a firm's hard capital assets.

synergy   The ability of the system to produce a result that is greater than the sum of individual components. In the context of knowledge management, synergy refers to the ability of the knowledge management system to allow different groups of users, representing different functional departments, to produce results exceeding those that they would produce working without the support of such a system.

team synergy   The process of working together as a team that creates synergy by combining each member's unique knowledge. The combination is capable of producing results exceeding those possible if each member's capabilities and productivity measures were summed up.

360° performance appraisal   The concept that smart knowledge workers regularly request mentors, team leaders, peers, and customers to appraise their performance by providing them formal and informal feedback.

virtual competence center   A virtual team of people organized around a specific knowledge domain. Also see Communities of Practice.

wrappers   Scripts and connection modules that allow personal computers and modern networks to access legacy data. Knowledge query modeling language (KQML) and TCL/TK are often used to write these wrappers.

Index

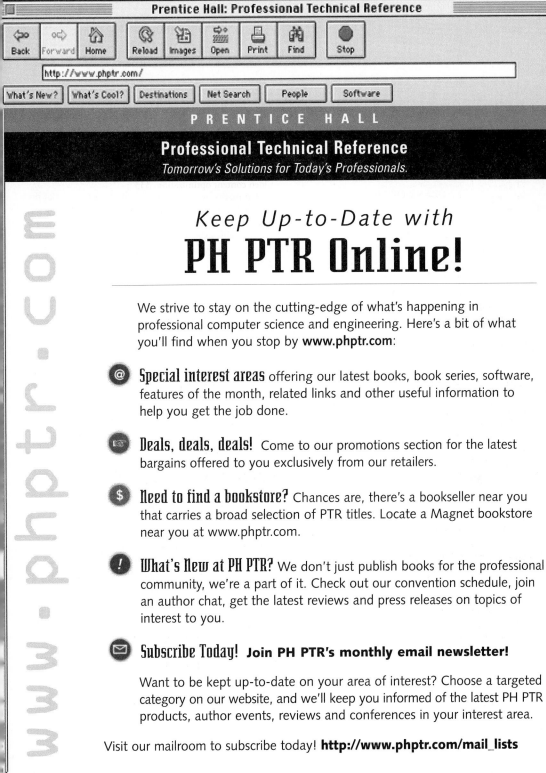

LICENSE AGREEMENT AND LIMITED WARRANTY

READ THE FOLLOWING TERMS AND CONDITIONS CAREFULLY BEFORE OPENING THIS DISK PACKAGE. THIS LEGAL DOCUMENT IS AN AGREEMENT BETWEEN YOU AND PRENTICE-HALL, INC. (THE "COMPANY"). BY OPENING THIS SEALED DISK PACKAGE, YOU ARE AGREEING TO BE BOUND BY THESE TERMS AND CONDITIONS. IF YOU DO NOT AGREE WITH THESE TERMS AND CONDITIONS, DO NOT OPEN THE DISK PACKAGE. PROMPTLY RETURN THE UNOPENED DISK PACKAGE AND ALL ACCOMPANYING ITEMS TO THE PLACE YOU OBTAINED THEM FOR A FULL REFUND OF ANY SUMS YOU HAVE PAID.

1. **GRANT OF LICENSE:** In consideration of your payment of the license fee, which is part of the price you paid for this product, and your agreement to abide by the terms and conditions of this Agreement, the Company grants to you a nonexclusive right to use and display the copy of the enclosed software program (hereinafter the "SOFTWARE") on a single computer (i.e., with a single CPU) at a single location so long as you comply with the terms of this Agreement. The Company reserves all rights not expressly granted to you under this Agreement.

2. **OWNERSHIP OF SOFTWARE:** You own only the magnetic or physical media (the enclosed disks) on which the SOFTWARE is recorded or fixed, but the Company retains all the rights, title, and ownership to the SOFTWARE recorded on the original disk copy(ies) and all subsequent copies of the SOFTWARE, regardless of the form or media on which the original or other copies may exist. This license is not a sale of the original SOFTWARE or any copy to you.

3. **COPY RESTRICTIONS:** This SOFTWARE and the accompanying printed materials and user manual (the "Documentation") are the subject of copyright. You may not copy the Documentation or the SOFTWARE, except that you may make a single copy of the SOFTWARE for backup or archival purposes only. You may be held legally responsible for any copying or copyright infringement which is caused or encouraged by your failure to abide by the terms of this restriction.

4. **USE RESTRICTIONS:** You may not network the SOFTWARE or otherwise use it on more than one computer or computer terminal at the same time. You may physically transfer the SOFTWARE from one computer to another provided that the SOFTWARE is used on only one computer at a time. You may not distribute copies of the SOFTWARE or Documentation to others. You may not reverse engineer, disassemble, decompile, modify, adapt, translate, or create derivative works based on the SOFTWARE or the Documentation without the prior written consent of the Company.

5. **TRANSFER RESTRICTIONS:** The enclosed SOFTWARE is licensed only to you and may not be transferred to any one else without the prior written consent of the Company. Any unauthorized transfer of the SOFTWARE shall result in the immediate termination of this Agreement.

6. **TERMINATION:** This license is effective until terminated. This license will terminate automatically without notice from the Company and become null and void if you fail to comply with any provisions or limitations of this license. Upon termination, you shall destroy the Documentation and all copies of the SOFTWARE. All provisions of this Agreement as to warranties, limitation of liability, remedies or damages, and our ownership rights shall survive termination.

7. **MISCELLANEOUS:** This Agreement shall be construed in accordance with the laws of the United States of America and the State of New York and shall benefit the Company, its affiliates, and assignees.

8. **LIMITED WARRANTY AND DISCLAIMER OF WARRANTY:** The Company warrants that the SOFTWARE, when properly used in accordance with the Documentation, will operate in substantial conformity with the description of the SOFTWARE set forth in the Documentation. The Company does not warrant that the SOFTWARE will meet your requirements or that the operation of the SOFTWARE will be uninterrupted or error-free. The Company warrants that the media on which the SOFTWARE is delivered shall be free from defects in materials and workmanship under normal use for a period of thirty (30) days from the

date of your purchase. Your only remedy and the Company's only obligation under these limited warranties is, at the Company's option, return of the warranted item for a refund of any amounts paid by you or replacement of the item. Any replacement of SOFTWARE or media under the warranties shall not extend the original warranty period. The limited warranty set forth above shall not apply to any SOFTWARE which the Company determines in good faith has been subject to misuse, neglect, improper installation, repair, alteration, or damage by you. EXCEPT FOR THE EXPRESSED WARRANTIES SET FORTH ABOVE, THE COMPANY DISCLAIMS ALL WARRANTIES, EXPRESS OR IMPLIED, INCLUDING WITHOUT LIMITATION, THE IMPLIED WARRANTIES OF MERCHANTABILITY AND FITNESS FOR A PARTICULAR PURPOSE. EXCEPT FOR THE EXPRESS WARRANTY SET FORTH ABOVE, THE COMPANY DOES NOT WARRANT, GUARANTEE, OR MAKE ANY REPRESENTATION REGARDING THE USE OR THE RESULTS OF THE USE OF THE SOFTWARE IN TERMS OF ITS CORRECTNESS, ACCURACY, RELIABILITY, CURRENTNESS, OR OTHERWISE.

IN NO EVENT, SHALL THE COMPANY OR ITS EMPLOYEES, AGENTS, SUPPLIERS, OR CONTRACTORS BE LIABLE FOR ANY INCIDENTAL, INDIRECT, SPECIAL, OR CONSEQUENTIAL DAMAGES ARISING OUT OF OR IN CONNECTION WITH THE LICENSE GRANTED UNDER THIS AGREEMENT, OR FOR LOSS OF USE, LOSS OF DATA, LOSS OF INCOME OR PROFIT, OR OTHER LOSSES, SUSTAINED AS A RESULT OF INJURY TO ANY PERSON, OR LOSS OF OR DAMAGE TO PROPERTY, OR CLAIMS OF THIRD PARTIES, EVEN IF THE COMPANY OR AN AUTHORIZED REPRESENTATIVE OF THE COMPANY HAS BEEN ADVISED OF THE POSSIBILITY OF SUCH DAMAGES. IN NO EVENT SHALL LIABILITY OF THE COMPANY FOR DAMAGES WITH RESPECT TO THE SOFTWARE EXCEED THE AMOUNTS ACTUALLY PAID BY YOU, IF ANY, FOR THE SOFTWARE.

SOME JURISDICTIONS DO NOT ALLOW THE LIMITATION OF IMPLIED WARRANTIES OR LIABILITY FOR INCIDENTAL, INDIRECT, SPECIAL, OR CONSEQUENTIAL DAMAGES, SO THE ABOVE LIMITATIONS MAY NOT ALWAYS APPLY. THE WARRANTIES IN THIS AGREEMENT GIVE YOU SPECIFIC LEGAL RIGHTS AND YOU MAY ALSO HAVE OTHER RIGHTS WHICH VARY IN ACCORDANCE WITH LOCAL LAW.

ACKNOWLEDGMENT

YOU ACKNOWLEDGE THAT YOU HAVE READ THIS AGREEMENT, UNDERSTAND IT, AND AGREE TO BE BOUND BY ITS TERMS AND CONDITIONS. YOU ALSO AGREE THAT THIS AGREEMENT IS THE COMPLETE AND EXCLUSIVE STATEMENT OF THE AGREEMENT BETWEEN YOU AND THE COMPANY AND SUPERSEDES ALL PROPOSALS OR PRIOR AGREEMENTS, ORAL, OR WRITTEN, AND ANY OTHER COMMUNICATIONS BETWEEN YOU AND THE COMPANY OR ANY REPRESENTATIVE OF THE COMPANY RELATING TO THE SUBJECT MATTER OF THIS AGREEMENT.

Should you have any questions concerning this Agreement or if you wish to contact the Company for any reason, please contact in writing at the address below.

Robin Short
Prentice Hall PTR
One Lake Street
Upper Saddle River, New Jersey 07458

ABOUT THE CD-ROM

The CD-ROM included with *The Knowledge Management Toolkit* contains
(restricted versions unless otherwise noted):

The Knowledge Management Toolkit (full version)
Contains an interactive 10-step road map, unrestricted, royalty-free, customizable electronic versions
of all KM evaluation forms in PDF and Word for Windows format
    AlphaCONNECT Suite
    Austin Hayne
    BrainForest for the PalmPilot
    Ferret Software
        Web Ferret
        Info Ferret
        Email Ferret
        Phone Ferret
        Ferret Toolbar
    HyperWave Information Server
    Intranetics 2.0 demo version
    Microsoft Frontpage 2000
    KeyFlow
    Mindmanager Personal (full version)
    MIS-AG DeltaMiner suite
    Opentext LiveLink Intranet
    Performance Now
    SmartDraw

The CD-ROM can be used on Microsoft Windows® 95/98/NT®. For best results, use
Internet Explorer.

Technical Support
Prentice Hall does not offer technical support for any of the programs on the CD-ROM.
However, if the CD-ROM is damaged, you may obtain a replacement copy by sending an email that
describes the problem to: disc_exchange@prenhall.com

License Agreement
Use of the software accompanying *The Knowledge Management Toolkit* is subject to the terms of
the License Agreement and Limited Warranty, found on the previous two pages.
This program was reproduced by Prentice Hall PTR under a special arrangement with
Microsoft Corporation. For this reason, Prentice Hall PTR is responsible for the product warranty. If
your diskette is defective, please return it to Prentice Hall PTR, which will arrange for its replace-
ment. PLEASE DO NOT RETURN IT TO MICROSOFT CORPORATION. PLEASE DO NOT
CONTACT MICROSOFT CORPORATION FOR PRODUCT SUPPORT. End users of this
Microsoft program shall not be considered "registered owners" of a Microsoft product and therefore
shall not be eligible for upgrades, promotions or other benefits available to "registered owners" of
Microsoft products.